'This insightful book explores the judicial turn in international environmental law through the lens of legitimacy, with an impressive group of scholars examining how international litigation is contributing, in a mostly positive way, to the norms and processes of global environmental governance. For scholars, practitioners, and judges, the book provides an indispensable and up-to-date account of environmental litigation in contemporary international law.'

Professor Tim Stephens, University of Sydney Law School

'The surge in international environmental adjudication that some foresaw a quarter of a century ago, on the eve of the Rio Conference on Environment and Development, has now become a widespread phenomenon, and one that is particularly challenging to keep abreast with, even for specialists. This volume presents the state of the art in international environmental adjudication, providing detailed treatment of the main developments from the analytical prism of "legitimacy", with its many faces. It is a significant contribution to knowledge and a necessary addition to the library of both international and environmental lawyers.'

Jorge E. Viñuales, Harold Samuel Professor of Law and Environmental
Policy, University of Cambridge

INTERNATIONAL JUDICIAL
PRACTICE ON THE ENVIRONMENT

More and more environmental cases are being heard and decided by international courts and tribunals that lack special environmental jurisdiction. This situation raises fundamental questions about the legitimacy of the environmental practice of international courts. This book addresses, inter alia, questions of who has legal standing to bring an environmental claim before an international court, on which legal norms the case is decided and whether judges have the necessary expertise to adjudicate environmental cases that are often of a complex nature. It analyses the challenges that international courts face, the possibilities that they have, and the advances that international judicial practice has been able to make in protecting the environment. Through the prism of legitimacy, important insights emerge as to whether international courts and tribunals are fit for addressing some of the most pressing global challenges of our time.

CHRISTINA VOIGT is Professor at the Department of Public and International Law, University of Oslo, Norway. She is an expert in international environmental law and works in particular on legal issues of climate change, environmental multilateralism, sustainability, and international courts and environmental protection. She is a member of the International Union for Conservation of Nature (IUCN) World Commission on Environmental Law, the chair of the Commission's Climate Change Specialist Group and a member of the IUCN Task Force on Climate Change. In 2009, she was awarded the first IUCN Academy of Environmental Law Junior Scholarship Prize. She is the author of *Sustainable Development as a Principle of International Law* (2009), numerous academic articles and several edited volumes. She also serves as principal legal advisor to the Government of Norway in the United Nations (UN) climate negotiations.

STUDIES ON INTERNATIONAL COURTS AND TRIBUNALS

General Editors
Andreas Føllesdal, University of Oslo
Geir Ulfstein, University of Oslo

Studies on International Courts and Tribunals contains theoretical and interdisciplinary scholarship on legal aspects as well as the legitimacy and effectiveness of international courts and tribunals.

Other books in the series

INTERNATIONAL JUDICIAL PRACTICE ON THE ENVIRONMENT

Questions of Legitimacy

Edited by

CHRISTINA VOIGT

University of Oslo

CAMBRIDGE
UNIVERSITY PRESS

CAMBRIDGE
UNIVERSITY PRESS

University Printing House, Cambridge CB2 8BS, United Kingdom

One Liberty Plaza, 20th Floor, New York, NY 10006, USA

477 Williamstown Road, Port Melbourne, VIC 3207, Australia

314–321, 3rd Floor, Plot 3, Splendor Forum, Jasola District Centre,
New Delhi – 110025, India

79 Anson Road, #06–04/06, Singapore 079906

Cambridge University Press is part of the University of Cambridge.

It furthers the University's mission by disseminating knowledge in the pursuit of
education, learning, and research at the highest international levels of excellence.

www.cambridge.org
Information on this title: www.cambridge.org/9781108497176
DOI: 10.1017/9781108684385

© Cambridge University Press 2019

First published 2019

Printed and bound in Great Britain by Clays Ltd, Elcograf S.p.A.

A catalogue record for this publication is available from the British Library.

Library of Congress Cataloging-in-Publication Data
Names: Voigt, Christina, 1971– editor.
Title: International judicial practice on the environment : questions of legitimacy / edited by
Christina Voigt, Universitetet i Oslo.
Description: Cambridge, United Kingdom ; New York, NY, USA : Cambridge University
Press, 2019. | Series: Studies on international courts and tribunals | Includes index.
Identifiers: LCCN 2018037699 | ISBN 9781108497176
Subjects: LCSH: Environmental law, International – Cases. | Environmental law – European
Union countries – Cases. | International courts. | Political questions and judicial power.
Classification: LCC K3585 .I582 2019 | DDC 344.04/6–dc23
LC record available at https://lccn.loc.gov/2018037699

ISBN 978-1-108-49717-6 Hardback

CONTENTS

CONTRIBUTORS

LISA CHAMBERLAIN is Acting Director of the Centre for Applied Legal Studies (CALS) at the School of Law, University of the Witwatersrand, in South Africa. She is an environmental justice activist, practising attorney and senior lecturer at the Wits School of Law. She has an LLM (University of Michigan) and a BA, LLB (Wits). Her areas of expertise include environmental justice, access to information, protest, mining and legislative drafting. Prior to joining CALS, she worked at Cheadle, Thompson and Haysom Inc. and clerked at the Constitutional Court of South Africa.

ARTHUR RODRIGUES DALMARCO is a PhD candidate at the Federal University of Santa Catarina Law School, Florianopolis, Brazil.

CRISTIANE DERANI is Professor of International, Environmental and Economic Law at the Federal University of Santa Catarina Law School, Florianopolis, Brazil, and Visiting Scholar at the Centre for Environment, Energy, Natural Resources and Governance (C-EENRG), University of Cambridge, UK.

KAZUKI HAGIWARA is Lecturer in Public International Law at the Faculty of Law, Fukuoka University, Japan. He holds an LLD (Yokohama National University), an LLM (Ottawa), and a Masters in International and Business Law (Yokohama National University). His research has a specific focus on the law of treaties, international economic law, and international environmental law. He currently teaches public international law and common law legal systems.

EVAN HAMMAN is Lecturer at the School of Law at Queensland University of Technology (QUT) in Brisbane, Australia. He holds Bachelors' degrees in law and commerce from the University of New South Wales, a Master's in Environmental Science and Law from Sydney

University and a PhD in law from QUT. His research focuses on civil society, biodiversity governance and environmental law. He has a particular interest in making environmental laws work 'on the ground', particularly in the Asia–Pacific region.

ANNA HUGGINS is Senior Lecturer in the Faculty of Law at the Queensland University of Technology, Brisbane, Australia. Her research interests include international environmental law, compliance, and global administrative law. She is the author of *Multilateral Environmental Agreements and Compliance: The Benefits of Administrative Procedures* (2018). Anna holds a PhD from the University of New South Wales (UNSW) Law School, for which she received a PhD Excellence Award. Before entering academia, Anna worked at the New South Wales Department of Environment and Climate Change.

TRACEY KANHANGA is a PhD candidate at the South African Research Chair in International Law (SARCIL), University of Johannesburg. She holds an LLM in International Law from the University of Johannesburg, which incorporates international environmental law, international human rights, international criminal law, and international humanitarian law. She is an expert in international environmental laws and international courts and tribunals. She graduated from the University of Zimbabwe with an LLB (Honours), and she is also a member of the South Africa International Law Association.

LUDWIG KRÄMER was a judge in Germany. For more than thirty years, he worked in the environmental department of the European Commission in Brussels. He has since retired from both positions. At present, he runs Derecho y Medio Ambiente, an environmental law consultancy, in Madrid.

ANDREW B. LOEWENSTEIN is Partner with the International Litigation and Arbitration Department of Foley Hoag LLP, where he specialises in representing states before international courts and tribunals, including in disputes concerning international environmental law. He served as counsel in several cases in which claims involving environmental impact assessments (EIAs) were litigated, including *Pulp Mills on the River Uruguay (Argentina* v. *Uruguay)*, *Aerial Herbicide Spraying (Ecuador* v. *Colombia)*, *Certain Activities Carried*

Out by Nicaragua in the Border Area (Costa Rica v. Nicaragua), Construction of a Road in Costa Rica Along the San Juan River (Nicaragua v. Costa Rica), and the *South China Sea Arbitration* case *(Philippines v. China).*

VOLKER MAUERHOFER holds Masters' degrees in law (1989–33), natural sciences (1992–9) and ecological economics (2002–3), and a Doctorate in Law (1993–8). Former positions include Attorney-at-Law, Senior Research Fellow and Visiting Professor at United Nations University (Japan), and Coordinating Lead Author of the United Nations' Intergovernmental Science-Policy Platform on Biodiversity and Ecosystem Services' (UN-IPBES's) Global Assessment (Chapter 6). Currently, he is an examiner and MSc theses supervisor at the University of Vienna, holding several visiting researcher positions in Japan. Besides being a member of different legal professional bodies, including the International Union for Conservation of Nature's (IUCN's) World Commission on Environmental Law (WCEL), he is also member of the Austrian United Nations Educational, Scientific and Cultural Organization Man and the Biosphere (UNESCO-MaB) Committee and a board member of the International Sustainable Development Research Society and the International Society for Ecological Economics.

DELPHINE MISONNE is Professor and Permanent Researcher (Fund for Scientific Research (FNRS), Belgium), specialising in environmental law. She holds an LLM from King's College London. She is the Head of the Environmental Law Centre (CEDRE) at Saint-Louis University, Brussels (USL-B). She teaches at Saint-Louis University, Brussels (environmental law; sectoral policies; law, governance and sustainable development) and at the Free University of Brussels (ULB) (environmental law for scientists). She is a member of the Belgian Federal Council for Sustainable Development.

HARI M. OSOFSKY is Dean of Penn State Law and the Penn State School of International Affairs, and Distinguished Professor of Law, Professor of International Affairs, and Professor of Geography. Dean Osofsky's more than fifty publications focus on improving governance and addressing injustice in energy and climate change regulation, and she has collaborated extensively with business, government, and non-profit leaders. Dean Osofsky received a JD from Yale Law School and a PhD in geography from the University of Oregon.

JACQUELINE PEEL is Professor of Law at Melbourne Law School, an Associate Director of its Centre for Resources, Energy and Environmental Law, and Associate Dean of Melbourne Law Masters. She is an international expert in international environmental law and climate law, and particularly the topic of climate litigation.

MARIE-CATHERINE PETERSMANN is a PhD fellow at the European University Institute (EUI), Florence, Italy.

KATJA RATH is Research Fellow and Lecturer in Law at Martin-Luther-University in Halle, Germany. Her areas of expertise are European environmental law and access to justice, as well as nature conservation and agri-environmental law. She is a member of the European Environmental Law Forum (EELF).

ZERRIN SAVAŞAN has a PhD from the Department of International Relations, Middle East Technical University (METU), a Master's degree from the Department of European Studies (METU) and a Bachelor's degree from Ankara University, Law Faculty. In her PhD thesis, she investigated the role of compliance mechanisms established under multilateral environmental agreements. Currently, she is Assistant Professor at Selcuk University and gives courses on Turkish law, EU law, international law and international environmental law. She is also a climate leader on the Climate Reality Project, and an International Network of Environmental Compliance and Enforcement (INECE) correspondent.

HENDRIK SCHOUKENS graduated as Master in Law at the Catholic University of Leuven in 2005. In 2007, he graduated as Master in Environmental Law at Ghent University. In 2010, he received a complementary Master's degree in Environmental Law at the Facultés Universitaires Saint-Louis and the Catholic University of Louvain. Since January 2006, he has been working as an environmental lawyer at LDR Advocaten, based in Ghent. In 2017, he successfully defended his PhD at Ghent University, on the legal aspects of ecological restoration within the context of EU environmental legislation. He is now a post-doctoral researcher at Ghent University.

MAHITO SHINDO is Assistant Professor (Legal Science Group) in the School of Social Sciences at Waseda University, Tokyo, Japan. His research interests include access to justice in environmental matters, ombudsmen, legal governance, and comparative administrative law. Mahito holds a PhD in law from Macquarie University. Before entering academia, he worked at both governmental and non-governmental organisations in the environmental field.

CHRISTINA VOIGT is Professor at the Department of Public and International Law, University of Oslo, Norway, and Environmental Coordinator for PluriCourts – Centre of Excellence. She is a member of the IUCN´s World Commission on Environmental Law (WCEL) and the Chair of the WCEL´s Climate Change Specialist Group as well as a member of the IUCN´s Climate Change Task Force. In her teaching and academic publications, she focuses on international climate change law, international courts and legal aspects of multilateralism and sustainable development. She also serves as principal legal advisor to the Government of Norway and as negotiator in the UN climate negotiations.

KURT WINTER is an Australian qualified lawyer. He holds as Master of Laws (specialising in international law) from the Australian National University, as well as a Bachelor of Laws and a Bachelor of Arts (Honours in International Relations) from the University of Queensland. He is currently Manager, Policy and Research, at AGL Energy, where he advises on climate change and energy policy.

ACKNOWLEDGEMENTS

This book is carried forward by the expectation that analysing and comparing practices and experiences from different regional and international courts and tribunals enhance mutual learning and understanding. The chapters combine various legal perspectives and traditions represented by judges, legal practitioners and academics from many different parts of the world, different ages and genders, and different career stages. Different as they are, they have a shared objective: to contribute, by the means available to courts, to protecting and conserving the environment, and to securing a dignified and environmentally sustainable life for all and an economy defined by safe ecological boundaries.

I would like to express my sincere gratitude to all who supported this book project. First and foremost, my thanks go to all the excellent authors who dedicated their time, efforts, knowledge and energy to writing the chapters and who shared their experiences, insights and reflections. I am deeply grateful for having had the privilege of working together with so many inspiring, great minds.

This project would have been impossible without the International Union for Conservation of Nature Academy of Environmental Law, the World Commission of Environmental Law and the generous support provided by PluriCourts, the Centre of Excellence for the Study of the Legitimate Roles of the Judiciary in the Global Order, at the University of Oslo, as well as the Bren School of Environmental Science and Management at the University of California Santa Barbara, and the W. S. Richardson School of Law and its Environmental Law Program at the University of Hawai'i at Mānoa, for hosting me during the editorial work on this book.

My special thanks also go to Karen Howatson for her editorial work, and to Tom Randall and Finola O'Sullivan at Cambridge University Press and the various anonymous reviewers for their support, trust and encouragement.

Christina Voigt
June 2018

TABLE OF CASES

A Permanent Court of International Justice

B International Court of Justice

C International Tribunal for the Law of the Sea

E   World Heritage Committee

F National Case Law

1 Australia

2 Japan

3 Netherlands

4   Pakistan

5   South Africa

6   United States of America

INTRODUCTION

International Courts and the Environment: the Quest for Legitimacy

CHRISTINA VOIGT

A   International Courts and the Environment: An Introduction

International courts and tribunals (ICs) are fascinating actors. They are supra-national institutions, tasked with upholding the rule of law in international affairs, and, as such, important wheels in the machinery of international law.

They are independent, while at the same time deriving their legitimacy from the establishment by states, as well as states' consent to exercising jurisdiction.[1] This means that ICs need to tread a thin line between adherence to state sovereignty on one side and protection of a common interests in the environmental asset at stake, on the other – or, more broadly, between being guarantors of stability and agents of change in the global public order.

ICs also exert political influence. They can change in domestic politics, for example, by providing legal, symbolic, and leverage (argumentative) resources that shift the political balance in favor of domestic and international actors who prefer policies more consistent with international law objectives. This (limited) power can translate into political influence and change state behavior.[2]

Because of their independence, ICs can ensure the strength, quality, and longevity of environmental protection against other interests pursued by parties. In that way, they can be defenders of existing norms. But they can also act proactively, at the forefront of norm development. This can happen in different ways. ICs could exercise a "quasi-legislative" function and develop the law by themselves. They may also suggest or request that states factor an appropriate legal response to an environmental challenge. Or they can point to ineffective or insufficient state

---

[1] K. Alter, *The New Terrain of International Law: Courts, Politics, Rights* (Princeton University Press, 2014).
[2] Ibid.

1

action, and – indirectly – identify the need for norm development. It is in the latter functions that ICs can act as proponents for a (stronger) environmental rule of law in states' international affairs – a legal framework that extends to the environment the procedural and substantive legal principles enshrined in the "rule of law".[3] However, this function may not be exercised without criticism. "Over-active" ICs could be perceived as providing obstacles to processes that may be better left to diplomatic exchanges and political decision-making.[4]

ICs play multiple roles in the global (judicial) order. Their primary role is to adjudicate disputes between states, or between states and other actors, arising out of the interpretation and application of international law. They legitimize states' claims, clarify legal positions, and announce consequences that arise from breaches of treaties or acts and omissions that do not correspond to legal duties. In doing so, they hold states accountable to their respective international legal obligations and help to ensure compliance by those subject to the rules.[5]

Some ICs, such as the International Court of Justice (ICJ) or the Seabed Disputes Chamber of the International Tribunal for the Law of the Sea (ITLOS), are also competent to give advisory opinions on questions of international law, depending on their jurisdiction. They determine what the law requires by providing authoritative interpretations, and adapt the law to new circumstances through dynamic and evolutionary interpretation.[6] By exercising such functions they play an important role in the contemporary functioning and dynamic development of international law.

Yet, ICs differ significantly in their functions, processes and outputs. Some ICs are open to states only, while others, such as the Permanent Court of Arbitration, also provide services to international organizations or private parties. Only one IC – the ICJ – has broad, general jurisdiction,

---

[3] C. Voigt (ed.), *Rule of Law for Nature* (Cambridge University Press, 2013); and C. Voigt and Z. Makuch (eds.), *Courts and the Environment* (Edward Elgar Publishing, 2018).

[4] D. Bodansky, *The Art and Craft of International Environmental Law* (Harvard University Press, 2009).

[5] See T. Squatrito et al. (eds.), *The Performance of International Courts and Tribunals* (Cambridge University Press, 2018); and O. Young, *Governing Complex Systems: Social Capital for the Anthropocene* (MIT Press, 2017).

[6] See A. von Bogdandy and I. Venzke, *In Whose Name?: A Public Law Theory of International Adjudication (International Courts and Tribunals Series)* (Cambridge University Press, 2014); and K. Alter, *The New Terrain of International Law: Courts, Politics, Rights* (Princeton University Press, 2014).

while most others are limited to particular subject areas regulated by specific treaties. Some ICs can adjudicate on punitive measures, fines and sanctions, while others are limited to making recommendations or noting inconsistencies with legal obligations. In some cases, treaty-based so-called "non-compliance" mechanisms exist, which provide additional fora for addressing inconsistencies between state behavior and international legal obligations. These mechanisms may exhibit some court-like features, but are primarily aimed at preventing, rather than punishing for, cases of potential non-compliance.

In this dispersed landscape of ICs, environmental claims are an interesting and important area to study. In the absence of a special international environmental court, disputes or claims with environmental relevance come up across a wide spectrum of ICs and in a wide range of circumstances.[7] Moreover, environmental cases hold a number of particular challenges that are not (all) present in other areas of law.

First, the main objective of an environmental claim may be to prevent, rather than seek redress for, environmental harm. Avoiding harm to occur, however, might apply only within a small window of time. Accordingly, environmental cases might be more time sensitive than other cases; a situation that sits uneasily with the slow-motion nature of international adjudication.

Secondly, there are difficulties in quantifying environmental harm once it has occurred. In general, courts have recognized material and moral damage, including environmental damage, as long as it is financially assessable.[8] For a long time, however, the question whether ICs would support the idea that environmental damage also encompasses damage to the intrinsic value of the environment, beyond resources of a direct economic value, remained an open one.[9] Only recently has the ICJ started to evaluate environmental harm in *Certain Activities Carried*

---

[7] T. Stephens, *International Courts and Environmental Protection* (Cambridge University Press, 2009).

[8] J. Crawford, *The International Law Commission's Articles on State Responsibility – Introduction, Text and Commentaries* (Cambridge University Press, 2002), p. 202. For a settlement on, inter alia, environmental damages, see: General Agreement between Iran and the United States on the Settlement of Certain ICJ and Tribunal cases of 9 February 1996, Award on Agreed Terms by order of the Iran–US Claims Tribunal, 20 February 1996, (1996) 32 Iran-U.S.C.T.R. 207, 213.

[9] P. Sands and J. Peel, *Principles of International Environmental Law*, 3rd edn. (Cambridge University Press, 2012), p. 706; and C. Voigt, "Climate Change and Damages" in C. Carlarne, K. Grey and R. Tarasofsky (eds.), *Oxford Handbook of International Climate Change Law* (Oxford University Press, 2016), pp. 464–94.

Out by Nicaragua in the Border Area (2018).[10] However, the final amount of compensation assessed against Nicaragua fell significantly short of what Costa Rica had demanded. The case is nonetheless an important precedent for recognizing conservation interests and ecosystem services; yet the question of how to quantify environmental harm is still far from settled.

Thirdly, environmental cases rely on scientific evidence of causes and effects: for example, which pollutants have which effects on ecosystem, animal or plant life or health. The science can be complex or unsettled. There might be uncertainties and loop-holes. In addition, there could be challenges in securing scientific experts who are willing to speak against vested commercial interests. Once scientific data are presented, the question arises of how to use them in order to decide a case.[11] In most cases judges are trained in law and are not experts in natural sciences. There is a need to translate complex technical data into a language that is accessible to judges. Environmental judicial practice provides some examples of how this can be done and which challenges exist.

These are only some of the circumstances that make the study of international judicial environmental practice relevant. In order to grasp international judicial practice on the environment, however, it is necessary to investigate the many various ways and means by which different international and regional courts and quasi-judicial bodies deal with environmental claims. This necessitates the study of different regional and international courts and tribunals, as well as a large variety of cases and claims. This is the aim of this book. It attempts to shed light on new developments, challenges, and possibilities and issues of legitimacy across a variety of ICs.

For the sake of clarity, it is not the intention of the book to promote the establishment of an environmental court; rather, it seeks to analyse both the procedural and substantive challenges and solutions as they arise in the context of environmental adjudication by various international and regional courts and tribunals.

---

[10] *Certain Activities Carried Out by Nicaragua in the Border Area (Costa Rica v. Nicaragua) Compensation Owed by the Republic of Nicaragua to the Republic of Costa Rica* (2018), available at: www.icj-cij.org/en/case/150

[11] C. Foster, *Science and the Precautionary Principle in International Courts and Tribunals: Expert Evidence, Burden of Proof and Finality* (Cambridge University Press, 2013); and J. Vinuales "Legal Technique for dealing with scientific uncertainty in Environmental law", *Vanderbilt Journal of Transnational Law*, 43 (2010), 438.

B The Quest for Legitimacy

Because no special IC exists for international environmental affairs, states and other actors seek to address environmental issues of a transboundary nature in different courts and tribunals on the international and regional stage. This situation gives rise to challenges and possibilities.

The possibilities lie in the fact that states can (and should) pursue various fora and strategies. In the absence of a specialist court, states and other actors may try different avenues in different courts and tribunals with the aim of achieving the desired outcome. While this situation has been criticized by some as "forum shopping",[12] such a fragmented approach can have constructive and healthy (side) effects.[13] Different courts may be asked to deal with similar legal questions pertaining to environmental issues. As a consequence, this situation could give rise to richer and more diverse judicial practice. Moreover, different courts dealing with similar issues might start referring to each others' judgments. This situation could become a counter-tendency to the fragmented structure of international law and could pave the way for a more coherent and consistent body of law. The diversity of ICs potentially available to address environmental claims should thus be seen as an advantage, rather than a constraint.

At the same time, there are challenges. In the absence of an international environmental court, environmental disputes are being addressed by ICs with either general jurisdiction (e.g. the ICJ) or ICs with other, special – but *non-environmental* – competence, such as the World Trade Organization (WTO) Dispute Settlement Body or regional Human Rights Courts.[14] In this context, environmental legal issues arise before those ICs either as questions of justified exceptions or extensions of legal rights and obligations, but in general not as the basis of claims.

This situation raises a number of legitimacy questions, which are addressed in the six parts of this book.

---

[12] G. Marceau, "Conflicts of Norms and Conflicts of Jurisdictions, The Relationship between the WTO Agreement and MEAs and other Treaties", *JWT*, 35(6) (2001), 1082.

[13] M. Koskenniemi, *The Gentle Civilizer of Nations – The Rise and Fall of International Law 1870–1960, Series: Hersch Lauterpacht Memorial Lectures (No. 14)* (Cambridge University Press, 2001/2004); M. Koskenniemi and P. Leino, "Fragmentation of International Law? Postmodern Anxieties", *Leiden Journal of International Law*, 15 (2002), 579.

[14] See, for example, E. Grant and C. Voigt, "The Legitimacy of Human Rights Courts in Environmental Disputes – Editorial", *Journal of Human Rights and the Environment* 2, 1 (2015), 131–38; and N. Hayashi and C. Bailliet (eds.), *The Legitimacy of International Criminal Tribunals* (Cambridge University Press, 2017).

1   Procedural Legitimacy of Judicial Environmental Practice: Access to Justice

First, there are issues of *procedural legitimacy* of judicial environmental practice, especially with regard to standing, access to courts and admissibility. Environmental law often concerns community interests. It is a field of international law in which public interest norms and environmental issues as common concerns are well recognized. Many of the challenges that ICs face are rife with externalities: Actions or omissions by one state can affect other states, areas beyond national jurisdiction or even the international community *per se*.[15] This situation leads to important and difficult questions of how to protect a general, public interest in the environment, of legal standing and access to courts for those states that are not directly injured, by individual persons or environmental organizations.[16]

2   Legitimacy and Scientific Certainty: Environmental Adjudication, Use of Experts and the Limits of Science

Secondly, another procedural aspect arises with respect to scientific evidence, expertise and the use of experts. Environmental cases often involve complex scientific data. Such scientific evidence might not always be easily accessible to judges; neither might it be conclusive. The use of independent experts is therefore often suggested to ICs. In the face of complex environmental challenges, there is often a lack of absolute knowledge about the causes and effects of changes in the environment, creating scientific uncertainties and controversies. These scientific

---

[15] J. Brunnée, "International Environmental Law and Community Interests: Procedural Aspects" in E. Benvenisti and G. Nolte (eds.), *Community Obligations in International Law* (Oxford University Press, 2017); J. Brunnee, "«Common Interests» – Echoes from an Empty Shell? Some Thoughts on Common Interest and International Environmental Law" *Max-Planck-Institut für ausländisches öffentliches Recht und Völkerrecht*, (1989), 793; D. Bodansky, "Global Public Goods, International Law, and Legitimacy" *European Journal of International Law*, 23 (2012), 651–68; and B. Simma, "From Bilateralism to Community Interest in International Law", in *Collected Courses of the Hague Academy of International Law*, The Hague Academy of International Law, 250 (1994).

[16] See Chapter 1 in this book: Ludwig Krämer, "The Environment before the European Court of Justice"; Chapter 2: Katja Rath, "The EU Aarhus Regulation and EU Administrative Acts Based on the Aarhus Regulation: The Withdrawal of the CJEU from the Aarhus Convention"; and Chapter 3: Hendrik Schoukens, "Access to Justice before EU Courts in Environmental Cases against the Backdrop of the Aarhus Convention: Balancing Pathological Stubbornness and Cognitive Dissonance?".

uncertainties are placing adjudicators in a difficult position. Kanhanga notes in this context:

> When faced with complex scientific evidence in environmental cases, adjudicators need the capacity to gain an accurate and deep understanding of the science behind the environmental case. If not, the likelihood of making an uninformed decision is more serious and inevitable. However, the insight needed to make sound legal decisions emanates from experts consulted by the courts. While the purpose of expert opinion is to assist the court in giving judgment upon the issues submitted to it for decision, the court must still discharge its judicial functions such as the interpretation of legal rules, the legal categorization of factual issues and the assessment of the burden of proof.[17]

Moreover, the judges and arbitrators on those ICs may not be too well versed in international environmental law and meet challenges in capacity and expertise in this regard, too.

A further procedural aspect applies to the burden of proof, which in general lies with the claimant of an environmental violation by the respondent. Where science is uncertain while there is a risk of harm, this (impossible) burden might challenge the fairness – and thus legitimacy – of judicial proceedings. In this context, the role and potential of the precautionary principle, and whether it could lead to a reversal to the burden of proof, are highly relevant.[18]

3 Judges as Law-Makers: Legitimate Development of Environmental Law

Thirdly, a legitimacy concern arises in situations when judges develop the law, rather than just applying it.[19] This can be referred to as a "*substantive legitimacy*". In other words, can courts be law-makers? Where does the judicial function end and a legislative function begin, and to what extent

---

[17] See Chapter 4: Tracey Kanhanga, "Scientific Uncertainties: A Nightmare for Environmental Adjudicators". See also: *Pulp Mills on the River Uruguay (Argentina v. Uruguay)*, Judgment, ICJ Reports 2010, 14, Joint Dissenting Opinion of Judges Al-Khasawneh and Simma, para. 6, at: www.icj-cij.org/files/case-related/135/135-20100420-JUD-01-01-EN.pdf,(last accessed on 03/06/2018).

[18] See Chapter 5: Volker Mauerhofer, "Ignorance, Uncertainty and Biodiversity: Decision Making by the Court of Justice of the European Union".

[19] T. Squatrito et al. (eds.), *The Performance of International Courts and Tribunals* (Cambridge University Press, 2018); K. Alter, *The New Terrain of International Law: Courts, Politics, Rights* (Princeton University Press, 2014); and J. Dunoff and M. Pollack (eds.), *Interdisciplinary Perspectives on International Law and International Relations: The State of the Art* (Cambridge University Press, 2013).

can the latter be exercised justifiably? While this is a long-standing concern regarding any judiciary body, it is more pronounced in environmental cases. Environmental challenges of a collective nature, such as climate change or the decline of biological diversity, require multilateral solutions by international environmental treaties that have a legitimate place in the public global order. This public (or community) interest is recognized by international environmental law, which makes it a particularly interesting area for studying the interaction between the global judiciary and legal advances. At the same time, international environmental treaty law may not be so concise or advanced as to provide a clear legal basis for a claim. It is often based on principles and/or legal obligations that grant significant discretion to the parties. Examples of such principles are good faith,[20] prohibition of transboundary harm[21] or a high level of environmental protection.[22] In a judicial setting, judges might be asked to concretize or specify these principles into legal rules which they apply, walking a tight-rope between application and development of the law. Moreover, in cases in which the treaty does not contain environmental rights, for example most human rights treaties,[23] or where environmental concerns are drawn in in the context of exception clauses,[24] judges might need to apply some legal creativity within their legal boundaries in order to accommodate legitimate environmental concerns.

Human rights law provides a particularly interesting case example. Despite the growing contemporary awareness of the intimacy between environmental quality and fundamental human rights and interests, it remains the case that very few international human rights agreements explicitly recognize the close interconnection between human rights and the environment. Even fewer recognize a human right to a healthy

[20] See Chapter 6: Kazuki Hagiwara, "Sustainable Development before International Courts and Tribunals: Duty to Cooperate and States' Good Faith".
[21] See Chapter 7: Kurt Winter, "The Paris Agreement: New Legal Avenues to Support a Transboundary Harm Claim on the Basis of Climate Change".
[22] See Chapter 8: Delphine Misonne, "The Court of Justice of the European Union and the High Level of Environmental Protection – Transforming a Policy Objective into a Concept Amenable to Judicial Review".
[23] Dinah Shelton, "Legitimate and necessary: adjudicating human rights violations related to activities causing environmental harm or risk", *Journal of Human Rights and the Environment*, 6(2), September 2015, 139–55; and E. Grant and C. Voigt, "The Legitimacy of Human Rights Courts in Environmental Disputes – Editorial", *Journal of Human Rights and the Environment*, 1 (2015), 2, 131–38.
[24] C. Voigt, *Sustainable Development as a Principle of International Law – Resolving Conflicts between Climate Measures and WTO Law* (Martinus Nijhoff Publishers, 2009).

environment. In fact, environmental rights have been proclaimed in only two regional human rights treaties: the African Charter of Human and Peoples' Rights[25] and the Additional Protocol to the American Convention on Human Rights.[26] Other human rights treaties contain no such explicit guarantees. The European Convention on Human Rights (ECHR), for example, does not provide for a right to a healthy environment and is thus dependent on the interpretation of other, explicitly enumerated, human rights to include or to extend to environmental matters. This is an interpretive strategy now widely recognizable in the practice of regional human rights courts, which have been increasingly active in applying existing general human rights norms to environmental issues – and environmentally sensitive interpretive strategies to existing human rights and jurisprudence. As a result, these human rights courts and bodies have begun to develop an important body of environment-related human rights jurisprudence in relation to procedural rights as well as to substantive rights. Taken together, such developments provide strong evidence of converging trends towards greater uniformity and certainty concerning human rights obligations relating to the environment.

4   Legitimacy of Outcomes: Performance, Effects (and Side-Effects)

Fourthly, adjudication can have legal or political effects beyond a particular case and/or outside the parties involved. These effects may not be intended or within the control of the judicial organ. The question is whether courts would be legitimately expected to consider such wider consequences or whether they are simply outside the realm of the deciding court. Courts, and ICs in particular, are organs that are sensitive to political and legal tensions and criticism. In particular, questions of conflict of norms,[27] normative development beyond the court[28] and

---

[25] Article 24, Organization of African Unity (OAU), African Charter on Human and Peoples' Rights ("Banjul Charter"), 27 June 1981, CAB/LEG/67/3 rev. 5, 21 I.L.M. 58 (1982), available at: www.refworld.org/docid/3ae6b3630.html (accessed 13 May 2018).

[26] Article 11, Organization of American States, Additional Protocol to the American Convention on Human Rights in the Area of Economic, Social, and Cultural Rights ("Protocol of San Salvador"), 17 November 1988, OAS Doc. OAS/Ser.L/V/I.4 rev. 13.

[27] See Chapter 9: Marie-Catherine Petersmann, "When Environmental Protection and Human Rights Collide: Four Heuristics of Conflict Resolution".

[28] See Chapter 10: Cristiane Derani and Arthur Rodrigues Dalmarco, "Silent Implications of US-Tuna II: Greening Market Behaviour through the WTO".

shifts in legal strategies by parties in response to previous judgments point to the issue of extended "judicial influence".

For example, states are increasingly invoking the jurisdiction of ICs and tribunals to adjudicate legal matters relating to the obligation to carry out an Environmental Impact Assessment (EIA). The increase in such disputes comes as a response to previous difficulties of ICs in granting compensation for environmental harm. Loewenstein notes that:

> Framing a dispute as one concerning EIA instead of – or in addition to – a claim for environmental harm may be advantageous. An EIA claim does not require a state, for example, to establish that harm occurred; nor must it prove a causal link between the respondent state's alleged delinquency and the harm it allegedly caused. Moreover, by putting its claim in terms of EIA, a claimant may challenge the respondent state's allegedly delin-quent actions before any harm has materialized or, indeed, even prior to the implementation of the project. The claimant can thus seek to influence the project through the adjudicative process.[29]

But where does the sphere of normative influence for which the court may assert responsibility end, and which implications of deci-sions simply lie outside the court's concern? The question is whether ICs can "ignite" change and transformation, where effective treaty law is missing or where parties do not comply with their obligations, or whether litigation before an IC is a limited tool to answer specific questions of international law. This is particularly opportune with regard to environmental goods of global common nature. Here, press-ing questions arise as to whether ICs, typically addressing issues between two parties, are well suited to dealing with problems of common concern. If they are, what is the effect of their findings on the collective ability to address the environmental problem at stake through the development of effective international norms?

Also, the repercussions of judgments of ICs on domestic law and domestic courts raise interesting questions. To what extent, if any, should ICs be familiar with and sensitive to domestic circumstances? Because (most) ICs are limited in their jurisdictional scope, national courts might provide an important avenue to pursue international environmental obligations. But what is the interplay, if any, between domestic and international environmental judicial practice? Could we foresee a stronger judicial interaction between national and international courts

---

[29] See Chapter 11: Andrew B. Loewenstein, "Adjudication of Environmental Impact Assessment Claims before International Courts and Tribunals".

in such matters? Can domestic courts pave the way for ICs on addressing new environmental challenges, such as climate change? Climate change raises complex questions of legal standing, scientific evidence, causality, multiplicity of actors etc. The accumulation of domestic case law and the crystallization of successful legal arguments could provide a stepping stone for ICs to follow.[30]

5   The Legitimacy of Non-Compliance Procedures

Fifthly, in some areas in international environmental law, so-called non-compliance mechanisms are established within treaties. These mechanisms first and foremost aim to prevent non-compliance by parties, to identify challenges that parties might experience and to address them in collaboration with the respective party. The rise of these mechanisms occurred as a result of the absence of an international environmental court, but mostly because of the multilateral set-up of defining the environmental obligations. The acceptance of compulsory jurisdiction by parties to a multilateral environmental agreement in order to oversee compliance might be to the detriment of the stringency of legal obligations contained in that agreement and/or the willingness of states to join the treaty.[31] It might, thus, be counter-productive to the overall effectiveness of the treaty in addressing the environmental challenge at stake. Finally, the need to prevent, rather than mitigate, environmental harm, speaks for in-house solutions that aim to avoid non-compliance in the first place, rather than *ex post factum* adjudication.

However, some of the features of non-compliance procedures are reminiscent of adjudication, while others clearly are not.[32] It is thus important to scrutinize the practice of those mechanisms from the perspective of comparative advantages to ICs,[33] as well as their legitimacy

---

[30] See Chapter 12: Jacqueline Peel and Hari M. Osofsky, "Litigation as a Climate Regulatory Tool".

[31] S. Barrett, *Environment and Statecraft: The Strategy of Environmental Treaty-Making* (Oxford University Press, 2003); R. B. Mitchell, 'Compliance Theory' in D. Bodansky, J. Brunnée and E. Hey (eds.), *The Oxford Handbook of International Environmental Law* (Oxford University Press, 2007), p. 893.

[32] See, for example, G. Ulfstein and J. Werksman, "The Kyoto Compliance System: Towards Hard Enforcement" in O. Schram Stokke, J. Hovi and G. Ulfstein (eds.), *Implementing the Climate Regime: International Compliance* (Earthscan, 2005), pp. 39–62.

[33] See Chapter 13: Anna Huggins, "Administrative Procedures and Rule of Law Values in the Montreal Compliance System".

in situations in which they act as "quasi-courts".[34] Huggins, for example, argues, that

> although the administrative procedures and mechanisms for non-compliance under the Montreal compliance system at times facilitate departure from binding legal rules, this administrative action is nevertheless constrained by administrative mechanisms for accountability, transparency, participation and reason giving … Such constraints are important as numerous scholars claim that procedural rigour and integrity enhance normative legitimacy in international law.[35] The adoption of administrative procedures is one way to promote right process, and thereby to address legitimacy concerns regarding MEA compliance decisions.[36]

6   The Limits of Environmental Justice through Courts: Balancing Legitimacy with the Need for Creativity

Sixthly, and finally, ICs face limits in granting environmental justice. Not all environmental claims can or should be addressed by ICs. Rather, this situation begs for creativity in ensuring states' compliance with their international environmental obligations. Suggestions made here include the establishment of an environmental ombudsman as an accountability mechanism in order to improve the legitimacy of administrative environmental decision-making.[37]

Another example is the increased use of non-governmental organizations (NGOs)[38] and communities[39] for collaborating in compliance monitoring of states and private commercial actors. For example, NGOs have used petitions as a mechanism for monitoring state behavior. In its most basic form, a petition is a written instrument given from an individual to a state to address a grievance. In the case of World Heritage,

---

[34] See Chapter 14: Zerin Savaşan, "Legitimacy Questions of Non-Compliance Procedures: Examples from the Kyoto and Montreal Protocols".

[35] See S. Cassese, "A Global Due Process of Law?" in G. Anthony, J.-B. Auby, J. Morison and T. Zwart (eds.), *Values in Global Administrative Law* (Hart Publishing, 2011), pp. 19–20; D. C. Esty, "Good Governance at the Supranational Level: Globalizing Administrative Law", *Yale Law Journal*, 115 (2006) 1490, 1509–14.

[36] See Chapter 13.

[37] See Chapter 15: Mahito Shindo, "Environmental Ombudsman: Its Role in the System of Accountability Mechanisms for Administrative Environmental Decision Making".

[38] See Chapter 16: Evan Hamman, "The Role of NGOs in Monitoring Compliance under the World Heritage Convention: Options for an Improved Tripartite Regime".

[39] See Chapter 17: Lisa Chamberlain, "Beyond Litigation: the Need for Creativity in Working to Realize Environmental Rights".

petitions have been used by NGOs to bring issues of non-compliance to the attention of the World Heritage Committee. While the Committee eventually accepted their petitions, the proceedings raise some legitimacy concerns. There is no formal process or format for their use, and thus the legal status and impact of petitioning are highly questionable.[40]

In this context, Chamberlain points out: "What is clear is that communities affected by environmental harm, and the lawyers who support them, will have to devise and experiment with creative strategies outside the conventional litigious box. The realization of environmental rights depends on it."[41]

All in all, the diffuse landscape of ICs dealing or potentially dealing with environmental claims together with the evolving legal substance, innovative use of principles, evolutionary interpretation of existing norms etc., are well worth watching and studying. They provide for a level of innovation, creativity and flexibility in judicial practice that certainly does not lag behind – while not being at the forefront of – legal developments in other areas of international law.

Studying international judicial practice with regard to environmental protection therefore means analyzing the practice of various, very different adjudicative bodies that are *not specialized* in environmental law. Such a wide spread of non-specialized adjudicative bodies involves the careful study and analysis of a significant amount of case law and invites a comparison of how different adjudicative and quasi-adjudicative bodies treat environmental issues. It also provides a basis for an analysis of common challenges and practices provided for in this book.

C Analyzing Judicial Practice on the Environment: Why Now?

If the reasons mentioned above were not already sufficiently compelling for analysis the practice of ICs on the environment, there are at least three further factors that make such study highly relevant and timely.

1 An "Environmental" Turn to Courts

First, as environmental pressure grows worldwide, we are witnessing a "turn to international courts" in environmental matters.[42] An increasing

---

[40] See Chapter 16.
[41] See Chapter 17.
[42] Stephens, *International Courts and Environmental Protection*.

number of claims concerning environmental aspects are being brought
before the ICJ, the WTO dispute settlement system (especially with
regard to renewable energy), the ITLOS, regional human rights
courts,[43] and investment treaty arbitration etc.[44]

Only within the last two years – 2017 and 2018 – several ground-
breaking environmental decisions were rendered by ICs. In 2017, the
International Court for the Settlement of Investment Disputes (ICSID)
tribunal decided to award US$39 million in damages to Ecuador for
environmental remediation costs.[45] On 23 September 2017, the ITLOS
issued an order in *Dispute Concerning Delimitation of the Maritime
Boundary between Ghana and Côte d'Ivoire in the Atlantic Ocean
(Ghana/Côte d'Ivoire)* (Case 23), prescribing provisional measures protecting the marine environment, *including* the suspension of all
ongoing oil exploration and exploitation operations in a disputed
area.[46]

On 2 February 2018, the in the conjoined *Costa Rica v. Nicaragua/
Nicaragua v. Costa Rica* cases the ICJ ordered Nicaragua to pay compensation to Costa Rica for environmental damage.[47] The compensation
granted to Costa Rica is for environmental damage which arose from
Nicaragua's activities in excavating a caño for navigation and removing
trees and vegetation. In 2010, Costa Rica had instituted proceedings with
the ICJ against the Republic of Nicaragua for unlawful incursion, occupation and use of Costal Rican territory, including claims of serious
environmental. Nicaragua responded by instituting proceedings against
Costa Rica in 2011, claiming violations of Nicaraguan sovereignty and
major environmental damage arising from a road construction works by
Costa Rica along the border area between the two countries. In 2013, the
Court joined the two cases.

---

[43] Grant and Voigt, "The Legitimacy of Human Rights Courts in Environmental Disputes –
Editorial".

[44] D. Behn and O. K. Fauchald, "Governments under Cross-Fire?", (2015) *Manch JIEcL*,
2 2(12).

[45] ICSID, *Burlington Resources, Inc. v. Republic of Ecuador*: www.italaw.com/sites/default/
files/case-documents/italaw8206.pdf (last accessed 3 June 2018).

[46] ITLOS, *Dispute Concerning Delimitation of the Maritime Boundary between Ghana and
Côte d'Ivoire in the Atlantic Ocean*, available at: www.itlos.org/fileadmin/itlos/docu
ments/cases/case_no.23/23_published_texts/2015_23_Ord_25_Avr_2015-E.pdf   (last
accessed 3 June 2018).

[47] ICJ, *Certain Activities Carried Out by Nicaragua in the Border Area (Costa Rica
v. Nicaragua) Compensation Owed by the Republic of Nicaragua to the Republic of Costa
Rica* (2018), available at: www.icj-cij.org/en/case/150 (last accessed 3 June 2018).

The Courts granted US$120,000 compensation, based on the principle that a breach of an obligation gives rise to an obligation to make reparation in adequate form. However, the ICJ failed to provide details as to how it calculated the value of the impairment or losses to the environmental services provided. The ICJ's way of quantifying environmental damages was criticized as an "'incrementalist' approach to quantification and empirical proof for every head of damage asserted – a methodologically ambiguous and context-sensitive approach which is not easily replicable for future environmental cases, given the complex nature of environmental damages in any given dispute."[48]

Although the final amount of compensation fell significantly short of what Costa Rica had demanded, the case is nonetheless an important precedent for recognizing conservation interests and ecosystem services. In her excellent analysis of the case, Oral notes: "There was no dispute between the parties that damage to the environment was compensable under international law. What is significant is that Court recognized ecosystem services as part of the compensable damage to the environment, including both direct and indirect services. The Court stated that "damage to the environment, and the consequent impairment or loss of the ability of the environment to provide goods and services, is compensable under international law," which may include indemnification for such impairment or loss or payment for restoration of the damaged environment.[49]

Oral summarizes the importance of the case in the following way: "Notably, it is the first time, that [. . .] the International Court of Justice has decided an environmental compensation case. Secondly, and most importantly it marks a clear affirmation that environmental damage includes ecosystem services."[50]

---

[48] D. Desierto, *Environmental Damages, Environmental Reparations, and the Right to a Healthy Environment: The ICJ Compensation Judgment in Costa Rica v. Nicaragua and the IACtHR Advisory Opinion on Marine Protection for the Greater Caribbean*, EJIL: Talk!, 14 February 2018: www.ejiltalk.org/environmental-damages-environmental-reparations-and-the-right-to-a-healthy-environment-the-icj-compensation-judgment-in-costa-rica-v-nicaragua-and-the-iacthr-advisory-opinion-on-marine-protection (last accessed 3 June 2018).

[49] N. Oral, "The ICJ renders it first environmental compensation decision: A summary of the judgment": www.iucn.org/news/world-commission-environmental-law/201804/icj-renders-it-first-environmental-compensation-decision-summary-judgment) (last accessed on 3/06/2018).

[50] Ibid.

On 7 February 2018, the Inter-American Court on Human Rights (IACtHR) Inter-American Court's Advisory Opinion (AO) on Environment and Human Rights released its latest and potentially most significant decision in this series of high-profile international judicial rulings, which acknowledge legal consequences for environmental harm. In its AO on Environment and Human Rights, the court focused on state obligations under international environmental law and human rights law in the transboundary context, in particular as concerns the construction and operation of infrastructure mega-projects, petroleum exploration and exploitation, maritime transportation of hydrocarbons, construction and enlargement of ports and shipping canals.

The AO has been characterized as a landmark in several respects.[51] It is the IACtHR's first pronouncement on State obligations concerning environmental protection under the American Charter on Human Rights (§ 46). Indeed, it is the first-ever ruling by an international human rights court that truly examines environmental law as a systemic whole, as distinct from isolated examples of environmental harm analogous to private law nuisance claims. As noted by Feria-Tinta: "Perhaps most importantly, it is a landmark in the evolving jurisprudence on 'diagonal' human rights obligations, i.e. obligations capable of being invoked by individual or groups against States other than their own. The AO opens a door – albeit in a cautious and pragmatic way – to cross-border human rights claims arising from transboundary environmental impacts."[52] Under existing international law, it was unclear whether a state may be obliged to require multinationals domiciled in its territory to adopt, at the headquarters level, policies and frameworks to ensure that subsidiaries or supply chain partners in the Global South do not infringe human rights in their places of operation. The reasoning in the AO supports such obligation at a general level. This has been done with great care in balancing between the fundamental

---

[51] G. Vega-Barbosa and L. Aboagye, "Human Rights and the Protection of the Environment: The Advisory Opinion of the Inter-American Court of Human Rights", *EJIL:Talk!*, 26 February, 2018, available at: www.ejiltalk.org/human-rights-and-the-protection-of-the-environment-the-advisory-opinion-of-the-inter-american-court-of-human-rights (last accessed 3 June 2018).

[52] M. Feria-Tinta, "The Rise of Environmental Law in International Dispute Resolution: Inter-American Court of Human Rights issues Landmark Advisory Opinion on Environment and Human Rights", *EJIL:Talk!*, 26 February 2018, available at: www.ejiltalk.org/the-rise-of-environmental-law-in-international-dispute-resolution-inter-american-court-of-human-rights-issues-landmark-advisory-opinion-on-environment-and-human-rights (last accessed 3 June 2018).

nature of the right to a healthy environment as a necessary condition for enjoyment of human rights generally, and continuing to treat extraterritorial obligations and claims as "exceptional".

Moreover, although the IACtHR in its AO does not address climate change, commentators have noted that some of the Court's observations on states' duties "are clearly pertinent to this ultimate example of transboundary harm. Moreover, the Court's reasoning on the 'jurisdiction' issue could be used to support an argument that a State's contribution to the accumulation of greenhouse gases in the atmosphere should result in State responsibility and accountability under the ACHR to victims living in other States, e.g. persons whose lands have become submerged or uncultivable due to rising sea levels."[53]

These cases are an example of a "turn to courts", as they are a challenge and chance for ICs to define, redefine or strengthen their role in the global public order. There is a need to understand the intricate dynamics of ICs "impacts" as actors embedded in the global public order.

The practice of ICs can go both ways: it could be inhibiting or facilitating legal development. Litigation may serve as a mechanism for defending the *status quo* or for promoting movement toward global environmental change. Court judgments may 'freeze' development, making it even more difficult to attain political progress or they might accelerate it. Both those wanting to protect their vested sovereign interest and those desiring to pursue a common concern for an environmental good may look to ICs as institutions that may prove useful in promoting their causes. Moreover, the judicial channel often provides a "last-resort"

---

[53] Ibid. For comparison and discussion of the ICJ case and the Advisory Opinion of the IACtHR, see D. Desierto, "Environmental Damages, Environmental Reparations, and the Right to a Healthy Environment: The ICJ Compensation Judgment in *Costa Rica v. Nicaragua* and the IACtHR Advisory Opinion on Marine Protection for the Greater Caribbean", *EJIL:Talk!*, 14 February 2018, available at: www.ejiltalk.org/environmental-damages-environmental-reparations-and-the-right-to-a-healthy-environment-the-icj-compensation-judgment-in-costa-rica-v-nicaragua-and-the-iacthr-advisory-opinion-on-marine-protection (last accessed 3 June 2018). Desierto notes, critically: "The Court's reasoning in its Judgment on compensation nowhere surveys the considerably evolved scientific landscape on short-term and long-term environmental damages assessment for complex environmental phenomena such as biodiversity, energy, air quality, and raw materials – as well as the climate change impacts that will also be felt in the affected area. This would have been a far more visionary Judgment – emulating the scientific bases for interlocking State responsibilities for prevention, remediation, and mitigation that were recognized in the IACtHR's Advisory Opinion – had the Court at least transparently discussed the evidence before it and any use it made, if any, of the highly developed scientific resources of the international community today."

when other political or diplomatic channel are blocked or exhausted. Environmental judicial practice of ICs may therefore exert a normative force beyond the particular claim at stake; it can impact on transnational, political issues and on the development of rules to protect the environment.[54] Yet, it can be a "double-edged sword": ICs could be conservative, guard stability and inhibit change or they could be proactive and promote change.

There is also another, procedural aspect to this: The turn to courts in environmental matters might concern both national and international courts. Could we foresee a stronger judicial interaction between national and international courts in such matters? Does the turn to ICs also open possibilities for non-state actors, which has traditionally been more difficult at the interstate level? The inclusion of non-state actors on the international level, however, might be a particularly important element in triggering legal changes.

2   The "Judicialization" of International Politics

We also see a recent phenomenon – sometimes referred to as "judicialization of politics" – of an increased reliance on courts and judicial means for addressing core moral predicaments, public policy questions, and political controversies.[55] This phenomenon has mainly been analyzed with respect to the influence of decisions of national courts, e.g. the US Supreme Court, on matters of national politics. A growing legislative deference to the judiciary, an increasing intrusion of the judiciary into the prerogatives of legislatures and executives, and a corresponding acceleration of the judicialization of political agendas has led to criticism, for instance concerning the anti-democratic role of judicial review.[56] Judicialization of this type arguably also applies to ICs, which raises similar concerns for their influence in international and domestic policy- and law-making.

---

[54] L. Vanhala, "The comparative politics of courts and climate change", *Environmental Politics*, 22 (2013), 3.

[55] T. Vallinder, "The Judicialization of Politics. La judicialisation de la politique", *International Political Science Review / Revue internationale de science politique*, 15 (2) (1994), 91–99.

[56] R. Hirschl, "The Judicialization of Mega-Politics and the Rise of Political Courts", *Annual Review of Political Science*, 1 (2008), 93–118.

3   Global Power Shifts

We are also witnessing global power shifts towards a more dispersed, pluri-centric global power structure. With the hegemonic power of the United States waning[57] and the European Union struggling to define its own role[58] emerging powers such as China, India and Brazil shift the balance of geo-political power. This has significant implications for the protection of common environmental goods and shared resources.[59] International regimes to address climate change, the protection of biological diversity outside national jurisdiction and the establishment of marine protected areas are particularly prone to being impacted by such political changes. Can we observe a relationship between global power structures and political, legal and institutional developments that seeks to establish and maintain the conditions for sustainable development and lasting access to common global resources?[60] It has been claimed that emerging powers from the Global South seem to largely agree with the goals and values that guide the international order, such as multilateral problem solving, state sovereignty, rule of law.[61] Yet, important questions arise as to whether they bring a certain criticism or even reluctance towards existing international institutions, including ICs and the many privileges often enjoyed by established great powers.[62]

Do the cases and findings of ICs reflect international power shifts, or are they neutral and independent from them? Are those changing structures based on globally coordinated responses with international and

[57] R. Falk, "American Hegemony and the Global Environment", *International Studies Review*, 7 (2005), 585–99; R. Falk, *Power Shift: On the New Global Order* (Zed Books, 2016); and R. Falk et al. (eds.), *International Law and the Third World – Reshaping Justice* (Routledge, 2008).

[58] R. Falkner and H. Anheier (eds.), "Special issue: Europe and the world: global insecurity and power shifts", *Global Policy*, (2017), 8.

[59] S. Alam et al. (eds.), *International Environmental Law and the Global South* (Cambridge University Press, 2015); and A. Anghie, *Imperialism, Sovereignty and the Making of International Law* (Cambridge University Press, 2005).

[60] K. Bosselmann, *The Principle of Sustainability: Transforming law and governance*,2nd edn. (Routledge, 2016); and C. Voigt, *Sustainable Development as a Principle of International Law – Resolving Conflicts between Climate Measures and WTO Law* (Martinus Nijhoff Publishers, 2009).

[61] O. Stuenkel, *Post-Western World: How Emerging Powers Are Remaking Global Order* (Polity Press, 2016); M. Sanwal, *The World's Search for Sustainable Development – A Perspective from the Global South* (Cambridge University Press, 2015); and Falk, *International Law and the Third World – Reshaping Justice*.

[62] A. Acharya, *The End of the American World Order* (Polity Books, 2014); and R. K. Betts, "Institutional Imperialism", *The National Interest*, 113 (2011).

regional organizations and non-state actors – or are these actors getting more marginalized?[63] The new geo-political reality affects ICs, especially when making decisions on legal questions that concern common environmental goods and shared resources. But the question is: in what way do changing political landscapes impact use of and compliance with ICs? Do we see more or less willingness to accept the compulsory jurisdiction of and active use of relevant ICs in newer practice and international environmental treaties?

This book does not attempt to trace the influence, either directly or indirectly, of the identified IC decisions on the development of international norms or principles, treaties or even regimes for environmental protection. It would be difficult to establish a causal, direct relationship. However, throughout the various chapters, the book establishes a case for a connection between ICs' jurisprudence and successive normative developments; and shows that some of the decisions by ICs had a transformative effect in the sense that they led to mobilization of state action. This happened in the form of initiating an international discourse of the matter addressed or by leading to regulatory changes in national legal systems beyond the ones of the parties to the dispute concerned.

D   Expectations and Outlook

This books analyzes recent cases with environmental aspects brought before international and regional courts and tribunals. It emerges that ICs engage in questions of environmental protection, for example on the question of appropriateness of level of environmental protection or in giving authoritative statements of the concrete obligations contained in treaty provisions that, more often than not, are of an ambiguous nature. Moreover, the book also reveals a tendency of courts to engage in dynamic treaty interpretation and the crystallization of new norms and principles to protect the environment. It shows that, to a large extent, ICs are responsive to the (high) expectations of the environmental community and go to great length in applying thorough care in clarifying, developing and extending the norms of environmental protection. ICs are also sensitive to criticism when they do not do so.

---

[63] R. Falk, *Power Shift: On the New Global Order* (Zed Books, 2016); C. Bailliet (ed.), *Non-State Actors, Soft Law and Protective Regimes: From the Margins* (Cambridge University Press, 2014); and J. Dunoff, S. Ratner and S. Wippman, *Law: Norms, Actors, Process* (Aspen Casebook, 2015).

Strong judicial statements by an IC can have a normative effect far beyond the state parties to the dispute concerned. It could, eventually, provide a normative building block in a greener global order.

In any case, the practice of ICs – whether it progresses the development of environmental norms or inhibits it – has repercussions for how states act and organize themselves in the area of environmental multilateralism.[64] Eventually, the quest of this book is to shed light on this intricate and complex relationship between the decisions by ICs and their rippling effects in the further development of the international legal framework to protect the environment.

Perhaps the book raises more questions than it answers. The hope, however, is that it stimulates more discussion and more research that contributes to the understanding of the intricate interplay between the global judiciary and norm development with regard to environmental protection at a time of globally shifting power structures. The expected effect is the emergence of *a new way of thinking* about ICs as agents of environmental change. Such novel understanding is urgently necessary so that we can fully grasp the powers and limitations of ICs as independent institutions of international governance in times of both political and environmental change. It might even be urgently *needed* to prevent irreversible global environmental harm.

---

[64] J. Dunoff and M. Pollack (eds.), *Interdisciplinary Perspectives on International Law and International Relations: the State of the Art* (Cambridge University Press, 2013); and A. Hurrell, *On Global Order: Power, Values, and the Constitution of International Society* (Oxford University Press, 2007).

PART I

Procedural Legitimacy of Judicial Environmental
Practice: Access to Justice

The Environment before the European Court of Justice

LUDWIG KRÄMER

A Introduction

This chapter will, in its first section, deal with standing in environmental matters before the courts of the European Union (EU), and in particular the standing of natural and legal persons (section B). The next section will address the role and activity of the European Commission in environmental matters (section C). A subsequent section will discuss issues of substantive environmental law (section D). A general evaluation will conclude the contribution (section E).

B Access of the Environment to the EU Courts (Standing)

1 General Questions on Standing

When the European Commission is of the opinion that an EU Member State failed to fulfil one of its obligations under the Treaty on European Union (TEU) or the Treaty on the Functioning of the European Union (TFEU) or flowing out of an EU regulation, directive or decision, it may bring the matter before the European Court of Justice (ECJ) under Article 258 TFEU. It has to comply with the pre-judicial requirements of that provision before applying to the Court. However, no further requirement with regard to standing is necessary. When the Commission takes up a case against a Member State, which case it takes up and whether it treats all Member States that failed to fulfil a specific legal obligation in the same way are not checked by the Court. Neither need the Commission prove any interest, of itself or of the EU as a whole, in order to bring a case.

Under Article 259 TFEU, a Member State may bring another Member State before the Court for its failure to comply with the requirements of EU environmental law. It would not have to demonstrate that it is affected by such a failure – or demonstrate any interest in the case. The objective fact of non-compliance is sufficient to allow the action to be brought forward. In practice, though, such a case has never occurred in environmental matters.

Also, when a Member State or the European Parliament brings an action against an EU institution for not having complied with environmental legal obligations (Article 263(2) TFEU), no interest need be proven. In order to have access to the General Court, it is sufficient for the applicant to argue that environmental provisions have not been complied with.

In preliminary cases under Article 267 TFEU, it is the national court that submits the request to the European Court for a preliminary ruling that assumes responsibility for deciding whether the question submitted to the Court is of relevance for its decision of the national litigation. This decision by the national court is controlled by the ECJ in only very limited circumstances: where it becomes obvious that the procedure before the national court was not a true litigation, but a fake one, in order to obtain an interpretative decision by the European Court, the taking of a preliminary decision may be refused. The same applies when it is obvious that the questions raised do not concern EU law, or do not have any bearing on the national litigation, or when the questions formulated, including the underlying national file that was submitted to the Court, are so unclear or controversial that they do not allow the Court to identify what kind of answer is sought by the national court. Such "unsuccessful" preliminary procedures are, however, very rare.

2   Standing of Natural and Legal Persons

The situation is completely different when an individual person or an environmental organization wants to defend the environment before the EU Court (General Court). Under Article 263(4) TFEU, access to the EU courts for parties other than EU institutions and Member States is possible only under precise conditions. Article 263(4) TFEU reads as follows:

> Any natural or legal person may, under the conditions laid down in the first and second paragraph, institute proceedings against an act addressed to that person or which is of direct and individual concern to them, and against a regulatory act which is of direct concern to them and does not entail implementing measures.

According to this provision, standing is limited to natural or legal persons. This means that the environment, as such, has no standing.

Consequently, the question whether trees should have standing has never even been discussed in procedures before the EU courts, so clear and unambiguous is Article 263(2) TFEU.

Natural or legal persons may institute proceedings before the General Court against an act that is addressed to them. This provision, though, is that of normal judiciary proceedings: where a public authority addresses an act to a person – for example, a decision on access to environmental information – and the person has the impression that this act is wrong, it is entitled to have the legality of the act checked by a court. In this regard, EU law is no different from any national law that deals with questions of access to justice.

However, in environmental matters, the EU institutions do not normally adopt acts that are addressed to individual natural or legal persons. Rather, they adopt regulations, directives or decisions that regulate a specific environmental issue or problem. The Commission also takes – or declines to take – actions when it becomes aware that a Member State or a specific economic operator in a Member State has not complied with EU environmental law. Such measures may be general measures, or addressed to a Member State, but they are not specifically addressed to a natural or legal person.

a)   Direct Concern

That then raises the question of when such an environmental measure is of "direct and individual concern" to a person. In the past, legal discussion concentrated on the question of what "individual concern" meant. Only after 2009, when the last alternative was inserted into Article 263(4) TFEU, did this term receive more attention. The General Court held that the "measure must directly affect the legal situation" of a person.[1] This interpretation means that an environmental organization will never be allowed to introduce an application, as a measure that impairs the environment does not affect its *legal* situation. According to the General Court, the affecting of the factual situation of an applicant is not sufficient.[2] The same problem exists for natural persons: the pollution of the air or of water, the construction of an installation in a protected area etc. does not affect the *legal* situation of a person.

---

[1] General Court, Case T-18/10, *Inuit Tapiriit Kanatami a.o.* v. *European Parliament and Council*, ECLI:EU:T:2011:419, para. 71, considering this to be "settled case-law." In the appeal procedure, the Court of Justice left this question open: Case C-583/11P, *Inuit Tapiriit Kanatami a.o.* v. *European Parliament and Council*, ECLI:EU:C:2013:625.

[2] General Court, Case T-18/10, para. 75.

In its judgment of 2011 (T-18/10), the General Court did not give any reasoning on why a person is directly affected only when its legal situation is changed by the measure. The Court's reference to earlier cases does not justify such a conclusion. Indeed, in the case quoted by the Court (T-127/05),[3] it only discussed whether the contested Council measure left some discretion to Member States as to its implementation. The same applies to all judgments (without exception!) that were quoted in Case T-127/05.[4] The standard formula that was examined in all these cases clearly refers to the question whether the contested measure left discretion to the implementing authorities.[5]

It can only be hoped that that the EU courts will soon find an opportunity to clarify precisely what is meant by "direct concern." For the time being, the case law interprets this provision in a way that bars almost any court action by an individual or an environmental organization.

b)   Individual Concern

As regards the question of "individual concern," the ECJ developed a general formula that it still applies today. In 1963, the Court had to decide a case in which Plaumann, a German fruit-importing company, sought the annulment of a Commission decision that refused to authorize Germany's suspension of customs duties for some imported products – among them, fruit. The Court stated:[6]

> Persons other than those to whom a decision is addressed may only claim to be individually concerned if that decision affects them by reason of certain attributes which are peculiar to them or by reason of circumstances in which they are differentiated from all other persons and by virtue of these factors distinguish them individually just as in the case of the person addressed.

In the Court's judgment, Plaumann was affected by reason of its commercial activity – namely the import of products – which could at any

---

[3] General Court, Case T-127/05, *Lotus v. Council*, ECLI:EU:T:2007:2.

[4] Court of Justice, Joined Cases 41/70 to 44/70, *International Fruit Co a.o. v. Commission*, ECLI:EU:C:1971:53; Case C-152/88, *Sofrimport v. Commission*, ECLI:EU:C:1990:259; Case T-69/99, *Danish Satellite TV v. Commission,* ECLI:EU:T:2000:302.

[5] See Court of Justice, Case C-386/96, *Dreyfus v. Commission*, ECLI:EU:C:1998:193, para. 43: "[to be of direct concern, the measure must] leave no discretion to the addressees of that measure who are entrusted with the task of implementing it, such implementation being purely automatic and resulting from Community rules without the application of other intermediate rules."

[6] Court of Justice, Case 25/62, *Plaumann v. Commission,* ECLI:EU:C:1963:17.

time be practiced by any other person; therefore, the company could not be distinguished from other persons who imported or could import products. The action was held to be inadmissible.

In the Greenpeace case,[7] this jurisdiction was, for the first time, applied to an environmental case. Greenpeace and sixteen local residents had asked for the annulment of a Commission decision that granted Spain financial assistance from the European Regional Development Fund for the construction of two power plants on the Canary Islands. EU legislation required that power plants had to be subjected to an environmental impact assessment before authorization could be given, but Spanish authorities had granted the authorization without undertaking an impact assessment. EU law further provided that measures financed by the Regional Development Fund had to comply with EU law. The Commission should thus have refused financial assistance to the construction of the power plants.

The General Court observed that the *Plaumann* case, and other cases previously decided by the Court, concerned, in principle, economic interests. It held, though, that the essential criterion applied in earlier judgments, and in particular in the *Plaumann* decision, "remains applicable whatever the nature, economic or otherwise, of those of the applicants' interests which are affected." As the General Court could not find any element that differentiated the sixteen applicants from any other local resident, their application was held to be inadmissible. Further, as an association, Greenpeace could not have more rights under the present Article 263(4) TFEU than its members, so that application was also thus inadmissible.

On appeal, the Court of Justice upheld the judgment of the General Court.[8] It held, in accordance with its earlier case law, that the decisive element against the admissibility of the application was that the Commission decision might affect "generally and in the abstract, a large number of persons who cannot be determined in advance in a way which distinguishes them individually in the same way as the addressee of a decision."

The unpleasant truth is that both the General Court and the Court of Justice apparently overlooked the fact that the environmental impact assessment directive, which was in force at the time of the judgments, sharply differentiated, in Article 6, between the "public," which is to be

---

[7] General Court, Case T-585/93, *Greenpeace v. Commission*, ECLI:EU:T:1995:147.
[8] Court of Justice, Case C-321/95, *Greenpeace v. Commission*, ECLI:EU:C:1998:153.

informed about a project, and the "public concerned," which has a *right* to participate in the impact assessment procedure and give its opinion on the project in question. It was therefore simply not correct to state that the persons who were particularly affected by the power plant projects – for example, because they lived close to the plants – could not be identified in advance and therefore be distinguished from other persons living on the Canary Islands. Thus, at least those of the applicants who were part of the "public concerned" should have been granted legal standing.[9]

c)   Present Application of the *Plaumann* Doctrine

The *Plaumann* doctrine was widely criticized as being overly restrictive. The General Court even tried once to reverse the doctrine,[10] but, on appeal, called it back.[11] The Court of Justice confirmed the *Plaumann* doctrine in settled case law[12] and stated:[13]

> While it is, admittedly, possible to envisage a system of judicial review of the legality of Community measures of general application different from that established, by the founding Treaties and never amended as to its principles, it is for the Member States, if necessary, in accordance with [Article 48 TEU] to reform the system actually in force ... (T)he courts of the European Union cannot, without exceeding their jurisdiction, interpret the conditions under which an individual may institute proceedings against a regulation in a way which has the effect of setting aside those conditions which are expressly laid down by the Treaty, even in the light of the principle of effective judicial protection.

d)   Inconsistent Judgments by the ECJ

The problem is that the Court of Justice itself had taken another line on the application of Article 263(4) TFEU in a number of decisions. For example, in the original EEC Treaty of 1958, the European Parliament,

---

[9] Directive 85/337 on the assessment of the effects of certain public and private projects on the environment, EU OJ 1985, L 175/40; this directive is now replaced by Directive 2011/92, EU OJ 2012, L 26/1. Directive 85/337 was not even mentioned by the General Court.

[10] General Court, Case T-177/01, *Jégo-Quére* v. *Commission*, ECLI:EU:T:2002:112, para. 49: "There is no compelling reason to read into the notion of individual concern ... a requirement that an individual applicant seeking to challenge a general measure must be differentiated from all others affected by it in the same way as an addressee."

[11] Court of Justice, Case C-263/02P, *Commission* v. *Jégo-Quére*, ECLI:EU:C:2004:210.

[12] See, for example, Joined Cases C-71/09P, C-73/09P and C-76/09P, *Venezia vuole vivere* v. *Commission*, ECLI:EU:C:2011:368.

[13] Court of Justice, Case C-50/00P, *Unión de Pequenos Agricultores*, ECLI:EU:C:2002:462, para. 40; in the same sense, Case C-583/11 P, para. 81.

which was then called the "Assembly," did not have the right, under Article 173 of the Treaty on the European Economic Community (EEC), the predecessor of Article 263 TFEU, to institute proceedings against another institution, nor was it possible to institute proceedings against the Parliament. In 1988, the Court found it impossible to give Parliament standing in a case against the Council, and explained that this was the law as laid down by the Treaty.[14] Less than two years later, the Court of Justice found that "(A)n interpretation of Article 173 of the Treaty which excluded measures adopted by the European Parliament from those which could be contested would lead to a result contrary both to the spirit of the Treaty and to its system."[15] In 1990, it also allowed the European Parliament itself to institute proceedings before the Court, as it held that this was required by the institutional balance in the Treaty provisions.[16] This interpretation of Article 173 EEC, which was obviously *contra legem*, demonstrated how the law may be interpreted, if one so wishes. The argument that the EEC Treaty's institutional balance *required* to give active and passive standing to the Parliament is not a legal argument, and no justification for this interpretation was given. Neither did the Court of Justice, with one word, discuss whether its interpretation exceeded its jurisdiction.

The Court also showed greater flexibility in cases in which the applicant defended economic interests, as some examples may demonstrate. In the *Codorníu* case,[17] the Court admitted that the applicant, the Codorníu company, was individually concerned by an EU regulation that reserved the term "crémant" to French and Luxembourg producers of sparkling wine. The Court's justification was that Codorníu had registered the term as a trademark. The Court did not examine or discuss whether other producers of sparkling wine also had registered trademarks, but just assumed that Codorníu distinguished itself from all other producers of sparkling wine.

In Case T-3/93, the General Court held an application of Air France to be admissible under the present Article 263(4) TFEU, because "the

---

[14] Court of Justice, Case C-302/87, *European Parliament* v. *Council*, ECLI:EU:C:1988:461.
[15] Court of Justice, Case 294/83, *Les Verts* v. *European Parliament*, ECLI:EU:C:1986:166, para. 25.
[16] Court of Justice, Case C-70/88, *European Parliament* v. *Council*, ECLI:EU:C:1990:373, para. 27. See also L. Krämer, "The EU courts and access to environmental justice" in Ben Boer (ed.), *Environmental law dimensions of human rights* (Oxford University Press, 2015), p. 107.
[17] Court of Justice, Case C-309/89, *DEP-Cordoníu* v. *Council*, ECLI:EU:C:1994:197.

competitive position of the Air France group has been affected in a manner which distinguishes it individually from any other carrier."[18] In other words, this means that any carrier's application against a Commission decision in competition law is admissible, because the competitive position of each carrier is unique. In Case C-169/84,[19] the Court of Justice again held an application to be admissible, because the competitive situation of the applicant was affected by a Commission decision.

In Case 264/82,[20] the application in a competition case was held admissible because the applying company had complained to the Commission, which had led to an investigation by the Commission; during that investigation, the company had been heard, and the conduct of the investigation had largely been determined by the company's observations. In what way the company distinguished itself from all other competitors is unclear; the introduction of a complaint and the way in which the Commission conducts its investigation do not individualize an applicant; neither can its consultation have been decisive, as this would mean that the EU institutions could decide whether an application will be admissible. It is also obvious that the market share of a company, its initiative in bringing a complaint or even the possession of a trademark have nothing to do with the *legal* situation of that company, so that the criterion of "direct" concern is not complied with; the decisions mentioned did not discuss the issue of direct concern, though.

The list of competition and other cases in which the ECJ showed great creativity in overcoming the standing problems of Article 263(4) TFEU could be enlarged. It can only be concluded that the Courts' continued recurrence to the *Plaumann* doctrine is determined not by legal but by ideological considerations: the Court of Justice does not wish to see environmental organizations or individuals raise the infringement of environmental provisions by EU institutions before the Court. It did not ever consider whether the application of the *Plaumann* doctrine, which was developed in 1963, is outdated in the meantime – in particular, because environmental protection requirements were, in 1986, inserted into the EU treaties in a very prominent place and progressively strengthened by Treaty amendments in 1993, 1998, and 2009;[21] in 2000, the EU

---

[18] General Court, Case T-3/93, *Air France* v. *Commission*, ECLI:EU:T:1994:36.
[19] Court of Justice, Case C-169/86, *COFAZ* v. *Commission*, ECLI:EU:C:1986:42.
[20] Court of Justice, Case C-264/82, *Timex* v. *Council and Commission*, ECLI:EU:C:1985:119.
[21] See Arts 3 and 21 TEU, and Arts 114 and 191–3 TFEU. A "high level" of environmental protection is required (Art 3 TEU; Arts 114 and 191 TFEU) and environmental protection

Charter of Fundamental Rights was adopted, which aims for a high level of environmental protection and effective judicial protection. On the contrary, the Court considered that, as the provision of the present Article 263(3) TFEU had not been amended since 1958, there was no reason to make another interpretation of it.

The Court was not impressed by the applicant's argument that its understanding of Article 263 TFEU was in conflict with the requirement of effective judicial protection laid down in the European Convention on Human Rights (ECHR) and the EU Charter of Fundamental Rights. It held that the EU had not adhered to the ECHR and that it therefore had not to examine the compatibility of Article 263 with that Convention.[22] Also, the requirement for effective judicial protection of the EU Charter could not go as far as setting aside the provision of Article 263(4) TFEU. The Court was of the opinion that the EU treaties, by introducing the possibility for natural and legal persons to resort to Article 263(4) TFEU and, furthermore, bring an action before a national court when they were of the opinion that an EU measure infringed their rights, had set up a complete system of access to justice. A national court could address a preliminary question to the ECJ when it was of the opinion that the EU measure was illegal. Any change of this system would require, so the Court said, an amendment of the EU treaties.

The Court of Justice did not discuss the point that the subject matters of a case before a national court and of one before the ECJ are different: the national litigation is aimed at the annulment of a national measure, and the EU litigation at the annulment of an EU measure. Furthermore, the national litigation is subject to the national rules of procedure (action available, standing, delays, burden of proof, etc.), and the national court is normally not obliged to submit a preliminary question to the EU Court;[23] the exact formulation of the questions to be submitted to the Court is in entirely its hands. It is thus more wishful thinking by the Court of Justice that Articles 263(4) and 267 TFEU together established a complete system of effective judicial protection.

---

is considered essential to reach a sustainable development of the EU (Art 3 TEU; Art 11 TFEU; Art 37 Charter of Fundamental Rights).

[22] According to Art 6 TEU, the European Union is to adhere to the ECHR. However, a draft agreement to adhere was vetoed by the Court of Justice under Art 218(11) TFEU (see Opinion 2/13, ECLI:EU:C.2014:2454); accession negotiations are ongoing.

[23] Such an obligation exists only when there is no judicial remedy against the national court's decision (see Art 267(3) TFEU).

e)   Different Treatment of National and EU Courts

In 2011, it became obvious that the ECJ applied different standards for national courts and for itself. The Court had to decide on a preliminary question that concerned Article 9(3)[24] of the Aarhus Convention[25] and the possibility of an environmental organization (a non-governmental organization (NGO)) relying on that provision before a national court. The Court rejected the direct application of Article 9(3),[26] but added:[27]

> it must be added that those provisions [of Article 9(3)], although drafted in broad terms, are intended to ensure effective environmental protection ... if effective protection of EU environmental law is not to be undermined, it is inconceivable that Article 9(3) of the Aarhus Convention be interpreted in such a way as to make it in practice impossible or excessively difficult to exercise rights conferred by EU law. It follows that ... it is for the national court, in order to ensure effective judicial protection in the fields covered by EU environmental law, to interpret the national law in a way which, to the fullest extent possible, is consistent with the objectives laid down in Article 9(3) of the Aarhus Convention. Therefore, it is for the referring court to interpret, to the fullest extent possible, the procedural rules relating to the conditions to be met in order bring administrative or judicial proceedings in accordance with the objectives of Article 9(3) of the Aarhus Convention and the objective of effective judicial protection of the rights conferred by EU law, so as to enable an environmental protection organization, such as zoskupenie, to challenge before a court a decision taken following administrative proceedings liable to be contrary to EU environmental law.

Neither before nor after that judgment did the Court ever consider applying this standard to itself and to interpret, to the fullest extent

---

[24] Article 9(3) Convention on access to information, public participation indecision-making and access to justice in environmental matters, Aarhus 1998 (Aarhus Convention): "each Party shall ensure that, where they meet the criteria, if any, laid down in its national law, members of the public have access to administrative or judicial procedures to challenge acts and omissions by private parties and public authorities which contravene provisions of national law relating to the environment."

[25] The EU adhered to the Aarhus Convention by Decision 2005/370, EU OJ 2005, L124/1. According to Art 216(2) TFEU, "(A)greements concluded by the Union are binding upon the institutions of the Union and on its Member States."

[26] In this author's opinion, the Court's decision to refuse direct effect to Art 9(3) is erroneous. However, this cannot be elaborated on here. See L. Krämer, *EU Environmental Law*, 8th edn (Sweet & Maxwell, 2015), paras. 12–22.

[27] Court of Justice, Case C-240/09, *Lesoochranárske zoskupenie*, ECLI:EU:C:2011:125, paras 46–51.

possible, the procedural rules relating to be met in order to bring administrative and judicial proceedings of EU law [this is Article 263(4) TFEU] with the objectives of Article 9(3) of the Aarhus Convention and the objective of effective judicial protection of the rights conferred by EU law, so as to enable an environmental organization to challenge before the EU Court of Justice an EU decision taken following administrative proceedings liable to be contrary to EU environmental law.

Thus, the Court requests national courts to interpret, to the fullest effect possible, Article 9(3) in favour of environmental organizations. However, it does not apply that standard to itself.

As an EU institution, also the Court is bound by the provisions of the Aarhus Convention which are an "integral part of the legal order" of the EU.[28] And the argument that the Aarhus Convention does not rank higher than the EU treaties and therefore cannot amend their provisions, is not relevant, because what is in question is another interpretation of Article 263(4) TFEU, not its amendment ("setting aside").

f)   Standing and Human Rights

The Court's restrictive interpretation of Article 263(4) TFEU also became very obvious, where human rights were at stake. In Case T-219/95, applicants who lived in Tahiti applied to the Court in order to have French nuclear tests in the South Pacific stopped. Their action was addressed against a Commission decision that had given green light to the tests, by stating that they were not particularly dangerous. The applicants argued that the tests risked affecting their health and life. The General Court held the action to be inadmissible, stating:[29]

> the contested decision concerns the applicants only in their objective capacity as residents of Tahiti, in the same way as any other person residing in Polynesia. Even on the assumption that the applicants might suffer personal damage linked to the alleged harmful effects of the nuclear tests in question on the environment or on the health of the general public, that circumstance alone would not be sufficient to distinguish them individually in the same way as a person to whom the contested decision is addressed.. since damage of the kind they cite could affect, in the same way, any person residing in the area in question.

---

[28] Ibid., para. 30.
[29] General Court, Case T-219/95R, *Danielsson* v. *Commission*, ECLI:EU:T:1995:219.

This statement means, in clear terms, that even the infringement of human rights of a person does not give to that person a right of standing.[30] The General Court recognized this in all frankness.[31] It is thus naive to believe that a breach of a person's human rights by an EU institution would give that person a right of access to the EU courts!

As to the question whether the application of Article 47 of the Charter of Fundamental Rights, which gives a fundamental right to effective judicial protection, would require or allow another interpretation of Article 263(4) TFEU, the Court of Justice was quite clear:

> Article 47 of the Charter is not intended to change the system of judicial review laid down by the Treaties. Accordingly, the conditions of admissibility laid down in the fourth paragraph of Article 263 TFEU must be interpreted in the light of the fundamental right to effective judicial protection, but such an interpretation cannot have the effect of setting aside the conditions expressly laid down in that Treaty.[32]

The Court does not discuss whether Article 47 of the Charter, while not allowing a "setting aside" of Article 263(4) TFEU, would allow or require to give to that provision a new interpretation. A discussion of this aspect would have been all the more appropriate as the societal circumstances, also and in particular with regard to the environment – climate change, loss of biodiversity, air, water and ocean pollution, eco-refugees etc. – have considerably changed during the fifty years since the development of the *Plaumann* doctrine.[33]

The ideological character of the Court's attitude towards environmental issues also becomes obvious from the declaration that the Court made

---

[30] See also the comment by Advocate General Jacobs in Case C-50/00P, ECLI:EU:C:2002:197, para 16: "On that reading, the greater the number of persons affected by a measure, the less likely it is that judicial review will be made available. The fact that a measure adversely affects a large number of individuals, causing wide-spread rather than limited harm, provides, however, to my mind a positive reason for accepting a direct challenge by one or more individuals."

[31] General Court, Case T-13/94, *Century Oil Hellas* v. *Commission*, ECLI:EU:T:1994:77, para.15: "The principles [of the case law] cannot be altered by the nature of the EC law infringement alleged. The fact that the applicant is alleging an infringement of his right to property is not relevant in assessing the admissibility of the action."

[32] Court of Justice, Case C-583/11P, paras. 97 and 98. In the *Codorníu* case (Case C-309/89), the Court of Justice implicitly recognized that the human right of property – trademark as intellectual property – gave standing to a company.

[33] The Court's decisions to give standing to the European Parliament, mentioned above, also followed a change in societal circumstances, namely the introduction of direct elections to the Parliament in 1979. Before that, members of the Parliament were appointed by Member State bodies.

when it declared that another interpretation of Article 263(4)TFEU would go beyond its competence and would require an amendment of the TFEU.[34] The Court had already made a very similar declaration in 1988, in a case that the European Parliament had brought against the Council. As mentioned, at that time, the then Article173 of the EC Treaty did not foresee that the Parliament could bring such actions. The Court examined the provision and concluded:[35] "the applicable provisions, as they stand at present, do not enable the Court to recognize the capacity of the European Parliament to bring an action of annulment." However, two years later, on October 4, 1991, and with five of the eight judges who gave the second judgment having already participated in the judgment of 1988, the Court changed its opinion and allowed the European Parliament to bring an action against the Council.[36]

Thus, in 1988, the Court thought that it was impossible to interpret Article 173 EC Treaty (the present Article 263 TFEU) in a sense that would be favourable to the European Parliament. Two years later, such an interpretation was possible, without the wording of Article 173 EC or any other factual circumstance having changed.[37]

3   Conclusion on Standing

Anyway, the result of this jurisdiction is that there is not one single case in which an action by an environmental organization against an EU measure was held admissible. The EU courts are of the opinion that the protection of the general interest "environment" is best ensured by the EU institutions and by Member States. Citizens and NGOs should interfere in this as little as possible. And it leads to the result that, for example, when a producer applies for the authorization of a pesticide, he may attack a negative decision in court. However, when the pesticide is authorized, an environmental organization may not bring an action before the court, because it is not directly and individually concerned.[38] It is not sufficient that the NGO argues that the pesticide constitutes a risk for humans or the environment. The authorizing EU institutions assume

---

[34] See above, text to n. 13.

[35] Court of Justice, Case 302/87, para. 28. This judgment was given on 27 September 1988.

[36] See above.

[37] One feels reminded of Goethe, *Faust*, Part I, lines 224 and 225: "What you the Spirit of the Ages call, is nothing but the spirit of you all."

[38] See General Court, Joined Cases T-214/04 and 236/04, *European Environment Bureau and Stichting Natuur en Milieu v. Commission*, ECLI:EU:T:2005:426.

that they alone know what is in the general interest, and the EU courts do not come in in order to weigh the public interest arguments against the producer's interests.

C The Commission as Defender of the Environment

1 The Commission's General Policy

De facto, thus, it is the European Commission that has a quasi-monopoly in bringing cases before the ECJ, in order to defend the environment. It has already been mentioned that the Commission has a very large discretion as to whether it brings a case before the Court. The Court of Justice refused to control this discretion directly or indirectly.[39]

The number of 550 cases decided by the Court in environmental matters on the request of the Commission since 1976 appears very impressive. And it demonstrates how EU environmental law is different from the enforcement of international environmental agreements; in international law, there is no body to call the contracting parties to an agreement to order and, if necessary, bring them before a court. Non-compliance with international agreements is thus rather normal.

However, these figures concerning Commission actions include numerous cases in which a Member State had not – or with delay, or incompletely or incorrectly – transposed provisions of EU environmental law into its national legal order. This delayed transposition became so regular that a provision was introduced into the TFEU according to which the Commission could bring the matter before the Court under Article 260 TFEU and ask for a penalty payment, without first having to recur to the procedure under Article 258 TFEU.[40] That measure was effective: since 2011, only one case has been decided by the Court for the reason that a Member State had not transposed environmental provisions in time.[41]

---

[39] Court of Justice, Case 247/87, *Star Fruit Co* v. *Commission*, ECLI:EU:C:1989:58; Case 371/ 89, *Emrich* v. *Commission*, ECLI:EU:C:1990:158; Case 416/85, *Commission* v. *United Kingdom*, ECLI:EU:C:1988:321: Case C-234/91, *Commission* v. *Denmark*, ECLI:EU: C1993:910. With this jurisdiction – which contradicts, as regards the pre-judicial stage, the wording of Art 258 TFEU – the Court has created an area in which public power is exercised without being controlled by the judiciary.

[40] See Art 260(3) TFEU).

[41] Court of Justice, case C-548/10, *Commission* v. *Austria*, ECLI:EU:C:2011:534. Article 260(3) TFEU was not yet applicable at the time of that judgment.

The Commission's policy to bring environmental (and other) cases before the Court is strongly influenced by political considerations, as the Commission is a political institution and also has tasks other than enforcing existing EU law, in particular to orient EU policy and to make proposals for legislation. There is no environmental enforcement agency at EU level.[42] The Commission does not have either environmental inspectors or other bodies that would inform it of the practical application or non-application of environmental provisions within the Member States. It mainly has to rely on reports concerning the implementation of EU environmental directives that Member States transmit; and such reports normally inform on the measures taken, but not on the practical application or the results obtained. Moreover, all Member States try to make the presentations look good, avoiding the demonstration of difficulties and breaches of the law.

In its cases brought before the Court, the Commission concentrates on the incomplete or incorrect transposition of EU environmental law into national law, or on the absence of adopting management or clean-up plans. Since 2002, it has very largely abandoned the practice of the years 1985 to 2000, to take environmental complaints, introduced by citizens or environmental organizations, as samples, examine the facts and, when it suspected that EU environmental law had not been respected, have the matter decided by the Court.[43] As such citizen complaints were almost the only source of information of the Commission on the practical application of EU environmental law at local, regional and national levels in the Member States, the Commission – deliberately – cut itself off its main source of information. This had the consequence that, between 2011 and 2015, the Court decided only seven cases that concerned poor application of EU environmental law in a specific case.[44]

---

[42] The European Environment Agency (EEA), established in 1990, only has the task of collecting, processing and distributing environmental information: see Regulation 401/ 2009, EU OJ 2009, L126/13.

[43] On which, see L. Krämer, "The environmental complaint in EU law". Journal of Environmental Law (2009), 13. With regard to the Commission's shift of policy in the treatment of complaints, see Commission, *A Europe of results – applying Community law* COM(2007) 502, in which the Commission declared that the following cases would be treated with priority: absence of national legislation transposing EU law into national law; systemic disregard of significant EU provisions; and non-compliance with a decision by the Court of Justice.

[44] Court of Justice, Case C-383/09, *Commission* v. *France*, ECLI:EU:C:2011:369; Case C-404/09, *Commission* v. *Spain*, ECLI:EU:C:2011:768; Case C-560/08, *Commission* v. *Spain*, ECLI:EU:C:2011:835; Case C-340/10, *Commission* v. *Cyprus*, ECLI:EU: C:2012:143; Case C-517/11, *Commission* v. *Greece*, ECLI:EU:C:2013:66; Case C-600/12,

There is no intention to criticize political decisions with regard to priorities that the Commission fixes. However, when the Commission has a quasi-monopoly in enforcing EU environmental law before the EU courts, this also implies some obligations to take this enforcement task seriously and try to ensure the practical application of environmental law.

2 Examples of Actions against Member States

This is not the place to review all sections of EU environmental law, in which serious problems of practical application exist. Some examples must suffice:

As regards air pollution, Directive 2008/50, which replaced earlier directives, fixed quality requirements for several air pollutants, which were not to be exceeded from 2010 onwards.[45] In 2015, the EEA stated:[46]

> The EU limit and target value for particulate matter continue to be exceeded in large parts of the European Union. The EU daily limit value for PM 10 was exceeded in 22 out of the 28 EU Member States and the target value for PM 2.5 was exceeded in 7 Member States ... The annual limit value for nitrogen dioxide (NO²) was widely exceeded in Europe, with 93 per cent of all exceedances occurring next to roads. A total of 19 out of the 28 EU Member States recorded exceedances of their limit value at one or more stations.

The EEA indicated that the PM 2.5 concentrations were, in 2012, responsible for some 403,000 premature deaths within the EU, and the exposure to NOx for 72,000 premature deaths. The Commission itself indicated that, in 2010, air pollution caused over 400,000 premature deaths and estimated the overall external costs of air pollution at 23 billion euros per year.[47] Between 2011 and June 2016, though, the Commission did not bring before the Court one single case concerning air pollution against a Member State. Directive 2000/60 required that, by 2015, the European surface and groundwater have good ecological status.[48] The EEA reported that, by 2015, only some 52 per cent of all

---

Commission v. Greece, ECLI:EU:C:2014:2086; Case C-677/13, Commission v. Greece, ECLI:EU:C:2014:2433.
[45] Directive 2008/50 on ambient air quality and cleaner air for Europe, EU OJ 2008, L152/1.
[46] EEA, Air quality in Europe – 2015 report (EEA Report 5/2015) (Copenhagen, 2015), pp. 7 and 8.
[47] Commission, A clean air programme for Europe, COM(2013) 718, p. 4.
[48] Directive 2000/60 establishing a framework for Community action in the field of water policy, EU OJ 2000, L327/1.

surface waters would reach this objective and asked for "radically different measures", if the EU wanted to respect the Directive's requirements.[49] Between 2011 and mid-2016, the Commission did not bring before the Court any case concerning the non-compliance with the ecological quality requirement.

Under Directive 92/43, species and habitats that were covered by this directive were to have good conservation status by 2007.[50] In 2015, the EEA found that the status of species was favourable for 17 per cent of the protected species, unfavourable in 40 per cent and unknown in 43 per cent; 5 per cent of the natural habitats had favourable conservation status, 78 per cent unfavourable conservation status, and the status of 17 per cent was unknown.[51] Between 2011 and mid-2016, the Commission had five cases on specific species or habitats decided by the Court of Justice, thus less than one case per year,[52] while Directive 92/43 concerns some 23,000 protected habitats and 1,200 protected fauna and flora species.

Under Directive 2002/49 on environmental noise,[53] Member States had to identify areas with high noise levels and develop strategic noise maps and, by 2008 and then every five years, action plans for reducing noise levels. In 2014, the EEA found that only 44 per cent of all information that was due under Directive 2002/49 was actually transmitted, "entirely due to late reporting by countries";[54] this lack of reporting made it difficult to draw conclusions and develop noise abatement strategies. The EEA estimated that noise within the EU causes annually at least 10,000 premature deaths, 900,000 cases of hypertension and 43,000 hospital admissions. Almost 20 million adults are annoyed by,

---

[49] EEA, *European waters – current status and future challenges* (EEA Report 9/2012) (Copenhagen, 2012), pp. 12 and 15.

[50] Directive 92/43 on the conservation of natural habitats and of wild fauna and flora, EU OJ 1992, L206/7. The exact date of compliance is not fixed. The year 2007 follows from the requirement to designate habitats (three years), the establishment of the EU list of habitats (six years) and the establishment of national protection measures (six years); see Art 4 of the directive.

[51] EEA, *EU biodiversity baseline – adapted to the MAES typology* (2015) (EEA Technical Report 9/2015) (Copenhagen, 2015), pp. 21 and 45.

[52] Court of Justice, Case C-383/09 (European hamster); Case C-404/09 (Alto Sil habitat); Case C-340/10 (Cypriot grass snake); Case C-517/11 (Koroneia lake); Case C-141/14 *Commission* v. *Bulgaria*, ECLI:EU:C:2016:8 (Kaliakra habitat).

[53] Directive 2002/49 relating to the assessment and management of environmental noise, EU OJ 2002, L189/12. There are also a number of EU legislative acts on noise emission limits of cars, motorcycles and trucks.

[54] EEA, *Noise in Europe* 2014 (Report 10/2014) (Copenhagen, 2014), p. 54.

and a further 8 million suffer sleep disturbance due to, environmental noise.[55] The Commission estimated the economic damage caused by noise at 40 billion euros per year.[56] The Commission did not undertake any action in court to enforce timely reporting or the reduction of noise levels by Member States.

3 Enforcing the Application of International Agreements

The biggest omission of the Commission in bringing cases is that of ensuring the full application of international environmental agreements to which the EU adhered. Such agreements are, as mentioned above, binding on the EU institutions *and* on the Member States (Article 216(2) TFEU). By its conclusion of such an agreement, the EU commits itself towards the other contracting parties to ensure that the agreement's provisions are respected all over the territory of the EU. Where an international environmental agreement concerns questions "which are in large measure covered" by EU legislation – such as water, nature conservation, air pollution, waste management etc. – the EU has to ensure that the international agreement is complied with by Member States, even when a specific, detailed measure had not (yet) been regulated by EU law.[57] The Commission thus has the obligation, flowing out of Article 17 TEU, to ensure that the provisions of the international environmental agreements are transposed into the national legal order and complied with; this obligation is, in procedures under Article 258 TFEU, independent from the questions of whether the provisions of the international agreement are directly applicable or not.[58]

Apart from one single case,[59] the Commission never took action against a Member State in order to ensure the full application of an

---

[55] Ibid., p. 2.

[56] Commission, *Report on the implementation of the environmental noise directive*, COM (2011) 321, p. 2.

[57] Court of Justice, Case C-239/03, *Commission v. France*, ECLI:EU:C:2004:598, para. 28.

[58] The cases that are normally quoted by the Court all concern procedures under Art 267 TFEU, where the issue of whether a natural or legal person could rely on the provisions of international (environmental) law was relevant, see Case 12/86 *Demirel*, ECLI:EU: C:1987:400, para. 14; Case C-213/03, *Etangs de Berre*, ECLI: EU:C:2004:464, para. 39; Case C-366/10, *Air Transport Association of America*, ECLI:EU:C:2011:864, paras. 50–53; Case C-240/09, para. 44. However, in cases under Art 258 TFEU, the question of the direct effect of a provision is not relevant.

[59] See Case C-239/03, which concerned a Protocol to the Barcelona Convention on the Protection of the Mediterranean against pollution from land-based sources.

international environmental agreement to which the EU had adhered. These agreements appear thus in the EU statute books, but are otherwise completely ignored – even when their subject matter is "in large measure" covered by EU environmental law,[60] unless the EU itself has transposed their provisions into an EU legislative act. The Commission's implementation activity then concerns this EU legislative act, but not the international convention.

4   Limits of the Commission's Actions

Of course, the Commission may have recourse to other means than applications to the Court in order to ensure that Member States comply with their obligations under EU environmental law; examples are bilateral or multilateral discussions, name-and-shame publications, requests for information, public denouncements etc. However, the examples above clearly show that compliance with legal requirements is not facilitated by such extrajudicial means. A number of Member States simply consider EU environmental legislation as recommendations that one follows or ignores, according to national or regional convenience. The example of the incorporation of Article 260(3) TFEU into the TFEU, which led to the disappearing of late transposition of EU legislation into national law, demonstrates that, next to the carrot of persuading Member States to follow EU environmental law, a stick – in the form of legal enforcement means – is also necessary.

The quasi-monopolistic position of the Commission in bringing cases before the Court is of no help. Member States frequently engage in political discussions with the Commission in order to deter it from bringing a case, often enough with the intervention at high political level (intervention by a prime minister or a minister). Of course, data on such policy interventions is not available.

Sometimes, the Commission turns a blind eye to breaches of EU environmental law through national activities. For example, the spring hunting of the tourterelle (*streptopelia*) in the Medoc (France) has a long tradition, though it has been prohibited since 1981, when the EU Birds

---

[60] Examples are the Rio Convention on Biological Diversity, the Bonn Convention on the Conservation of Migratory Species of Wild Animals, the Salzburg Convention on the Protection of the Alps, the Stockholm Convention on Persistent Organic Pollutants, and even, with regard to access to justice issues, the Aarhus Convention.

Directive[61] became applicable. This hunting continues to be practiced today, but the Commission has never taken any legal action against France for more than thirty-five years.

Another example is the nitrate concentration in surface waters in Bretagne (France) which is due to excessive livestock holding; the concentrations very regularly exceed the level of 50 mg per liter that is allowed under EU law.[62] The Commission took several judicial actions against France,[63] but carefully avoided bringing before the Court a case under Article 260 TFEU that might have led France to have to pay a penalty payment and/or a lump sum. Instead, the Commission has tolerated the disregard of EU environmental law for several decades.

Cases of this kind also concern the Volkswagen scandal of 2015, in which the Commission omitted to enforce the prohibition of safety devices in cars, which had existed since 2001[64] or the omission to control, whether indeed industrial installations apply the best available techniques for their emissions into air or water.[65]

Other issues are less important: when new states accede to the EU, they should, in theory, respect existing EU environmental law from the first day onwards. In practice, the Commission waits several months, if not years, before it tries fully to enforce EU environmental law in a recently acceded country. And before the Brexit-referendum in the United Kingdom (UK) in June 2016, the Commission did not start new infringement procedures against the UK in order not to influence the voting. Sometimes, also, procedures against some countries are simply not started for linguistic or staff-resource reasons: as the procedure under Article 258 TFEU must be carried out in the language of the Member State in question, the Commission might have to make extensive translations of national legislation, studies and administrative papers.

---

[61] Directive 2009/147 on the conservation of wild birds, EU OJ 2010, L20/7, which replaced Directive 79/409 of 1979.

[62] Directive 91/676 on the protection of waters against pollution caused by nitrates from agricultural sources, EU OJ 1991, L375/1.

[63] Court of Justice, Case C-266/99, *Commission* v. *France*, ECLI:EU:C:2001:142; Case C-258/00, *Commission* v. *France*, ECLI:EU:C:2002:400; Case C-183/12, *Commission* v. *France*, ECLI:EU:C:2013:369; Case C-237/12 *Commission* v. *France*, ECLI:EU: C:2014:2152.

[64] See Regulation 715/2007 on type-approval of motor-vehicles with respect to emissions from light passenger and commercial vehicles (Euro 5 and Euro 6) and on access to vehicle repair and maintenance, EU OJ 2007, L171/1, Art 5; for more details, see L. Krämer, "The Volkswagen scandal – air pollution and administrative inertia", *elni-Review* (2016), 64.

[65] Directive 2010/75 on industrial emissions, EU OJ 2010, L334/17.

All these aspects are, at the end of the day, normal for an institution that is a political body and has a political mandate. However, as one of the main principles of the EU is the government of the "rule of law," contradictory, inconsistent or unequal treatment of breaches of environmental law by Member States inevitably undermine the credibility of the EU. When citizens, associations, regions or even Member States get the feeling that they are being treated differently from others, they lose the confidence in the rule of law as a governing principle within the EU. Frustrations, cynicism and objections to the whole EU unification undertaking are the consequence.

From the Commission's point, it is only consequent that it makes the greatest possible secret of Member States' compliance with EU environmental law and, hence, also of its role as enforcing authority. National reports on the implementation of EU directives or regulations are normally not made public. Commission implementation reports – published at irregular intervals – remain general and do not blame and shame. Conformity studies by external consultants, which examine the compliance of national law with EU directives, are either not published or published only several years later. Letters of formal notice and reasoned opinions, sent by the Commission under Article 258 TFEU, are confidential, and so on.

All this could have been softened, if not completely avoided, when citizens or environmental organizations obtained the practical right to contribute, through their action, to the enforcement of existing EU environmental law. Another interpretation of the provision of Article 263(4) TFEU would thus have impacts that reach far beyond legal quarrels and affect important democratic decisions of a European Union that claims that "decisions are taken as openly as possible and as closely as possible to the citizen."[66]

In conclusion, the Commission is not a reliable guardian of the environment when it comes to court actions to defend the environment.

D   Substantive Law

It would be presumptuous to select, out of the more than a thousand environmental cases, some that are considered particularly important,[67]

---

[66] Art 1(2) TEU.

[67] See L. Krämer, *European environmental law casebook* (Sweet & Maxwell, 1993) (27 judgments); L. Krämer, *Casebook on EU environmental law* (Hart Publishing, 2002) (50 judgments); J. Jans, "The effect of the ECJ judgments in environmental cases for other

even though several of these court decisions concern routine questions, such as the absence or late transposition of legislation, or the omission to adopt a plan or programme or to transmit implementation reports to the Commission.

A number of Court decisions in environmental matters had, in this author's opinion, a clear political touch. For example, in the judgment in Case 252/85, the Court refused to declare France's traditional hunting methods contrary to EU law;[68] in Case 302/86, the Court held that Denmark was allowed to introduce an effective recycling system for bottles, but not a very effective system;[69] in Case 2/90, the Court authorized a Belgian import ban for hazardous waste, based on an debatable legal principle that the Court interpreted rather arbitrarily;[70] in the cases on access to documents concerning court proceedings;[71] or in the refusal to take a precise position with regard to the prolonged disregard of air pollution requirements by the UK.[72]

In the majority of cases, the Court of Justice – except, in this author's opinion, the General Court – has tried to interpret EU environmental law in a sense that is favourable to the environment, and to be creative and innovative in its interpretation; this remark more concerns the years between 1976 and 1990 than the last fifteen years. Generally, the Court has favoured EU environmental law over Member States' rights to regulate, and held a balance between diverging economic and environmental interests. The interpretation of some directives, such as those on environmental impact assessments[73] or on the protection of birds, habitats and species,[74] is very largely influenced by the numerous Court decisions in these areas.

---

areas of EU law" in G. Bándi (ed.), *The impact of ECJ jurisprudence on environmental law* (Budapest, 2009), p. 83.

[68] Court of Justice, Case 252/85, *Commission v. France*, ECLI:EU:C:1988:202.

[69] Court of Justice, Case C-302/86, *Commission v. Denmark*, ECLI:EU:C:1988:421.

[70] Court of Justice, Case C-2/90, *Commission v. Belgium*, ECLI:EU:C:1992:310.

[71] See Case C-514/07P, *Sweden v. API and Commission*, ECLI:EU:C:2010:541.

[72] Court of Justice, Case C-404/13, *The Queen ex parte ClientEarth v. Secretary of State*, ECLI:EU:C:2014:2382.

[73] Directive 2011/92; on which, see Agustín García Ureta (ed.), *La directiva de la Unión europea de evaluación de impacto ambiental de proyectos: balance de treinta años* (Madrid, 2016); Directive 2001/42 on the assessment of certain plans and programmes on the environment, OJ 2001, L197/30.

[74] Directive 2009/147; Directive 92/43; together, these directives have been the subject of 120 Court decisions since 1976 (author's own reckoning). See generally, on the implementation and application of Directive 92/43: Charles-Hubert Born a.o. (eds.), *The habitats directive in its EU environmental law context. European nature's best hope?* (Abingdon – New York, 2015).

On the rare occasions on which the Court of Justice touched on the objective of a high level of environmental protection, laid down in Article 3 TEU and Articles 114 and 191 TFEU, the Court satisfied itself with the reasoning that a high level did not require to reach the highest possible level.[75] It then went into the argument that the weighing of different interests in situations that required political, economic or social assessments made it necessary to allow the EU institutions a broad discretion that could be controlled by the Court only to the extent that this discretion was obviously exceeded[76] – which never occurred, according to the Court, in an environmental case. The Court of Justice never tried to specify what a high level in a concrete case meant. The General Court followed that line, disregarding an applicant's (Sweden's) arguments in very few words and concluding that the Commission had not compromised the requirement of a high level of protection.[77]

The Court encouraged the rights of citizens and environmental organizations by holding that EU air and water limit values also intended to protect human health and therefore allowed natural and legal persons to invoke the disregard of those provisions in court.[78] Its jurisdiction – and even more so that of the General Court – on access to environmental information was, though, rather conservative, trying to shield the EU institutions as far as possible from openness, transparency and accountability. Both courts ignored the fact that, since 2005, the TEU and TFEU have requested openness not less than five times[79] and, in doing so, have tried to establish the model of an open society for the EU.

Environmental law principles played only a subordinate role in the Courts' decisions. The four principles mentioned in Article191(2) TFEU – precaution, prevention, fighting environmental damage at source, and the "polluter pays" principle – were mentioned in different decisions, without gaining too much importance. The Court of Justice held that citizens could not rely on those principles alone, without further concretization in directives or regulations.[80] This general approach did not prevent it from deriving far-reaching conclusions from the principle

---

[75] Court of Justice, Case C-284/95, *Safety Hi-Tech*, ECLI:EU:C:1998:772, para. 49.
[76] Court of Justice, Case C-127/07, *Arcelor*, ECLI:EU:C:2008:728 (settled case law).
[77] General Court, Case T-229/04, *Sweden v. Commission*, ECLI:EU:T:2007:217, para. 187s.
[78] Court of Justice, Cases 131/88, *Commission* v. *Germany*, ECLI:EU:C:1991:87; Case 361/88, *Commission* v. *Germany*, ECLI:EU:C:1991:224; Case C-237/07, *Janecek*, ECLI:EU:C:2008:447.
[79] Arts 1, 10 and 11 TEU and Arts 15 and 298 TFEU.
[80] Court of Justice, Case C-534/13, *Fipa Group*, ECLI:EU:C:2015:140.

of fighting damage at source.[81] The precautionary principle was recognized as a determining principle to deal with situations of scientific uncertainty.[82]

In contrast, principles of international law[83] – the common heritage of humankind, common concern for humanity, sustainable development (unless this is seen as an objective instead of a principle), respect for all life forms, equity, common but differentiated responsibilities, non-regression and consideration for future generations – were not discussed at all and mostly not even mentioned by the EU Courts.

The judgments are marked by the interpretation of EU law, rather than exploring or developing environmental long-term effects or impacts. There is no consideration in any decision that the environment may well survive without humans (without the EU), but that humans (the EU) will not be able to survive without the environment. There is no consideration in any judgment that the environment is an interest without a vested group behind it – in contrast with competition (competitors as group), trade (trade and industry), social affairs (employers groups and trade unions), transport (people who transport or are transported), energy (energy producers) etc. – and that this might influence the balancing of environmental (general) interests against other (vested) interests. And there is no consideration in any judgment of whether there is a right of the individual EU citizen to live in a clean and healthy environment.

Since 2009, the combating of climate change has been identified as one of the objectives of EU environmental policy (Article 191(1) TFEU). The EU Courts discussed several pieces of EU legislation which had the objective of reducing the emission of greenhouse gases, or saving of energy or energy efficiency measures. However, until now, they have never discussed climate change issues and their implications for the EU and its environment in any detail, but have limited themselves strictly to the interpretation of the law. In this author's opinion, the ECJ will sooner or later have to decide whether the individual citizen has a right to claim (more) effective measures to combat climate change and whether Article 263(4) TFEU gives him standing for such an action. This will then decide whether the right to health and to life, which were given standing in cases

---

[81] Court of Justice, Case C-653/13, *Commission v. Italy*, ECLI:EU:C:2015 478.

[82] Court of Justice, Case C-157/96, *The Queen ex parte National Farmers Union*, ECLI:EU:C:1998:191; Case C-180/96, *United Kingdom v. Commission*, ECLI:EU:C:1998:192.

[83] On these principles, see IUCN, *Draft International Covenant on Environment and Development*, 5th edn (Gland, 2015).

of air and water pollution, also extend to lacking or insufficient measures on climate change.

E   General Evaluation

In the 1950s, the protection of the environment was not an issue, and the word "environment" did not appear in the EEC Treaty of 1958, the predecessor of the EU Treaties of today. Environmental organizations did not exist.[84] It was thus normal that the protection of the environment at that time – including the right to bring cases before the ECJ – was placed into the hands of the European Commission and that the present Article 263(4) TFEU was conceived to play just a subordinate role. The interpretation of that provision – the *Plaumann* doctrine – might have had its justification in the 1960s and perhaps beyond.

However, it is much less acceptable that this doctrine continues to govern the relationship between citizens and the Court of Justice even more than fifty years later, despite all the very considerable societal changes – the rise of democracy in Europe, the evolution of human rights, the rise of civil society movements, the recognition of the need to preserve and protect the environment, the move of the EEC to the EU etc. – which has occurred since the 1960s. These changes make the perseverance of the Court in its jurisdiction of 1963 traditional and conservative.

It is understandable that the small number of judges at the Court of Justice provokes attempts to limit, as far as any possible, the right of access to the EU courts. However, first, the Court has apparently never had such concerns with regard to competition or trademark cases, which are also very numerous and in which the Court has been more flexible and creative in interpreting Article 263(4) TFEU. Secondly, if this were really one of the hidden considerations of the Court, it would mean that the judges place their personal-professional interests above the general interest to ensure an appropriate protection of the environment. All empirical evidence shows that the fear of an inflationary number of environmental cases being brought forward, if

---

[84] Greenpeace was founded in 1971, WWF as a foundation in 1961 and Friends of the Earth in 1969. Rachel Carson's book *The Silent Spring* appeared in 1962. The Club of Rome published its *Limits to Growth* in 1969. And the first conference that drew global attention to the problems of the environment took place in Stockholm 1972 under the auspices of the United Nations.

the standing of NGOs in environmental matters is improved, is unjustified.[85]

Indeed, another interpretation of Article 263(4) TFEU than that given by the Court is possible, and the Court itself has proven it in a number of cases mentioned above. It is therefore simply not correct to state, as the Court does in settled case law, that another interpretation would require an amendment of the EU Treaties. A different interpretation of the provision does not constitute a "setting aside" of the provision, as the Court argues, but works within the context of the Treaty and does therefore not need its amendment.

The Court of Justice could thus eliminate the biggest obstacle to a proper representation of the environment in the EU Courts, if it had the political will to change its conservative and outdated interpretation of Article 263 TFEU and allow NGOs to represent the environment in court.

The Aarhus Convention Compliance Committee stated in 2016:[86] "The Committee finds that [the European Union] fails to comply with Article 9, paragraphs 3 and 4 of the Convention with regard to access to justice by members of the public because neither the Aarhus Regulation [this is Regulation 1367/2006[87]] nor the jurisprudence of the ECJ implements or complies with the obligations arising under those paragraphs".

The fact that the European Commission is capable of bringing environmental cases before the Court is not sufficient. Often enough, the Commission does not take action, either because of pressure from Member States or vested interest groups, or because it has other priorities or lacks sufficient information about what really happens at local level. There remains unanswered the question of who protects the environment against passivity or inertia by the Commission or other EU

---

[85] See, for example, Jonas Ebbesson (ed.), *Access to justice in environmental matters in the EU* (The Hague-London-New York, 2002); Nicola de Sadeleer, Gerhard Roller and Miriam Dross (eds.), *Access to justice in environmental matters and the role of NGOs; empirical findings and legal appraisal* (Groningen, 2005).

[86] Aarhus Convention Compliance Committee, Draft findings and recommendations of the Compliance Committee with regard to Communication ACCC/C/2008/32, part II, concerning compliance by the European Union: www.unece.org/fileadmin/DAM/env/pp/com pliance/C2008-32/From_Party/ToPartyC32_draft_findings.pdf (accessed 13 March 2017). The drafts findings still need to be finalized by the Compliance Committee itself and then approved by the Conference of the Parties.

[87] Regulation 1367/2006 on the application of the provisions of the Aarhus Convention on Access to Information, Public Participation in Decision-making and Access to Justice in Environmental Matters to Community institutions and bodies, EU OJ 2006, L264/13.

institutions. The Commission is aware of its bad record with regard to the enforcement of EU environmental law all over the EU territory, though its half-hearted measures to improve the situation[88] do not get away from its basic concept that the protection of the environment should be handled by public authorities and not also by civil society.

Once the environment has overcome the hurdle of access to the European courts, it may, generally, hope to find adequate protection. This, though, is also due to the existence of extensive EU environmental legislation. Neither the General Court nor the Court of Justice has, so far, recognized the unique role and function of the environment for the wellbeing of the EU and of the whole planet. For the EU courts, the preservation and protection of the environment is just one element of assessment among others. They have not accepted that the environment is a non-renewable resource.

As the EU is a regional globalization organization, the number of economic, social and environmental standards that are adopted at EU level, will increase in future, also because economic operators need bigger than national markets. Bad enforcement of existing EU environmental legislation is the cause of the very considerable discrepancy in the level of environmental protection within the EU, despite rather uniform EU standards; examples are, on the one hand, countries such as Sweden, the Netherlands, Denmark or Finland, and on the other hand, countries such as Portugal, Spain, Greece and the countries of central and Eastern Europe. Allowing civil society to contribute to the enforcement of EU environmental provisions is thus capable of reducing these discrepancies, give civil society a voice at EU and not only national level. This would finally increase democracy at EU level, contribute to further European integration and take away the image of the EU that it is just an organization for big business (vested interests).

---

[88] See, most recently, Commission, *Delivering the benefits of EU environmental policies through a regular Environmental Implementation Review*, COM(2016) 316 and COM (2017) 63.

2

The EU Aarhus Regulation and EU Administrative Acts Based on the Aarhus Regulation: the Withdrawal of the CJEU from the Aarhus Convention

KATJA RATH

A Introduction

The European Union (EU) is a contracting party to numerous bilateral and multilateral international treaties. The United Nations Economic Commission for Europe (UNECE) Convention on Access to Information, Public Participation in Decision-making and Access to Justice in Environmental Matters (the 'Aarhus Convention'[1]) is one of them. The EU is therefore an actor in the international community, which not only shapes the international system, but also has impacts the internal legal order of the Union. When the EU ratified the Aarhus Convention in 2005, a commitment to guarantee broad access to justice in environmental matters at both national and EU levels was made. One of the aims of the EU, as stated in art 3(5) of the 2007 Treaty on European Union (TEU), is to contribute 'to the strict observance and the development of international law'. While there is no doubt that the EU is bound as a party to the Aarhus Convention, the commitment to international law by the Court of Justice of the European Union (CJEU) differs tremendously. In particular, the tendency of the Court in recent years to give environmental associations more rights to obtain information and appeal in court has recently suffered a setback if EU institutions have been involved. This chapter debates whether EU secondary legislation, such as the Aarhus Regulation and decisions by EU institutions, may be reviewed against the criteria of the provisions of an international treaty

---

[1] UNECE Convention on Access to Information, Public Participation in Decision-making and Access to Justice in Environmental Matters, signed on 25 June 1998, entered into force on 30 October 2001 (Aarhus Convention).

like Aarhus. The European General Court (EGC) endorsed this and overturned decisions of the European Commission that were found to be incompatible with the Aarhus Convention. In contrast, the CJEU decided, in several cases in 2015, that environmental non-governmental organisations (NGOs) have no right to access information from EU authorities when withholding requested information is acceptable by provisions of the EU Aarhus Regulation, or when the challenged act of the EU institution is not an 'administrative act' as defined by the Aarhus Regulation. It is remarkable that in comparable cases in which NGOs requested information from Member State authorities or sought access to court, the CJEU was quick to rule that such behaviour was not compatible with provisions of the Aarhus Convention. It appears as though the Court wishes to avoid challenges to decisions of EU institutions, which would be in blatant conflict with international law, namely the Arhus Convention, as well as the public demand for a more transparent and accountable EU. The EU's commitment to international law cannot be taken for granted, and, accordingly, this chapter will investigate the reasons that the CJEU has given for its behaviour.

The selected case law will thus mainly focus on the question of whether European secondary law, such as Regulations and Directives transforming the Aarhus Convention, must be measured against the Aarhus Convention, and specifically art 9(3) thereof. To get to the bottom of this contentious jurisdiction, it is crucial to understand the general relationship between international law and EU secondary law (B). In a second step, the relevant case law on the matter of the Aarhus Convention will be explored (C), and finally possible reasons for the different outcomes will be discussed (D).

B   Relationship between International Law and EU Secondary Law

1   The Adoption of Aarhus within the Multi-level-Governance System

The Aarhus Convention currently has forty-seven parties, forty-six of them states and the remaining one the EU.[2] It is a multilateral environmental agreement, which strengthens three pillars: access to information, public participation in decision-making and access to justice in

---

[2] When using the term 'EU', the former EC is meant if the reference relates to the European Community before the Treaty of Lisbon 2009.

environmental matters.[3] One of the cornerstones of the Aarhus Convention is art 9(3), which reads that '[...] each Party shall ensure that, where they meet the criteria, if any, laid down in its national law, members of the public have access to administrative or judicial procedures to challenge acts and omissions by private persons and public authorities which contravene provisions of its national law relating to the environment'.

With the European Community's Decision on the conclusion of the Aarhus Convention, the EU acceded to the Convention in 2005.[4] As with most multilateral environmental agreements (MEAs), the EU and the Member States signed the Aarhus Convention as a mixed agreement. Nevertheless, unlike other MEAs, the Aarhus Convention commits the EU to guarantee compliance not only within its Member States, but also within its own institutions, as they are, by definition, public authorities in the sense of the Convention, art 2(2)(d).[5] Upon signature of the Aarhus Convention, the EU made a statement underlining its commitment, declaring that '[its] institutions will apply the Convention ... in the field covered by the Convention'.[6] In the post-Aarhus era, environmental NGOs gained better standing requirements for direct actions in environmental cases, at least when the EU court had to decide on the standing of national courts of the Member States (see Section C.I.).

By 2003, two Directives concerning the first and second pillars of the Aarhus Convention had already been adopted to establish the legal framework for the transformation of the three pillars into European legislation: Directive 2003/4/EC on public access to environmental information[7] and Directive 2003/35/EC on public participation.[8]

---

[3] J. Wates, 'The Aarhus convention: a driving force for environmental democracy', JEEPL [2005], 2.

[4] Council Decision 2005/370/EC of 17 February 2005 on the conclusion, on behalf of the European Community, of the Convention on access to information, public participation in decision-making and access to justice in environmental matters [2005] OJ L124/1.

[5] V. Rodenhoff, 'The Aarhus convention and its implications for the "Institutions" of the European Community', RECIEL [2002], 343; S. Kravchenko, 'The Aarhus convention and innovations in compliance with multilateral environmental law and Policy', CJIELP [2007] 1.

[6] For the full text of the declaration see: https://treaties.un.org/Pages/ViewDetails.aspx?src=TREATY&mtdsg_no=XXVII-13&chapter=27&lang=en accessed 15 July 2017.

[7] Directive 2003/4/EC of 28 January 2003 on public access to environmental information and repealing Council Directive 90/313/EEC [2003] OJ L41/26.

[8] Directive 2003/35/EC of 25 June 2003 providing for public participation in respect of the drawing up of certain plans and programmes relating to the environment and amending with regard to public participation and access to justice [2003] OJ L156/17; for a critical

The third pillar, though – access to justice – was not so easy to incorporate into the EU *acquis*. For years, environmental NGOs struggled to obtain direct access to EU courts in environmental matters.[9] The European Courts refused to reconsider its well-established *Plaumann* approach,[10] but stated that the *Plaumann* test remained good law regardless of 'the nature, economic or otherwise, of those of the applicants' interests which are affected'.[11] After a long legislative quarrel about another Directive on access to justice,[12] Regulation 1367/2006 (the 'Aarhus Regulation'[13]) finally adopted provisions of the Aarhus Convention relating not only to European institutions, but also to bodies, offices or agencies established by or based on the TEU.

These EU institutions need to adapt their internal procedures and practices to the provisions of the new Regulation. Article 1(1) of the Aarhus Regulation states that the 'objective of this Regulation is to contribute to the implementation of the obligations arising [. . .] by laying down rules to apply the provisions of the Convention to Community institutions and bodies [. . .]'. Article 2(1) of the Aarhus Regulation defines an 'administrative act' as 'any measure of individual scope under environmental law'. As a central issue, art 10(1) of the Aarhus Regulation provides that NGOs that fulfil certain criteria are permitted to request an internal review to the EU institution or body that has adopted an administrative act under environmental law. Article 10(1) can be understood as implementing the obligations resulting from art 9(3) of

---

view on this Directive, see M. Mason, 'Information disclosure and environmental rights: The Aarhus Convention', GEP [2010] 10.

[9] Case T-585/93, *Stichting Greenpeace Council v. Commission* [1995] ECR II-2205; Case C-321/95P, *Stichting Greenpeace Council and Others v. Commission* [1998] ECR I-1651; Case T-219/95R, *Marie-Thérèse Danielsson, Pierre Largenteau and Edwin Haoa v. Commission of the European Communities* [1995] ECR II-3051; Case C-294/83, *Parti écologiste 'Les Verts' v. European Parliament* [1986] ECR 1339.

[10] Case 25/62, *Plaumann & Co v. Commission* [1963] ECR 95.

[11] See also on the topic H. Schoukens, 'Access to Justice in Environmental Cases after the Rulings of the Court of Justice of 13 January 2015: Kafka Revisited?' *Utrecht Journal of International and European Law* [2015] 46; N. Gérard, 'Access to the European Court of Justice: A Lost Opportunity' JEL [1998] 331; D. L. Torrens, 'Locus Standi of Environmental Associations under EC Law – Greenpeace – A Missed Opportunity for the CJEU', RECIEL [1999] 336; C. Poncelet, 'Access to Justice in Environmental Matters – Does the European Union Comply with Its Obligations?', JEL [2012] 287.

[12] See details on the legislative procedure: Procedure 2003/0246/COD.

[13] Regulation (EC) 1367/2006 of 25 September 2006 on the application of the provisions of the Aarhus Convention on Access to Information, Public Participation in Decision-making and Access to Justice in Environmental Matters to Community institutions and bodies [2006] OJ L264/13.

the Aarhus Convention, which should have made obsolete the *Plaumann* formula for NGOs in environmental cases. Many welcomed the Aarhus Regulation as a substantial milestone in the pursuit of better access to justice at EU level.[14] But, as the case law in section C.II. will show, the internal review procedure of the Aarhus Regulation cannot be seen as a great triumph in changing the difficulty of environmental NGOs in obtaining better access to justice. In many instances, controversial acts by EU institutions do not – at least as far as the CJEU is concerned – constitute measures for which internal review is foreseen.[15] It is thus not surprising to see that the Aarhus Compliance Committee concluded that, if the rigid jurisprudence of the EU courts continues, the EU will fail to comply with art 9(3) of the Aarhus Convention.[16]

2   The Influence of International Law on the EU Acquis

For a better comprehension of the upcoming case law and the dispute over the possible effects of the Aarhus Convention on the EU legal order, some context on the influence of international law is necessary.[17] Traditionally, international law does not regulate the question of the legal status of an international agreement within the internal legal order of a contracting party. This principle also applies to the EU, and it is thus up to EU law to define how an international agreement gains legal relevance in EU law.

The general framework concerning the relationship between international treaties to which the EU is a contracting party and European law is governed by the TEU[18] and the Treaty on the Functioning of the European Union (TFEU).[19] Article 47 of the TEU provides the EU with international legal personality, and thus the ability to become a party to

[14] T. Crossen and V. Niessen, 'NGO Standing in the European Court of Justice – Does the Aarhus Regulation Open the Door?', RECIEL [2008] 332.

[15] J. H. Jans and G. Harryvan, 'Internal Review of EU Environmental Measures. It's True: Baron Van Munchausen Doesn't Exist! Some Remarks on the Application of the So-Called Aarhus Regulation', Rev Eur & Ad L [2010] 53.

[16] Communication ACCC/C/2008/32 [Part I] (European Union), para. 93.

[17] For a more detailed account of the matter, see: C. Tietje, 'The Status of International Law in the European Legal Order: The Case of International Treaties and Non-Binding International Instruments' in Jan Wouters, André Nollkaemper and Erika de Wet (eds.), *The Europeanisation of International Law – The Status of International Law in the EU and Its Member States* (The Hague: TMC Asser Press, 2008).

[18] Treaty on European Union [2012] OJ C326.

[19] Treaty on the Functioning of the European Union [2012] OJ C326.

an international agreement governed by international law as defined in the Vienna Convention on the Law of Treaties[20] and the Vienna Convention on the Law of Treaties Between States and International Organizations or Between International Organizations.[21] Article 216(2) of the TFEU states that 'agreements concluded by the Union are binding upon the institutions of the Union and on its Member States'. However, the status of an international treaty as an integral part of Community law does not say anything about its hierarchical status within the EU *acquis*. International treaties to which the EU has acceded must comply with the constitutional framework of the EU (art 218(11) of the TFEU). Accordingly, if the EU acceded to an international agreement, the provisions of that specific international contract generally prevail over acts laid down by institutions of the EU. In simplified terms, international law is higher ranking than EU secondary law, and EU primary law is superior to international law.[22] This means that the CJEU, at least from an international law perspective, does not have the power to void a treaty that is in conflict with EU law.[23] At the same time, the CJEU may very well declare the act of an EU institution invalid.

In its past jurisdiction, the European Court of Justice (ECJ) has established a wide-ranging jurisprudence on what effect is to be given to provisions of international agreements on EU law. Individuals may directly rely on provisions of an international agreement to which the EU is a contracting party, if the conditions for 'direct effect' or 'direct applicability' are fulfilled.[24] In this context, the ECJ usually applies a two-tier assessment. It first asks whether the respective international treaty is of such a nature that it might create directly effective rights and obligations for individuals. If this can be answered positively, the ECJ goes on to determine whether the specific provision is sufficiently 'legally perfect' to accord individual rights. With regard to the wording, purpose and nature of the agreement, a provision is directly applicable if it 'contains a clear, precise and unconditional obligation, which is not subject, in its

---

[20] 1155 UNTS 331, No. 18232.

[21] Not yet in force. For text, see: http://legal.un.org/ilc/texts/instruments/english/conventions/9_1_1961.pdf accessed 15 July 2017.

[22] A. Peters, 'The Position of International Law within the European Community Legal Order', GYIL [1997] 36.

[23] Tietje, 'The Status of International Law', p. 55.

[24] On the problems of confusing terminology in this regard, see Peters, 'The Position of International Law'; for the link between environment and human rights, see E. Morgera, 'An Update on the Aarhus Convention and its continued global relevance', RECIEL [2005] 138.

implementation or effects, to the adoption of any subsequent measure'.[25] It should be noted, though, that the ECJ established this type of assessment by referring to preliminary rulings (art 267 of the TFEU). Hence, the ECJ only dealt with the possibility of invoking provisions of an international treaty before the judge of a Member State.

Furthermore, the ECJ clarified that because international treaty law is an integral part of European law, there is an obligation for national courts 'when called upon to apply national rules' related to a respective international agreement 'to do so, as far as possible, in the light of the wording and purpose' of the applicable provisions of an agreement.[26] If the ECJ applies this principle of interpretation in conformity with international law to the Member States, then it must also apply it to secondary EU law relating to an international treaty. The ECJ stated explicitly that 'the primacy of international agreements concluded by the Community over provisions of secondary Community legislation means that such provisions must, so far as is possible, be interpreted in a manner that is consistent with those agreements'.[27] In order to answer the question of whether provisions from the Aarhus Convention have a direct effect or need to be at least interpreted in the light of the international agreement, it would be beneficial to look at some case law of the ECJ on other international agreements and their effect on European and national law.

3   Previous Jurisdiction of the ECJ on International Treaties

First, it is important to clarify that the ECJ in its permanent jurisprudence denies direct effect to World Trade Organization (WTO) law before national courts or the courts of the Community.[28] It ruled that individuals could only appeal provisions that conferred rights before courts if

---

[25] See Case 12/86, *Meryem Demirel* v. *Stadt Schwäbisch Gmünd* [1987] ECR 3719, para. 14; Case C-162/96, *A. Racke GmbH & Co.* v. *Hauptzollamt Mainz* [1998] ECR I-3655, para. 31; Case C-300/98, *Parfums Christian Dior SA* v. *TUK Consultancy BV and Assco Gerüste GmbH and Rob van Dijk* v. *Wilhelm Layher GmbH & Co. KG and Layher BV* [2000] ECR I-11307, para. 42.

[26] Case C-53/96, *Hermès International* v. *FHT Marketing Choice BV* [1998] ECR I-3603, para. 28; and Tietje, 'The Status of International Law'.

[27] Case C-61/94, *Commission of the EC* v. *Federal Republic of Germany* [1996] ECR I-3989, para. 52.

[28] See Cases C-53/96 and C-76/00, *Petrotub SA and Republica SA* v. *Council of the European Union* [2003] ECR I-79; Case C-93/02, *Biret International SA* v. *Council of the European Union* [2003] ECR I-10497; Case C-377/02, *Léon Van Parys NV* v. *Belgisch Interventie- en Restitutiebureau (BIRB)* [2005] ECR I-1465.

the international treaty at issue can be seen as being 'capable of having direct effect and if the provision at issue was sufficiently precise and unconditional'.[29] The main reason for this argumentation and the refusal of direct effect was, of course, to maintain political flexibility. Nonetheless, the Court also established two exemptions whereby individuals could actually rely on provisions of WTO law to question provisions of EU secondary law: first, where the EU act at issue referred explicitly to specific provisions of WTO law (the *Fediol* exception[30]), and, second, where the EU anticipated the implementation of a specific requirement assumed under WTO law (the *Nakajima* exception[31]).

In its *Biotechnology* judgment,[32] the ECJ started to differentiate further between situations in which an international treaty created directly effective individual rights and where it could be used more broadly by courts to assess the EU's compliance. An example for the first interpretation is the application of provisions of the Rio Convention on Biological Diversity.[33] Unlike typical WTO law, it is not based on 'reciprocal and mutually advantageous arrangements'.[34] Rather, it works more like a human rights treaty, since it primarily establishes obligations of one treaty party towards its citizens.[35] It therefore does not preclude review by the courts of compliance with the obligations incumbent on the Community as a party to that agreement.[36] An example for the latter reading is the case of *Intertanko*,[37] which dealt with the International Association of Independent Tanker Owners. In that case, the ECJ again applied the firm reasoning of WTO case law to an international agreement – namely, the United Nations Convention on the Law of the Sea.

[29] Case C-149/96, *Portuguese Republic* v. *Council of the European Union* [1999] ECR I-8425.

[30] Case C-70/87, *Fédération de l'industrie de l'huilerie de la CEE (Fediol)* v. *Commission of the European Communities* [1989] ECR 1781.

[31] Case C-69/89, *Nakajima All Precision Co. Ltd* v. *Council of the European Communities* [1991] ECR I-2072.

[32] Case C-377/98, *Kingdom of the Netherlands* v. *European Parliament and Council of the European Union* [2001] ECR I-7149.

[33] The Rio de Janeiro Convention on Biological Diversity; Council Decision 93/626/EEC of 25 October 1993 concerning the conclusion of the Convention on Biological Diversity [1993] OJ L309/1.

[34] Case C-149/96, *Portugal* v. *Council* [1999] ECR I-8395, paras. 42–46.

[35] L. Ankersmit and B. Pirker, 'Review of EU legislation under EU international agreements revisited: Aarhus receives another blow' (European Law Blog, 17 November 2015) http://europeanlawblog.eu/?p=2999 accessed 15 July 2017.

[36] Case C-377/98 [2001] ECR I-7149, para. 54.

[37] Case C-308/06, *The Queen, on the application of International Association of Independent Tanker Owners (Intertanko) and Others* v. *Secretary of State for Transport* [2008] ECR I-4057.

The Court specified that the Convention does not 'in principle' grant independent rights to individuals and ruled that the 'nature and broad logic' of the Convention prohibited the Court from assessing the legality of EU acts in the sense of its provisions.[38]

A further fine-tuning for the Courts 'direct effect' application was reached in the judgment in *Air Transport Association of America*.[39] In that case, the Court allowed review of EU legislation in light of an international agreement, since the treaty did not specifically preclude this and because the agreement created directly and immediately applicable rules that conferred rights and freedoms to individuals. So the ECJ examined whether an agreement does not as a whole preclude any effect as a benchmark for review in the EU legal order and whether the provision to be applied regulated individuals in a sufficiently direct way.

Following this development, it seems only logical that the ECJ would most likely give direct effect to, or at least interpret, national and European legislation and acts in the light of the following Aarhus provisions. While art 4(1) of the Aarhus Convention states that 'public authorities in response to a request for environmental information, make such information available to the public', art 9(3) specifies that 'members of the public have access to administrative or judicial procedures to challenge acts and omissions'.

C   Selected Case Law on the Effect of the Aarhus Convention on Member States

1   ECJ Judgments concerning NGOs' Requests for Access to Court in Member States

a)   Case C-240/09 *Slovak Brown Bear*

This case concerned the request of a Slovak NGO called Lesoochranárske zoskupenie VLK ('LZ') to participate as a party to a number of administrative proceedings concerning the protection of nature and the environment. At the beginning of 2008, LZ was informed of a number of pending administrative proceedings brought by various hunting associations regarding the grant of derogations to the system of protection for species such as the brown bear.[40] LZ's attempts at becoming a party to the

---

[38] Ibid., paras. 64–65.
[39] Case C-366/10, *Air Transport Association of America and Others* v. *Secretary of State for Energy and Climate Change* [2011] ECR I-13755.
[40] Case C-240/09, *Lesoochranárske zoskupenie VLK* v. *Ministerstvo životného prostredia Slovenskej republiky* [2011] ECR I-1285, para. 20.

administrative proceedings, and for that purpose relying directly on the Aarhus Convention, were rejected by the national Ministry.[41] Furthermore, the Ministry stated that the Aarhus Convention was an international treaty that needed to be implemented in national law before it could take effect.[42] LZ then brought an appeal against the decisions of the Ministry, arguing that the provisions in art 9(3) of the Aarhus Convention had direct effect ('self-executing-effect'). The Slovak Supreme Court asked the ECJ for a preliminary ruling.

First, the Court considered whether it had the jurisdiction to interpret the provisions of art 9(3) of the Aarhus Convention. It stated that the Aarhus Convention was signed by the EU and the Member States based on joint competence. It follows that it is within the Court's competence to define the obligations of the Member States concerning the interpretation of the Aarhus Convention, on the one hand, and the obligations that the Community has assumed, on the other hand.[43] 'Where a provision can apply both to situations falling within the scope of national law and to situations falling within the scope of EU law, [it is important], in order to forestall future differences of interpretation, that the provision should be interpreted uniformly [. . .]'.[44] In the next step, the CJEU determined whether, in the field covered by art 9(3) of the Aarhus Convention, the EU has exercised its powers and adopted provisions to implement the obligations that derive from it. If not, art 9(3) of the Aarhus Convention would be assigned to the jurisdiction of the national legislators of the Member States.[45] The Court argued that, in the field of environmental protection, the EU has explicit competences (now art 191 of the TFEU).[46] The Court concluded that the dispute fell within the scope of EU law.[47] In this case, the affected species of the granted derogations, the brown bear, is mentioned in Annex IV(a) to Directive 92/43/EEC (the 'Habitats Directive').[48] Under art 12 thereof, it is subject to a system of strict protection from which derogations may be granted only under the conditions laid down in art 16 of the Habitats Directive. After the ECJ affirmed both the interpretation sovereignty of the Aarhus Convention as

---

[41] Ibid., para. 21.
[42] Ibid., Opinion of AG [Sharpston], para. 23.
[43] Ibid., para. 31.
[44] Ibid., para. 42.
[45] Ibid., paras. 32–34.
[46] Ibid., para. 35.
[47] Ibid., paras. 37–38.
[48] Council Directive 92/43/EEC of 21 May 1992 on the conservation of natural habitats and of wild fauna and flora [1992] OJ L206/7.

a mixed international agreement and its jurisdiction to interpret art 9(3) of the Aarhus Convention, despite the lack of a Community act, it devoted itself to the actual question of whether art 9(3) of the Aarhus Convention has direct effect. The Court denied the direct applicability of art 9(3) because 'it does not contain any clear and precise obligation capable of directly regulating the legal position of individuals'.[49] Rather, it requires an adoption of a subsequent measure of some kind. The ECJ then gave the national court orders on the interpretation of its national procedural law to comply with the Aarhus Convention. Accordingly, 'it is for the national court, in order to ensure effective judicial protection in the fields covered by EU environmental law, to interpret its national law in a way which, to the fullest extent possible, is consistent with the objectives laid down in art 9(3) of the Aarhus Convention'.[50]

The essential statement of the *Slovak Brown Bear* decision was not the finding that art 9(3) of the Aarhus Convention does not have direct effect. Rather, the remarks concerning how national law should be interpreted in the light of art 9(3) of the Aarhus Convention form the very core of the *Slovak Brown Bear* decision, which is apparent in the fact that they find themselves in the operative part of the decision. Additionally, the statement that the purpose of the generally formulated art 9(3) of the Aarhus Convention lies in ensuring effective environmental protection was decisive and formative. From this basic assumption, as well as the combination of art 9(3) of the Aarhus Convention and the principles of effectiveness and equivalence, the ECJ gives extensive legal specifications to Member States on how to embellish the structure of national law concerning the environmental protection. The Court clarified that it did not tolerate restrictions on 'wide access to justice' as well as actions restricting the possibility of challenging legal errors.

b) Case C-115/09 *Trianel*

Trianel, the intervener, intended to build a coal-fired power station in Lünen, Germany.[51] Within eight kilometres of the project site, there were designated areas per the definition of those in the Habitats Directive, which were also officially declared conservation zones under national German law. After the environmental impact assessment, the German

---

[49] Case C-240/09, paras. 44–45.
[50] Ibid., para. 51.
[51] Case C-115/09, *Bund für Umwelt und Naturschutz Deutschland, Landesverband Nordrhein-Westfahlen eV* v. *Bezirksregierung Arnsberg* [2011] ECR 3715 f.; Case C-115/09 Opinion of A G Sharpston, p. 3683 f.

authority issued a preliminary decision, stating that there were no legal concerns in relation to the project site, and a partial permit for the project was issued. The environmental NGO BUND,[52] recognised under paragraph 3 of the German Environmental Appeals Act, initiated proceedings against the German authorities. The proceedings aimed both at the withdrawal of the preliminary decision and at the permit. *Trianel* claims that these decisions contain formal and substantive defects (project infringes, violation of the protective and precautionary principles as well as violations of the German nature protection laws, which implement the Habitats Directive, especially art 6 thereof). The local Administrative Court referred the case to the ECJ and asked for a preliminary ruling on the interpretation of art 10a of the Public Participation Directive 85/337/EEC,[53] i.e. the EIA-Directive 2003/35/EC.[54] To obtain *locus standi* in German administrative law, the impairment of a substantive individual right is essential, following the German Environmental Appeals Act as well as the more general German Code of Administrative Court Procedure.

First, the Court underlined that the first paragraph of art 10a of Directive 85/337 provided that the decisions, acts or omissions referred to in that article must be actionable before a court of law through a review procedure 'to challenge [their] substantive or procedural legality'.[55] The Court further noted that it did not matter if the admissibility of an action might be conditional on a 'sufficient interest in bringing the action'[56] or on the applicant alleging 'the impairment of a right'.[57] This implementation, as well as the definition of a sufficient interest and impairment of a right, is left to the national legislation. With the objective of giving the public 'wide access to justice'[58] in applying the Aarhus Convention to environmental NGOs, the ECJ established that national statutes, by setting up additional prerequisites, obstruct access to justice as guaranteed by EU law and the Aarhus Convention.[59] The concept that a case can be brought to court only if individual rights explicitly granted by legislation are at stake is a major principle of German procedural law.

---

[52] The Nordrhein-Westfalen branch of Friends of the Earth Germany.
[53] Council Directive 85/337/EEC of 27 June 1985 on the assessment of the effects of certain public and private projects on the environment [1985] OJ L175/40.
[54] Council Directive 2003/35/EC of 26 May 2003.
[55] Case C-115/09, para. 37.
[56] Ibid., para. 38.
[57] Ibid.
[58] Ibid., para. 39.
[59] Ibid., paras. 41, 42.

However, in the field of environmental conservation, legislation often does not confer rights to individuals but provides for nature protection as such or for the public interest.[60] The Court then states that 'although it is the right of the Member State (...) what rights can give rise when infringed, but they cannot deprive environmental protection organisations which fulfil the conditions laid down in Directive 85/337 of the opportunity of playing the role granted to them both by Directive 85/337 and by the Aarhus Convention'.[61]

The key question was whether the German obligation of an impairment of individual rights valid in the environmental context is compatible with international and EU law, and in particular with art 9(3) of the Aarhus Convention and art 10a of Directive 85/337. The Court emphasised the importance of the Aarhus Convention. The special role accorded to environmental NGOs under the Convention and the Directives strengthens the quality and the legitimacy of decisions taken by the authorities and stimulates the machinery for preventing environmental damage. As a consequence of the judgment, Germany had to change its Environmental Appeals Act accordingly. Until this was done, the ECJ declared the Directive on Public Participation to be directly applicable. After two leading cases of the Court (*Slovak Brown Bear* and *Trianel*) confirmed the importance of the accessibility of courts in environmental law, especially for environmental protection organisations, the German legislators modified both paragraphs so that they are now in conformity with the Aarhus Convention.

2   CJEU Judgments concerning NGOs' Requests towards EU Institutions

a)   Joined Cases C-401/12P to C-403/12P and C-404/12P to C-405/12P

In joined cases C-401/12P to C-403/12P,[62] the NGO applicants Vereniging Milieudefensie and Pesticide Action Network Europe submitted a request to the Commission for internal review under art 10 of the Aarhus Regulation. The NGOs specifically demanded an internal

---

[60] ERA, 'Module 3: Environmental Impact Assessment (EIA) Directive – EIA procedure, Public Participation' http://ec.europa.eu/environment/legal/law/2/module_3_11.htm accessed 15 July 2017.

[61] Case C-115/09, para. 44.

[62] Joined Cases C-401/12P to C-403/12P, *Council of the European Union and Others v. Vereniging Milieudefensie and Stichting Stop Luchtverontreiniging Utrecht*, ECLI:EU: C:2015:4.

review of the decision of the Commission to grant the Netherlands an exemption under Directive 2008/50 on ambient air quality. The Commission rejected the NGOs' request as inadmissible, on the ground that its decision was not a measure of individual scope and that it could therefore not be considered an 'administrative act' within the meaning of art 2(1)(g) of the Aarhus Regulation. Only an administrative act could be the subject of an internal review procedure provided under art 10(1) of the Aarhus Regulation.

In joined cases C-404/12P to C-405/12P,[63] the Commission previously accepted that the Netherlands had postponed the deadline for attaining annual limit values for nitrogen dioxide in certain zones as laid down in Regulation 149/2008.[64] In 2008, the NGO Stichting Natuur en Milieu requested an internal review of Regulation 149/2008 itself. The European Commission rejected the requests for an internal review with the same reasoning as in C-401/12P to C-403/12P.

In all cases, the General Court annulled the Commission's decision and determined at the beginning that 'pursuant to art 300(7) EC,[65] international agreements concluded by the European Union bind its institutions and consequently prevail over the acts laid down by those institutions'.[66] The General Court ruled that an internal review in both cases was possible, following the so called *Nakajima* exception.[67] It determined that 'an internal review procedure which covered only measures of individual scope would be very limited (which) is not justified'.[68] Article 10(1) of the Aarhus Regulation has to be applied in the light of art 9(3) of the Aarhus Convention. This finding was based on the fact that art 10(1) of the Regulation was an implementation of art 9(3) of the Convention and expressly referred to the latter.[69] 'In consequence, in so far as art 10(1) (. . .) limits the concept of "acts" in art 9(3) of the

---

[63] Joined Cases C-404/12P to C-405/12P, *Council of the European Union and European Commission* v. *Stichting Natuur en Milieu and Pesticide Action Network Europe* [2011] ECR I-13755.

[64] Commission Regulation (EC) 149/2008 of 29 January 2008 amending Regulation (EC) No 396/2005 of the European Parliament and of the Council by establishing Annexes II, III and IV setting maximum residue levels for products covered by Annex I thereto [2008] OJ L58/1.

[65] Now art. 216(2) TFEU.

[66] Case T-338/08, *Stichting Natuur en Milieu and Pesticide Action Network Europe* v. *European Commission* [2012] ECR, para. 51.

[67] Ibid.; and Case T-396/09, *Vereniging Milieudefensie and Stichting Stop Luchtverontreiniging Utrecht* v. *European Commission* [2012] ECR, paras. 54–57.

[68] Case T-338/08, para. 76.

[69] Case T-396/09, paras. 54, 58.

Aarhus Convention to "administrative act[s]" defined (. . .) as "measure-[s] of individual scope", it is not compatible with art 9(3) of the Aarhus Convention'.[70] For the second case, it stated that the adoption of Regulation 149/2008 fell within the scope of the Commission's regulatory activities and could not be considered 'legislative' activity, which would be excluded from art 9(3) of the Aarhus Convention.[71]

All things considered, the reasoning of the General Court follows WTO case law (Cases C-70/87 and C-69/89). The General Court declares the partial incompatibility of the Regulation, which opens the way for a review of legality. For the very first time, EU judges were willing to assess the legality of EU rules on access to justice at the European level in the light of the third pillar of the Aarhus Convention. By considering the impact of art 9(3) of the Aarhus Convention on EU rules, it seemed as though the General Court began to move toward more accountability in environmental matters.[72] Nevertheless, the Commission, the Council and the Parliament appealed the ruling, claiming that the General Court erred in holding that art 9(3) of the Aarhus Convention might be relied on in order to assess the compliance of art 10(1) of the Aarhus Convention with that provision.

The CJEU annulled the judgments of the General Court in its decisions for both of the joined cases. According to its own judicature, the CJEU stressed that provisions of an international agreement to which the EU is a party need 'to be unconditional and sufficiently precise' to be relied upon in support of an action for annulment of an act of secondary EU law.[73] It held that art 9(3) of the Aarhus Convention does 'not contain any unconditional and sufficiently precise obligation capable of directly regulating the legal position of individuals',[74] '[s]ince only members of the public who "meet the criteria, if any, laid down in (. . .) national law" are entitled to exercise the rights provided for in art 9(3)'.[75] This required the adoption of a subsequent measure and was not, therefore, unconditional and sufficiently precise.[76] The CJEU rejected the application of the Fediol and the Nakajima cases, holding that 'those two exceptions were justified solely by the particularities of the agreements [WTO and the

---

[70] Ibid., para 69.
[71] Case T-338/08, paras. 68–70.
[72] Schoukens, 'Access to Justice in Environmental Cases' .
[73] Cases C-401/12P to C-403/12P, para. 54.
[74] Ibid., para. 55.
[75] Ibid., para. 55.
[76] Ibid., paras. 54–55.

General Agreement on Tariffs and Trade (GATT)] that led to their application.'[77] Article 10(1) of the Aarhus Regulation 'neither made direct reference to specific provisions of the Aarhus Convention nor (conferred rights on individuals to rely on art 9(3))'.[78] In addition, art 10(1) did not implement specific obligations stemming from art 9(3) of the Convention, since the parties to the Convention had 'a broad margin of discretion when defining the rules for the implementation of "the administrative or judicial procedures"'.[79] Finally, the Court ruled that, by adopting the Aarhus Regulation, the EU did not intend to implement obligations that derive from art 9(3) of the Aarhus Convention.[80] It further stated that 'with respect to national administrative or judicial procedures, which as EU law now stands, fall primarily within the scope of member State law',[81] and refers to the *Slovak Brown Bear* case.[82]

The lack of specifics within the Aarhus Convention (determined in Case C-240/09) is now the main argument for its inapplicability, along with the non-existent intention of the EU to implement the obligations that derive from art 9(3) of the Aarhus Convention. Remarkably, the CJEU does not discuss the findings from Case C-240/09 in either of the judgments in the joined cases. While, for the Member States, national rules need to be brought into accordance with the Aarhus Convention, the EU institutions apparently are not required to follow the set outline. Herein lies the main shortcoming of the two decisions. Advocate General Jääskinen specified that 'the CJEU has adopted an approach that is highly protective of the effectiveness and objectives of the Aarhus Convention in relation to the implementation obligations mandatory for the Member States (and) it does not therefore appear to be conceivable for a different approach to be adopted with regard to the European Union itself'.[83] The tendency of the CJEU in recent years to give environmental associations more and more rights concerning access to justice is clearly not maintained in the decisions from early 2015.

b)   Case C-612/13P *ClientEarth*

Case C-612/13P dealt with the request by the NGO ClientEarth to receive access to studies relating to the conformity of national legislation with the

---

[77] Ibid., para. 57.
[78] Ibid., para. 58.
[79] Ibid., para. 59.
[80] Ibid., paras. 60–61.
[81] Ibid., para. 60.
[82] Case C-240/09, paras. 41, 47.
[83] Cases C-401/12P to C-403/12P, Opinion of AG Jääskinen, para. 132.

EU environmental acquis in several Member States. The Commission had granted only partial access to the documents, and stated that it needed to withhold information as its release would weaken its ability to monitor and enforce EU environmental law through infringement proceedings (art 258 of the TFEU). The Commission claimed that this information fell within the exception of art 4(2) (third indent) of Regulation 1049/2001 (Public Access to Documents).[84] That provision allows the Commission to refuse access to a document 'where disclosure would undermine the protection of the purpose of inspections, investigations, and audits, unless there is an overriding public interest in disclosure'. ClientEarth argued that the Commission could not rely on that exception because it was incompatible with art 4(4)(c) of the Aarhus Convention: 'a request for environmental information may be refused if the disclosure would adversely affect the course of justice (...) or the ability of a public authority to conduct an enquiry of a criminal or disciplinary nature'.

After mentioning the case law on the requirements for challenging the validity of EU acts under EU international agreements (mainly the joined cases from January 2015),[85] the CJEU applied the requirements to the case, and in particular art 4(4)(c) of the Aarhus Convention. The Court found art 4(4) (c) not sufficiently precise and unconditional. It then reasoned that Aarhus could not be relied upon, first, because 'the reference, in art 4(1) of the Aarhus Convention, to national legislation indicates that that convention was obviously designed with the national legal orders in mind, and not the specific legal features of institutions of regional economic integration, such as the European Union. This is even true where those institutions can sign and accede to the Aarhus Convention, under art 17 and 19 thereof'.[86] Secondly, it pointed out the context in which Aarhus had been concluded by the EU. It referred to the EU's statement, which said that 'the Community institutions will apply the Convention within the framework of their existing and future rules on access to documents and other relevant rules of Community law in the field covered by the Convention'.[87] Thirdly, and more specifically to the text of art 4(4)(c) of the Aarhus Convention, it stated that 'neither the reference, in art 4(4)(c), to enquiries "of a criminal or disciplinary

---

[84] Regulation 1049/2001/EC of 30 May 2001 regarding public access to European Parliament, Council and Commission documents [2001] OJ L145/43.
[85] Cases C-401/12P to C-403/12P and C-404/12P to C-405/12P.
[86] Case C-612/13P *ClientEarth* v. *European Commission*, ECLI:EU:C:2015:486, para. 40.
[87] Ibid., para. 41.

nature"', nor the obligation laid down in the second paragraph of art 4(4) to interpret in a restrictive way required release of the documents. 'A fortiori, a prohibition on giving to the concept of "enquiry" a meaning which takes account of the specific features of the Union, and in particular the task incumbent on the Commission to investigate any failures of Member States to fulfil their obligations which might adversely affect the correct application of the Treaties and the EU rules adopted pursuant to the Treaties, cannot be inferred from those provisions.'[88]

The first controversial point was reading the reference to national legislation in art 4(1) of the Aarhus Convention as indicating that the Convention's terms should not apply to EU legislation.[89] But, apart from this very formal argument, the crucial point was whether the Aarhus Regulation was in compliance with the Aarhus Convention, since infringement proceedings are not mentioned within the exception of art 4(4) (c) of the Aarhus Convention. It almost seems as though the CJEU is only incidentally protecting Regulation 1049/2001 from review under the Aarhus Convention's art 4(4)(c).[90] Infringement proceedings are aimed at simultaneously policing compliance with EU law by Member States and more generally as an instrument for securing performance of EU policies. But, aside from this, the rejection of direct effect for art 4(4) of the Aarhus Convention follows in the footsteps of the joined cases establishing case law that is not Aarhus friendly.

D   Conclusion

The initial question – whether EU secondary legislation such as the Aarhus Regulation and decisions by EU institutions may be reviewed against the criteria set down in art 9(3) and art 4(1) of the Aarhus Convention – must be answered in the affirmative, despite the recent rulings by the CJEU.

First and foremost, the hierarchical level of international law favours this view. The Aarhus Convention concluded by the EU is binding upon the institutions of the Union and on its Member States (art 216(2) of the TFEU). Within the multi-level governance system, international law, namely international agreements to which the EU is a contracting

---

[88] Ibid., para. 42.
[89] Mason, 'Information disclosure and environmental rights'.
[90] L. Ankersmit and B. Pirker, 'Aarhus receives another blow' (European Law Blog, 17 November 2015) http://europeanlawblog.eu/?p=2999 accessed 15 July 2017.

party, has far-reaching effects on European law. Pursuant to the established case law of the ECJ and the CJEU, the EU courts may review the
legality of a regulation in the light of an international agreement only
when the nature and the broad logic of the agreement do not preclude
such an assessment and where, in addition, the provisions of the treaty
appear, as regards their consent, to be unconditional and sufficiently
precise (direct effect). At first it seemed to be only consequent to deny
direct effect to art 9(3) of the Aarhus Convention, as in the *Slovak Brown
Bear* decision. Still, the decision from the Grand Chamber of the CJEU
stated that, although it had been drafted in broad terms, the provision
aimed to ensure effective environmental protection at national level. This
begs the question why a similar rationale has not prevailed in a case
concerning internal review at EU level. There is no visible reason for the
CJEU's being progressive at national level and conservative at EU level,
except to guard the decisions of EU institutions. This shows that the
Court apparently believes that international environmental law is still, at
least in part, 'soft law', and not of a comprehensive constitutional nature
in the interest of the international community. For international environmental treaties, such as the Aarhus Convention or the Biodiversity
Convention, which are not based on mutually advantageous arrangements such as WTO, this selective view of the Court can make or – as in
the recent case law – break the effectiveness of international environmental law.

The concept of direct effect could be a strong instrument that the CJEU
can use to overcome the line of the European legal order and enhance the
rights of individuals or NGOs when European secondary law falls short,
even though the provisions in art 4(1) and art 9(3) of the Aarhus
Convention do not contain clear and precise obligations capable of
directly regulating the legal position of individuals but rather require
an adoption of a subsequent measure. The denial of direct effect of these
provisions is questionable. At the least, the CJEU's rejection of the *Fediol*
and *Nakajima* exceptions to the criteria of direct effect do not seem
reasonable. The CJEU ruled that those two exceptions were justified
solely by the particularities of the agreements (WTO and GATT) that
led to their application. At first glance, the CJEU makes a reasonable
choice in opting for a restrictive application of the *Fediol* and *Nakajima*
exceptions. On the other hand, when an EU act such as the Aarhus
Regulation, in its Recital 18, refers directly to art 9(3) of the Aarhus
Convention in stating that 'provisions on access to justice should be
consistent with the Treaty', then the application of the *Nakajima*

exception does not seem too far-fetched. However, it remains unclear whether the Court's take remains convincing when it is considered that the CJEU's strict reading of the exceptions is not compensated for by a more lenient approach towards direct effect as a precondition for international law. Then major differences in the level of judicial protection exist for individuals in cases that relate to the EU's international obligations.

Even if the provisions in question cannot be qualified for direct effect, this does not release the CJEU from interpreting European secondary law in the light of the Aarhus Convention. This is especially true if the implementing legislation narrows access to courts and access to information by putting up stricter criteria than Aarhus, as has been done in art 10(1) of Aarhus Regulation and in the exception for access to documents in art 4(2) of the Public Access to Documents Regulation. Although, in the cases *Slovak Brown Bear* and *Trianel*, the Court argued that, by setting up additional national requirements to obtain standing for a NGO in court, suitable access to justice as assured by EU law and the Aarhus Convention had been violated, it nevertheless seemed oblivious as to whether European secondary law added additional requirements.

The CJEU's weak grounds in the joined cases decisions for the strict requirement of an 'administrative act' in art 10(1) of the Aarhus Regulation were as follows: by adopting the Aarhus Regulation, the EU did not intend to implement obligations that derive from art 9(3) of the Aarhus Convention. The main question is: if the Aarhus Regulation does not implement the Aarhus Convention, what, then, does it do?[91] The Court started its line of argumentation by explaining that the Aarhus Convention is designed for Member States of the Aarhus Convention and not for the EU. It refers to the *Slovak Brown Bear* case, completely ignoring art 216(2) of the TFEU and art 1(1) of the Aarhus Regulation. Clearly, the EU intended (at least in 2006) to implement art 9(3) of the Aarhus Convention when drafting the incompatible art 10(1) of the Aarhus Regulation. Consequently, it is for the CJEU to review the legality of the measure in question in the light of the obligations laid down in the Aarhus Convention. Currently, the Aarhus Regulation offers only a restricted scope, namely by limiting access to an internal review procedure only where the EU acts being challenged are 'measures of

---

[91] To the point: B. Pirker, 'Cases C-401 to 403/12 and C-404 to 405/12: No review of legality in light of the Aarhus Convention' (European Law Blog, 29 January 2015) http://europeanlawblog.eu/?p=2674#sthash.tAx3qXTc.dpuf accessed 15 July 2017.

individual scope'. As a result of these discretions accorded to the EU institutions, the Aarhus Regulation is currently applicable to only a very few decisions adopted in environmental matters. The CJEU missed a unique opportunity to fill the gaps in the EU system of judicial protection in environmental cases. It is very likely that the weaknesses of the current EU implementing rules as to access to justice in environmental matters will persist in the next years.

Apparently, the CJEU plans to defer the possibility of challenging decisions of the European institutions back to the Member States and what legal protection can be afforded by national courts. This conclusion considers the context of the latest study on the implementation of art 9(3) and (4) of the Aarhus Convention – a daring venture, as the study describes national implementation as 'diverging, random and inconsistent'.[92] During national proceedings, the CJEU might be involved. But preliminary proceedings often last several years, during which, in order to safeguard the effectiveness of the legality review before the CJEU, the national proceedings are suspended.[93] It remains highly uncertain whether national proceedings can, in cases in which national implementing measures are present, serve as a useful and practical back-up option for the CJEU.[94] The strategy of the CJEU might just be that the delays and financial burden involved with proceedings that start at the national courts make them disadvantageous and therefore seldom used.

When interpreting art 4(2) of the third indent of Regulation 1049/2001 in light of art 4(4)(c) Aarhus Convention in the *ClientEarth* judgment, the CJEU ignored the general rule that exceptions to a rule (here, the right to access public documents) are to be interpreted in a restrictive manner. The second paragraph of art 4(4) of the Aarhus Convention specifically states this narrow rule of interpretation, as well as art 6(1) of the EU Aarhus Regulation, which refers to the provision that was in question (art 4 of Regulation 1049/2001). They all claim that 'the grounds for refusal shall be interpreted in a restrictive way, taking into account the public

---

[92] J. Darpö, 'Effective Justice? Synthesis Report of the Study on the Implementation of Articles 9.3 and 9.4 of the Aarhus Convention in the Member States of the European Union' [2013] http://ec.europa.eu/environment/aarhus/access_studies.htm accessed 15 July 2017.

[93] P. Wennerås, 'The Enforcement of EC Environmental Law', *Oxford Studies in European Law* [2007] 213.

[94] H.Schoukens, 'Access to Justice in Environmental Matters on the EU Level After the Judgements of the General Court of 14 June 2012: Between Hope and Denial' [2014] Nordic Envtl LJ http://nordiskmiljoratt.se/haften/NMT%252c%2022%20aug%20(2).pdf accessed 15 July 2017.

interest served by disclosure and whether the information requested relates to emissions into the environment'. The CJEU then again used the formality that art 4(1) of the Aarhus Convention refers specifically to the framework of national legislation and not to the specific legal features of the EU. However, due to the historic development of international treaties and the special nature of the EU, international agreements will often speak of their Member 'States' and then of 'national' legislation and not include an extra sentence so the EU is reminded of their obligation.

E   Outlook

The non-application of direct effect and the denial of the *Fediol-* and *Nakajima* exceptions shield the European legal order from international environmental law. The practice of when direct effect of international law is applied by the CJEU exposes how the Court plays a critical political function at the intersection of legal orders. Accordingly, the CJEU might indeed be criticised for not taking into account the official aim of the EU to contribute to the strict observance and development of international law (art 3(5) of the TEU). Altogether, the reasons for decisions by EU institutions and secondary EU legislation not being measured against the benchmark of the Aarhus Convention are protective, obvious and, frankly, a confession that the CJEU favours the EU over the Member States. While the Court is not hesitant to enforce strict requirements on the Member States whenever it is asked to interpret the Aarhus Convention, EU institutions are let off easy, and with dubious reasons. The unjustified lenience towards EU institutions might easily lead to less engagement of the EU legal order with international law and therefore a weakened influence for international environmental law. Despite this negative outlook, the recent CJEU decisions, together with a future non-compliance finding by the Aarhus Compliance Committee, might serve as a wake-up call for the EU legislator.

3

Access to Justice before EU Courts in Environmental Cases against the Backdrop of the Aarhus Convention: Balancing Pathological Stubbornness and Cognitive Dissonance?

HENDRIK SCHOUKENS

A General Introduction: Environmental Accountability in Times of Mass Extinction

In recent times, the concrete manifestations of the impending ecological crisis that is currently taking place on our planet have become increasingly harder to ignore. The shrinking sea ice cover in the Arctic Ocean as well as in Antarctica, while partly dependent on yearly weather conditions, represents probably one of the most worrisome illustrations of unprecedented global warming.[1] Likewise, the advent of industrial agriculture, at the beginning of the twentieth century, skyrocketed human-induced nitrogen emissions, significantly disrupting the natural nitrogen cycle.[2] Nitrous oxide concentrations in the atmosphere are currently higher than at any other time during the last 800,000 years.[3] In turn, the massive extent of the current biodiversity crisis, which results from human impacts such as habitat destruction and poaching, in 2000 led Crutzen to dub the time period in which we live, and which is officially labeled the "Holocene," the "Anthropocene."[4]

---

[1] See M.-J. Viñas, "Sea ice extent sinks to record lows at both poles," 2017, https://phys.org/news/2017–03-sea-ice-extent-lows-poles.html (accessed 20 October 2017).

[2] See also Live Science Staff, "Nitrogen Fingered as Latest Ecosystem Evildoer", 2010: www.livescience.com/8720-nitrogen-fingered-latest-ecosystem-evildoer.html (accessed 20 October 2017).

[3] A. Schilt et al., "Glacial–interglacial and millennial-scale variations in the atmospheric nitrous oxide concentration during the last 800,000 years," *Quaternary Science Reviews*, 29 (2010), 182.

[4] P. J. Crutzen and E. F. Stroermer, "The 'Anthropocene'," *Global Change Newsletter*, (2000), 12. See, more recently, A. Zlasiewic et al., "The new world of the Anthropocene," *Environmental Science Technology* (2010), 2228.

Scientific research now suggests that, given current extinction rates, the world is witnessing a so-called sixth mass extinction event, with species being lost 1,000 to a staggering 10,000 times faster than the natural rate.[5] Even in the European Union (EU), which is often regarded as one of the regions in the world with the most progressive environmental legislation, biodiversity is not necessarily faring any better.[6] And while there are some remarkable success stories, such as the relatively recent recovery of endangered large carnivore species, such as gray wolves, throughout some parts of their former range, other studies have revealed that the populations of so-called common species, such as toads[7] and farmland species,[8] have suffered significant losses. The predicament of the EU's biodiversity was further exposed by a 2017 German report, which found that, in just a couple of decades, insect populations in German nature reserves have plummeted by more than 75 percent.[9]

Engaged and well-informed citizens and non-governmental organizations (NGOs) are seminal for achieving a more sustainable environment. In the aftermath of the Rio Declaration on Environment and Development, and in particular its Principle 10, the term "environmental democracy" has gained increasing traction among scientists and policy makers as a new paradigm.[10] This concept aims to reverse the well-vested approach to environmental decision-making procedures, which used to be exclusively determined by the economic aspirations of the governmental and industrial sectors concerned, by offering more procedural guarantees for the citizens concerned and environmental NGOs in this context. The increased levels of participation and the better access to court review were expected gradually to step up the level of

---

[5] A. Barnosky et al., "Has the Earth's sixth mass extinction already arrived?" *Nature*, 473 (2011), 51.

[6] European Environment Agency, *State of nature in the EU. Results from reporting under the nature directives 2007–2012* (EEA Technical Report, No. 2/2015).

[7] S. O. Petrovan and B. R. Schmidt, "Volunteer Conservation Action Data Reveals Large-Scale and Long-Term Negative Population Trends of a Widespread Amphibian, the Common Toad (*Bufo bufo*)," *PLoS ONE*, 11(10) (2016), e0161943, DOI: 10.1371/journal.pone.0161943.

[8] See, among others: A. Gamero et al., "Tracking Progress Towards EU Biodiversity Strategy Targets: EU Policy Effects in Preserving its Common Farmland Birds," *Conservation Letters* (2016): DOI: 10.1111/conl.12292.

[9] C. A. Hallman et al., "More than 75 percent decline over 27 years in total flying insect biomass in protected areas", *PLoS ONE*, 12(10) (2017), e0185809.

[10] J. Watts, "The Aarhus Convention: a Driving Force for Environmental Democracy", *Journal of European Environmental and Planning Law*, (2005), 3, 4.

environmental protection, which might ultimately lead to a better environmental quality on the ground. By any measure, environmental democracy presupposes that the wider public is able freely to access information around environmental impacts, participate meaningfully in decision making, and demand enforcement of environmental laws or compensation for environmental damage. These rights – often coined "procedural rights" – are traditionally grouped into three areas: access to information, public participation, and access to justice. With the adoption of the 1998 Convention on Access to Information, Public Participation in Decision making and Access in Environmental Matters (hereafter the "Aarhus Convention") within the framework of the United Nations Economic Commission for Europe (UNECE) these rights were further translated into more clear-cut international duties.[11] The entry into force of the Aarhus Convention, which has now been ratified by forty-seven parties,[12] gradually turned "environmental democracy" into one of the bedrock principles of environmental governance.

In that regard, the quintessential third pillar of the Aarhus Convention has come to the fore as one of the main tools used by environmental NGOs and the wider public to enforce environmental law before courts. In particular, Article 9(3) of the Aarhus Convention seeks to implement the "rule of law", of which effective judicial protection and judicial review are intrinsic components, in the specific context of environmental decision making. By ratifying the Aarhus Convention in 2005, the EU – which is a self-declared progressive player in the domain of environmental governance – explicitly committed itself to guaranteeing wide access to justice in environmental matters for environmental NGOs.[13] The EU Member States explicitly pledged to foster "responsible environmental citizenship", acknowledging that "an engaged, critically aware public is essential to a healthy democracy."[14] Even so, the initial enthusiasm soon gave way to mild opposition when the precise consequences became apparent, among others, in terms of more bothersome

---

[11] Convention on Access to Information, Public Participation in Decision-making and Access to Justice in Environmental Matters, done at Aarhus, Denmark, 25 July 1998 ("Aarhus Convention") (1999) 2161 UNTS 447; 38 ILM 517.

[12] See: www.unece.org/env/pp/ratification.html (accessed 20 October 2018).

[13] Council Decision 2005/370/EC of 17 February 2005 on the conclusion, on behalf of the European Community, of the Convention on access to information, public participation in decision-making and access to justice in environmental matters [2005] OJ L124/1.

[14] M. Pallemaerts, "Introduction" in M. Pallemaerts (ed.), *The Aarhus Convention at Ten. Interactions and Tensions between Conventional International Law and EU Environmental Law* (Europa Law Publishing, 2011), p. 3.

administrative procedures and an augmented number of lawsuits in environmental cases. Many business people and politicians became increasingly wary about the important impediments to economic development caused by the increased eagerness of environmental NGOs to go to court. Fears for flood of appeals and increased administrative burdens led to a shifted perception of the international commitments incumbent upon the EU in terms of access to justice in environmental matters.

B   Judicial Review at EU Level after the Aarhus Convention: Ambitious Pledges versus Half-Hearted Implementation Efforts?

Whereas the EU relatively quickly implemented specific legislation pertaining to access to justice in relation to decisions that fall within the ambit of the second pillar of the Aarhus Convention,[15] which relates to specific activities and project that are subject to public participation requirements, it faltered in enacting specific measures to ensure effective access to justice at national level in the broader context of Article 9(3) of the Aarhus Convention, at both national and EU levels. Until then, limited attention had been paid to providing more direct accountability in environmental matters at EU level, which in any event was perceived by the ordinary citizen as a non-transparent decision-making structure. Yet, as the EU had committed itself to providing access to justice in environmental matters, the decision-making procedures at EU level also had to be scrutinized in view of Article 9(3) of the Aarhus Convention. For, while the power to grant planning permits for concrete activities and projects is situated at the Member State level, the EU institutions themselves are also empowered to take decisions that can have a significant impact on the environment. One of the most evident illustrations thereof is the EU's exclusive competence for fisheries matters. In addition, institutions such as the European Commission also possess important competences for authorizing genetically modified organisms (GMOs) throughout the EU, approving "active substances" in pesticides, and so forth. Therefore, the EU could not simply point to the national remedies when pondering its implementation duties within the framework of Article 9(3) of the Aarhus Convention.

---

[15] Directive 2003/35/EC of the European Parliament and of the Council providing for public participation in respect of the drawing up of certain plans and programmes relating to the environment and amending with regard to public participation and access to justice Council Directives 85/337/EEC and 96/61/EC [2003] OJ L257/26.

That said, the longstanding, quasi-constitutional *Plaumann*-doctrine, established by the European Court of Justice (ECJ) back in 1963, which put forward a rather stringent interpretation of the standing of private individuals and legal entities when directly challenging EU acts, proved to constitute a formidable obstacle for environmental litigation.[16] In order to mitigate the well-known rigidity of the jurisprudential approach to legal standing in cases in which the legality of EU acts was directly challenged before the EU courts, the EU institutions were pondering the creation of an additional administrative review procedure for environmental decisions passed at EU level. With the adoption of the Aarhus Regulation[17] in 2006, one hoped to reconcile the rigid *Plaumann*-rationale with the requirements of Article 9(3) of the Aarhus Convention. The creation of additional review procedures against EU decisions, open to environmental NGOs, was believed to be satisfactory in view of the EU's duties under Article 9(3) of the Aarhus Convention. In spite of its ambitious goals, though, the Aarhus Regulation has been applied so restrictively by the EU institutions that it has offered no real "cure" for the persistent lack of access to direct judicial review against EU acts in environmental matters.[18]

Moreover, these limited expectations were quickly confirmed by the outcome of the first comprehensive legal challenges that had been launched against the Aarhus Regulation back in 2010. Whereas the General Court was found willing to reaffirm at least some part of the criticism vis-à-vis the limited scope of the Aarhus Regulation in 2012,[19] this modest opening towards more environmental accountability at the EU level was quickly denounced in the subsequent appeal proceedings. In its renowned 2015 rulings in the *Vereniging Milieudefensie* and *Stichting Natuur en Milieu*-cases, in which the compliance of the Aarhus Regulation with the EU's international commitments was reassessed; the Court of Justice of the EU (CJEU) overruled the allegedly progressive

---

[16] Case 25/62 *Plaumann* [1963] ECR 95.
[17] Regulation (EC) No. 1367/2006 of the European Parliament and the Council of 6 September 2006 on the application of the provisions of the Aarhus Convention on Access to Information, Public Participation in Decision-making and Access to Justice in Environmental Matters to Community institutions and bodies ("Aarhus Regulation") [2006] OJ L264/13.
[18] See, more extensively, H. Schoukens, "Access to Justice in Environmental Cases after the Rulings of the Court of Justice of 13 January 2015: Kafka Revisited?", *Utrecht Journal of International and European Law*, 31(81) (2015), 50–51.
[19] Case T-396/09 *Stichting Natuur en Milieu* (GC, 14 June 2012) ECLI:EU:T:2012:301; Case T-338/08 *Vereniging Milieudefensie* (GC, 14 June 2012) ECLI:EU:T:2012:300.

stance that had been adopted by the General Court.[20] Well aware of the limitations of internal review mechanisms and the limited chances of achieving any success before the EU courts situated in Luxembourg, a coalition of environmental NGOs, headed by ClientEarth, and a private individual had submitted a claim to the Aarhus Compliance Committee pending the abovementioned lawsuits. In this specific context, it was argued that the EU was failing to abide by its obligations under Article 9(3) of the Aarhus Convention by not granting wider access to the EU courts in environmental matters. Reiterating its 2011 findings, which were deemed to be of a preliminary nature in view of the ongoing court cases,[21] in its final 2017 findings the Committee came to the conclusion that the EU had failed to observe Article 9(3) of the Aarhus Convention by not granting more substantive procedural rights to the wider public in environmental matters.[22]

Against the backdrop of the long-running dispute concerning access to justice in the field of environmental law at EU level, which gradually evolved into a sort of Mexican standoff between the EU institutions and the environmental movement from which there was no easy escape, this chapter aims to discuss the different legal arguments at play, and addresses several solutions for overcoming the existing deadlock-scenario. In doing so, the latest jurisprudential evolutions, which were tagged by some commentators as a "lost opportunity for improving access to justice in environmental matters,"[23] are taken into account, as well as the recent findings and recommendations of the Aarhus Compliance Committee. In doing so, potential alternative scenarios in order to deal with this major flaw in the EU legal order are sketched out and critically assessed against the backdrop of the EU's international commitments.

---

[20] Joined Cases C-404/12P and C-405/12 P *Council and Others* v. *Vereniging Stichting Natuur en Milieu and Milieu and Pesticide Action Network Europe* (CJEU, 13 January 2015) ECLI:EU:C:2015:5; Joined Cases C-401/12P and C-403/12P *Council and Others* v. *Vereniging Milieudefensie and Stichting Stop Luchtverontreiniging Utrecht* (CJEU, 13 January 2015) ECLI:EU:C:2015:4.

[21] Communication ACCC/C/2008/32 (Part I) (European Union), adopted on 14 April 2011.

[22] Communication ACCC/C/2008/32 (Part II) (European Union), adopted on 17 March 2017.

[23] A. J. C. Roger, "A lost opportunity for improving access to justice in environmental matters: the CJE on the invocability of the Aarhus Convention" (15 February 2015): http://eulawanalysis.blogspot.be/2015/02/a-lost-opportunity-for-improving-access.htm (accessed 20 October 2018).

C   Article 9(3) of the Aarhus Convention versus the EU's Constitutional Order: *Plaumann* as a Perennial Obstacle Block?

In order better to come to grips with the legal conundrum that the EU institutions had to face when implementing their commitments under Article 9(3) of the Aarhus Convention, a thorough understanding of the precise extent of this provision is in order, as well as a basic knowledge of the major jurisprudential evolutions in the field of access to justice in environmental cases prior to 2005, i.e. the date of entry into force of the Aarhus Convention in the EU.

1   Article 9(3) of the Aarhus Convention as a Surprisingly 'Vague' Yet Decisive Yardstick

Article 9(3) of the Aarhus Convention puts forward a so-called "citizen suit" approach, thereby ensuring that standing in environmental cases would no longer be exceptional but rather the norm. However, it does so in a notoriously unclear manner. To be more precise, pursuant to Article 9(3) of the Aarhus Convention, parties to the Convention have to ensure that "members of the public have access to administrative or judicial procedures to challenge acts and omissions by private parties and public authorities which contravene provisions of its national law relating to the environment."

At first glance, this provision grants a larger margin of appreciation for the contracting parties, especially when compared with the more clear-cut duties that are enshrined in Article 9(2) of the Aarhus Convention. Indeed, the latter provision lays down more concrete requirements regarding review procedures for project-type decisions that are subject to public participation requirements.

For instance, Article 9(2), when read together with Article 2(5) of the Aarhus Convention, grants a form of legal standing *de lege* to environmental NGOs on the assumption that they meet the general requirements set out by national law. However, the alleged vagueness of the provision should not come as a surprise either, especially taking into account the rather troublesome drafting process.[24] At the time, the majority of the contracting parties was of the opinion that no change to national

---

[24] J. Ebbesson, "Impact of the Aarhus Convention and European Union Law" in M. Pallemaerts (ed.), *The Aarhus Convention at Ten. Interactions and Tensions between Conventional International Law and EU Environmental Law* (Europa Law Publishing, 2011), p. 269.

procedural rules was required in order to implement Article 9(3) of the Aarhus Convention. Eventually, the supporters of the provision succeeded, and the provision ended up in the Convention, albeit in a weakened version.[25]

Be that as it may, it should be pointed out that the scope *ratione personae* of Article 9(3) is at any rate very broad, entailing that any act or omission by private parties and/or public authorities that contravenes environmental law must be challengeable. Only decisions enacted by bodies or institutions acting in their legislative or judicial capacity seem to be excluded by virtue of Article 2(2)d of the Aarhus Convention. Pertaining to the nature of the review procedures that need to be provided, Article 9(3) of the Aarhus Convention stipulates that the public should have access to administrative or judicial proceedings. So, while Article 9(3) does not spell out any specific quality requirements in this regard, the generally applicable quality standards laid down by Article 9(4) have to be taken into account. This entails that, irrespective of the specific nature of the available review procedures, contracting parties need to ensure that the review options are "adequate and effective," which requires, among other things, that the available remedies should be capable of real and efficient enforcement. In the Aarhus Implementation Guide, it is further highlighted that parties should try to eliminate any potential barriers to the enforcement of injunctions and other remedies in order to ensure the intended effect of the review procedure.[26]

Lastly, Article 9(3) of the Aarhus Convention urges the contracting parties to provide for access to the aforementioned review procedures for "members of the public" where they meet the criteria, if any, laid down in national law. Given the broad definition of "the public."[27] it can be upheld that it effectively covers any natural or legal persons, including, among others, environmental organizations. On the other hand, the referral to "the criteria, if any, laid down in national law" seems to allow a great deal of flexibility to the Convention parties in delimiting the scope of the review procedures. Indeed, from the outset it was already

---

[25] M. Zschiesche, "The Aarhus Convention – more citizens' participation by setting out environmental standards?", *ELNI Review*, (2002), 27–28.

[26] United Nations Economic Commission for Europe (UNECE), *The Aarhus Convention: An Implementation Guide*, 2nd edn (2014), pp. 200–202.

[27] See Art. 2(4) of the Aarhus Convention: "one or more natural or legal persons, and, in accordance with national legislation or practice, their associations, organizations or groups".

clear that the Convention parties are not obliged to establish a system of popular action (*actio popularis*) in their national laws with the effect that anyone can challenge any decision, act or omission relating to the environment. Nonetheless, as evidenced by later findings and recommendations of the Aarhus Compliance Committee, contracting parties cannot use the clause "where they meet the criteria, if any, laid down in national law" as a justification for introducing or maintaining such strict criteria that they effectively bar all or almost all environmental organizations from challenging acts or omissions that contravene national law relating to the environment.[28]

2 The Rigid Plaumann Doctrine: Consistently Reinforced in the Context of Environmental Cases

The relatively wide review options that have to be put in place by virtue of Article 9(3) of the Aarhus Convention stand in stark contrast to the notoriously limited options for direct judicial review against EU acts. As such, the rule of law is one of the fundamental principles of EU law. It is among others reflected in Article 47 of the Charter of Fundamental Rights, which is reminiscent of Articles 6 and 13 of the European Convention on Human Rights (ECHR) and puts forward in its first paragraph the right to an effective remedy, providing that "Everyone whose rights and freedoms guaranteed by the law of the Union are violated has the right to an effective remedy before a tribunal in compliance the conditions laid down in this Article." However, in practice, direct access to EU courts against EU acts in the context of public interest litigation is extremely limited due to the relatively strict interpretation given by the EU courts to the existing standing requirements enshrined in EU primary law. To be more precise, legal challenges in environmental matters are inhibited by the prevailing interpretation of what is of "individual concern," one of the two conditions that need to be fulfilled pursuant to Article 263(4) of the Treaty on the Functioning of the European Union (TFEU) for private entities in order to be able to challenge in an admissible manner an act originating from a EU institution. This is what is generally known as the so-called "*Plaumann*-doctrine," referring to the landmark decision of the ECJ in which this interpretation

---

[28] Communication ACCC/C/2005/11 (Belgium), ECE/MPPP/C.1/2006/4/Add.2 (28 July), para. 35.

standard has been laid down.[29] Pursuant to *Plaumann*, a private party has standing to challenge an EU act directly only if it can be established that he or she is in a unique position to the contested administrative or legislative act. Not surprisingly, this rigid approach to *locus standi* in court cases revolving around the legality of EU acts, which has been consolidated ever since, considerably bars public interest organizations, such as environmental NGOs, from directly challenging EU acts before EU courts.

A notorious illustration of the limited standing for environmental NGOs and private individuals in environmental cases was offered by the rulings of the Court of First Instance (CFI) and, on appeal, the ECJ in the *Greenpeace*-case.[30] In refuting the arguments raised by the applicants against an EU decision subsidizing the construction of two power stations on the Canary Islands, the CFI ultimately held that the *Plaumann*-test remained good law in environmental cases regardless of "the nature, economic or otherwise, of those of the applicants' interests which are affected."[31] On appeal, a similar reasoning was upheld by the EU judges, thereby debunking pleas for a more liberalized approach to the standing requirements.[32] When confronted with the supplementary argument that rejecting the direct actions created a legal vacuum, the ECJ maintained that the necessary remedies were still available at the level of the national courts, in which EU legislative acts and EU acts of a general nature that entail implementing measures can be challenged indirectly.[33]

Unsurprisingly, the outcome of the *Greenpeace*-case – which was the first in which individuals and NGOs advocated for broader access to direct judicial review against EU acts – was met with fierce criticism in the legal literature.[34] It was discarded as a flawed response to what was regarded to constitute a "perennial flaw" in the EU's system of legal remedies in the field of environmental law. Many commentators openly questioned whether the so-called standard of a "complete" system of judicial remedies in the EU/EC legal order, which had been put forward by the ECJ itself in

---

[29] Case 25/62 *Plaumann* [1963] ECR 95.

[30] Case T-585/93 *Stichting Greenpeace Council (Greenpeace International)* [1995] ECR II-2205; Case C-321/95P *Stichting Greenpeace Council* [1998] ECR I-1651. For a more recent critical assessment of this case law, see: C. Poncelet, "Access to Justice in Environmental Matters – Does the European Union Comply with Its Obligations?", *Journal of Environmental Law*, (2012), 287.

[31] Case T-585/93 *Stichting Greenpeace Council (Greenpeace International)* [1995] ECR II-2205, para. 38

[32] Case C-321/95P *Stichting Greenpeace Council* [1998] ECR I-1651.

[33] Ibid., para. 32.

[34] Case C-321/95P *Stichting Greenpeace Council* [1998] ECR I-1651.

its landmark ruling in *Les Verts*,[35] had been lived up to.[36] Thus, the bigger the environmental impact of an EU decision, the less likely that it can be challenged before an EU court. The 2005 decisions of the CFI in the *European Environmental Bureau*-case starkly exemplified that access in environmental matters was – in spite of novel lines of argumentation submitted by the environmental NGOs – still as remote in 2005 as it had been in the mid-1990s.[37] Also, after the entry into force of the Aarhus Convention in 2005, direct actions against EU acts in environmental matters did not fare better.[38] Among other things, the subsequent jurisprudence in the *World Wildlife Fund UK*-case, in which annulment was sought of a fisheries regulation laying down quotas and total allowable catches for cod, aptly illustrates the limited impact that the Aarhus Convention has had so far on the *locus standi* of environmental NGOs.[39] Even relying on the Aarhus Convention could not sway the EU judges to relax their stance on the application of the standing rules. Thus, the case law is to be read in conjunction with the decision of the CFI in the *Região autónoma dos Açores*-case, in which the CFI reasserted that Article 9(3) of the Aarhus Convention referred to the criteria laid down in the national law, and that in EU law such criteria were set by ex Article 230(4) of the Treaty on the European Community (TEC) and the related jurisprudence.[40]

The quasi-constitutional status of the jurisprudential definition of "individual concern" persistently prevailed over pledges for a more open approach for environmental NGOs and concerned individuals. It should be noted, though, that in 2002, the CFI famously revolted against the well-established *Plaumann*-doctrine in the *Jégo-Quéré*-case, a legal action in which, rather ironically, the legality of an EC measure aimed at recovering the stock of hake in the waters south of Ireland was at stake. With reference to the principle of effective judicial protection, the CFI

---

[35] Case C-294/83 *Les Verts* [1986] ECR 1339, para. 23.

[36] A. Ward, *Judicial Review and the Rights of Private Parties in EC Law* (Oxford University Press, 2000), p. 154.

[37] Case T-94/04 *European Environmental Bureau (EEB)* [2005] ECR II-4419; Joined Cases T-236/04 and T-241/04 *European Environmental Bureau (EEB)* [2005] ECR II-4945.

[38] For a more extensive overview, see: H. Schoukens, "Access to Justice in Environmental Matters on the EU Level after the Judgements of the General Court of 14 June 2012: Between Hope and Denial?", Nordic Environmental Law *Journal* (2014), 13.

[39] Case T-91/07 *WWF-UK Ltd* [2008] ECR II-00081, para. 81–82; Case C-355/08P *WWF-UK Ltd* [2009] ECR I-00073.

[40] Case T-37/04 *Região autónoma dos Açores* v. [2008] ECR II-00103, para. 93. The view of the CFI was also upheld by the ECJ on appeal: Case C-444/08P *Região autónoma dos Açores* [2009] ECR I-00200.

held that "there (was) no compelling reason to read into the notion of individual concern a requirement that an individual applicant seeking to challenge a general measure (had to be) differentiated from all others affected by it in the same way as an addressee."[41] As is generally known, the revolt by the CFI was only short lived, as it was effectively struck down by the ECJ in its subsequent decision in the *Unión de Pequeños Agricultores (UPA)* case in 2002.[42]

D The Limited Added Value of the Aarhus Regulation: Back to Square One after the Rulings of 15 January 2015?

1 *The 2006 Aarhus Regulation: a Simple Solution that Gives Rise to Additional Hurdles?*

By all means, it had become clear that, in order to in order to fulfill its obligations under the third pillar of the Aarhus Convention, the EU had to establish new rules regarding administrative and/or court review of decisions of its own institutions. Those new rules were ultimately laid down by the Aarhus Regulation.[43] The underpinnings of the Aarhus Regulation are not hard to grasp. It was assumed that, by granting environmental NGOs the right to seek an internal review of EU administrative acts, the issue of standing could be solved without having to revise the strict *Plaumann*-doctrine. Within the context of the newly established internal review procedure, environmental NGOs could then easily challenge the reply given by the EU institution to which a request has been made, as it would be addressed only to the applicant.[44] Seeing that a reform of the EC treaties in order to allow for a more generous *locus standi* for environmental NGOs had been ruled out from the very beginning, the only option left was the creation of a preliminary administrative review procedure that would then, indirectly, be sufficient to grant the environmental NGOs in question access to justice.[45] Accordingly, the review procedure was hoped to provide for a more down-to-earth

---

[41] Case T-177/01 *Jégo Quéré* [2002] ECR I-5137.

[42] Case C-50/00P *Unión de Pequeños Agricultores (UPA)* [2002] ECR I-6677.

[43] See, more extensively, M. Pallemaerts, *Compliance by the European Community with its obligation on access to justice as a party to the Aarhus Convention* (Institute for European Environmental Policy, 2009), p. 26.

[44] Proposal for a Regulation of the European Parliament and of the Council of the application of the provisions of the Århus Convention on Access to Information, Public Participation in Decision-Making and Access to Justice in Environmental Matters to EC Institutions and Bodies, COM (2003) 622 final.

[45] Schoukens, "Access to Justice in Environmental Matters on the EU Level after the Judgements of the General Court of 14 June 2012: Between Hope and Denial?", 16–17.

solution to what was deemed to be a fundamental shortcoming of the EU's constitutional order.

The exact material scope of this internal review procedure, which is determined by Article 10(1) of the Aarhus Regulation, lies at the heart of the current debate on access to justice in environmental cases at EU level. Article 10(1) of the Aarhus Regulation stipulates that environmental NGOs meeting certain criteria are entitled to request an internal review to the EU institution or body that has adopted a certain administrative act under environmental law or, in the case of an alleged administrative omission, that should have adopted such an action.[46] However, a major additional constraint was created by the requirement that limits the substantive scope of the internal review procedure to "an administrative act adopted under environmental law, or an alleged administrative omission (to adopt such an act)." By referral to Article 2(1) (g) of the Aarhus Regulation, administrative acts are further defined as "any measure of individual scope under environmental law, taken by a Community institution or body, and having a legally binding and external effect," restricting the material scope of the internal review procedures in a significant manner.[47] By inserting the word "individual," the majority of environmental decisions, such as implementing measures adopted by the European Commission in the field of the Common Fisheries Policy, authorisations in the field of pesticides law or decisions directed towards Member States in the field of air quality policy, seemed to fall outside the scope of the internal review procedure.[48]

And this is exactly what happened in practice.[49] Of the more than thirty or so requests for internal review that have been submitted by environmental NGOs before the EU institutions so far, the bulk have been rejected because they did not amount to a "measure of individual scope."[50] For instance, in several decisions regarding national plans that contain temporary exemptions from the obligations to comply with the

---

[46] See, more extensively, Pallemaerts, *Compliance by the European Community*, pp. 26–27.

[47] Common Position (EC) No 31/2005 adopted by the Council on 18 July 2005 (2005) OJ C264E/18.

[48] P. Wennerås, *The Enforcement of EC Environmental Law* (Oxford Studies in European Law, 2007), p. 234.

[49] For an overview, see J. Jans and G. Harryvan, "Internal Review of EU Environmental Measures. It's True: Baron Van Munchausen Doesn't Exist! Some Remarks on the Application of the So-Called Aarhus Regulation", *Review of European Administrative Law*, 3(2) (2010), 53.

[50] All the decisions taken by the European Commission in the context of the internal review procedure can be consulted at: http://ec.europa.eu/environment/aarhus/requests.htm (accessed 20 October 2018).

emission ceiling set by Directive 2010/75 for certain pollutants, the Commission reached the conclusion that, since the authorizations did not approve specific individual obligations for the operators of combustion plants, they did not qualify as measures of individual scope.[51] Only decisions to authorize the placing of the market of products of GMOs under the scope of Regulation 1829/2003 eventually qualified as "administrative acts" within the meaning of the Aarhus Regulation, according to the European Commission.[52]

2 A Pyrrhic Victory before the General Court in 2012: False Hope?

The many admissibility hurdles surrounding the practical application of the internal review procedure soon became a matter for the EU judges in Luxembourg when several Dutch environmental NGOs decided to sue the European Commission over its restricted approach to the internal review procedure enshrined in the Aarhus Regulation. In the *Stichting Milieu en Natuur*-case, two Dutch environmental NGOs requested an internal review of Regulation 149/2008, amending Regulation (EC) 396/2005 of the European Parliament and the Council by setting maximum residue levels for listed products. The second legal challenge, the *Vereniging Milieudefensie*-case, revolved around the persisting unsatisfactory air quality in the Netherlands. In particular, two Dutch environmental NGOs had launched a request for internal review against a Commission Decision, made on the basis of a derogation clause enshrined in the Air Quality Framework Directive, which granted the Netherlands a temporary exemption from the applicable air quality standard. In both cases the European Commission declined to review the contested decisions on the merits, by holding that the latter did not amount to "administrative acts" meeting the criteria of Article 2(1)(g) of the Aarhus Regulation.[53]

Chiefly, the environmental NGOs contended that, if it would turn out that the strict interpretation of the internal review procedure upheld by the European Commission was indeed compatible with the explicit wording of the Aarhus Regulation, Article 10(1) of the Aarhus Regulation would contravene Article 9(3) of the Aarhus Convention.

---

[51] See, for instance: Reply of the Commission services to European Environmental Bureau of 11 April 2014.

[52] Reply of the Commission services to TestBioTech of 8 January 2013.

[53] Reply of the Commission services of 1 July 2008 to Stichting Natuur en Milieu en Pesticide Action Network; Reply of the Commission services of 28 July 2009 to Vereniging Milieudefensie en Stichting Stop Luchtverontreiniging Utrecht.

The General Court sided with the central part of the argumentation submitted by the NGOs in its rulings of 14 June 2012.[54] Even so, this claim was not as evident as it may seem, seeing that the Grand Chamber had held, in its 2009 landmark ruling in the *Lesoochranárske zoskupenie I*-case, that Article 9(3) of the Aarhus Convention was devoid of direct effect. The latter ruling ostensibly precluded the General Court from using Article 9(3) of the Aarhus Convention as an "international" standard for review of secondary EU legislation, such as the Aarhus Regulation.[55] In order to bypass the lack of direct effect linked to Article 9(3) of the Aarhus Convention, the General Court held that Article 10(1) explicitly aimed at implementing a particular obligation under an international agreement. Interestingly, the Court grounded its reasoning on the so-called *Fediol*-[56] and *Nakajima*[57] exceptions. In both cases, which also related to legality review of EU decisions in view of international agreements, the ECJ had decided still to carry out a substantive review of the legality of EU legislation in light of international commercial law, despite its apparent lack of direct effect. A similar approach appeared possible within the context of the present legal proceedings, seeing that the Aarhus Regulation clearly sought to implement the EU's commitments under the Aarhus Convention. In its rulings of 14 June 2012, the General Court quickly reached the conclusion that the conditions for applying the latter exception had been complied with since the Aarhus Regulation explicitly referred to the Aarhus Convention and thus no doubts could persist as to whether this was a typical "implementation" case.[58]

As to the substance, General Court held that the limitation of the concept of "acts" to "administrative acts" in the sense of Article 2(1)(g) of the Aarhus Regulation, was clearly incompatible with Article 9(3) of the Aarhus Convention. While recognizing that, under Article 9(3) of the Aarhus Convention, the contracting parties retained a certain measure of discretion with regard to the definition of the persons who have a right of recourse to administrative or judicial procedure and as to the nature of

---

[54] Case T-396/09 *Stichting Natuur en Milieu* (GC, 14 June 2012) ECLI:EU:T:2012:301, para. 52; Case T-338/08 *Vereniging Milieudefensie* (GC, 14 June 2012) ECLI:EU:T:2012:300, para. 52.
[55] Case C-240/09 *Lesoochranárske zoskupenie VLK I* (2011) ECR I-01255.
[56] Case C-70/87 *Fediol* [1989] ECR 1781.
[57] Case C-69/89 *Nakajima* [1991] ECR I-2069, para. 31.
[58] Case T-396/09 *Stichting Natuur en Milieu* (GC, 14 June 2012) ECLI:EU:T:2012:301, paras. 57–58; Case T-338/08 *Vereniging Milieudefensie* (GC, 14 June 2012) ECLI:EU:T:2012:300, paras. 57–58.

the procedure (whether administrative or judicial), the General Court ultimately held that the Aarhus Convention does not offer the same discretion as regards the definition of "acts" that are open to challenge.[59] And thus a more liberal interpretation of the concept of "individual act" – also covering acts of a general nature – ultimately prevailed, opening up new review mechanisms in the context of the EU's fisheries and pesticides law.

3 Back to Square One with the Rulings of 15 January 2015: No (Indirect) Access after All?

The rulings of the General Court were hailed by environmental activists as a grand victory for environmental democracy. And indeed, one could dub the 2012 rulings of the General Court as the first explicit endorsement for more accountability in environmental matters at EU level by the EU courts. Even more so, the General Court also rejected the referral to indirect legality review of the contested EU acts before the national courts.[60] By doing so, the General Court seemed cautiously to step away from the much-debated dual track-nature of the EU system of legal protection, which was often used to justify the limited review options against EU acts before EU courts. Instead of pointing to the "national courts" as the ordinary courts to enforce EU environmental law, the General Court was found ready to focus exclusively on access to EU courts in environmental cases.[61]

In spite of the General Court's readiness to scrutinize the internal review procedure in light of Article 9(3) of the Aarhus Convention and the liberal interpretation given to the latter provision, the rulings of 14 June 2012 still left unaddressed many substantial loopholes relating to legal protection in environmental cases.[62] Even leaving aside the very limited practical effect of the rulings,[63] the General Court still reiterated that, regardless of the exact scope of the internal review procedure under the Aarhus Regulation, the conditions for admissibility laid down by Article 263(4) of the TFEU must always be observed if an action is brought before the EU courts. This served as an important reminder of the unwillingness of the EU judges to reconsider their strict standing

---

[59] Case T-396/09 *Stichting Natuur en Milieu* (GC, 14 June 2012) ECLI:EU:T:2012:301, para. 77; Case T-338/08 *Vereniging Milieudefensie* (GC, 14 June 2012) ECLI:EU:T:2012:300, para. 66.

[60] Case T-338/08 *Vereniging Milieudefensie* (GC, 14 June 2012) ECLI:EU:T:2012:300, para. 76.

[61] See, among others: Case C-50/00P *Unión de Pequeños Agricultores (UPA)* [2002] ECR I-6677.

[62] Schoukens, "Access to Justice in Environmental Matters on the EU Level after the Judgements of the General Court of 14 June 2012: Between Hope and Denial?", 29–34.

[63] See, more extensively: ibid., 33–34.

approach in the context of direct actions against EU acts.[64] That said, even the limited progress towards environmental democracy at EU level that resulted from the 2012 rulings of the General Court was not certain to last. The EU institutions, among which were the European Commission and the Council, were vigorously opposing the unexpected progressive approach to Article 9(3) of the Aarhus Convention and lodged appeals against the decisions before the CJEU. In its rulings of 13 January 2015, the Grand Chamber of the CJEU ultimately dismissed the rationale used by the General Court and refused to carry out a legality review of the Aarhus Regulation in the light of Article 9(3) of the Aarhus Convention.

The rationale used for this dismissal was procedural by nature. Even so, it is vital briefly to exhibit its main building blocks in order better to understand the complex nature of the EU's commitments under the Aarhus Convention. Returning to the basic legal principles underlying the invocability of provisions of an international agreement in the EU legal order, the CJEU set out that provisions of an international agreement can be relied upon to review an act of EU secondary legislation only where the nature and broad logic of that agreement did not preclude it and, additionally, the provisions at issue were, as regards their content, unconditional and sufficiently precise. With reference to its previous decision in the *Lesoochranárske zoskupenie I* case,[65] the CJEU stated that Article 9(3) of the Aarhus Convention does not contain any unconditional and sufficiently precise obligation capable of directly regulating the legal position of individuals. By explicitly allowing only members of the public who "meet the criteria, if any, laid down in (. . .) national law," the latter provision is subject, in its implementation or effect, to the adoption of a subsequent measure.[66] Consequently, the provision could not be relied upon to review the validity of the Aarhus Regulation.

In order fully to understand the Court's reasoning, we need to return briefly to the procedural arguments by the General Court to use Article 9(3) of the Aarhus Convention as a yardstick in the first place. For one, the CJEU firmly rejected the use of the so-called *Fediol-* and *Nakajima*

---

[64] Case T-396/09 *Stichting Natuur en Milieu* (GC, 14 June 2012) ECLI:EU:T:2012:301, para. 80; Case T-338/08 *Vereniging Milieudefensie* (GC, 14 June 2012) ECLI:EU:T:2012:300, para. 72.

[65] Case C-240/09 *Lesoochranárske zoskupenie VLK I* (2011) ECR I-01255.

[66] Case T-396/09 *Stichting Natuur en Milieu* (GC, 14 June 2012) ECLI:EU:T:2012:301, para. 48; Case T-338/08 *Vereniging Milieudefensie* (GC, 14 June 2012) ECLI:EU:T:2012:300, para. 55.

exceptions, which had been used by the General Court as gateways for the legality review against the backdrop of the Aarhus Convention. In the *Fediol*-exception, the ECJ held that it would conduct a legality review of an EU act in light of WTO law in which the EU act at issue referred explicitly to specific provisions of WTO law, whereas the *Nakajima*-exception referred to a case of legality review in which the EU intended to implement a particular obligation assumed under WTO law. Although the lawsuits filed by the environmental NGOs in the present cases had no direct linkages with WTO law, these "exceptions" had been brought up by the General Court in its 2012 rulings in order for it to proceed with the legality review of the Aarhus Regulation in light of the requirements set out by Article 9(3) of the Aarhus Convention. In the absence of such case law, it would have been impossible for the General Court to carry out the requested legality review of the Aarhus Regulation in the first place.

However, the Grand Chamber of the CJEU ultimately held that "those two exceptions were justified solely by the particularities of the agreements that led to their application." In other words, they could not be transposed to the context of the Aarhus Convention. In addition, in the CJEU's view, the vague and ambiguous wording of Article 9(3) of the Aarhus Convention rendered it unsuitable as a reference criterion for the purpose of legality review of EU secondary legislation. As an important reminder, the CJEU also recalled that Article 9(3) of the Aarhus Convention leaves too much leeway and discretion to the contracting parties when defining the rules for the implementation of administrative or judicial procedures in the context of environmental cases. In addition, the CJEU underlined that the EU clearly could not have intended to implement the obligations arising from Article 9(3) of the Aarhus Convention, since the mentioned administrative or judicial procedures predominantly fell within the competences of the Member States. Having rejected both vested exceptions to the rigid direct effect-approach of EU courts towards international agreements, the CJEU concluded that the General Court had erred in law in both cases by reviewing the Aarhus Regulation in the light of Article 9(3) of the Aarhus Convention.[67] And thus the CJEU ultimately declined from reinforcing the more favourable approach towards the Aarhus Convention, as reflected in the first instance-rulings of the General Court. As ii is demonstrated below, the rationale used by the court when

---

[67] Case T-396/09 *Stichting Natuur en Milieu* (GC, 14 June 2012) ECLI:EU:T:2012:301, para. 54;
Case T-338/08 *Vereniging Milieudefensie* (GC, 14 June 2012) ECLI:EU:T:2012:300, para. 61.

it comes to the legal repercussions of article 9(3) of the Aarhus Convention in the EU legal order, will also be reflected in the subsequent case law of the EU courts as regards direct access to justice in environmental cases.

E   Alternative Approaches within the EU Legal Order: Ensuring the Effectiveness of International Environmental Law without Touching upon the Fundamental Underpinnings of EU Law?

By vehemently rejecting the possibility of reviewing the Aarhus Regulation against the backdrop of Article 9(3) of the Aarhus Convention, the CJEU made life easy for itself. For, as a result, the CJEU did not have to pronounce on the substance of the arguments raised by the environmental NGOs in their original claims. Hence the CJEU missed a unique opportunity to pronounce on the loopholes in the EU system of judicial protection in environmental cases. However, the question arose how this new "procedural stance" would be appraised in view of the provisional outcome of the complaints that had been lodged by several environmental NGOs and a private individual before the Aarhus Compliance Committee in 2008. In 2011, the Aarhus Compliance Committee decided to defer further consideration of the communication to a subsequent point in time. While it refused to issue a non-compliance statement, in its partial findings it did not refrain from openly critizising the reluctant stance of the EU courts on standing in environmental cases.[68] Here, it was held that the omnipresence of the strict standing requirements was deemed to be in violation of the assumptions underpinning the Aarhus Convention.[69] Still, the Aarhus Compliance Committee was hesitant to issue a clear-cut condemnation of the EU system of legal remedies in environmental cases back in 2011.[70] This was specifically linked to the fact that, at the time of the promulgation of the first findings and recommendations, several lawsuits, among which the prominent lawsuits in the *Stichting Natuur en Milieu-* and *Vereniging Milieudefensie* cases, were pending before the EU courts.

The Aarhus Compliance Committee seemed inclined to believe that the 2006 Aarhus Regulation, which had been adopted to amend the limited standing for environmental NGOs at EU level, if interpreted in an Aarhus-friendly way, would offer ample review options, at least for

---

[68] Communication ACCC/C/2008/32 (Part I) (European Union), adopted on 14 April 2011.
[69] Communication ACCC/C/2006/18 (Denmark) ECE/MP.PP/2008/5/Add.4, paras. 31, 35 and 41.
[70] Communication ACCC/C/2008/32 (Part I) (European Union), adopted on 14 April 2011. para. 97.

environmental NGOs. And thus it concluded that only in the hypothesis in which no adequate administrative review procedures are put in place in order to offset the rigid standing rules before the EU courts, a non-compliance scenario would arise.[71]

While no explicit reference is to be found in the rulings of the CJEU to the provisional findings of the Aarhus Compliance Committee, the Grand Chamber must have certainly been aware of the fact that its reserved approach towards the Aarhus Convention might further the ongoing non-compliance at EU level with the access to justice requirements set out by Article 9(3). The evident question now arises whether the CJEU's approach towards the Aarhus Convention is sound, legally speaking. At first sight, the rationale underpinning the CJEU landmark rulings of 13 January 2015 appears plausible when approached from EU law perspective. Article 216 (2) of the TFEU states that agreements concluded by the EU are binding on the institutions of the Union and its Member States. Still, the binding effect of a provision of international law is not sufficient in itself to ensure review of the legality or validity of EU acts. Pursuant to steadfast case law of the ECJ/CJEU, EU courts may review the legality of a Regulation in the light of an international Convention only when the nature and the broad logic of the Convention do not preclude such an assessment and where, in addition, the provisions of the international Convention or Treaty appear, as regards their consent, to be unconditional and sufficiently precise.[72] This case law is described in the relevant legal literature as a two-tiered test.[73] First, the EU courts examine the nature and broad logic of an agreement as to whether it intends to accord direct effect to its provisions, or at least considers them capable of having self-executing character. Secondly, the EU courts check the wording of the provision at stake as to whether it is sufficiently clear and precise and does not require the adoption of subsequent measures to be fully implemented.[74]

Given the fact that the CJEU had, as already mentioned above, explicitly declined to accord direct effect to Article 9(3) of the Aarhus Convention in its *Lesoochranárske zoskupenie I*-decision, the CJEU's refusal to proceed with the requested legality review is certainly not to be treated as a major surprise. Still, the relatively straightforward line of

---

[71] Ibid., para. 93.
[72] Case C-121/06 P *FIAMM* [2008] ECR I-6513, para. 110.
[73] See also, more extensively: B. Pirker, "Access to Justice in Environmental Matters and the Aarhus Convention's Effects in the EU Legal Order: No Room for Nuanced Self-executing Effect?", RECIEL (2015), DOI: 10.111/reel.12124.
[74] Case C-308/06 *Interanko* [2008] ECR I-04057, para. 45.

argumentation used by the CJEU when rejecting a substantive legality review is certainly not flawless. As such, the reliance on *Lesoochranárske zoskupenie I* – which centered on access to justice at national level – seems to lay bare a certain ambiguity in the Court's reasoning. Whereas the CJEU refused to accord direct effect to Article 9(3) of the Aarhus Convention in the latter case, it still went on noting that the latter provision, albeit drafted in broad terms, clearly aimed to ensure effective environmental protection at national level. This eventually prompted the EU judges to oblige national courts, with reference to the principle of effectiveness, to interpret the national procedural rules in light of Article 9(3) of the Aarhus Convention.[75]

So why are the EU judges not prepared to reach a similar conclusion in the context of secondary EU legislation and accord indirect effect to Article 9(3) of the Aarhus Convention in the context of access to justice at EU level? Are EU courts then not bound to ensure effective judicial protection within their own realm of competences, just as the EU courts required the national courts to do so?

1   Nakajima *Revisited: Towards More Accountability in the Context of the EU's International Commitments?*

In order to explore the alternatives available to the CJEU when handling the legal effects of Article 9(3) of the Aarhus Convention, we need to go back to the core of the reasoning used by the General Court in order for it to use Article 9(3) of the Aarhus Convention as a benchmark for legality review. As explained above, the General Court refused to use the so-called implementation exceptions, which allowed it to bypass the lack of direct effect of Article 9(3) of the Aarhus Convention. The CJEU's approach confines the application of the *Fediol-* and *Nakajima* exceptions to the specific context of the GATT and WTO agreements.[76] In itself, the CJEU might have common sense at its side in opting for a restrictive application of the *Fediol-* and *Nakajima* exceptions outside the context of international commercial policy. However, it remains unclear whether the CJEU's take is still persuasive and sound when approached from a broader perspective. Several arguments can be submitted that repudiate the remarkably strict approach of the CJEU to the so-called implementation exception.

---

[75] Case C-240/09 *Lesoochranárske zoskupenie VLK I* (2011) ECR I-01255, para. 49.

[76] This reasoning was also reasserted by Advocate-General Jääskinen: see Joined Cases C-401/12P, C-402/12P and C-403/12P *Vereniging Milieudefensie* [2014] Opinion AG Jääskinen, paras. 52–57.

For one, by confining both exceptions exclusively to the realm of the GATT and WTO agreements or, alternatively, by limiting the principle of EU law implementing international rules to scenarios in which the provision at stake explicitly refer to the international provision, the CJEU can be accused of having raised the bar for legality review so high that one might wonder whether the exceptions might ever be applied again.[77] As was rightly stated by Pirker, the CJEU's apparent scrutiny towards the implementation principle renders "review scenarios" almost non-existent.[78] Yet, when also assessed within the specific context of Aarhus Regulation, the Court's reasoning is not immaculate. Indeed, it remains uncontested that the Aarhus Regulation deliberately intended to implement the EU's obligations under the Aarhus Convention. This is, among others, illustrated by Recital 18 and Article 1(1)(d) of the Aarhus Regulation, which explicitly acknowledge that the objective of that Regulation was to contribute to the implementation of the obligations arising under the Aarhus Convention by granting, inter alia, "access to justice in environmental matters at European level under the conditions laid down by this Regulation."

By opting for a rigid interpretation of the implementation principle – essentially requiring a specific mention of the international agreement in the provision at stake – the CJEU sends out the message that review of an EU act in the light of international law will remain exceptional, which would again lead to double standards and complications in view of the enforceability of the EU's international commitments. In a more recent ruling in respect of Regulation 1429/2001 on Access to Public Documents, the CJEU adopted a seemingly similar strict stance when reasserting the General Court's refusal to take into account the *Nakajima-* and *Fediol* exceptions as a means of carrying out a legality review in light of the Aarhus Convention.[79] However, in sharp contrast to the former cases, Regulation 1429/2001 did not contain an express reference to the Aarhus Convention, either in its preamble or in its provisions. Thus the latter ruling might be less questionable in this respect. However, as demonstrated, the Aarhus Regulation did contain explicit references to the Aarhus Convention, which should have led to a different, more favourable outcome in light of the objectives of the Aarhus Convention.

---

[77] B. Pirker, "Cases C-401 to 403/12 and C-404 to 405/12: No legality review in the light of the Aarhus Convention" (29 January 2015) http://europeanlawblog.eu/?p=2674 (accessed 20 October 2017).

[78] Ibid.

[79] Case C-612/13P *ClientEarth* (CJEU, 16 July 2015), ECLI:EU:C:2015:486, paras. 36–38.

Most importantly, though, the CJEU's implicit premise might be subject to criticism on a more fundamental level. While it is certainly true that the context of WTO-related cases is to be distinguished from environmental cases, the sharp dichotomy between both policy spheres does not appear wholly justified. Critics could advance that most international environmental agreements are the result of difficult negotiations. Not surprisingly, given the major impact that the adoption of stricter environmental rules might have on national economic policies, many provisions of international environmental agreements lack precise and unconditional wording. Under the CJEU's rigid approach, however, such Conventions could almost never be used as a yardstick for the purpose of the legality review of the EU's implementing measures. Therefore, it might be feared that, absent any threat of legality review by EU courts, EU institutions will feel virtually immunized from legal challenges when implementing international obligations. It remains questionable whether such repercussions are desirable in view of the already existing enforcement troubles in the context of international environmental agreements.

2   Different Shades of Grey: the Lack of Direct Effects Does Not (Necessarily) Hinder Legality Review

What makes the CJEU's obstinate refusal to carry out a legality review in the light of the Aarhus Convention even more unsettling from the point of view of the Aarhus Convention was the fact that it had before it a possible alternative argumentation line. This "novel" approach was presented to it by Advocate-General Jääskinen in the Opinion of 8 May 2014 in the *Vereniging Milieudefensie*-case. He proposed a more nuanced approach towards the invocability of norms of international law in the EU legal order. Advocate–General Jääskinen grounded his reasoning on earlier jurisprudence, in which the ECJ seemed to apply a less rigid approach, and made a distinction between the situation in which an individual wishes to invoke an act of international law directly by relying on a right laid down in that law for his benefit, on the one hand, and that of the review of the discretion enjoyed by the institutions of the EU during the process of alignment of an act of EU law with an act of international law, on the other.[80]

---

[80] Joined Cases C-401/12P, C-402/12P and C-403/12P *Vereniging Milieudefensie* [2014] Opinion AG Jääskinen, para. 77.

Advocate-General Jääskinen reasoned that, in order to avoid creating an area free of judicial review, the lack of direct effect of a provision of an international agreement should not rule out an examination of an EU act in the light of the former, provided that the characteristics of the said Convention in question do not preclude this.[81] For a provision of international law to serve as a yardstick for the purpose of legality review, it must necessarily include sufficiently clear, intelligible, and precise elements. However, most importantly, the Advocate-General underlined that such a provision does not need an exhaustive rule, allowing that such a provision may be also mixed in nature. Whenever it would remain possible to isolate parts of the content of that provision that satisfy that requirement, it must be possible to use it in the specific context of a legality review.[82] It was found that Article 9(3) of the Aarhus Convention fulfills the said requirements and thus qualifies as a "mixed provision." Whereas the Advocate-General concedes that Article 9(3) of the Aarhus Convention requires the adoption of subsequent acts and that therefore individuals could not rely upon it, it does contain a clear-cut obligation on the part of the contracting parties to ensure that there is a clearly identifiable outcome.[83] This ultimately led the Advocate-General to the conclusion that, having regard to its objective and its broad logic, Article 9(3) of the Aarhus Convention is in part a sufficiently clear rule that is capable of serving as the basis of a legality review of the Aarhus Regulation.[84]

The above-presented considerations are inevitably of a procedural nature, with limited appeal to people that are less acquainted with EU law. However, a sound appraisal thereof is necessary in order to evaluate the outcome of the *Stichting Milieu en Natuur-* and *Vereniging Milieudefensie* cases. For one, the Advocate-General's take would have offered a more satisfactory solution for the detected loopholes to which the traditional case law of the CJEU on the legal effects of international Conventions in the EU legal order has led. Be that as it may, in its rulings of 13 January 2015, the CJEU did not elaborate on why it did not take into account this more nuanced approach to the usage of norms of international law in the context of legality review. Rather ironically, the Court might have had some procedural reasons not to delve into the solution presented by the Advocate-General. As such, the limited competences of the CJEU on appeal might have barred it from expressing its view on the

[81] Ibid., para. 78.
[82] Ibid., para. 80.
[83] Ibid., para. 93.
[84] Ibid., para. 94.

additional observation provided to it by the Advocate-General, which had not been presented by the applicants in the original proceedings. Absent further motivation in this respect, it evidently remains challenging to second-guess the motivation of the CJEU for not treating the alternative pathway suggested by the Advocate-General.[85]

Having said this, the CJEU's approach clearly reveals that it was not really prepared to consider the more lenient, and nuanced, approach to legality review in light of international obligations. In light of other, more recent rulings, such as the above-referenced decision of 16 July 2015, it becomes clear that there exists a clear reluctance in the heads of the EU judges to use Article 9(3) of the Aarhus Convention as a yardstick for the legality of secondary legislation. In the latter case, the CJEU once again ruled that the Aarhus Convention could not be relied upon in order to challenge the legality of EU secondary legislation. While this case did not concern the Aarhus Regulation – it related to Regulation 1049/2001 concerning Public Access to Documents – the CJEU held that the Aarhus Convention, and Article 4(4)(c) to be precise, was not sufficiently precise and unconditional to serve as a yardstick for legality control. In addition, the CJEU also held, albeit in the context of the specific wording of Article 4(1) of the Aarhus Convention, that "the convention was manifestly designed with the national legal orders in mind, and not the specific legal features of institutions of regional economic integration, such as the European Union, even where those institutions can sign and accede to the Aarhus Convention, under Articles 17 and 19 thereof."[86] This hands-off approach to the Aarhus Convention appears to be the common thread of the recent jurisprudential evolutions pertaining to the enforceability of the Aarhus Convention vis-à-vis EU institutions.

F   The Aarhus Compliance Committee Strikes Again: a Deeper Analysis of the 2017 Findings and Recommendations

From the findings and recommendations handed down in 2011, it could already have been inferred that the Aarhus Compliance Committee was not satisfied with options for judicial review which were, at the time, available for the members of the public. However, as previously stated, the Aarhus Compliance Committee explicitly refrained from examining

---

[85] See, more extensively: Schoukens, "Access to Justice in Environmental Cases after the Rulings of the Court of Justice of 13 January 2015: Kafka Revisited?", 59–61.

[86] Case C-612/13P *ClientEarth* (CJEU, 16 July 2015), ECLI:EU:C:2015:486, paras. 36–38.

whether the Aarhus Regulation or any other internal review procedure at EU level, was in compliance with the Aarhus Convention in view of the pending procedures in, among others, the *Stichting Milieu en Natuur*-case. Seeing that these proceedings had been completed by the beginning of 2015, the Aarhus Compliance Committee was subsequently asked to shed light on the whole package of judicial review mechanisms available in environmental matters at EU level. In its findings and recommendations of 17 March 2017, the Aarhus Compliance Committee could no longer refrain from presenting its final evaluation of the EU system of legal remedies in environmental cases, also taking in account the outcome of the *Stichting Milieu en Natuur*-case, in view of Article 9(3) and (4) of the Aarhus Convention.

As to the latter, the Aarhus Compliance Committee devotes a distinct section to the outcome of the *Stichting Natuur en Milieu*-case before the General Court. In this respect, it is concluded that the General Court's analysis, relating both to the effect of Article 9(3) of the Aarhus Convention as well as to the inadequacy of Article 10(1) of the Aarhus Regulation in implementing Article 9(3) of the Aarhus Convention, appears viable in view of Article 9(3). The Aarhus Compliance Committee contends that Article 10(1) of the Aarhus Regulation, as currently interpreted by the EU institutions, fails to implement Article 9(3) of the Aarhus Convention correctly in so far as the former covers merely acts of an individual scope.[87]

Pertaining to the outcome of the appeal proceedings before the CJEU, the Aarhus Compliance Committee evidently refrains from criticizing the CJEU's stance on EU law. Even so, the Compliance Committee did not hold back from pointing out that "by setting aside the judgment of the General Court in this way the ECJ left itself unable to mitigate the flaws correctly identified by the General Court. In other words, the Aarhus Compliance Committee remained convinced that Article 9, paragraph 3, of the Convention is not adequately implemented by Article 10(1) of the Aarhus Regulation."[88] After having expressed its views on the outcome of the *Stichting Natuur en Milieu* case, the Aarhus Compliance Committee further proceeded with its substantive analysis of the set of judicial remedies available within the context of EU law. Below, I outline the major conclusions of the Aarhus Compliance Committee and assess

---

[87] Communication ACCC/C/2008/32 (Part II) (European Union), adopted on 17 March 2017, paras. 52–53.
[88] Ibid., para. 56.

to what extent they are valid in view of the recent case-law developments at EU level.

1   Direct Annulment Actions under Article 263(4) of the TFEU: a Road to Nowhere?

In order to be able to assess the full picture as regards effective judicial protection in environmental matters, the Aarhus Compliance Committee was asked to give due regard to the modifications introduced by the Treaty of Lisbon. The EU institutions had submitted that the amendments introduced into the EU treaties as regards standing before EU courts significantly improved the position of the environmental NGOs and thus ensured compliance in view of the Aarhus Convention. And, indeed, it is to be recalled that, when drafting the TFEU, the Member States included, to a certain extent, the remarks pertaining to the limited standing rules before the EU courts that had been made by the CFI in its highly contested decision in the *Jégo-Quéré* case, back in 2002.[89] For one, the TFEU did not limit itself to merely copying the framework of remedies set out in the EC Treaties, but also revised the *locus standi* requirements for private applicants. Hence, as of 2009, the provision on direct actions for annulment by natural or legal persons, which is now present in Article 263(4) of the TFEU, now allows: "Any natural or legal person (...) (to)institute proceedings against an act addressed to that person or which is of direct and individual concern to them, and against a regulatory act which is of direct concern to them and does not entail implementing measures."

By excluding the so-called *Plaumann*-test in the hypothesis of a regulatory act not entailing implementing measures, the Treaty of Lisbon clearly sought to remedy the lack of judicial review in situations such as those outlined in the *Jégo-Quéré* case. Due to the lack of a clear definition of the notion of "regulatory act" in the Treaty of Lisbon, the exact meaning thereof became the subject of a lively debate among scholars, ever since it was included in the draft Treaty Establishing a Constitution for Europe.[90] Even more so, Article 263(4) of the TFEU does not lay down any special provisions that would guarantee access to judicial

---

[89] See, more extensively on this topic: T. Corthaut and F. Vanneste, "Waves between Strasbourg and Luxemburg: The Right of Access to a Court to Contest the Validity of Legislative or Administrative Measures", *Yearbook of European Law* (2006), 475.

[90] See, among others: R. Barents, "The Court of Justice after the Treaty of Lisbon", *Common Market Law Review* (2010), 709.

review in environmental matters in accordance with Article 9(3) of the Aarhus Convention.[91]

That said, as the EU institutions consistently pointed to the latter provision as an argument partly to justify the stringent application of the Aarhus Regulation, the Aarhus Compliance Committee could not refrain from expressing its view on the recent jurisprudential evolutions in this regard. As is also implicitly acknowledged by the Aarhus Compliance Committee, the recent case-law developments before the EU courts have revealed that that "regulatory acts" must be understood as covering all acts of general application apart from legislative acts.[92] In October 2013, this view was reasserted by the CJEU in its highly anticipated ruling in the *Inuit* case.[93] However, these promising case-law evolutions notwithstanding, the Aarhus Compliance Committee is still of the opinion that the CJEU's interpretation remains too narrow in view of the broad scope of Article 9(3) of the Aarhus Convention, among other provisions, because at least some acts and measures would not be reviewable.[94]

As was rightly pointed out by the Aarhus Compliance Committee, other more important elements might equally undermine the effectiveness of Article 263(4) of the TFEU as a means of providing wider access to justice in environmental cases. One of the most obstructive issues in this respect is the requirement of "direct concern," which was interpreted in a very stringent manner by the General Court in the *Microban*-case of 2013. In the context of this legal proceeding, the General Court pointed out that only if the applicant's economic situation is directly economically impacted by a measure will he or she be considered "directly concerned" within the meaning of Article 263(4) of the TFEU.[95] In line with the previous literature on this topic,[96] the Aarhus Compliance

---

[91] For a first analysis, see: J. Jans, "Did Baron von Munchausen ever Visit Aarhus? Some Critical Remarks on the Proposal for a Regulation on the Application of the Provisions of the Aarhus Convention to EC Institutions and Bodies" in R. Macrory, *Reflections on 30 Years on EU Environmental Law: A High Level of Protection* (Europa Law Publishing, 2005), pp. 478–480, 485.

[92] See also: Joined Cases C-401/12P, C-402/12P and C-403/12P *Vereniging Milieudefensie* [2014] Opinion AG Jääskinen, para. 56.

[93] See, for instance, Case C-583/11P *Inuit Tapiriit Kanatami and Others* v. *European Parliament and Council of the European Union* (CJEU, 3 October 2013), para. 60.

[94] Communication ACCC/C/2008/32 (Part II) (European Union), adopted on 17 March 2017, paras. 70–71.

[95] Case T-262/10 *Microban* [2011] ECR II-07697, para. 22.

[96] Schoukens, "Access to Justice in Environmental Matters on the EU Level after the Judgements of the General Court of 14 June 2012: Between Hope and Denial?", 35–37.

Committee concluded that, if this stance were to be confirmed in sub-sequent case law relating to environmental matters, it would constitute a major obstacleto public-interest litigation. The Aarhus Compliance Committee held that, against the backdrop of this case-law development, "an NGO promoting environmental protection would not be directly concerned with a contested measure unless the measure in question directly affected the organisation's legal position. Such an organization would always be excluded from instituting proceedings under the third limb of Article 263(4) when it acted purely for the purposes of promoting environmental protection."[97] It needs little consideration to understand that such outright exclusion is to be considered a clear violation of Article 9(3) of the Aarhus Convention.[98] As a last point, the Committee high-lighted that the jurisprudential interpretation of the third limb of Article 263(4), according to which the contested acts should not entail imple-menting measures, is equally not in line with Article 9(3) of the Aarhus Convention.[99]

Taken at face value, this view appears to be rather harsh. However, the Committee's appraisal was reaffirmed by a recent order of the General Court, in which it held that, among other factors, *Pesticide Action Network Europe* did not possess the required standing to directly chal-lenge the validity of a decision concerning the approval of the active substance sulfoxaflor, a systemic pesticide, under the framework of the EU regulations on the placing of plant protection products on the market. The General Court, among others, refuted the reference to the impact of the decision on the environmental objectives of the NGOs. In this respect, the General Court held that "it should be pointed out that, according to settled case-law, environmental protection organisations, such as *Pesticide Action Network (PAN) Europe* and *Bee Life*, are entitled to effective judicial protection of the rights they derive from the EU legal order, but the right to such protection cannot call into question the conditions laid down for all natural or legal persons in the fourth para-graph of Article 263 TFEU."[100]

Even more worrisome in terms of access to justice in environmental cases at EU level is the General Court's refutation of the reference to

---

[97] Communication ACCC/C/2008/32 (Part II) (European Union), adopted on 17 March 2017, para. 75.
[98] Ibid.
[99] Ibid., paras. 77–80.
[100] Case T-600/15 *Pesticide Action Network Europe (PAN Europe)* (GC, Order, 28 September 2016) ECLI:EU:T:2016:601, para. 40.

either Article 47 of the EU Charter of the Fundamental rights or Article 9(3) of the Aarhus Convention.[101] When it came to the impact of Article 9(3) of the Aarhus Convention, the Court recalled that international agreements concluded by the EU, such as the Aarhus Convention, do not have primacy over EU primary law. Thus, a derogation from the strict standing requirements set out by Article 263(4) of the TFEU cannot be accepted on the basis of the Aarhus Convention.[102] After having reiterated the CJEU's stance on the lack of direct effect of Article 9(3) of the Aarhus Convention, the General Court stated that its stringent interpretation of the requirement of direct concern is deemed to be in line with Article 9(3) of the Aarhus Convention. For, to quote the General Court's explicit rationale, "(i)t is, in fact, the Aarhus Convention itself, when it refers to members of the public who 'meet the criteria, if any, laid down [in] national law', which makes the rights that Article 9(3) is supposed to give to members of the public conditional upon meeting the eligibility criteria arising under the fourth paragraph of Article 263 TFEU."[103]

While the decision of the General Court in the *PAN*-case was not explicitly referenced by the Aarhus Compliance Committee in its decision of 17 March 2017, it nevertheless clearly reaffirms the stance of the Aarhus Compliance Committee vis-à-vis the limited added value of Article 263(4) of the TFEU in providing additional effective judicial protection at the EU level. In other words, the reluctance on the part of the Aarhus Compliance Committee is certainly not unwarranted in view of the outcome of the above-featured lawsuits.

2   The National Courts as Ordinary Courts: No Fundamental Cure for Blocked Access at EU Level?

As has become apparent from the previous analysis, EU courts have consistently tried to justify the rather limited access to direct annulment actions by pointing to the dual-track-nature of the system of legal remedies within the EU. It is thus no surprise to see the representatives of the EU institutions persistently drawing the attention to a number of progressive rulings of the CJEU as regards access to justice at the national level. It was submitted that, as the national courts are to be treated as the "ordinary courts" for implementing EU law, allowing them to provide

---

[101] Ibid., paras. 49–52.
[102] Ibid., para. 56.
[103] Ibid., para. 58.

access to justice against EU acts in an indirect manner, through Article 267 of the TFEU. The latter provision sets up the system of preliminary rulings before the CJEU, which provides the opportunity to private individuals to seek an indirect legality review of EU acts through national legal proceedings, that might be referred via a preliminary ruling to the EU courts in Luxemburg. In order to be relied upon as a proper justification for the narrow direct access before EU courts, though, national law needs to provide for sufficient access to national courts in the first place. As such, the recent shift towards a more liberalized reading of national procedural rules in environmental cases cannot be denied. As evidenced by its decision in the *Lesoochranárske zoskupenie I*-case, the CJEU certainly did not shy away from urging national courts to reconsider their traditional strict approach towards standing for environmental NGOs in its case law. And, indeed, the latter ruling was by no means exceptional. In its 2011 decision in the *Bund für Umwelt und Naturschutz Deutschland* case, the CJEU also compelled German courts to reconsider their well-rooted '*Schutznormtheorie*', under which individuals and environmental NGOs only have standing to invoke legal proceedings that are designed to protect their specific interest, in light of the Aarhus Convention.[104] The case law recently culminated in the CJEU holding in the *Lesoochranárske zoskupenie II* case that the right to an effective remedy and to a fair hearing set out in Article 47 of the Charter of Fundamental Rights, when read in combination with Article 9(2) and (4) of the Aarhus Convention, should oblige national courts to grant effective access to justice to environmental NGOs in environmental cases.[105] Yet, reiterating its previous stance,[106] the Aarhus Compliance Committee pointed out that judicial review in national courts cannot fully offset the lack of access to justice at EU level. In doing so, it recalled that the system of preliminary ruling does not constitute in itself a means of redress available to the parties to a case pending before a national court or tribunal.[107] And hence, while the evolution towards better access to national courts was certainly applauded by the

---

[104] Case C-115/09 *Trianel* [2011] ECR I-03673, para. 46. See also, more recently: Case C-137/14 *Commission v. Germany* [2015] ECLI:EU:C:2015:683.
[105] Case C-243/15 *Lesoochranárske zoskupenie VLK II* [2016] ECLI:EU:C:2016:838.
[106] Communication ACCC/C/2008/32 (Part I) (European Union), adopted on 14 April 2011, para. 90.
[107] Communication ACCC/C/2008/32 (Part II) (European Union), adopted on 17 March 2017, para. 59.

Aarhus Compliance Committee, it could therefore not serve as offset for the lack of direct access to EU courts in environmental cases.

3   The Aarhus Regulation: Fundamental Shortcomings in Light of the Aarhus Convention?

Not surprisingly, especially in light of its already critical appraisal of the outcome of the *Stichting Natuur en Milieu* case, the Committee equally found the Aarhus Regulation to be incompatible with the wide access to justice requirements set out by Article 9(3) of the Aarhus Convention at several points. Aside the restricted material scope of the Aarhus Regulation, since it wrongly covers only acts of an individual nature,[108] the Aarhus Compliance Committee also pointed to the limited personal scope of the former. Article 10(1) of the Aarhus Regulation indeed grants access to the internal review procedure only to environmental NGOs that meet particular criteria, whereas Article 9(3) of the Aarhus Convention, as indicated above, requires "members of the public" to be given access to judicial or administrative review procedures. The latter concept is, as such, not limited to environmental NGOs.[109]

Interestingly enough, the Aarhus Compliance Committee equally held that the limitation, included in the Aarhus Regulation, that only acts formally adopted under environmental law are open to internal review under the terms of Aarhus Regulation, is too narrowly construed when assessed in the light of Article 9(3) of the Aarhus Convention.[110] For, indeed, also acts that have not been formally adopted within what Article 2(1)(f) of the Aarhus Regulation defines as "environmental law," might contravene laws relating to the environment. While the definition enshrined in Article 2(1)(f) is rather broad – including all EU legislation that, irrespective of its legal basis, contributes to the pursuit of the EU's environmental objectives – it is not hard to imagine acts falling outside the scope of the latter framework that still might breach environmental laws.

Further, the requirements that the contested measure under the internal review procedures also need to have "legally binding and external effects" as well as the automatic exemption of decisions taken by EU bodies in their capacity as administrative review body are ruled to be

---

[108] Ibid., paras. 93–94
[109] Ibid., paras. 85–86.
[110] Ibid., paras. 96–101.

incompatible with Article 9(3) of the Aarhus Convention. As to the former, the Aarhus Compliance Committee notes that the concept of "acts" in Article 9(3) of the Aarhus Convention should not be construed as covering only acts that have legally binding and external effects,[111] whereas the exemption provided for in Article 2(2) of the Aarhus Regulation, which excludes EU institutions acting as an administrative review body, does not find support in the explicit wording of the Aarhus Convention. As such, Article 2(2) of the Aarhus Convention merely excludes from the definition of "public authorities" "bodies acting in a judicial or legislative capacity" but not bodies acting in the capacity of an administrative review body.[112]

More fundamentally, the environmental NGOs claimed that the internal review procedure should not be considered a review procedure that met the requirements of Article 9(3) of the Aarhus Convention.[113] In this respect, the Aarhus Compliance Committee adopted a more nuanced stance, which might be subject to even further criticism. While it recognized that, if the internal review procedure had constituted the only available remedy, there might have been doubts as to its adequacy in light of Article 9(3) of the Aarhus Convention, it highlighted that due regard needs to be given to the subsequent legal proceedings that can be instituted before the EU courts in accordance with Article 12 of the Aarhus Regulation. Accordingly, the subsequent legal proceedings, launched against a written reply, might still allow the EU institutions to comply with Article 9(3) of the Aarhus Convention whenever they also allowed for a more general debate upon the legality of the underlying decision against which a request for internal review had been launched. In this respect, ClientEarth had claimed that legal proceedings pursuant to the latter provision might relate only to the written reply and thus would not touch upon the underlying substantive act of which review had been sought. The Aarhus Compliance Committee, however, seems to differ from the communicants on this point. In the light of Recitals 20 and 21 of the Aarhus Regulation, in which the relevance of the subsequent judicial proceedings before the EU courts is highlighted, the Committee does not rule out the possibility that EU courts would still be found ready to

---

[111] Communication ACCC/C/2008/32 (Part II) (European Union), adopted on 17 March 2017, paras. 102–105.

[112] Ibid., paras. 106–112.

[113] See also, in this respect: Schoukens, "Access to Justice in Environmental Matters on the EU Level after the Judgements of the General Court of 14 June 2012: Between Hope and Denial?", 34–36.

look into the substance of the underlying act.[114] In any event, the Committee points out that new jurisprudence might shed light on this aspect and possibly might leave open the possibility of challenging the underlying act in the context of the subsequent legal proceedings launched by virtue of Article 12 of the Aarhus Regulation.[115]

When taken at face value, the reserved optimism of the Aarhus Compliance Committee as to the effectiveness of subsequent legal proceedings before EU courts, is surprising in itself, especially since the EU courts had already struck down hopes for a more Aarhus-friendly interpretation in other instances. Even more so, recent case law of the General Court has shed new light on the latter issue and seems to reaffirm the fears expressed by the environmental NGOs in this regard. For, in its judgment of 16 December 2016 in the *TestBioTech eV* case, in which the Court had to assess the substantive points raised against an internal review decision, a more stringent reading of Article 12 of the Aarhus Regulation clearly prevailed.[116]

In the latter lawsuit before the General Court, the contested act at issue was a decision from the European Commission dismissing a request for internal review on the placing of the market of foods, food ingredients and feed containing, consisting of, or produced from modified soybeans. Whereas no action for annulment had been launched against the underlying authorization decision, which, as a result, had become definitive, the question was raised whether, in the context of a subsequent legal action by virtue of Article 12 of the Aarhus Regulation, arguments could be invoked that related to the legality of the underlying decision (i.e. the authorization). As a matter of principle, the General Court underlined that, when the arguments raised in the context of internal review appear well founded, the EU institution concerned might still ponder any other measure that it deems necessary to amend the original decision, such as amendment, suspension, and repeal of the authorization.[117] While the latter approach might be in line with the stance of the Aarhus Compliance Committee on this point, the General Court also added that, when it comes to the specific scope of the legal review action that is launched against the outcome of an internal review request by virtue of Article 12 of the Aarhus Regulation, an environmental NGO cannot rely on substantive arguments that have not been raised in the initial internal

---

[114] Communication ACCC/C/2008/32 (Part II) (European Union), adopted on 17 March 2017, para. 119.

[115] Ibid., para. 120.

[116] Case T-177/13 *TestBioTech ev* (GC, 15 December 2016), ECLI:EU:T:2016:736.

[117] Ibid., paras. 52–53.

review request. Neither is an environmental NGO permitted to put forward an argument aimed at directly challenging the lawfulness or merits of the authorization decision.[118]

Thus, the General Court does not seem inclined to allow, at least within the context of a legal review of the decision on an internal review request, claims aimed at reconsideration of the substance of the underlying act. Such submissions therefore need to be raised in the course of an "ordinary" annulment action launched within the framework of Article 263(4) of the TFEU. Yet, in view of the recent jurisprudential evolutions regarding "direct concern," it remains very unlikely that environmental NGOs will ever be able to surpass the existing standing requirements in the context of "simple" annulment actions before the General Court against the underlying EU decisions. Ultimately, a direct court review action in environmental cases is still lacking at EU level. And it turns out that the Aarhus Regulation, as such, even when reinterpreted in view of the standards set out by the Aarhus Convention, might still be incapable of offering environmental NGO effective access to judicial review at EU level against decisions of EU institutions in the realm of environmental law.

G   Persisting Issues and More Lasting Solutions: What Options Are Left?

The previous analysis has laid bare the fact that the conclusions of the Aarhus Compliance Committee, as reflected in its 2017 findings and recommendations, were inevitable in view of recent case-law developments before the EU courts. With its obstinate refusal to review the internal review procedure in light of the Aarhus Convention, which lies at the heart of the running dispute, the CJEU has made itself vulnerable to many criticisms.[119] While some might credit the CJEU for sticking to its well-established traditional jurisprudence on the direct effect of provisions of international law in the EU legal order and, in addition, to preserve the so-called autonomy of the EU legal order, one can certainly criticize the CJEU for having opted for a rather formalistic approach to the Aarhus-related claims and not having seized the opportunity to reverse its previous stance on Article 9(3) of the Aarhus Convention.[120]

---

[118] Ibid., para. 56.

[119] See, for instance: Roger, "A lost opportunity for improving access to justice in environmental matters: the CJEU on the invocability of the Aarhus Convention".

[120] See also, more extensively: H. Schoukens, "Articles 9(3) and 9(4) of the Aarhus Convention and Access to Justice before EU Courts in Environmental Cases:

Rather, the EU judges chose to exploit the allegedly vague formulations of Article 9(3) as an argument for avoiding a substantive review. In doing so, the EU judges cautiously managed to avoid the so-called "elephant in the room." The recent findings and recommendations of the Aarhus Compliance Committee, while non-binding in themselves, have not made matters less complicated by reiterating the substantive shortcomings of the EU system of legal system in view of the access to justice-requirements set out by the Aarhus Convention. Seeing that an amendment of the EU Treaties in view of the EU's international commitments under the Aarhus Convention is to be set aside as highly improbable, there remains the question what other options are left. The Aarhus Compliance Committee basically listed two options in order to remedy the ongoing non-compliance: revising the existing case law regarding the Aarhus Convention and/or adopting new legislation or amending the existing Aarhus Regulation so as to provide more legal remedies in environmental cases.[121] Even so, the practical implementation thereof might be more troublesome than ever, in view of the well-established case-law developments of the past years.

1   The Less Evident Route: Reversing the Well-Established Jurisprudence?

Even if amending the EU Treaties in view of the limited access to justice in environmental cases appears unlikely, it still needs to be borne in mind that the Aarhus Convention is an integral part of the EU legal order by virtue of Article 216(2) of the TFEU. Hence, EU courts are bound to observe it, also in respect of their own competences. Thus, while the decisions of the Aarhus Compliance Committee are non-binding as such, EU courts are nonetheless required to observe international law. In this respect, the decisions of the Aarhus Compliance Committee cannot simply be put aside as irrelevant. Furthermore, whereas one might be inclined to follow the EU courts' reasoning that international agreements cannot prevail over the primary EU law, such as the provision on standing in direct annulment actions enshrined in Article 263(4) of the TFEU, the *Plaumann* doctrine is obviously not written in stone. In this regard, it is important that, as such, nothing bars the EU courts from softening

Balancing On or Over the Edge of Non-Compliance", *European Energy and Environmental Law Review*, (2016), 178.
[121] Communication ACCC/C/2008/32 (Part II) (European Union), adopted on 17 March 2017, paras. 125–126.

their stance on the standing requirements enshrined in Article 263(4) of the TFEU. Thus, while it is often assumed that the *Plaumann* doctrine constitutes a part of the EU's constitutional order, judges can always decide to opt for a more environmentally friendly interpretation in view of the EU's more recent international commitments in this regard. For one, the *Plaumann* doctrine itself is but an interpretation given to a requirement of individual concern that is mentioned in the TFEU. The same goes for the requirement of direct concern.

However, recent case law attests to the well-entrenched willingness on the part of EU judges to stick to the quasi-constitutional nature of the strict interpretation of the standing rules present within primary EU law. As highlighted above, though, the reluctance of the EU courts to address the flaws of the system of legal review against the backdrop of Article 9(3) of the Aarhus Convention stands in sharp contrast to the CJEU's recent progressive stance on access to justice before national courts in environmental matters. It is therefore not precluded from trying to pursue a litigation strategy in which the discrepancy between both approaches is further underscored. As is widely known, the CJEU has recently revealed itself as a strong advocate of wide access to justice in environmental cases at national level. As is evidenced by its decision in the *Lesoochranárske zoskupenie I* case, the CJEU did certainly not shy away from urging national courts to reconsider their traditional strict approach towards standing for environmental NGOs in its case law.

This decision was by no means exceptional. In its 2011 decision in the *Bund für Umwelt und Naturschutz Deutschland* case, the CJEU also compelled German courts to reconsider their well-rooted "*Schutznormtheorie*," under which individuals and environmental NGOs have standing only to invoke legal proceedings that are designed to protect their specific interest, in light of the Aarhus Convention.[122] Likewise, the decisions of the CJEU in the *Boxus*-[123] and *Solvay* cases[124] aptly illustrate that both the Aarhus Convention and the EIA Directive require national courts to trump well-established principles of national procedural and even constitutional law whenever this would be necessary to review legislative acts in light of the substantive requirements set out by the EU environmental directives.[125] To an inattentive observer, these findings might be puzzling: the admittedly

---

[122] Case C-115/09 *Trianel* [2011] ECR I-03673, para. 46.
[123] Joined Cases C-128/09 to C-131/09, C-134/09 and C-135/09 *Boxus* [2011] ECR I-09711.
[124] Case C-182/10 *Marie-Noëlle Solvay* (CJEU, 16 February 2012).
[125] Joined Cases C-128/09 to C-131/09, C-134/09 and C-135/09 *Boxus* [2011] ECR I-09711, para. 54; Case C-182/10 *Marie-Noëlle Solvay* (CJEU, 16 February 2012), para. 50.

progressive case-law developments at national level are seemingly hard to reconcile with the Court's strict scrutiny when assessing national procedural laws in the context of environmental litigation.

Environmental NGOs, such as ClientEarth, have consistently accused the EU courts and institutions of applying double standards[126] – and rightly so. Whereas the European Commission is a virulent propagator of wide access to justice at the national level, which recently led to the issuance of an interpretative guidance to the Member States on how to implement the access to justice provisions of Article 9(2)–(4) of the Aarhus Convention within their own jurisdictions, they have persistently declined to adopt a similar liberal stance to judicial review in environmental cases at the national level.[127] The same goes for the standpoint of the EU courts, which has been extensively treated above, and consistently underlined the role of the EU courts as gatekeepers of the special legal order and the constitutional principles of EU law.[128] While national courts are increasingly forced by the CJEU to relinquish their well-vested traditional approaches to standing for environmental NGOs, the CJEU itself seems unwilling to reconsider its well-entrenched *Plaumann* doctrine for direct actions or even consider a more liberal approach to the direct concern requirement in environmental cases.

However, as indicated above, the outcome of the Aarhus Regulation-inspired proceedings before the CJEU is not, as such, extraordinary. In line with its earlier case law, in which the CJEU consistently dismissed pleas for a more lenient interpretation of the standing requirements before the EU courts, the CJEU again referred to the dual-track nature of the so-called "complete system of judicial protection" upon which the EU legal order is based. In its rulings of 13 January 2015, the CJEU indeed held that the Aarhus Regulation concerns "only one of the remedies available to individuals for ensuring compliance with EU environmental law" and, in addition, underscored that the implementation of Article 9(3) of the Aarhus Convention is primarily a competence of the Member States.[129] Whereas the latter view might lack persuasiveness in itself, it remains at best improbable that the EU

---

[126] See: www.clientearth.org/compliance-committee-aarhus-convention-rules-eu-breach-access-justice/ (accessed 20 October 2018).

[127] Communication from the Commission, Commission Notice on Access to Justice in Environmental Matters, Brussels, 28 April 2017 C(2017) 2016 final.

[128] Roger, "A lost opportunity for improving access to justice in environmental matters: the CJE on the invocability of the Aarhus Convention".

[129] Case T-396/09 *Stichting Natuur en Milieu* (GC, 14 June 2012) ECLI:EU:T:2012:301, para. 53; Case T-338/08 *Vereniging Milieudefensie* (GC, 14 June 2012) ECLI:EU:T:2012:300, para. 60.

courts will be found ready to review their position on this point anytime soon. Yet, while the national courts have a crucial role to play in filling gaps in the system of judicial protection, they will not be able to provide an all-encompassing solution to the loopholes that are present at EU level, where, in spite of the clear-cut rulings of the CJEU, a lot of barriers still prevent environmental NGOs and individuals from having broad access to justice in conformity with the requirements set out in Article 9(3) of the Aarhus Convention.[130] In some cases, for instance in the context of Regulations, no national decisions will be challengeable before a national court, thereby also rendering indirect legality review of underlying EU decisions very bothersome.

Moreover, the preliminary ruling procedure under EU law, which could in certain cases lead to an indirect legality review of an EU act that had been transposed into national law, is not available as a matter of right, since it is up to the national courts to refer a question relating to the legality of a contested EU act to the CJEU.[131] The Committee rightly pointed out that indirect legality review through national courts cannot be a basis for generally denying members of the public access to the EU courts to challenge EU acts.[132] The latter criticism appears all the more poignant since there is no general directive on access to justice in environmental cases that fall within the scope of Article 9(3) of the Aarhus Convention. And even while the recent promulgation of guidance on access to justice in environmental matters before national courts might lead to wider access to justice at the national level, it certainly does not serve as a comprehensive replacement for more explicit legal court review schemes in this regard. However, for now, the CJEU seems to ignore the many obstacles that have to be faced within national review procedures in environmental cases, especially in the context of preliminary proceedings. The very fact that the CJEU is still often tasked with clarifying the relevance of the Aarhus Convention in the context of national court proceedings indirectly highlights the often unsatisfactory nature of the available national remedies in the context of EU environmental law. And, even when no strict standing requirements are present at national level, such lawsuits often last several years and involve large

---

[130] See, most interestingly J. Darpö, *Effective Justice?, Synthesis report of the study on the Implementation of Articles 9.3 and 9.4 of the Aarhus Convention in the Member States of the European Union* (Brussels, 2013).

[131] Communication ACCC/C/2008/32 (Part I) (European Union), adopted on 14 April 2011, para. 89.

[132] Ibid., para. 90.

delays and costs.[133] They will therefore never be presented as effective legal remedies in the context of environmental cases.

2 Thinking Outside the Box: Towards More Adequate Forms of Administrative Review?

Given the limited options for improving the current EU system of legal remedies against the backdrop of the international environmental obligations incumbent upon the EU, a number of commentators blame the CJEU for having missed out on a unique chance for an "easy fix" of its blatant inadequacies.[134] As was aptly pointed out by Advocate-General Jääskinen in his Opinion of 8 May 2014, the European Commission could come up with only a single example of the specific application of the internal review procedure, namely the authorization to place a GMO on the market. Consequently, the field of GMOs and the placement on the market of chemicals in accordance with the REACH Regulation appear to be the main area in which the internal review procedure will be applied by the EU institutions in the near future.[135]

As highlighted, the Aarhus Compliance Committee, among others, suggested that the EU institutions amend the existing Aarhus Regulation in view of its findings and/or adopt new legislation in order to come forward to Article 9(3) of the Aarhus Convention. Yet it remains at best doubtful if merely opening up the scope of the internal review procedure is sufficient adequately to implement Article 9(3) of the Aarhus Convention at the EU level. Indeed, for now, the Aarhus Compliance Committee seems to presuppose that the existing internal review procedure, provided that its material scope is further widened and all its other listed shortcomings are addressed, might still be capable of fulfilling the requirements of Article 9(3) and (4) of the Aarhus Convention.

Be that as it may, a number of observers, including myself, questioned this attractive premise in earlier writing.[136] In itself, Article 9(3) of the Aarhus Convention does not lay down many specific requirements as to

---

[133] "Access to Justice in Environmental Matters on the EU Level after the Judgements of the General Court of 14 June 2012: Between Hope and Denial?", 37–39.

[134] Roger, "A lost opportunity for improving access to justice in environmental matters: the CJE on the invocability of the Aarhus Convention".

[135] Joined Cases C-401/12P, C-402/12P and C-403/12P *Vereniging Milieudefensie* [2014] Opinion AG Jääskinen, para. 129.

[136] Schoukens, "Access to Justice in Environmental Matters on the EU Level after the Judgements of the General Court of 14 June 2012: Between Hope and Denial?", 34–37.

the substantial guarantees that have to be provided in the context of the available administrative *or* judicial procedures to challenge acts or omissions that might contravene the applicable provisions of environmental law. Still, it remains uncontested that Article 9(3) of the Aarhus Convention should be read in conjunction with Article 9(4) and (5) of the Aarhus Convention, which requires that the procedures chosen must provide adequate and effective remedies, must be fair, equitable and timely and must not be prohibitively expensive. As such, even if the internal review mechanism would also encompass acts of a general nature, it cannot qualify as an "adequate and effective" legal remedy. The question must even be raised whether merely amending the existing internal review procedure in view of the inadequacies detected by the Aarhus Compliance Committee would make much of a difference as far as effective legal protection is concerned.

The internal review procedure merely allows environmental NGOs to request that EU bodies and institutions reconsider the contested acts. In itself, an internal review does not offer a review track that qualifies as impartial, adequate, and fair. Admittedly, widening the personal and material scope of the internal review mechanism, as well as opting for a broader understanding of notions such as "environmental law," might significantly improve effective judicial protection. However, it does not touch upon the more fundamental shortcoming of the internal review mechanism. Obviously, EU institutions and bodies will not be very keen on frequently reviewing their own acts, which are often the result of long and hard negotiations and political compromises. This is also illustrated by the above-analysed administrative practice of the internal review to date. So far, not a single EU act has been reconsidered by the EU institutions under the internal review procedure.

Admittedly, an eventual finding that a written reply is vitiated by an error of law will inevitably reflect on the legality of the underlying decisions. In addition, environmental NGOs might also request an examination of the substance of matter by means of a plea of illegality. However, as has been demonstrated by recent case-law developments before the General Court, EU courts are very reluctant to carry out indirect legality review of the underlying decisions of requests for internal review. For now, Article 12 of the Aarhus Regulation is indeed constructed rather narrowly, which again seems to compromise the effectiveness of subsequent legal proceedings launched within the context of Article 12 of the Aarhus Regulation. This conclusion is in itself incompatible with the underpinnings of Article 9(3) of the Aarhus

Convention. Yet, let us assume – for the sake of argument – that it might still be possible to raise substantive claims vis-à-vis the underlying decision when challenging the legality of a dismissal of a request for internal review by virtue of Article 12 of the Aarhus Convention. Even in such a scenario, it still remains doubtful whether such indirect legality review would suffice in the light of the Aarhus Convention, especially in light of Article 9(4). In fact, one might hardly entertain the notion that the limited changes of an indirect legality review of the underlying decision might suffice as an effective remedy in view of Article 9(4) of the Aarhus Convention.[137]

H   Conclusions and Outlook

The pursuit of better access to justice in environmental cases at EU level has given rise to a scenario with distinct Kafkaesque features, in which procedural arguments have so far succeeded in blocking access to EU courts for environmental NGOs and the wider public in environmental cases.[138] Even with the application of the Aarhus Regulation – which was explicitly aimed at curing the existing defects – the woes of the environmental NGOs are definitely far from over.

The EU institutions are left with two options: either revising the existing Aarhus Regulation and/or adopting new legislation on administrative review that does comply with the quality requirements set out by the Aarhus Convention, or, as far as the EU courts are concerned, reassess their position on the legal effects of the Aarhus Convention. Since, pursuant to Article 216(2) of the TFEU, the EU courts themselves are bound by the international agreements that are concluded by the EU, they have a good reason to revisit their "old habits." As a result, it might be submitted that the CJEU will now be obliged to rethink its well-vested *Plaumann* approach towards the admissibility requirements for direct actions. For, indeed, the relevant provisions of the TFEU are drafted in such a way that they can be interpreted in line with the standards enshrined in the Aarhus Convention. Rather than sticking to a flawed and outdated internal review procedure, a reconsideration of the quasi-constitutional status of the *Plaumann* doctrine by the EU courts probably constitutes the most comprehensive

---

[137] Schoukens, "Access to Justice in Environmental Cases after the Rulings of the Court of Justice of 13 January 2015: Kafka Revisited?", 65.
[138] Ibid., 66.

solution to the decade-long stand-off between the environmental NGOs and the EU judges.

For now, however, the EU institutions and courts appear inclined to continue the ongoing stalemate with the environmental NGOs instead of pondering new legislation to cure the loopholes. As for the other EU institutions, they persisted in submitting that the EU's "special legal order" is not sufficiently recognized in the findings of the Aarhus Compliance Committee. Moreover, it is held that the separation of powers is invoked by the EU institutions as additional argument. This principle bars the EU institutions from forcing the EU courts to reconsider their approach to Article 9(3) of the Aarhus Convention. As of today, the risk of a flood of litigation before EU courts, which for now seems unsubstantiated and could also be used by national courts to reject the EU Commission's liberal understanding of standing in environmental cases at the national level, still has the upper hand. Instead of considering a reform of the existing regulatory framework to review environmental matters at EU level, the European Commission initially wanted to put additional effort into explicitly rejecting the formal endorsement of the findings and recommendations vis-à-vis the EU by the Meeting of the Parties (MOP) in Montenegro in September 2017.[139] This unprecedented move prompted the Aarhus Compliance Committee to issue an open statement, in which it not only highlighted that its recent 2017 decision does not call into question the constitutional underpinnings of the EU legal order – thereby refuting the Commission's viewpoint that it is "impossible" to comply with the Committee's findings and recommendations – but also referred to Article 27 of the Vienna Convention on the Law of Treaties, which, by any measure, precludes a contracting party to a Treaty from invoking its constitutional order as an excuse for not observing its duties under the said convention.[140] Yet in spite of the widespread denouncement by the environmental NGOs of this

---

[139] European Commission, Proposal for a Council Decision on the position to be adopted, on behalf of the European Union, at the sixth session of the Meeting of the Parties of the Aarhus Convention regarding compliance case ACCC/C/2008/32, Brussels, 26 June 2017, COM (2017) 366 final. See: www.consilium.europa.eu/en/press/press-releases/2017/07/17/aarhus-convention/ (accessed 20 October 2017).

[140] Compliance Committee to the UNECE Convention on Access to Information, Public Participation in Decision-Making and Access to Justice in Environmental Matters, Open statement by the Aarhus Compliance Committee regarding its findings on communication ACCC/C/2008/32 (part II) concerning compliance by the European Union, 30 June 2017. See: www.unece.org/fileadmin/DAM/env/pp/compliance/CC-57/ACCC_statement_on_Commission_proposal_on_C32_30.06.2017.pdf (accessed 20 October 2017).

unprecedented move[141] and the decision of the Council not to reject the principal findings and recommendations of the Aarhus Compliance Committee,[142] the European Commission's strict approach still prevailed at the end of the day. For, the 2017 MOP eventually decided, by consensus, to postpone the decision making in this matter to the next ordinary MOP, to be held in 2021.[143]

Be that as it may, at some point the EU institutions will have to come to terms with their international commitments as regards environmental justice and accountability. While the initial reluctance of the EU courts and institutions in dealing with the concrete implications of Article 9(3) of the Aarhus Convention is understandable, they have gradually run out of excuses for their continued unwillingness to fix the current short-comings as regards access to justice at EU level in environmental cases. As has been demonstrated, there exist numerous legal pathways to reconcile the implementation of Article 9(3) of the Aarhus Convention with the constitutional principles underpinning the EU legal order. The recurring reference to the "special nature" of the EU legal order only goes that far. In times of unprecedented environmental decline and complaints about the allegedly non-transparent nature of the decision-making procedures at EU level, there exists no satisfactory explanation for not directly applying the "rule of law" in the context of environmental litigation at EU level and ensuring effective judicial protection in this context. The persisting unwillingness to come forward with an Aarhus-friendly solution might ultimately backfire, since it will ultimately also affect the environmental credentials of the EU on the international plane. For, how seriously can one take the environmental commitments of the EU, if it appears to be incapable of providing adequate judicial protection in environmental cases before its own courts? At some point, this march of folly will have to stop.

---

[141] See, among others, the Open Letter that was published by several environmental NGOs in response to the original proposal of the European Commission: https://eeb.org/publications/106/environmental-democracy/27068/letter-to-environment-ministers-addressing-the-eus-non-compliance-with-the-aarhus-convention-4-july-2017.pdf (accessed 20 October 2017).

[142] Council Decision of 17 July 2017 on the position to be adopted, on behalf of the European Union, at the sixth session of the Meeting of the Parties to the Aarhus Convention as regards compliance case ACCC/C/2008/32.

[143] For more information, see: www.unece.org/env/pp/aarhusmop6&prtrmopp3/main .html (accessed 20 October 2017).

PART II

Legitimacy and Scientific Certainty:
Environmental Adjudication, Use of Experts and
the Limits of Science

4

Scientific Uncertainties: a Nightmare for Environmental Adjudicators

TRACEY KANHANGA

A Introduction

The adjudication of international environmental law cases is facing two major challenges: lack of scientific expertise among judges and vague norms. When the challenge of lack of expertise is examined, one observes that the most frequent obstacle to scientific expertise is uncertainty. At another level, there is the challenge of vagueness in normative text, unclear principles that judges must apply in uncertain environmental law cases. Vague norms are also a result of scientific uncertainties in matters of environmental law. The dilemma associated with vague norms easily comes to the fore when adjudicators are called upon to interpret them. This often results in inconsistent decisions and conflicting case law on similar facts. These two issues are clear obstacles to effective environmental law adjudication.

The aim of this chapter is to show that there is a connecting thread between the issue of lack scientific expertise among judges, which is sometimes exacerbated by scientific uncertainties in environmental issues, on the one hand, and the issue of vague norms in international environmental law also a result of scientific uncertainty, on the other hand. The chapter asserts that scientific uncertainties are the root cause of the obstacles faced by judges in settling international environmental law disputes. I argue that, apart from the lack of scientific expertise, scientific uncertainties in environmental cases are what make judges ill equipped to make an informed ruling in an environmental dispute. In this regard, this chapter supports the view that there is insufficient competence among judges with regard to the complex nature of environmental law cases.

With the aid of case law, Section B of the chapter will examine the issue of lack of scientific expertise among judges, which is often exacerbated by scientific uncertainty. Furthermore, this section will examine two major issues. One is whether there is credibility in the claim that judges lack sufficient competence regarding uncertain environmental law cases, and the second is the procedural solutions that are available to adjudicators when faced with complex environmental law cases. Section C will analyse the relationship between scientific uncertainty and vague norms, while bearing in mind that such norms also pose a challenge to adjudicators.

The chapter concludes that adjudicators may not possess scientific expertise, but they do have expertise in law, and the law has provided them with both procedural and substantive recourse when faced with complex environmental law cases. Vague norms are a result of scientific uncertainty, and they will be a permanent feature of international environmental law notwithstanding other factors such as language complexities, including linguistic conventions.

B   Lack of Scientific Expertise Exacerbated by Scientific Uncertainties in Environmental Issues

Viñuales observes that, since the inception of international environmental law in the late 1960s, proponents of the international regulations on environmental issues have struggled with scientific uncertainties.[1] The legal regimes that address climate change, protection of the ozone layer and atmospheric pollution provide examples of how international environmental law is muddled by scientific uncertainties. Hence, Article 4(1)(g) of the United Nations Framework Convention on Climate Change urges all the State parties to cooperate in scientific research to "reduce or eliminate uncertainties regarding the causes, effects, magnitude ... of climate change ... ". These uncertainties are due to the complex nature of the environment and its natural processes.

In the face of complex environmental challenges, there is often a lack of absolute knowledge about the causes and effects of changes in the environment, creating scientific uncertainties and controversies. These scientific uncertainties and controversies do not remain within the science and legal scholarship but extend to the bench, placing adjudicators in a difficult position. When faced with complex scientific evidence in environmental cases, adjudicators need the capacity to gain an accurate and deep understanding of the science behind the environmental case. If not, the likelihood of making an uninformed decision is more

---

[1] J. E. Vinuales "Legal Technique for dealing with scientific uncertainty in Environmental law", *Vanderbilt Journal of Transnational law*, 43 (2010), 438.

serious and inevitable. However, the insight needed to make sound legal decisions emanates from experts consulted by the courts. While the purpose of expert opinion is to assist the court in giving judgment upon the issues submitted to it for decision, the court must still discharge its judicial functions such as the interpretation of legal rules, the legal categorization of factual issues and the assessment of the burden of proof.[2]

1 Evidence from the Court Room

Adjudicators lack the scientific expertise required to adjudicate upon complex environmental cases muddled by scientific uncertainties. It can be argued that, apart from the lack of scientific expertise, scientific uncertainty in environmental law cases is what makes judges ill equipped to make an informed decision in an environmental law dispute, for scientific uncertainties make environmental adjudication more arduous. Weinberg observes that the judge's dilemma originates from the law, which "expects a judge to decide cases when science is uncertain, when science can't help him".[3] In these regards, the judge is expected to discharge their judicial functions "outside the limits of scientific certainty".[4] However, as challenging as it might be, "judicial decisions require putting scientific information into a form appropriate for legal application so that fair and well-reasoned decisions are the result".[5]

Admittedly, judges are not scientists but, as a rule, they must aim for decisions that properly evaluate scientific evidence and approximately reflect the scientific knowledge behind the environmental dispute. The competence of judges to address complex scientific evidence in environmental matters can evidently be measured against their work. In that regard, the evidence is within the case law. A few international environmental law cases entailing scientific aspects before the International Court of Justice (ICJ) have been analyzed in this article to answer the

---

[2] *Pulp Mills on the River Uruguay (Argentina v. Uruguay)*, Judgment, ICJ Reports 2010, p. 14, Joint Dissenting Opinion of Judges Al-Khasawneh and Simma, para. 6 at www.icj-cij.org/files/case-related/135/135-20100420-JUD-01-01-EN.pdf (accessed on 09/02/2018).

[3] A. M. Weinberg, "Science and Its Limits: The Regulator's Dilemma", *Issues in Science and Technology*, 2(1) (1985), 60.

[4] Ibid., 59.

[5] M. Mangel "Whales, Science, and Scientific Whaling in the International Court of Justice" (2016), available at www.pnas.org/content/113/51/14523.full (accessed on 20/03/2018).

question: Do judges have the sufficient competence with regard to the nature (complex, uncertain) of environmental cases? In this regard, this chapter examines cases such as *Gabcikovo-Nagymaros (Hungary v. Slovakia)* ICJ 1997,[6] the *Pulp Mill case (Argentina v. Uruguay)* ICJ 2010,[7] *Whaling in the Antarctic (Australia v. Japan)* ICJ 2014,[8] and *Construction of a road in Costa Rica along the San Juan River (Nicaragua v. Costa Rica)* joined together with *Certain Activities Carried Out by Nicaragua in the Border Area (Costa Rica v. Nicaragua)* ICJ 2015 (twin case).[9]

a)   Gabcikovo-Nagymaros

The case arose out of a 1977 bilateral treaty between Hungary and Slovakia relating to the construction and operation of the Gabcikovo-Nagymaros barrage system on the Danube River. The treaty outlined the principal works to be constructed; one in Gabcikovo in Slovakia, the other in Nagymaros in Hungary. The joint project was thus aimed at the production of hydroelectricity, the improvement of the river navigational system and the protection of areas along the banks against flooding. The parties to the treaty also undertook to ensure that the quality of the water in the Danube was not impaired as a result of the project. Being the second-longest river in Europe, flowing along and across the borders of nine countries, the project became the subject of public and scientific controversy. Uncertainty and apprehension grew as to the economic viability of the operation, and more so on the environmental impact of the project. For these reasons, in 1989 the government of Hungary suspended the operations of the project, citing that, as per scientific studies they had undertaken, issues of ecological necessity or ecological risk existed. Slovakia, in contrast, argued that

---

[6] *Gabcikovo-Nagymaros Project (Hungary v. Slovakia)*, Judgment, ICJ Reports 1997, p. 7, available at: www.icj-cij.org/files/case-related/92/092–19970925-JUD-01–00-EN.pdf (accessed on 09/02/2018).

[7] *Pulp Mills on the River Uruguay (Argentina v. Uruguay)*, Judgment, ICJ Reports 2010, p. 14, available at: www.icj-cij.org/files/case-related/135/135–20100420-JUD-01–00-EN.pdf (accessed on 09/02/2018).

[8] *Whaling in the Antarctic (Australia v. Japan: New Zealand intervening)*, Judgment, ICJ Reports 2014, p. 226, available at: www.icj-cij.org/files/case-related/148/148–20140331-JUD-01–00-EN.pdf (accessed on 09/02/2018).

[9] *Certain Activities Carried Out by Nicaragua in the Border Area (Costa Rica v. Nicaragua)* and *Construction of a Road in Costa Rica along the San Juan River (Nicaragua v. Costa Rica)*, Judgment, ICJ Reports 2015, p. 665, available at: www.icj-cij.org/files/case-related/152/152–20151216-JUD-01–00-EN.pdf (accessed on 09/02/2018).

there were no such issues of ecological necessity based on its own scientific studies. Moreover, the issue of ecological necessity could not, in relation to the law of state responsibility, constitute a circumstance precluding the wrongfulness of an act.

It is a known fact that environmental issues might raise competing scientific claims, which a judge must decide based on their merits.[10] While science prefers to wait until it has conclusive proof, courts must reach a decision even in the face of uncertainties,[11] and proving science in a court of law can be a challenge for the adjudicators. This reality is evident in the *Gabcikovo-Nagymaros* case, in which the court had to assess conflicting scientific reports presented by Hungary[12] and Slovakia[13] on the existence or nonexistence of an ecological state of necessity, and this proved not to be an easy task. In this case the environmental legal argument the court had to address was based on the question of whether there was, in 1989, a state of necessity which would have permitted Hungary, without incurring international responsibility, to suspend and abandon works that it was committed to perform in accordance with the 1977 Treaty and related instruments.[14]

Hungary was uncertain about the ecological impacts of putting in place the Gabcikovo-Nagymaros barrage system, hence it took time out of the project to conduct further scientific studies.[15] Based on its own scientific studies, Hungary concluded that a "state of ecological necessity" did exist in 1989.[16] To refute this claim, Slovakia "denied that there had been any kind of 'ecological state of necessity' in this case either in 1989 or subsequently. It invoked the authority of various scientific studies when it claimed that Hungary had given an exaggeratedly pessimistic description of the situation".[17]

---

[10] T. S. Ndiaye and R. Wolfrum *Law of the Sea, Environmental law and Settlement of Disputes: Liber Amicorum Judge Thomas A. Mensah* (2000), p. 315.

[11] H. Mcleod-Kilmurray, "Placing and Displacing Science: Science and the Gates of judicial power in Environmental Case", *University of Ottawa Law and Technology Journal*, 6(1–2) (2009), 25.

[12] *Gabcikovo-Nagymaros Project (Hungary v. Slovakia)*, Judgment, ICJ Reports 1997, p. 7, para. 40; available at: www.icj-cij.org/files/case-related/92/092–19970925-JUD-01-00-EN.pdf (accessed on 09/02/2018).

[13] Ibid., para. 44.

[14] Ibid., para. 49.

[15] Ibid., paras. 33 and 54.

[16] Ibid., para. 40.

[17] Ibid., para. 44.

In its assessment the court considered that the "state of necessity is a ground recognized by customary international law for precluding the wrongfulness of an act not in conformity with an international obligation".[18] However, the court rejected Hungary's state of ecological necessity claim because it was established that no grave and imminent risk existed to the environment and there were other measures available to Hungary to protect its interest. Hence the court opined that "with respect to both Nagymaros and Gabcikovo, the perils invoked by Hungary, without prejudging their possible gravity, were not sufficiently established in 1989, nor were they 'imminent'; and that Hungary had available to it at that time means of responding to these perceived perils other than the suspension and abandonment of works with which it had been entrusted".[19]

As noted above, the case concerned several issues such as the implementation of the law of treaties, questions concerning the international responsibility of state and issues pertaining to the protection of the environment. The case also bares the court's unfortunate history of failing to engage with sophisticated scientific and technical evidence in support of legal claims made by states before it. This is evident when one critically analyzes the court's opinion, in which it notes that:

> Both the parties have placed on record an impressive amount of scientific material aimed at reinforcing their respective arguments. The court has given most careful attention to this material, in which the parties have developed their opposing views as to the ecological consequences of the project. It concludes, however, that, as will be shown below, *it is not necessary in order to respond to the question put to it in the Special Agreement for it to determine which of the points of view is scientifically better founded*.[20] (Italics author's own emphasis)

In consideration of the above, in the same case Judge Herczegh, in his dissenting opinion, notes that:

> The court only grants a very modest place to ecological consideration in the "declaratory" part of its judgment. As a judicial organ, the court was admittedly not empowered to decide questions touching on biology, hydrology and so on, or questions of a technical type which arose out of the G/N Project; but it could – and even should – have ruled on the legal consequences of certain facts alleged by one party and either or not

[18] Ibid., para. 51.
[19] Ibid., para. 57.
[20] Ibid., para. 54.

addressed by the other, in order to assess their respective conduct in this case.[21] (Italics author's own emphasis)

In my opinion, the two quotations above clearly bring to the fore two issues: first, the unassertive nature of the court with regard to environmental issues, and, secondly, the inability of the judges to tackle complex scientific matters. On the former point, the statement "it is not necessary in order to respond to the question put to it in the Special Agreement for it to determine which of the points of view is scientifically better founded" might convey different implications than what can ordinarily be deduced from it. It can be argued that it exposes the judges' timid nature, which inhibits them from engaging with scientific complex environmental cases. The judges' lack of confidence may be caused by their lack of scientific expertise, which is exacerbated by scientific uncertainties in environmental issues. The latter point, on the inability of judges to tackle complex scientific matters, is substantiated by the point that Judge Herczegh makes when he notes that, "As a judicial organ, the court was admittedly not empowered to decide questions touching on biology, hydrology and so on, or questions of a technical type which arose out of the G/N Project". It can be argued that the quotation means that the court lacked the authority and qualifications to address questions on science. In my opinion it is not the judges' role to be science experts in complex legal scientific matters such as most environmental law cases involve;[22] that role is for expert witnesses. Yet it is not the role of experts to decide court cases, for it still remains the adjudicator's role in such cases to evaluate the claims of parties before them and weigh whether such claims presented by the parties are well founded so as to constitute evidence of a breach of a legal obligation.[23] In my view, the court failed to utilize scientific expertise and gave an excuse that "it was not necessary in order to respond to the question . . . points of view is scientifically better found" quoted above.

Against the backdrop of the above case, it is therefore arguable that complex scientific matters are better left in the capable hands of scientific experts. The court can engage the experts to handle complex and

[21] *Gabcikovo-Nagymaros* case dissenting Opinion of Judge Herczegh 176 available at: www .icj-cij.org/files/case-related/92/092–19970925-JUD-01–08-EN.pdf (accessed on 09/02/ 2018).

[22] Ibid., 177, Judge Herczegh states that the court was not empowered (by experts' advice) to adjudicate upon questions touching on biology, hydrology and so on, or questions of a technical type that arose out of the G/N Project.

[23] Ibid. (Dissenting Opinion of Judges Al-Khasawneh and Simma, para. 4).

scientific material submitted before it. This does not undermine the judicial function of the court; instead, it assists the court in elucidating the facts and clarifying the validity of the methods used to establish the scientific data presented to it.[24]

b) Pulp Mills

In 2006, Argentina filled a case against Uruguay in respect of a dispute concerning the breach, allegedly committed by Uruguay, of obligations under the 1975 Statute of the River Uruguay. The latter State had unilaterally authorized the construction of two pulp mills on the river that bordered the two States. Argentina argued that this act violated the procedural as well as the substantive obligations of Uruguay under the treaty.[25] Both parties placed before the court a vast amount of scientific and technical opinion regarding the potential transboundary pollution of the river because of pollutants emitted from the pulp mill. The court took it upon itself to weigh and evaluate the data, rather than relying on what it referred to as "conflicting interpretation given to it by the parties or their experts or consultants".[26] It was the court's consideration of the scientific and technical material that elicited the strong criticism from the judges in this case.

In their dissenting opinion, Judges Al-Khasawneh and Simma note that the court had evaluated the scientific evidence brought before it by the parties in ways that they considered flawed methodologically. Furthermore, they note that, on its own, the court is in no position adequately to assess and weigh complex scientific evidence of the type presented by the parties. Their observation enjoins Judge Owada's sentiments delivered in the *Whaling* case subsequently. Furthermore, their opinion is a testament to the claim that judges are not competent to decide upon complex environmental law cases. In complex scientific matters, science becomes inseparable from law, and to this Al-Khasawneh and Simma suggest that:

---

[24] *Pulp Mills on the River Uruguay (Argentina v. Uruguay)*, Judgment, ICJ Reports 2010, p. 14, available at: www.icj-cij.org/files/case-related/135/135–20100420-JUD-01-00-EN.pdf (accessed on 09/02/2018). Declaration by Judge Yusuf, para. 10, available at: www.icj-cij .org/files/case-related/135/135–20100420-JUD-01-05-EN.pdf (accessed on 09/02/2018).

[25] On the allegations of breach of procedural obligations, see ibid., paras. 57–158; and on the issue of breach of substantive, see paras. 159–266.

[26] Ibid., para. 236. See also J. Klabbers, *Finnish Yearbook of International Law*, vol. 20 (2009), 250.

The adjudication of disputes in which the assessment of scientific questions by experts is indispensable, as the case here, requires an interweav-
ing of legal process with knowledge and expertise that can only be drawn
from experts properly trained to evaluate the increasingly complex nature
of the facts put before the court.[27]

Throughout their dissenting opinion, the judges were corroborating the
view that judges are incapable of handling complex environmental law
cases. However, they assert that the court system does not require them to
be competent to tackle scientifically uncertain environmental issues,
because of two major reasons. The first is that the role of the court in
such matters is not to give scientific assessment of what transpired within
the dispute before them, but to consider all the evidence placed before it
by the parties and determine which facts are relevant and assess which
evidence has probative value. Secondly, the court system made available a
recourse that judges can exploit when faced with uncertain environmental law disputes. In this regard Simma and Al-Khasawneh note that: "it is
certainly compatible with the court's judicial function to have recourse,
when necessary, to experts".[28] To elaborate on the latter point, the judges
consider that the court should have made use of general principles of
procedure available to it under its constitutive instruments in order
properly to assess scientific evidence placed before it. The general principles of procedure that they referred to are within the ICJ Statute and the
Court's Rules.

c)   Whaling in Antarctica

In 2010, Australia instituted proceedings against Japan, alleging that the
latter's whaling programme in the Antarctic (JARPA II) breached certain
provisions of the 1946 International Convention for the Regulation of
Whaling (ICRW), Article VIII.[29] To conserve and regulate whale stock,
the International Whaling Commission (IWC) had issued a prohibition
on commercial whaling.[30] Australia alleged that, contrary to the prohibition, the Japanese government had indiscriminately hunted whales in the

---

[27] *Pulp Mills on the River Uruguay (Argentina v. Uruguay)*, Judgment, ICJ Reports 2010,
available at: www.icj-cij.org/files/case-related/135/135–20100420-JUD-01–00-EN.pdf
(accessed on 09/02/2018); Judges Al-Khasawneh and Simma joint Dissenting Opinion,
para. 3.

[28] Ibid., para. 5.

[29] *Whaling in the Antarctic (Australia v. Japan: New Zealand intervening)*, Judgment, ICJ
Reports 2014, p. 226, available at: www.icj-cij.org/files/case-related/148/148–20140331-
JUD-01–00-EN.pdf (accessed on 09/02/2018), para. 48.

[30] Ibid., para. 100.

Antarctic Ocean, under the disguise of carrying out scientist research. Moreover, according to Australia's final submissions, when authorizing JARPA II, Japan also failed to comply with procedural requirements, set out in paragraph 30 of the schedule, for proposed scientific permits. However, Japan contended that JARPA II had been undertaken "for the purpose of scientific research" and it was therefore covered by the exception provided in Article VIII of the Convention, which authorized contracting governments to issue special permits to its nationals to kill whales "for the purpose of scientific research".[31]

In November 2012, New Zealand filed a declaration of intervention in the case. In its declaration New Zealand cited that it had legitimate legal interest in the interpretation of Article VIII of the ICRW because it was a member State of the ICRW. By an order dated 6 February 2013, the court admitted its declaration to intervene.

The legal question that the court had to answer in this case was whether the special permits granted by Japan from 2005 under the JAPAR II programme were issued "for the purpose of scientific research" within the meaning of Article VIII of the 1946 Convention.[32]The court observed that "the two elements of the phrase 'for the purpose of scientific research' are cumulative".[33] Hence the court analyzed the content of the terms "scientific research" and "for the purpose of" separately. In this regard, the court stressed that "even if a whaling programme involves scientific research, the killing, taking and treating of whales pursuant to such a programme does not fall within Article VIII unless the activities are 'for the purposes of' scientific research".[34]

In order to ascertain whether JARPA II was "for the purpose of scientific research", the court had to evaluate issues pertaining to science, such as the role of a testable hypothesis in scientific research,[35] appropriate sample size,[36] how models and data are connected, adjusting field work according to circumstances,[37] and the importance of peer review in scientific research.[38] As a result, the parties presented to the

---

[31] Ibid., para. 49.
[32] Ibid., Dissenting Opinion of Judge Abraham, para. 16, available at: www.icj-cij.org/files/case-related/148/148–20140331-JUD-01–02-EN.pdf (accessed 09/02/2018).
[33] Ibid., para. 71
[34] Ibid.
[35] Ibid., paras. 73–78.
[36] Ibid., paras. 160–98.
[37] Ibid., paras. 201, 206–12.
[38] Ibid., paras. 84, 126.

court a vast amount of factual and scientific data in support of their cases, on which the court had to rely in order to render a ruling.

Based on the evidence from the parties, the court held that JARPA II involved activities that could be characterized as scientific research.[39] However, the evidence before the court did not establish that the programme's design and implementation are reasonable in relation to achieving Japan's objectives.[40] Many aspects of JARPA II discredited the programme as one for purposes of scientific research, such as its limited scientific output and the lack of co-ordination between the programme and other related research projects.[41] The court therefore concluded that the special permits granted by Japan under the JAPAR II programme were not issued "for the purpose of scientific research" within the meaning of Article VIII, paragraph 1 of the 1946 Convention.[42]

On the question of what constitute activities "for the purpose of scientific research", Judge Owada in his dissenting opinion notes that:

> it must first of all be said in all frankness that this court, as a court of law, is not professionally qualified to give a scientifically meaningful answer, and should not try to pretend that it can, even though there may be certain elements in the concept that the court may legitimately and usefully offer a salient from the viewpoint of legal analysis.[43]

This observation by Judge Owada substantiates the point that judges do lack the required ability holistically to settle scientifically uncertain environmental law cases without the aid of scientific experts. Furthermore, Judge Owada emphasizes his sentiments above by noting that, with regard to scientifically uncertain matters, the court should not attempt to decipher techno-scientific examinations of which it has no sufficient knowledge; rather, it must rely on experts. He notes that:

> it is the point that when the court of law or a judicial body is engaged in the legal assessment of a scientific matter where scientist hold divergent views, *the judicial institution is under an intrinsic limitation on its power and must not exceed its competence as the administrator of the law, by straying into an area which lies beyond its delimited function.*[44] (Italics author's own emphasis).

---

[39] Ibid., para. 127.
[40] Ibid., para. 227.
[41] Ibid., paras. 223–26.
[42] Ibid., para. 227.
[43] Ibid., Dissenting Opinion of Judge Owada, paras. 24 and 25, available at: www.icj-cij.org/files/case-related/148/148-20140331-JUD-01-01-EN.pdf (accessed 09/02/2018).
[44] Ibid., para. 37.

Clearly, judging from Judge Owada's submission, there was a lack of certainty and apprehension among the judges as to whether this case was an issue within the purview of the court's judicial functions.[45]

The judges' anxiety is justifiable because, in the two preceding cases, the court had been criticized for the way that it handled scientific evidence. In the *Gabcikovo-Nagyamros* case, the court was denounced for being too reluctant to engage with the scientific aspects of the dispute. Moreover, the court had categorically declined to assess the scientific evidence before it.[46] In the *Pulp Mills* case, the court assessed complex scientific evidence without consulting with science experts who had acted as counsel for the parties. This resulted in a backlash from individual judges who questioned the court's capacity to render a scientific assessment. Apart from Judges Al-Khasawneh and Simma's criticisms, Judge Viñuales also criticized the way in which the court had independently assessed the scientific data presented to it. He notes that the court did not possess the proper expertise or knowledge to draw the expert conclusions that it made in the *Pulp Mills* case.[47] In the *Whaling* cases the court endeavored to prove to the international community its ability and preparedness to approach scientifically complex disputes in a contemporary manner, hence it adopted a divergent approach. Instead of having experts appear before the court as counsel, as in the *Pulp Mills* case, the experts appeared as expert-witnesses and were submitted to cross-examination.[48]

The ICJ revised the way that it handles scientific data. Guillaume observes that the court developed a three-part special method of handling scientific data. He addresses in detail how the court first made use of experts, secondly, how it adopted the standard review method described as "objective" and, thirdly, how it developed an innovative approach to evidentiary issues with a possible reversal of the burden of proof.[49]

---

[45] Ibid., Dissenting Opinion of Judge Abrahams, para. 36, Dissenting Opinion of Judge Yusuf, para. 44. Separate opinions of Judge Xue, para. 15, and Judge Sebutinde, para. 9.

[46] G. Guillaume, "The ICJ's Handling of science in the Whaling in the Antarctic Case: A Whale of a Case?", *Journal of International Dispute Settlement*, 6 (2015), 579.

[47] *Pulp Mills* case, Dissenting Opinion of Judge Viñuales, para. 72, available at: www.icj-cij .org/files/case-related/135/135-20100420-JUD-01-08-EN.pdf (accessed on 22/03/2018). See also Guillaume, "The ICJ's Handling of science", 580

[48] P. Sands, "Climate Change and the Rule of Law; Adjudicating the Future in International Law" in T. Maluwa et al., *The Pursuit of a Brave New World in International Law : Essays in Honor of John Dugard* (2017), p. 127. See also Guillaume, "The ICJ's Handling of science", 581.

[49] Guillaume, "The ICJ's Handling of science", 581–619.

Regarding the issue of experts, Judges Simma and Al-Khasawneh in the *Pulp Mills* case had examined ways in which the ICJ could make use of experts. Furthermore, they had advised the court on how to utilize the procedures available to it under its constitutive instruments, so as properly to assess scientific evidence placed before it. They noted that such procedures are within the bounds of the ICJ Statute and the Court's Rules.

2   Procedural Solutions Available to Adjudicators When Faced with Scientific Uncertainty

The chapter addresses two approaches of which the court can make use in handling scientific uncertainties within environmental law disputes. On the one hand, we have the procedural route via the rules and statute of the court. On the other hand, the courts may utilize the substantive measure by simply applying the precautionary principle. This study concentrates on the first approach and generally examines the second approach at the end of the chapter.

In *Certain Activities Carried Out by Nicaragua in the Border Area Costa Rica* v. *Nicaragua* (*Costa Rica* v. *Nicaragua* case), joined with *Construction of a Road in Costa Rica along the San Juan River Nicaragua* v. *Cost Rica* (*Nicaragua* v. *Costa Rica* case), 16 December 2015 judgment (twin case), the court adhered to the rules and statute of the court in handling scientific evidence. In the former case, in its application Costa Rica alleged that Nicaragua had invaded and occupied its territory, and that it had dug a channel thereon. Moreover, it reproached Nicaragua for conducting works (notably dredging the San Juan River) in violation of its international obligations.[50] In a twist of events in the latter case *Nicaragua* v. *Costa Rica*, Nicaragua instituted proceedings against Costa Rica. In its application, Nicaragua stated that the case related to "violations of Nicaraguan sovereignty and major environmental damages on its territory", contending, that Costa Rica was carrying out major road construction works in the border area between the two countries along the San Juan River, in violation of several international obligations, and that these works had grave environmental consequences.[51]

---

[50] *Certain Activities Carried Out by Nicaragua in the Border Area (Costa Rica v. Nicaragua)* and *Construction of a Road in Costa Rica along the San Juan River (Nicaragua v. Costa Rica)*, Judgment, ICJ Reports 2015, p. 665, available at: www.icj-cij.org/files/case-related/152/152–20151216-JUD-01–00-EN.pdf (accessed on 09/02/2018), para. 1.

[51] Ibid., para. 9.

During the hearings, the parties presented to the court a vast amount of factual and scientific material in support of their respective contentions. They also submitted numerous reports and studies prepared by experts and consultants commissioned by each of them on questions such as technical standards for road construction; river morphology; sedimentation levels in the San Juan River, their causes, and effects; the ecological impact of the construction of the road; and the status of remediation works carried out by Costa Rica.[52]

In this matter, the court took some insight from the *Pulp Mill* case above, on the use of scientific experts available to it under the rules of procedure. The court made use of Article 57 and 64 of the ICJ Rules,[53] implying that the specialists appearing before the Court to give evidence did so in their capacity as experts as opposed to counsel in accordance with the rules. These two articles, among others, address procedural issues in the court. Article 57 of the ICJ Rules provides for a procedure to be followed when producing documents before the court. It states that:

> each party shall communicate to the registrar, in sufficient time before the opening of the oral proceedings, information regarding any evidence which it intends to produce or which it intends to request the court to obtain . . . This communication shall be transmitted to the court and the other party and it shall contain a list of witnesses and experts amongst other items.

The purpose of this provision is to ensure sound administration of justice, transparency, procedural fairness and the protection of the other party from an ambush in court.[54] Article 57, read together with Article 63(1) of the Rules, would mean that a witness or experts not included in the list cannot appear before the court except "if the other party makes no objection or if the court is satisfied that his/her evidence seems likely to prove relevant".[55] An expert who appears before the court under Article 57 has to make a solemn declaration under Article 64(b). Article 64, in general, provides for the procedure of swearing in of witnesses and experts.

The court had previously observed Articles 57 and 64 in the *Pulp Mill* case. The court notes that scientific experts should not have been used as

---

[52] Ibid., para. 175.
[53] Ibid.
[54] C. Zengerling, *Greening International Jurisprudence: Environmental NGOs before the International Courts, Tribunals and Compliance Committees* (2013), p. 192.
[55] A. Zimmermann et al. (eds.), *The Statute of the ICJ A Commentary* (2006), p. 1123.

counsel on behalf of the parties.[56] Furthermore the court observed that it would have been more useful to the court if the experts had presented their testimony before the court as experts or witnesses under Articles 57 and 64 of the Court's Rules, rather than have them present written and oral "reports" that did not allow for cross-examination or judicial questioning by the other party and the court. While Simma and Al Khasawneh agreed with the court's observation in this regard, they did not agree on the court's unassertive approach to the parties' conduct, and they suggested several procedural options under the Court's Rules and Statute that the court could have applied.[57] These procedural rules enable the court to outsource the help of experts in handling complex scientific disputes.

One route of which the court can make use is available under Article 62 of its Rules. Article 62 provides for an avenue that allows the court to call upon the parties to produce evidence or explanations that it considers necessary for understanding the issues under dispute. Article 62(2) seems to open the way for the court to make its own inquiry on a given matter.[58] By making use of the procedure under Article 62, the court would trigger Article 64(b), which addresses the procedure of swearing in an expert, and Article 65, which reads:

> Witnesses and experts shall be examined by the agents, counsel or advocates of the parties under the control of the president. Questions may be put to them by the President and the judges. Before testifying, witnesses shall remain out of court.

The Article clarifies that the examination of experts, and the evidence that they give, can be done by the parties, with the court (through the President) exercising control, the process and reserving a right to put questions.[59] These procedural safeguards do not exist for experts who appear under Article 43 of the Statute, who speak to the courts as counsel.

---

[56] *Certain Activities Carried Out by Nicaragua in the Border Area (Costa Rica v. Nicaragua)* and *Construction of a Road in Costa Rica along the San Juan River (Nicaragua v. Costa Rica)*, Judgment, ICJ Reports 2015, p. 665, available at: www.icj-cij.org/files/case-related/152/152-20151216-JUD-01-00-EN.pdf (accessed on 09/02/2018), para. 168

[57] *Pulp Mills on the River Uruguay (Argentina v. Uruguay)*, Judgment, ICJ Reports 2010, p. 14, Joint Dissenting Opinion of Judges Al-Khasawneh and Simma, para. 6, at: www.icj-cij.org/files/case-related/135/135-20100420-JUD-01-01-EN.pdf (accessed on 09/02/2018).

[58] S. Rosenne, *Procedure in the International Court: A Commentary on the 1978 Rules of the ICJ*, p. 135.

[59] A. Zimmermann et al. (eds.), *The Statute of the ICJ A Commentary* (2006), p. 1123.

The second route would be an alternative route provided for in Article 50 of the Statute, read together with Article 67 of the Court Rules. Article 50 reads:

> The court may, at any time, entrust any individual, body, bureau, commission or other organization that it may select, with the task of carrying out an enquiry or giving expert opinion,

whereas Article 67 of the Rules, which complements it, notes that:

> If the court considers it necessary to arrange for an enquiry or an expert opinion, it shall, after hearing the parties, issue an order to this effect defining the subject of the enquiry or expert opinion.

Article 50 has proven to be a useful provision applicable in cases involving complex technical, scientific, or other issues beyond the judges' expertise. In the *Corfu Channel* case, the court appointed independent experts or a commission of inquiry under Article 50, which enabled it to solve intricate issues of fact in a satisfactory manner.[60] The procedure governing Article 50 in the present context will be Article 67 of the rules. Article 67(1), cited above, regulates the procedure of appointing experts or setting up a commission. The decision thus takes the form of an order, which is preceded by a hearing. This order can either appoint the experts directly or set out a procedure by which they are to be appointed.[61]

A literal interpretation of Article 50 of the Statute of the Court, in my opinion, would mean that the judiciary may entrust any other entities more suited to fact finding to state a case for the court to determine. Such entities may include specialized international organizations or agencies that are scientifically equipped and capable of dealing with complex environmental issues.

Up to now, it appears that the court has not made use of the procedural routes advocated by Al-Khasawneh and Simma. They could have applied the procedure in the twin cases, however, they opted not to, maybe because of the disadvantages associated with following such procedure. For example, the downside of following route Articles 50 and 67 of the Statute and Rules respectively is that this procedure disregards procedural rights of the parties – namely, the right to comment on the results

---

[60] See *Corfu Channel Case (UK v. Albania)*, judgment of 9 April 1949, ICJ Reports 1949, p. 4, available at: www.icj-cij.org/files/case-related/1/001–19490409-JUD-01–00-EN.pdf (accessed on 09/02/2018).
[61] A. Zimmermann et al. (eds.), *The Statute of the ICJ A Commentary* (2006), p. 1115.

of independent expert advice.[62] However, it grants the court the chance to assess the opinions that such experts might produce and also grants parties to the dispute a chance to comment on the expert opinion.[63]

3   Contemporary Approach

Apart from making use of experts, judges may appoint assessors under the Court's Rules. The assessors may sit on the bench under Article 9 and take part in the deliberations of the court under Article 21(2). The role of the assessor is to ensure that the decisions of the court do not contain technical errors and conform to the latest scientific knowledge with respect to the matter in dispute.[64]

Above are procedural steps available to courts when faced with scientific uncertainty in environmental law cases. The court has to simply make use of experts who appear before the court under (a) Articles 57 and 64 of the ICJ Court Rules, (b) Articles 62, 64 and 65 of the ICJ Court Rules and (c) Article 50 of the Statute of the ICJ read together with Article 67 of the Court Rules. Alternatively, the court can make use of assessors under Articles 9 and 21(2) of the Rules. There is another substantive measure that the court can apply when faced with scientific uncertainty: it can apply the precautionary principle. The court may invoke the precautionary principle when assessing the facts of a case if it is uncertain about any scientific issues in any given case.[65]

C   A Substantive Solution Available to Adjudicators When Faced with Scientific Uncertainty

1   Law and Science

In complex environmental disputes, a clear line should be drawn between law and science. However, science is in many cases the basis around which environmental law is organized; to separate it from environmental law is difficult. To view science as distinct from environmental law is incomprehensible because of two major reasons submitted by Sadeleer.

---

[62] International Court of Justice Rules of the Court, Art. 67(2). See also ibid., p. 1118.

[63] *Pulp Mills on the River Uruguay (Argentina v. Uruguay)*, Judgment, ICJ Reports 2010, p. 14, Joint Dissenting Opinion of Judges Al-Khasawneh and Simma, para. 8, at: www.icj-cij .org/files/case-related/135/135–20100420-JUD-01–01-EN.pdf (accessed on 09/02/2018).

[64] Zimmermann et al. (eds.), *The Statute of the ICJ A Commentary*, p. 1111.

[65] N. Sadeleer *Implementing the Precautionary Principle: Approach from the Nordic Countries, the EU and USA* (2007), p. 107.

First, he observes that science detects, identifies, and sets out the ecological problems to which the law must respond; secondly, he notes that science is often called upon to play a decisive role in judicial procedures as highlighted above from the case law analysis.[66] The relationship between science and law is often in conflict. The variance between the two emanates from the fact that legal rules are meant to provide predictability, yet nature is unpredictable; while the jurist seeks certainty, the scientist points to the uncertainty inherent in ecological risk.[67]

2 The Law's Response to Ecological Problems

Policy makers had anticipated the challenging dynamics presented by science and law in international environmental law. Accordingly, precaution came to the center stage in the field of environmental policy in response to the limitations of science in assessing environmental risks.[68] The precautionary principle aims to provide guidance in the development and application of international law where there is scientific uncertainty,[69] and a number of multilateral environmental agreements have the precautionary provision as provided for in the *Rio* Declaration in a greater or lesser form.[70] Nevertheless, the essence of the rule is captured in the 1992 Rio Declaration on Environment and Development, Principle 15, which states that:

> In order to protect the environment, the precautionary approach shall be widely applied by states according to their capabilities. Where there are threats of serious or irreversible damage, the lack of scientific certainty shall not be used as a reason for postponing cost –effective measures to prevent environmental degradation.[71]

---

[66] N. Sadeleer, "The Principles of Prevention and Precaution in International Law: Two Heads of the Same Coin?" in M. Fitzmaurice, *Research Handbook in International Environmental Law* (2010), p. 185.

[67] Ibid., p. 186.

[68] Ibid., p. 185.

[69] P. Sands et al., *Principles of International Environmental Law*, 3rd edn. (2012), p. 218.

[70] See also United Nations Framework Convention on Climate Change (adopted 9 May 1992, entered into force 21 March 1994), Art. 3. Montreal Protocol on Substances that Deplete the Ozone Layer (adopted 16 September 1987, entered into force I January 1989), preamble. Both have a provision on the application of the precautionary principle in cases of uncertainty.

[71] Rio Declaration on Environment and Development of 1992 (adopted on 14 June 1992), Principle 15.

Sands observes that, in the past decade, the status of the precautionary principle has evolved in the international environmental field.[72] Even though there has been an evolution of the principle, there exists some confusion in the international community with regard to the principle as it has been provided for in many conventions, though in a different language.[73] Certain conventions couch this principle in terms similar to the progressive realization of enhanced scientific capabilities and available knowledge,[74] while others consider that it provides the basis for early international legal action to address highly threatening environmental issues such as chemical pollution and climate change.[75] It is also a principle that is accorded a range of possible interpretation that renders the principle vague.

The terms in which principle 15 of the Rio Declaration is drafted are so vague as to make it difficult to regard it as a legal rule. Scholtz raises several questions with regard to the principle, such as "what does full scientific certainty" entail and whether it should relate to the cause of the harm or the probability of occurrence.[76] Lowe asks what the relevant capabilities of states are. In what context should the precautionary principle be applied? How can one know whether a proposed measure is "cost effective" if one lacks full "scientific certainty" concerning it and the risk against which they are directed?[77] All these questions are just an indication of how vague the principle is.

The problem associated with vague norms comes to the fore when adjudicators are called upon to interpret vague norms; an adjudicator faces a situation of real difficulty when asked to apply the law to particular facts of a case.[78] This is not an easy task, as the ICJ recognized in the

[72] Sands, *Principles of International Environmental Law*, p. 218.
[73] *Construction of a road in Costa Rica along the San Juan River (Nicaragua v. Costa Rica)*, proceedings joined with *Certain Activities Carried Out by Nicaragua in the Border Area (Costa Rica v. Nicaragua)* (judgment) [25 December 2015], Judge Bhandari, Separate Opinion, para. 18, at: www.icj-cij.org/files/case-related/148/148–20140331-JUD-01–10-EN.pdf (accessed on 09/02/2018).
[74] International Convention for the Regulation of Whaling 161, United Nations Treaty Series (UNTS) 1946 signed at Washington D.C.
[75] See also J. Cameron and J. Abouchar, "The Status of the Precautionary principle in International law" in D. Freestone and E. Hey (eds.), *The Precautionary Principle and International Law: The Challenge of Implementation* (1996), p. 45.
[76] W. Scholtz, "Legal Protection of the Environment" in H. Strydom et al. (eds.), *International Law* (2015), p. 519.
[77] V. Lowe, *Clarendon Law Series International Law* (2007), p. 96.
[78] P. Sands, "Litigating Environmental Disputes: Courts, Tribunals and the Progressive Development of International Environmental Law" in T. M. Ndinaye et al. (eds.), *Law*

Gabcikovo-Nagymaros case, and one can understand the court's reluctance to descend into detail if to do so was to adjudicate upon a dispute that had a broader context and that might have elicit the conclusion that the court was legislating.[79] In the face of complex environmental matters with scientific uncertainties the approach of international courts is to apply the precautionary principle. This was the case in the *Pulp Mill* case, in which the court notes that the principle may be relevant in the interpretation of the legal text.[80] Judges also refer to the precautionary principle as part of their legal reasoning to justify decisions that are aligned with the rule. A good example is in the *Southern Bluefin Tuna* case, which was settled by the International Tribunal for the Law of the Sea. The court noted that it could not conclusively assess the scientific evidence presented by the parties, hence it applied the precautionary approach to avert further deterioration of the Southern blue tuna stock.[81]

While the challenge of lack of scientific expertise, exacerbated by scientific uncertainty, seems to have a ready fix in applying the substantive law by making use of the precautionary principle, one quickly realizes that even the application of the principle is a challenge to adjudicators, for the principle is vague.

It is important to note that the precautionary principle is not the only one in international environmental law (IEL) that is vague. Fitzmaurice also states that the concept of sustainable development is vague and its normative value is ill defined.[82] In addition, she notes that the concept of intergenerational equity is equally elusive. Many principles in IEL embodied in the treaties are vague and amorphous and require clarification and explanation in relation to specific issues and fact situations before they can be implemented and enforced.[83]

---

of the Sea, Environmental Law and Settlement of Dispute: Liber Amicorum Judge Thomas Menash (2007), pp. 313–25, 315.

[79] Ibid.

[80] *Pulp Mills on the River Uruguay (Argentina v. Uruguay)*, Judgment, ICJ Reports 2010, p. 14, available at: www.icj-cij.org/files/case-related/135/135–20100420-JUD-01–00-EN.pdf (accessed on 09/02/2018), para. 164.

[81] *Southern Bluefin Tuna Cases (New Zealand v. Japan; Australia v. Japan)* (Provisional Measures, Order of 27 August 1999; Separate Opinion. Laing, para. 13); ITLOS at www .itlos.org/fileadmin/itlos/documents/cases/case_no_3_4/published/C34-O-27_aug_99-SO_L.pdf (accessed on 09/02/2018).

[82] M. Fitzmaurice, *Contemporary Issues in International Law*, p. 177.

[83] C. Peck and R. S. Lee, *Increasing the Effectiveness of the ICJ. Proceedings of the ICJ Uniter Colloquium to Celebrate 50th Anniversary of the Court*, p. 423.

The challenge presented by vague norms also extends to the adjudication of international environmental law matters. Vague norms pose a particular challenge to international courts and tribunals faced with resolving disputes having an environmental component.[84] In identifying features that distinguish environmental law matters from other cases, Sands stated, as noted above, that the problem associated with vague norms comes to the fore when adjudicators are called upon to interpret vague norms; an adjudicator faces a situation of real difficulty when asked to apply the law to particular facts of a case. Furthermore, he seems to be explaining the reasons why vague norms manifest in international law. The question of why we have vague norms in IEL is of importance to this chapter because it certainly has a connection to the issue of scientific uncertainties.

3 Are Scientific Uncertainties the Reason We Have Vague Norms?

For the law to achieve its purpose, as Fisher observes, rules, principles and norms should be coherent, certain, consistent, and predictable.[85] Fisher's observation is not the reality in the field of international environmental law. Rather, international environmental law is often reflected in international treaties that involve a high degree of compromise, or "fudge".[86] This, in turn, results in international norms that tend to be couched in rather broad (even vague) terms, making it difficult and impossible to settle international environmental matters.[87]

Sands notes that

> international courts and tribunals are faced with a particular, but by no means unique, difficulty: the development of international law is often reflected in international treaties that involve a high degree of compromise, or "fudge" In other words, the legislative body has presented the international judiciary with a set of rules and principles that can be vague.[88]

---

[84] Sands, "Litigating Environmental Disputes", 315.

[85] D. Fisher, *Legal Reasoning in Environmental Law A study of Structure, Form and Language* (2013), p. 42.

[86] U. Beyerlin, "Different Types of Norms in International Environmental law: Policies, Principles and Rule" in D. Bodansky et al. (eds.), *The Oxford Handbook of International Environmental Law* (2014), pp. 227–28.

[87] P. M. Dupuy and J. E. Vinuales, *International Environmental law* (2015), p. 387.

[88] See also ibid., p. 246; Sands "Litigating Environmental Disputes", 315. See generally N. Klein, "Settlement of International Environmental Disputes" in M. Fitzmaurice et al. (eds.), *Research Handbook on International law* (2010), p. 382; E. Fisher et al., *Environmental law Text, Cases and Material* (2013), pp. 192–93.

Sands appear to be suggesting that the reason environmental law norms are vague is because there is a high degree of compromise and fudge, also known as constructive ambiguity during policy making. Constructive ambiguity is a theory pioneered by Henry Kissinger.[89] It refers to the deliberate use of ambiguous language on a sensitive issue to advance some political purpose.[90] Such ambiguity allows each party to read its own interpretation and allows progress on other, less contentious issues to continue. This way of negotiation has potential benefits, for it allows consensus around sensitive issues by deliberately using ambiguous language. However, if ambiguous language is used to explain a central concept, then ambiguity only delays or prohibits difficult decisions and tough political choices.[91]

In his work *Relative Normativity in International law* Fastenrath observes that such vagueness is a necessity in the case of multilingual international legal texts, which come into existence because of the use of different national languages. He analyses the issue of vague norms under the subheading of what he terms "Linguistic conventions". He observes that these conventions are neither completely clear nor fully homogeneous and may also change over time.[92] There are several debates on the status, role, and effects of these norms in international environmental law and there seems to be not much research among scholars as to why these norms are vague. Is the problem inherent language or the wording that these principles are structured in? *Fitzmaurice* and others see language as an inherently defective way of communication because of its limitations and various interpretations that can be leveled at a norm in international law. They note that "in practice language is always more or less vague, so that what we assert is never quite precise".[93]

This chapter agrees with Fastenrath and Fitzmaurice who subscribe to the notion that language is the least effective way of communication and may be the cause of vague norms, and with *Sands* who suggests that the reason that norms are vague is because of the degree of compromise and fudge during the treaty-making phase. However, I contend that the

[89] J. Peel and D. Fisher, *The Role of International Environmental Law Disaster Risk Management* (2016), p. 121.
[90] Ibid., pp. 120–21
[91] Ibid., p. 121.
[92] U. Fastenrath, "Relative Normativity in International Law", *European Journal of International Law*, 4 (1993), 312.
[93] M. Fiitzmaurice et al. (eds.), *Treaty Interpretation and the Vienna Convention on the Law of Treaties 30years on* (2010), p. 6.

reason vague norms are unclear is – also – because of scientific uncertainty. International policy makers try to regulate that which is uncertain and cannot be fully comprehended, i.e. nature.

The problem on the international agenda is that international environmental issues are generally difficult to address due to their high political nature. Hence international environmental law comes into being through a high degree of compromise, as Sands suggests. International environmental law issues also pose a challenge to treaties, due to their highly dynamic nature and the resulting interrelation with scientific findings. Hence, Bondansky et al. note that international environmental issues turn into "moving targets" for regulation.[94] To corroborate Bodansky's point of view, Schiele states that: "international environmental issues are especially challenging as they constantly evolve with advancing physical and technological knowledge".[95]

Even though environmental issues are difficult to address, environmental issues need to be addressed even amid uncertainty. Lawmakers must regulate even when based on uncertainties. Weinberg observes that "uncertainties still remain because we can never be certain that we have identified [and understood] every relevant [components of the natural environment]".[96] Hence scientific uncertainties "should be accepted as a basic element of environmental decision making at all levels and be better communicated".[97] In his separate opinion in the *Whaling* case, Judge Trindade notes that, in the absence of corresponding scientific proof the precautionary principle must be applied.[98] The precautionary principle offers a solution to environmental lawmakers for how to deal with the problem of uncertainty. The principle states that, rather than await certainty, lawmakers "should act in anticipation of any potential environmental harm to prevent it".[99] The precautionary principle is prevalent and "frequently endorsed in environmental resolutions that it has come

---

[94] D. Bodansky et al., *International Environmental Law* (2007), p. 7.

[95] S. Schiele, *Evolution of International Environmental Regimes: The Case of Climate change* (2014), p. 28.

[96] A. M. Weinberg, "Science and its Limits: The Regulator's Dilemma", *Issues in Science and Technology*, 2(1) (1985), 62.

[97] R. Constanza and L. Cornwell, "The 4P Approach to Dealing with Scientific Uncertainty", *Environmental Science and Policy for Sustainable Development*, 34(9) (1992),15.

[98] *Whaling* case, Separate Opinion of Judge Trindade, para. 71, available at: www.icj-cij .org/files/case-related/148/148-20140331-JUD-01-05-EN.pdf (accessed on 22/03/2018).

[99] Constanza and Cornwell, "The 4P Approach".

to be seen by some as a basic normative principle of international environmental law".[100]

Based on the above, I submit that the role of the precautionary principle in treaty making is that of a bridge; it acts as a link between science and law. Since much of environmental legislation is based on scientific study, information gained from these studies is only certain to a degree because science is a moving target and can never be certain – it is always changing. For instance, the knowledge that we have now about climate change is not the same knowledge from 60 years ago. Faced with such a conundrum, how else could best available science (which is a moving target) be considered? I propose that, in an event of scientific advancement, the law should be amended accordingly.

Scientific uncertainty may cause environmental adjudication to be more arduous for adjudicators and may be the determinate factor to vague norms. Nevertheless, it is important to be mindful of the fact that in science there is often no absolute certainty. However, research reduces uncertainty. In matters pertaining to environmental law, scientific knowledge is our greatest ally.

D   Conclusion

Scientific expertise and expertise in international environmental law is a prerequisite for adjudicators to enable them to make sound legal decisions in disputes in which environmental science is an inseparable component. Adjudicators may not possess scientific expertise, but they do have expertise in law, and the law has provided them with both procedural and substantive recourse when faced with complex environmental law cases. In complex environmental law disputes the legal knowledge of judges is no longer sufficient to substantiate and legitimize a decision.[101] A legitimate judgment must stem from the combination of expert and legal knowledge in the adjudication procedures.[102]

Commentators have often emphasized the passive nature of the court regarding environmental issues. Hence, adjudicators need to be more assertive. Certainly, there is scope for fuller use of the procedural and substantive recourse available to the court. The court needs to reconsider

---

[100] Ibid.
[101] D. Piet, "The Use of Court- Appointed Experts by the International Court of Justice!, *British Yearbook of International Law*, 84(1) (2013), 271–303.
[102] Ibid.

adopting more progressive approaches such as the use of experts, assessors, 'special masters' and even procedures allowing other tribunals who
are more suited to fact finding, sometimes to state a case for the court to
determine.[103] On the issue of the use of experts in environmental cases,
the changes made by the court are noteworthy. Over the years, the court
has revised the way that it handles scientific evidence, as is observable in
the *Gabcikovo-Nagyamros* case and the *Pulp Mills* case, and more
recently in the *Whaling* case.

With regard to vague norms, scientific uncertainty will remain an
obstacle to the elaboration of clear and efficient environmental regulations, mainly because of the uncertain science behind most environmental matters.

---

[103] C. E. Foster, *Science and the Precautionary Principle in International Courts and
Tribunals: Expert Evidence, Burden of Proof and Finality* (2013), p. 29.

5

Ignorance, Uncertainty and Biodiversity: Decision-Making by the Court of Justice of the European Union

VOLKER MAUERHOFER*

A   Introduction

This chapter aims to highlight patterns of practical solutions for dealing with ignorance and uncertainty in conservation conflicts dealing with different interests[1] regarding species protection and habitat conservation. It does so through a structured and comprehensive assessment of more than 100 cases adjudicated since 1985 by the Court of Justice of the European Union (CJEU).

The intensity of the regional integration within the EU is unique in the world. In acceding to this regional integration organization, Member States gave up a large part of their sovereignty. Nowadays, they are subject to the jurisdiction of the CJEU in EU-related environmental matters. The EU also deals with conservation issues in its autonomous legislation. Among the most striking examples are the Birds Directive[2]

---

* This chapter constitutes a partly modified and widely amended version of V. Mauerhofer, 'Ignorance, Uncertainty and Biodiversity: Decision Making By the Court of Justice of the European Union', Nicolas de Sadeleer's Jean Monnet Working Paper Series Environment and Internal Market (2014), vol. 2014/8, 10, at www.tradevenvironment.eu/uploads/Mauerhofer_on_Ignorance_and_Uncertainty_and_ECJ_WITH_TRACKS_citat_proposal_NEW_VM_1.pdf (accessed 30 April 2016). The author wishes to thank Ms. Felister Nyakuru for her valuable contribution and Nicolas de Sadeleer as well as Christina Voigt for their thoughtful corrections of an earlier version of this chapter. All remaining errors are the author's.

[1] A conflict of interests, in which two groups want different things from the same habitat or species, is one of six types of conservation conflicts identified by J. C. Young et al., 'The emergence of biodiversity conflicts from biodiversity impacts: characteristics and management strategies', *Biodiversity and Conservation*, 19 (2010), 3973–90.

[2] EEC (1979) Council Directive 79/409/EEC of 2 April 1979 on the conservation of wild birds [1979] OJ L103/1–18 and its amending acts, replaced by Directive 2009/147/EC of

and the Habitats Directive[3] which cover species protection and habitat conservation, including the protected area network Natura 2000, respectively.[4] This specific legislation has already been the subject of more than 100 cases since its adoption, and the subject of interpretation by the CJEU.[5] In several of them the CJEU has already had to deal with ignorance, uncertainty and risk.

For the purpose of this chapter, three terms are interpreted in the following manner:[6]

Ignorance: *if not all results of a future happening are known* (e.g. future adaptations/genetic modifications of species)

Uncertainty: *if potential results are known, but probabilities are not known* (e.g. new species discovered during an expedition into a yet unexplored rainforest site)

Risk: *if all potential results are known, and also their probabilities* (e.g. in a horse race).

These definitions refer to the results of future happenings. Thus, the future happening, such as any activity or inactivity in terms of a plan or project, is known as such. Differences in the definitions consist in terms of the results therefrom and the probabilities of these results occurring.

If a species protection norm obliges, for example, public authorities to take requisite measures to establish a system of strict protection for certain wild species in their natural range, prohibiting deterioration or

the European Parliament and of the Council of 30 November 2009 on the conservation of wild birds (codified version); [2010] OJL20/7 and its amending acts.

[3] EEC (1992) Council Directive 92/43/EEC of 21 May 1992 on the conservation of natural habitats and of wild fauna and flora [1992] OJ L206/7–50 and its amending acts.

[4] J. Paavola, 'Environmental justice and governance: Theory and lessons from the implementation of the European union's habitats directive', Working Paper – Centre for Social and Economic Research on the Global Environment 01/2003, 1–19; V. Mauerhofer, 'Missing links: how individuals can contribute to reserve policy enforcement on the example of the European Union', *Biodiversity and Conservation*, 19 (2010), 601–18; A. Hochkirch et al., 'Europe Needs a New Vision for a Natura 2020 Network', Conservation Letters, 6.6.(2013), 462–7; G. Winkel et al., 'The implementation of Natura 2000 in forests: A trans- and interdisciplinary assessment of challenges and choices', *Environmental Science & Policy*, 52 (2015), 23–32; S. Winter et al., 'The impact of Natura 2000 on forest management: a socio-ecological analysis in the continental region of the European Union', *Biodiversity and Conservation*, 23 (2014), 3451–82.

[5] See also L. Cashmen, 'Commission Compliance Promotion and Enforcement in the Field of Environment', *Journal for European Environmental and Planning Law*, (2006), 5, 385–94.

[6] Based on M. Faber, R. Manstetten and J. Proops, 'Humankind and the Environment: An Anatomy of surprise and ignorance' in M. Faber and J. Proops (eds.), *Ecological Economics: Concepts and Methods* (Edward Elgar, 1996), pp. 205–30, 212.

destruction of breeding sites or resting places,[7] the subjective side does not matter. Thus, these "results" are forbidden no matter what kind (purposely, deliberatively, consciously etc.) of intention or (gross, slight or slightest etc.) negligence was involved, if at all. Ignorance or uncertainty about this subjective side does not matter.

On the objective side, any deterioration or destruction of breeding sites or resting places establishes certainty that public authorities have failed to take requisite measures.[8] An event or process might have taken place of which the public authority was not aware and that had not been contemplated by science. This would constitute a case of ignorance in the abovementioned sense. But it would not relieve the public authority from the obligation to take restoration measures as a consequence of not fulfilling its original obligation. If potentially harmful events were known by the public authority but wrongfully underestimated in its probability of occurrence or – contrary to the available science – erroneously considered not to be harmful, this would constitute a case of uncertainty. But, again, if deterioration or destruction were to occur, restoration duties are the obvious sort of trade-off. If all options in the sense of actions or inactions and the probability of their harm or lack of harm are known, the public authority would be obliged to choose the option without the deteriorative or destructive effect mentioned above and so act in a "risk-averse" way.[9]

In the sections that follow, this chapter deals with ignorance and uncertainty in habitat conservation and later with uncertainty in species protection, both particularly in connection with the Habitats Directive as well as the Birds Directive and the related jurisdiction of the CJEU.

B   Ignorance and Uncertainty on Habitat Conservation

Articles 3 and 4 of the Birds Directive place several conservation duties on Member States, requiring them to protect areas for birds, be they inside or outside Special Protection Areas (SPAs).[10] These duties include

---

[7] In this sense, see the wording of Article 12(1)d of the Habitats Directive.

[8] If at all and how far this conclusion is restricted by the application of the principle of proportionality, also inherent in EU, cannot be discussed further within the scope of this article.

[9] The – very unlikely – case that there is no option without harm cannot be assessed further within the scope of this (short) contribution.

[10] Mauerhofer, 'Missing links', 601–18. C. I. Iojă et al., 'The Efficacy of Romania's Protected Areas Network in Conserving Biodiversity', *Biological Conservation*, 143 (11) (2010), 2468–76

actions[11] and – as there is no reason for a visible differentiation – also inactions "to adopt both measures intended to avoid external man-caused impairment and disturbance and measures to prevent natural developments that may cause the conservation status of species and habitats ... to deteriorate".[12]

In this way the CJEU dismissed in the arguments of the UK that suggested alleged insufficient transposition of the Habitats Directive that "only 'non-natural' deterioration, resulting, for example, from poor husbandry, is to be avoided and not natural deterioration, for example climate change or flooding due to a rise in sea level."[13] Thus, in my opinion, the effects of climate change – often an issue of uncertainty[14] – also ought to be addressed by Member States when implementing the Birds and Habitats Directives. This appears to be valid not only for the conservation of natural habitats and habitats of species but also for protection under both Directives as all contributes to the common goal of a favourable conservation status.

On the other side of the litigation table, the Commission was asked in an infringement procedure against Ireland to bring forward not only any claims but proof, even regarding illegal measures of individuals, that, through the alleged behaviour, a breach of EU-law by the Member State occurred. In this case the Commission referred, by means of an example of an activity that infringes Article 6(2) of the Habitats Directive, to unauthorized mechanical cockle harvesting in an area protected under this Directive.[15] Whereas the CJEU found that "as noted by the Advocate General in point 140 of her Opinion, that this is mere illustrative use which is not the subject-matter of the application. In any event, the Commission has not adduced any evidence such as to establish the failure to fulfil obligations on this point."[16]

---

[11] Reactive not only to actual damage but even to preventive ones, as was expressed by the CJEU in C–183/05 (para. 30): 'Similarly, the system of strict protection presupposes the adoption of coherent and coordinated measures of a preventive nature (Case C–518/04 *Commission* v. *Greece*, not published in the ECR, paragraph 16).'

[12] C–6/04, para. 34. In this sense, see also the recommendations of AG Kokott in this case at para 20ff of her Opinion delivered on 9 June 2005.

[13] Quoted from the description of the UK-arguments within the Opinion of AG Kokott, 9 June 2005, in C–6/04 at para. 17.

[14] J. De Koning et al, 'Natura 2000 and climate change-Polarisation, uncertainty, and pragmatism in discourses on forest conservation and management in Europe', *Environmental Science & Policy*, 39 (2014), 129–38.

[15] C–418/04, para. 202.

[16] Ibid., para. 211.

Regarding the alleged illegal mechanical mollusc fishing in that site, the Commission submitted that the Irish Government had informed it that prohibiting this activity would require comprehensive public consultation, but that, in subsequent communications, the Irish Government had stated that the competent authorities had intervened without delay and the mollusc fishing had been terminated within twenty-four hours.[17] The Advocate General formulated that the Commission would "have at least to put forward evidence, such as witnesses, to support its version of events."[18]

1 Ignorance of Conservation Status Outside and Inside of Sites

The SPAs mentioned previously play a major role in the EU bird site conservation policy.[19] This can be exemplified by the infringement action brought by the Commission against Spain,[20] in which the designation and management of SPAs in that country in accordance with Articles 3 and 4 of the Birds Directive was the matter in dispute. In this case, the CJEU stated that "The obligations on Member States under Articles 3 and 4 of the directive therefore exist before any reduction is observed in the number of birds or any risk of a protected species becoming extinct has materialized."[21]

This interpretation was confirmed explicitly in Case C–117/00 (paragraph 15) for all species in areas outside wild bird sites protected under Article 3 of the Birds Directive. This clearly shows an (early judicial) expression of the (later legislatively introduced) precautionary principle[22] in the face of ignorance, as it concerns yet unknown reasons of future reductions. Effective conservation measures have to be taken even in order to address yet unknown threats, leading to a reduction in

---

[17] See point 139 of the Opinion of AG Kokott in Case C–418/04.

[18] See AG Kokott at point 141 of her Opinion in Case C–418/04.

[19] P. F. Donald et al., 'International conservation policy delivers benefits for birds in Europe', *Science*, 317 (2007), 810–13; V. Mauerhofer, 'Conservation of Wildlife in the European Union with a focus on Austria' in R. Panjwani (ed.), *Wildlife Law: A Global Perspective* (American Bar Association (ABA) Publishing, 2008), pp. 1–55; Mauerhofer, 'Missing links', 601–18.

[20] See Case C–355/90.

[21] Ibid., para. 15.

[22] The Birds Directive was launched in 1979, while the precautionary principle was introduced by the Treaty of Maastricht to the primary law of today's EU; for further information, see, e.g., Communication from the Commission on the precautionary principle (COM(2000) 1 final of 2 February 2000).

the number of birds.[23] Of course, this raises the question of how to react to unknown threats and therefore how to counteract ignorance. The role of science could be twofold here: (1) to help to identify hypothetical threats that have not yet occurred or that have already occurred but have not yet had any impact, but could negatively affect the number of birds in the future, and (2) to help to develop potentially effective countermeasures. Of course, whether such threats will materialize and whether the countermeasures will be needed is uncertain.

Nevertheless, the CJEU has repeatedly used the phrase cited above[24] regarding ignorance, most recently in 2016, and thus emphasized its continuous validity.[25] In Case C–141/14, for example, the Court used it regarding ignorance, to condemn Bulgaria's approval of a wind farm in a wrongfully undesignated SPA. The Court found, first "that the operation of wind-power installations may lead to significant disturbances and deterioration of the habitats of protected bird species".[26] The CJEU stated that "[T]he fact that, according to the results of observations made by the wind farm 'AES Geo Energy', to which the Republic of Bulgaria refers, red-breasted geese still use the areas in question and that, when the wind conditions are favourable, migratory birds are concentrated in the Kaliakra site does not stand in the way of that finding".[27] The Court justified this alone with reference to "the obligations to protect exist before any reduction in the number of birds has been observed or before the risk of a protected species becoming extinct has materialised".[28] The Court did not try to point out the specific effect(s) that "may lead to significant disturbances and deterioration". This could be seen as being an element of ignorance, for science to fill up. In fact, the wind farm might even keep out birds of prey and, thus, positively affect the habitats, but this is also something not known (yet?) and has to be scientifically assessed. The CJEU mentioned additionally ("Furthermore") that "the data in question appear

---

[23] As has been mentioned, for the purpose of this chapter 'risk' is defined as 'if all potential results of a future happening are known, and also their probabilities', based on Faber, Manstetten and Proops, 'Humankind and the Environment', 212. In the interpretation just quoted, the CJEU also used the word 'risk', but in a way that such a risk is not known yet (which would – otherwise – call for the application of the principle of prevention). Thus, the Court refers to a much earlier phase. The future happening does not refer to the extinction itself, but factors – known or unknown (yet) – that can lead to extinction.

[24] See Case C–355/90, para. 15.

[25] See, e.g., C–186/06, para. 36 and C–141/14, para. 76

[26] C–141/14, para. 75.

[27] Ibid.

[28] Ibid.

to indicate a loss of attractiveness, since they show that red-breasted geese use the site less often than when peak values were recorded before the wind turbines were built".[29] Due to the order of arguments it is likely that even without this indication a condemnation by the Court would have happened. This case, as well as the other site-related cases mentioned,[30] deals with both the designation and the implementation of protective measures of bird sites. It will have to be seen in the future how far this judicial interpretation about ignorance will be used additionally in cases dealing with sites solely or also protected for species and/or habitat types falling under the regime of the Habitats Directive. In the Bulgarian Case mentioned, a site designated under this Directive was at least covering almost all the areas of the SPA designated under the Birds Directive.[31]

2   Uncertainty in Selecting Sites

The CJEU also addressed uncertainty in the sense described above in cases regarding the selection of SPAs. There, the duty to designate was clear, but uncertainty took place regarding the number and size of areas to be designated. The related judgments started with very general prescriptions on the overall number of sites to be designated under Article 4 of the Birds Directive and have been continuously fleshed out at the level of individual species.

Basically, Article 4 of the Birds Directive obliges Member States to classify in particular the most suitable territories in number and size as SPAs for the conservation of migrating species and species listed in Annex I to the Directive. Therefore, their protection requirements have to take into account the geographical sea and land area in which the Birds Directive applies.

The first case was brought against the Netherlands.[32] As a matter of factual evidence, the CJEU applied as a benchmark the so-called Important Bird Area (IBA) – n inventory that was published by a non-governmental organization (NGO) for how much the defending Member State had failed to provide relevant evidence as to the suitability of the sites to be designated. Regarding such an inventory from the year 1989 (IBA89), the CJEU stated in this case that:

---

[29] Ibid., para. 77.
[30] Ibid., para. 76; and Commission against Spain, C–355/90, para. 15.
[31] But apparently not the area that was, in an unlawful manner, not designated; see C–141/14, para. 10.
[32] C–3/96.

(i)n the circumstances, IBA 89 has proved to be the only document containing scientific evidence making it possible to assess whether the defendant State has fulfilled its obligation to classify as SPAs the most suitable territories in number and area for conservation of the protected species. The situation would be different if the Kingdom of the Netherlands had produced scientific evidence in particular to show that the obligation in question could be fulfilled by classifying as SPAs territories whose number and total area were less than those resulting from IBA 89.[33]

In this way, uncertainty about the number and size of areas to be designated under the Birds Directive was clarified for the first time by the Court, and it was done based on available scientific evidence while leaving the door open for improved evidence. Afterwards, the Court used similar terms in its judgments on the Birds Directive – for instance in Case C–240/00, *Commission* v. *Finland* as well as in Cases C–378/01 and C–235/04, *Commission* v. *Italy and Spain*, respectively. Partly, it arrived at the evidence provided for in the successor inventory, namely IBA 2000.

In all these cases, the CJEU did not delve into detail. However, this changed in Case C–334/04, *Commission* v. *Greece* regarding the failure of that Member State, alleged by the Commission, to classify areas of importance for the conservation of birds. In this case the CJEU ruled – beside the well-known general formulation first used in the case against the Netherlands – down to species level. Thus, besides an overall failure by Greece to abide by the duty to designate the relevant bird sites, the CJEU also stressed that one species was not represented in any SPA area and that eleven species were insufficiently represented.[34] This shows that the CJEU does not refrain from entering into the "battlefield of scientific facts." This was even more surprising in particular with regard to the different evidence that was produced by both the Commission and Greece concerning lingering uncertainty about the extent of occurrence of the eleven species, finally considered by the CJEU to be insufficiently represented. However, the fact that some evidence produced by Greece was unfinished and some was not properly notified to the Commission,[35] was the main influence for the final decision of the Court.

Recently, the European Commission also successfully claimed against the Republic of Cyprus regarding the Habitats Directive the inclusion of one site for one specific species into the national list of sites of community

---

[33] Ibid., para. 69f.
[34] C–334/04, para. 59.
[35] Ibid.

importance (SCIs) while the uncertainty concerning the extension of the
site was (unfortunately) not addressed during the pre-litigation stage.[36]

3   Uncertainty about Changing Boundaries of Designated Sites

Once protected areas have been designated within the framework of the
Natura 2000 network, Member States have continuously intended to
reduce or alter their boundaries. In a judgment against Portugal, the
CJEU made it clear that a Member State is not endowed with the same
discretion that it has in the course of the selection process. The rationale
is that the Member State is required to bring evidence that suitability for
conservation has faded away and/or that the site was not suitable any
more.[37] However, an appropriate assessment based on Article 6(3) of the
Habitats Directive can be implemented regarding the question whether
the alteration of the site's borders is possible. The uncertainty in this case
lies in the question which of the two options – to reduce or not to reduce –
is allowed under which circumstances and whether the probability for
both options to occur is the same: something that the Court neglected.

The more recent preliminary ruling in the case *Cascina Tre Pi Ss*[38] – in
which the Court had to decide about national legislation not providing for
persons concerned to request a review of status in the event of pollution or
degradation of the environment of SCIs under the Habitats Directive – did
not bring significant modifications of the criteria for changing sites'
demarcation developed by the Court in the Portuguese case[39] described.

4   Uncertainty on Implementing an Appropriate Assessment

The CJEU took a similar view to that in its case law on reducing and
altering SPAs, in cases in which it had to assess the level of uncertainty
triggering an appropriate assessment under the Habitats Directive. With
respect to Article 6(3) of the Habitats Directive, the Court decided in
a preliminary ruling that:

> any plan or project not directly connected with or necessary to the
> management of the site is to be subject to an appropriate assessment of
> its implications for the site in view of the site's conservation objectives if it

[36] It could therefore not be judged upon by the CJEU; see C–340/10, para. 22.
[37] C–191/05, para. 13.
[38] C–301/12.
[39] C–191/05.

cannot be excluded, on the basis of objective information, that it will have a significant effect on that site, either individually or in combination with other plans or projects.[40]

Again, any discretion of the authority is excluded. Without any objective information proving the opposite, the authority is called on to implement an appropriate assessment.[41]

5   Uncertainty in Granting Permission

The situation just described concerns the question whether an appropriate assessment should be implemented. One must also deal with another procedural step in which the appropriate assessment has already been implemented. Now, the authority has to decide whether the licence should be granted. The legal basis for that decision is clearly set forth in Article 6(3) of the Habitats Directive. According to this paragraph, the competent national authorities, taking account of the appropriate assessment of the implications of certain plans and/or projects for the site concerned in the light of the site's conservation objectives, are to permit such an activity in so far as they can ascertain that it will not adversely affect the integrity of that site. According to the CJEU in the case against the Netherlands mentioned previously, this authorization criterion 'integrates the precautionary principle'.[42] In the same judgment, the CJEU stated, concerning the absence of such adverse effects, that 'no reasonable scientific doubt [should] remain'.[43] Hence, the mere fact that uncertainty lingers precludes the public authority from granting the licence (apart from the next steps of that procedure set forth in Article 6(4) of the Habitats Directive). Article 7 of the Habitats Directive applies this interpretation in line with the precautionary principle even on those sites that have been designated as SPAs under Article 4 of the Birds Directive.

Furthermore, this interpretation of the Court has recently been reconfirmed, namely in the preliminary ruling case *Peter Sweetman*.[44] Therein,

---

[40] C–127/02, para. 45.

[41] See also, in relation to this case, P. F. M. Opdam, M. E. A. Broekmeyer and F. H. Kistenkas, 'Identifying uncertainties in judging the significance of human impacts on Natura 2000 sites' Environmental Science & Policy, 12 (2009), 912–1; and J. R. Floor, C. S. A. van Koppen and J. P. M. van Tatenhove, 'Uncertainties in the assessment of "significant effect" on the Dutch Natura 2000 Wadden Sea site – The mussel seed fishery and powerboat race controversies', *Environmental Science & Policy*, 55 (2016), 380–92.

[42] C–127/02, para. 58.

[43] Ibid., para. 61.

[44] C-258/11, para. 12.

the CJEU explicitly and similarly applied the precautionary principle in an appropriate assessment regarding a project that would have led to a permanent loss of 1.47 hectares of a total of 270 hectares of the priority habitat type "8240 * Limestone pavements" in one SCI.[45] The Court did so by referring to the definition of a favourable conservation status[46] in the Habitats Directive[47] and therefore applied a quantitative measurable and absolute benchmark especially on the appropriate assessment step of Article 6(3) of the Habitats Directive.

In fact, the CJEU stated:

> The competent national authorities cannot therefore authorise interventions where there is a risk of lasting harm to the ecological characteristics of sites which host priority natural habitat types. That would particularly be so where there is a risk that an intervention of a particular kind will bring about the disappearance or the partial and irreparable destruction of a priority natural habitat type present on the site concerned (see, as regards the disappearance of priority species, Case C–308/08, Commission v. Spain, paragraph 21, and Case C–404/09, Commission v. Spain, paragraph 163).[48]

This interpretation should not lead to the assumption that other habitat types or species than the priority ones are excluded from this interpretation of the precautionary principle. As the CJEU highlighted in one of the previous paragraphs, "Such an appraisal applies *all the more* in the main proceedings, since the natural habitat affected by the proposed road scheme is among the priority natural habitat types".[49]

The use of the term "all the more" seems to indicate clearly that not only priority assets are covered.

C   Uncertainty on Effective Implementation of Strict Species Protection Systems

All the cases treated so far dealt with the maintenance or restoration of habitats of wild species. That being said, the Birds and the Habitats

---

[45] Ibid., para. 27.
[46] According to Article 1(e) of the Habitats Directive, the conservation status of a natural habitat is taken to be 'favourable' when, in particular, its natural range and areas that it covers within that range are stable or increasing and the specific structure and functions that are necessary for its long-term maintenance exist and are likely to continue to exist for the foreseeable future.
[47] C–258/11.
[48] Ibid., para. 43.
[49] Ibid., para. 42 (highlights by the author).

Directives of the EU also address the issue of uncertainty regarding the protection of wild species in their own rights. Articles 5–9 of the Birds Directive and Articles 12–16 of the Habitats Directive are particularly relevant. They mainly cover the concrete protection of wild bird species and other wild animal species as well as wild plants respectively. In several judgments, the CJEU was called on to interpret these provisions.

1   Uncertainty about the Existence of a Strict Species Protection System

Article 12(1) of the Habitats Directive requires Member States to take all the requisite specific measures with the aim of effectively implementing the regime of strict protection. Interpreting this article, the CJEU found in the case against Ireland[50] that a Member State bears the burden of proving "the adoption of coherent and coordinated measures of a preventive nature" enhancing effective protection, and not merely "the existence of a network of full-time rangers and officers responsible for monitoring and protecting species". Furthermore, the CJEU ruled that "(a)s noted by the Advocate General in point 24 of his Opinion, the transposition of Article 12(1) of the Directive requires the Member States not only to adopt a comprehensive legislative framework but also to implement concrete and specific protection measures ... ".[51] Finally, the CJEU highlighted the precautionary principle in this case against Ireland in the following way: "(s)imilarly, the system of strict protection presupposes the adoption of coherent and coordinated measures of a preventive nature (Case C–518/04, Commission v. Greece, not published in the ECR, paragraph 16)".[52] By emphasizing the "preventive nature" of the measures to be taken, it can be assumed that the CJEU applies a similar benchmark to that in the habitat-related cases cited above. Thus, measures have to be taken before any quantitative or qualitative decline is observed and any threat or risk has materialized.

2   Uncertainty due to Unsubstantiated Assumptions

The case law annotated with regard to unsubstantiated assumptions seems to indicate that the European Commission does not bear the

---

[50] C–183/05, para. 30.
[51] Ibid., para. 29.
[52] Ibid., para. 30.

burden of too strict proof requirements such as is shown in the following. First of all, it can be concluded that the Commission has to provide more than assumptions regarding the circumstances threatening wild species. This was stated in the case *Commission v. Spain* concerning the Iberian Lynx,[53] in which the Iberian lynx, a priority species indigenous to Spain, is listed in Annex IV(a) to the Habitats Directive. The facts of the case concerned the incidental killing of the Iberian Lynx by vehicles along a road in Spain.[54] Spain was able to prove that it was continuing to study new measures capable of improving the conditions for conservation and improvement of species as provided under Article 12(4) of the Habitats Directive.[55] The CJEU interpreted the provisions of that article. This norm provides that "Member States shall establish a system to monitor the incidental capture and killing of the animal species listed in Annex IV (a). In the light of the information gathered, Member States shall take further research or conservation measures as required to ensure that incidental capture and killing does not have a significant negative impact on the species concerned." Thus, the Court concurred with the reasoning of the Spanish authorities and dismissed the case. Similarly, in an earlier judgment handed down against Ireland,[56] the Court ruled out unsubstantiated assumptions put forward by the Commission by holding that "(I)n that regard, it must be borne in mind that, according to settled case-law, in an action for failure to fulfil obligations brought under Article 226 EC it is for the Commission to prove that the obligation has not been fulfilled without being able to rely on any presumption (Case C–221/04, Commission v. Spain [2006] ECR I–4515, paragraph 59 and the case-law cited)." Concrete evidence is also required to prove a breach of the provisions above: "(I)n the present case, it must be held that the Commission has not put forward any concrete evidence to substantiate the seventh part of its second complaint".[57]

3   Uncertainty on Deliberativeness of Species Killing/Catching

Another case brought by the Commission against Spain[58] concerned the deliberativeness of killing/catching of wild species prohibited also by

---

[53] C–308/08.
[54] Ibid., para. 57.
[55] Ibid., para. 59.
[56] C–183/05, para. 39.
[57] Ibid., para. 40.
[58] C–221/04.

Article 12(1)(a) of the Habitats Directive. Therein the Commission had to prove deliberate action regarding the killing of a protected species through a specific hunting method (snares) mainly targeting a non-protected species. Although the Commission failed even to prove that the protected species occurred in the area in which the hunting method was used, the Court required nonetheless that "it must be proven that the author of the act intended the capture or killing of a specimen ... or, at the very least, accepted the possibility of such capture or killing".[59] Although the CJEU consequently dismissed the infringement action, the broad interpretation of deliberativeness can be considered important. In comparison with the Austrian Criminal Law Act, that concept covers even the slightest extent of intentional behaviour, whereas, in accordance with this Act, "deliberativeness" is only the middle of three gradual forms of intentional behaviours. Thus, the proof of deliberativeness in the CJEU's interpretation could be achieved rather easily.

4 Uncertainty on Deliberativeness in Species Disturbance

In the following, there is provided another example in which the European Commission succeeded in producing the extent of proof required by the CJEU.

This happened in a case brought against Greece.[60] The Commission asked the CJEU to condemn Greece for infringing Article 12(1)(b) and (d) of the Habitats Directive by failing to offer strict protection to the sea turtle *Caretta caretta* so as to avoid disturbance of the species during its breeding season. The Commission could produce evidence – based on a field visit – on the presence of pedalos and small boats around two breeding beaches, coupled with the presence of illegal buildings on another breeding beach. The Greek Government did not dispute the accuracy of those findings.

The CJEU then concluded that the use of mopeds, as well as the presence of pedalos and small boats, deliberately disturbed the species in question during its breeding season for the purposes of Article 12(1)(b) of the Directive.[61] By the same token, the existence of illegal buildings was considered to be liable to lead to the deterioration or destruction of

---

[59] Ibid., para. 71.
[60] C–103/00.
[61] Ibid., paras. 32–6.

the breeding site within the meaning of Article 12(1)(d) of the Directive.[62] Deliberativeness is not required within this provision.

5 Derogation from Species Protection and the Burden of Proof

Article 12(1) (a) of the Habitats Directive prohibits all forms of deliberate capture or killing of specimens of the species in the wild, whereas Article 16(1) allows Member States to derogate from the strict provisions of Articles 12, 13, 14 and 15 subject to certain preconditions such as to prevent serious damage to crops, livestock and other types of property. An explicit precondition laid down in Article 16(1) of the Habitats Directive is that "the derogation is not detrimental to the maintenance of the populations of the species concerned at a favorable conservation status in their natural range". Despite this clear wording, the CJEU ruled differently in an infringement case brought by the Commission against Finland.[63] This case was brought against Finland under Articles 12(1) (a) and 16(1) of the Habitats Directive for hunting wolves, which was considered to be in breach of the said provisions. Therein, the CJEU ruled that a Member State that wants to hunt a certain species despite its "unfavourable conservation status"[64] bears the burden of proof that the grants of such derogations "are not such as to worsen the unfavourable conservation status of those populations or to prevent their restoration at a favourable conservation status".[65] Nevertheless, the CJEU found that "by authorising wolf hunting on a preventive basis, without it being established that the hunting is such as to prevent serious damage within the meaning of Article 16(1)(b) of the Habitats Directive, the Republic of Finland has failed to fulfil its obligations under Articles 12(1)(a) and 16(1)(b) of that directive;".[66] Though Finland managed to prove that the derogation did not worsen the unfavourable conservation status of those populations, or to prevent their restoration towards a favourable conservation status, it failed to provide sufficient evidence for another precondition, namely the effectiveness of the hunting in order to really prevent these serious damages.

[62] Ibid., para. 38.
[63] C–342/05.
[64] For a definition of the 'Favourable Conservation Status', see Article 1(e) of the Habitats Directive, quoted in n. 46 above.
[65] C–342/05, para. 29.
[66] Ibid., para. 47.

In summary, according to the CJEU, the burden of proof shifts to the Member State in the face of uncertainty as to the impact of the derogation on the unfavourable conservation status. Finland was in that case not able to come forward with such proof prior to granting the derogation permit.

6 Uncertainty on Numbers of Derogations from Species Protection

As already mentioned, Article 9 of the Birds Directive provides the basis for granting derogations from the species protection obligations laid down by this Directive. Important criteria are therein the restriction of derogations to "small numbers" and "affected populations". In this connection, the Member States are increasingly challenged by the findings of the CJEU, given that the Court has already defined "small numbers" and "affected populations" based on recommendations of the so-called ORNIS-Committee.[67] This Committee for the Adaptation to Technical and Scientific Progress was instituted under Article 16 of the Birds Directive, consists of representatives of the Member States and is chaired by a representative of the European Commission.

In all these cases, the CJEU decided that the definitions of the ORNIS Committee are not legally binding. However, in recognizing the scientific value of the work of the ORNIS Committee and in as much as the defending Member States are unable to contradict this evidence, ORNIS Committee analyses are taken into consideration.[68] Thus, the Member States bear the burden of proof in challenging the definitions brought forward by the ORNIS Committee.

D Conclusions

Conflicts of different interests in conservation often include aspects of ignorance and uncertainty. This chapter concentrated on such conservation conflicts dealing with at least one of these aspects and occurring in connection with the Birds Directive and the Fauna-Flora-Habitat-Directive of the European Union. It offers practical examples of such conflicts regarding species protection as well as habitat conservation based on several judgments of the CJEU.

The methodology applied is an in-depth analysis of more than 100 judgments handed down by the CJEU since 1984. These judgments are in

---

[67] See, e.g., C–79/03, para. 36; and C–344/03, para. 53.
[68] C–79/03, para. 36; and C–344/03, para. 53.

particular analysed with regard to situations in which the Court was facing a lack of information about future environmental developments as well as on withstanding opinions on technical matters. Cases are also distinguished according to habitat conservation and species protection.

The analysis shows regarding ignorance in habitat conservation that the Court applied the precautionary principle on conflicts inside and even outside protected areas in order to prevent any deterioration of the species and their biotopes. Concerning ignorance in species conservation no such application as yet been found.

Regarding uncertainty, the Court allocated the burden of proof to the proposer of a potential deterioration of habitat as well as species protection and while doing so referred partly to the precautionary principle. Thereby, the CJEU relies on existing formal rules as well as – if no such rules are available – creating innovative new rules in order to allocate the burden of proof and its extent among litigating parties. This allocation of the burden of proof is based on criteria such as the narrow interpretation of exemptions, the general availability of scientific proof concerning the asserted theme, the effectiveness of conservation, and the absolute lack of any means to prevent damage. The CJEU also handed down judgments regarding uncertainty in cases relating to the selection by Member States of protected sites. This started with very general prescriptions on the overall number of sites to be designated under Article 4 of the Birds Directive and has recently been concretized down to the level of individual species.

The CJEU has already applied "ignorance" in the perspective of the precautionary principle inside and outside protected sites in four cases and adjudicates cases under uncertainty mostly "*in dubio pro natura*" (when in doubt, favour nature). Similarly, de Sadeleer[69] states that "pursuant to the precautionary principle, authorities are prepared to tackle risks for which there is no definitive proof that the damage will materialize." The CJEU has continued to apply the principle even in instances in which there has been no concrete knowledge of any perceived risks to the protected sites.

The same is true of the CJEU's rulings on whether, for Natura 2000 sites, an appropriate assessment pursuant to Article 6 of the Habitats Directive for certain plans and projects has to be implemented and

---

[69] N. de Sadeleer N., 'Origin, Status and Effects of Precautionary Principle' in N. de Sadeleer (ed.), *Implementing the Precautionary Principle, Approaches from the Nordic Countries, the EU and USA* (Earthscan, 2007), pp. 3–6, p. 3.

whether such activities can be approved afterwards by the authorities. Also in these two cases the CJEU puts "*in dubio*" the burden of proof respectively on the shoulders of the developer, which reflects again the precautionary principle in cases of uncertainty.[70]

Regarding species protection, the European Commission bears at least the burden of proving mostly the probability/likeliness of damage and deliberativeness in each case. With the wide meaning of deliberativeness discussed above, it should be quite easy for the Commission to establish such evidence. Thus, the Commission should be usually able to put forth a watertight case that fosters the implementation of the provisions of Article 12(1) of the Habitats Directive.

According to the CJEU, a Member State has to produce mostly the full scientific and factual evidence of effective protection as provided for under Article 9 of the Birds Directive, with no negative impact. Where a Member State is unable to provide such scientific evidence, the ORNIS Committee's work forms the basis of the Court's findings. This is in line with de Sadeleer,[71] who states that "absence of scientific certainty as to the existence or the extent of a risk should henceforth no longer delay the adoption of preventive measures to protect the environment."

In summary, the CJEU has already ruled in a wide range of cases on issues of ignorance and especially uncertainty. These decisions cover both habitat conservation and species protection. In the habitat conservation cases the issue of ignorance is dealt with to some extent, whereas uncertainty receives broad attention by the CJEU in habitat conservation as well as species conservation. Regarding both issues, the precautionary principle is widely applied by the CJEU. The allocation and the extent of the burden of proof are main elements in all cases in which the CJEU has to deal with ignorance and uncertainty.

Based on several practical examples, the findings of this chapter summarize main problems and solutions relating to ignorance and uncertainty in CJEU case law on species protection and habitat protection. The approaches applied in these judgments by the CJEU can widely serve as a pattern for parties and decision-makers during similar conflicts, as well as for legislative bodies in providing the legislative basis for such decisions.

---

[70] V. Mauerhofer, '3-D Sustainability: an approach for priority setting in situation of conflicting interests towards a sustainable development', *Ecological Economics*, 65 (2008), 496–506.

[71] De Sadeleer, 'Origin, Status and Effects of Precautionary Principle', p. 3.

PART III

Judges as Law-Makers: Legitimate Development
of Environmental Law

6

Sustainable Development before International Courts and Tribunals: Duty to Cooperate and States' Good Faith

A Introduction

This chapter focuses on the principle of good faith in performing a duty to cooperate in the context of sustainable management of shared resources. The main objective of the current research is to illustrate that a state's good faith occupies a positive role in fulfilling a duty to cooperate. In conventional interstate disputes, under the concept of sovereign equality, a state's good faith in exercising treaty rights or obligations is presumed unless its bad faith has been established by the other party. Such presumption has been challenged in the context of the international law of cooperation. A state's good faith can be objectively assessed by international courts and tribunals when reviewing the state's domestic decision-making processes in accordance with international standards. This review function takes a monistic approach, making a state's discretion an object of evaluation in light of international law and soft law materials. Therefore this monistic approach may raise tensions between state sovereignty on domestic policy making and the review function of international courts and tribunals, and it may entail a matter of legitimacy in international law.

The notion of good faith reflects legal and extra legal elements, such as honesty, fairness, and reasonableness.[1] Although the meaning of the principle of good faith in international law is ambiguous and

* This work was supported by JSPS KAKENHI Grant Number JP17H02456.
[1] J. F. O'Connor, *Good Faith in International Law* (Dartmouth, 1991), pp. 122–4.

controversial in theory and practice, good faith in international law has manifold roles in the creation, interpretation, and performance of treaties as well as in the creation and performance of international obligations derived from other sources of international law. In this sense, good faith is a fundamental principle of international law.[2]

In comparison with municipal legal systems that have centralized governance structures, the processes of law-making and implementation of international law considerably rely on states' good faith due to the decentralized structure of the community of states.[3] In a somewhat modest manner, Fitzmaurice suggested that in the context of the international law of cooperation "the accepted obligation of good faith [...] requires something more than the merely negative avoidance of action in bad faith."[4] Such a good faith obligation contains three components: recognition of a common or general interest; participation in measures for the promotion of that common interest; and refraining from impairing such a common interest.[5] Schwarzenberger systematically elaborated the function of coordination of the *bona fide* principle in *jus aequum*, in which reasonableness and good faith work to balance conflicting interests.[6] Good faith is a regulative element in treaty interpretation that reduces subjectivity, and rationalizes interpreters' "views of what, in concrete instance, good faith requires."[7]

---

[2] Bin Cheng, *General Principles of Law as Applied by International Courts and Tribunals* (Cambridge University Press, 1953), pp. 103 ff. Cf.Paul Guggenheim, *Traité de droit international public*, tome I, 2e éd (1967), pp. 27–9 (stating that "inhérente à tout système consensuel").

[3] E.g. Manfred Lachs, "Some Thoughts on the Role of Good Faith in International Law" in R. J. Akkerman et al. (eds.), *Declarations on Principle: A Quest for Universal Peace* (A. W. Sijthoff, 1977), pp. 47–55, especially p. 48; Alfred Verdross, "Die bona fides als Grundlage des Völkerrechts" in D. S. Constantopolos and H. Webber (Hrsg.), *Gegenwartsprobleme des internationalen Rechtes und der Rechtsphilosophie, Festschrift für Rudolf Laun zu seinem siebzigsten Geburtstag* (Girardet, 1953), pp. 29–33, especially pp. 29–30.

[4] Gerald Fitzmaurice, "The Future of Public International Law and of International Legal System in the Circumstances of Today" in Institut de Droit International, *Liver du Centenaire 1873-1973* (Karger, 1973), pp. 319–20.

[5] Ibid.

[6] Georg Schwarzenberger, *A Manual of International Law*, 6th edn. (Fred B. Rothman & Co, 1976), pp. 118–19; Georg Schwarzenberger, "The Fundamental Principles of International Law," *Recueil des Cours*, 1955-I, 323–5.

[7] Schwarzenberger, "Fundamental Principles", 301.

B Cooperation and Good Faith in Recent ICJ Cases

Recent cases brought before the International Court of Justice ("ICJ" or "the Court") have elaborated the principle of good faith in fulfilment of a duty of cooperation, and have revealed the substance of the principle under concrete circumstances related to sustainable development and, more specifically, to sustainable management of shared resources in international law.

In the *Gabčikovo-Nagymaros Project Case*, within the realm of cooperation in the use of the shared water resources contemplated by the 1977 Treaty between the parties, the Court called upon the parties to re-negotiate and re-establish the joint regime in good faith under the rule of *pacta sunt servanda*, taking into consideration newly developed environmental norms even after the construction began. The Court indicated that "[w]hat is required in the present case by the rule *pacta sunt servanda*, as reflected in Article 26 of the Vienna Convention of 1969 on the Law of Treaties, is that the Parties find an agreed solution within the co-operative context of the Treaty."[8] The Court construed good faith under Article 26, such that "[t]he principle of good faith obliges the Parties to apply [the 1977 Treaty] in a reasonable way and in such a manner that its purpose can be realized."[9] For the Court, the cooperative context of the 1977 Treaty was meant to re-establish the joint regime for the common utilization of the shared water resources.[10] The Court called for the parties to resume their cooperation for the utilization of the shared water resources of the Danube as a form of reparation, wiping out all the consequences of the illegal act.[11] In re-establishing the joint regime in pursuit of the 1977 Treaty purposes, the Parties should renegotiate to find an agreed solution in good faith. For their negotiation, the wording of Articles 15 and 19 of the 1977 Treaty obliged the parties to take into account newly

---

[8] *Gabčikovo-Nagymaros Project* (Hungary/Slovakia), Judgment, ICJ Reports 1997, pp. 78–9, para. 142.

[9] Ibid.

[10] Ibid., p. 77, para. 147. The Court referred to Article 5(2) of the Convention on the Law of the Non-Navigational Uses of International Watercourses, which reads as follows:

> "Watercourses States shall participate in the use, development and protection of an international watercourse in an equitable and reasonable manner. Such participation includes both the right to utilize the watercourse and the duty to cooperate in the protection and development thereof, as provide in the present Convention."

[11] Ibid., p. 80, para. 150.

generated environmental norms not only for new activities but also for activities begun in the past.[12]

The Court found that the principle of good faith was the foundation of the mechanism for cooperation between the parties in the *Pulp Mills on the River Uruguay Case (Pulp Mills Case)*.[13] The object and purpose of the 1975 Statute regulating the use of the river for the Parties, set forth in Article 1, was "for the Parties to achieve 'the optimum and rational utilization of the River Uruguay' by means of the 'joint machinery' for co-operation, which consists of both [Comisión Administradora del Río Uruguay] and the procedural provisions contained in Articles 7 to 12 of the Statute."[14] The Court observed the relationship between cooperation and the obligations stipulated in the 1975 Statute, and noted that the cooperation between the Parties for the joint management of the environmental risks was realized through the performance of the procedural and substantive obligations laid down by the 1975 Statute.[15] In this respect, the Court noted as follows:

> The Court notes, moreover, that the 1975 Statute is perfectly in keeping with the requirements of international law on the subject, since the mechanism for co-operation between States is governed by the principle of good faith. Indeed, according to customary international law, as reflected in Article 26 of the 1969 Vienna Convention on the Law of Treaties (...).[16]

---

[12] Ibid., p. 77, para. 140. In this regard, the Court pointed out that the purpose of the 1977 Treaty and the intentions of the parties in concluding it should prevail over its literal application. However, there is criticism over the construction of the meaning of good faith under Article 26 taken by the Court that it contained "far-reaching and controversial implications" regarding the rule of *pacta sunt servanda* based on the specific circumstances attached to the 1977 Treaty: flexibility of the objectives aimed at in the Treaty and in its terms reflecting the parties' intention and its nature of a territorial regime. Malgosia Fitzmaurice and Olufemi Elias, *Contemporary Issues in the Law of Treaties* (Eleven International Publishing, 2005), p. 370.

[13] *Pulp Mills on the River Uruguay*, ICJ Reports 2010, p. 14.

[14] Ibid., p. 48, para. 75.

[15] Ibid., p. 49, para. 77. The Court mentioned as follows:

> [I]t is by cooperation that the States concerned can jointly manage the risks of damage to the environment that might be created by the plans initiated by one or other of them, so as to prevent the damage in question, through the performance of both the procedural and the substantive obligations laid down by the 1975 Statute. (...) the two categories of obligations mentioned above complement one another perfectly, enabling the parties to achieve the object of the Statute which they set themselves in Article 1.

[16] Ibid., p. 67, para. 145.

Within the cooperative scheme, the parties had to negotiate in good faith regarding the construction of the mills and the port terminal. Authorization and initiation of the construction of these facilities before the end of the negotiation period would defeat the object and purpose of the 1975 Treaty.[17] Thus, the Court held as follows:

> In the view of the Court, there would be no point to the co-operation mechanism provided for by Articles 7 to 12 of the 1975 Statute if the party initiating the planned activity were to authorize or implement it without waiting for that mechanism to be brought to a conclusion. Indeed, if that were the case, the negotiations between the parties would no longer have any purpose.[18]

In the case of *Whaling in the Antarctic* (*Whaling Case*)[19] the Court elaborated the duty of cooperation of the States parties to the International Convention on Regulation of Whaling (ICRW) and good faith as an essential factor in performance of that duty.

The dominant issue in the *Whaling Case* was whether the special permits issued by Japan for the whaling programme (JARPA II) were accordance with the term "for purposes of scientific research" under Article VIII(1) of the ICRW. Assessing that question, the Court set up the standard of review, which translated the treaty terms into "whether, in the use of lethal methods, the programme's design and implementation are reasonable in relation to achieving its stated objectives."[20] Applying the standard of conduct, the Court examined several facets surrounding JARPA II. As a result, the Court found that Japan did not provide convincing evidence establishing that the programme was designed for scientific research.[21] It concluded that Japan had not considered non-lethal methods in designing and implementing its whaling programme in an adequate manner and had failed to satisfy requirements under "an obligation to give due regard to [International Whaling Commission (IWC)] resolutions and Guidelines" that was derived from the duty to cooperate with the IWC and the Scientific Committees.[22]

---

[17] Ibid., pp. 60–70, paras. 123–58

[18] Ibid., p. 67, para. 147.

[19] *Whaling in the Antarctic*, ICJ Reports 2014, p. 226 ff.

[20] Ibid., p. 254, para. 67.

[21] Ibid., pp. 292–3, paras. 224–7.

[22] Ibid., p. 271, para. 144.

The Court specified the duty to cooperate as involving a procedural obligation under paragraph 30 of the Schedule to the ICRW,[23] according to which parties to the ICRW were required to submit specific information regarding the whaling programme to the Scientific Committee for review.[24] In this regard, the Court observed that the implementation of JARPA II differed in significant respects from the original design of the programme, therefore "consideration by a State party of revising the original design of the programme for review would demonstrate co-operation by a State party with the Scientific Committee."[25] On the other hand, the Court found that Japan had not violated paragraph 30 in light of the practice of the Scientific Committee.[26]

Furthermore, the Court inferred an "obligation to give due regard to IWC resolutions and Guidelines" from the duty to cooperate.[27] The Court confirmed that these resolutions and Guidelines themselves were not legally binding on the States parties to the ICRW and they could not even be regarded as subsequent agreement or as subsequent practice establishing interpretation of Article VIII within the meaning of Article 31(3)(a) and (b) of the Vienna Convention on the Law of Treaties (Vienna Convention).[28] The Court considered that these resolutions and Guidelines contained certain legal standards for assessing whether Japan appropriately considered availability of non-lethal methods in designing JARPA II. The Court pointed out that JARPA II should have included "some analysis of the feasibility of non-lethal methods."[29] However, Japan could not prove that it had appropriately taken into account non-lethal methods. Therefore, the Court concluded that "this is difficult to reconcile with Japan's obligation to give due regard to IWC resolutions and Guidelines and its statement that JARPA II uses lethal methods only to the extent necessary to meet its scientific objectives."[30]

---

[23] The most recent amendment of the Schedule was made in 2016 and contained text identical to that of paragraph 30, which was adopted in 1979. Available at the IWC website: https://archive.iwc.int/pages/view.php?ref=3606&k. The text of paragraph 30 of the Schedule adopted in 1979 appears also in the Memorial of Australia, p. 148, para. 4.23.

[24] *Whaling in the Antarctic*, ICJ Reports 2014, p. 248, para. 47.

[25] Ibid., p. 297, para. 240.

[26] Ibid., p. 297, para. 239.

[27] Ibid., p. 271, para. 144.

[28] Ibid., p. 256, para. 80 and p. 257, para. 83.

[29] Ibid., pp. 269–70, para. 137.

[30] Ibid., p. 271, para. 144.

In this regard, Judge Bennouna criticized the Court's reasoning as inadequate because it did not provide evidence of the existence of the requirement that the non-lethal methods should have priority over lethal methods. The inadequacy of the reasoning was due to the fact that the Court relied on non-legally binding IWC resolutions and Guidelines to remedy the lack of legal obligation.[31] To the contrary, Judge *ad hoc* Charlesworth inferred the obligation to prioritize non-lethal methods from resolutions adopted by consensus in the IWC.[32] For Judge *ad hoc* Charlesworth, "[t]he concept of a duty of co-operation is the foundation of legal régimes dealing (*inter alia*) with shared resources and with the environment."[33] The resolutions adopted by the IWC with consensus or a large majority vote represent the shared interest in regulation of whaling; therefore States parties are "required to consider these resolutions in good faith."[34] Thus, the purpose of paragraph 30 is to deter abuse of Article VIII(1) by States parties in authorizing commercial whaling in the guise of scientific research.[35] Judge Greenwood pointed out that since the IWC had power to amend the Schedule adopting to changing circumstances, to consider that recommendations had the same effects as legally binding regulations would "destroy the balance of the Convention."[36]

In the *Whaling Case*, as a matter of definition, the Court mentioned that "the States parties to the *ICRW* have a duty to co-operate with the IWC and the Scientific Committee," therefore, the cooperation in the judgment signified institutional cooperation.[37] According to Wolfrum, cooperation in international law is defined as "the voluntary coordinated action of two or more States which takes place under a legal régime and serves a specific objective."[38] However, recent developments in international human rights, environmental, and economic law have shown that there is another form of cooperation, in addition to cooperation between States, which is cooperation between Member States and international organizations or treaty bodies, i.e. institutional cooperation. This form of cooperation is more important in effective accomplishment of common

---

[31] Ibid., dissenting opinion of Judge Bennouna, p. 344.
[32] Ibid., separate opinion of Judge *ad hoc* Charlesworth, p. 454, para. 5.
[33] Ibid., separate opinion of Judge *ad hoc* Charlesworth, p. 457, para. 13.
[34] Ibid., separate opinion of Judge *ad hoc* Charlesworth, p. 458, para. 14.
[35] Ibid.
[36] Ibid., separate opinion of Judge Greenwood, p. 408, para. 7.
[37] Ibid., p. 257, para. 83.
[38] Rüdiger Wolfrum, "International Law of Cooperation" in R. Bernhardt (ed.), *Encyclopedia of Public International Law*, vol. II (North-Holland, 1995), p. 1242.

and shared goals.[39] Interstate cooperation may fall into the conventional realm of reciprocity and concession between states with positive behavior; however, functioning institutional cooperation often entails inherent difficulties in international law. It is undesirable for states to lose a part of their sovereignty in decision-making at municipal level.[40] This aspect of institutional cooperation brings about the issue of legitimacy. When international courts and tribunals considered non-legally binding recommendations taken by international institutions or treaty bodies as having any legal effects affecting the domestic power of decision-making of states, the problem of legitimacy might be related to the role of consent of states in international law-making and the rule of *pacta sunt servanda*.

As discussed above, on one hand, the judgment denied taking the view that resolutions and Guidelines of the IWC and the Scientific Committee occupy formal positions in the treaty interpretation rule codified in Article 31(3)(a) and (b) of the Vienna Convention. On the other hand, the majority of the bench took the position that States parties to the ICRW are required to respect those non-legally binding recommendations. To explain this inconsistency in the nature of the recommendations adopted by the IWC and the Science Committee, the Court employed the duty to cooperate and the obligation to give due regard to such non-legally binding documents.

Finding the duty to cooperate with treaty organs in the *Whaling Case* was heavily dependent upon Japan's declaration that it accepted the duty to cooperate with the IWC and the Scientific Committee. Certainly, in its counter-memorial, Japan clearly stated that "even in the absence of binding effect, there is a duty on the part of the Contracting Governments to consider a recommendation in good faith and, if requested, to explain their action or inaction."[41] Japan's confirmation of the existence of the duty to cooperate put emphasis on the non-obligatory character of those recommendations the Court required

---

[39] On cooperation in international human rights law and international economic law, see Jost Delbrück, "The International Obligation to Cooperate – An Empty Shell or A Hard Law Principle of International Law? – A Critical Look at A Much Debated Paradigm of Modern International Law" in H. P. Hestermeyer et al. (eds.), *Coexistence, Cooperation and Solidarity: Liber Amicorum R. Wolfrum*, vol. I (Martinus Nijhoff Publishers, 2012), pp. 8, 10.

[40] On environmental law, see Rüdiger Wolfrum and Nele Matz, *Conflicts in International Environmental Law* (Springer, 2003), p. 163.

[41] *Whaling Case*, Japan, Counter-Memorial, p. 373, para.8.63. Online: www.icj-cij.org/files/case-related/148/17384.pdf (last accessed 2 August 2017).

Japan to explain its action or inaction in terms of the non-legally binding recommendations and Guidelines.

For Young and Sullivan, these resolutions and Guidelines have possessed a certain legal influence in the cooperation of States parties with treaty organs. Among others, Young and Sullivan consider that the normative influence attached to the monitoring and reviewing functions of international organizations as soft law having consequences of "[r]equiring states parties to 'give due regard' to non-legally binding recommendations of the IWC, even if they had not been adopted with consensus or unanimity."[42] And, they suggest the possibility of evolution of international law-making that is not strictly dependent upon the consent of States parties.[43]

However, it is doubtful whether such non-legally binding instruments adopted by treaty organs acquire certain legal effects by themselves. In the *Whaling Case* the resolutions and Guidelines adopted by the IWC are referred to not as legally binding but as legally to be considered for reassessing actions that have been taken.[44] As Japan asserted, and the majority of the Court supported, the obligation to "give due regard" is derived from the duty to cooperate with international organizations; however it does not mean that these recommendations themselves (per se) may possess legally binding force. This view is taken also by Judge Greenwood's formalistic approach that such resolutions do not obtain any normative grounds for substantive duty for cooperation.[45]

Despite the importance of the duty to cooperate in the judgment, it is not clear where it derived from.[46] Japan quoted Judge Lauterpacht's separate opinion in the *Voting Procedure Case*, which presupposed that "[t]he State in question, while not bound to accept the recommendation, is bound to give it due consideration in good

---

[42] Margaret A. Young and Sebastian R. Sullivan, "Evolution through the Duty to Cooperate: Implications of the *Whaling Case* at the International Court of Justice", *Melbourne Journal of International Law*, 16(2) (2015), 30.

[43] Ibid.

[44] Jeffrey J. Smith, "Evolving to Conservation?: The International Court's Decision in the Australia/Japan Whaling Case", *Ocean Development and International Law*, vol. 45(4) (2014), 318.

[45] *Whaling* in *the Antarctic*, ICJ Reports 2014, separate opinion of Judge Greenwood, pp. 407–8, paras. 6–7. See Smith, "Evolving to Conservation?", 315.

[46] See also Hironobu Sakai, "After the *Whaling in the Antarctic Judgment*: Its Lessons and Prospects from a Japanese Perspective" in Malgosia Fitzmaurice and Dai Tamada (eds.), *Whaling in the Antarctic: Significance and Implications of the ICJ Judgment* (Brill Nijhoff, 2016), p. 332–4.

faith".[47] The Court was rather dependent upon Japan's argument at this point and did not clarify the ground(s) for the legal basis of that duty. In this regard, it should be noted that Judge Klaestad submitted his doubt concerning the legal nature of the duty to consider non-legally binding recommendations in his Separate Opinion in the very same case. He mentioned as follows:

> the Union of South Africa is in duty bound to consider in good faith a recommendation adopted by the General Assembly under Article 10 of the Charter and to inform the General Assembly with regard to the attitude which it has decided to take in respect of the matter referred to in the recommendation. But a duty of such a nature, however real and serious it may be, can hardly be considered as involving a true legal obligation, and it does not in any case involve a binding legal obligation to comply with the recommendation.[48]

The Court reviewed the reasonableness of JARPA II in considering seven elements, and it referred to the recommendations and Guidelines adopted by the IWC and the Science Committee regarding the use of lethal methods and the scale of lethal sampling. The standard of review provided a practical justification for the Court's evaluating objectively whether the design and implementation of the whaling programme were reasonable in achieving its stated objectives without assessing a controversial subjective element of state's good faith in exercising the right to issue a special permit under Article VIII(1).[49] Regarding the review methodology that the Court used, Judge Greenwood cautioned that it was somewhat unusual to consider recommendations as having significant effects, where the IWC has the capacity to adjust the ICRW to changing circumstances by amending the Schedule and thus to apply that convention as a "living instrument."[50] It is certain that there is a tendency

---

[47] *Whaling Case*, Japan, Counter-Memorial, p. 373, para. 8.63.

[48] *Voting Procedure Case*, ICJ Reports 1955, separate opinion of Judge Klaestad, p. 88. See also comment by Alan Boyle for Japan, Public sitting held on Thursday 4 July 2013, at 3 p.m., at the Peace Palace, President Tomka presiding, in *Case concerning Whaling in the Antarctic* (*Australia* v. *Japan*: New Zealand intervening), VERBATIM RECORD, CR 2013/16, p. 35, para. 22.

[49] See also Caroline E. Foster, "Methodologies and Motivations: Was Japan's Whaling Programme for Purposes of Scientific Research?" in Fitzmaurice and Tamada (eds.), *Whaling in the Antarctic*, p. 19.

[50] *Whaling in the Antarctic*, ICJ Reports 2014, separate opinion of Judge Greenwood, p. 408, para. 7. He also warned that to permit such a methodology for adopting the ICRW to the current situation by means of recommendations would destroy the balance of the Convention.

to decrease the importance of consent of a state in law-making process in international law inter alia in the fields of environmental protection.[51] If it is the case in the *Whaling Case*, one could see the evolution of international law that "is never strictly dependent upon the consent of states, but is instead a multiplicious process."[52] This could lead to questioning whether non-legally binding instruments are an adequate source that could erode States parties' sovereignty in decision-making that relates to the power of states conferred by the treaty provision.

On the other hand, it is possible to see that the *Whaling Case* is not one in which the adopted recommendations themselves had certain legal influence. The Court introduced a vague duty of cooperation and an obligation to give due respect to non-legally binding documents. In a circumlocutory way it reviewed JARPA II in terms of non-legally binding recommendations as though they were of an obligatory nature.[53] However, it took a traditional position in respect of the legal effect of recommendatory decisions taken by treaty organs. Thus, by inducing an obligation to give due regard to non-legally binding recommendations

---

[51] Rüdiger Wolfrum, "Legitimacy of International Law from a Legal Perspective: Some Introductory Considerations" in Rüdiger Wolfrum and Volker Röben (eds.), *Legitimacy in International Law* (Springer, 2008), pp. 10–12. See also, e.g., Andrew D. Finkelman, "The Post-Ratification Consensus Agreements of the Parties to the Montreal Protocol: Law or Politics? An Analysis of Natural Resources Defense Council v. EPA", *Iowa Law Review*, 93 (2008), 665ff; Annecoos Wiersema, "The New International Law-Makers?: Conferences of the Parties to Multilateral Environmental Agreements", *Michigan Journal of International Law*, 31 (2009), 231ff; Jacob Werksman, "The Conference of Parties to Environmental Treaties" in Jacob Werksman (ed.) *Greening International Institutions* (Earthscan Publications Ltd, 1996), p. 55; Nikolaos Lavranos, "Multilateral Environmental Agreements: Who Makes the Binding Decisions?", *European Environmental Law Review*, 11 (2002), 44ff; Jutta Brunnée, "COPing with Consent: Lawmaking Under Multilateral Environmental Agreements", *Leiden Journal of International Law*, 15 (2002), 1ff; Christopher C. Joyner, "The Legal Status and Effect of Antarctic Recommended Measures" in Dinah Shelton (ed.), *Commitment and Compliance: The Role of Non-Binding Norms in the International Legal System* (Oxford University Press, 2000), pp. 163ff.

[52] Young and Sullivan, "Evolution through the Duty to Cooperate", pp. 30–1. They observe that some international organizations, such as the WTO, the EU, and the COP of the UNFCCC, have gained the power to adopt certain decisions that function standard-setting without States parties' agreement or consensus. In order to maintain the legitimacy of their decisions some requirements are to be fulfilled by the organizations, such as transparency, openness, impartiality and consensus, relevance and effectiveness, coherence, development dimension, clarity, consistency, etc.

[53] See Mika Hayashi, "The Whaling Judgment and the Challenges of Dynamic Treaty Regimes" in Fitzmaurice and Tamada (eds.), *Whaling in the Antarctic*, pp. 229–36.

adopted by the treaty organs from the duty to cooperate, the Court enabled itself to examine the state's domestic decision-making from a perspective of international standards. This reasoning may also involve an issue of legitimacy on the methodology taken by the Court for its judicial review function.[54]

C   Current Status of Good Faith

In the *Whaling Case* the Court reviewed whether Japan's domestic decision-making contemplated "meaningful co-operation" by taking into consideration the non-legally binding recommendations and Guidelines adopted by the Science Committee and the IWC. The Court did not use the term "good faith" in its judgment. Neither did it hold that Japan had acted in bad faith.[55] However, the judgment implicitly assessed the subjective element of Japan's good faith in issuing the special permits to JARPA II in an objective manner.[56]

The question whether Japan appropriately considered, in good faith, the feasibility of the use of non-lethal methods when issuing special permits in its whaling programmes or not was a crucial issue of the assessment of the duty to cooperate in this case. Should parties' good faith be presupposed when a treaty provision grants a right to act under a certain requirement set by the treaty? In the *Whaling Case* the judges, expressed by either separate or dissenting opinions, suggested three conceptions of good faith: first, it is the principle of good faith under the law of treaties; second, it is represented in procedural requirements that prove the existence of a party's cooperation with IWC and Scientific Committee; and, third, it is embodied in substantial requirements that establish meaningful cooperation with them.

Judge Xue observed that the principle of good faith under the law of treaties provided limitations on the authorizing party's exercising the power to issue a special permit granted under Article VIII(1) within

---

[54] Foster, "Methodologies and Motivations", pp. 11ff.

[55] Ibid., p. 34.

[56] In this regard, as Foster pointed out, Judge Yusuf considered that the judgment implicitly found Japan's bad faith in finding the JARPA II as not convincing scientific whaling: ibid., p. 35 and n. 121.

properness and reasonableness.[57] In the Vienna Convention, good faith appears explicitly in five provisions: Preamble, Article 26, Article 31(1), Article 46(2), and Article 69(2)(b).[58] Although Judge Xue did not mention exactly what was the content of the principle of good faith under the law of treaties, it probably related to the rule of *pacta sunt servanda* under Article 26 of the Vienna Convention.

Regarding Article 26 of the Vienna Convention, the concept of reasonableness seems to be a central element for determining whether a party is considered to have performed treaty obligations in good faith.[59] Reasonableness is a criterion establishing good faith. According to the *Gabčíkovo-Nagymaros Project Case*, performance in good faith was assessed in terms of reasonableness towards achieving the purpose of the treaty reflecting the intentions of the parties in concluding it. It is said that the reasonableness test in the *Whaling Case* was a synonym of good faith.[60]

The second concept of good faith is identified in Judge Abraham's dissenting opinion. He emphasized two facts surrounding JARPA II. First, the judgment found that JARPA II was considered "broadly [to] be characterized as 'scientific research'"; and the second finding was that Japan submitted the whaling plan for examination to the Scientific Committee before issuing the first permit in pursuance of its obligations under paragraph 30 of the Schedule. According to his dissenting opinion, fulfilment of these requirements suggests that Japan had acted in good faith until proof of the contrary.[61]

---

[57] *Whaling* in *the Antarctic*, ICJ Reports 2014, separate opinion of Judge Xue, p. 422, para. 9.

[58] Article 18 of the Vienna Convention also embodies the good faith principle. Commentary to Draft Article 15 (current Article 18), *Yearbook of the International Law Commission*, 1966, vol. II, p. 202, para.(1); Mark E. Villiger, *Commentary on the 1969 Vienna Convention on the Law of Treaties* (Martinus Nijhoff Publishers, 2009), p. 247; Laurence Boisson de Chazournes, Anne-Marie La Rosa, and Makane Moïse Mbengue, "Article 18 Convention of 1969" in Olivier Corten and Pierre Klein (eds.), *The Vienna Convention on the Law of Treaties: A Commentary*, vol. I (Oxford University Press, 2011), pp. 397–402.

[59] *Gabčíkovo-Nagymaros Project* (Hungary/Slovakia), Judgment, ICJ Reports 1997, pp. 78–9, para. 142.

[60] Young and Sullivan, "Evolution through the Duty to Cooperate", p. 29.

[61] *Whaling* in *the Antarctic*, ICJ Reports 2014, dissenting opinion of Judge Abraham, p. 330, para. 34: "I believe that the permits granted under JARPA II should have been presumed to have been issued 'for purposes of scientific research' – for a State's word cannot lightly be challenged, and its good faith must be presumed until proof of the contrary – and only very strong evidence could have justified a finding unfavourable to the Respondent." For a critical view of this point, see Julian Wyatt, "Should We Presume that Japan Acted in

Judge Abraham's dissenting opinion points to an inconsistency in the Court's reasoning. While the Court held that Japan did not breach the procedural obligation under paragraph 30, it doubted its good faith in cooperation with the IWC and the Scientific Committee. In principle, a sovereign state's good faith should be presupposed until the contrary is established.[62]

Such a presumption of good faith on the part of a state acting under international law has traditionally been maintained by international tribunals in the context of the doctrine of abuse of right. For instance, in *Case Concerning Certain German Interests in Polish Upper Silesia (The Merits)* the Permanent Court of International Justice clearly mentioned as follows:

> Germany undoubtedly retained until the actual transfer of sovereignty the right to dispose of her property, and only a misuse of this right could endow an act of alienation with the character of a breach of the Treaty; such misuse cannot be presumed, and it rests with the party who states that there has been such misuse to prove his statement.[63]

In *Case of the Free Zones of Upper Savoy and the District of Gex* the PCIJ emphasized that "[a] reservation must be made as regards the case of abuses of a right, since it is certain that France must not evade the obligation to maintain the zones by erecting a customs barrier under the guise of a control cordon. But an abuse cannot be presumed by the Court."[64]

In the *Whaling Case*, according to Judge Greenwood, the presumption of good faith of a party acting under the Convention was simply proved through examining the performance of the procedural obligation under paragraph 30 and was distinct from compliance with the duty to give due regard to recommendations of the IWC and the Scientific Committee. While Judge Greenwood denied Japan's violation of the procedural obligation under paragraph 30, he found that it had infringed the substantive obligation under the duty to cooperate. Thus, in his opinion, Japan had not acted in bad faith under paragraph 30 and Australia could not prove that Japan's bad faith in this regard, however since Japan had

---

Good Faith?: Refractions on Judge Abraham's Burden of Proof Based Analysis", *Australian Year Book of International Law*, 32 (2014), 145ff.

[62] *Whaling in the Antarctic*, ICJ Reports 2014, dissenting opinion of Judge Abraham, pp. 327–8, para. 28.

[63] Series A, No 7, p. 30.

[64] Series A/B, No 46, p. 167.

failed to consider the review of the IWC and the Scientific Committee in a positive manner, it had breached the duty to cooperate.[65]

The third conception of good faith is submitted by Judge *ad hoc* Charlesworth. She considered that the principle of good faith was not presumed to be in performance of the procedural obligation by simply submitting a whaling plan to the Science Committee but was requiring parties to "show genuine willingness to reconsider its position in light of [the IWC and the Scientific Committee] views."[66] Thus, for Judge *ad hoc* Charlesworth that obligation was not procedural but substantive:

> In this context, the duty of co-operation at the heart of paragraph 30 requires a permit-authorizing State to provide the IWC with the permits "before they are issued and in sufficient time to allow the Scientific Committee to review and comment on them"; to provide specified information about the proposed scientific permits; to engage and promote the participation of the international scientific community in the research; and to give consideration in good faith to the views of the IWC and the Scientific Committee. This means that, although a State is not bound to accept the Committee's assessment of proposed permits, it must show genuine willingness to reconsider its position in light of those views. The duty entails keeping the Scientific Committee apprised of the results of scientific research on an annual basis. The duty also implies that permit-authorizing States should provide the Scientific Committee with timely and accurate information about modifications in the implementation of scientific research programmes already reviewed by the Committee and the implications for the authorization of special permits. States may not take a narrow or formalistic approach to the duty of cooperation. It is a substantive duty to consider the views of the IWC and the Scientific Committee and to co-operate with the international scientific community in any research on whales.[67]

Judge Sebutinde also elaborated in her separate opinion on the duty to cooperate under paragraph 30 of the Schedule to the ICRW. In her words, "[t]he obligation entails a substantive duty of meaningful co-operation with the IWC and its subordinate organs such as the Scientific Committee."[68] She suggests a set of requirements determining a substantive duty of meaningful cooperation and, besides some procedural requirements, considers parties to have a duty "to give due

---

[65] *Whaling* in *the Antarctic*, ICJ Reports 2014, separate opinion of Judge Greenwood, p. 410, para. 11 and p. 416, para. 29.

[66] Ibid., separate opinion of Judge *ad hoc* Charlesworth, p. 458, para. 15.

[67] Ibid.

[68] Ibid., separate opinion of Judge Sebutinde, pp. 434–5, para. 15.

consideration, in good faith, to the views and recommendations of the
IWC, with a readiness to modify the terms of the special permits or the
decision to issue them, taking into account such recommendations."[69]

Inducing the obligation to give due regard to non-binding recommendations from the duty to cooperation with the treaty organs may provide
confirmation of Schwarzenberger's anticipation of the function of good
faith, which requires a party to "rationalise their views of what, in
concrete instance, good faith requires" in cooperation.[70] In the
Whaling Case the Court carefully avoided mentioning good faith and
evaluating a controversial issue of a subjective and psychological aspect
of State's behaviour. Rather, the Court exploited the duty to cooperate for
the extensive procedural obligation under paragraph 30 and of the substantive obligation to "give due regard" to non-binding instruments
adopted within the Convention for meaningful cooperation.

In this respect, recent jurisprudence shows the possibility that the
principle of good faith may contain such substantive requirements.
In an advisory opinion, the International Tribunal for the Law of the
Sea (ITLOS) observed that the obligations provided under Articles 63(1)
and 64(1) of the United Nations Convention on the Law of the Sea
(UNCLOS) are both "due diligence" obligations which

> require the States concerned to consult with one another in good faith,
> pursuant to article 300 of the [UNCLOS]. The consultations should be
> meaningful in the sense that substantial effort should be made by all States
> concerned, with a view to adopting effective measures necessary to coor-
> dinate and ensure the conservation and development of shared stocks.[71]

However, as Judge Paik considered, in the event of lack of cooperation
between the parties and the international organization concerned, the
ITLOS should clarify the meaning and scope of the duty to cooperate.[72]
Judge Paik observed that the duty to cooperate did not require parties to
reach an agreement, but they were obliged to negotiate in good faith with
a view to agreeing upon cooperative arrangements for sustainable

---

[69] Ibid., p. 436, para. 18.
[70] Schwarzenberger, "The Fundamental Principles of International Law", 301.
[71] Request for an advisory opinion submitted by the Sub-Regional Fisheries Commission
(SRFC), ITLOS, Advisory Opinion, [hereinafter, "*SRFC Advisory Opinion*"], para. 210.
Online: https://www.itlos.org/fileadmin/itlos/documents/cases/case_no.21/advisory_opi
nion_published/2015_21-advop-E.pdf
[72] *SRFC Advisory Opinion*, separate opinion of Judge Paik, p. 116, para. 34. Online: https://
www.itlos.org/fileadmin/itlos/documents/cases/case_no.21/advisory_opinion_pub
lished/2015_21_SO_Paik-E.pdf

management of their shared resources.[73] Thus, this implies that at least certain arrangements for an agreed solution are to be made by parties to prove their fulfilment of the duty to cooperate.

D Extensive Scope of Good Faith and the Rule of *Pacta Sunt Servanda*

The rule of *pacta sunt servanda* embodies good faith in international law. The rule of is codified in Article 26 of the Vienna Convention as existing customary international law. However, the precise content and scope of the rule in that article are not necessarily clear.[74] Article 26 reads: "Every treaty in force is binding upon the parties to it and must be performed by them in good faith." There are two elements in the text; the former refers to the binding force of a treaty, and the latter element includes good faith performance of treaty obligations and exercise of rights conferred under a treaty.[75]

As the *Gabčikovo-Nagymaros Project* Case presented, for the parties to a treaty to perform their obligations under that treaty, the principle of good faith as embodied in Article 26 of the Vienna Convention obliges them to apply the treaty terms "in a reasonable way and in such a manner that its purpose can be realized."[76]

The function of the principle of good faith may be enhanced in the context of cooperation.[77] In this regard, Principle 4 of the Declaration on Principles of International Law concerning Friendly Relations and Cooperation among States in accordance with the Charter of the United Nations (2625 (XXV)) provides a duty of interstate cooperation as "the duty of States to co-operate with one another in accordance with the Charter." This clause contains the

---

[73] Ibid., p. 17, para. 37.
[74] O'Connor, *Good Faith in International Law*, p. 37.
[75] *Yearbook of the International Law Commission 1966*, vol. II, p. 211.
[76] *Gabčikovo-Nagymaros Project* (Hungary/Slovakia), Judgment, ICJ Reports 1997, p. 79, para. 142.
[77] *Nuclear Tests Case (Australia v. France)* (Merits), *ICJ Reports 1974*, p. 473, para. 49. The Court held as follows:

> "One of the basic principles governing the creation and performance of legal obligations . . . is good faith. Trust and confidence are inherent in international co-operation, in particular in an age when this cooperation in many fields is becoming increasingly essential. Just as the very rule of *pacta sunt servanda* in the law of treaties is based on good faith, so also is the binding character of an international obligation assumed by unilateral declaration."

term "in accordance with the Charter," such that it should be read in the context of the UN Charter. Chapter IX of the UN Charter is titled "International Economic and Social Cooperation" and explicitly stipulates the duty of Members to cooperate "with the Organization" in Article 56. In this context, different structures of cooperation seem to be set out in Principle 4 and in Article 56: interstate cooperation and cooperation between Member States and the UN.[78]

Beyond cooperation between states, the rules of *pacta sunt servanda* and good faith constitute an underpinning of cooperation between Member States and the UN. Article 2(2) of the UN Charter reads: "All Members, in order to ensure to all of them the rights and benefits resulting from membership, shall fulfil in good faith the obligations assumed by them in accordance with the present Charter." This provision confirms the rule of *pacta sunt servanda* in the context of the law of international organizations.[79] According to the introductory sentence of Article 2 of the Charter, good faith under Article 2(2) directs Member States to act so as to achieve the purposes of the UN and reconciles with state sovereignty.[80]

The duty to "fulfil in good faith the obligations assumed by them in accordance with the Charter" is addressed not only in the relationship

---

[78] Reading these two cooperation structures reconcilably in the context of the UN Charter, we shall recall Article 2(2) of the Charter providing that "[a]ll Members, in order to ensure to all of them the rights and benefits resulting from membership, shall fulfil in good faith the obligations assumed by them in accordance with the present Charter." International cooperation is one of prominent aims of the UN as laid down in Article 1. Duties of members are directed in pursuit of these main purposes of the UN. Article 2(2) of the Charter combines international cooperation and good faith. Good faith as contained in that provision is considered to be a requirement for how to establish and fulfil obligations imposed upon members under the UN Charter. Also, good faith gives a foundation for flexibility in terms of effective implementation in determining what and how members shall do under the Charter in concrete situations, which allows interpreters go beyond textual interpretation of the Charter (Jörg P. Müller and Robert Kolb, "Article 2(2)" in Bruno Simma (ed.), *The Charter of the United Nations: A Commentary*, 2nd edn., vol. I (Oxford University Press, 2002), pp. 96–7).

[79] Albrecht Randelzhofer, "Article 2" in Simma (ed.), *The Charter of the United Nations*, p. 65. Randelzhofer points out that the English version of the text "constitutes not only a confirmation of *pacta sunt servanda* but also an undertaking to comply with the whole of public international law, in so far as it is not amended by the UN Charter." In this regard, see also Müller and Kolb, "Article 2 (2)", p. 93.

[80] Müller and Kolb, "Article 2 (2)", p. 94.

between the Member States, but also in the relationship between a Member State and UN organ.[81] The country's membership of the organization "entails certain mutual obligations of co-operation and good faith incumbent upon [the country] and upon the Organization."[82]

The question is how far such a general duty to cooperate with international organizations extends its scope. A formulation of a general duty to cooperate with international organizations was submitted by Judge Lauterpacht in his separate opinion on the *Voting Procedure Case*. According to that, a general obligation incumbent upon states to cooperate with international organizations generates a duty to respect recommendatory resolutions taken by the organizations.[83] Regarding the refusal to pay due regard to the recommendatory resolutions, he explained as follows:

> Although there is no automatic obligation to accept fully a particular recommendation or series of recommendations, there is a legal obligation to act in good faith in accordance with the principles of the Charter and of the System of Trusteeship. An administering State may not be acting illegally by declining to act upon a recommendation or series of recommendations on the same subject. But in doing so it acts at its peril when a point is reached when the cumulative effect of the persistent disregard of the articulate opinion of the Organization is such as to foster the conviction that the State in question has become guilty of disloyalty to the Principles and Purposes of the Charter. Thus an Administering State which consistently sets itself above the solemnly and repeatedly expressed judgment of the Organisation, in particular in proportion as that judgment approximates to unanimity, may find that it has overstepped the imperceptible line between impropriety and illegality, between discretion and arbitrariness, between the exercise of the legal right to disregard the recommendation and the abuse of that right, and that it has exposed itself to consequences legitimately following as a legal sanction.[84]

As to the other aspect of the principle of good faith in exercising rights conferred by international law, we will turn to consider the doctrine of abuse of rights and good faith.[85] Under the doctrine of abuse of rights,

---

[81] Ibid., pp. 93–4.

[82] *Interpretation of the Agreement of 25 March 1951 between the WHO and Egypt*, Advisory Opinion, ICJ Reports 1980, p. 93, para. 43.

[83] *South-West Africa-Voting Procedure*, Advisory Opinion, ICJ Reports 1955, separate opinion of Judge Lauterpacht, p. 119 (stated that "[t]he State in question, while not bound to accept the recommendation, is bound to give it due consideration in good faith").

[84] Ibid., p. 120.

[85] Anthony D'Amato, "Good Faith" in R. Bernhardt (ed.), *Encyclopedia of Public International Law*, vol. II (Elsevier, 1992), p. 600; Bin Cheng, *General Principles of Law*

a state that intends to exercise its rights under international law "is obliged not to cause a legally cognizable injury to another State."[86] Therefore, when a state exercises its right "in an arbitrary manner in such a way as to inflict upon another state an injury which cannot be justified by a legitimate consideration of its own advantage," that state's behaviour would be considered as violating the rule prohibiting abuse of rights.[87] In a conventional context, good faith of a state has been reviewed in a passive manner in which it was considered that the state exercised its rights appropriately and its good faith was presumed unless the other state proved that there was legal injury to the latter.[88] Under the concept of sovereign equality, the presumption of good faith on the part of a State in exercising its rights has been strongly maintained, and the burden of disproving good faith of the state lies with the state that insists that there has been abuse of rights.[89] Contrary to such conventional cognizance, good faith of a state in fulfilling a duty to cooperate is reviewed from reasonableness in light of the spirit of a convention by assessing actual behaviour presented through domestic administrative and judicial decisions of a state.

as Applied by International Courts and Tribunals (Cambridge University Press, 1953), p. 121 (stating that "[t]he theory of abuse of rights, abus de droit, recognised in principle both by the Permanent Court of International Justice and the International Court of Justice, is merely an application [of the principle of good faith] to the exercise of rights.") (Footnote omitted).

[86] Anthony D'Amato, "Good Faith" in R. Bernhardt (ed.), Encyclopedia of Public International Law, vol. II (Elsevier, 1992), p. 600.

[87] Hersch Lauterpacht, Oppenheim's International Law, 8th edn. (Longmans, 1955), p. 345.

[88] Andreas R. Ziegler and Jorun Baumgartner, "Good Faith as a General Principle of (International) Law" in John H. Jackson et al. (eds.), Good Faith and International Economic Law (Oxford University Press, 2015), p. 33 and cases cited in n. 165. In this regard, see also Nottebohm Case (second phase), ICJ Reports 1955, dissenting opinion of Judge Read, p. 37 (insisting that "The doctrine of abuse of right cannot be invoked by one State against another unless the State which is admittedly exercising its rights under international law causes damage to the State invoking the doctrine"); Foster, "Methodologies and Motivations", p. 34 and n. 119.

[89] The Electricity Company of Sofia and Bulgaria (Preliminary Objection), PCIJ Series A/B, No 77 (1939), separate opinion by Anzolotti, p. 98 (stating that "[t]he theory of abuse of right is an extremely delicate one, and 1 should hesitate long before applying it to such a question as the compulsory jurisdiction of the Court. The old rule, a rule in such complete harmony with the spirit of international law, Qui iure suo utitur neminem ladit, would seem peculiarly applicable)"; Case Concerning Certain German Interests in Polish Upper Silesia (Merits), PCIJ Series A, No 7 (1926), p. 30 (upholding that "Germany undoubtedly retained until the actual transfer of sovereignty the right to dispose of her property, and only a misuse of this right could endow an act of alienation with the character of a breach of the Treaty; such misuse cannot be presumed, and it rests with the party who states that there has been such misuse to prove his statement").

E Concluding Remarks

Good faith of a state in performing a duty to cooperate is assumed when the state's behaviour indicates substantial conduct towards cooperation in a specific context confined by a concrete case. Under the doctrine of abuse of rights, conventionally, a state's good faith is presumed if there is no damage on part of the other party or no proof of bad faith. The *Whaling Case* avoided referring to the subjective element of good faith in reviewing the manner of exercising the right to issue special permits to whaling programmes under Article VIII(1). Rather, it transferred the subjective element into the problem of commitment in the decision-making process to consider non-legally binding recommendations and guidelines for making "meaningful cooperation."

Conventionally, international judicial bodies have simply evaluated a state's conduct on the international plane with a presumption of state's good faith in its domestic decision-making process. This attitude is coincident with the dualism of international law emphasizing the difference between municipal law and international law. The methodology of standard of review taken by international courts and tribunals would introduce a monistic approach by which international judicial bodies are allowed to evaluate a state's domestic decision-making in light of international standards, including not only hard law but also soft law instruments, thereby substantializing the subjective element of good faith in a way that can be objectively assessed.

7

The Paris Agreement: New Legal Avenues to Support a Transboundary Harm Claim on the Basis of Climate Change

KURT WINTER

> In Paris we have seen many revolutions.
> The most beautiful, most peaceful has been achieved: a climate revolution.
>
> – François Hollande[1]

> The term 'Grotian Moment,' is a relatively recent creation [. . .] here I use it to denote a transformative development in which new rules and doctrines of customary international law emerge with unusual rapidity and acceptance.
>
> – Michael P. Scharf[2]

A Introduction

Launching an international transboundary harm claim on the basis of climate change and the principles of state responsibility presents significant challenges in terms of jurisdiction, jurisprudence and, not least, the availability of compelling evidence to prove attribution and causation. It equally raises the question of the legitimacy of international adjudication on states' efforts to address the harmful effects of climate change.

In the COP21 negotiations that ultimately led to the adoption of the Paris Agreement,[3] the issue of loss and damage constituted a 'red line' between the Alliance of Small Island States (AOSIS) and the developed-country negotiating groups. As Burkett and Doelle observe, while AOSIS

---

[1] President of France, on the adoption of the Paris Agreement at the United Nations Climate Change Conference in Paris, December 2015 (COP21).

[2] M. P. Scharf, 'Seizing the Grotian Moment: Accelerated Formation of Customary International Law During Times of Fundamental Change'. *Cornell International Law Journal*, 43 (2010), 439.

[3] Paris Agreement (adopted 12 December 2015, entered into force 4 November 2016).

would not accede to an agreement without a standalone loss-and-damage mechanism, developed-country parties, notably the United States and Australia, sought to exclude loss and damage altogether, for fear of unlimited liability.[4] The compromise was in part a standalone article on loss and damage in Article 8 of the Paris Agreement, but also an explicit exclusion of compensation for loss and damage articulated in Decision 1/CP.21, paragraph 51.[5]

Substantial questions remain, however, as to the effect of the exclusion of liability for loss and damage and the legal significance of the Paris Agreement more broadly, as understood against existing international law that may support a transboundary harm claim on the basis of climate change. This chapter considers some of these questions.

While a detailed discussion on jurisdiction is beyond the scope of this chapter, it should be noted that establishing the jurisdiction of an international court or tribunal to adjudicate a transboundary harm claim remains a difficult prospect.

As a court of general jurisdiction, the International Court of Justice (ICJ) remains the most credible court to adjudicate such a claim. In order to commence a contentious dispute before the ICJ, a claimant state would need to establish a jurisdictional basis, which necessarily entails determining whether the states in dispute consented to the Court's jurisdiction consistent with the Statute of the International Court of Justice.[6] Consent may be established through agreement to a treaty specifically referring to ICJ jurisdiction for the settlement of disputes, via a *compromis* referring a particular dispute for determination, or through states' advanced declarations on jurisdiction.

Although the Paris Agreement provides for dispute settlement in the form of voluntary submission to the ICJ, and/or arbitration, consistent with the United Nations Framework Convention on Climate Change (UNFCCC),[7] only Cuba and the Netherlands have accepted the ICJ's jurisdiction under the UNFCCC, and only the Solomon Islands and

---

[4] See M. Burkett, 'Reading between the Red Lines: Loss and Damage and the Paris Outcome', *Climate Law*, 6 (2016), 118, 122; M. Doelle, 'The Paris Agreement: Historic Breakthrough or High Stakes Experiment?', *Climate Law*, 6 (2016), 1.

[5] See further M. J. Mace, 'Mitigation Commitments Under the Paris Agreement and the Way Forward', *Climate Law*, 6 (2016), 21, 24.

[6] Statute of the International Court of Justice (adopted 26 June 1945, entered into force 24 October 1945), Article 36(1). In some circumstances, states may also rely upon states' advanced declarations of jurisdictions in accordance with Article 36(2).

[7] Paris Agreement (adopted 12 December 2015, entered into force 4 November 2016), Article 24; UNFCCC, Article 14.

Tuvalu have accepted compulsory arbitration. In the vast majority of cases, therefore, claimant states may need to establish jurisdictional grounds through alternative applicable treaties, the existence of a *compromis* and/or declarations. As Sands[8] observes, although a contentious dispute would be a highly political decision, a claimant state that has accepted the compulsory jurisdiction of the ICJ may also bring proceedings against another state in relation to a failure to meet an obligation under general international law, as was illustrated in the ICJ's decision on jurisdiction in the *Whaling in the Antarctic Case.*[9]

Political momentum could also build for the United Nations (UN) General Assembly, Security Council or an authorised specialised agency of the UN to seek an Advisory Opinion from the ICJ on state responsibility for transboundary harm resulting from anthropogenic climate change. Such a request could seek the Court's clarification on the content of states' evolving due diligence obligations in relation to climate change. In 2011, the former President of the Republic of Palau, Johnson Toribiong, initiated a campaign at the UN General Assembly to seek such an Advisory Opinion from the ICJ.[10] The case for an ICJ advisory opinion was recently reinvigorated in a speech given by Philippe Sands QC.[11]

There may also be scope for a range of courts with more limited jurisdiction to address questions associated with transboundary harm and climate change. These include regional courts such as the Court of Justice of the European Union and the Inter-American Commission on Human Rights and specialised tribunals such as the World Trade Organization (WTO) Dispute Settlement Body as well as investor–state dispute settlement arbitral tribunals. It is also conceivable that the International Tribunal for the Law of the Sea (ITLOS) could adjudicate

---

[8] Philippe Sands QC, 'Climate Change and the Rule of Law: Adjudicating the Future in International Law', *Journal of Environmental Law*, 28 (2016), 19.

[9] *Whaling in the Antarctic Case (Australia* v. *Japan; New Zealand intervening)* (Judgment) [2014] ICJ Rep 226, [30]–[41].

[10] In 2011, the former President of the Republic of Palau, Johnson Toribiong, initiated a campaign at the UN General Assembly to seek such an Advisory Opinion from the ICJ. See further A. Korman and G. Barcia, 'Rethinking Climate Change: Towards an International Court of Justice Advisory Opinion', *Yale Journal of International Law*, 37 (2012), 40.

[11] See Philippe Sands QC, 'Public Lecture' (Climate Change and the Rule of Law: Adjudicating the Future in International Law, The Dickson Poon School of Law, King's College London, The Supreme Court and HM Government, London, 17 September 2015) available at: www.supremecourt.uk/docs/professor-sands-lecture-on-climate-change-and-the-rule-of-law.pdf (accessed 10 June 2016).

upon a contentious dispute or advisory opinion. As Sands observes,[12] ITLOS may be well placed to address issues such as the prevention of sea-level rise. While these alternative forums may present advantages in terms of establishing jurisdiction, claimants would face the added complexity of establishing an appropriate nexus between the Paris Agreement standards and the specialised jurisprudence of such tribunals.

Having regard to the provisions of the Paris Agreement, this chapter will consider the applicable law and avenues through which to develop supporting evidence to support a transboundary harm claim on the basis of climate change. Beyond launching a contentious dispute or seeking an advisory opinion from an international court or tribunal, such considerations could also inform diplomatic efforts to secure greater mitigation efforts from laggard states.

Part B of this chapter assesses the extent to which the exclusion of compensation for loss and damage, articulated in paragraph 51 of Decision 1/CP.21, may prohibit a transboundary harm claim on the basis of climate change. Part C evaluates the nature of some of the new legal standards articulated in the Paris Agreement, as a matter of treaty law and customary international law. Finally, from an evidentiary perspective, Part D considers the ways in which the enhanced transparency framework and compliance committee could assist potential claimants in developing evidence upon which to base a claim, as economies are increasingly opened up to international scrutiny.

B An Illusionary Shield against Claims for Liability and Compensation

In a significant progression from the UNFCCC, in Article 8 of the Paris Agreement, the parties recognised loss and damage associated with the adverse effects of climate change as distinct from adaptation. On its face, the explicit exclusion of compensation for loss and damage articulated in Decision 1/CP.21 appears to foreclose the prospect of a claim for liability or compensation in respect of loss and damage.[13] The Decision text appears intrinsically tied to the international community's determination to move forward on loss and damage as well as the understanding that the Warsaw International Mechanism on Loss and Damage should be the

---

[12] Philippe Sands QC, 'Climate Change and the Rule of Law'.
[13] Decision 1/CP.21, para. 51 provides: '*Agrees* that Article 8 of the Agreement does not involve or provide a basis for any liability or compensation.'

only legitimate avenue through which to address loss and damage. For example, Lees argues that the way in which the Paris Agreement distinguishes between responsibility and liability liberates us 'to consider how responsibility can be allocated without fear of immediate liability'.[14] However, an analysis of the legal structure and wording of the exclusion, as well as its relationship with existing international environmental law, reveals that a range of actionable legal obligations remain that give rise to state responsibility. Moreover, as will be discussed further below, the Paris Agreement also establishes new primary legal obligations that provide potential new legal avenues for accountability.

For a number of reasons, the purported exclusion of liability and compensation for loss and damage is of limited legal weight. While the international community's recognition of the need to avert, minimise and address loss and damage associated with the adverse effects of climate change is articulated in Article 8 of the Paris Agreement, the purported exclusion of liability is expressed in Decision 1/CP.21. As Brunée[15] underscores, from a formal legal perspective, COP decisions are not legally binding on parties without explicit authorisation. Rajamani[16] also observes that while COP decisions are relevant factors in interpreting treaties, their legal status depends upon the enabling clause. Bodansky[17] has similarly noted that COP decisions will not be legally binding unless there is a legal hook in the treaty that gives it legal force. As Burkett observes, 'there is no identifiable provision in the UNFCCC that would lend legal force to the prohibition of claims for compensation based on Article 8 of the Agreement'.[18]

On another level, as Rajamani highlights, COP decisions cannot create substantive new legal obligations because of the nature of conventional international lawmaking, which requires state consent through signature and ratification or accession.[19] A provision that effectively shields a state from liability must also enter into international law through the same

---

[14] E. Lees, 'Responsibility and liability for climate loss and damage after Paris', *Climate Policy*, 17(1) (2017), 59, 60.

[15] J. Brunée, 'COPing with consent: Law Making under Multilateral Environmental Agreements', *Leiden Journal of International Law*, 15(1) (2002), 32.

[16] L. Rajamani, 'The Devilish Details: Key Legal Issues in the 2015 Climate Negotiations', *Modern Law Review*, 78(5) (2015), 826.

[17] D. Bodansky, 'Legally Binding Versus Non-Legally Binding Instruments' in S. Barrett, C. Carraro and J. de Melo (eds.), *Towards a Workable and Effective Climate Regime* (CEPR Press and Ferdi, 2015).

[18] See M. Burkett, 'Reading between the Red Lines', 127.

[19] L. Rajamani, 'The Devilish Details', 840.

conventional means, either as a validly enacted treaty or attaining the status of customary international law. Given the stark negotiating positions on this point, there is limited scope to argue that the exclusion has any status under custom.

The precise wording of the exclusion also points to its limitations. The draft text contemplated its relationship with existing international law in the wording 'in a manner that does not involve or provide a basis for liability or compensation *nor prejudice existing rights under international law*' (emphasis added).[20] By contrast, the agreed exclusion is silent as to existing international law or indeed other provisions of the Paris Agreement. Even if the exclusion were effective as against Article 8, a state would still be entitled to rely upon the weight of existing international law to pursue a transboundary harm claim on the basis of climate change. In particular, claimants could still rely upon the 'no harm', precautionary, prevention and 'polluter pays' principles as cornerstones of international environmental law.[21] As will be discussed further below, a state could also draw upon the primary legal obligations contained elsewhere in the Paris Agreement, including the obligation to submit nationally determined contributions pursuant to Article 4.2 (the nationally determined contribution (NDC) obligation).[22] Under the principles

---

[20] UNFCCC, Draft decision/CP.21, 'Draft Paris Agreement', COP 21 Agenda item 4(b), 10 December 2015.

[21] *Trail Smelter Case (US v. Canada)* (1941) 3 RIAA 1905, reprinted in 35 AJIL 684; 1992 Rio Declaration on Environment and Development (adopted 14 June 1992) 31 ILM 874, Principle 2, Convention on Biological Diversity (adopted 5 June 1992, entered into force 29 December 1993) 1760 UNTS 79, Art. 3; UNFCCC, preamble, Recital 8; Declaration of the United Nations Conference on the Human Environment, U.N. Doc. A/Conf.48/14/ Rev. 1(1973) (Stockholm Declaration), Principle 21; ICJ, *Legality of the Threat or Use of Nuclear Weapons* (Advisory Opinion) [1996] ICJ Rep 226, [29]; *Case Concerning the Gabčíkovo-Nagymaros Project (Hungary v. Slovakia)* (Judgment) [1997] ICJ Rep 41, [53]; *Case Concerning Pulp Mills on the River Uruguay (Argentina v. Uruguay)* (Judgment) [2010] ICJ Rep 1, 38; International Law Commission, 'Report of the International Law Commission on the Work of its 5th Session: Draft Articles on Prevention of Transboundary Harm from Hazardous Activities, with Commentary' (2001) UN Doc A/56/10; International Law Association Committee on the Legal Principles Relating to Climate Change, 'Legal Principles Relating to Climate Change' Third Report of the Committee to the ILA (International Law Association, Washington 2014).

[22] While the NDC obligation is the primary focus of this article, the Paris Agreement contains a range of other primary legal obligations that could be drawn upon, including: the obligation to engage in adaptation planning processes and implementation (Art. 7(9)); the obligation for Developed Country Parties to provide financial resources to assist Developing Country Parties with respect to mitigation and adaptation (Art. 9(1)); the obligation for each Party to provide information to the enhanced transparency framework (Art. 13(7)); and the obligation for Parties to update and enhance their actions

of state responsibility, it would still be open for a state to seek injunctive relief and/or compensation for transboundary harm caused by anthropogenic greenhouse gas emissions.[23] Moreover, the exclusion would not affect the ability to seek an Advisory Opinion from the ICJ on the question of state responsibility for transboundary harm caused by greenhouse gas emissions.

At best, the exclusion appears to have an *operational* significance for the development of the Warsaw International Mechanism on Loss and Damage, and a *political* significance in the parties' agreement not to use Article 8 as a basis for any claims for liability and compensation in connection with loss and damage. As Doelle and Burkett observe, while this compromise may not necessarily impede upon the ability to pursue liability claims, it could make the inevitable discussions on responsibility for loss and damage more difficult.[24]

C New Legal Standards to Support a Transboundary Claim on the Basis of Climate Change

Looking beyond Article 8, other provisions of the Paris Agreement arguably articulate new primary legal obligations and associated standards that strengthen existing international environmental law. The principles of state responsibility provide that a state may be held responsible for an action or omission where the conduct of the state constitutes a breach of a primary international legal obligation, whether that primary obligation exists under treaty or customary international law.[25] Both under the law of treaties and as codifications of emerging customary law obligations, the Paris Agreement arguably articulates new legal standards that could support an actionable claim.

---

and support, informed by the outcome of the global stocktake, which shall occur in 2023 and every five years thereafter unless otherwise decided (Art. 14(3)).

[23] International Law Commission, 'Report of the International Law Commission on the Work of its 53rd Session: Draft Articles on the Responsibility of States for Internationally Wrongful Acts, with commentaries' (2001) UN Doc A/56/10, Articles 2, 29, 30, 31 (Draft Articles on State Responsibility); *Case Concerning the Factory at Chorzów (Germany v. Poland) (Jurisdiction)* [1927] PCIJ Rep Series A No 9, 21.

[24] See M. Burkett, 'Reading between the Red Lines', 122; M. Doelle, 'The Paris Agreement'.

[25] International Law Commission, *Draft Articles on Responsibility of States for Internationally Wrongful Acts*, November 2001, Supplement No. 10 (A/56/10).

1   The Paris Agreement and the Law of Treaties

In the first instance, it is worth considering the extent to which the legal standards articulated in the Paris Agreement constitute actionable obligations that could give rise to state responsibility.[26]

In Articles 2.1 and 4.1, the parties agreed to important new standards, reflecting the best available science on crucial temperature tipping points, their projected impacts, as well as the economic and financial transformations required to realise the core objective of the UNFCCC.[27] These include:

1. temperature stabilisation;[28]
2. climate resilient financial flows;[29]
3. global peaking of greenhouse gas emissions;[30]
4. rapid reductions of greenhouse gas emissions;[31] and
5. net zero emissions in the second half of the century.[32]

Although these standards cannot constitute primary legal obligations in their own right due to their framing as goals, in an interpretational sense, they provide content to the core legal obligations articulated elsewhere in

---

[26] Draft Articles on State Responsibility; *Phosphates in Morocco Case* (Judgment) [1938] PCIJ Series A/B No 74, 10, 28; *Case Concerning United States Diplomatic and Consular Staff in Tehran (United States of America v. Iran)* (Judgment) [1980] ICJ Rep 3, 29, [56]; *Case Concerning Military and Paramilitary Activities in and against Nicaragua (Nicaragua v. United States of America)* (Merits) (Judgment) [1986] ICJ Rep 14, 117–118; *Case Concerning the Gabčíkovo-Nagymaros Project (Hungary v. Slovakia)* (Judgment) [1997] ICJ Rep 41, 54, [78]; *Dickson Car Wheel Company (USA) v. United Mexican States* (1931) UNRIAA, vol. IV (Sales No 1951.V.1) 669, 678. Article 2 of the Draft Articles on State Responsibility provides the key elements of an internationally wrongful act of a State: 'There is an internationally wrongful act of a State where conduct consisting of an action or omission: a) is attributable to the State under international law; and b) Constitutes a breach of an international obligation of the State.'

[27] Article 2 provides: 'The ultimate objective of this Convention and any related legal instruments that the Conference of the Parties may adopt is to achieve, in accordance with the relevant provisions of the Convention, stabilization of greenhouse gas concentrations in the atmosphere at a level that would prevent dangerous anthropogenic interference with the climate system. Such a level should be achieved within a time frame sufficient to allow ecosystems to adapt naturally to climate change, to ensure that food production is not threatened and to enable economic development to proceed in a sustainable manner.'

[28] Paris Agreement (adopted 12 December 2015, entered into force 4 November 2016), Art. 2.1(a).

[29] Ibid., Art. 2.1(c).

[30] Ibid., Art. 4.1.

[31] Ibid., Art. 4.1.

[32] Ibid., Art. 4.1.

the Paris Agreement. Most notably, these standards provide interpretational value vis-à-vis the NDC obligation. That view is consistent with the general rule of interpretation under Article 31(1) of the Vienna Convention on the Law of Treaties (VCLT),[33] which provides that treaties be interpreted 'in good faith in accordance with the ordinary meaning given to the terms of the treaty in their context and in light of its object and purpose'.[34]

The requisite standard of the NDC obligation is elaborated further in Articles 4.3 and 4.4. Article 4.3 subjects the content of NDCs to the complex standard of 'common but differentiated responsibilities and respective capabilities, in the light of different national circumstances'. While some commentators have suggested that this wording widens the parameters of differentiation, others have noted an array of criteria that could frame NDCs, including past, current and projected future emissions as well as cost, capacity and population.[35] Article 4.3 sets forth two further standards against which to measure the adequacy of compliance: 'upward only progression' and 'highest possible ambition'.

The NDC obligation, when read in conjunction with the standards articulated in Articles 2.1, 4.1, 4.3 and 4.4 could be understood as a primary rule establishing a wrongful act when breached. Prima facie, the wording of the NDC obligation suggests that the content of NDCs is a matter of sovereign discretion. On the other hand, as Viñuales has suggested, because NDCs are 'anchored' in a provision of the Paris Agreement, they may qualify as a binding unilateral act or as a 'subsequent agreement' that interprets the UNFCCC and the Paris Agreement.[36] On that reading, the wording 'intends to achieve' may come to also mean states' intention to be bound to the content of their NDCs.

---

[33] United Nations, Vienna Convention on the Law of Treaties, 23 May 1969, United Nations, Treaty Series, vol. 1155.

[34] In *Case Concerning Kasikili/Sedudu Island (Botswana v. Namibia)* [1999] ICJ Rep 1045, the ICJ applied Art. 31 of the VCLT on the basis that it constitutes customary international law.

[35] C. Voigt and F. Ferreira, 'Differentiation in the Paris Agreement', *Climate Law*, 6 (2016), 58; L. Rajamani, 'Differentiation in a 2015 Climate Agreement' [June 2015] *Centre for Climate and Energy Solutions*; H. Winkler et al., 'What factors influence mitigation capacity', *Energy Policy*, 35(1) (2007), 692.

[36] J. Viñuales, 'The Paris Climate Agreement: An Initial Examination (Part II of III)' (*EJIL Talk*, 8 February 2016): www.ejiltalk.org/the-paris-climate-agreement-an-initial-examination-part-ii-of-iii/ (accessed 10 June 2016).

The 'anchoring' of the NDC obligation in the Paris Agreement presents significant implications as to the requisite level of ambition and implementation of NDCs. Interpreted in a teleological way in accordance with Article 31(1) of the VCLT, the NDC obligation arguably imposes an 'obligation of conduct' or due diligence obligation to *implement* measures towards achieving the goals articulated in Articles 2.1 and 4.1, and in a manner consistent with Articles 4.3 and 4.4. In a similar manner, Voigt has found that Article 4.2 of the UNFCCC sets forth an 'obligation of conduct' upon Annex I parties 'to reverse the long-term trend of ever-increasing greenhouse gas emissions'.[37]

The understanding that the NDC obligation is to be measured against the international standards in the Paris Agreement is reinforced by the International Law Association's (ILA's) analysis of due diligence under international law. As the ILA Study Group on Due Diligence noted in 2014, while the intellectual foundations for the concept of due diligence were laid by Grotius in the seventeenth century, it was not until the nineteenth century that due diligence began to take shape and was applied as both a duty and a constraint upon state behaviour.[38] Having regard to early jurisprudence, the Study Group made a number of relevant observations on the content of the due diligence obligation. The Study Group opined that 'while the content of due diligence cannot be precisely defined, a series of objective factors may be taken into account in determining [its] content'.[39] The Study Group also observed that 'the content of due diligence is made by reference to international, rather than domestic, standards'.[40]

The interpretational link between the primary NDC obligation and its associated standards is arguably stronger in the Paris Agreement than in the UNFCCC. Article 4.1 specifically cross-references the temperature stabilisation goal. Moreover, the articulation of the NDC obligation in the same section of the Agreement as the 'rapid reductions' goal supports the conclusion that the primary obligation and associated standards are intrinsically linked.

The international standards articulated in the Paris Agreement arguably strengthen states' existing due diligence obligations under

---

[37] C. Voigt, 'State Responsibility for Climate Change Damages', *Nordic Journal of International Law*, 77 (2008), 1, 6.

[38] International Law Association, *Report of the Seventy-Sixth Conference* (2014), pp. 937, 948.

[39] Ibid., pp. 937, 949–950.

[40] Ibid., pp. 937, 950.

international environmental law and provide new avenues to establish a breach of state responsibility in circumstances in which a state party has not done enough within its capability to act on climate change. As Stephens observes, the due diligence obligation under international environmental law is 'not an absolute guarantee against the occurrence of harm'.[41] Stephens refers to the International Law Commission's (ILC's) commentary to the Draft Articles on State Responsibility, which relevantly state:

> Due diligence is manifested in reasonable efforts by a State to inform itself of factual or legal components that relate foreseeably to a contemplated procedure and to take appropriate measures in timely fashion, to address them.[42]

As Stephens continues:

> [The commentary] reflects state practice generally, in which there has been great reluctance to accept a stricter standard. Indeed, in the *Trail Smelter* case it was accepted that a due diligence standard was to apply having regard to the capacity of Canada, via improving emissions control technologies, to limit transboundary damage.[43]

The international standards articulated in the Paris Agreement do not go as far as guaranteeing against the occurrence of harm. However, the NDC obligation, understood in light of its associated standards, requires that states apply a particular *quality* of due diligence that is more precise and considered, and which is both referable to the goals articulated in Articles 2.1 and 4.1, and done in a manner consistent with Articles 4.3 and 4.4. It is in this respect that states could be held to account.

The adequacy of a state's NDC, and its implementation, will need to be assessed in a highly nuanced manner, having regard to the individual economic and demographic circumstances of that state. Nevertheless, it is conceivable that a state could be in breach of state responsibility where, for example, its NDC does not align with or build upon its previously submitted one (in accordance with the standard of 'upward only progression'). The extent to which that may be possible will depend on the way in which the international community comes to understand the

---

[41] T . Stephens, *International Courts and Environmental Protection* (Cambridge University Press, 2009), p. 158.
[42] Report of the International Law Commission, 53rd Session, UN Doc. A/56/10 (2001), p. 154.
[43] Stephens, *International Courts and Environmental Protection*, p. 158.

meaning of 'in light of different national circumstances' and its relationship with the obligation of 'upward only progression'.

It may be more challenging to measure compliance with the other standards that are associated with the NDC obligation – for example, the 'global peaking of emissions' and their subsequent 'rapid reductions'. Nevertheless, as will be discussed below, the Paris Agreement also establishes new evidentiary avenues that could enable tribunals to draw more evidence-based assessments. Indeed, the technical expert reviews[44] and the compliance committee's assessments[45] could position tribunals to assess whether a state's actions accords with its 'highest possible ambition' with a degree of objectivity.

2   The Paris Agreement and Customary International Law

The treaty-making process that culminated in the Paris Agreement may also signify an element of universality that speaks to the formation of new customary international law. An unprecedented level of support was expressed at the Paris Agreement signing ceremony, involving by far the largest number of countries ever to sign a treaty in a single day.[46] As Patricia Espinosa, Executive Secretary of the UNFCCC, remarked upon the Paris Agreement reaching the thresholds for entry into force,[47] 'the speed at which countries have made the Paris Agreement's entry into force possible is unprecedented in recent experience of international agreements'.[48] The universality of the Paris Agreement is also reinforced by the diversity of states that comprised the first movers, including the biggest and smallest emitters, and the richest and most vulnerable nations.

---

[44] Paris Agreement (adopted 12 December 2015, entered into force 4 November 2016), Art. 13.

[45] Ibid., Art. 15.

[46] See UN News Centre, '"Today is an historic day" says Ban, as 175 countries sign Paris climate accord' (22 April 2016): www.un.org/apps/news/story.asp?NewsID=53756#.V2PoIyMrLAc (accessed 10 June 2016).

[47] Article 21(1) provides that the Paris Agreement 'shall enter into force on the thirtieth day after the date on which at least 55 Parties to the Convention accounting in total for at least an estimated 55 per cent of the total greenhouse gas emissions have deposited their instruments of ratification, acceptance, approval or accession'. It entered into force on 4 November 2016; at the time of writing, 153 parties have ratified the Paris Agreement.

[48] See UN News Centre, 'Over 55 Parties covering more than 55 per cent of global greenhouse emission ratify the Paris Climate Change Agreement' (5 October 2016): http://newsroom.unfccc.int/unfccc-newsroom/landmark-climate-change-agreement-to-enter-into-force/

While any conclusions as to the customary nature of the provisions contained in the Paris Agreement will ultimately depend upon evidence of state practice and *opinio juris*, if that conclusion were reached, provisions of the Paris Agreement may be actionable even against non-parties. Such a conclusion would have significant political and diplomatic utility, especially in the context of the United States' announcement of its intention formally to withdrawal from the Paris Agreement.[49]

A context of fundamental change can accelerate the formation of customary international law.[50] Scharf describes this phenomenon as the 'Grotian Moment' – a term first coined by Professor Richard Falk.[51] Notably, during his service at the Extraordinary Chambers in the Courts of Cambodia, Scharf applied the concept of the 'Grotian Moment' to the way in which the Nuremberg trials crystallised into customary international law joint criminal enterprise liability. Despite the dearth of state practice, Scharf successfully contended that Nuremberg must be understood as 'an instance in which there was such fundamental change to the international system that a new principle of customary international law could arise with exceptional velocity'.[52] Scharf applies the same analysis to a range of other disciplines, including the law of the sea and space law. As each of these disciplines illustrates, the rapid expansion of customary international law tends to reflect the 'urgency of coping with new developments of technology … or widespread sentiments of moral outrage'.[53]

The nature of the climate change issue, coupled with the extent of state support for the Paris Agreement, begs the question whether the

---

[49] On 1 June 2017, the President of the United States announced that it would withdraw from the Paris Agreement. See UNFCCC, 'UNFCCC Statement on the US Decision to Withdraw from the Paris Agreement' (1 June 2017), available at: http://newsroom .unfccc.int/unfccc-newsroom/unfccc-statement-on-the-us-decision-to-withdraw-from-paris-agreement/. At the time of writing, some commentators have suggested that the US administration may be reconsidering its withdrawal. See, for example, Tessa Berenson, 'Macron, "something could happen" with Paris Agreement' (14 June 2017), available at: http://time.com/4858221/donald-trump-emmanuel-macron-paris-climate-agreement/

[50] See M. P. Scharf, 'Accelerated Formation of Customary International Law', *ILSA Journal of International and Comparative Law*, 20(2) (2014), 305; M. P. Scharf, *Customary International Law in Times of Fundamental Change: Recognizing Grotian Moments* (Cambridge, 2013).

[51] Scharf 'Accelerated Formation of Customary International Law', 308.

[52] Ibid., 332.

[53] T. Treves, 'Customary International Law', *Max Planck Encyclopedia of Public International Law*, 25 (2006), [24].

agreement might similarly be characterised as a 'Grotian Moment' of the accelerated formation of customary international law. In particular, it is worth considering the extent to which the NDC obligation and its associated international standards may constitute the codification of emerging principles of customary international law.

The NDC obligation and its associated standards, particularly the goals articulated in Article 2.1, speak directly to the prevention principle that is already well-established under customary international law.[54] These provisions arguably elaborate states' due diligence obligations in more concrete terms with the benefit of the best available science and economic foresight. Elements of the preamble to the Paris Agreement also support the conclusion that the NDC obligation should be interpreted in a progressive manner.[55]

Although the preparation of conventions may contribute favourably to the accelerated development of custom, it is important to recall that a conventional text has a stimulating function only in the generation of custom; it is state practice and *opinio juris* that give rise to the customary rule.[56] More than the passage of time, the uniformity of state practice will be determinative of the existence of a particular customary rule.[57]

---

[54] *Trail Smelter Case (US v. Canada)* (1941) 3 RIAA 1905, reprinted in 35 AJIL 684; 1992 Rio Declaration on Environment and Development (adopted 14 June 1992) 31 ILM 874, Principle 2, Convention on Biological Diversity (adopted 5 June 1992, entered into force 29 December 1993) 1760 UNTS 79, Art. 3; UNFCCC, preamble, Recital 8; Declaration of the United Nations Conference on the Human Environment, U.N. Doc. A/Conf.48/14/ Rev. 1(1973) (Stockholm Declaration), Principle 21; ICJ, *Legality of the Threat or Use of Nuclear Weapons* (Advisory Opinion) [1996] ICJ Rep 226, [29]; *Case Concerning the Gabčíkovo-Nagymaros Project (Hungary v. Slovakia)* (Judgment) [1997] ICJ Rep 41, [53]; *Case Concerning Pulp Mills on the River Uruguay (Argentina v. Uruguay)* (Judgment) [2010] ICJ Rep 1, 38; International Law Commission, 'Report of the International Law Commission on the Work of its 5th Session: Draft Articles on Prevention of Transboundary Harm from Hazardous Activities, with Commentary' (2001) UN Doc A/56/10; International Law Association Committee on the Legal Principles Relating to Climate Change, 'Legal Principles Relating to Climate Change' Third Report of the Committee to the ILA (International Law Association, Washington 2014). While the *Trail Smelter* arbitration adjudicated upon pollution between neighbouring states, subsequent agreements, in particular the Stockholm Declaration, evidence that the principle also applies to the global commons.

[55] The following wording is informative: 'recognizing the need for an effective and *progressive response* to the urgent threat of climate change on the basis of the best available scientific knowledge'.

[56] M. Villiger, *Customary International Law and Treaties*, 2nd edn. (Kluwer Law International, 1997).

[57] *North Sea Continental Shelf Cases (Federal Republic of Germany v. Denmark; Federal Republic of Germany v. Netherlands)* (Judgment) [1969] ICJ Rep 3, 43 [74].

Evidence of state practice prior to the adoption of the Paris Agreement suggests that the NDC obligation was an emerging customary rule though it had not yet attained the status of customary law. By its Decision 1/CP.19, the COP invited all parties 'to initiate or intensify domestic preparations for their intended nationally determined contributions towards achieving the objective of the Convention as set out in its Article 2, without prejudice to the legal nature of the contributions'.[58] By its Decision 2/CP.20, the COP reiterated its invitation that parties communicate their intended nationally determined contributions 'well in advance of the twenty-first session of the Conference of the Parties (by the first quarter of 2015 by those Parties ready to do so) in a manner that facilitates the clarity, transparency and understanding of the intended nationally determined contributions'.[59] Although the parties were only *invited* to submit intended nationally determined contributions (INDCs), state practice was so widespread that it was virtually uniform. By 15 December 2015, 160 INDCs had been submitted, representing 187 countries.[60] In the same way that Denmark and the Netherlands contended that the delimitation article had crystallised into custom in the *North Sea Continental Shelf Cases*,[61] it is arguable that the NDC obligation that emerged from customary due diligence obligations was subsequently consolidated through the COPs and widespread state practice, and eventually crystallised into a rule of customary international law through its articulation in the Paris Agreement.

The crystallisation thesis may prove to be more compelling in the case of the NDC obligation than in respect of the delimitation article in the *North Sea Continental Shelf Cases*. The ICJ could not accept that the delimitation article reflected or crystallised a customary rule, in part because 'the principle of equidistance, as it now figures in Article 6 of the Convention, was proposed by the Commission with considerable hesitation, somewhat on an experimental basis, at most *de lege ferenda*, and not at all *de lege lata* or as an emerging rule of customary international law'.[62] In contrast, the universal obligation to communicate efforts towards prevention that is contained in the NDC obligation evidences

---

58 Report of the Conference of the Parties on its nineteenth session, held in Warsaw from 11 to 23 November 2013, para. 2(b).
59 Lima call to climate action, para. 13.
60 Climate Action Tracker, 'Tracking INDCs' (15 December 2015): http://climateaction tracker.org/indcs.html (accessed 10 July 2016).
61 *North Sea Continental Shelf Cases*, 38 [61].
62 Ibid., 38, [62].

a fair degree of consistency with existing customary law on the prevention of transboundary harm.[63] The fact that the Paris Agreement does not permit reservations provides further support to this argument.[64] Claimants could also draw upon a wider body of evidence of state practice, including the United States–China joint announcement on climate change, to establish the rule's emergence.[65]

Conversely, the wording of the Warsaw and Lima COP Decisions may undermine the customary law interpretation in the sense that parties were invited to prepare INDCs *without prejudice* to their legal nature and content.[66] Any conclusive interpretation of state practice and *opinio juris* would need to weigh the possibility that states may have been willing to submit INDCs strictly on the understanding that such submissions would not impinge upon the legal significance of those contributions.

Even if customary international law supports the submission of NDCs, it is difficult to conclude that custom yet supports that NDCs should reflect a particular level of ambition. As the UN's Synthesis Report[67] revealed, the collective effect of INDCs submitted in the lead-up to COP21 were not ambitious enough to meet what are now the Paris Agreement goals. At best, state practice supported an emerging customary rule on the articulation of NDCs, notwithstanding their level of ambition.

It is conceivable that, with the passage of time, subsequent state practice may come to evidence more certainty on the requisite ambition of national contributions. As MacGibbon[68] highlights, the subsequent practice of parties to a treaty plays an important role in international

---

[63] Consider, in particular, the ICJ's reasoning in *Case Concerning Pulp Mills on the River Uruguay (Argentina v. Uruguay)* (Judgment) [2010] ICJ Rep 1, 38: 'A State is thus obliged to use all the means at its disposal in order to avoid activities which take place in its territory, or in any area under its jurisdiction, causing significant damage to the environment of another State.'

[64] Paris Agreement (adopted 12 December 2015, entered into force 4 November 2016), Art. 27; *North Sea Continental Shelf Cases*, 39, [63].

[65] US–China Joint Announcement on Climate Change (Beijing, China, 12 November 2014): www.whitehouse.gov/the-press-office/2014/11/11/us-china-joint-announcement-climate-change (accessed 10 July 2016).

[66] Report of the Conference of the Parties on its nineteenth session, held in Warsaw from 11 to 23 November 2013, para. 2(b); Lima call to climate action, para. 8.

[67] UNFCCC Secretariat, Synthesis report on the aggregate effect of the intended nationally determined contributions' (30 October 2015): http://unfccc.int/resource/docs/2015/cop21/eng/07.pdf (accessed 10 July 2016).

[68] I. MacGibbon, 'The Scope of Acquiescence in International Law', *British Yearbook of International Law*, 31 (1954), 144.

lawmaking, interpretation, estoppel and the development of rules of customary international law. In the COP21 decision, parties were invited 'to communicate, by 2020 . . . mid century, long-term low greenhouse gas emission development strategies'.[69] Indeed, Christiana Figueres described the INDCs as a kind of 'down-payment on a new era of climate ambition'.[70] It remains to be seen whether states will revise their national contributions to reflect a higher level of ambition. If states were to do so, as a matter of custom, it may become possible to argue that the NDC obligation entails a particular standard of ambition that directly corre-lates to the international standards articulated in the Paris Agreement, namely temperature stabilisation, climate resilient financial flows, global peaking of greenhouse gas emissions, rapid reductions of greenhouse gas emissions and net zero emissions in the second half of the century.

While Article 31(1)(b) of the VCLT accords interpretational relevance to subsequent practice, international jurisprudence demonstrates a high threshold for the establishment of the existence of subsequent practice in contentious cases. Because judges' interpretation and indeed jurisdiction in these cases is based on the will of the parties as manifested in the past, the ICJ has been reticent to find that there was sufficient knowledge of subsequent practice such that it could conclude that there was an inter-pretive agreement between the parties.[71]

The nature of the climate change issue and the way in which the international community has reframed its commitments in the Paris Agreement could inspire international adjudicators to adopt a more dynamic mode of interpretation. Generally, in cases in which judges have acted more as guardians of a common institution (for example, in adjudicating on treaties that establish international organisations), they have tended towards a more dynamic approach.[72] As Dupuy observes, in such cases, interpretation is 'not simply an exercise of memory [but]

---

[69] Decision 1/CP.21, para. 36.

[70] See UN Press Office, 'Global Response to Climate Change Keeps Door Open to 2 Degrees C Temperature Limit: New UN Report Synthesizes National Climate Plans from 146 Countries' (30 October 2015): http://newsroom.unfccc.int/unfccc-newsroom/indc-synth esis-report-press-release/ (accessed 10 July 2016).

[71] See, for example, *Case Concerning Kasikili/Sedudu Island (Botswana v. Namibia)* [1999] ICJ Rep 1014; *Case Concerning the Temple of Preah Vihear (Cambodia v. Thailand)* [1962] ICJ Rep 6; *Case Concerning Maritime Delimitation in the Area Between Greenland and Jan Mayen (Denmark v. Norway)* [1993] ICJ Rep 38; *Sovereignty over Pulau Ligitan and Pulau Sipadan (Indonesia/Malaysia)* [2002] ICJ Rep 625.

[72] P. Dupuy, 'Evolutionary Interpretation of Treaties' in E. Cannizzaro (ed.), *The Law of Treaties Beyond the Vienna Convention* (Oxford University Press, 2011), p. 126.

tends towards prophesy'.[73] Consequently, judges are less bound by the consent of state parties and are more inclined to interpret the treaty so as to ensure the furtherance of a collective plan.[74]

The collective and reciprocal nature of the legal obligations contained in the Paris Agreement means that the climate regime is inherently different to the territorial disputes in respect of which international adjudicators have adopted a cautious interpretational approach. Any contentious dispute on the question of transboundary harm on the basis of climate change would also entail an adjudication aimed at protecting the integrity of humanity's collective plan to stem the harmful effects of climate change. Arguably, that adjudication would need to engage directly with the core global compact articulated in Articles 2 and 4. Indeed, as Mace observes:

> [P]eaking as soon as possible, rapid reductions thereafter, net zero emissions in the second half of the century, in pursuit of a limit in temperature increase to 1.5°C. From these elements, consistent emission-reduction pathways can be identified, and what is in effect a carbon budget can be determined, though with many uncertainties.[75]

3 The United States' Intended Withdrawal from the Paris Agreement

The United States' intended withdrawal from the Paris Agreement presents an interesting case study against which to test the observations made above. It is difficult to downplay the significance of the withdrawal, given the long and tumultuous path that finally led to a near unanimous agreement,[76] as well as the United States' own significant contribution to emissions,[77] which must be addressed to achieve temperature

---

[73] Ibid.

[74] See, for example, *Legal Consequences of the Construction of a Wall in the Occupied Palestinian Territory* (Advisory Opinion) [2004] ICJ Rep 136; *Certain Expenses of the United Nations (Article 17, paragraph 2, of the Charter)* (Advisory Opinion) [1962] ICJ Rep 151.

[75] Mace, 'Mitigation Commitments Under the Paris Agreement and the Way Forward', 24.

[76] See, for example, D. Campbell, 'After Doha: What Has Climate Change Policy Accomplished?', *Journal of Environmental Law*, 25(1) (2013), 125; L. Rajamani, 'The Changing Fortunes of Differential Treatment in the Evolution of International Environmental Law', *International Affairs*, 88 (2012), 605; C. Carlarne, 'The Glue That Binds Or The Straw That Broke The Camel's Back?: Exploring the Implications of US Reengagement in Global Climate Change Negotiations', *Tulane Journal of International and Comparative Law*, 19 (2010), 113.

[77] See L. Rajamani, 'Reflections on the US withdrawal from the Paris Climate Change Agreement', *EJIL Talk* (5 June 2017), available at: www.ejiltalk.org/reflections-on-the-

stabilisation. Some commentators suggest that climate action will instead be driven by American states, cities and businesses, or indeed domestic litigation.[78] Other commentators have suggested that international climate policy would benefit from the United States' withdrawal. As Kemp observes, continued United States participation 'would reveal the weaknesses of the agreement, prevent new opportunities from emerging and gift greater leverage to a recalcitrant administration'.[79] Kemp asserts that 'money matters, not legality', referring to the Paris Agreement's 'difficult-to-enforce legal obligations'.[80] On another view, however, it is the very existence of the Paris Agreement that provides the legal hook to challenge the current United States Administration's change of direction. While enforcement may not be straightforward, the Paris Agreement contains primary legal obligations that continue to bind the United States and may continue to do so beyond withdrawal, as a matter of customary international law.

As a matter of treaty law, having announced its intention, the United States cannot withdraw from the Paris Agreement until at least November 2020.[81] As Rajamani[82] and Bodansky[83] highlight, as long as the United States remains a party to the Paris Agreement, at least until 2020, it is bound to perform its commitments under the treaty in good faith, in accordance with Article 26 of the VCLT. In that intervening period, any backsliding in the United States' actions in connection with its primary legal obligations could be subjected to international legal

---

us-withdrawal-from-the-paris-climate-change-agreement/. As Rajamani notes, 'the US is responsible for 27% of cumulative historic emission, 15% of cumulative current emissions and has per capita GHG emission that are double the global average': ibid., 1–2.

[78] See, for example, H. Tabuchi and L. Friedman, 'US Cities, States and Businesses Pledge to Measure Emissions', *New York Times* (11 July 2017), available at: www.nytimes.com/2017/07/11/climate/cities-states-businesses-emissions-climate-pact.html;   United Nations Environment Programme, *The Status of Climate Change Litigation - A Global Review*, (May 2017), available at: http://columbiaclimatelaw.com/files/2017/05/Burger-Gundlach-2017–05-UN-Envt-CC-Litigation.pdf

[79] L. Kemp, 'Better out than in', *Nature Climate Change*, 7 (July 2017), 458.

[80] Ibid., 459.

[81] Paris Agreement, (adopted 12 December 2015, entered into force 4 November 2016), Art. 28 provides that: '1) At any time after three years from the date on which this Agreement has entered into force for a Party, that Party may withdraw from this Agreement by giving written notification to the Depositary. 2. Any such withdrawal shall take effect upon expiry of one year from the date of receipt by the Depositary of the notification of withdrawal, or on such later date as may be specified in the notification of withdrawal.'

[82] Rajamani, 'Reflections on the US withdrawal from the Paris Climate Change Agreement'.

[83] D. Bodansky, 'Sound and Fury on the Paris Agreement – But Does it Signify Anything?', *Opinio Juris* (2 June 2017), available at: http://opiniojuris.org/2017/06/02/33147/

scrutiny. Having regard to the preceding analysis of the NDC obligation and its associated standards, close attention should be paid to the *ambition* contained in the United States' current NDC,[84] and the means by which the current administration is seeking to unravel it.[85] In the absence of formal treaty withdrawal, actions contrary to the United States' NDC commitment may constitute contraventions of international law.

More controversially, if it could be established that any of the primary legal obligations contained in the Paris Agreement has attained the status of customary international law, then, regardless of withdrawal from the treaty, such obligations would continue to bind the United States as a matter of custom. The obligation of good faith or *bona fides* would equally apply to those customary legal obligations.[86]

D New Evidentiary Avenues through which to Pursue Accountability

Although the Paris Agreement establishes new legal standards under both the law of treaties and customary international law, these standards present significant interpretational and evidentiary challenges in attributing acts or omissions to a state and then establishing a breach pursuant to the principles of state responsibility.

While the 'no harm' principle does not prohibit a particular act or omission of a state *per se*, NDCs will become an important measure of a particular state's compliance with its due diligence obligations. As noted above, this will be a highly nuanced assessment. Turning to Article 4.3 of the Paris Agreement, a tribunal may consider whether a state's NDC is consistent with the achievement of Paris Agreement goals, having regard to that particular state's economy and opportunity to act. Indeed, as Voigt and Ferreira observe:

---

[84] See UNFCCC NDC Registry (Interim), *United States of America, First NDC Submission*, available at: www4.unfccc.int/ndcregistry/PublishedDocuments/United%20States%20of%20America%20First/U.S.A.%20First%20NDC%20Submission.pdf

[85] See, for example, R. Meyer, 'The Giant Trump Climate Order is Here', *The Atlantic* (28 March 2017), available at: www.theatlantic.com/science/archive/2017/03/trump-climate-eo/520986/; M. Pengelly, 'Trump to sign executive order undoing Obama's clean power plan', *Guardian* (27 March 2017), available at: www.theguardian.com/environment/2017/mar/26/trump-executive-order-clean-power-plan-coal-plants

[86] M. Kotzur, 'Good faith (bona fide)', *Max Planck Encyclopedia of Public International Law* (January 2009), available at: http://opil.ouplaw.com.ezp.lib.unimelb.edu.au/view/10.1093/law:epil/9780199231690/law-9780199231690-e1412?rskey=djS5dg&result=1&prd=EPIL

It is only when article 4.3 and article 4.4 are read together that a comprehensive picture emerges of differentiation in the context of mitigation commitments. Differentiation applies both to the content (i.e. ambition, or 'how much') and to the form (i.e. type of target, or 'what') of parties' mitigation efforts.[87]

Nevertheless, at the most basic level, a party's failure to put forward any NDC altogether, or a contribution that does not progress from previous commitments, may be found to constitute an internationally wrongful act or omission. A tribunal could also be minded to interpret the temperature stabilisation and global peaking goals in reciprocal and therefore several terms so as to enable a more comprehensive assessment of efforts.

The extent to which a tribunal may be able to make evidence-based assessments of NDCs could also be enhanced by the review mechanisms and data metrics that are being developed through the Paris Agreement. The technical expert reviews to be undertaken through the enhanced transparency framework[88] as well as the compliance committee's assessments[89] will be particularly informative.

In attributing liability for transboundary harm on the basis of climate change, a major evidentiary hurdle arises in accounting and comparing states' relevant mitigation contributions in a fair manner, when states use different baselines and accounting methodologies. The ongoing work of the Ad Hoc Working Group on the Paris Agreement (APA) in developing guidance on the features of NDCs, and information to facilitate clarity, transparency and understanding of NDCs, as well as accounting for parties' NDCs, could lead to crucial accounting metrics.[90] In turn, adjudicators could more readily assess the adequacy of particular measures undertaken by state parties.

The views expressed by the technical expert review and the compliance committee could also serve to inform adjudicators' ultimate legal determinations on the adequacy of a particular state's compliance, although the mode of operation of these institutions is still under negotiation. While it is envisaged that both mechanisms would operate in an expert-based and non-punitive manner, in an evidentiary manner their findings

---

[87] Voigt and Ferreira, 'Differentiation in the Paris Agreement', 68.
[88] Paris Agreement (adopted 12 December 2015, entered into force 4 November 2016), Art. 13.
[89] Ibid., Art. 15.
[90] Decision 1/CP.21, paras. 26, 28 and 31 See, further, UNFCCC, 'Ad Hoc Working Group on the Paris Agreement', available at: http://unfccc.int/bodies/apa/body/9399.php

and recommendations could inform an independent tribunal's interpretation of compliance, for example with the NDC obligation.

The way in which this could occur is illustrated in the recent *Whaling in the Antarctic Case*.[91] Of particular interest is the way in which the ICJ drew upon the views of the Commission and Scientific Committee in its conclusion that Japan's granting of permits for the killing, taking and treating of whales in connection with the whaling program at issue was not 'for purposes of scientific research' in accordance with the Convention.[92] The Commission, which was established under the Convention, was mandated to make recommendations to the Contracting Parties on matters relating to whales and whaling and to the objectives and purposes of the Convention. As the Court observed, while its recommendations, which take the form of resolutions, are not binding, 'when adopted by consensus or by a unanimous vote, they may be relevant for the interpretation of the Convention and its Schedule'.[93] The Scientific Committee, which was established to assist the Commission in discharging its obligations, had elaborated particular guidelines, which were then endorsed by the Commission.

While the ICJ reasoned that the use of lethal sampling *per se* was not unreasonable, it found that the design and implementation of Japan's particular program was unreasonable in achieving the program's stated objectives. The Court observed that Japan had given insufficient attention to the possibility of using non-lethal research methods to achieve the research program's outcomes. In prosecuting the use of lethal methods, Australia had sought to rely upon certain resolutions and guidelines from the Commission that had been approved by consensus. The ICJ found that while the instruments did not prohibit the use of lethal methods, they required that state parties take into account whether non-lethal research methods could be employed.[94] In light of Japan's expanded use of lethal methods in its whaling program, the ICJ concluded that Japan had not given sufficient attention to the potential use of non-lethal methods, in accordance with the Commission resolutions and guidelines.

In a similar manner, it is conceivable that, in the context of a transboundary harm claim on the basis of climate change, a tribunal could scrutinise advice emanating from the technical expert review and

[91] *Whaling in the Antarctic Case (Australia v. Japan; New Zealand intervening)* (Judgment) [2014] ICJ Rep 226.
[92] Ibid., 292–293.
[93] Ibid., 248.
[94] Ibid., 257.

the compliance committee, to assess, for example, whether a state had given due regard to the implementation of appropriate measures to encourage transition toward clean energy technologies. A tribunal could build upon these assessments to draw particular inferences as to the proportionality of a state's efforts to prevent transboundary harm.

E   Conclusion

The United States' announcement of its intention to withdraw from the Paris Agreement underscores that political will may be fickle. Nevertheless, the law of nations is a force that binds political will and survives beyond political administrations. As has been discussed, the Paris Agreement architecture is not as weak as some would suggest. The legal obligations and evidentiary avenues that it establishes not only reinforce existing international environmental law but also establish new legal avenues to support a transboundary harm claim on the basis of climate change.

Vulnerable populations should not lose sight of their existing legal rights, which, if anything, have been reinforced by new legal standards articulated in the Paris Agreement. The COP21 negotiations have been characterised as a kind of 'schizophrenia', given the tension between the 1.5 degree temperature goal, which will directly impact upon the severity of climate-related loss and damage, and the corresponding attempt to circumvent legal remedies.[95] However, as has been discussed, the Paris Agreement arguably further legitimises international adjudication of states' environmental obligations. As international climate law continues to evolve, the increasing precision of states' due diligence prevention obligations bears a direct correlation with the corresponding rights of populations to seek redress where those standards are not met. Indeed as Scharf observes:

> [C]ontemporary international law suggests . . . [that] the traditional ben-eficiaries of international charity have become creditors, and their requests for support and development aid concern the settlement of a debt. States responsible for causing climate change that do not comply with their preventative duties carry the risk of liability for future compensation payments at unprecedented levels.[96]

[95] See Burkett, 'Reading between the Red Lines', 123.
[96] C. Schwarte and W. Frank, 'The International Law Association's Legal Principles on Climate Change and Climate Liability Under Public International Law', *Climate Law*, 4 (2014), 201, 216.

The Paris Agreement supports a very small window of opportunity for climate action. As Christiana Figueres emphasised in the 2016 Grantham Institute Lecture,[97] the physical urgency of preventing irreparable damage is embodied in the temperature stabilisation goal of the Paris Agreement. In order to achieve that goal, however, global peaking of emissions would need to occur by 2020. As evidence comes to light that states are backsliding in their climate mitigation commitments, or seeking to walk away from the fragile deal that was struck in Paris, vulnerable populations should look to the standards articulated in the Paris Agreement and assess the ways in which these principles may support existing jurisprudence on the duty to prevent transboundary harm.

---

[97] C. Figueres, 'Transforming Growth: Climate policy today for a sustainable tomorrow' (Grantham Institute Annual Lecture, London, 11 April 2016).

8

The Court of Justice of the European Union and the High Level of Environmental Protection: Transforming a Policy Objective into a Concept Amenable to Judicial Review

DELPHINE MISONNE

A Introduction

Among the new conceptual developments that broaden the range of possible avenues for advancing the effectiveness of environmental law, the objective of a 'high level of environmental protection', as far as it governs the environmental competence of the European Union (EU), is certainly worth consideration. The notion is deeply enshrined into the EU Treaties but, for a long time, remained in a sort of shadow zone. It is only quite recently that it stepped up into the limelight of the European case-law scene, by virtue of various – not always coherent – developments in which the Court of Justice of the European Union (CJEU) plays a paramount role.

It is already well known that the CJEU[1] has the capacity, through adjudication, to consolidate the legitimacy and the legality of European legislation and regulatory measures that opt for a strong message, as far as environmental protection is concerned. This is how, back in 1985, environmental protection was acknowledged as being one of the European Community's essential objectives – one that could impact the principle of freedom of trade – and that even before any official insertion of that dimension into the Treaty of Rome.[2] The Court's decision was a decisive trigger factor in

---

[1] The Court of Justice of the European Union, which has its seat in Luxembourg, consists of two courts: the Court of Justice (ECJ) and the General Court. The Court constitutes the judicial authority of the European Union and, in cooperation with the courts and tribunals of the Member States, it ensures the uniform application and interpretation of European Union law. All cases are available online at: http://curia.europa.eu

[2] Treaty of Rome of 25 March 1957 establishing the European Economic Community.

formalizing the incorporation of an environmental dimension into the European integration process.[3]

In terms of judicial control, as far as environmental measures are concerned, the Court is now fundamentally supported by various primary law requirements, for which a certain capacity has now been firmly proven: that of acting as a shield in order to strengthen the legality of EU acts or to reinforce their interpretation towards a stricter protection of the environment. Among these requirements, the precautionary principle, the 'polluter pays' principle and the '*effet utile*' doctrine have already notoriously been pinpointed.[4]

But the effect of the 'high-level of protection' objective, which, as the reader may know, the European Treaties[5] ascribe to the way in which the environment should be protected under EU law, still remains quite confidentially discussed in scholarship, while the ECJ already welcomes the requirement both as a possible ground for judicial review and as a convenient rhetorical boost to its interpretations.[6]

In a recent Opinion, dated 8 September 2016, Advocate General Kokott stipulates that various provisions mentioning that objective 'are not to be interpreted or examined independently of each other', as 'they give expression to the common principle of a high level of environmental protection, to which particular importance must be attached given the number of provisions of EU law in which it is enshrined'.[7]

The policy space that is being occupied by the requirement is indeed quite vast. It is firmly embedded in various Treaty provisions – the

[3] Case 240/83 *Procureur de la République* v. *ADBHU* [1985] ECR 531.

[4] See, for instance: R. Macrory (ed.), *Principles of European Environmental Law, Europa law Publishing*, Avosetta series (2004), p. 256; N. de Sadeleer, *Environmental Principles: From Slogans to Political Rules* (Oxford: OUP, 2003), p. 482.

[5] Treaty on European Union (TEU), Treaty on the Functioning of the European Union (TFEU) and Charter of Fundamental Rights.

[6] On the high level of protection requirement in EU law, see D. Misonne, *Droit européen de l'environnement et de la santé. L'ambition d'un niveau élevé de protection* (Limal: Anthemis, 2011), p. 450; A. Aragao, 'Le fondement européen de la prohibition de la régression : le niveau élevé de protection de l'environnement' in M. Prieur and G. Sozzo (ed.), *La non régression en droit de l'environnement* (Bruylant, 2012), pp. 347–364; N. de Sadeleer, 'The Principle of a High Level of Environmental Protection in EU Law: Policy Principle or General Principle of Law?' in *Mijörättsliga Perspektiv Och Tankevändor* (Iustus Förlag, 2013), pp. 447–65; D. Misonne, 'The Importance of Setting a Target – The EU Ambition of a High Level of Protection' in *Transnational Environmental Law*, vol. 4/1 (Cambridge, April 2015), pp. 11–36; A. Sikora, 'The Principle of a High Level of Protection as a Source of Enforceable Rights', *Cahiers de droit européen* (2016), 1, 399–418

[7] Opinion of A.G. Kokott, Case 444/15, *Associazione Italia Nostra Onlus* v. *Comune di Venezi* ECLI:EU:C:2016:665, 24–25.

highest level in the hierarchy of norms under EU law – such as Article 3 of the TEU ('The Union shall establish an internal market. It shall work for the sustainable development of Europe based on balanced economic growth and price stability, a highly competitive social market economy, aiming at full employment and social progress, and a high level of protection and improvement of the quality of the environment'), Article 114 ('The Commission, in its proposals envisaged in paragraph 1 concerning health, safety, environmental protection and consumer protection, will take as a base a high level of protection, taking account in particular of any new development based on scientific facts. Within their respective powers, the European Parliament and the Council will also seek to achieve this objective'), Article 168 ('A high level of human health protection shall be ensured in the definition and implementation of all Union policies and activities') and Article 191 ('Union policy on the environment shall aim at a high level of protection taking into account the diversity of situations in the various regions of the Union. It shall be based on the precautionary principle and on the principles that preventive action should be taken, that environmental damage should as a priority be rectified at source and that the polluter should pay') of the TFEU and Article 37 ('A high level of environmental protection and the improvement of the quality of the environment must be integrated into the policies of the Union and ensured in accordance with the principle of sustainable development') of the Charter of Fundamental Rights.

The purpose of the present chapter is to highlight and explain the decisive role that the CJEU is performing in granting more weight to a notion that has long been inactive.

It also recalls and briefly explains the legitimacy of such an ambition, when one understands that a high level of ambition can lead to restrictions on other rights and interests.

Our intention is to pay attention to the attitude of the Court, when faced with issues testing the legality of environmental measures that could have a strong economic impact on private interests – for example, banning a substance. The assessment of the degree of balance between environmental protection and corporate interests can turn out to be quite different, depending on the courts and tribunals involved, even if they control the same type of regulation. Much depends on the dimensions that the said institutions are in charge of verifying – the impact on an investment, for instance. This is also reflected in the type of claims that are allowed to be brought before the ECJ.

The context and field of this chapter is the EU. The Union has been conferred the 'shared' competence[8] to adopt environmental legislation that shall be applicable to the territory of the 28 (soon to be 27) Member States. By virtue of the principle of primacy, the Member States must abide by such legislation and do not benefit from a generic possibility of opting out. Under some circumstances – for instance, when the main purpose of the proposed measure is environmental protection – Member States always have the power to strengthen the harmonized scheme.[9] But this is not the case when the main objective of the measure is to ease the integration of the internal market; such integration has the opposite effect, imposing that differentiation is made much more difficult. In all circumstances, so-called 'secondary legislation', which can be either a Regulation (directly applicable) or a Directive (imposing an implementation process within each Member State), must comply with 'primary law' – which refers to the European Treaties that govern the functioning of EU institutions and the adoption of their acts.

In that kind of scenario, one of the main roles of the CJEU is to review the legality of EU legislative acts and of the legality of delegated acts, when adopted by the European Commission on the basis of a mandate provided for by the legislator. If the action is founded, the Court is to declare the act concerned to be void.[10] The Court also has jurisdiction to give a preliminary ruling concerning the interpretation of the Treaties and the validity and interpretation of the acts of the institutions that make up the Union,[11] including when Member States question the meaning or scope of such acts in their implementation processes.

B   Fit for Judicial Review?

A close observation of recent European case law demonstrates that the CJEU welcomes the 'high level of protection' ('HLP') requirement as a possible ground for judicial review and as a convenient boost to its interpretations. This stands in contrast to the long-lasting total

---

[8] 'When the Treaties confer on the Union a competence shared with the Member States in a specific area, the Union and the Member States may legislate and adopt legally binding acts in that area. The Member States shall exercise their competence to the extent that the Union has not exercised its competence. The Member States shall again exercise their competence to the extent that the Union has decided to cease exercising its competence': Art. 2. 2. TFEU.

[9] Art. 193 TFEU.

[10] Art. 264 TFEU.

[11] Art. 267 TFEU.

indifference – or at most scepticism – of scholarship towards that dimension, which was thought of as being far too simplistic or intrusive on the
decision-maker's margin of discretion, especially when one knows how
difficult a negotiation process can be.[12]

Still, case law has now evolved sufficiently to consider that the concept
has grown some teeth, in relation to the judicial control of the EU's
environmentally related acts, and that it could even grow more.

For the sake of clarity, I divide my observations into two categories.
The first category of cases, to which I refer via the image of a shield,
reveals the potential as well as the limits of the high level of protection
requirement as a means of insulating European acts from legal challenge.
In contrast, the image of a 'sword' then characterizes a second category of
cases in which the HLP requirement is used as a direct ground to petition
the annulment of a legal measure, or to contest the legitimacy of the
measure. Importantly, the Court considers that the argument is admissible for judicial review, but it rarely finds it to have sufficient merit. Still,
these cases are important as they clarify what constitutes a high level of
protection.

1   The Shield

I observe that the HLP requirement will more easily be deployed to affirm
EU authority than to dismantle it, as far as legislative acts are concerned.
This is mostly due to what I call 'a special alchemy'.

a)   The Special Alchemy

It is when three specific ingredients meet and melt that the full potential
of the HLP requirement can crystallize before the Court, when applied to
the judicial control of EU legislative acts and in relation to a very specific
question: 'Does this legislation goes too far in favour of environmental
protection?'

This alchemy occurs via a combination of three dimensions, all linked
to the specificity of the concept of an HLP in its condition of 'target' –
understood as the target of either a legislative measure or of the whole EU

---

[12] P. Pescatore, 'Some Critical Remarks on the Single European Act', *Common Market Law
Review*, 9 (1986), 18; H. J. Glaesner, 'L'Acte Unique Européen', *Revue du Marché
Commun*, (1986), 238, 312. L. Krämer, *EC Environmental Law*, 5th edn. (Thomson-
Sweet & Maxwell, 2003), p. 12: '(The) institutions use the formula of a high level in its
reversed order: whatever is proposed or adopted is considered to be a high level of
environmental protection.'

policy at large: a) the marginal control, b) the pivotal element of the proportionality test and c) the teleological approach.

i) **The Marginal Control**   In environmental- or health-related issues, and similarly in agricultural matters, the ECJ often considers that the EU legislature must be allowed a broad discretion in an area that entails complex political, economic and social choices on its part.[13] The Court shall, as a consequence, adopt a self-restraining attitude and limits its review to the question whether a manifest error of appraisal has been committed.[14] In that configuration, challenging the legality of an EU legislative act that entails an ambitious protection of the environment means controlling whether a manifest error of appraisal has been committed, and this often takes place through the use of a proportionality test.

ii) **The Target is the Pivotal Element of the Proportionality Test**   When applying the proportionality principle, which is one of the general principles of Community law, the Court tends to consider that the legality of a measure adopted in that sphere can be affected only if the measure is manifestly inappropriate with regard to the objective that the competent institutions are seeking to pursue;[15] when there is a choice between several appropriate measures, recourse must be had to the least onerous, and the disadvantages caused must not be disproportionate to the aims pursued.[16]

It is worth highlighting that the pivotal element of that specific configuration of the proportionality test is very explicitly 'the aims pursued', 'the objective', the target of the measure at stake. The objectives or aims pursued are truly deciding factors in the review of proportionality; they are the steady elements, like beacons in a sea of various possibilities, against which the acceptability of restrictive measures shall be tested.

In that regard, being associated with that aim is being on the right side, especially when judicial review is limited to the search of measures that

[13] Case C–425/08 *Enviro Tech (Europe)* [2009] ECR, para. 47.
[14] Case C–284/95 *Safety Hi-Tech* [1998] ECR I–4301; Case C–341/95 *Bettati* [1998] ECR I–4355. Case C–444/15, *Associazione Italia Nostra Onlus*, [2016],para 46; Case C–549/15 *E.ON Biofor* [2017], para. 50.
[15] Case C–549/15 *E.ON Biofor* [2017],para. 50; Case C–444/15, *Associazione Italia Nostra Onlus*, [2016],para. 46.
[16] Case C–343/09 *Afton Chemical* [2010] ECR I–7027, para. 45; Case C–189/01 *Jippes and Others* [2001] ECR I–5689, para. 81; Case C–558/07 *S.P.C.M. and Others* [2009] ECR, para. 41; and Joined Cases C–379/08 and C–380/08 *ERG and Others* [2010] ECR, para. 86.

are manifestly inappropriate with regard to the objective pursued. F. Jacobs considers it 'safe to say that if the set objective involves a high level of protection, the restraints will inevitably be also higher. So, endorsing higher levels implies a readiness to accept more restrictive measures, as that is the very nature of proportionality'.[17]

iii) **The Teleological Approach**   As expressed by Advocate General Bot in 2003,[18] both the Lisbon Treaty and the Charter of Fundamental Rights[19] raise the general interest of a high level of environmental protection to the status of an EU target. The target of a piece of legislation or of a policy is a decisive factor in a European jurisprudence that is very keen on teleological interpretations, a purpose-driven interpretation. The target – of a specific provision but also of the whole EU order – very often guides the reasoning of the judge in order to avoid diluting interpretations that would weaken the strength of EU law, or in appreciating limits to delegations stemming from a basic act, by helping to highlight the essential elements which are the realm of the legislature.[20] In that regard, mentioning an ambitious target to environmental protection in all important parts of primary law is not devoid of consequences.

   In that threefold configuration, dismantling the legality of an EU act – due to its being too unbalanced or too far reaching regarding its impact on economic interests – becomes a less straightforward avenue. Still, it will remain necessary to ascertain whether, in exercising its discretion, the EU legislature attempted to achieve a degree of balance between, on the one hand, environmental protection, and, on the other hand, the economic interests of traders, and this 'while pursuing the objective assigned to it by the Treaty to ensure a high level of health and environmental protection'.[21]

b) An Interpretation Guide

There is quite an extensive body of case law demonstrating that the HLP functions as an interpretative tool that can consolidate the ambition of EU acts, without always necessarily endorsing a true attempt to reach a higher level of protection. It is, of course, already well known that

---

[17] F. Jacobs, 'The Role of the European Court of Justice in the Protection of the Environment', *Journal of Environmental Law*, 18-2 (2006), 195–205, 195.

[18] Opinion in Case C–195/12 *Bois de Vielsam* [2013], para. 82.

[19] Article 191 TFEU and even Art. 37 of the Charter

[20] Case C–303/94 *Parliament* v. *Council* [1996] ECR I–2943, paras. 25–31.

[21] Case C–343/09, *Afton* [2010] ECR I–07027, para. 56.

a Directive or a Regulation must be interpreted in the light of its objective and in such a way as to ensure that it is fully effective (the '*effet utile*' doctrine). Still, the HLP dimension further helps to fend off attempts to dilute the stringency of some EU requirements, as it insists on the need to pursue a certain degree of ambition in the area of environmental protection. Altogether, where precaution and the HLP requirement both deal with ambition (what level of protection to pursue), precaution under EU law always implies situations in which risks and uncertainty are combined,[22] where this is not intrinsic to the HLP requirement. The peculiarity of the HLP concept lies rather in its bold questioning of the ambition as such, with no necessary link to issues of scientific uncertainty.

The HLP requirement proves to be useful as a shield in enhancing the legitimacy of EU acts and defending them against a wide array of claims. It has contributed to the inclusion of quails, partridges, pigeons[23] and gilts[24] within the scope of the Directive on Integrated Pollution Prevention and Control (IPPC). It consolidated the right to bring an action to prevent pollution, including the availability of an injunction against a permit as a remedy, where necessary.[25] It helped to ward off attempts made by Member States to narrow the scope of the Strategic Environmental Assessment Directive[26] and of the Waste Framework Directive.[27] It helped to firm up the threshold of compliance: if a legislative act pursues an HLP, a Member State (and its industrial installations) must comply with it fully.[28]

---

[22] 'Where it proves to be impossible to determine with certainty the existence or extent of the alleged risk because of the insufficiency, inconclusiveness or imprecision of the results of studies conducted, but the likelihood of real harm to public health persists should the risk materialise, the precautionary principle justifies the adoption of restrictive measures, provided they are non-discriminatory and objective': Case C–333/08 *Commission v. France* [2010] ECR, paras. 92–93.

[23] Case C–473/07 *Association nationale pour la protection des eaux et rivières and OABA* [2009] ECR I–319, paras. 25–27.

[24] Case C–585/10 *Møller* [2011] ECR, paras. 29 and 33.

[25] Case C–416/10 *Križan and Others* [2013] ECR, paras. 108–109.

[26] Case C–567/10 *Inter-Environnement Bruxelles et al.* v. *Région de Bruxelles-Capitale* [2012] ECR I–159, para. 30: an interpretation of the scope of the Directive, which would exclude plans and programmes whose adoption is regulated by national legislative or regulatory provisions, 'by appreciably restricting the directive's scope, would compromise, in part, the practical effect of the directive, having regard to its objective, *which consists in providing for a high level of protection of the environment*'. This was recently confirmed in Case C–290/15 *Patrice D'Oultremont*, [2016], para. 40.

[27] Case C–270/03 *Commission v. Italy* [2005] ECR I–5233, paras. 19–22.

[28] Case C–158/12, *Commission v. Ireland* [2013], not yet reported (electronic only), para. 22.

In the cases just mentioned, the ECJ's references to the HLP emanate directly from the wording of the secondary legislation under scrutiny. However, if the HLP requirement is not expressly mentioned in the Directive or Regulation at issue, the Court will introduce it by directly invoking the Treaty and affirming the HLP in relation to the legal basis or even to the fundamental objectives of the Treaty. In such cases, it is the aim governing the policy itself, as laid down in the TFEU, that helps to avoid restrictive interpretations.

The process is decisive in a consistent series of cases[29] that deal with the concept of waste and, particularly, what it means to 'discard' an item. That is so even if the reference is enshrined in a package of provisions that also often includes the precautionary principle. The HLP is also a key element when assessing room for manoeuvre for the Member States regarding the power to restrict movements of waste and keep them on their territory, should they consider that recovery in the state of destination could harm human health and the environment.[30] It plays an important role in the Court's refusal to accept weak interpretations of the Waste Water Directive[31] and in its confirmation that treatment is an obligation for all urban waste water, and not only for water that is directly discharged into a sensitive area.[32]

But the trend is not fully consistent, and may still evolve in a range of different directions. In some cases, the HLP wording could have reinforced or even changed interpretations in favour of a stricter environmental protection framework, but it was not even mentioned.[33] In other cases, the requirement plays the role of a convenient tiebreaker that helps to close difficult debates without any attempt to enhance environmental goals, using peremptory statements such as 'this means that the measure is not capable of compromising the objective of a high level of protection'.[34]

---

[29] Joined Cases C–418/97 and C–419/97 *ARCO Chemie Nederland and Others* [2000] ECR I–4475, para. 39; Case C–9/00 *Palin Granit and Vehmassalon kansanterveystyön kuntayhtymän hallitus* [2002] ECR I–3533, para. 23; Case C–1/03 *Van de Walle and Others* [2004] ECR I–7613, para. 45.

[30] Case C–277/02 *EU-Wood-Trading* [2004] ECR I–11957, para. 47.

[31] Directive 91/271/EC concerning urban waste-water treatment [1991] OJ L135/40.

[32] Case C–396/00 *Commission v. Italy* [2002] ECR I–3949, paras. 29–32; Case C–335/07 *Commission v. Finland* [2009] ECR I–9459, para. 29; Case C–438/07 *Commission v. Sweden* [2009] ECR I–9517, para. 30.

[33] Case C–237/07 *Janecek* [2008] ECR I–6221, para. 46.

[34] Case C–358/11 *Lapin* [2013] ECR, paras. 31 and 62.

2   The Sword

a   The Systemic Approach

The second category of cases – the 'sword' one, – includes cases in which the HLP requirement is used as a direct ground to petition the annulment of a legal measure, or to contest the legitimacy of the measure. These cases demonstrate that the Court is much less equipped for contesting the legitimacy of EU measures that would impose a low level of protection, except where the authority commits a manifest error of assessment, where it blatantly exceeds its powers or, due to other reasons, public health issues are at stake.

Again, the concrete level of ambition deemed acceptable for society in a specific EU act, in areas such as the environment or health protection, results from a complex political choice, which lies with the competent authority and not with the Court. Judicial review of the substance is therefore often confined to examining whether the authority's exercise of its powers is vitiated by an evident error of assessment, or whether it exceeded the limits of discretion.

As a consequence, establishing that an institution did not commit an evident error or exceed its powers is easier than establishing the inverse scenario. The 'sword' path is not conclusively barred, but it must be used selectively. The ECJ case law shows that at least two avenues are worth considering.

The first avenue involves a conformity testing of the relationship between a basic act (a Directive or a Regulation, adopted by the Council and Parliament) and its delegations or executory measures, often made in favour of the European Commission. When a mandate has been given, the delegate's margin of discretion is necessarily limited: delegated acts must remain in conformity with the essential elements of a basic act, including the aims thereof. In this regard, the HLP dimension has already proven useful for annulling Commission decisions[35] or revealing a breach of an obligation to act.[36] 'In determining the level of risk deemed unacceptable for society, the institutions are bound by their obligation to ensure a high level of protection of public health, safety and the environment in order to be compatible with the Treaty.'[37]

---

[35] Case T–229/04 *Sweden* v. *Commission* [2007] ECR II–2437, para. 54; Joined Cases C–14/06 and C–295/06 *Parliament* v. *Commission* [2008] ECR I–1649, paras. 75–76.

[36] Case T–521/14 *Sweden* v. *Commission* [2016], not yet reported, paras. 71–77.

[37] Mentioning here the health provisions; Case T–31/07 *Du Pont de Nemours* [2013].

The second avenue relates to the harmonization of measures based on Article 114 TFEU, the Treaty legal basis for all measures that aim to build the internal market further. Here, the HLP requirement can be interpreted as a specific duty that limits the discretion of the decision-maker, especially where the harmonization deals with health issues. This needs some explanation, bound to institutional reasons.

According to the Treaties, in health matters, the EU can only 'complement' but not 'harmonize' national legislation, except in a few limited areas.[38] Notwithstanding this restriction, the ECJ has used two tools that expand the potential for EU harmonization. First, the Court referred to the integration principle, as expressed in the health policy chapter,[39] according to which a high level of human health protection *is to be ensured* in the definition and implementation of all EU policies and activities. Secondly, the Court read Article 114 TFEU expansively and interpreted it to mean that the Article *explicitly* requires that a high level of protection of human health 'is to be ensured'[40] or 'should be guaranteed'[41] in achieving harmonization. This is not the exact wording of the Treaty.[42] The Court considers that because a high level of human health protection is to be ensured in the definition and implementation of all EU policies and activities, one can safely say that Article 114-based proposals encompass that dimension just as one can accept the possibility of harmonization in health-related areas.[43]

Such logic certainly entails that 'a manifest neglect to address the protective quality of the harmonized rule or a manifest error of appraisal regarding the applicable conditions would provide a basis for annulment of an adopted act'.[44] Generalising the lowest level of protection, or

---

[38] Art.168 TFEU.

[39] Ibid.

[40] Case C–376/98 *Germany* v. *Parliament and Council (Tobacco Advertising)* [2000] ECR I–8419, para. 88 (italics added).

[41] Case C–491/01 *British American Tobacco (Investments) and Imperial Tobacco* [2002] ECR I–11453, para. 62.

[42] The exact wording of today's Art. 114 TFEU is: 'The Commission, in its proposals envisaged in para. 1 concerning health, safety, environmental protection and consumer protection, will take as a base a high level of protection, taking account in particular of any new development based on scientific facts. Within their respective powers, the European Parliament and the Council will also seek to achieve this objective.'

[43] Case C–434/02 *Arnold André* [2004] ECR I–11825, para. 32; Case C–210/03 *Swedish Match* [2004] ECR I–11893, para. 32; and Joined Cases C–154/04 and C–155/04 *Alliance for Natural Health and Others* [2005] ECR I–6451, para. 30.

[44] S. Weatherill, 'Union Legislation Relating to the Free Movement of Goods' in P. Oliver (ed.), *Oliver on Free Movement of Goods in the European Union* (Hart Publishing, 2010), p.441.

adopting a standard that would result in a real reduction of protection at Union level may well be an indicator of such a manifest neglect or error of appraisal. Admittedly, this would impact on only the most obvious situations.

Paradoxically, challenging the legality of the level of protection of an EU act adopted on the basis of the environmental chapter of the TFEU[45] is a near dead-end, except for testing whether and how far that EU policy objective is amenable to judicial review. This is because the possibility of correction towards of a higher level of protection afforded in Article 193 TFEU.

That specific chapter creates a 'system' in achieving the target of the EU environmental policy, by combining, on the one hand, the protection that the harmonized rule crystallizes and, on the other hand, the broad and generic possibility left to the Member States to strengthen that protection. In this area, legally speaking, the possibility is always left to Member States to reinforce the standard of protection,[46] even if this is not an easy political choice.[47]

The criterion against which the compatibility of an individual act of EU legislation with the level of environmental protection required under Article 191(2) TFEU must be reviewed was defined by the Court in two old judgments – Safety Hi-Tech and Bettati[48] concerning bans on the use of substances harmful to the ozone layer – that have very recently been confirmed, in 2016, in a case concerning the lagoon of Venice: 'whilst it is undisputed that Article 191(2) TFEU requires EU policy in environmental matters to aim for a high level of protection, such a level of protection, to be compatible with that provision, does not necessarily have to be the highest that is technically possible. Article 193 TFEU authorises the

---

[45] Art. 193 TFEU.
[46] Case C–284/95 Safety Hi-Tech [1998] ECR I–4301; Case C–341/95 Bettati [1998] ECR I–4355 ; Fornasar and Others, para. 46; Case C–6/03 Deponiezweckverband Eiterköpfe [2005] ECR I–2753, para. 27.
[47] P. Pagh, 'The Battle on Environmental Policy Competences; Challenging the Stricter Approach; Stricter Might Lead to Weaker Protection' in R. Macrory (ed.), Reflections on 30 Years of EU Environmental Law: a High Level of Protection? (Europa Law Publishing, 2005), pp. 1–16; J. H. Jans, 'Minimum Harmonisation and the Role of the Principle of Proportionality' in M. Führ, R. Wahl and P. von Wilmowsky (eds.), Umweltrecht und Umweltwissenschaft; Festschrift für Eckard Rehbinder (Erich Schmidt Verlag, 2007), pp. 705–717. On that dimension of 'gold-plating', see J. H. Jans et al., 'Gold Plating of Environmental Measures?', Journal of European Environment and Planning Law, 6(4) (2009), 417–435.
[48] Case C–284/95 Safety Hi-Tech [1998] ECR I–4301; Case C–341/95 Bettati [1998] ECR I–4355

Member States to maintain or introduce more stringent protective measures'.[49]

The justification is important: if the level of protection needs not necessarily be the highest that is technically possible, it is because, as a result of the specific provisions of the environmental chapter on which the measure is based, Member States may always introduce more stringent protective measures. The broad possibility of correction towards a higher level of protection that characterizes the environmental chapter of the EU Treaty must be read into the objective of the policy. If the EU does not necessarily need to opt for the highest possible level of protection, technically, it is because the Treaty allows Member States to go even further and raise the level of protection as they wish. Although slightly contrived, the logic makes sense. In this manner, the Court avoids creating a sword of Damocles that might have jeopardized any European environmental legislation that does not meet the most stringent standards possible.

In such a system, identifying a breach of the high level of protection objective becomes quite difficult. There are some narrow possibilities – at the interface with international law, for instance. As observed by Advocate General Kokott, a level of environmental protection must be considered 'high' when it exceeds the EU's obligations under international environmental law,[50] – so, does it mean that the level is (too) low when it does not comply with the EU's obligations under international environmental law?

The Court did not follow Advocate General Kokott when she asserted, in 2016, that the objective of EU environmental policy does not stop at exceeding external standards and that 'rather, it requires continuous efforts to be made to increase and improve environmental protection,

---

[49] Case C–444/15 *Associazione Italia Nostra Onlus* [2016], para. 44.

[50] Opinion of Advocate General Kokott in Case 444/15 *Associazione Italia Nostra Onlus* v. *Comune di Venezi* [2016], paras. 24–25, by reference to the two old cases *Bettati* and *Safety*. The link to international law is also observed in 'shield cases', such as Case C–366/10 *ATAA,* [2011], para. 128: 'It must be pointed out that, as European Union policy on the environment seeks to ensure a high level of protection in accordance with Article 191(2) TFEU, the European Union legislature may in principle choose to permit a commercial activity, in this instance air transport, to be carried out in the territory of the European Union only on condition that operators comply with the criteria that have been established by the European Union and are designed to fulfil the environmental protection objectives which it has set for itself, in particular where those objectives follow on from an international agreement to which the European Union is a signatory, such as the Framework Convention and the Kyoto Protocol.'

even if there is no higher level of protection available internationally . . . After all, a level of protection ceases to be high in any event if an even higher level is readily achievable – a fact which must not, of course, be confused with the requirement to achieve the highest level of environmental protection technically possible, whatever the circumstances. The foregoing imposes on the EU legislature the requirement, when formulating environmental legislation, to improve environmental protection at least in areas where this can be accomplished with a reasonable degree of effort and is not precluded by any legitimate interests'.[51]

b   The Limits to Delegation

As already mentioned, the HLP requirement plays a part in assessing the bounds of the executive power and in questioning measures adopted by the European Commission that would lead to mitigate the protected standards decided by the legislature, 'this without it being necessary to rule on the extent of the Commission's discretion'. It is worth highlighting, in that regard, that a clear divide exists between the judicial review of the ambition of a basic legislative act and the judicial review of the ambition of an executive or delegated act. The intensity of the review is considerably higher in the latter than in the former scenario, as it is at the level of the legislator that the proper balancing of opposite interests is being made.

In a recent case on the adoption of a list of scientific criteria allowing the identification of substances that must be classified as endocrine disruptors, the powers of the Commission, in its decision not to adopt a delegated act, were harshly reframed by the Tribunal, in a diatribe in which the 'high level of protection' objective of the basic act is central. Given that the legislative act, a Regulation on biocides, had already struck the balance between the objective of an HLP and the necessity to protect

[51] Opinion of Advocate General Kokott in Case 444/15 *Associazione Italia Nostra Onlus* v. *Comune di Venezi* [2016], para. 32; Case C–444/15 *Associazione Italia Nostra Onlus,* [2016],paras. 44 et al. The Court does not follow her, either, when she breaks new ground in concluding that, in combination with the marginal control limitation that is a necessity in the appraisal of environmental measures, and viewed in conjunction with the variety of objectives that the EU legislature may legitimately pursue when making provisions for environmental protection: 'the principle of a high level of protection laid down in Article 191(2) TFEU is therefore clearly infringed where there is nothing to indicate the existence of legitimate interests precluding a higher level of protection. It should be noted in this regard that, in accordance with the general EU-law principle of proportionality, "precluding" interests include those the weight of which is disproportionate to any potential improvement in the level of protection' (para. 34).

the internal market, the Commission was not permitted to use the argument of additional free market-related objections in order to reach a decision not to adopt the list within the set deadline. Further claims according to which the pre-existing level of protection was already high enough were to no avail.[52]

3   Judicial Review of National Measures

Another question is whether the HLP plays a role in assessing the legality of national measures related to environmental protection and adopted in the European territory. Here, also, we can proceed in two categories.

The first one is very obvious and brings us back to some our above-mentioned 'shield' cases. They concern the manner in which Member States interpret harmonized EU legislation. That interpretation must take due consideration of the objective being pursued by such legislation. Manifold cases raise issues on the way in which Member States implement EU law, in which one finds blunt assertions of the type: 'such a (high) level of protection could, however, be seriously jeopardised if classification as biocidal products were to be reserved solely for those products containing, etc.'[53]

But the interesting question is rather to identify how far that objective of an HLP, which is mentioned in Article 3 TEU, can govern the acceptability of national measures that would, outside any harmonized framework, impact some Treaty provisions – such as one of the four freedoms, among which we find the free movement of goods.

Various steps have already been taken in that regard, in the area of health protection and education, with an impact on the burden of proof and the assessment of proportionality. National measures that have an impact on the freedom of establishment or equal access to education may be justified if they meet a certain threshold. According to the ECJ, proactive national measures that restrict the freedom of establishment may indeed be justified, in so far as they satisfy a new criterion – that of making a 'contribution to achieving a high level of protection' of health,[54] without going beyond what is necessary to attain that goal.[55] Moreover,

---

[52] Case T–521/14 *Sweden* v. *Commission* [2016], paras. 72–78.

[53] Case C–420/10 *Söll* v. *Tetra* [2012], not reported, para. 27.

[54] Case C–169/07 *Hartlauer* [2009] ECR, para. 47; Case C–73/08 *Bressol and Others* [2010] ECR I–2735, para. 62.

[55] With reference to Case C–158/96 *Kohll* [1998] ECR I–1931, para. 50; Case C–157/99 *Smits and Peerbooms* [2001] ECR I–5473, para. 74; Case C–385/99 *Müller-Fauré and van Riet* [2003] ECR I–4509, para. 67; Case C–372/04 *Watts* [2006] ECR I–4325, para. 105.

any difference in access to education that could be indirectly discriminatory on the basis of nationality may also be justified by the objective of maintaining a balanced, high-quality medical service open to all, 'in so far as it contributes to achieving a high level of protection of health'.[56]

Along the same lines, one could wonder whether the HLP requirement might also soften, in the future, the acceptance of national measures having an impact on the free movement of goods, in so far as environmental protection is concerned, and in situations in which the Member States are not implementing a specific EU legislation but are acting upon their own initiative. This might help to reverse the presumption. Instead of considering that the proposed national measures are suspect *per se* – for they would necessarily be incompatible with the specific provisions of primary law expounding the essentials of free movement, and that in contrast to the way in which national measures in the area of moral values or public health are taken on –[57] such measures would rather be viewed through the more serene prism of the global EU project to ensure a high level of environmental protection. This would, of course, not circumvent the review of the proportionality of these national measures, which is generally much tougher than the test applied to EU acts,[58] but might slightly ease the burden of proof resting on Member States, on the basis of the consideration that such national measures do indeed contribute to the overall EU objective of 'ensuring a high level of protection' and are proposed pursuant to the principle of sincere cooperation, as imposed by Article 4 TEU, in order to facilitate the achievement of other equally important Union tasks and objectives.

---

[56] Bressol and Others, para. 62.

[57] This is indeed the fate of most environmental initiatives of the Member States, in contrast with measures in the field of public morals or even health protection that, without prejudice to the difficult questions linked to the scientific evidence regarding health issues, are usually welcomed by the phrase 'in the absence of harmonisation, it is for each Member State to determine in those areas, in accordance with its own scale of values, what is required in order to ensure that the interests in question are protected'. See, among others, Case C-42/07 Liga Portuguesa de Futebol [2009] ECR I-7633, para. 57; Case C-333/08 *Commission* v. *France* [2010] ECR, para. 85.

[58] The proportionality test is not a uniform test but an open-textured principle that is used in different contexts to protect different interests, and it entails different degrees of scrutiny, as expressed by T. Tridimas, 'Proportionality in European Community Law : Searching for the Appropriate Standard of Scrutiny' in *The Principle of Proportionality in the Laws of Europe* (Hart Publishing, 1999), pp. 65–84. On the proportionality of national measures, see: J. Jans, 'Proportionality revisited', *Legal Issues of Economic Integration*, 27 (3) (2000), pp. 239–265.

A recent case demonstrates that the trend might be on the move. In *Canadian Oil*, where the question raised was to know whether Sweden could impose complementary registration requirements on top of the procedures that are already imposed on importers and producers by the REACH Regulation, the Court explained

> that the registration required by national legislation such as that at issue in the main proceedings seeks to obtain data which, on the one hand, are essentially complementary to those falling within the relevant scope of the REACH Regulation and which, on the other, contribute, in the Member State concerned, particularly to the implementation of a control system for safe management of the chemical products covered by that regulation and to the evaluation of that management in order, in particular, to propose any useful improvements to it at EU level.

It therefore decides, without any further ado, that 'such an objective linked to that of the regulation, which seeks to ensure a high level of protection of human health and the environment, *is capable of justifying any hindrance to the free movement of goods'.*[59]

C   The Importance of the Target

While not discussed so frequently, the status of being a 'target' is very significant under EU law – for various reasons.

For instance, as shown in the analysis of the 'shield' case law above, the target of a legislative act or of a policy is a decisive factor where case law embraces teleological interpretations: the target often guides the reasoning of the judge in order to avoid diluting interpretations that would weaken EU law.[60]

The target is also decisive in appreciating limits to the delegation stemming from a basic act: the target helps to distinguish what is essential from what is not, and therefore what can or cannot be lawfully delegated.[61] The target of the basic act helps in determining the margin

---

[59] Case C–472/14, *Canadian Oil Company Sweden AB, Anders Rantén* v. *Riksåklagaren* [2016], para. 46. The French translation is, however, more moderate, in the sense of the acceptance of possible hindrance ('est susceptible de justifier d'éventuelles entraves à la libre circulation des marchandises').

[60] This teleological method leading to a creative jurisprudence has proponents but also detractors. See, among others, G. Conway, *The Limits of Legal Reasoning and the European Court of Justice* (Cambridge University Press, 2012); A. Albors Llorens, 'The European Court of Justice, More Than a Teleological Court' in *The Cambridge Yearbook of European Legal Studies* (Hart Publishing, 2000), pp. 373–398.

[61] See *Parliament* v. *Council*, paras. 25–31.See also nn. 62 and 68 above.

of discretion of the delegate, and curtails discretion when the basic act directly fixes a mandate that, because of the aim pursued, must be interpreted strictly.

Additionally, as already mentioned, the target is a decisive pivotal element in the review of proportionality of EU legislation. Extremely often, even if not always, EU acts are expected to be proportionate to the aim that they pursue. They must not exceed the limits of what is appropriate and necessary to attain their objectives.[62]

Furthermore, in other types of discussion, the objective of a measure also plays a crucial role in the justification of possible restrictions to protected rights, such as the right to property, as far as it corresponds to the general interest and as far as the measure impairs the very substance of the right.

A target is nonetheless rarely isolated and must often be read in combination with another. Still, concurrent targets are not necessarily conflicting; they can reinforce each other.[63] The Court sometimes organizes targets hierarchically and gives precedence to the protection of health and the environment, as it did with regard to the REACH Regulation on chemical substances.[64] Even when the Court decided that it was necessary to ascertain whether, in exercising its discretion, the EU legislature had attempted to achieve a degree of balance between the protection of health, the environment and the consumer on the one hand and the economic interests of traders on the other, the Court clarified that such a balance must be struck 'while pursuing the objective assigned to it by the Treaty to ensure a high level of protection of health and environmental protection', therefore adding particular weight to the last dimension.[65]

---

[62] C–379/08 and C–380/08 *ERG and Others* EU:C:2010:127, para. 80

[63] Case C–558/07 *SPCM and Others* [2009] ECR, paras. 44–45.

[64] Regulation 1907/2008 of the European Parliament and of the Council of 18 December 2006 concerning the Registration, Evaluation, Authorisation and Restriction of Chemicals (REACH), [2006] OJ L396/1.

[65] *Afton Chemical*, para. 56: 'The objectives of the REACH Regulation, set out in Article 1 thereof, are to "ensure a high level of protection of human health and the environment [...] as well as the free circulation of substances on the internal market while enhancing competitiveness and innovation". However, regard being had to Recital 16 in the preamble to the REACH Regulation, it must be stated that the Community legislature established, as the main purpose of the obligation to register laid down in Article 6(3) thereof, the first of those three objectives, namely to ensure a high level of protection of human health and the environment.'

It is also settled case law that although some freedoms and rights form part of the general tenets of EU law, such as the freedom to pursue a trade or a business and the right to own property, they do not amount to unfettered prerogatives but must be seen in the light of their social functions. Consequently, they may be restricted, provided that these restrictions correspond in fact to objectives of general interest pursued by the EU.[66] In that regard also, the target that is being pursued by the restrictive measure plays a crucial role. Where it often happens that the ECJ, when confronted with conflicting rights or freedoms of equal value, considers that the interests involved must be weighed with regard to all the circumstances of the case in order to determine whether a fair balance was struck,[67] one cannot find such an explicit review of a 'fair balance' in situations where the ECJ observes, on the contrary, that the '*the importance of the objective pursued* by the disputed regulation may justify adverse consequences, even substantial adverse consequences, for certain traders'.

The Court, in notorious cases such as *Fedesa* (hormones) or *Arcelor* (emissions trading),[68] affirms that the importance of the public interest objectives pursued, including health and environmental protection, is such that it justifies even substantial negative economic consequences for certain operators. This remains applicable even if it has also been made clear that the EU legislature's exercising of discretion must not produce results that are 'manifestly less appropriate than those that would be produced by other measures that were also suitable for those objectives',[69] or must pursue a 'certain balance', as in the *Afton* case.[70]

The fact that a disputed regulation entails serious economic consequences therefore does not suffice to conclude that it is disproportionate or unbalanced for the purpose of judicial review.

---

[66] Case 44/79 *Hauer* [1979] ECR 3727, para. 23; Case 265/87 *Schräder* [1989] ECR 2237, para. 15; Case C–293/97 *Standley and Others* [1999] ECR I–2603, para. 54; Joined Cases C–402/05P and C–415/05P *Kadi and Al Barakaat International Foundation* v. *Council and Commission* [2008] ECR I–6351, para. 355.

[67] Case C–112/00 *Schmidberger* [2003] ECR I–5659, para. 81.

[68] See, to that effect, Case C–331/88 *Fedesa and Others* [1990] ECR I–4023, paras.15–17; *United Kingdom* v. *Commission*, para. 93; Case C–183/95 *Affish* [1997] ECR I–4315, para. 42; *Industrias Químicas del Vallés* v. *Commission*, para. 134; *Pfizer Animal Health* v. *Council*, paras. 456 and 457; Case C–86/03 *Greece* v. *Commission* [2005] ECR I–10979, para. 96; Case C–127/07 *Arcelor Atlantique et Lorraine and Others* [2008] ECR I–9895, para. 57.

[69] *Arcelor Atlantique et Lorraine and Others* [2008] ECR I–9895, para. 57.

[70] As mentioned in *Afton*.

The General Court recently linked this quite radical statement to the HLP *target*, at least in relation to the public health dimension of the TFEU: By requiring the maintenance of a high level of human health protection, Directive 91/414 applies Article 152(1) EC, which provides that a high level of human health protection is to be ensured in the definition and implementation of all Community policies and activities. That protection of human health takes precedence over economic considerations, with the result that it may justify adverse economic consequences, even those which are substantial, for certain traders.[71]

D   Added Value

The assessment of the degree of balance between environmental protection and corporate interests can turn out to be quite different, indeed, when made by other courts or tribunals in charge of the verification of other dimensions, even if controlling the same type of rules. This is also reflected in the type of claims that are allowed to be brought before the ECJ. The *Afton* case,[72] already mentioned above, can be referred to in that light, in comparison with an old Ethyl arbitration attempt which took place in the 1990s, under the North American Free Trade Agreement (NAFTA).

In a preliminary ruling released in 2010, the ECJ was asked to assess the legality of regulatory limits that are being imposed under EU law, on the use of a specific metallic additive in fuel(the so-called MMT) in order to protect human health and the environment. The company claimed a breach of the proportionality principle. The Court recalled that the EU legislature must be allowed a broad discretion in an area that entails political, economic and social choices on its part, and in which it is called upon to undertake complex assessments. The legality of a measure adopted in that sphere can be affected only if the measure is manifestly inappropriate having regard to the objective that the competent institutions are seeking to pursue.[73] The Court stated that the objectives of protection of health, environmental protection and consumer protection are referred to both in Article 114 TFEU, under which the legislature is to take as a base a high level of protection, taking account, in particular, of any new developments based on scientific facts, and in Article 191 TFEU,

---

[71] Case T–31/07 *Du Pont de Nemours* [2013], paras. 131–132.
[72] Case C–343/09 *Afton* v. *Secretary of State for Transport* [2010].
[73] Case C–558/07 *SPCM and Others* [2009] ECR, para. 42.

which provides that the Community policy on the environment is to be based on, inter alia, the precautionary principle. As a consequence, the Court decided that the setting of a limit for the presence of MMT in fuel that makes it possible thereby to reduce the quantities of that substance that might potentially damage health, was not manifestly inappropriate for attaining the objectives of protection of health and environmental protection pursued by the EU legislature. However, it also decided to verify that the legislature had not gone beyond what was necessary to attain those objectives but concluded that the EU could justifiably take the view that the appropriate manner of reconciling the *high level of health and environmental protection* and the economic interests of producers of MMT was to limit the content of MMT in fuel on a declining scale while providing for the possibility, in Article 8a(3) of Directive 98/70, of revising those limits on the basis of the results of future assessment.

So far, nothing unusual: the judgment remained within the classical canons of European jurisprudence.

However, there are other entries in the same type of subject matter, revealing the importance of the paradigm, such as were observed in former approaches to investment protection.

On the occasion of a claim submitted before an arbitration tribunal, alleging that Canada breached its obligations under Chapter Eleven of NATFA as a result of introducing legislation banning the importation of and interprovincial trade in MMT,[74] the outcome turned out to be radically different. This even though it concerned the same kind of ban, the same substance (MMT), the same link to public health issues, and even related companies (Ethyl and Afton are parent companies), but fifteen years earlier.

In that action brought in 1996 against Canada, the legal grounds are not identical to those tested in the European arena. They relate to the protection of Ethyl property as an investor. The industry believes that the Canadian ban is to be assimilated to an indirect expropriation of its investment: the production activity of the substance (produced in the United States but imported to Canada in order to be mixed with gasoline), but also the profits to be expected and even its reputation (due to debates in Parliament on the dangerousness of the substance) were all imperilled. The industry claimed significant compensation of about US$251 million. The story ended in Ethyl's favour without ever being

---

[74] Available at: www.international.gc.ca/trade-agreements-accords-commerciaux/topics-domaines/disp-diff/ethyl.aspx?lang=eng

heard by that arbitration court, except for a preliminary decision on the competence of the tribunal. Canada withdrew its restrictive measure, issued a statement about the safety of the substance and is said to have paid US$13 million to the company. The threat impacted a measure that had been discussed and decided in Parliament.[75]

Such a threat would be of no avail under current EU law (the possible impact of CETA is not being discussed here).[76] As regards infringement of the right to property, the Court has consistently held that, while the right to property forms part of the general principles of Community law, it is not an absolute right and it must be viewed in relation to its social function. Consequently, its exercise can be restricted, provided that those restrictions correspond to objectives of general interest pursued by the EU and do not constitute a disproportionate and intolerable interference, impairing the very substance of the rights guaranteed.[77] As regards the objectives of general interest referred to above, established case-law shows that the protection of the environment – I add: streamlined

[75] J. A. Soloway, 'Environmental Trade Barriers Under Nafta : the MMT Fuel Controversy', *Minn. J.Global Trade*, 8 (1999), pp. 55–95; A. Aslam, Corporations Use Trade Pact to Sue Countries, *Global Policy Forum,* September 1998, available at: www.globalpolicy.org/component/content/article/221/47001.html

[76] We are not assessing here the application of the brand-new Comprehensive Economic and Trade Agreement (CETA) that entered into force provisionally (without awaiting the agreement of Parliaments) in July 2017, with the exception of some of its provisions, between the EU and Canada. CETA is a sort of junction point between different worlds – or legal orders: the trade and investment law sphere versus the environmental law sphere – that for a long time evolved in a compartmentalized manner but find there a fresh opportunity to intersect with each other. In order to prevent possible conflicts between investment protection and environmental protection, the Parties insert a guarantee, in Art. 8.9.1., that they, for the purpose of that chapter only, '*reaffirm their right to regulate within their territories*'.(See, for instance, L. Wandahl Mouyal, *International Investment Law and the Right to Regulate* (Routledge, 2016), pp. 1–264, p. 231). Furthermore, an Art. 8.9.2 states that, for the purpose of the section on investment protection only, that 'the mere fact that a Party regulates, including through a modification to its laws, in a manner which negatively affects an investment or interferes with an investor's expectations, including its expectations of profits, does not amount to a breach of an obligation under this Section' and a remote Annex 8.A even adds that 'For greater certainty, except in the rare circumstance when the impact of a measure or series of measures is so severe in light of its purpose that it appears manifestly excessive, non-discriminatory measures of a Party that are designed and applied to protect legitimate public welfare objectives, such as health, safety and the environment, do not constitute indirect expropriations'.

[77] Case C–379/08 and C–380/08, *ERG and Others* [2010] ECR I–127, para. 80; Case 44/79 *Hauer* [1979] ECR 3727, para. 23; Case 265/87 *Schräder HS Kraftfutter* [1989] ECR 2237, para. 15; Case C–293/97 *Standley and Others* [1999] ECR I–2603, para. 54; and Joined Cases C–402/05P and C–415/05P *Kadi and Al Barakaat International Foundation v. Council and Commission* [2008] ECR I–6351, para. 355.

towards its target to achieve a high level of protection – is certainly one of those objectives.[78]

E   Prospects

The origin and developments of the HLP requirements are closely linked to the process of European integration. They were germinated not in serenity but in fear – fear of the lowering of pre-existing levels of protection. Neither do they do emanate from prior or parallel developments that occurred at the international level and that could keep up their dynamism. They are deeply linked to the conferral of competences from the national to the transnational – in this case, European, level – and to the questions regarding harmonization and the appropriate standard of protection that emerged through this process.

HLP requirements were at first not solid enough to exist as autonomous principles that emerge 'beyond the texts',[79] but recent developments demonstrate that the dimension is resolutely 'on the move'. Advocate General Kokott states that these various provisions give expression to the common *principle* of a high level of environmental protection, 'to which particular importance must be attached given the number of provisions of EU law in which it is enshrined'.[80]

The importance to be given to that concept or principle remains for now tethered to the Treaties and, as a consequence, could still quite easily be jeopardized, were it not to be maintained explicitly in primary EU law. Such a removal would raise important questions on the legitimacy of EU powers regarding environmental protection. Bringing such requirements into light – and there are actually even others to mention, such as the fresh boost given by the Court to the requirement of an HLP, as inserted in Article 37 of the Charter of Fundamental Rights of the European Union, which it inserts into the category of 'rights',[81] or its possible

---

[78] Case 240/83 ADBHU [1985] ECR 531, para. 13; Case C–302/86 *Commission v. Denmark* [1988] ECR 4607, para. 8; and Case C–213/96 *Outokumpu* [1998] ECR I–1777, para. 32.

[79] D. Misonne, *Droit européen de l'environnement et de la santé: L'ambition d'un niveau élevé de protection* (Anthemis, 2011), pp. 286–287; N. de Sadeleer, 'The Principle of a High Level of Environmental Protection in EU Law: Policy Principle or General Principle of Law?' in *Mijörättsliga Perspektiv Och Tankevändor* (Iustus Förlag, 2013), pp. 447–465, p. 450.

[80] Case 444/15 *Associazione Italia Nostra Onlus v. Comune di Venezi* [2016], 24–25.

[81] Case 444/15 *Associazione Italia Nostra Onlus v. Comune di Venezi* [2016], 62: 'In that regard, it must be pointed out that Article 52(2) of the Charter provides that rights recognised by the Charter for which provision is made in the Treaties are to be exercised

relation to the dynamics of an emerging principle of 'no-regression'[82] –
helps to consolidate and develop their potential and relevance, should
one care to give flesh to new conceptual developments that broaden the
range of possible avenues for advancing the effectiveness of environmental law, in the framework of substantial large-scale legislative and regulatory integration.

under the conditions and within the limits defined by those Treaties. Such is the case with
Article 37 of the Charter.' The Court explicitly inserts Art. 37 into the category of 'rights',
and not in that of 'principles', as suggested by the text of the Charter itself.

[82] D. Misonne and I. Hachez, 'Simplifier Le droit européen de l'environnement : un
processus liberé de toute exigence de non-régression?' in I. Doussan, *Les futurs du droit
de l'environnement* (Bruylant: Bruxelles, 2016).

PART IV

Legitimacy of Outcomes: Performance, Effects
(and Side-Effects)

.

9

When Environmental Protection and Human Rights Collide: Four Heuristics of Conflict Resolution

MARIE-CATHERINE PETERSMANN*

A Introduction

Legal scholars have traditionally defined environmental protection and human rights as mutually reinforcing legal fields. This synergistic approach is grounded on the idea that 'the goals of environmental protection and human rights are both aimed at ensuring human well-being'.[1] Although many examples of synergies prove that a better protected environment usually enhances specific human rights (such as the right to private and family life[2] or the right to life[3]), the jurisprudence of regional human rights courts instantiates numerous cases of conflicts between these two

---

* I would like to thank Professor Nehal Bhuta and Dimitri Van den Meerssche for their insightful feedback on an earlier draft of this chapter. I also thank Professor Christina Voigt for her comments and her editorial work throughout this book's publication.

[1] E. de Wet and J. Vidmar, 'Conflicts between International Paradigms: Hierarchy versus Systemic Integration', *Global Constitutionalism*, 2 (2013), 196, 213.

[2] See *Lopez-Ostra* v. *Spain*, App no. 16798/90 (ECHR, 9 December 1994), para. 51: '[n]aturally, severe environmental pollution may affect individuals' well-being and prevent them from enjoying their homes in such a way as to affect their private and family life adversely'. The pollution caused by a waste treatment facility was recognized as violating Article 8 of the European Convention on Human Rights (ECHR).

[3] See *Social and Economic Rights Action Center (SERAC) and another* v. *Federal Republic of Nigeria*, Comm. 155/96, African Commission on Human and Peoples' Rights (27 October 2001), in which the oil pollution in the Niger Delta was recognized as violating the Ogoni people's right to freedom from discrimination (Article 2); right to life (Article 4); right to property (Article 14); right to health (Article 16); right to family life (Article 18(1)); right to free disposal of wealth and natural resources (Article 21) and right to a general satisfactory environment (Article 24) of the African Charter on Human and Peoples' Rights.

legitimate objectives.[4] The purpose of this chapter is to delve into these largely overlooked conflicts.

The objectives of the chapter are twofold. First, it maps out the existing conflicts between EU environmental protection laws and fundamental rights and freedoms protected under the EU Charter of Fundamental Rights (EUCFR). Secondly, the chapter induces and analyses certain patterns in the legal reasoning of the Court of Justice of the European Union (CJEU) when managing such conflicts.

More specifically, by analysing the case law of the CJEU from a conflict-based approach, three main areas of tension between EU environmental protection laws and fundamental rights and freedoms emerge. Conflicts mostly occur between EU environmental protection laws and (i) fundamental freedoms and rights of private companies,[5] (ii) property rights and (iii) indigenous peoples' rights.

A careful analysis of cases that belong to these three main areas of tension reveals four legal argumentative *topoi*[6] employed by the CJEU when solving the conflict of norms. First, the struggle for autonomy and normative independency in assessing conflicts between environmental protection and human rights sheds light on, I argue, the 'legal solipsism' of the CJEU.[7] By refusing to be guided by external legal sources of law, the CJEU claims its supremacy in normatively shaping both environmental protection and fundamental rights, and in regulating the interface between the two legal fields.

Secondly, when EU environmental protection and human rights collide, environmental protection is granted strong protection by the CJEU and commonly recognized as a general interest capable of limiting relative fundamental rights and freedoms. The content of this general

---

[4] M.-C. Petersmann, 'The Integration of Environmental Protection Considerations within the Human Rights Law Regime: Which Solutions Have Been Provided by Regional Human Rights Courts?' (2015) 24 *Italian Yearbook of International Law* 1, 191–218.

[5] Although private companies' fundamental freedoms are not *stricto sensu* human rights, they are recognized as fundamental freedoms under the EUCFR. As the CJEU analyses those freedoms by interpreting provisions of the EUCFR and employs the legal hermeneutics of human rights adjudication in doing so, those cases fall under the scope of this chapter.

[6] *Topoi* are used in this chapter in a general sense and refer to the various legal arguments and judicial techniques that are made and employed by the CJEU in support or against the interpretation of a legal problem.

[7] From the Latin *solus*, meaning 'alone', and *ipse*, meaning 'self': that nothing external to one's own mind can be ascertained. I refer to solipsism loosely, in the sense that only the CJEU's internal normative structures seem relevant to its adjudication, banning the external as being either non-existent or irrelevant.

interest, however, is nowhere defined. This allows the CJEU to use the general interest criterion as a vehicle for the systemic integration of new environmental protection concerns that align with current social expectations. Thereby, the CJEU substantively and normatively engages with the content of EU environmental law, which it constantly redefines and sharpens.

Thirdly, the CJEU engages with the content of EU environmental law by interpreting its impact on fundamental rights and freedoms even when it does not have the competence to do so. In this process, the CJEU contributes to the proliferation of environmental protection and its integration within the human rights *corpus*, thereby acting as a quasi 'law-maker'.

Finally, methods of scientific policy-balancing are observed in the cases. These methods express pragmatism over legal rigidity. Thus, the case law analysis reveals how the CJEU developed, I argue, a 'managerial approach' to solve conflicts between environmental protection and human rights.

B   The CJEU and the Outside World: a History of Solipsism

The case law analysis of conflicts between EU environmental protection laws and fundamental rights and freedoms sheds light on the solipsistic nature of the legal reasoning of the CJEU. When interpreting alleged human rights violations on environmental protection grounds, the CJEU refers solely to EU law in determining legal validity, instead of taking into account specific legal sources situated outside the EU legal framework. By either disregarding exogenous sources when parties explicitly invoke them, or merely referring to them *pro forma* but refuting their validity, the CJEU engages in a struggle for normative autonomy when substantively delineating its internal fundamental rights regime.

The recent *Inuit* case provides an example.[8] This case concerns a conflict between, on the one hand, an EU Regulation aimed at protecting seals by forbidding the trade of seal products on the EU market,[9] and, on the other hand, the effectiveness of a legal exception inserted into the Regulation, aimed at protecting the right of indigenous peoples to continue hunting seals and to sell the derived products on the EU market.

---

[8] See Case T–526/10 *Inuit Tapiriit Kanatami and Others* v. *Commission* [2013] ECR. These conclusions were confirmed on appeal in Case C–398/13P *Inuit Tapiriit Kanatami and Others* v. *Commission* [2015] EU:C:2015:535.

[9] Council Regulation (EC) 1007/2009 on Trade in Seal Products [2009] OJ L286.

The indigenous peoples affected by the Regulation claimed that the Inuit exception did not guarantee their rights, since the requirements to obtain the attesting documents from a certified body to allow them to sell seal products derived from traditional hunting on the EU market allowed only one indigenous people, namely the Kalaallit from Greenland (Denmark), to access the EU market.[10] All the other indigenous peoples affected by the Regulation were unable to trade their seal products in the EU. To determine whether the exception was or was not violating indigenous peoples' rights, the CJEU based its interpretation *solely* on EU law, thereby turning away from the European Convention on Human Rights (ECHR) and its interpretation by the European Court of Human Rights (ECtHR). While the applicants explicitly relied on the ECHR and invoked a violation of their right to property under Article 1 of Protocol 1 to the ECHR, their right to private and family life under Article 8 of the ECHR, as well as their fundamental right to be heard, the CJEU held that the protection conferred by these articles are implemented in EU law by Articles 17, 7, 10 and 11 of the EUCFR respectively. Therefore, it held, it is 'appropriate to refer *only* to those provisions'.[11] In doing so, the CJEU discarded the cases in which the ECtHR showed, to some extent, sensitivity towards indigenous peoples' rights. It appears, thus, that the applicants intentionally chose to invoke rights protected under the ECHR before the CJEU, rather than the EUCFR, as, under the 'hegemony clause'[12] of Article 52(3) of the EUCFR, the CJEU is required to grant *at least* the same meaning and scope to the provisions of the EUCFR as the ECtHR grants to the corresponding rights protected under the ECHR.[13]

---

[10] See S. K. Elfving, 'The European Union's Animal Welfare Policy and Indigenous Peoples' Rights: the case of Inuit and Seal Hunting in Arctic Canada and Greenland' (March 2014) http://ethos.bl.uk/OrderDetails.do?uin=uk.bl.ethos.656320 (last accessed 16 March 2018).

[11] Case T–526/10 *Inuit Tapiriit Kanatami and Others* v. *Commission* [2013] ECR, para. 105 (emphasis added).

[12] As referred to by AG Kokott in Case C–109/10P *Solvay* v. *Commission* [2011] ECR I-10329, para. 252.

[13] Article 52(3) of the EUCFR provides that '[i]n so far as this Charter contains rights which correspond to rights guaranteed by the European Convention on Human Rights, the meaning and scope of those rights shall be the same as those laid down by the said Convention. This provision shall not prevent Union law providing more extensive protection'. The explanation of Article 52 specifies that '[t]he meaning and the scope of the guaranteed rights are determined not only by the text of those instruments, but also by the case law of the European Court of Human Rights and by the Court of Justice of the European Communities'. See Note from the Praesidium: Text of the Explanations relating to the Complete Text of the EUCFR of 12 December 2000, Brussels, 11 October 2000, Charter 4473/00.

Although there is no landmark case within the jurisprudence of the ECtHR that has been decided in favour of indigenous peoples, the ECtHR has recognized a certain degree of protection to indigenous peoples. In this context, the CJEU should have granted to the indigenous peoples a right to private and family life at least to the same level of protection as that granted by the ECtHR under Article 8 of the ECHR in *G and E v. Norway*,[14] and a right to property with at least the same level of protection as that granted by the ECtHR under Article 1 of Protocol 1 to the ECHR in the *Hingitaq* case.[15] By framing *en passant* that it is appropriate to refer only to the EUCFR, the CJEU's hermeneutics actually have a substantial negative impact on the rights of indigenous peoples, as the CJEU avoids granting them the minimum standards of protection recognized by the ECtHR. Indeed, precisely this point was appealed by the applicants. Relying on Article 52(3) of the EUCFR, they argued that 'the provisions of the ECHR must prevail if they confer broader protection than those of the EUCFR'.[16] The CJEU, however, held that the ECHR 'does not constitute, as long as the EU has not acceded to it, a legal instrument which has been formally incorporated into EU law'.[17] In doing so, the CJEU emancipated itself from the normative authority of the ECtHR.

The same reasoning holds with regard to the UN Declaration on the Rights of Indigenous Peoples (UNDRIP). While acknowledging the protection that it grants to indigenous peoples, the CJEU stressed that the UNDRIP is only a declaration and that it 'cannot be considered that a declaration can grant the Inuit autonomous and additional rights over and above those provided for by EU law'.[18] The applicants appealed against the CJEU's position. They held that by not obtaining the

---

[14] The ECtHR granted protection to the right to private life of the Saami people of Norway by recognizing that the construction of a hydroelectric plant interfered with their rights to move their herds and deers around a considerable distance, thereby infringing their right to private and family life under Article 8 of the ECHR: *G. and E. v. Norway*, App nos. 9278/81 and 9415/81, Commission decision of 3 October 1983, Decisions and Reports (DR) 35, 36.

[15] The ECtHR recognized natural heritage and resources of the Thule Tribe Inughuit and their descendants as forming part of the right to property under Article 1 of Protocol 1 to the ECHR: *Hingitaq 53 and others v. Denmark*, App no. 18584/04 (ECtHR, 12 January 2006).

[16] Case C–398/13P *Inuit Tapiriit Kanatami and Others v. Commission* [2015] EU: C:2015:535, para. 43.

[17] Ibid., para. 45.

[18] Case T–526/10 *Inuit Tapiriit Kanatami and Others v. Commission* [2013] ECR, para. 112.

appellants' prior consent before the Regulation was adopted, the EU institutions violated Article 19 of the UNDRIP,[19] which was recognized as a norm of customary international law by the International Law Association in 2012.[20] However, as the appellants had not pleaded any breach of a rule of customary international law resulting from Article 19 of the UNDRIP in the original proceedings, the CJEU dismissed the plea as inadmissible in the appeal.[21] Additionally, the CJEU did not refer to other existing valid sources of law – for instance, the International Covenant on Civil and Political Rights (ICCPR), to which all EU Member States are parties.[22] By refusing to engage with competing sources of law, more specialized with regard to this specific legal conflict, the CJEU denied the normative importance of external sources of law, and affirmed its belief that only EU law is valid. The 'structural bias' of the CJEU towards EU law renders the Court oblivious to the outside world.[23]

Another example of solipsism can be seen in the *Križan* case.[24] This case illustrates a conflict between environmental protection and property rights. A company's right to property was allegedly violated when Mr Križan and forty-three other applicants successfully invoked their environmental procedural rights against a permit to construct a landfill site for

[19] Article 19 of the UNDRIP provides that '[s]tates shall consult and cooperate in good faith with the indigenous peoples concerned through their own representative institutions in order to obtain their free, prior and informed consent before adopting and implementing legislative or administrative measures that may affect them'.

[20] Case C–398/13P *Inuit Tapiriit Kanatami and Others* v. *Commission* [2015] EU: C:2015:535, para. 50. See also Resolution No. 5/2012 on 'Rights of Indigenous Peoples' adopted at the 75th Conference of the International Law Association held in Sofia, Bulgaria, on 26–30 August 2012.

[21] Case C–398/13P *Inuit Tapiriit Kanatami and Others* v. *Commission*, para. 58.

[22] The 168 States Parties to the ICCPR are bound by Article 27 to ensure that 'persons belonging to [ethnic, religious or linguistic] minorities shall not be denied the right, in community with the other members of their group, to enjoy their own culture (...)'. See UN General Assembly, International Covenant on Civil and Political Rights, 16 December 1966, United Nations, Treaty Series, vol. 999, p. 171.

[23] This relates to Koskenniemi's theory on the 'structural bias' of judicial institutions, which varies depending on their 'mission' or 'special mandate'. According to Koskenniemi, judicial institutions are 'mechanised producers of outcomes that are internally validated by their embedded hierarchies of preference – their structural biases'. See M. Koskenniemi, 'Hegemonic Regimes' in M. A. Young (ed.), *Regime Interaction in International Law: Facing Fragmentation* (Cambridge University Press, 2012), pp. 305–24, 317. See also M. Koskenniemi, *From Apology to Utopia: the Structure of International Legal Argument* (Cambridge University Press, reissue with a new epilogue, 2005), pp. 600–15.

[24] See Case C–416/10 *Jozef Križan and Others* v. *Slovenská inšpekcia životného prostredia* [2013] ECR.

waste granted by the Slovak Environment Inspection to that company. In this case, the CJEU once again excluded the ECHR, and its interpretation by the ECtHR, from its legal reasoning, despite the requirement under Article 52(3) of the EUCFR. Noticeably, in its question referred to the CJEU, the Slovak Supreme Court referred *solely* to the right to property as guaranteed under Article 1 of Protocol 1 to the ECHR.[25] In its answer to that question, however, the CJEU referred *only* to the right to property under Article 17 of the EUCFR.[26] Thus, the CJEU substituted Article 1 of Protocol 1 to the ECHR with Article 17 of the EUCFR, regardless of the question referred to it by the parties, thereby voluntarily detaching itself from the jurisprudence of the ECtHR.[27] The solipsistic reasoning of the CJEU becomes even more explicit through its lack of reference to the argumentation of Advocate General (AG) Kokott in her Opinion delivered on 19 April 2012 in relation to this case. In the latter, AG Kokott based her argumentation on precedents of the CJEU, but referred even more extensively to the jurisprudence of the ECtHR.[28] This demonstrates AG Kokott's explicit and important reliance on the authoritative fundamental rights' protection as established by the ECtHR in Europe today. The CJEU, however, avoided any reference to these cases and to AG Kokott's Opinion.

Finally, this legal solipsism can be traced back to the very first case of conflict between environmental protection and human rights ever decided by a European court. In the *Hauer* case,[29] in which the applicant was refused permission to use her land for winegrowing, thereby allegedly violating her right to property for inter alia environmental protection purposes, the Court relied *solely* on EU law to interpret the conflict at hand. In this case, the CJEU's strategy to free itself from the authoritative

---

[25] Ibid., paras. 43 and 47.

[26] Ibid., para. 111.

[27] This praxis was confirmed in the *Siragusa* case, which concerned the alleged violation by a landscape conservation measure of the right to property of the applicant. The CJEU rejected again the legal authority and validity of the ECHR and its interpretation by the ECtHR, despite its existing jurisprudence with regard to landscape conservation in relation to the right to private property. See Case C–206/13 *Cruciano Siragusa* v. *Regione Sicilia – Soprintendenza Beni Culturali e Ambientali di Palermo* [2014] ECLI: EU:C:2014:126; and the existing case law of the ECtHR on landscape conservation, which the CJEU disregarded: *Chapman* v. *United Kingdom,* App. no. 27238/95 (ECtHR, 18 January 2001) and *Herrick* v. *United Kingdom,* App. no. 11185/84 (ECHR, 11 March 1985).

[28] See Opinion of AG Kokott, delivered on 19 April 2012, in relation to *Križan* v. *Slovenská inšpekcia životného prostredia,* para. 185 and especially n. 82.

[29] See Case C–44/79 *Liselotte Hauer* v. *Land Rheinland-Pfalz* [1979] ECR 3727.

interpretations of the ECtHR is subtler and requires a careful analysis of the semantics used by the Court. First, the Court stated that in accordance with the 'ideas' common to the constitutions of the Member States, which are also 'reflected' in Article 1 of Protocol 1 to the ECHR, the right to property is guaranteed in the Community legal order.[30] The reference to a mere 'reflection' of fundamental rights within the ECHR seems intentional, creating a sense of vagueness that legitimizes its own more precise analysis at a further stage. The Court, then, explicitly refers to Article 1 of Protocol 1 to the ECHR and acknowledges the two conditions of necessity and general interest for restrictions upon the right to private property to be lawful. Following this observation, however, it directly concludes that Article 1 of Protocol 1 to the ECHR 'does not enable a sufficiently precise answer to be given to the question'.[31] The lack of any reference to the extensive case law of the ECtHR with regard to the provision at hand leaves the interpretation of the Court incomplete, as the meaning of the ECHR is complemented by the interpretations of the ECtHR. It is, thus, not surprising that by merely referring to the black letter of the provision, the Court considers it as too imprecise to answer the question at hand. The supposed legal gap that the Court subsequently aims to fill is therefore created by its own neglect of the jurisprudence of the ECtHR. In short, it is not the lack of legal clarity, but rather the assertive claim for normative autonomy vis-à-vis the ECtHR that underlies the Court's reasoning. Hence, the key elements to understand the *Hauer* case are once more questions of normative independency and jurisdiction. The Court uses an intentional language to distance itself from the jurisdiction of the ECtHR.[32]

To conclude, the *Hauer* case shows that, already in 1979, the Court considered itself as the sole source of legitimacy in determining the compatibility of a Community environmental protection measure with fundamental rights. The recent *Inuit* and *Križan* cases prove that this praxis has only exacerbated since the EUCFR's entry into force in 2009. Since then, the CJEU has referred even less to the provisions of the ECHR and, most importantly, to the case law of the ECtHR, and this despite Article 52(3) of the EUCFR.[33] The legal solipsism of the CJEU is hereby

---

[30] Ibid., para. 17.

[31] Ibid., para. 19.

[32] See also J. Weiler, 'Human Rights: Member State, EU and ECHR Levels of Protection' (*EJIL: Talk!*, 7 June 2013) www.ejiltalk.org/human-rights-member-state-eu-and-echr-levels-of-protection/ (last accessed 16 March 2018).

[33] Indeed, 'statistics on the practice of the European Court since the Charter of Rights acquired binding force indicate that the frequency of citations of the European Court to

put in focus: when assessing the impact of EU environmental protection laws on fundamental rights or freedoms, the CJEU has constructed and continues to construct an internal fundamental rights system that is validated, from a Hartian perspective, by its own 'rule of recognition' that stands independently from any external criteria of validity.[34]

C   The General Interest and the CJEU: a Hermeneutic Mantra

The case law analysis demonstrates how the CJEU uses the general interest criterion as a way of systemically integrating environmental protection concerns into the EU legal order.

The very first time that the Court recognized environmental protection as a general interest was in the 1979 *Hauer* case.[35] As environmental protection had not yet been integrated into the Treaties,[36] the Court had to derive this general interest from the domestic constitutions and legislations of its Member States. In doing so, however, it explicitly relied on the constitutions of only three of the then nine Member States (Germany, Italy and Ireland). For the other countries, the Court relied on domestic laws and recognized that 'the legislature [can] control the use of private property in accordance with the general interest' and that 'in all the Member States there is legislation on ... the protection of the environment ... which imposes restrictions ... on the use of real

the European Convention on Human Rights has declined, and that whereas the Court used to cite the ECHR significantly more often than the Charter in cases involving human rights claims, the reverse is now the case'. See G. de Búrca, 'After the EU Charter of Fundamental Rights: The Court of Justice as a Human Rights Adjudicator?', *Maastricht Journal of European and Comparative Law*, 20 (2013), 168, 175.

[34] An analogy can be constructed between Koskenniemi's view on functional regimes of international law and the judicial institutions of these specialized regimes. For Koskenniemi, 'like states, functional regimes operate as clusters of interest and knowledge, and like states they act in solipsistic and imperial ways – they are coded so as to perceive only themselves and their own preferences and to translate those mechanically into the preferences of everyone'. This is also observable in the case law of judicial mechanisms operating within these legal regimes, as hereby proved with the case law of the CJEU. See Koskenniemi, 'Hegemonic Regimes', p. 318. See also G. Teubner and A. Fischer-Lescano, 'Regime-Collisions: The Vain Search for Legal Unity in the Fragmentation of Global Law', *Michigan Journal of International Law*, 25 (2004), 999–1046.

[35] See *Hauer* v. *Land Rheinland-Pfalz* .

[36] The first explicit legal integration of an environmental protection provision within a European Treaty saw the light of day in 1987, with the entry into force of the Single European Act, of which Title VII is entitled 'Environment'. See Single European Act [1987] OJ L169.

property'.[37] On this ground, the Court concluded that the limitation of
the right to property for environmental protection is 'a type of restriction which is known and accepted as lawful, in identical or similar
forms, in the constitutional structure of *all* the Member States'.[38]
A textual analysis sheds light on the active role taken by the Court,
ahead of the EU legislature, to grant a level of protection to the
environment that is higher than the one granted to it by most of
the Member States at that time. Noticeably, the Court presented the
normative argument that the general interest in environmental protection can interfere with private property as supposedly being induced
from an analysis of the constitutional traditions of the Member States.
In reality, however, the Court went further than many of the Member
States (six out of nine) in constitutionally recognizing environmental
protection as a general interest capable of limiting the fundamental
right to property. The lack of explicit environmental protection provisions in six out of nine constitutions illustrates this reality. Thus, at
a time where environmental protection issues were not yet at the
centre of the debate but were only beginning to be discussed at
international level,[39] it is noteworthy how the Court overcame this
legal weakness and legally integrated environmental protection within
the EU legal framework by recognizing it as a general interest that can
trump property rights.

Ever since 1979, the legitimacy of environmental protection's interference with fundamental rights has been established by mere reference
to the vague and substantively indeterminate heuristic of 'general interest' in the Court's own legal precedents. This practice has allowed judges
to grant ever-stronger protection to the environment without being
bound by the rather general and weak protection granted to it by the

---

[37] See *Hauer* v. *Land Rheinland-Pfalz*, para. 20.
[38] Ibid., para. 22 (emphasis added).
[39] It is commonly recognized that modern international environmental law finds its origins
in the *Zeitgeist* of the 1970s. The 1972 Stockholm Declaration on the Human
Environment aimed at 'inspiring and guiding the peoples of the world in the preservation
and enhancement of the human environment'. The same year, the 1972 Conference of the
European Economic Community Heads of State was held in Paris, and the first
Environment Action Programme was created in 1973. See the Preamble of the
Declaration of the United Nations Conference on the Human Environment, adopted in
Stockholm on 16 June 1972: U.N. Doc. A/Conf.48/14/Rev. 1 (1973) 11 ILM 1416 (1972).
See also C. Knill and D. Liefferink, 'The Establishment of EU Environmental Policy' in
A. Jordan and C. Adelle (eds.), *Environmental Policy in the European Union: Contexts,
Actors and Policy Dynamics*, 3rd edn. (Routledge, 2013).

Treaties.[40] In other words, the use of this generic term allows the CJEU progressively to include new environmental protection concerns as forming part of the indefinite general interest in environmental protection, thereby granting an ever-stronger protection to the environment. In 1985 in the *ADBHU* case, for instance, the Court recognized that restrictions on the fundamental freedoms of trade and competition for environmental protection purposes are 'justified by the pursuit of the objective of environmental protection, which is in the general interest'.[41] Thereby, the CJEU expanded the normative content of the general interest in environmental protection by recognizing specific measures (here, treatment of waste oils) as part of it and as capable to justify restrictions, this time, on freedoms of trade and competition. In doing so, the judges adopted a proactive approach to environmental protection even before it was explicitly integrated within the Single European Act (SEA) in 1987, thereby acting as 'quasi-legislators'.

The quasi 'law-making' powers of the Court are made even more explicit when analysing how it recognized environmental protection as, in 1979, an 'object of general interest';[42] and shortly after, in 1985, as a 'Community's essential objective';[43] in 1988, as a 'mandatory requirement';[44] and finally, in 1998, as an 'imperative requirement'.[45] This shows how the Court has constantly strengthened the degree of importance of environmental

---

[40] EU environmental law is characterized by a principle-based approach. Under the current constitutional arrangements, only Article 11 of the Treaty on the Functioning of the European Union (TFEU) and Article 37 of the EUCFR are formulated as legal obligations. On the one hand, Article 11 of the TFEU provides that '[e]nvironmental protection requirements must be integrated into the definition and implementation of the Union's policies and activities, in particular with a view to promoting sustainable development'. The objective of sustainable development, however, is based on the three equally important objectives of environmental care, social justice and economic growth. Thus, Article 11 of the TFEU already entails a policy-balancing requirement at its core. Article 37 of the EUCFR, on the other hand, is only a principle and does not grant any substantive or procedural right to a healthy environment. The other core provisions on environmental protection, namely Article 3(3) of the Treaty on European Union (TEU) (which recognizes environmental protection as one of the five general objectives of EU law) and Articles 191–3 of the TFEU (which set out the EU's objectives in the field of environmental policies) are all formulated as programmatic policy-objectives. Thus, none of these provisions recognizes any rights; rather, they are only formulated as policy competences.

[41] See Case 240/83 *Procureur de la République* v. *Association de défense des brûleurs d'huiles usagées (ADBHU)* [1985] ECR 531, para. 42.

[42] See *Hauer* v. *Land Rheinland-Pfalz*, para. 2.1.

[43] See *Procureur de la République* v. *ADBHU*, para. 13.

[44] See Case 302/86 *Commission* v. *Denmark (Danish Bottles)* [1988] ECR 4607, para. 8.

[45] See Case C–341/95 *Gianni Bettati* v. *Safety Hi-Tech Srl* [1998] ECR I–04355, para. 63.

protection, characterized as 'mandatory' from 1987 on, when it was explicitly included in the SEA (although subject to the principle of subsidiarity), and as 'imperative' from 1992 on, when it became legally binding upon the EU institutions.[46] It appears, thus, that it is the EU legislature that followed the judges' proactive role in legally integrating environmental protection within the EU legal framework in 1987, after the Court had already recognized it as an object of general interest and then a Community essential objective in, respectively, 1979 and 1985.

More recently, in the *Križan* case,[47] the CJEU recognized that the procedural rights to consultation and participation in the decision-making process of Mr Križan and forty-three other applicants, as guaranteed under the EU Aarhus Directives,[48] are exercised in, and therefore part of, the general interest in environmental protection. The violation of the exercise of such rights was therefore recognized as rendering unlawful the grant of a permit to construct a landfill site for waste. In this context, the CJEU recalled once more that 'established case law has shown that protection of the environment is one of those objectives [of general interest] and is therefore capable of justifying a restriction on the use of the right to property'.[49] To come to this conclusion, the CJEU relied on four legal precedents in which it had already recognized the necessity to protect the environment as a general interest.[50] Hence, by simply recalling its settled case law, the CJEU seemingly only repeated what former AG Jacobs has framed as its 'mantra on environmental protection'.[51] The use of the word 'mantra' underlines the CJEU's repetitiveness in recognizing environmental protection as a general interest. Although these cases all cover different facts, the CJEU refers to the general interest in environmental protection as

---

[46] See Consolidated Version of the Treaty Establishing the European Community [1992] [2002] OJ C325/33.

[47] See *Križan v. Slovenská inšpekcia životného prostredia.*

[48] See Parliament and Council Directive 2003/4/EC on public access to environmental information on the environment [2003] OJ 1990 L158/56; and Council Directive 85/337/EEC on the assessment of the effects of certain public and private projects on the environment [1985] OJ 1985 L175/40, as amended by Parliament and Council Directive 2003/35/EC [2003] OJ 2003 L156/17.

[49] See *Križan v. Slovenská inšpekcia životného prostredia*, para 114.

[50] See *Procureur de la République v. ADBHU*, para. 13; *Danish Bottles*, para. 8; Case C–213/96 *Outokumpu* [1998] ECR I–1777, para. 32; and Joined Cases C–379/08 *Raffinerie Mediterranee (ERG) SpA, Polimeri Europa SpA and Syndial SpA v. Ministero dello Sviluppo economico and Others* and C–380/08 *ENI SpA v. Ministero Ambiente e Tutela del Territorio e del Mare and Others* [2010] ECR I–2007, para. 81.

[51] F. Jacobs, 'The Role of the European Court of Justice in the Protection of the Environment', *Journal of Environmental Law*, 18 (2006), 185–205, 203.

a generic term, without further substantive engagement with its content. This mantra is, thus, supposedly non-substantive. In reality, however, we can see from the cases that the repetition of this mantra masks the CJEU's normative engagement with the substance of this general interest. By recognizing procedural features of environmental protection as constitutive elements of the general interest in environmental protection, the CJEU clearly expanded the meaning of this general interest. In other words, the CJEU ingeniously integrated environmental procedural rights that stem from the EU Aarhus Directives into the general interest in environmental protection. Thereby, the CJEU granted specific normative weight to these Directives in relationship to the fundamental rights enshrined in the EUCFR.

To conclude, the general interest is used by the CJEU normatively to engage with EU environmental law and its relationship with EU fundamental rights and freedoms. This hermeneutic entails specific consequences, as the CJEU thereby implicitly shapes the content of this general interest in environmental protection without being restricted to the limited content of Article 3(3) of the TEU, Articles 11 and 191–193 of the TFEU and Article 37 of the EUCFR.[52] The non-delineated content of the general interest in environmental protection allows the CJEU systemically to integrate new components as part of this general interest, capable of restricting fundamental rights or freedoms. Inside the 'black box' of the general interest criterion, a substantive expansion and refinement of EU environmental protection laws occurs, with the CJEU as a pivotal normative actor.

D   On the Borders of Competence: the CJEU as Quasi 'Law-Maker'

A third feature of the CJEU's legal reasoning induced from the cases is its normative engagement with the content of EU environmental protection laws even when it lacks the jurisdiction to do so.

In the *Inuit* case,[53] the CJEU overcame the legal *lacunae* on animal welfare protection[54] by seemingly disguising the rationale of the

---

[52] See n. 40.
[53] See Case T–526/10 *Inuit Tapiriit Kanatami and Others* v. *Commission* [2013] ECR. These conclusions were confirmed on appeal in Case C–398/13P *Inuit Tapiriit Kanatami and Others* v. *Commission* [2015] EU:C:2015:535.
[54] Article 13 of the TFEU is the only provision that touches upon animal welfare. Under this provision, EU institutions are invited to take animal welfare into consideration only when formulating and implementing other matters of EU law.

legislation as an internal market harmonisation measure. Indeed, the CJEU concluded that the objective of the Regulation on trade in seal products 'is not to safeguard the welfare of animals but to improve the functioning of the internal market'.[55] And yet, the CJEU conceded that it was initially '[i]n response to concerns of citizens and consumers about ... animal welfare ... because of the suffering caused to those animals when they were killed and skinned' that the Regulation was adopted.[56] Thus, in the absence of specific competences to legislate on animal welfare protection, the EU legislature seems to have ingeniously handled the concerns of EU citizens by using former Article 95 of the Treaty Establishing the European Community (EC)[57] (today, Article 114 of the TFEU) as a legal basis for adopting measures to protect seals. Since the objective of Article 95 of the EC is limited to market integration, however, it argued that the objective of the Regulation was to avoid disharmonized trade regulations in seal products.[58] The instrumental use of Article 95 of the EC had already been criticized for this reason, and the EU legislature had been accused of using it as a pretext to implement policy goals other than harmonizing the internal market.[59] By bypassing the lack of legal competence to legislate on animal welfare, however, the EU legislature found a creative way to answer to EU citizens' concerns by using Article 95 of the EC as a 'mask'. This sheds light on the integration of animal welfare concerns within EU environmental policies despite the restricted legislative leeway in that regard. Hence, the case demonstrates how the absence of explicit animal welfare competences in the hands of the Commission is compensated for by the CJEU's proactive (and instrumental) interpretation of other treaty provisions. In doing so, the CJEU normatively contributes to the proliferation of environmental protection in the EU legal space.

---

[55] Case C–398/13P *Inuit Tapiriit Kanatami and Others* v. *Commission* [2015] EU: C:2015:535, para. 35.

[56] Ibid., para. 38.

[57] Article 95 of the EC provides that ' ... [t]he Council shall ... adopt the measures for the approximation of the provisions laid down by law, regulation or administrative action in Member States which have as their object the establishment and functioning of the internal market'.

[58] Case C–398/13P *Inuit Tapiriit Kanatami and Others* v. *Commission* [2015] EU: C:2015:535, para. 40.

[59] See H.-W. Liu, 'Harmonizing the internal market, or public health? – revisiting Case C–491/01 (British American Tobacco) and Case C–380/03 (Tobacco advertising II)', *Columbia Journal of European Law* 15 (2009), 41–45.

The ingenious feature of the CJEU's legal reasoning substantively to engage with EU environmental protection laws and their limits on fundamental rights or freedoms, despite its limited competence, is illustrated even more explicitly in the *Siragusa* case.[60] There, the CJEU was asked to determine whether a provision under the Italian Code of Cultural Heritage and Landscape is precluded in accordance with the right to property under Article 17 of the EUCFR and the principle of proportionality. The CJEU, however, lacked the jurisdiction to answer the question referred to it by the Italian court, as the national legislation had not been adopted with the objective of implementing EU law. Thus, the CJEU had no competence to review the conflict at hand, as, under Article 51 of the EUCFR, it can interpret domestic measures in the light of the EUCFR *only* when Member States are implementing EU law. Despite its lack of jurisdiction, however, the CJEU substantively engaged with the conflict at hand. First, the CJEU reaffirmed that 'no specific obligations to protect the landscape ... are imposed on the Member States by [the Treaties]; nor are such obligations imposed by the legislation relating to the Aarhus Convention, nor by Directives 2003/4 [on public access to environmental information] and 2011/92 [on the assessment of the effects of certain public and private projects on the environment]'.[61]

These conclusions confirm the previous findings of the Court in the *Annibaldi* case, in which it recognized that a piece of national legislation that established a nature and archaeological park in order to protect and enhance the 'value' of the environment and the 'cultural heritage' of the area concerned, did not fall within the scope of Community law.[62] In the *Siragusa* case, however, the CJEU *in fine* provided a specific place for landscape protection with regard to procedural environmental rights, by stating that 'the landscape is one of the factors to be taken into consideration in assessing the impact of a project on the environment ... and ... part of the environmental information referred to in the Aarhus Convention'.[63] In other words, while the CJEU confirmed that there is no specific obligation of landscape protection under EU law, it did

---

[60] See Case C–206/13 *Cruciano Siragusa* v. *Regione Sicilia – Soprintendenza Beni Culturali e Ambientali di Palermo* [2014] ECLI:EU:C:2014:126.

[61] Ibid., para. 27.

[62] See Case C–309/96 *Daniele Annibaldi* v. *Sindaco del Comune di Guidonia and Presidente Regione Lazio* [1997] ECR I–07493, para. 24. Importantly, the CJEU also lacked jurisdiction in this case as the question referred was not directly a matter of Community law.

[63] *Cruciano Siragusa* v. *Regione Sicilia*, para. 28.

normatively expand the scope of protection to be granted to the environment by recognizing landscape protection as part of the procedural
environmental rights that are safeguarded under the Aarhus
Convention. In doing so, the CJEU creatively overcame the lack of
explicit legislative provision on landscape protection in order to expand
the normative content of what, under EU law, procedural environmental
protection entails.

Notably, this normative expansion of procedural environmental protection standards took place despite the CJEU's lack of jurisdiction to
interpret the referred question at hand. The same was true in the
Annibaldi case. Thus, the CJEU first substantively engaged with the
content of landscape protection in 1997, when it recognized that
the 'value' and 'cultural heritage' of the land were *not* part of EU environmental protection policies. In 2014, it again substantively engaged with
the question of landscape protection, but this time it specified that it *is*
one of the factors to be taken into consideration in undertaking environmental impact assessments. Thereby, the CJEU expanded the normative
content of procedural environmental protection, despite no specific legal
provision having been adopted in the meantime, to include landscape
protection into EU environmental law. Remarkably, the CJEU proactively contributes to the legitimization, definition and proliferation of EU
environmental law, although it lacks the strict competence to do so.
The lack of jurisdiction demonstrates that the CJEU does not perceive
itself as being merely an organ of conflict-resolution, but also as an
important agent in the substantive development of EU environmental
law.[64]

To conclude, these cases illustrate how the CJEU often acts as
a proactive normative agent when introducing and shaping EU environmental protection laws, even when it is, *de jure,* not entitled to do so.
The CJEU innovatively bypasses its lack of jurisdiction to interpret both
EU environmental law and its infringement of fundamental rights,
thereby substantively shaping the rule on environmental protection and
contributing to its progressive expansion. This analysis demonstrates
how important the CJEU has been in the normative proliferation and
refinement of environmental protection in the EU legal space. It allows us

---

[64] This was also observed in the *Leth* case, in which the CJEU, while lacking jurisdiction,
defined the scope of the EU Directive on Assessment of the Effects of Certain Public and
Private Projects on the Environment, and interpreted the conflict between this Directive
and the right to property of the applicant in favour of environmental protection. See Case
C–420/11 *Jutta Leth* v. *Republik Österreich and Land Niederösterreich* [2013] ECR.

to understand how the contours of EU environmental protection policies are legitimized and defined, sometimes by adding content to it (such as landscape conservation in the *Siragusa* case) and at other times by denying its supposed content (as in the *Annibaldi* case with regard to the value and cultural heritage of the land). In short, the quasi 'law-making' role of the CJEU has been pivotal in legitimizing, structuring and refining environmental protection in EU law. The Court has shown itself to be a proactive normative player for EU environmental protection.

E   A Managerial Approach to Legal Conflict Resolution

Finally, the cases demonstrate how, in solving conflicts between environmental protection laws and fundamental rights and freedoms, the CJEU adopts a managerial approach based on the assessment of experts, thereby stepping away from strict (formal) legal reasoning. By adopting economic, technical and scientific vocabularies, the CJEU handles legal problems as managerial problems. This corresponds to deference from law to the 'politics of expertise'.[65]

The *Arcelor* case provides a straightforward example.[66] In this case, the CJEU had to determine whether Directive 2003/87/EC establishing a Scheme for Greenhouse Gas Emission Allowance Trading within the Community (2003 Directive on EU Emission Trading System (ETS))[67]

---

[65] See M.-C. Petersmann, 'Rights and Expertise: Assessing the CJEU's Managerial Approach to Conflict Adjudication' in F. Baetens (ed.), The Legitimacy of Unseen Actors in International Adjudication (Cambridge University Press, in press). On the 'politcs of expertise', see M. Koskenniemi, 'The Fate of Public International Law: Between Techniques and Politics', *Modern Law Review*, 70 (2007), 10.

[66] See Case C-127/07 *Société Arcelor Atlantique et Lorraine and Others* v. *Premier ministre, Ministre de l'Écologie et du Développement durable and Ministre de l'Économie, des Finances et de l'Industrie* [2008] ECR I-09895.

[67] The EU Emissions Trading System (ETS) enables the EU and the Member States to meet the commitments to reduce greenhouse gas (GHG) emissions made in the context of the Kyoto Protocol to the United Nations Framework Convention on Climate Change. The ETS works on the 'cap and trade' principle. A 'cap', or limit, is set on the total amount of certain GHGs that can be emitted by the factories, power plants and other installations in the system. The cap is reduced over time so that total emissions fall. Within the cap, companies receive or buy emission allowances that they can trade with one another as needed. The limit of the total number of allowances available ensures that they have a value. After each year, a company must surrender enough allowances to cover all its emissions, as otherwise heavy fines are imposed. If a company reduces its emissions, it can keep the spare allowances to cover its future needs or else sell them to another company that is short of allowances. See 'The EU Emissions Trading System (EU ETS)' http://ec.europa.eu/clima/policies/ets/index_en.htm (last accessed 16 March 2018).

breached the principle of equal treatment of Arcelor. Arcelor, a private company in the steel sector, claimed that it was victim of unjustifiable different treatment in comparison with companies from the plastics and aluminium sectors not yet included in the Directive. In interpreting the latter, the CJEU held that 'in the exercise of the powers conferred on it, the Community legislature has a broad discretion where its action involves political, economic and social choices and where it is called on to undertake complex assessments and evaluations'.[68] Notably, environmental protection had, already back in the 1990s, been attributed the status of a 'complex' issue, which grants the EU legislature wide discretion.[69] Thus, when the EU legislature has to balance 'political, economic and social choices' based on 'complex assessments and evaluations' in the light of environmental protection, it enjoys a wide margin of discretion to develop these rules. Hence, the EU legislature can develop environmental legislation capable of interfering with fundamental freedoms and rights, but the CJEU does not review these choices, and national authorities have to abide by them. The EU's political, economic and social choices, however, must be based on 'objective criteria appropriate to the aim pursued', and take into consideration 'all the facts and the technical and scientific data available at the time of adoption of the act in question'.[70] In trying objectively to justify the difference in treatment, the Parliament, Council and Commission submitted claims on the basis of the 'novelty', 'complexity' and 'necessity' of the Directive, and grounded this justification on statistics and scientific data prepared by expert bodies.[71] The reliance on statistics and scientific data illustrates how the EU institutions' role in adopting environmental laws is largely expert driven and stands far from the traditional

---

[68] Société Arcelor Atlantique et Lorraine v. Premier ministre, para. 57.

[69] See Bettati v. Safety Hi-Tech Srl. See also Case C–284/95 Safety Hi-Tech Srl v. S. & T. Srl. [1998] ECR I–04301, which covers mutatis mutandis the same factual matrix and conflict.

[70] Société Arcelor Atlantique et Lorraine v. Premier ministre, para. 58. The need to base environmental policies on scientific data had already been recognized in the Safety Hi-Tech case in 1998: '[a]rticle 130r(3) of the Treaty requires the Community, in preparing its policy on the environment, to take account in particular of available scientific and technical data' (ibid., para. 51). This condition still holds under the current Article 191(3) of the TFEU (ex Article 130(r) of the EC).

[71] Ibid., paras. 49–54. In this case, the scientific data was based on a report entitled 'Economic Evaluation of Sectoral Emission Reduction Objectives for Climate Change. Top-down Analysis of Greenhouse Gas Emission Reduction Possibilities in the EU. Final Report, March 2001', written by P. Capros, N. Kouvaritakis and L. Mantzos (para. 52) and on statistics from the European Pollutant Emission Register for 2001 (para. 55).

patterns of legal reasoning that characterize fundamental rights doctrine. Policy choices grounded in scientific data and developed by technocrats[72] are granted the presumption of legality, provided by the legal hermeneutic of 'margin of discretion'. As recognized by Nele Matz-Lück, the 'enhanced need for interaction between different actors involved in policy- and law-making, standard-setting and interpretation corresponds to a decline of formalism in international law'.[73] This decline of formalism is observable at the EU level in the practice and legal reasoning of the CJEU. Once more, the creative and innovative interpretative praxis of the CJEU is hereby illustrated.

Albeit without referring back to the arguments of the EU legislature, the CJEU picked up the adjectives used by the latter and aligned its reasoning with the EU institutions by defining the Directive as 'novel and complex'.[74] By referring to the step-by-step approach adopted by the EU legislature, and to the technical and scientific information submitted by the experts, the CJEU rightfully recognized that the difference in treatment was 'objectively justified'.[75] Thus, no breach of the principle of equal treatment was found. In contrast to a formal interpretation, technical arguments have replaced legal arguments and represent 'that which is "true"'[76] or, in other words, objective scientific findings. Implicitly, the CJEU confirmed the managerial competences of the EU legislature by granting it a broad discretion in that regard, and by reviewing its measures only in the event of a manifest lack of objective criteria appropriate to achieve the aim of environmental protection.

This *topos* is observable in a number of cases. In the *Inuit* case,[77] in order to assess the animal welfare aspects of the practice of killing and skinning seals, the Commission mandated the Panel on Animal Health

---

[72] When analysing the EU's managerial approach to solving problems, Klabbers refers to 'expert bodies of limited composition that have the task to define and implement technical issues', while Koskenniemi refers to 'specialized elite of managerial experts [that] carries out strategic choices'. See J. Klabbers, 'Two Concepts of International Organization', *International Organizations Law Review*, 2 (2005), 281; and Koskenniemi, 'Hegemonic Regimes', p. 305. Both these definitions illustrate how technical reasoning determines legal outcomes.

[73] N. Matz-Lück, 'Norm Interpretation across International Regimes: Competences and Legitimacy' in M. A. Young (ed.), *Regime Interaction in International Law: Facing Fragmentation* (Cambridge University Press, 2012), p. 204.

[74] *Société Arcelor Atlantique et Lorraine* v. *Premier ministre*, para. 60.

[75] Ibid.

[76] See Koskenniemi, 'Hegemonic Regimes', p. 313.

[77] See Case T–526/10 *Inuit Tapiriit Kanatami and Others* v. *Commission* [2013] ECR.

and Welfare to write a report.[78] This practice was proved to be inherently inhumane, supported by scientific evidence.[79] The scientific, technical and expert driven policy calculus that led to the adoption of the Regulation were backed by the CJEU, which followed the position of the Commission by granting it a wide margin of policy discretion, given the complexity of the issue at hand.

Similarly, in the *Romonta* case, the CJEU also granted a wide discretion to the Commission for adopting complex environmental protection policies based on scientific and technical data collected by expert bodies.[80] More specifically, the CJEU had to assess whether the Commission infringed the freedom to choose an occupation (Article 15 of the EUCFR), the freedom to conduct a business (Article 16 of the EUCFR) and the right to property (Article 17 of the EUCFR) of a private company, Romonta, by refusing to grant it supplementary free allowances as provided for in the German law implementing the 2003 Directive on EU ETS. In doing so, the CJEU granted a 'wide discretion' to the Commission in areas entailing 'political, economic and social choices' and in which the Commission is called upon to undertake 'complex assessments and evaluations' to reduce GHG emissions by means of a 'cost-effective' and 'economically efficient' trading scheme.[81] As in the *Arcelor* case, the policy trade-offs were left in the hands of the Commission, and the rights entailed in the EUCFR were hereby again subordinated to the policy discretion exercised by the Commission. Once more, the CJEU reviewed the balancing exercise of the Commission on the basis of technical and scientific data, and concluded that, in accordance with the 'polluter pays' principle, and as the benefit for the environment depends on the stringency of the total quantity of allowances allocated, the Commission was right not to adopt a hardship clause as

---

[78] Scientific institutions were commissioned to research on the animal welfare aspects of methods for killing and skinning of seals. It is based on the results of these researches that the EU institutions approved the adoption of the Regulation. See 'Scientific Opinion of the Panel on Animal Health and Welfare on a request from the Commission on the Animal Welfare aspects of the killing and skinning of seals', *The EFSA Journal*, 610 (2007), 1–122. See also D. Cambou, 'The Impact of the Ban on Seal Products on the Rights of Indigenous Peoples: A European Issue', *The Yearbook of Polar Law*, (2013), 389–415, 392.

[79] Case T–526/10 *Inuit Tapiriit Kanatami and Others* v. *Commission* [2013] ECR, para. 38.

[80] See Case T–614/13 *Romonta GmbH* v. *European Commission* [2014] ECLI:EU: T:2014:835, currently under appeal before the CJEU.

[81] Ibid., para. 63.

provided for in the German law. In the opposite scenario, operators would have less of an incentive to reduce their emissions through 'economic or technical adjustment measures'.[82] This line of argumentation again illuminates how managerial arguments supplement a strict legal reasoning in the policy-oriented adjudication of the CJEU. Technical and scientific examinations are the grounds on which legal and judicial decisions are taken: the Commission's policy is justified by an 'effective' and 'efficient' outcome aimed at achieving an optimal result.

A specific mode of governance and adjudication is highlighted here: one that facilitates expert-based methods of administrative decision-making to interfere with fundamental freedoms and rights at any time. Interestingly, we notice in the CJEU's argumentation how the administrative and managerial features of environmental protection are given legal weight in its judicial reasoning. All in all, the 'management of the allowance trading scheme' and the 'administrative complexity', 'burden' or 'feasibility' of the Directive are referred to seven times in the case.[83]

A clear managerial approach to conflict resolution is discernible, with a noticeable shift from tools of legal reasoning to methods of scientific or administrative policy balancing. Thereby, the CJEU allows for a process of legal reasoning that stands far from the traditional legalistic concept of law and adjudication and seems to embrace a much more policy-based or managerial understanding of the conflict within the EU legal order. This policy-oriented adjudication mirrors the policy-oriented formulation of EU environmental law in general, and the balance of interests as political calculus in search of optimal outcomes that emerge when EU environmental protection laws and fundamental rights and freedoms collide.

F Conclusion

By analysing the case law of the CJEU with regard to conflicts between EU environmental protection laws and fundamental rights and freedoms, four main characteristics of the legal reasoning of the CJEU unfold.

The first feature of the CJEU's reasoning in solving conflicts between environmental protection laws and human rights is its 'legal solipsism'. In normatively engaging with the conflict at hand, the CJEU structurally discards other applicable sources of international law. Its struggle for

---

[82] Ibid., para. 92.
[83] Ibid., paras. 53, 55, 65, 66, 71.

normative independency, and for developing an autonomous interpretation of the fundamental rights and freedoms enshrined within the EUCFR, is put under the spotlight. This is especially true with regard to the ECtHR: the cases translate the hostility from the part of the CJEU towards the idea of subordination or compliance to the authority of the ECtHR.[84] In short, the CJEU's internal rule of recognition only acknowledges EU law as valid. In doing so, however, it contributes to the pluralism, fragmentation and competition of human rights protection in the European legal space.

The second feature of the CJEU's reasoning is its ingenious recognition of environmental protection as a general interest capable of limiting relative fundamental rights or freedoms. The specific content of this general interest in environmental protection, the cases demonstrate, is prone to permanent substantive revision and expansion in the jurisprudence of the CJEU. By recognizing some normative and procedural attributes as forming part of the general interest in environmental protection, the CJEU has proven to be an important actor in the normative expansion of environmental protection in the EU. In short, the 'mantra' of the general interest in environmental protection is employed as a vehicle for systemic legal integration of new social concerns as constitutive elements of environmental protection. The general interest criterion thus plays an essential role in the normative development of environmental protection in the case law of the CJEU.

A third feature that characterizes the CJEU's practice in solving conflicts between EU environmental protection laws and fundamental rights and freedoms is the role that it sometimes plays as a quasi 'law-maker'. The cases demonstrate how the CJEU creatively engages with the content of EU environmental law by interpreting its impact on fundamental rights and freedoms even when it does not have the competence to do so. In these circumstances, the CJEU disregards what is expected from it *de jure* and deems its interpretation as being too crucial not to be given. The normative engagement with EU environmental law is hereby reaffirmed, since even when it is not explicitly required to do so, the CJEU

---

[84] This legitimizes the concerns raised by Weiler on the struggle for hegemony and the 'historic' competition between the CJEU and the ECtHR. See Weiler, 'Human Rights'www.ejiltalk.org/human-rights-member-state-eu-and-echr-levels-of-protection/ (last accessed 16 March 2018). See also V. Tzevelekos, 'When Elephants Fight it is the Grass that Suffers: "Hegemonic Struggle" in Europe and the Side-Effects for International Law' in K. Dzehtsiarou et al., *Human Rights Law in Europe, The Influence, Overlaps and Contradictions of the EU and the ECHR* (Routledge, 2014), pp. 9–34.

redefines and reshapes the contours of EU environmental protection laws and the extent to which they can interfere with fundamental rights or freedoms.

Finally, the cases illustrate how the CJEU's reliance on scientific and technical data has given rise to a specific mode of legal reasoning that closely aligns with modes of 'managerial' governance. The cases demonstrate how questions of ultimate legal validity in the CJEU's fundamental rights jurisprudence are determined by managerial assessments undertaken by the EU legislature and based on experts' studies. Technical and scientific examinations are the grounds on which legal decisions are adopted by the EU legislature. These decisions are in turn backed by the CJEU through the wide discretion it grants to the EU legislature. Given today's proliferation of environmental protection concerns, the EU institutions and the CJEU must balance complex policies that determine the level of restriction of fundamental freedoms and rights that are legitimized for the general interest in environmental protection. This informs us on the nature of the 'general interest' in environmental protection, and how its normative structures are shaped by administrative procedures, scientific research, planning programmes, complex assessments and evaluations. A technical regulatory exercise undertaken by EU institutions on the basis of non-legal managerial assessments of environmental protection are prone to restrict relative freedoms and rights in the EU. In short, the case law analysis signals a shift from the traditional, hierarchical processes of fundamental rights jurisprudence to managerial processes of policy balancing, based on scientific expertise on environmental protection. The authority of the CJEU's judgments is found in the scientific and technical expertise on which it bases its policy-oriented reasoning.

10

Silent Implications of *US-Tuna II*: Greening Market Behaviour through the WTO

CRISTIANE DERANI AND ARTHUR RODRIGUES
DALMARCO

A Introduction

International law, as we see it today, is a creation from the end of the eighteenth century. At that time, the world was amply occupied by colonial structures, linked by commercial trade, having Europe, and especially England, at the epicentre of this colonial trade system thanks to the flourishing Industrial Revolution and extremely well-developed trade routes. We take this historical background as a single thread of the juridical and economic considerations in this chapter. The central idea of this chapter follows the Benthamian perspective, which relies on taking international regulation as a source of individual and collective welfare. Although the creator of the expression "international law" bears in mind a law among nations, he argues on a moral basis that he called a "principle of utility."[1]

Briefly, for Bentham, the legally based relationship between nations aims at having better utility for nations and peoples. Bentham's utilitarianism strengthens the idea of a normative positivism of international

---

[1] "The principle of utility is that which approves or disapproves every action whatsoever, according to the tendency it appears to have to augment or diminish the happiness of the party whose interest is in question; in other words, to promote or oppose that happiness. I say of every action whatsoever, and therefore not only of every action of a private individual, but of every measure of government. Utility is that property in any object, whereby it tends to produce benefit, advantage, pleasure, good, or happiness, (all this in the present case comes to the same thing) or (what comes again to the same thing) to prevent the happening of mischief, pain, evil, or unhappiness to the party whose interest is considered: if that party be the community in general, then the happiness of the community: if a particular individual, then the happiness of that individual." (Jeremy Bentham, *An Introduction to the Principles of Morals and Legislation* (first published in 1781), p. 15).

law. This idea from the nineteenth century will be decisive for international juridical reconstruction after World War II.

Notwithstanding, as will be described in the first part of this chapter, the twentieth century brought an overwhelming complexity to Bentham's concepts and the idea of happiness or welfare. As such, the arrangement of elements in order to build the wealth of nations was much more diversified and controversial. This new situation was reflected by the development of the norms and decisions of the General Agreement on Tariffs and Trade (GATT) and the World Trade Organization (WTO). From initial concepts aimed at controlling trade tariffs and raising wealth, a new type of regulation appeared during the Uruguay Round of negotiations that closed with the Marrakesh Agreement in 1994.[2]

Conscious of the immanent relationship between law, economics, and environment in GATT/WTO, this chapter acknowledges that, once environmental regulation is there, it provokes a change in the meaning of the primeval idea of what raising wealth is. For a clear comprehension of that statement, it is necessary to take the trade law regime as part of international law, and for this reason the former absorbs the fundamental structure and principles from the latter. It means, for example, that the Trade Related Environmental Agreements (TREA) and the Vienna Convention on the Law of Treaties (VCLT) express themselves in the trade law regime.

Subsequently, the second part of this chapter presents the *US-Tuna II* case, highlighting the decision of the WTO Appellate Body (AB) on labeling of environmentally friendly production methods and technical barriers to trade. The debate about different labeling schemes for dolphin-safe fisheries is much more market driven than environment oriented[3] – a fact that dislocates the discussions toward arguments related to technical barriers to trade – instead of consistent considerations about adopting environmental measures.

Positive labeling that indicates responsible practice, internalizing some of its costs, shows a company's awareness of environmental production risks and publicizes its care for the common good. Such a decision, taken within the companies' own interests, is welcomed by *US-Tuna II*; mindful of its inconsistency with the Agreement on Technical Barriers to

---

[2] See, for example, the multiplicity of provisions encompassed in Annex 1's Agreements.
[3] We argue that although both elements can be identified in different labeling schemes, the generally predominant characteristic in labeling solutions – such as the one presented above – is their market nature, which is collaterally aimed at environmental results.

Trade (TBT Agreement), this chapter argues that WTO decisions can induce future effects that transcend disputes and reach those at the forefront of production. A WTO decision on production and process methods, with its juridical, economic, and environmental ingredients, is a gateway for technical changes and adoption of new technologies that are more accountable to society. Thus, the WTO remains an influential dynamic core of decision-making and market-shaping standards for international trade, and, unquestionably in more recent times, for environmental law.

Furthermore, we argue that, in the contemporary global economy, global environmental damage is much more frequent than local damage. Despite the production forces' territorial migration due to transnational companies[4] or production rearrangements in clusters spread worldwide, the WTO juridical relationship is limited to empowered territorial subjects, meaning the member states. Disputes between the nations have results for these nations' behaviour. Although the issues dealt with by the Dispute Settlement Body are directly related to nations, indirectly, decisions cause effects on the conduct of corporations that are located in the nations involved – if we assume that firms' behaviour is affected by the legal framework that surrounds their decision-making process.

Within this ambivalence of WTO decisions, which produces direct and indirect effects, we reach the third part of this chapter. Corporations are very sensitive to government regulation and can choose less regulatory regimes rather than those more concerned with environmental problems. Nevertheless, in a global market, despite government regulation, consumers are interested in environmentally accountable products. For this reason, WTO dispute settlement about labeling of green technology will directly concern the nations as parties, but the corporations of the sector will be aware of the discussion. In other words, there is an informational effect, beyond the dispute settlement itself. This effect is sometimes much more important for the market, since it fosters a web of technological modification. The potential behavioural change[5] of

---

[4] Intra-firm trade characterizes the movement of capital. For a concise overview, see Rainer Lanz and Sébastien Miroudot, "Intra-Firm Trade: Patterns, determinants and policy implications" (2011) OECD Trade Policy Papers n. 114: dx.doi.org/10.1787/5kg9p39lrwnn-en (accessed 15 March 2016).

[5] Considering the known advances in decision theory, especially those which study the "bounded rationality" aspects of individual decision-making and the so-called "behavioural theory of the firm," as first described in Richard Cyert and James Merch's 1963 seminal work by the same name, it is safe to assume that such decisions are, by definition, influenced by legal constraints and contingencies.

investors and consumers by WTO decisions cannot be ignored as it presents a good possibility in the competition for profits.

A juridical approach has to consider the ways in which market players change their behaviour, which is evidently more important to the health of the market than WTO decisions. Dispute settlement carries out an ex-post analysis. It examines the past in order to provide a decision. Consequently, a decision on an economic issue can be considered as a sign indicating how society and "judges"[6] see the activity. Past experience by a competitor will indicate whether an investment in new green technology is worthwhile, given that such a commitment would involve a considerable amount of time and money. In contrast to new regulations, judicial decisions are more specific and concretely show what behaviour is expected from market actors.

As stated by the Agreement Establishing the World Trade Organization,[7] in its Annex 2, Article 3, "the dispute settlement system of the WTO is a central element in providing security and predictability to the multilateral trading system." That particular sentence, which clearly presupposes a close relationship with market actors, is fine tuned with the declared functions and jurisdiction of the Dispute Settlement System, such as (i) the preservation of rights and obligations under the WTO's covered agreements; and (ii) the clarification of the agreements' provisions, regarding their accordance with customary rules of interpretation of public international law.

Environmental regulation may be considered a hypothesis of behavioural conditioning for an uncertain result that should ultimately benefit society. It is a projection into the future, and therefore has fallibilities. A judicial decision is a result based on real actions that occurred in the past. The decision is a turning point between past and future behaviour. The present concentrates all the possibilities of change, both for the directly affected (states as litigating parties) and the economic agents from the sector that detects a gap between technology used and factors that could boost and steer production towards consumer preferences.

In a competitive market, technological change can simply define the maintenance or exclusion of a player. Not only the difficulty of financing but also the perception of the right moment to initiate a technological transformation is decisive for being in or out of the market. Hence

---

[6] The term "judges" is used here in a broad sense, meaning the members of the Appellate Body.

[7] See: www.wto.org/english/docs_e/legal_e/04-wto.pdf

judicial decisions provide an important sign in order to foresee the future of market preferences as well as new patterns to be adopted by the rule of law.

B   GATT/WTO – From Ricardian Liberalism to Sustainable Development

> The merchants knew perfectly in what manner it enriched themselves. It was their business to know it. But to know in what manner it enriched the country was no part of their business. This subject never came into their consideration but when they had occasion to apply to their country for some change in the laws relating to foreign trade. It then became necessary to say something about the beneficial effects of foreign trade, and the manner in which those effects were obstructed by the laws as they then stood.[8]

The heading above may suggest that there is a divide between liberalism and sustainable development, but this is not how GATT/WTO conducts itself. There is no intention here to trace the history of GATT and the WTO. Nonetheless, it is important to emphasize the main reasons that led to the dawn and development of this international compromise. Signed on July 22, 1944, before the end of World War II, the Breton Woods Agreement was the first initiative for creating an international economic order for finance, after which the United States engaged in organizing a free market for the entire world. Almost concurrent with a United Nations (UN) meeting on development and trade held in Havana, the United States organized meetings with invited nations in Geneva, for looking towards an agreement on tariffs for imported products. This apparently limited aim encapsulated an aspiring ideal – to warm up commercial relations among nations and diminish protectionism. The *pax perpetua* rebuilt by the United States had its roots in the *pax mercatoria*, which meant keeping free market working and promote economic integration.

Even before the final surrender of Nazi Germany and Japan, economists and heads of state were having talks in order to avoid what is considered one of the most significant causes of World War II. The first half of the twentieth century was a time of high import tariffs and protectionism, imports quotas, unilateralism, and bilateralism. As the

---

[8] Adam Smith, *An Inquiry into the Nature and Causes of the Wealth of Nations* (first published in 1776), IV [1.10]: www.econlib.org/library/Smith/smWN.html accessed 16 March 2016.

heat of battle intensified at the beginning of World War II, discussions between US President Franklin D. Roosevelt and British Prime Minister Winston Churchill led to the Atlantic Charter, approved on August 14, 1941, a document that shaped the future of world trade relations.[9] Although motivated by concerns other than environmental issues, access to natural resources and world trade came together as the mainspring for commercial activities: "Endeavor with due respect for their existing obligations, to further enjoyment by all States, great or small, victor or vanquished, of access, on equal terms, to the trade and to the raw materials of the world which are needed for their economic prosperity."

Even if environmental concerns were set aside, this has to be mentioned as it demonstrates the unavoidable relationship between economics and natural resources inasmuch as it builds a legal framework in which there is a clear understanding that economic practice is inseparable from the existence (maintenance) of natural resources. Access is essential, and so maintenance is seen as vital to the system. At the root of contemporary business practices is a pivotal need for an ongoing relationship of access to natural resources, which is introduced as sustainable development in the UN documents at the end of the 1980s.

Six years after the Atlantic Charter, in 1947, the United States organized a meeting in Geneva at which twenty-three founder nations had discussions on a system aimed at removing barriers to trade. It is the beginning of a worldwide process of economic integration. The ideological basis of GATT 47 was the same as that of the Bretton Woods Agreement, with Adam Smith and David Ricardo as intellectual inspiration. It is understood that the wealth of nations is built on broad-based free trade. Monetary and non-monetary barriers have to be banished in order to install peace among nations. An international organization was envisaged, and an international regulation to foster global free trade was created at that moment.

Although corporations are the entities actually generating trade, nations are involved and reflect the interests of these entities, which provide the same nations with their wealth. Nations search for internal benefits such as generally increased economic activity and productivity, as well as leverage of comparative advantages.[10] Seen from this

---

[9] José Augusto Fontoura Costa, *Decidir e julgar: um estudo multidisciplinar sobre a solução de controvérsias na Organização Mundial do Comércio* (USP, 2013), p. 159.

[10] Comparative advantage is a known concept developed by David Ricardo, who stated that a country that trades products that it can get at lower cost from another country is better off than if it had made the products domestically. Benefits are accrued in terms of

perspective, economic integration consequently forges an international division of work and production.

Over time, GATT became a much more complex system than just a mechanism for the construction of the free market. The Uruguay Round of negotiations is a milestone. During its eight-year existence (September 1986 to April 1994), it passed through a worldwide political, geographic, economic, and environmental transformation – a 'great transformation', perhaps as big as the one after World War II. The Uruguay Round started in 1986. In the same year, the UN General Assembly approved the Declaration on the Right to Development (A/Res/41/128 of 04/12/1986), which recalls the right of peoples to exercise sovereignty over all their natural wealth and resources. This document, thus, adds to the already established principle of permanent sovereignty over natural resources (AG/Res 1803 (XVII) 1962), the right of peoples over their natural resources that, according to GATT 47, are also necessary to the development of trade and the raising of standards of living.

The world opened to free trade in bigger proportions than those of 1947, as did the corporations, who were eager to gain new markets. Nations depending on private wealth became mouthpieces of corporations that were intent on expanding their wealth and were affected with what Krugman defined as the "wrong and dangerous obsession with competitiveness."

Against this backdrop, we must note the gigantic transnational corporations of the late twentieth and early twenty-first centuries that are extremely skilled in accumulating capital and moving it around the world from one country to another. The concentrated volume and power of mobility are equivalent to political and economic domination by corporations, a dependency of nations that, fearing a flight of capital, succumb to the demands of those corporations and act as their representatives. These are the hidden circumstances behind most disputes that take place in the GATT/WTO system nowadays. A decision between nations is actually an investment indicator for corporations that have interests in specific matters being in dispute. New decisions from dispute settlement bodies, initially arbitrations between contending nations, reverberate directly on corporate decisions. These corporations have to interpret the juridical messages and translate them into economic

marginal cost (the cost of producing an additional unit of a commodity) and opportunity costs (the value of the next-best alternative use of an asset), creating trade gain even if a country has absolute advantages to all commodities: Fontoura Costa, *Decidir e julgar:*.

practices, the implications of which extend beyond the scope of state sovereignty.

A new GATT arose from the Uruguay Round of Multilateral Trade Negotiations. Expressions such as "raising standards of living," "steadily growing volume of real income and effective demand," and "expanding the production of and trade in goods and services" are able to show how frontiers tumble in favour of the expansion of trade. This document revises GATT 47, with the 1986 development declaration and the 1992 UN declaration on environment and development leaving their imprints on the final agreement: the Marrakesh Agreement.

The maximization of the use of natural resources receives a Paretian design, tailored to the novel environmental economy. Slightly different from that of 1947, the Agreement establishing the WTO acknowledges that nations, "while allowing for the optimal use of the world's resources in accordance with the objective of sustainable development," shall also be "seeking both to protect and preserve the environment and to enhance the means for doing so in a manner consistent with their respective needs and concerns at different levels of economic development."

A big organization emerges from the Uruguay Round negotiations, and the GATT/WTO system conquers the world and spreads a one-sided idea of economic production as well as a globalized concept of sustainable development. This notion in the preamble of the Agreement points toward the birth of a juridical principle that bridges economic and environmental law. International trade has to pass the proof of the sustainable use of natural resources. From GATT 47 to GATT 94, the idea of "the full use of the resources of the world" turns into "the objective of sustainable development, seeking to protect and preserve the environment." Sustainability is a point of reference for international trade. It orients the trade and is one of the aims of trade. Although it may sound provocative, it is juridically true.

Also in Marrakesh, on April 14, 1994, a ministerial decision acknowledges the UN declaration on environment and development and states "that there should not be, nor need be, any policy contradiction between upholding and safeguarding an open, non-discriminatory and equitable multilateral trading system on the one hand, and acting for the protection of the environment, and the promotion of sustainable development on the other." Undoubtedly, the GATT/WTO system reinvents itself and introduces, in the wake of environmental economics, the privatization of common goods and the optimal private use of natural resources aimed at maximizing social gains.

Sustainable development has become an economic, political, and legal cornerstone, which is confirmed in the Doha Declaration of 2001, in which, at the conclusion of the fourth Ministerial Conference of the WTO, it was declared that trade envisages the environment and the principle of sustainable development to be mutually supportive. Even considering that WTO is chiefly a free-trade oriented treaty with limited environmental concerns, the text of the relevant documents implies a necessary integration of the trade related environmental agreements to its dispute settlement mechanism. After Marrakesh, the Doha Declaration in 2001 reaffirms the sustainable development principle. More recently, in 2015, there is the tenth Ministerial meeting recalling the Nairobi Declaration. Its preamble adjusts the action of WTO towards achievement of the 2030 Sustainable Development Goals.[11]

Since 1994, there has been a steadily convergence between GATT/WTO legal texts and UN environmental agreements. This approach confirms that the GATT/WTO system is a part of international law and follows its primary and methodological norms as well as its general principles. As such, the economic and legal principles stated in the WTO texts and decisions have to be in accordance with the general legal principles of international law and those principles that relate to activities regulated by the WTO. In the end, this is a structuring movement in which principles reflect the search for common aims.[12]

C.   *US-Tuna II* and the Process of Market Greening as a Source of Institutional Change

1   *Initial Considerations about the Case*

It is possible to summarize the core of the *US-Tuna II* case by its own description: the dispute concerns the labeling regime of the United States for "dolphin-safe" tuna products. In the original proceedings, in 2008, Mexico raised claims under the General Agreement on Tariffs and Trade

---

[11]   We recognize the role that the WTO can play in contributing towards the achievement of the 2030 Sustainable Development Goals, insofar as they relate to the WTO mandate, and bearing in mind the authority of the WTO Ministerial Conference.

[12]   "International law governs relations between independent States. The rules of law binding upon States therefore emanate from their own free will as expressed in conventions or by usages generally accepted as expressing principles of law and established in order to regulate the relations between these co-existing independent communities or with a view to the achievement of common aims" (*SS Lotus* case (*France v. Turkey* [1927] ICJ Rep 18)).

1994 (GATT 1994) and the TBT Agreement that challenged the consistency of certain measures imposed by the United States on the importation, marketing, and sale of tuna and tuna products with these agreements.[13]

The original tuna measure specified the conditions to be fulfilled in order for tuna products sold in the United States to be labeled "dolphin-safe" or to make similar claims on their labels. The specific conditions varied depending on the fishing method by which tuna contained in the tuna product was harvested, the area of the ocean where the tuna was caught, and the type of vessel used.[14]

Thus, the dispute arose because of a US regulation related to the duty to provide labeling of tuna and tuna products that could stimulate consumers to buy these goods and, simultaneously, constrain practices that may harm dolphins, specifically in the Tropical Pacific Area.

Although the WTO AB has the task of assessing whether the US measures are consistent with the GATT/WTO regulation, its arguments include in-depth considerations in terms of economic matters, and consumer and retailer preferences, as well as its effects on the market. It is worth noting a comment resulting from its decision:

> the original tuna measure did not make the use of a dolphin-safe label mandatory for the importation or sale of tuna products in the United States, although the preferences of retailers and consumers are such that the dolphin-safe label has "significant commercial value", and access to that label constitutes an "advantage" on the US market for tuna products.[15]

According to the AB statement, it remains clear that the adoption of such a "green technology" attested by a label constitutes a "significant commercial value."[16] The AB is not ignorant of economic arguments even though it is a legal dispute settlement body. This kind of argument has relevance for investors in the related segment of the market.

---

[13] WTO, *United States – Measures Concerning the Importation, Marketing, and Sale of Tuna and Tuna Products – Recourse to Article 21.5 of the DSU – Report of the Appellate Body* (20 November 2015) WT/DS381/AB/RW [1.2].

[14] Ibid., [1.3].

[15] Ibid., [1.3].

[16] Ibid., [7.60], as stated: "We further recall that, as was found in the original proceedings and as both parties have acknowledged in these compliance proceedings, access to the dolphin-safe label constitutes an 'advantage' on the US market for tuna products by virtue of that label's 'significant commercial value'."

It indicates the importance of such new technology and its potential for increasing capital gains.

The AB considers the facts and circumstances in order to "assess any implications for competitive conditions discernible from the design, structure, and expected operation of the measure." Such examination must also "take account of all the relevant features of the market, which may include the particular characteristics of the industry at issue, the relative market shares in a given industry, consumer preferences, and historical trade patterns" – that is, "the operation of the particular technical regulation at issue in the particular market in which it is applied." Thus, a panel conducting a *de facto* detrimental impact analysis under Article 2.1 of the TBT Agreement ought to take into account both the design and structure of the measure at issue and the way in which the measure operates (or can be expected to operate) in the light of the relevant features of the concerned market.[17]

It is noticeable that there is a real apprehension about how the market will react to an obligation of adoption of "green technologies." It also accepts the possibility of a label as a source of commercial value, as indeed it is. Nonetheless, the search for this value could exclude players that do not have the means to invest in technological change during the "greening competition" that is already taking place. Furthermore, this is the moment of a legal decision – the primary task to analyse an existing situation. In terms of the WTO framework, this has great relevance since the consequences of its decisions mostly affect the future, referring to succeeding steps to be made by governments. It is quite different from traditional courts' decision-making, which usually involves mitigation, resolving conflicts by repairing prior faults.

Another point of the decision is that it considered "even-handedness" as an "analytical tool" that serves as a proxy to determine the extension of "legitimate regulatory distinctions" under Article 2.1. Therefore, its results must show the adequacy of the decision to the precise configuration of market behaviour as a whole. In that sense, the fundamental aspect is not to harm the participants in a reciprocal manner, whether they are competitors or consumers.

As the AB states:

> the measure applied by regulation has to be inquiry by pointing out that examining whether a measure involves "arbitrary discrimination" is *one way* of demonstrating that a measure is not even-handed, but that

---

[17] Ibid., [7.59].

ascertaining whether the detrimental impact stems exclusively from a legitimate regulatory distinction "may involve examination of more than just the existence (or not) or 'arbitrary discrimination'".[18]

Notwithstanding:

> In conclusion, in the absence of a proper assessment by the Panel of the respective risks posed to dolphins inside and outside the ETP large purse-seine fishery, we are unable to complete the legal analysis and assess fully whether all of the regulatory distinctions drawn under the amended tuna measure can be explained and justified in the light of differences in the relative risks associated with different methods of fishing for tuna in different areas of the oceans.[19]

The analysis of the legal and economic elements that constituted the GATT 47 system clearly reveals a response to the limits established by a certain period in history. Its institutional structure was guided towards the resolution of less complex (although relevant) problems in international trade, such as protectionism and asymmetrical trade barriers and policies in general.

Under an evolutionary movement, rarely marked by severe moments of inflection, certain characteristics remain central to the current multilateral trade paradigm. In different terms, the profound modification to GATT 47 through the addition of new agreements, and the ensuing GATT/WTO system, reflects stability and continuity, aimed at the maintenance of certain core aspects of the original regime. Within that statement, we include the political–economical, transparency, product differentiation, creation of new markets, and capital concentration aspects.

Contrary to a common belief in that particular period of time, between both agreements (1947–94), international trade rarely subjected itself to a mere "tariffs game." Rather, international trade was shaped by a wide array of elements, such as different producers, different environmental characteristics, consumers' mentality, access to technology and, above all, diverse domestic legal frameworks related to production factors. Examples of that fact appear in the variety of shapes that indispensable legal institutes assumed across different countries, such as property rights, labour law, environmental restrictions, and so forth.

Another point of key importance that also concerns the central preoccupation with tariffs in the system's first moments is the equilibrium

[18] Ibid., [7.85].
[19] Ibid., [7.359].

regarding production costs. In a hypothetical extreme, the complete elimination of tariffs would imply exposure to the existing imbalance of production factors between related countries.

In other words, tariffs on imported goods generally imply the imposition of an *ex-post* cost to international producers, unrelated to their domestic production factors (which could otherwise grant to those countries comparative advantages in an international free trade scenario). On the other hand, dumping and domestic subsidies imply an international devaluation of domestic products, making it "more competitive" by reducing the costs of the same factors of production *ex ante*, and therefore generating an equal distortion in market prices of tradable goods.

In that sense, a common feature of these classical forms of artificial creation of comparative advantages involves the inequitable use of such financial–legal instruments. Nowadays the predominance of indirect forms of creating the same kind of artificial interference manifests itself through a subtler devaluation of production costs – mostly through under-regulation of labour or environmental protection in certain jurisdictions, usually bringing about the noticeable effect of displacing entire production chains around the globe (besides the capital flows related to the effect).

Therefore, although it is partially true that the GATT 47 system has been historically important in the process of tariffs' asymmetry reduction between nations, only with the signal emitted by the agreements of 1994 have other important elements been brought to the debate's core (i.e. non-tariff barriers to trade, sanitary, and phytosanitary considerations, and so on), complementing necessary aspects of a more complex free trade environment.

2   Markets, Legal Design and Environmental Issues

If literature review is rich in using a more institutional perspective over trade dilemmas in the system's adaptation process, there is a persistent lack of consistent studies that analyse the influence that multilateral decisions of dispute settlement bodies have over particular markets on which their effects are expected to be felt.

As such, we shall explore the specific interface between trade and social goals (whether environmental, consumer oriented, or behavioural), as well as perspectives about internal relations produced by the current WTO legal framework regarding this interface.

Among many objectives around which such an interface may be oriented, the known debate over production and process related measures (PPMs) is one that illustrates appropriately the kind of limitations – anachronistic at times – that the current dispute settlement model might produce. In general, the system is designed to focus on tradable goods per se, such as materials, features, and physical attributes. Conversely, the existence of non-physical aspects (NPAs) is, by itself, a problem, as these might imply restrictions on international trade. Examples are the importation of wood illegally harvested or harvested in regions that do not possess any reforestation policy,[20] or even fish imports that are associated with negative externalities over a certain ecosystem due to the fishing methods.

PPMs are the most common subset of NPAs, regarding the production process and methods used in the production and trade of a certain good. The paradigm used in this chapter to illustrate restrictions based in a certain kind of PPM is the prohibition of tuna trade when the tuna were not caught by methods that do not harm dolphins. Although the case highlights many features, it is important to note the legal and economic context in which restrictions of such nature are introduced and, above all, in what measure the WTO's position in the case indicates the necessity of further considerations about the free market rationale that orients the organization's existence.

In any event, the above mentioned debate is placed in a broader context – the growing importance of socially relevant considerations (in this case, environmental) within international trade relations, including the WTO.

The relationship between the economy and the environment at international level is rather complex and, as such, constitutes an endless source of legal disputes.[21] Although more robust considerations about this particular relationship came about only in the 1960s, it is safe to say that, between then and now, the most common way to deal with a legal approach to emerging problems was, and still is, through treaties or agreements on international environmental law that contain provisions about trade. As a notable exception of a primarily trade-oriented agreement, we outline the North American Free Trade Agreement (NAFTA), with its subsidiary environmental agreement.[22]

---

[20] Christiane Conrad, *Processes and Production Methods in WTO Law* (Cambridge University Press, 2011), p. 298.

[21] The *US-Tuna I* and *II* cases, for instance, are adequate examples of such legal controversies.

[22] See www.cec.org/

Moreover, still under GATT 47, the paradigm of this particular controversy was the 1991 decision in the case *US-Tuna I*,[23] in which the Panel stated that the restrictions imposed by the United States on tuna captured by foreign companies was in clear non-compliance with its domestic rules and could not be justified as an exception under Article XX(b) and (g).

A few years later, in 1998, under the GATT/WTO system, the AB's decision in the *Shrimp-Turtle* case[24] implied the recognition of the applicability of Article XX(g) to similar circumstances, which brought about a new comprehension of the subject-matter and set aside the *US-Tuna I* decision.

In that sense, we agree with Goyal[25] that one of the reasons for there being such a profusion of treaties and other environmental agreements with trade provisions, and not many trade agreements with environmental clauses, is a fact connecting both areas: it is not necessary to protect the environment to foster trade; however, it is certainly necessary to regulate trade in order to protect the environment.

Therefore, we consider it necessary to highlight certain elements in order to understand fully not only the legal rationale behind the WTO's decisions, but also its economic rationale, through the reanalysis of those same decisions. From that point of view, it will be possible to assess the consistency and compatibility of trade related environmental measures (TREM) with the GATT/WTO system.

First of all, we understand that in order to analyze the compatibility of TREMs with the GATT/WTO system, it is imperative to verify the extension of meaning attributed to "like-products," a common concept in the provisions of the Agreements (i.e. Articles I:1, II:2, III:2, III:4, and others).

This need stems from the AB's conclusion in the *Asbestos* case[26] that stressed the criteria and main features defining "like-products" within the WTO legal framework, in a case-by-case approach: (i) the physical properties of the products; (ii) the extent to which the products are

---

[23] GATT, *United States – Restrictions on Imports of Tuna* (September 1991). See: www.wto.org/english/tratop_e/envir_e/edis04_e.htm

[24] WTO, *United States – Import Prohibition of Certain Shrimp and Shrimp Products – Recourse to Article 21.5 of the DSU – Report of the Appellate Body* (22 October 2001) WT/DS58/AB/RW.

[25] Anupam Goyal, *The WTO and International Environmental Law* (Oxford University Press, 2006).

[26] WTO, *European Communities – Measures Affecting Asbestos and Products Containing Asbestos – Appellate Body Report* (12 March 2001) WT/DS135/AB/R [101].

capable of serving the same or similar end-uses; (iii) the extent to which consumers perceive and treat the products as alternative means of performing particular functions in order to satisfy a particular want or demand; and (iv) the international classification of the products for tariff purposes.

Nonetheless, in the process of outlining the features to define "likeness," the AB highlights a systematic and unidirectional internal logic that has as its background considerations focused on the product per se and not on PPMs that appear as a new development frontier to environmental considerations in trade forums.

In a second stance, from the definition held by criterion (iii) of the AB's conclusions, it is possible to extract the important role held by the consumer in international trade dynamics; however, if it is true that the GATT/WTO system is historically preoccupied by limiting the possibility of restrictions to producers, such restrictions mostly focus on products as such, usually under the spectrum of clauses such as most-favored nation (MFN) or national treatment (NT).

Apparently, the system positions itself as a structure that craves equilibrium in trade relations between nations, in search for a more harmonic context of comparative advantages and macroeconomic trade relations. Conversely, nations are direct actors but necessary representatives of companies whose goals are to introduce their products in a broader market (investors), as well as of those whose first aspirations are to obtain the best products at lowest prices (consumers).

This particular shift in perception and rationality allows one to observe that, deep down, there should not be a differentiation within the system of trade oriented by GATT/WTO regarding product-related processes and production methods (PR-PPMs) and non-product-related ones[27] (NPR-PPMs). The foundation of PR-PPMs is associated with the idea

---

[27] As Steve Charnovitz defines it, "Analysts often divide PPMs in two categories – product-related and non-product-related. Product-related PPMs are used to assure the functionality of the product, or to safeguard the consumer who uses the product. Food safety may be the best example on how regulators rely on process-based sanitary rules. [...] Thus, they are *related* to the product, even though adherence to a particular process may not be directly detectable in the product. By contrast, the non-product-related PPM is designed to achieve a social purpose that may or may not matter to a consumer. For example, prohibiting the use of a driftnet to catch fish may achieve an ecological goal but has no effect on a fish as such or on its nutritional and gustatory value for the consumer. Hence, such PPMs are referred to as *non-product-related.*" See: Steve Charnovitz, "The Law of Environmental PPMs' in the WTO: Debunking the Myth of Illegality", YJIL, 27 (59) (2002), 65.

of "likeness," once the system directs itself to the idea of assessing whether certain practices are discriminatory and illegal under trade agreements related to products per se or elements that have been incorporated in products (be it under MFN or NT requirements under GATT or the requirements of other trade agreements, such as TBT and Sanitary and Phytosanitary Measures). Unfortunately, only in a few occasions such 'equal' approach was recognized as appropriate regarding NPR-PPMs.[28]

We firmly argue that from criterion (iii) established in *Measures Affecting Asbestos Products* to assess "likeness" between products, with the purpose of analyzing a possible unjustified discrimination based on an NPR-PPM, a whole new branch of problems arises, involving consumer preferences and the intrinsic rationale of the GATT/WTO system.

If we assume that in today's global economy a large portion of the branding process involves the social responsibility of companies' actions, usually based on sustainability or sustainable development initiatives, it is relevant to recognize that, even if it is intangible in some cases, such preoccupation has already transmuted to a relevant financial asset and, as such, pertains to the market in terms of comparative advantages.

To explore this point further, we argue that many of those actions and initiatives might not represent or produce a great impact in terms of carbon emissions, discharge of pollutants, among others.[29] However, it is clear that they are "enough" to shape the perception and tastes of consumers in relation to certain products, services, or even the image of corporations.

It must be acknowledged that these elements reveal the existence of a potential market share related to branding based on PPMs, whether incorporated into the final product or not. A strong evidence for that argument is that some of the most troublesome cases brought to the dispute settlement mechanism involve considerations about PPMs, namely *US-Tuna II* and *Shrimp/Turtle* regarding ecolabels, whose main aim is to provide clear and trustworthy information about products to consumers.

---

[28] See, for instance: *Auto Taxes, U.S Alcoholic Beverages* and *Reformulated Gasoline Appellate Decision*.

[29] If we assume that a relevant part of the companies' incentives to promote such initiatives is not necessarily focused on concrete and positive environmental impacts, but rather on "green marketing" efforts, it becomes clear that, despite direct results, there is nonetheless a potential net effect that is related to consumers' behavioral change as an indirect result.

That aim also relates to the processes and production methods being valuable characteristics that consist of the right to information of consumers, about elements that exceed the physical features of a given product (i.e. the use of safety devices that do not capture or harm dolphins or turtles, but also related to energy efficiency, non-use of slave work, respect to basic labor rights, and so forth).

In *US-Tuna II*, the tension becomes visible when the AB states that the analysis of detrimental impacts to the environment is "realistic,"[30] meaning that the simple assessment of the formal legal treatment given to different products, such as structure, design and expected effects, is somewhat incomplete. The assessment of the measures' impacts should therefore be *de facto*, based on the totality of facts and circumstances presented to the Dispute Settlement Understanding.

Paradoxically, it is also stated by the AB that, even in the assessment made by Panels, such as the one reviewed in this case, it is not mandatory to derive conclusions from the whole set of evidences about real effects on trade produced by technical regulations, but from the arguments and evidence brought to analysis by the parties.[31]

Even so, it becomes evident by the reasons presented by the AB that the restrictions to trade addressed in Article 2.1 of the TBT Agreement do not constitute per se a prohibition of measures based in product characteristics or even processes and production methods,[32] particularly when these PPMs are based exclusively on a legitimate regulatory distinction.[33]

Regarding the specific aspect of legitimacy, the AB states that the creation of an eco-labeling system, doubtless and necessarily, imposes a difference in the competition process in the analysed market (North American), by affecting consumer behaviour towards products that do or do not receive the label.[34] The legal discussion would thus consist in

---

[30] WTO, *United States – Measures Concerning the Importation, Marketing, and Sale of Tuna and Tuna Products – Recourse to Article 21.5 of the DSU – Report of the Appellate Body* (20 November 2015) WT/DS381/AB/RW [7.28].

[31] Ibid., [7.29].

[32] See: WTO, *United States – Clove Cigarettes, Report of the Appellate Body* [169], *United States–Measures Concerning the Importation, Marketing, and Sale of Tuna and Tuna Products* [211] and *United States– Certain Country of Origin Labelling (COOL) Requirements* [268].

[33] See: Appellate Body's Reports in *US–COOL* [271], *US–Clove Cigarettes* [182] and *US–Tuna II* [215].

[34] WTO, *United States – Measures Concerning the Importation, Marketing, and Sale of Tuna and Tuna Products – Report of the Appellate Body* (16 May 2012) WT/DS381/AB/R [298].

identifying whether the regulation to provide for the imposition of the labeling requirements is legitimate as to its targeted aims (in this case, environmental ones).

The AB considered the Panel analysis as insufficient to determine whether the regulation was legitimate under such perspective, since the United States was not able to demonstrate that the parameters used by the eco-label program were consistent with Article 2.1 of the TBT Agreement in every fishing area that provided tuna to US markets.

The differences that existed between various regions of the world that commercialized tuna in the United States and the specific region with Mexican producers that was under scrutiny was so relevant, according to the AB, that the simplistic assessment made by the Panel was inadequate to determine the legitimacy of the measure, which implied for the AB the revision of the Panel's original decision and, consequently, the declaration of inconsistency with the provisions of TBT Agreement's Article 2.1.[35]

Successively, on the occasion of analysing the arguments in light of Article 2.2 of the TBT Agreement, the AB furthers its considerations as to the necessity of legitimate goals for the establishment of technical regulations that create restrictions to trade, recognizing that the provision does not set out a closed list of legitimate objectives, but rather lists several examples of legitimate objectives – human health or safety, animal and plant life or health, or the environment.[36]

In its analysis regarding the consistency of the United States eco-labeling scheme with the provisions of Article 2.2 of the TBT Agreement, the Panel originally considered the regulation to be inconsistent with this provision. It is interesting to note that the Panel considered the United States' declared aims (information regarding consumers, and directives regarding equipment and fishery practices) as compatible and protected by the provision; however, the AB's assessment came to the conclusion that there could be less restrictive solutions available to reach the same goals, rendering the measures, by that consideration, inconsistent with the provisions of the TBT Agreement.

---

[35] *In verbis:* "For these reasons, we reverse the Panel's finding, in paragraphs 7.374 and 8.1(a) of the Panel Report, that the US 'dolphin-safe' labelling provisions are not inconsistent with Article 2.1 of the TBT Agreement. We find, instead, that the US 'dolphin-safe' labelling provisions provide 'less favorable treatment' to Mexican tuna products than that accorded to tuna products of the United States and tuna products originating in other countries and are therefore inconsistent with Article 2.1 of the TBT Agreement."

[36] Ibid., [314].

The AB, once more, stated that the Panel's assessment was only partially correct, since the analysis required by Article 2.2 regarding less restrictive measures was conducted in an inappropriate manner. According to the AB's established proceeding in cases such as *US Wool Shirts and Blouses* and *EC Sardines*, the duty to indicate *prima facie* inconsistency with the mentioned article lies with the complainant (Mexico), and thus the proof presented ought to be sufficient to conclude that there are other ways to pursue "legitimate goals" in a less trade-restrictive form.[37]

On this basis, the AB concluded that the less restrictive solution presented by Mexico (the use of another eco-label with similar objectives), was neither equivalent nor less restrictive to trade if compared with the United States' scheme, which presented several well-documented limitations in the decision's assessment.

However debatable the internal consistency of these eco-labeling schemes might be, it is undeniable that the producers' preoccupation regarding consumer perception of their products goes beyond "what is visible" in the purchase moment. This perception has thus acquired the shape of a valuable market asset.

Such an argument becomes even stronger and more "visible" in particular market segments in which the diffusion of new technologies represent the core of the activity, as in the renewable energies sector and R&D in energy efficiency. Additionally, it is important to note that beyond the immediate effect produced by regulatory environments that foster such enquiries and sectors (which would fall under WTO jurisdiction in the case of disputes involving "international standards," for instance), there is also an unmeasured positive externality related to well-designed regulatory models in the medium to long term to be taken into account.

---

[37] Ibid., [322], *in verbis*: "In sum, we consider that an assessment of whether a technical regulation is 'more trade-restrictive than necessary' within the meaning of Article 2.2 of the TBT Agreement involves an evaluation of a number of factors. A panel should begin by considering factors that include: (i) the degree of contribution made by the measure to the legitimate objective at issue; (ii) the trade-restrictiveness of the measure; and (iii) the nature of the risks at issue and the gravity of consequences that would arise from non-fulfilment of the objective(s) pursued by the Member through the measure. In most cases, a comparison of the challenged measure and possible alternative measures should be undertaken. In particular, it may be relevant for the purpose of this comparison to consider whether the proposed alternative is less trade restrictive, whether it would make an equivalent contribution to the relevant legitimate objective, taking account of the risks non-fulfilment would create, and whether it is reasonably available."

We also argue that positive externalities that might arise from legal-regulatory structures are the key to evaluate the design, creation, and assessment of more stable and goal-oriented regulatory environments. This approach allows the continuous improvement and fine-tuning of institutions towards goals such as sustainable development, both locally (adapting domestic legal structures to local specificities) and globally (by aiming at the improvement of environmental indicators, regarding biodiversity loss, diversification in the energy matrix with greater shares for renewables, and so forth).

Nevertheless, we reject a 'naive' approach that excludes the importance of international law in domestic regulatory improvement, or that discards economic considerations that might emerge from the still most prominent trade discussion forum – the WTO. That very reality, by itself, exposes the limitations of a more traditional approach in market regulation that still exists within the GATT/WTO system.

In a world where the frontiers for a clear definition of "likeness" have assumed many different tones, along with the changes in perception and preferences of consumers based on progressively more mainstream concepts such as green consuming,[38] corporations are perceiving that scenario as an opportunity, modeling their way to grasp the attention of well-informed consumers, and reinforce environmentally adequate patterns based on their preferences.[39]

Moreover, it seems adequate to argue that the current changes already in place within the market towards green technologies and goal-oriented institutional mechanisms will impose great pressure on the regulatory framework in which the WTO is placed. A major shift in that regulatory paradigm, which exceeds the mere incorporation of new interpretations to the current paradigm, wat today's pace, will be inevitable, even if their future shape is yet uncertain.

---

[38] See the macro-level structure on the promotion of green consumerism proposed by Sonya Sachdeva, Jennifer Jordan, and Nina Mazar in "Green Consumerism: Moral Motivations to a Sustainable Future", COP, 2015 6, 60.

[39] Additionally, about the relationship between firms and consumers in different market scenarios, see Dominic Hauck, Erik Ansink, Jetske Bouma and Daan van Soest, "Social Network Effects and Green Consumerism", Tinbergen Institute Discussion Paper 14–150 (2014).

D   WTO and the Effects of Technological Change among Competitors

The WTO regime still sends unclear signals to market agents about the extent and limits of an ideal trade-environment framework that, in an ideal approach, would be expected for informational purposes. Nevertheless, the developing relationship between international trade and environmental law echoes beyond GATT/WTO DSM and influences the "behavioral shaping" of market agents. Considering the extension of the discussion, it is important to adopt a more integrated approach towards the relationship between the trade system and market behaviour.

Considering PPMs and the preferences for products the production methods of which embody new green technologies on the one hand, and uncertainties about GATT/WTO conformity on the other, creates a stimulus in the market for a technological externality.[40]

The choice for investment obeys a variety of options. The neoclassical idea of the agents' rationality being linked to immediate gains is simplistic and unreal.[41] This rationale would not explain the great technological innovation that occurred in the production process during the last three centuries, let alone the last two decades. Nevertheless, the technological innovation process has a key importance in order to explain the development of this production process being driven to maximize private wealth based on the use of social resources while concurrently maintaining social approval. In other words, technological innovation is the antidote to the cyclical characteristic of market production. It is the tool that operates the capitalist revitalization, since the rupture with the feudal structures, as stated by Schumpeter.[42]

---

[40] "The so called technological external economies involve the spill over of knowledge between firms: to the extent that firms can learn from each other, a strong national industry can give rise to a national knowledge base that reinforces the industry's advantage." (Paul Krugman, *Pop Internationalism* (MIT, 1996), p. 96).

[41] See Florian Knobloch and Jean-François Mercure, *The behavioural aspect of green technology investments: a general positive model in the context of heterogeneous agents* (Elsevier, 2016), p. 11. *In verbis:* "Not adopting a green technology deemed profitable, however, constitutes a gap between classical theory and reality. It can be explained either by assuming that agents act rationally, but don't invest in seemingly profitable technologies due to economic factors that are omitted in engineering studies – so called market barriers. Or, agents systematically violate the rationality axioms of expected utility theory – which would constitute *irrational* behaviour from a neoclassical perspective."

[42] "The economist Joseph Schumpeter (1942) famously characterized this process as one of 'creative destruction' in which technological innovation and entrepreneurship not only created waves of innovation but also swept away previous forms of capital accumulation

The option for a new technology is based on complex objective and subjective evaluations related to the findings and expectations of a firm that go beyond the rational choice, especially considering that each decision is embedded in cultural and historical elements.

Technological transformation towards a more resilient pattern of production and consumption is not only necessary for sustainable development; it is a requirement of international economic and environmental law. Furthermore, ensuring competitiveness in the global market and avoiding monopolistic behaviour caused by assuming upfront costs in new green technologies demands a major technological upgrade from high pressure natural resources' sectors as a whole. Without such transforming investments, nations will probably stall in this period of economic transition, with negative development consequences.

The landmark report on the Green Economy by NEP recognizes this challenge and highlights the "growing recognition that achieving sustainability rests almost entirely on getting the economy right"[43] This has been echoed by subsequent reports by other key international institutions, including the Organisation for Economic Cooperation and Development, the World Bank and UN-DESA/UNEP/UNCTAD, which prepared a report specifically for the UN Rio+20 Conference.[44] All these and other expert reports highlight the urgency of advancing large-scale investments to redirect the trajectory of today`s US$70 trillion global economy towards a sustainable pathway, and the risks and challenges in so doing.

It is important to consider that, in the pursuit of their own interests, investors must be aware of society's demands. Adopting new technological patterns, greening production and consumption, certainly will

and natural resources. Although 'creative destruction' has been celebrated by free market economists as central to economic efficiency and human progress, it is worth remembering, Schumpeter's prescience. Crucially, he cautioned that the activity he described also involved systemic risks: In breaking down the pre-capitalist framework of society, capitalism thus broke not only barriers that impeded its progress but also flying buttresses that prevented its collapse ... " (Christopher Wright and Daniel Nyberg, *Climate Change, Capitalism, and Corporations – Processes of Creative Self-Destruction* (Cambridge University Press, 2015), p. 32).

43 UNEP, *Towards a Green Economy: Pathways to Sustainable Development and Poverty Eradication* (2011), 17: http://web.unep.org/greeneconomy/sites/unep.org .greeneconomy/files/field/image/green_economyreport _final_dec2011.pdf (accessed 30 April 2016).

44 UN, UNEP and UNCTAD, *Transition to a Green Economy* (2012): www.uncsd2012.org/ rio20/content/documents/Transition%20to%20a%20Green%20Economy_summary.pdf (accessed 30 April 2016).

make consumers consider the reasons underlying such change. In doing so, they might change their perception and behaviour toward products apparently similar to others but different in its green appeal. Of course, the existence of a proper label should outline the difference between products more efficiently. Nonetheless, in times of greening ideology, a simple mention of the product might be able to change consumers' preferences, creating incentives for companies to move toward green technologies as soon as possible.

Green technologies are, therefore, also an intangible capital, beyond products and innovation. In other words, they can also be considered a positive social contribution once they are adopted, if we consider the possibility of internalizing social costs caused by pollution and other externalities.[45] Even considering, as Mercure does, that there is limited knowledge of what drives the behaviour of people and corporations, and how this influences aggregate outcomes, we are convinced that technological change adopted by significant economic agents might serve as benchmarking, and is, therefore, relevant.[46]

This is particularly important in the perspective of sustainability transitions studies, in which the process of decision-making by agents is rarely emphasized, but is at least as important as cultural, regulatory, and other contextual factors that influence or limit the formation of new sociotechnical regimes.[47]

Technology diffusion describes the gradual adoption of innovations by firms and consumers, which involves decision-making processes. Adopters first have to learn about the new technology's existence and benefits, and then decide whether to adopt it or not. In order to foster new consumers and further develop competition, technological change for a green market creates a sort of "race to the top" scenario.

Entrepreneurial activity, in turn, is not exempt from risk – which is itself a component of the rational choice process. One of the important aspects of such activity is the agent's risk-taking consideration in new technologies' upfront costs, considered to be uncertain investments to be compensated in future market competition.

---

[45] "A green technology is one that *generates or facilitates a reduction in environmental externalities relative to the incumbent*" (Knobloch and Mercure, *The behavioural aspect of green technology investments*, p. 1).

[46] Ibid., p. 2.

[47] Frank W. Geels, *Technological transitions as evolutionary reconfiguration processes: a multi-level perspective and a case-study* (Elsevier, 2002), RP 1257–74.

Insufficient information about the changes in technological and market preferences, or the difficulty of accessing capital in order to allocate investments in new technologies, are also considered to be imperfections, that may lead to the creation of monopolistic markets. This is not, however, an outcome that is desired by nations or consumers. Considering that the WTO is a system that aims to promote the welfare of nations and consumers, something is missing in its regulation when its decisions may leave room for the enhancement of market failures.

Governments are somewhat expected to provide trade rules and mechanisms conducive to their citizens developing economic activities across borders so as to pursue their economic interests. In *US – Section 301 Trade Act*, the WTO Panel also declared that

> it would be entirely wrong to consider that the position of individuals is of no relevance to the GATT/WTO legal matrix. Many of the benefits to members which are meant to flow as a result of the acceptance of various disciplines under the GATT/WTO depend on the activity of individual economic operators in the national and global market places. The purpose of many of disciplines, indeed one of the primary objects of the GATT/WTO as a whole, is to produce certain market conditions which would allow this individual activity to flourish.[48]

WTO law establishes trade rules and mechanisms for individuals to conduct trade across frontiers that have been negotiated in advance by their governments. These trade rules and mechanisms are created based on the intention of all WTO members to conduct free trade and economic activities with a view to raising standards of living for all individuals, by expanding trade in goods and services and reducing barriers to trade.[49]

Taking the *US-Tuna II* case as an example, it is important to outline that, in times of real ocean desertification and diminishing fish stocks, the search for conservation of global commons as a path to food security is consistent with sustainability goals and the raising of standards of living. Since it is undeniable that a better environment, and especially the conservation of global commons, is a very important and desirable thing for consumers, labeling is an important element of that equation.

---

[48] WTO, *US – Section 301–310 Trade Act of 1974 – Panel Report* (22 December 1999) WT/DS152/R [7.73].

[49] Interpretation of WTO Objective by the Panel in *Ecuador: Bananas III – Recourse to Appellate Body Under Article 21.5* (26 November 2008) WT/DS27/AB/RW2/EC, *US: EC – Bananas III Recourse to Appellate Body under Article 21.5* (19 May 2008) WT/DS27/RW/USA [433].

The AB's decision in *US-Tuna II* partially rejects labeling both as an instrument of consumer preference and as an indication to competitors of new technology adoption. Nonetheless, it does not prevent a "race to the top" incentive for entrepreneurs who wish to assume upfront costs as investments for a future *greener* market.

Finally, we conclude with two sets of statements: one being environmental-legal and the other environmental-economical. In our opinion, the legality of labeling processes and production methods not related to the product, when designed to protect global commons, is consistent with the WTO regime if we consider the objectives and principles of GATT/WTO along with the Doha Declaration and Article XX(g) of GATT – even more so if we consider the Doha Mandate regarding the creation of green jobs and increase in the diffusion of green products.[50]

Furthermore, labeling is a fair instrument to correct the "natural" failures of the market, such as information asymmetry and production negative externalities. It provides better information to both consumers and competitors, product related or not; stimulates corporations to internalize environmental costs and captivate consumers' preferences; and enables economic investors to analyse better the behaviour of consumers and assume an entrepreneurial position, taking upfront costs for technological change, considering the consumer sensitivity for global commons' protection.

Ultimately, the AB's decisions not only inform nations, but indirectly shake the global markets related to the disputes it addresses. Yet, the effectiveness of its *statements* for the global markets depends on its ability to recognize the nuanced rationality of market agents, capable of comprehending the WTO's debates within their own particular market-driven mindset – which might be nurtured adequately toward *green* legitimate objectives.

---

[50] "Portrayed as one of the areas where 'triple win' outcomes (i.e. good for trade, the environment and development) could be achieved, the negotiations on EGS have, however, been stalled at the WTO level. The main reason is that there is no agreement as to what should be treated as an 'environmental good' or as related 'environmental service'. There are of course some guiding definitions, such as the one provided by the European Commission and taken up by the OECD: goods and services capable of measuring, preventing, limiting or correcting environmental damage such as the pollution of water, air, soil, as well as waste and noise-related problems. They include clean technologies where pollution and raw material use is being minimized." (Jorge E. Viñuales, *International Environmental Law* (Cambridge University Press, 2016), pp. 395–96.)

11

Adjudication of Environmental Impact Assessment Claims before International Courts and Tribunals

ANDREW B. LOEWENSTEIN

A Introduction

Environmental impact assessment (EIA) is the process by which projects that are under consideration are evaluated to determine their likely impacts on the environment. As a planning tool, EIA assists both the project's proponent and the state's regulatory authorities in making decisions such as where the project should be located, how it should be designed, and what restrictions should be put into place to eliminate, reduce or mitigate potential adverse impacts.[1] Both customary international law and a network of treaties require states to undertake EIAs where projects could adversely impact the environments of other states or the marine environment.[2]

The obligation to carry out an EIA inevitably gives rise to disputes between states over its alleged breach. As a result, states are increasingly invoking the jurisdiction of international courts and tribunals to adjudicate matters such as whether an EIA should have been carried out; whether an EIA was adequate in light of the project's characteristics

---

[1] For general discussion of EIA, see, e.g., K. Hanna, 'A Brief Introduction to Environmental Impact Assessment' in K. Hanna (ed.), *Environmental Impact Assessment: Practice and Participation* (Oxford University Press, 2015); and C. Wood, *Environmental Impact Assessment: A Comparative Review* (Prentice Hall, 2002).

[2] See, e.g., N. Craik, *The International Law of Environmental Impact Assessment: Process, Substance and Integration* (Cambridge University Press, 2008); K. Bastmeijer and T. Koivurova, 'Transboundary Environmental Impact Assessment: An Introduction' in K. Bastmeijer and T. Koivurova (eds.), *Theory and Practice of Transboundary Environmental Impact Assessment* (Brill/Martinus Nijhoff Publishers, 2008); J. Knox, 'The Myth and Reality of Transboundary Environmental Impact Assessment', *American Journal of International Law*, 96 (2002), 291.

and the sensitivity of the receiving environment; and whether the project's ultimate location and design satisfactorily address the risks that were identified and evaluated.

Framing a dispute as one concerning EIA instead of – or in addition to – simply a claim for environmental harm may be advantageous. An EIA claim does not require a state, for example, to establish that harm occurred; nor must it prove a causal link between the respondent state's alleged delinquency and the harm it allegedly caused. Moreover, by putting its claim in terms of EIA, a claimant may challenge the respondent state's allegedly delinquent actions before any harm has materialized or, indeed, even prior to the implementation of the project. The claimant can thus seek to influence the project through the adjudicative process.

To date, inter-state cases involving EIAs have concerned a wide array of industrial and other activities, ranging from nuclear fuel reprocessing and dredging to aerial spraying of herbicides, land reclamation and the construction of transportation infrastructure. The types of potentially impacted environments have been equally diverse: terrestrial, riverine, and marine ecosystems, including specially designated reserves and areas set aside for use by indigenous peoples, have all been the subject of EIA-related litigation or arbitration.

This chapter evaluates the approach of international courts and tribunals to the adjudication of disputes concerning EIA. It first provides an overview of the development of EIA as a legal obligation and the jurisdictional bases under which courts and tribunals can be seized of inter-state claims for alleged failure to discharge that obligation. The chapter then examines how courts and tribunals have responded to the challenges posed by adjudicating EIA-related disputes in the inter-state dispute settlement context. In particular, the chapter focuses on the interplay between the fact-finding and decision-making processes at the domestic and international levels, and the means by which international courts and tribunals have dealt with the complex scientific and technical evidence that EIA disputes often involve.

B   The Obligation to Carry Out an Environmental Impact Assessment

As a regulatory tool, EIA is of recent vintage; its roots lie in domestic laws, dating to the enactment in 1969 in the United States of the National

Environmental Policy Act.[3] Requirements to undertake EIA were soon adopted in other domestic environmental regimes as well, including in Australia, Canada, New Zealand, Thailand, France, West Germany and the Netherlands.[4] In 1985, the European Commission adopted its EIA Directive in recognition of the fact that 'consent for public and private projects which are likely to have significant effects on the environment should be granted only after prior assessment of the likely significant environment effects of these projects has been carried out'.[5] The increasingly widespread acceptance of EIA as a planning tool was reflected in the 1992 Rio Declaration, Principle 17 of which states that 'Environmental impact assessment, as a national instrument, shall be undertaken for proposed activities that are likely to have a significant adverse impact on the environment and are subject to a decision of a competent national authority'.[6]

1   EIA in Treaties

Parallel developments on the international plane closely followed with the codification of EIA-related obligations in numerous treaties.[7] Some are of general application. For instance, the 1991 Espoo Convention on Environmental Impact Assessment in a Transboundary Context, which was concluded under the auspices of the UN Economic Commission for Europe, establishes an especially sophisticated EIA regime for its 45 states Parties, specifying the circumstances in which projects must be subjected to EIA, and the minimum requirements for the evaluation.[8]

Other treaties address EIA in particular contexts. For example, the Convention on Biological Diversity requires, among other things, that, 'as far as possible and as appropriate', the Parties shall '[i]ntroduce

---

[3] 42 U.S.C. § 4321 *et seq.* (1969).
[4] Wood, *Environmental Impact Assessment: A Comparative Review*, p. 4.
[5] Council Directive of 27 June 1985 on the assessment of the effects of certain public and private projects on the environment (85/337/EEC).
[6] United Nation Conference on Environment and Development, Rio Declaration on Environment and Development (14 June 1992), Principle 17.
[7] The 1972 Stockholm Declaration, although not referring explicitly to EIA, reflects its underlying approach; Principle 21 provides that states have 'the responsibility to ensure that activities within their jurisdiction or control do not cause damage to the environment of other states or of areas beyond the limits of national jurisdiction'.
[8] Other regional conventions also establish obligations concerning EIA. An early example is Art. 6 of the 1974 Nordic Environmental Protection Convention, which sets out a rudimentary EIA regime.

appropriate procedures requiring environmental impact assessment of its proposed projects that are likely to have significant adverse effects on biological diversity'.[9] Similarly, reflecting the fact that EIA is of particular importance for shared watercourses,[10] the Convention on the Protection and Use of Transboundary Watercourses and International Lakes and the Convention on the Law of Non-navigational Uses of International Watercourses both establish EIA-related obligations.[11]

The marine environment is another such area. Article 206 of the United Nations Convention on the Law of the Sea (UNCLOS) requires that states Parties must, 'as far as practicable, assess the potential effects' of planned activities when there is 'reasonable grounds for believing' that they 'may cause substantial pollution of or significant and harmful changes to the marine environment'.[12] This obligation, which has been invoked in a number of cases, is particularly significant because it pertains to any activities that could significantly impact the marine environment, even if confined to a state's own national jurisdiction, or fall outside the jurisdiction of any state. EIA-related obligations regarding the marine and coastal environment have also been codified in regional treaties, including those covering west and central Africa; eastern Africa; the Red Sea and Gulf of Aden; the South Pacific; the South-East Pacific; the Baltic Sea; and the Caribbean.[13]

---

[9] Convention on Biological Diversity, Art. 14(1)(a)–(b). The parties must also '[i]ntroduce appropriate arrangements to ensure that the environmental consequences of its programmes and policies that are likely to have significant adverse impacts on biological diversity are duly taken into account'.

[10] Bastmeijer and Koivurova, 'Transboundary Environmental Impact Assessment', p. 19. For discussion of transboundary EIA in regard to international watercourses, see generally A. Cassar and C. Bruch, 'Transboundary Environmental Impact Assessment in International Watercourse Management', *N.Y.U. Environmental Law Journal*, 12 (2003–05), 169; C. Bruch *et al.*, 'Assessing the Assessments: Improving Methodologies for Impact Assessment in Transboundary Watercourses', *Water Resources Development*, Sept. 2007, 391.

[11] Convention on the Protection and Use of Transboundary Watercourses and International Lakes, Art. 3(1); Convention on the Law of Non-navigational Uses of International Watercourses, Arts. 7(1) and 12.

[12] UNCLOS, Art. 206.

[13] Convention for Co-operation in the Protection and Development of the Marine and Coastal Environment of the West and Central African Region, Art. 13(2); Convention for the Protection, Management and Development of the Marine and Coastal Environment of the Eastern African Region, Art. 13; Regional Convention for the Conservation of the Red Sea and Gulf of Aden, Art. XI(1); Convention for the Protection of the Natural Resources and Environment of the South Pacific Region, Art. 16(2); Convention for the Protection of the Marine Environment and Coastal Area of the South-East Pacific, Art. 8; Convention on the Protection of the Marine Environment of the Baltic Sea Area, Art. 7;

2   EIA in Customary International Law

Apart from treaty-based obligations, in 2010, the International Court of Justice (ICJ) in the *Pulp Mills* case recognized that states are under a customary international law obligation to undertake transboundary EIAs prior to carrying out projects that may cause significant adverse transboundary impacts. The Court held:

> a practice, which in recent years has gained so much acceptance among States that it may now be considered a requirement under general international law to undertake an environmental impact assessment where there is a risk that the proposed industrial activity may have a significant adverse impact in a transboundary context, in particular, on a shared resource. Moreover, due diligence, and the duty of vigilance and prevention which it implies, would not be considered to have been exercised, if a party planning works liable to affect the regime of the river or the quality of its waters did not undertake an environmental impact assessment on the potential effects of such works.[14]

The Court reaffirmed this holding in its 2015 judgment in two joined cases concerning Nicaragua's San Juan River, in which it ruled:

> Although the Court's statement in the *Pulp Mills* case refers to industrial activities, the underlying principle applies generally to proposed activities which may have a significant adverse impact in a transboundary context. Thus, to fulfil its obligation to exercise due diligence in preventing significant transboundary environmental harm, a state must before embarking on an activity having the potential adversely to affect the environment of another state, ascertain if there is a risk of significant transbondary harm, which would trigger the requirement to carry out an environmental impact assessment.[15]

Other courts and tribunals have similarly held in the context of adjudicating EIA-related cases under the law of the sea. The Seabed Disputes Chamber of the International Tribunal for the Law of the Sea (ITLOS), in its 2011 Advisory Opinion on *Responsibilities and Obligations of States Sponsoring Persons and Entities with Respect to Activities in the Area*, 'stressed' that not only is 'the obligation to conduct an environmental

---

Convention for the Protection and Development of the Marine Environment of the Wider Caribbean Region, Art. 12.

[14] *Pulp Mills on the River Uruguay (Argentina v. Uruguay)*, Judgment, 20 April 2010 ('*Pulp Mills*'), para. 204.

[15] *Certain activities Carried Out by Nicaragua in the Border Area (Costa Rica v. Nicaragua)*, joined with *Construction of a Road in Costa Rica Along the San Juan River (Nicaragua v. Costa Rica)*, Judgment, 16 December 2015 ('*Costa Rica v. Nicaragua*'), para. 104.

impact assessment' a 'direct obligation under' UNCLOS, it is also 'a general obligation under customary international law'.[16] Commenting on the ICJ's holding in *Pulp Mills*, the Chamber observed that '[a]lthough aimed at the specific situation under discussion by the Court, the language used seems broad enough to cover activities in the Area' and that '[t]he Court's reasoning in a transboundary context may also apply to activities with an impact on the environment in an area beyond the limits of national jurisdiction'.[17] Likewise, the arbitral tribunal in the *South China Sea* arbitration observed that Article 206 of UNCLOS 'ensures that planned activities with potentially damaging effects may be effectively controlled and that other States are kept informed of their potential risks'. Quoting the Seabed Disputes Chamber, the tribunal 'emphasised that the obligation to conduct an environmental impact assessment is a direct obligation under the Convention and a general obligation under customary international law'.[18]

In so holding, these courts and tribunals have followed the International Law Commission's 2001 Articles on Prevention of Transboundary Harm from Hazardous Activities, Article 7 of which provides: 'Any decision in respect of the authorization of an activity within the scope of the present articles shall, in particular, be based on an assessment of the possible transboundary harm caused by that activity, including any environmental impact assessment.'[19] The ILC's Commentary explains:

> ... a State of origin, before granting authorization to operators to undertake activities referred to in article 1, should ensure that an assessment is undertaken of the risk of the activity causing significant transboundary harm. This assessment enables the State to determine the extent and the

---

[16] *Responsibilities and Obligations of States Sponsoring Persons and Entities with Respect to Activities in the Area*, Advisory Opinion, 1 February 2011, ITLOS Reports 2011 ('*Responsibilities and Obligations of States*'), para. 145. The 'Area' is defined in Art. 1(1) of UNCLOS as 'the seabed and ocean floor and subsoil thereof, beyond the limits of national jurisdiction'. Article 191 provides that the Seabed Disputes Chamber of ITLOS 'shall give advisory opinions at the request of the Assembly or the Council [of the International Seabed Authority] on legal questions arising within the scope of their activities'.

[17] *Responsibilities and Obligations of States*, para. 148. The Seabed Disputes Chamber also noted that 'the Court's references to "shared resources" may also apply to resources that are the common heritage of mankind'.

[18] *South China Sea Arbitration (Philippines v. China)*, Award of 12 July 2016 ('*South China Sea*'), para. 948.

[19] Articles on Prevention of Transboundary Harm from Hazardous Activities, Art. 7.

nature of the risk involved in an activity and consequently the type of
preventive measures it should take.[20]

Although the customary legal obligation to carry out an EIA appears to
have crystallized relatively recently, it is grounded in the well-established
principles of due diligence and prevention. The ICJ has long recognized
that it is 'part of the corpus of international law relating to the environment' that states are 'obliged to use all the means at its disposal in order to
avoid activities which take place in its territory, or in any area under its
jurisdiction, causing significant damage to the environment of another
state'.[21] This 'principle of prevention', the Court observed in *Pulp Mills*:
'has its origins in the due diligence that is required of a state in its
territory,' and mandates that it is '"every state's obligation not to allow
knowingly its territory to be used for acts contrary to the rights of other
states"'.[22]

There is debate over whether the need to conduct an EIA is a stand-
alone obligation, or whether it is a means to fulfil the more general
obligation of due diligence. Judge Donoghue, in her Separate Opinion in
the *San Juan River* cases, observed that although the ICJ in *Pulp Mills* 'is
widely understood' as having held that there is an obligation under customary international law to undertake an EIA where there is a risk of
significant transboundary environmental harm, she nonetheless is 'not
confident' that 'state practice and *opinio juris* would support the existence
of such a specific rule, in addition to the underlying obligation of due
diligence.'[23] Judge Owada shares this view; he conceptualizes EIA as 'one
important constituent element of the process that emanates from the
international obligation of states to act in due diligence to avoid or mitigate
significant transboundary harm, rather than a separate and independent
obligation standing on its own under general international law'.[24]

Regardless, commentators have noted that '[i]t would be hard for
a state to argue that it had acted in due diligence if it had not even studied
what the impacts of a proposed project on another state's environment
would be'.[25] Judge Donoghue herself has observed that her scepticism

---

[20] ILC, Draft Articles on Prevention of Transboundary Harm from Hazardous Activities,
with commentaries, Commentary on Art. 7 ('ILC, Draft Articles'), para. 1.

[21] *Pulp Mills*, para. 101.

[22] *Ibid.*, (quoting *Corfu Channel (United Kingdom v. Albania), Merits*, Judgment, I.C.J.
Reports 1949, p. 22).

[23] *Costa Rica v. Nicaragua*, Separate Opinion of Judge Donoghue, para. 13.

[24] *Ibid.*, Separate Opinion of Judge Owada, para. 18.

[25] Bastmeijer and Koivurova, 'Transboundary Environmental Impact Assessment', p. 7.

that EIA is itself a specific rule of customary international law 'does not mean that [she is] dismissive of the importance of environmental impact assessment in meeting a due diligence obligation' since '[i]f a proposed activity poses a risk of significant transboundary environmental harm, a State of origin would be hard pressed to explain a decision to undertake that activity without prior assessment of the risk of transboundary environmental harm'.[26] Judge Owada similarly accepts that '[i]n the process of carrying out the obligation to act in due diligence under international environmental law, the requirement of conducting an environmental impact assessment becomes a key element for determining whether certain activities may cause significant transboundary harm'.[27]

In any event, the jurisprudence is clear that states are under an obligation to carry out a transboundary EIA where there is a risk that a project might cause significant adverse environmental impacts to other states, regardless whether that is because EIA is the means by which the general due diligence obligation is fulfilled, or because the obligation to undertake an EIA is a stand-alone rule of customary international law.

C   The Jurisdiction of International Courts and Tribunals to Adjudicate EIA Disputes

The foundational principle that a state may be subjected to binding third-party dispute resolution procedures only if it has so consented is no less true for disputes concerning EIA. That consent may be located in a treaty's dispute settlement provisions. Treaties concerned with the regulation of shared resources, or the rights of riparian states, may be particularly relevant, as was the case in *Pulp Mills*, where the Court was asked by Argentina to determine the adequacy of the EIA that Uruguay had carried out in connection with its authorization of two pulp mills sited on the Uruguay River, a shared watercourse that forms the international border. The Court's jurisdiction was based on the Statute of the River Uruguay, a bilateral treaty Article 60 of which provides: 'Any dispute concerning the interpretation or application of ... the Statute which cannot be settled by direct negotiations may be submitted by either Party to the International Court of Justice.'[28]

---

[26]   *Costa Rica* v. *Nicaragua*, Separate Opinion of Judge Donoghue, para. 13.

[27]   *Ibid.*, Separate Opinion of Judge Owada, para. 14. See also *ibid.*, para. 18.

[28]   *Pulp Mills*, para. 48.

A bilateral treaty's compulsory dispute resolution procedures similarly provided the basis for jurisdiction in the *Indus Waters Kishenganga* arbitration, where a Court of Arbitration was constituted pursuant to Article IX and Annexure G of the Indus Waters Treaty to resolve a dispute between Pakistan and India concerning India's diversion of a river and other works undertaken in connection with the construction of a hydroelectric project. Among the issues the Court of Arbitration was required to determine was the adequacy of India's assessment of the project's downstream environmental impacts.[29]

Multilateral conventions may also establish jurisdiction for disputes concerning EIA. The dispute settlement procedures established in Part XV of UNCLOS have been the most frequently invoked. Article 287 allows states to choose from among ITLOS, the ICJ and arbitral tribunals constituted in accordance with Annex VII of the Convention as the means for settling disputes concerning UNCLOS's interpretation or application. These procedures are available for, *inter alia*, disputes over alleged breach of the EIA requirements set out in Article 206.[30]

ITLOS has adjudicated two such cases, both involving requests for provisional measures pending the constitution of arbitral tribunals pursuant to Annex VII.[31] In *MOX Plant*, Ireland sought provisional measures in relation to its claims concerning, *inter alia*, the United Kingdom's alleged failure to have 'properly and fully ... assess[ed]' the 'potential effects' of the operation of a mixed-oxide plant on the marine environment of the Irish Sea, as well as the possible effects of 'international movements of radioactive materials to be transported to and from

---

[29] *Indus Waters Kishenganga Arbitration, Pakistan/India*, Partial Award, 18 February 2013.

[30] If the parties to the dispute have not selected the same procedure, the dispute may be submitted to arbitration only in accordance with Annex VII; parties to disputes not covered by a declaration in force are deemed to have accepted Annex VII arbitration. See UNCLOS, Art. 287.

[31] Article 290(1) of UNCLOS allows for provisional measures to be prescribed to preserve the respective rights of the parties to the dispute or to prevent serious harm to the marine environment, pending the final decision. See UNCLOS, Art. 290(1). ITLOS may prescribe provisional measures pending constitution of an Annex VII arbitral tribunal 'if the Tribunal considers that the urgency of the situation so requires in the sense that action prejudicial to the rights of either party or causing serious harm to the marine environment is likely to be taken before the constitution of the Annex VII arbitral tribunal'. *The MOX Plant Case (Ireland v. United Kingdom)*, ITLOS, Request for Provisional Measures, Order of 3 December 2001, para. 64.

the MOX plant'.[32] Similarly, in the *Land Reclamation* case, ITLOS was called upon to address EIA in the context of a provisional measures request by Malaysia that Singapore had failed adequately to assess the environmental impacts of a land reclamation project. Among other things, Malaysia requested an order that Singapore 'suspend its current land reclamation activities until it has conducted and published an adequate assessment of their potential effects on the environment and on the affected coastal areas'.[33]

The subsequently constituted Annex VII arbitral tribunals in the *Mox Plant* and *Land Reclamation* cases are not the only ones to have had EIA-related disputes placed before them.[34] In the *South China Sea* arbitration, China's alleged failure to carry out an EIA in regard to artificial islands that it has built on submerged coral reefs in the South China Sea numbered among the claims asserted by the Philippines.[35]

Jurisdiction over EIA-related disputes may also be established by states *ex ante* accepting the compulsory jurisdiction of the ICJ, which can be done pursuant to Article 36(2) of the Statute of the Court, or by Article XXXI of the American Treaty on Pacific Settlement (Pact of Bogotá). Disputes in regard to transboundary EIA plainly fall within the scope of these articles. The Pact of Bogotá was the jurisdictional basis in the joined

---

[32] *MOX Plant Case (Ireland v. United Kingdom)*, ITLOS, Request for Provisional Measures, Order of 3 December 2001, para. 26(4). In particular, Ireland sought an order that the United Kingdom 'refrain from authorizing or failing to prevent (a) the operation of the MOX plant and/or (b) international movements of radioactive materials into and out of the United Kingdom related to the operation of the MOX plant or any preparatory or other activities associated with the operation of the MOX plant until such time as', *inter alia*, 'there has been carried out a proper assessment of the environmental impact of the operation of the MOX plant as well as related international movements of radioactive materials': *Ibid.*, para. 26(5).

[33] *Land Reclamation by Singapore in and around the Straits of Johor (Malaysia v. Singapore)*, Provisional Measures, Order of 8 October 2003, ITLOS Reports 2003, para. 22 (*citing* Notification and Statement of Claim).

[34] *Case concerning Land Reclamation by Singapore in and around the Straits of Johor (Malaysia v. Singapore)*, Decision of 1 September 2005; *The MOX Plant Case (Ireland v. United Kingdom)*, Order No. 3, 24 June 2003.

[35] Other treaties have a variety of dispute settlement procedures which, depending on the treaty, may enable disputes concerning EIA to be subjected to compulsory third-party dispute resolution. See, e.g., Convention on Environmental Impact Assessment in a Transboundary Context, Art. 15; Convention on the Law of the Non-navigational Uses of International Watercourses, Art. 33; Convention on Biological Diversity, Art. 27; Convention on the Protection and Use of Transboundary Watercourses and International Lakes, Art. 22; Convention for Co-operation in the Protection and Development of the Marine and Coastal Environment of the West and Central African Region, Art. 24.

Certain Activities and *Construction of a Road* cases, both of which concerned EIA-related disputes involving Nicaragua's San Juan River. The former involved a claim by Costa Rica that Nicaragua's dredging of the river had caused adverse impacts in Costa Rica in the form of diversion of flow and related changes to fluvial geomorphology, and that the project had been undertaken without adequate assessment of the risks allegedly posed to Costa Rica. The latter involved a claim by Nicaragua that Costa Rica had constructed a highway in close proximity to the river without having first evaluated the project's impacts to Nicaragua, including the effects of sedimentation caused by road-related erosion.[36] Jurisdiction under the Pact of Bogotá was likewise invoked in the *Aerial Herbicide Spraying* case, in which Ecuador asked the ICJ to determine whether Colombia had breached its international environmental obligations, including with respect to EIA, by authorizing the spraying of herbicides near the border without having adequately assessed its transboundary impacts, including on human health, agricultural crops, and the natural environment.[37]

States may also refer disputes concerning EIA to courts and tribunals by concluding special agreements. This mechanism was used by Hungary and Slovakia in the *Gabčikovo-Nagymaros* case, in which the Court addressed EIA in connection with a hydroelectric project on the Danube River.[38] In the *Iron Rhine* arbitration, the impact assessments carried out in connection with a railway rehabilitation project formed the basis for claims which Belgium agreed to arbitrate with the Netherlands. The parties' consent to jurisdiction was based on an arbitration agreement effectuated through an exchange of diplomatic notes.[39]

D   Procedural and Evidentiary Challenges Posed by Disputes Concerning EIA

Adjudicating EIA-related disputes presents international courts and tribunals with procedural and evidentiary challenges. These include having to review critically, and against the standards imposed by international

---

[36] See, e.g., *Costa Rica v. Nicaragua*, paras. 100–120, 146–162.
[37] As a supplemental source of jurisdiction, Ecuador invoked Art. 32 of the 1988 United Nations Convention against Illicit Traffic in Narcotic Drugs and Psychotropic Substances.
[38] *Gabčikovo-Nagymaros (Hungary/Slovakia)*, Judgment, ICJ Reports 1997, p. 7.
[39] *Iron Rhine ('Ijzeren Rijn') Railway between the Kingdom of Belgium and the Kingdom of the Netherlands*, Decision of 24 May 2005 (*'Iron Rhine'*), paras. 1–2.

law, the scientific analyses and decision-making of domestic regulatory authorities in regard to such matters as whether a particular project, in light of the sensitivity of the receiving environment, creates a level of risk that necessitates EIA; whether an EIA adequately evaluated such risks; and whether sufficient measures have been adopted by a State to prevent, reduce, or mitigate those risks. These adjudicative challenges are compounded by the fact that the evidence that an international court or tribunal must consider is invariably of a complex scientific and technical nature.

1 Disputes Concerning Whether EIA Is Required

The process for determining whether a project must be subjected to an EIA is known as 'screening'.[40] It 'answers the basic question, is an EIA required?'[41]

Disputes can arise over whether an EIA is required for a particular project. Not all cases present this issue since, in many, a state accepts that a risk assessment is necessary. For instance, in *Pulp Mills*, Uruguay did not contest that it had to evaluate the risks posed to Argentina by the proposed project. Likewise, in the *MOX Plant* and *Kishenganga* cases, the United Kingdom and India, respectively, accepted that EIA was required. In each, the dispute concerned whether the EIA's scope and content was adequate, not whether a risk assessment was needed. Nonetheless, courts and tribunals must sometimes adjudicate disputes concerning whether a project requires an EIA.

Some EIA regimes, such as the one established by the Espoo Convention, require EIAs for certain listed types of projects and/or where projects are located in or near pre-determined environmentally sensitive areas. For cases decided under customary international law, however, the ICJ explained in *Pulp Mills* that an EIA must be undertaken where there is a 'risk that the proposed industrial activity may have a significant adverse impact in a transboundary context'.[42] The Court confirmed this approach in the joined *San Juan River* cases, holding that

---

[40] Decision Adopted by the Conference of the Parties to the Convention on Biological Diversity at its Eighth Meeting, Curitiba, Brazil, 20–31 March 2006, VIII/28, Impact Assessment: Voluntary Guidelines on Biodiversity-Inclusive Impact Assessment, UNEP/CBD/COP/DEC/VIII/28 ('Voluntary Guidelines on Biodiversity-Inclusive Impact Assessment'), para. 5.

[41] Hanna, 'A Brief Introduction to Environmental Impact Assessment', p. 9.

[42] *Pulp Mills*, para. 204.

states must, 'before embarking on an activity having the potential adversely to affect the environment of another state, ascertain if there is a risk of significant transbondary harm, which would trigger the requirement to carry out an environmental impact assessment'.[43]

An international court or tribunal may be called upon to apply this standard against a prior determination by the relevant domestic regulatory authorities, which may have overseen the carrying out of an 'initial environmental examination or preliminary environmental assessment' that decided whether an EIA was needed.[44] The ILC's Commentary explains:

> The question of who should conduct the assessment is left to States. Such assessment is normally conducted by operators observing certain guidelines set by the States. These matters would have to be resolved by the States themselves through their domestic laws or as parties to international instruments. However, it is presumed that a State of origin will designate an authority, whether or not governmental, to evaluate the assessment on behalf of the Government and will accept responsibility for the conclusions reached by that authority.[45]

For the purposes of international law, the determination of whether there exists a 'risk' of transboundary harm is 'to be taken objectively', based on 'an appreciation of possible harm resulting from an activity which a properly informed observer had or ought to have had'.[46] Whether the threshold of risk of significant transboundary harm is crossed is often highly fact-specific:

> The term 'significant' is not without ambiguity and a determination has to be made in each specific case. It involves more factual considerations than legal determination. It is to be understood that *'significant' is something more than 'detectable' but need not be at the level of 'serious' or 'substantial'.* The harm must lead to a real detrimental effect on matters such as, for example, human health, industry, property, environment or agriculture in other States. Such detrimental effects must be susceptible of being measured by factual and objective standards.[47]

---

[43] *Costa Rica* v. *Nicaragua*, para. 104. See also *ibid.*, para. 153 ('a State's obligation to exercise due diligence in preventing significant transboundary harm requires that State to ascertain whether there is a risk of significant transboundary harm prior to undertaking an activity having the potentially adversely to affect the environment of another State. If that is the case, the State concerned must conduct an environmental impact assessment').

[44] Voluntary Guidelines on Biodiversity-Inclusive Impact Assessment, para. 10.

[45] ILC, Draft Articles, Commentary on Art. 7, para. 5.

[46] *Ibid.*, Commentary on Art. 1, para. 14.

[47] *Ibid.*, Commentary on Art. 1, para. 4. See also *ibid.*, para. 9.

The jurisprudence suggests that robust proof is required to convince an international court or tribunal that a state is justified in not undertaking a transboundary EIA. In the *Certain Activities* case, the ICJ ruled that Nicaragua had not been required to carry out an EIA in connection with its project to dredge the San Juan River only after finding that Nicaragua had 'conducted a study of the impact that the dredging programme would have on its own environment' which had also found 'that the programme would not have a significant impact on the flow of [Costa Rica's] Colorado River'.[48] The Court also relied on the fact that the conclusions of Nicaragua's regulatory authorities in this regard had been confirmed not only by the expert testimony which Nicaragua had presented to the Court, but also by Costa Rica's own expert.[49] The Court thus held that '[i]n light of the absence of risk of significant transboundary harm, Nicaragua was not required to carry out an environmental impact assessment'.[50]

In other cases, courts and tribunals have ruled that an EIA was required. In *Construction of a Road*, the ICJ held that Costa Rica's failure to present evidence that it had, prior to constructing a highway near Nicaragua's San Juan River, carried out at least a preliminary assessment of potential transboundary impacts, meant that it had not discharged its EIA obligations. The Court held that 'to conduct a preliminary assessment of the risk posed by an activity is one of the ways in which a state can ascertain whether the proposed activity carries a risk of significant transboundary harm', and Costa Rica had 'not adduced any evidence that it actually carried out such a preliminary assessment'.[51]

Further, the Court rejected Costa Rica's argument that an EIA was not required because 'the construction of the road did not create a risk of significant transboundary harm through the discharge of harmful substances into the San Juan River or otherwise into Nicaraguan territory'.[52] The Court evaluated this claim by reference to 'the nature and magnitude of the project and the context in which it was to be carried out'.[53] In so doing, the Court took account of the fact that 'the scale of the road project was substantial' – nearly 160 km long, 108.2 km of which was alongside the river – with approximately half located within 100 metres of the

---

[48] *Costa Rica v. Nicaragua*, para. 105.
[49] *Ibid.*
[50] *Ibid.*
[51] *Ibid.*, para. 154.
[52] *Ibid.*, para. 147.
[53] *Ibid.*, para. 155.

riverbank, including stretches within five metres. In light of this proximity, the Court determined that 'any harm caused by the road to the surrounding environment could easily affect the river, and therefore Nicaragua's territory'.[54]

When evaluating the significance of those potential impacts, the Court explained that 'the geographic conditions of the river basin where the road was to be situated must be taken into account'.[55] In that connection, the Court observed that '[t]he road would pass through a wetland of international importance in Costa Rican territory' and would be 'located in close proximity to another projected wetland' in Nicaragua. It thus held that '[t]he presence of Ramsar protected sites heightens the risk of significant damage because it denotes that the receiving environment is particularly sensitive'.[56]

The *South China Sea* arbitration, in which the Philippines argued that China had failed to carry out an EIA for its artificial island-building project, likewise required the tribunal to determine whether the threshold for carrying out an EIA had been crossed. Following the ICJ's approach, the tribunal observed that 'simple assertions as the existence of a preliminary assessment' do not 'equate to having "adduced any evidence that it actually carried out such a preliminary assessment"'.[57] Nor, the tribunal held, was there doubt that the scale of the project, which involved deploying 'a large fleet of vessels' to seven coral reefs and the use of 'heavy "cutter-suction dredge" equipment' to create more than 12.8 million square metres of artificial land,[58] was sufficient to trigger the obligation to perform an EIA, in light of the fact that China's 'construction and dredging activities' could:

> impact reef systems in three ways: (a) direct destruction of reef habitat through burial under sand, gravel and rubble; (b) indirect impacts on benthic organisms such as corals and seagrasses via altered hydrodynamics, increased sedimentation, turbidity, and nutrient enrichment; and (c) indirect impacts on organisms in the water column, such as fishes and larvae, from sediments, chemical and nutrient release, and noise.[59]

---

[54] *Ibid.*
[55] *Ibid.*
[56] *Ibid.* The Court also observed '[t]he possibility of natural disasters in the area caused by adverse events such as hurricanes, tropical storms and earthquakes, which would increase the risk of sediment erosion'.
[57] *South China Sea*, para. 989.
[58] *Ibid.*, para. 854.
[59] *Ibid.*, para. 857.

The tribunal thus ruled that 'given the scale and impact of the island-building activities', China 'could not reasonably have held any belief other than that the construction "may cause significant and harmful changes to the marine environment". Accordingly, China was required, "as far as practicable" to prepare an environmental impact assessment.'[60]

2 Disputes Concerning an EIA's Scope, Content and Implementation

Since respondent states often accept the need to carry out an EIA, many cases center on whether an EIA was adequate in scope and content, and/or over whether the project's design or location sufficiently addresses the risks identified and evaluated in the EIA.

The process for determining what a EIA should cover is known as 'scoping'. The Conference of the States Parties to the Biological Diversity Convention explains:

> During scoping relevant impacts are identified resulting in the terms of reference for the actual impact study. The scoping stage is considered critical in the process as it defines the issues to be studied and it provides the reference information on which the review of the study results will be based ... During scoping promising alternatives can be identified that may significantly reduce or entirely prevent adverse impacts on biodiversity.[61]

Disputes may arise over whether an EIA complied with the international law standard. The inquiry is inherently project-specific, a fact emphasized by the ICJ when it explained that the '[d]etermination of the content of the environmental impact assessment should be made in light of the specific circumstances of each case'.[62] This follows from the overarching principle that '[t]he standard of due diligence against which the conduct of the state of origin should be examined is that which is generally considered to be appropriate and proportional to the degree of risk of transboundary harm *in the particular instance*'.[63] Thus, for example, 'activities which may be considered ultrahazardous require a much higher standard of care in designing policies and a much higher degree of vigour on the part of the state to enforce them'.[64] Put simply, 'the

---

[60] *Ibid.*, para. 988.
[61] Voluntary Guidelines on Biodiversity-Inclusive Impact Assessment, para. 2. See also *Ibid.* at para. 5.
[62] *Costa Rica* v. *Nicaragua*, para. 104.
[63] ILC, Draft Articles, Commentary on Art. 3, para. 11 (emphasis added).
[64] *Ibid.*

assessment of risk of an activity can only be meaningfully prepared if it relates the risk to the possible harm to which the risk could lead'.[65]

Indeed, what is required for an adequate EIA may not only vary in accordance with the specifics of the project and the receiving environment, it may also vary over time. As ITLOS's Seabed Disputes Chamber has observed:

> The content of 'due diligence' obligations may not easily be described in precise terms. Among the factors that make such a description difficult is the fact that 'due diligence' is a variable concept. It may change over time as measures considered sufficiently diligent at a certain moment may become not diligent enough in light, for instance, of new scientific or technological knowledge. It may also change in relation to the risks involved in the activity.[66]

The determination of an EIA's scope and content is largely a function of a state's domestic environmental laws. According to the ILC, '[t]he specifics of what ought to be the content of assessment is left to the domestic laws of the state conducting such assessment'.[67] As the ICJ held in *Pulp Mills*, 'it is for each state to determine in its domestic legislation or in the authorization process for the project, the specific content of the environmental impact assessment required in each case'.[68]

Nonetheless, states do not enjoy unconstrained discretion in determining the content of an EIA. Although *Pulp Mills* held that an EIA's content is a matter that is left to a state's domestic legal regime, this is subject to an important caveat: the EIA must 'hav[e] regard to the nature and magnitude of the proposed development and its likely adverse impact on the environment as well as to the need to exercise due diligence in conducting such an assessment'.[69] The Court's Judgment in the *San Juan River* cases confirmed this approach. Judge Donoghue explained in her Separate Opinion:

> Today's Judgment makes clear that the above-quoted passage from the *Pulp Mills* case does not give rise to a *renvoi* to national law in respect of the content and procedures of environmental impact assessment (as one of the Parties had asserted). Instead, the '[d]etermination of the content of the environmental impact assessment should be made in light of the specific circumstances of each case' (paragraph 104). Thus, the Court

---

[65] *Ibid.*, Commentary on Art. 7, para. 6.
[66] *Responsibilities and Obligations of States*, para. 117.
[67] ILC, Draft Articles, Commentary on Art. 7, para. 7.
[68] *Pulp Mills*, para. 205.
[69] *Ibid.*

does not presume to prescribe details as to the content and procedure of transboundary environmental impact assessment. This leaves scope for variation in the way that States of origin conduct the assessment, so long as the State meets its obligation to exercise due diligence in preventing transboundary environmental harm.[70]

There is good reason why international courts or tribunals should not simply defer to the determination of a state agency in regard to the scope or content of an EIA. As one commentator has observed, 'agencies are not wholly neutral to the issues presented in an [Environmental Impact Statement]; they have their own institutional culture and sense of mission, and they typically attract administrators who share those values. Even if they are not willfully ignoring ecological factors, they may be biased in favor of their own *raison d'être* when forced to decide between defending the environment and furthering their project'.[71]

This is not to say that compliance with the domestic EIA regime is necessarily irrelevant; the fact that a state has failed to carry out an EIA in accordance with the requirements of its own domestic laws may be particularly probative of failure to comply with a state's international EIA obligations. In the *South China Sea* arbitration, the tribunal considered whether China had breached Article 206 of UNCLOS in light of China's domestic EIA obligations. It held:

> By China's own legislative standards, an EIA must be 'objective, open and impartial, comprehensively consider impacts on various environmental factors and the ecosystem they form after the implementation of the plan or construction project, and thus provide scientific basis for the decision-making.' Additionally, the 'state shall encourage all relevant units, experts and the public to participate in the EIA in proper ways.' With respect to construction projects, Chinese law require an EIA to include, *inter alia*, analysis, projection and evaluation on the potential environmental impacts of the project, and suggestions on implementation of environmental monitoring.[72]

Given the requirements of China's EIA law, the fact that publicly available Chinese documents purporting to describe China's risk assessments 'fall short of these criteria' was found by the tribunal to indicate that China had not discharged its EIA obligations under Article 206 of

---

[70] *Costa Rica* v. *Nicaragua*, Separate Opinion of Judge Donoghue, para. 15.
[71] C. Kersten, 'Rethinking Transboundary Environmental Impact Assessment', *Yale Journal of International Law*, 43 (2009), 181.
[72] *South China Sea*, para. 990 (quoting People's Republic of China, *Law of the People's Republic of China on Evaluation of Environmental Effects* (28 October 2002)).

UNCLOS.[73] At a minimum, the tribunal held, China was required to 'have assessed possible effects on the marine ecosystem of the South China Sea, the coral reefs at issue, the biodiversity and sustainability of living resource there and endangered species'.[74] The available evidence, however, suggested that China had fallen short of meeting this standard.[75]

Even if carried out, EIA cannot be an empty formality; its conclusions must be evaluated and taken into account in the implementation of the project. As the arbitral tribunal in the *Iron Rhine* arbitration held, international law requires 'the integration of appropriate environmental measures in the design and implementation of economic development activities'.[76] Such '[r]emedial action can take several forms, i.e., avoidance (or prevention), mitigation (by considering changes to the scale, design, location, siting, process, sequencing, phasing, management and/or monitoring of the proposed activity, as well as restoration or rehabilitation of sites, and compensation, (often associated with residual impacts after prevention and mitigation)'.[77] Indeed, 'EIA should be an

---

[73] *Ibid.* See also para. 989 ('Despite China's repeated assertions by officials at different levels, that it has undertaken thorough environmental studies, neither the Tribunal, the Tribunal-appointed experts, the Philippines, nor the Philippines' experts have been able to identify any report that would resemble an environmental impact assessment that meets the requirements of Article 206 of the Convention, or indeed under China's own Environmental Impact Assessment Law of 2002').

[74] *Ibid.*, para. 911.

[75] The tribunal ultimately determined that it was unable to 'make a definitive finding that China has prepared an environmental impact assessment, but nor can it definitively find that it has failed to do so in light of the repeated assertions by Chinese officials and scientists that China has undertaken thorough studies'. However, such a finding was 'not necessary in order to find a breach of Article 206' since under that provision 'a State must not only prepare an EIA but also must communicate it'. The tribunal had 'directly asked China for a copy of any EIA it had prepared; China did not provide one' even though, despite its non-participation in the arbitral proceedings, in respect of other matters, China had 'found occasions and means to communicate statements by its own officials, or by others writing in line with China's interests'. The tribunal determined that had China 'wished to draw attention to the existence and content of an EIA, the Tribunal has no doubt it could have done so'. Further, the tribunal observed that 'the obligation to communicate is, by the terms of Article 205, to "competent international organizations, which should make them available to all states." Although China's representatives have assured the state parties to the Convention that its "construction activities followed a high standard of environmental protection," it has delivered no assessment in writing to that forum or any other international body as far as the Tribunal is aware. Accordingly, the Tribunal finds that China has not fulfilled its duties under Article 206 of the Convention.' *Ibid.*, para. 991.

[76] *Iron Rhine*, para. 59.

[77] Voluntary Guidelines on Biodiversity-Inclusive Impact Assessment, para. 23.

iterative process of assessing impacts, re-designing alternatives and comparison'.[78]

The obligation to undertake an EIA is thus a continuing one, such that:

> EIA does not stop with the production of a report and a decision on the proposed project. Activities that have to make sure the recommendations from the [EIA] are implemented are commonly grouped under the heading of 'EIA follow-up.' They may include activities related to monitoring, compliance, enforcement and environmental auditing.[79]

As the ICJ has observed, 'new norms have to be taken into consideration, and such new standards given proper weight, not only when States contemplate new activities but also when continuing with activities begun in the past'.[80] In that connection, both the ICJ and ITLOS have held that 'an obligation to act with due diligence' 'entails not only the adoption of appropriate rules and measures, but also a certain level of vigilance in their enforcement and the exercise of administrative control applicable to public and private operators, such as the monitoring of activities undertaken by such operators'.[81] Thus, 'the obligation to carry out an environmental impact assessment is a continuous one, and that monitoring of the project's effects on the environment shall be undertaken, where necessary, throughout the life of the project'.[82]

3   The Challenge of Adjudicating Scientific and Technical Issues

Adjudication of EIA-related disputes, whether concerning screening, scoping or implementation, requires a court or tribunal to evaluate the sufficiency of a state's regulatory actions in a manner that forces it to address issues that are fact-intensive and, as Judge Owada has observed, 'essentially of a technical nature'.[83] The challenge this presents is compounded by the fact that the parties often disagree about the underlying scientific evidence and its significance. The Joint Declaration of seven ITLOS judges could have described most, if not all, EIA cases when it observed in *MOX Plant* that Ireland's dispute with the United Kingdom was 'characterized by an almost total lack of agreement on the scientific

---

[78] *Ibid.*, para. 28.
[79] *Ibid.*, para. 44.
[80] *Gabcikovo-Nagymaros*, para. 140.
[81] *Responsibilities and Obligations of States*, para. 115; *Pulp Mills*, para. 197.
[82] *Costa Rica v. Nicaragua*, para. 161 (*citing Pulp Mills*, para. 205).
[83] *Costa Rica v. Nicaragua*, Separate Opinion of Judge Owada, para. 21.

evidence with respect to the possible consequences' of the plant's operation on the marine environment.[84]

Some judges have expressed unease about their ability to resolve highly
technical issues. In *Pulp Mills*, Judges Al-Khasawneh and Simma
observed that this 'exceptionally fact-intensive case' was 'unlike most
cases submitted to the Court and raise[d] serious questions' about the
'role that scientific evidence can play in an international judicial institution'. They expressed concern that '[t]he traditional methods of evaluating evidence' were 'deficient in assessing the relevance of such complex,
technical and scientific facts'.[85]

There has thus been a preference in EIA cases for relying, where
possible, upon the conclusions of independent experts. In the *Land
Reclamation* case, after ITLOS determined that Singapore had not
assessed the project's impacts on waters under Malaysian jurisdiction,
and found that it could not exclude the possibility that it might adversely
impact the marine environment, ITLOS ruled that the parties should
'establish mechanisms for exchanging information and assessing the
risks or effects of the land reclamation, and devising ways to address
them.[86] Malaysia and Singapore were therefore ordered to 'cooperate'
and to study, on agreed terms, the land reclamation's effects, and to
propose, as appropriate, measures to deal with any adverse impacts.
ITLOS further directed Singapore 'not to conduct its land reclamation
in ways that might cause irreparable prejudice to the rights of Malaysia or
serious harm to the marine environment, taking especially into account
the reports of [a] group of independent experts' that would be
assembled.[87] Singapore and Malaysia ultimately settled the dispute
when Singapore agreed to modify the reclamation project based on the
experts' findings.[88]

In the *Iron Rhine* arbitration, the tribunal observed that it was not 'the
task of this Tribunal to investigate questions of considerable scientific

---

[84] *The MOX Plant Case (Ireland v. United Kingdom)*, ITLOS, Request for Provisional
Measures, Order of 3 December 2001, Joint Declaration of Judges Caminos,
Yamamoto, Park, Akl, Marsit, Eiriksson, and Jesus.

[85] *Pulp Mills*, Joint Dissenting Opinion of Judges Al-Khasawneh, and Simma, para. 3. For
contrary views, see Separate Opinion of Judge Keith, para. 1; Separate Opinion of Judge
Greenwood, para. 24.

[86] *Land Reclamation by Singapore in and around the Straits of Johor (Malaysia v. Singapore)*,
Provisional Measures, Order of 8 October 2003, ITLOS Reports 2003, para. 99.

[87] *Ibid.*, para. 106(1)–(2).

[88] *Land Reclamation by Singapore in and around the Straits of Johor*, Award on Agreed
Terms, 1 September 2005, Annex, sec. A.

complexity as to which measures will be sufficient to achieve compliance with the required levels of environmental protection', and that those matters were 'appropriately left to technical experts'. It therefore recommended that the parties, within four months, 'put into effect the conditions necessary for a committee of independent experts to be set up within the same time frame, unless the Parties agree otherwise, to engage in the task of determining' various technical matters. The experts' findings, the tribunal directed, should be 'used by the Parties in determining their respective share for the costs and risks associated with' the railroad's upgrade.[89]

Independent experts also appear to have played an important role in the *Pulp Mills* case. There, the Court had the benefit of external review and evaluation by technical experts who had been retained by the International Finance Corporation in connection with the project's financing, whose conclusions Uruguay presented to the Court.

Recent cases indicate that the ICJ may be becoming increasingly willing to engage directly with scientific and technical evidence. In that regard, the Court has shifted away from the procedure used in the *Pulp Mills* case, in which the parties' experts addressed the Court as advocates, which insulated them from cross-examination. Now, the Court is encouraging experts to give live testimony, with cross-examination by the opposing party and questioning from the bench. This procedure was used in the *Whaling* case, in which, although it was not a case that concerned EIA, matters of science were nonetheless at the forefront. It would also have been employed in the *Aerial Herbicide Spraying* case, in which Ecuador asked the ICJ to determine whether Colombia had unlawfully authorized the spraying of herbicides near the border without having assessed its transboundary impacts. Since the case presented complicated technical issues centered around predicting the dispersal of sprays released from aircraft flying at different speeds, heights, and weather conditions, and applying predicted deposition rates to the dose responses of various plants, it was well suited to the Court's new approach to expert evidence. However, the case settled shortly before oral hearings were scheduled to begin.

The Court's current practice was utilized in the joined *San Juan River* cases. Not only were the parties' experts cross-examined about complicated topics such as fluvial geomorphology; hydrology; highway engineering, design, and rehabilitation; and the impact of sediment on

---

[89] *Iron Rhine*, para. 235.

aquatic biota – there was extensive questioning from the bench. No fewer than nine judges posed sophisticated and nuanced questions.

The tribunal in the *South China Sea* arbitration was particularly proactive in engaging with the scientific and technical evidence presented in connection with the Philippines' environmental claims, including with respect to China's failure to carry out an EIA. Not only did the tribunal pose to the Philippines' experts questions that it required to be answered; the tribunal appointed its own team of scientific experts on coral reef ecology, which it commissioned to provide an 'independent review of the factual record, scientific literature, and other publicly available documents, including from China'.[90] Further, the tribunal directed its independent experts to identify and analyze 'any documents concerning China's assessment of the environmental impact of its activities'.[91]

D Conclusion

A state's obligation to undertake an EIA that evaluates potential environmental impacts to other states or to the marine environment is firmly established in both treaties and customary international law. To date, a diversity of EIA-related disputes have been placed before the ICJ, the ITLOS, and a variety of *ad hoc* arbitral tribunals. The procedural mechanisms that enabled these international courts and tribunals to exercise jurisdiction remain available. In light of the frequency of industrial projects being sited near international borders, or in proximity to marine ecosystems, one can anticipate that many more such cases will be brought in the future, when they will be litigated before courts and tribunals that are becoming increasingly adept at adjudicating scientifically and technically complex disputes.

---

[90] *South China Sea*, para. 821.
[91] *Ibid.*, para. 916 (quoting Terms of Reference for Expert, Dr. Sebastian Ferse, paras. 3.1.2, 3.1.4 (18 March 2016)).

12

Litigation as a Climate Regulatory Tool

JACQUELINE PEEL AND HARI M. OSOFSKY

A   Introduction

Environmental advocacy groups have a long history of using courts as a forum for promoting social and policy change.[1] Climate change has been an emerging frontier for strategic environmental lawsuits of this kind over the last decade, with a focus on how court action can assist efforts to reduce greenhouse gas (GHG) emissions and adapt to climate change impacts. This turn to the courts has been encouraged by uncertainty regarding the implementation of international climate change treaty requirements, and the inadequacy of government and business efforts to curb GHG emissions sufficiently to avoid dangerous levels of global warming.[2] Court actions addressing questions of climate change mitigation and adaptation have grown exponentially since the

---

[1] This kind of litigation is generally known as 'strategic', 'public interest' or (in the United States) 'impact' litigation, and is used by advocacy groups in many areas of social policy, including human rights and labour law. See, further, A. D. Freeman and J. E. Farris, 'Grassroots Impact Litigation: Mass Filing of Small Claims', *U.S.F. Law Review*, 26 (1992), 261; S. Cummings and D. Rhode, 'Public Interest Litigation: Insights from Theory and Practice', *Fordham Urban L.J.*, 36 (2009), 603; A. Chen and S. Cummings, *Public Interest Lawyering: A Contemporary Perspective* (New York, NY: Wolters Kluwer, 2013); A. Durbach et al., 'Public Interest Litigation: Making the Case in Australia', *Alternative L.J.*, 38(4) (2013), 219; A. R. Lucas, 'Participatory Rights and Strategic Litigation: Benefits Forcing and Endowment Protection in Canadian Natural Resource Development' in L. Barrera-Hernández et al. (eds.), Sharing the Costs and Benefits of Energy and Resource Activity: Legal Change and Impact on Communities (Oxford: Oxford University Press, 2016), p. 339.

[2] The Paris Agreement – a universal climate change treaty that will impose obligations on all parties to contribute to the global climate change response – was concluded in December 2015 and came into force on 4 November 2016: see Paris Agreement, Paris (France), 13 December 2015, in force 4 November 2016 (in UNFCCC, Report of the Conference of the Parties on its Twenty-First Session, Addendum, UN Doc. FCCC/CP/2015/10/Add.1, 29 January 2016). Despite conclusion of this Agreement, it comes into effect only from 2020, and at present parties' 'nationally determined contributions' to emissions reduction, adaptation and financing fall well short of what is needed to meet the Agreement's objectives:

mid-2000s.[3] Globally, climate change cases have been brought in more than twenty-nine countries across six continents, as well as in regional and international tribunals.[4]

While the international 'climate justice' movement continues to grow,[5] the majority of the climate change cases brought to date have been launched in a handful of countries.[6] With more than 900 claims filed, climate change litigation in the United States far exceeds that in any other country.[7] Other major developed country emitters, such as Australia, have also seen significant climate-related lawsuits focused on emissions-intensive activities, such as coal-fired power stations and coal mines, as well as issues of adaptation planning.[8] In other parts of the world, such as

see Decision 1/CP.21, 'Adoption of the Paris Agreement', 12 December 2015, FCCC/CP/2015/L.9/Rev.1, available at: http://unfccc.int/documentation/documents/advanced_search/items/6911.php?priref=600008865, para. 17 (last accessed 22 February 2017). President Donald J. Trump's notification of the United States' intention to withdraw from the Paris Agreement has also cast a cloud over its future: R. Eckersley, 'The view from Marrakech: climate talks are battling through a Trump tsunami', *The Conversation*, 11 November 2016, at: https://theconversation.com/the-view-from-marrakech-climate-talks-are-battling-through-a-trump-tsunami-68597 (last accessed 22 February 2017).

[3] Mitigation-related litigation is that addressing the GHG emissions that cause the climate change problem, whereas adaptation-related litigation focuses on the predicted impacts of climate change on ecosystems, communities, and infrastructure.

[4] For details, see R. Lord et al. (eds.), *Climate Change Liability: Transnational Law and Practice* (Cambridge: Cambridge University Press, 2011), Arnold and Porter LLP, 'U.S. Climate Change Litigation Chart' and 'Non-U.S. Climate Change Litigation Chart', available at: www.climatecasechart.com, and Climate Justice Programme, 'Cases', www.climatelaw.org/cases (websites last accessed 22 February 2017).

[5] See, generally, International Bar Association, Climate Change Justice and Human Rights Taskforce, *Achieving Justice and Human Rights in an Era of Climate Disruption* (London: IBA, 2014). International organisations with a climate justice focus include the Mary Robinson Climate Justice Foundation (www.mrfcj.org), the Climate Justice Project (www.fahamu.org/Climate-Justice-Project) and the Climate Justice Programme (http://climatejustice.org.au) (websites last accessed 22 February 2017).

[6] M. Wilensky, *Climate Change in the Courts: An Assessment of Non-U.S. Climate Litigation*, Sabin Center for Climate Change Law, Columbia Law School, February 2015, available at: https://web.law.columbia.edu/sites/default/files/microsites/climate-change/white_paper_-_climate_change_in_the_courts_-_assessment_of_non_u.s._climate_litigation.pdf (last accessed 22 February 2017).

[7] A comprehensive database of climate change cases filed and decided in U.S. courts, including links to judgments, is maintained by the Columbia Climate Change Law Center. See further, Arnold and Porter LLP, 'U.S. Climate Change Litigation Chart', available at: www.climatecasechart.com (last accessed 22 February 2017).

[8] For details of Australian climate change cases, see the database maintained by the Centre for Resources, Energy and Environmental Law (CREEL) at Melbourne Law School. Jacqueline Peel, 'Australian Climate Change Litigation', CREEL, available at: http://law.unimelb.edu.au/centres/creel#research. Judgments in many of the cases are freely

Europe, climate change litigation is more nascent,[9] but there are indications of increasing interest in its development, fostered by high-profile cases such as the 2015 decision in *Urgenda* v. *Netherlands*.[10]

This chapter considers climate change litigation as an expanding area of environmental adjudication across the world. It particularly examines whether such litigation is an effective tool for bringing about better regulation of climate change risks. In this regard, the chapter takes stock of the regulatory impact of climate change cases decided by courts in leading climate litigation jurisdictions such as the United States and Australia,[11] and discusses the lessons that this experience offers for how groups or individuals interested in using this tool can do so strategically.

B   Emergence and Growth of Climate Change Litigation

Courts at the international, regional and domestic levels are increasingly being asked to hear cases about issues of climate change risk posed by anthropogenic GHG emissions. Such 'climate change litigation' can encompass a wide range of claims with differing degrees of connection

available online from the Austlii website: www.austlii.edu.au (websites last accessed 22 February 2017).

[9] For a discussion of earlier European case law, mostly focused on the European Union Emissions Trading Scheme, see S. Bogojević, 'EU Climate Change Litigation, the Role of the European Courts, and the Importance of Legal Culture', *Law and Policy*, 35(3) (2013), 184. See also, on climate litigation in the United Kingdom, C. Hilson, 'UK climate change litigation: between hard and soft framing' in S. Farrall, T. Ahmed and D. French (eds.), *Criminological and legal consequences of climate change* (Oxford: Hart Publishing, 2012), p.47; C. Hilson, 'Climate Change Litigation in the UK: An Explanatory Approach (or Bringing Grievance Back In)' in F. Fracchia and M. Occhiena (eds.), *Climate Change: La Riposta del Diritto* (Naples: Editoriale Scientifica, 2010), p. 421.

[10] *Stichting Urgenda* v. *Government of the Netherlands (Ministry of Infrastructure and the Environment)*, ECLI:NL:RBDHA:2015:7145, Rechtbank Den Haag, C/09/456689/HA ZA 13-1396 (*Urgenda* case). The Dutch government's appeal against the decision was unsuccessful. See *Urgenda Foundation v Kingdom of the Netherlands* [2015] HAZA C/09/ 00456689, available at: http://climatecasechart.com/non-us-case/urgenda-foundation-v-kingdom-of-the-netherlands/

[11] This part of the chapter draws on research published in our book, *Climate Change Litigation: Regulatory Pathways to Cleaner Energy* (Cambridge: Cambridge University Press, 2015) which focused on the United States and Australia as the two jurisdictions with the greatest number of climate change cases, and the extent to which that litigation was influencing regulatory outcomes. In this chapter we seek to extend those findings in two ways: (1) by looking at climate change litigation emerging in other parts of the world; and (2) by expanding on the question of evaluating the impact or effectiveness of environmental adjudication as a tool for achieving particular regulatory goals – in this case, climate change mitigation and adaptation.

to climate change and related issues, such as energy transition, renewable energy use, adaptation policy or climate damage. This section focuses on cases in which climate change is a central issue in the litigation, in the sense that there is a deliberate framing of the parties' arguments and/or the ensuing judgment in climate change terms.[12] The aims of litigants bringing these cases tend to be strategic – that is, they are seeking to influence regulatory outcomes and behaviours, whether in a positive (pro-regulatory) or negative (anti-regulatory) fashion.[13]

Reflecting the strategic orientation of many claimants, climate change litigation has employed a diverse range of legal causes of action, including statutory interpretation; common law tort and public trust; and constitutional and international human rights avenues.[14] In the countries with the most climate-related court actions, the majority of litigation has involved public law claims using statutory pathways.[15] In these cases, litigants have generally focused on the interpretation of existing planning and environmental laws and their capacity to extend to issues of climate change. In the United States, for example, high-profile climate change litigation, such as the *Massachusetts* v. *EPA* case and subsequent Supreme Court challenges to the Obama administration's efforts to regulate transportation and power plant emissions, has focused on the scope for regulation of GHG emissions under the Clean Air Act. This line of litigation will likely continue to evolve under President Trump, depending on how he changes the current regulatory approach of federal agencies and whether Congress alters the underlying statutory framework.

Litigation under federal environmental statutes has played a key role in shaping the U.S. regulatory response to climate change at multiple levels.

---

[12] As Hilson comments, in n. 9 above, framing of litigation in climate change terms is a relatively new phenomenon.

[13] This is not to suggest that cases that do not directly engage with climate change issues cannot also be part of a strategic climate change litigation programme. However, in the main, cases that have the most impact on climate change regulation tend to be those that have climate change at their 'core': D. Markell and J. B. Ruhl, 'An Empirical Survey of Climate Change Litigation in the United States', Environmental Law Reporter, 40(7) (2010), 10644, 10647.

[14] B. J. Preston, 'Climate Change Litigation (Part 1)', *Carbon and Climate Law Review*, 5(1) (2011), 3; B. J. Preston, 'Climate Change Litigation (Part 2)', *Carbon and Climate Law Review*, 5(2) (2011), 244.

[15] J. Peel and H. Osofsky, *Climate Change Litigation: Regulatory Pathways to Cleaner Energy* (Cambridge: Cambridge University Press, 2015), p. 40.

Most significantly, the Obama administration justified Clean Air Act regulation of motor vehicle and power plant emissions as flowing from the U.S. Supreme Court's 2007 decision in *Massachusetts* v. *EPA*.[16] In that case, petitioners challenged the U.S. Environmental Protection Agency's (EPA's) denial of a petition requesting that it regulate motor vehicles' GHG emissions under section 202(a)(1) of the Clean Air Act. The Supreme Court decided that the Clean Air Act's broad definition of 'air pollutant' applied to GHG emissions despite their substantial differences from the types of pollutants, such as those contributing to smog, that were the Act's initial focus.[17] It found that the EPA had abused its discretion through the manner in which it justified not regulating GHG emissions, and required it to 'ground its reasons for action or inaction in the statute'.[18] Shortly after the Obama administration came into office, the EPA issued an Endangerment Finding (that GHG emissions from motor vehicles endangered public health)[19] and went on to create substantial new regulations for both motor vehicles[20] and major stationary sources of GHG emissions under the Clean Power Plan.[21] These regulations survived industry challenge in the *Coalition for Responsible Regulation* v. *EPA* litigation[22] and, despite being partially struck down by the Supreme Court in *Utility Air Regulatory Group* v. *EPA*,[23] retained practical effect for the regulation of the vast majority of GHG emissions from stationary energy sources.[24] In February 2016, the U.S. Supreme Court issued a decision staying the EPA's implementation of the Clean Power Plan pending the resolution of other challenges to the rules currently

---

[16] *Massachusetts* v. *EPA*, 549 U.S. 497 (2007).

[17] Ibid., 528.

[18] Ibid., 535.

[19] EPA, Endangerment and Cause and Contribute Findings for Greenhouse Gases under Section 202(a) of the Clean Air Act, Final Rule, 15 December 2009, 74(239) F.R. 66496

[20] See Peel and Osofsky, Climate Change Litigation, pp. 65–68.

[21] Alongside a 'Carbon Pollution Standard' for new power plants under Clean Air Act, section 111(b), the Clean Power Plan proposes 'emission guidelines for states to follow in developing plans to address greenhouse gas emissions from existing fossil fuel-fired electric generating units': see Clean Power Plan Final Rule, 23 October 2015, 80 F.R. 64965.

[22] *Coalition for Responsible Regulation* v. *EPA*, 684 F.3d 102 (D.C. Cir. 26 June 2012).

[23] *Utility Air Regulatory Group* v. *EPA*, 134 S. Ct. 2427, 2449 (2014).

[24] The Supreme Court struck down the so-called Tailoring Rule (concerning application of the Clean Air Act's Prevention of Significant Deterioration (PSD) provisions to GHG emissions) as exceeding the EPA's statutory authority, but allowed the EPA to regulate stationary sources that were already subject to PSD permitting requirements for other air pollutants (covering around 83 per cent of U.S. stationary-source GHG emissions).

before the D.C. Circuit.[25] This decision effectively delayed further administrative action to implement the Clean Power Plan until after the November 2016 U.S. federal election. The victory of Donald Trump in the election and the President's subsequent actions to roll back the climate policies of the Obama administration, such as the Clean Power Plan, [26] have created significant uncertainty for that litigation, and for future regulation pursuant to *Massachusetts* v. *EPA*. Unless the U.S. Congress eliminates the EPA's authority to regulate GHG emissions under the Clean Air Act, President Trump will still have obligations pursuant to *Massachusetts* v. *EPA*. If Congress were to eliminate that authority, the federal public nuisance litigation pathway – which the Supreme Court in *AEP* v. *Connecticut* said was displaced by the existence of statutory regulatory authority[27] – may become viable.

Similar pro-regulatory statutory actions have been brought in the United States regarding state legislation, such as the case of *Kain & Ors* v. *Department of Environmental Protection*.[28] There, the Massachusetts Supreme Court concluded that a state statutory mandate calling for emissions reductions of 80 per cent below 1990 levels required the Department of Environmental Protection, which was charged with implementing the mandate, to 'set actual limits' for sources of GHG emissions rather than merely specifying aspirational targets.[29] Other statutes that have generated significant case law in the United States include the National Environmental Policy Act (NEPA) and its state equivalents,[30] as well as

---

[25] Order in Pending Case, *West Virginia* v. *EPA* (9 February 2016), available at: www .scotusblog.com/wp-content/uploads/2016/02/15A773-Clean-Power-Plan-stay-order .pdf (last accessed 22 February 2017).

[26] For details .of the ongoing filings in these cases, see Arnold and Porter LLP.

[27] See n. 47 below and accompanying text.

[28] For details of other climate change cases brought under state legislation, see Arnold and Porter LLP.

[29] *Kain & Ors* v. *Department of Environmental Protection* (2016) 474 Mass 278, 290 (available at http://masscases.com/cases/sjc/474/474mass278.html) (last accessed 22 February 2017). The Court went on to hold that the 'plain language' of the statutory provision required 'the department to promulgate regulations that address multiple sources or categories of sources of emissions, impose a limit on emissions that may be released, limit the aggregate emissions released from each group of regulated sources or categories of sources, set emissions limits for each year, and set limits that decline on an annual basis' (at 292). The Court found the department's piecemeal regulations for sulphur hexafluoride, participation in the Regional Greenhouse Gas Initiative carbon trading scheme and a low emission vehicle programme did not fulfil the statutory mandate (at 300).

[30] National Environmental Policy Act, 42 U.S.C. § 4321 (1969); significant climate change litigation has also been brought under state environmental impact assessment legislation – 'little NEPAs' – such as the California Environmental Quality Act, Cal. Pub. Res. Code §

other federal and state legislation applicable to permitting of coal-fired power stations that may be challenged in environmental review actions.[31] The targets of these actions are generally governments who are tasked with implementing the relevant legislation in respect of which claims are brought.

Australia, the jurisdiction in the world with the second most climate change lawsuits, similarly has largely seen statutory-based claims. Australian courts and tribunals have decided a significant number of climate change cases – addressing issues of both mitigation and adaptation – under environmental statutes at both the state and federal levels. Among the most well known of these cases are the decisions in *Australian Conservation Foundation* v. *Latrobe City Council* (the 'Hazelwood case')[32] and *Gray* v. *Minister for Planning* (the 'Anvil Hill case').[33] The former case, decided in 2004, targeted plans for expansion of Australia's dirtiest coal-fired power station located in the Latrobe valley in the State of Victoria. It was decided by the Victorian Civil and Administrative Tribunal (VCAT), which held that, under the applicable planning legislation, the decision on a planning scheme amendment necessary to enable the expansion should consider the 'indirect' effects of the amendment in terms of the environmental impacts of the GHGs likely to be emitted if the life of the Hazelwood plant were to be extended.[34] A similar approach to including the 'indirect' environmental effects of fossil fuel projects in assessment processes was taken up and expanded by the New South Wales Land and Environment Court (NSWLEC) in the Anvil Hill case. In that case, the Court construed objectives relating to 'ecologically sustainable development' (ESD) in state environmental planning legislation so as to find that indirect, downstream emissions from burning of the extracted coal were a relevant factor in environmental assessment of a coal mine. While similar challenges under federal environmental legislation have not been as successful (see further below), Australian courts have shown willingness to extend environmental legislation to cover issues of climate change

---

21000 (1970). See Arnold and Porter LLP, n. 7 above, 'Stop Government Action' – 'NEPA' and 'State NEPAs'. See also D. Markell and J. B. Ruhl, 'An Empirical Assessment of Climate Change in the Courts: A New Jurisprudence or Business as Usual', *Florida Law Review*, 64 (2012), 15.

[31] See Arnold and Porter LLP, 'Stop Government Action' – 'Project challenges'.

[32] (2004) 140 LGERA 100.

[33] (2006) 152 LGERA 258.

[34] (2004) 140 LGERA 100, 109.

adaptation as well as mitigation. For instance, in the NSWLEC case of
Walker v. *Minister for Planning*,[35] the Court held that, in assessing a large
residential development proposal located in a low-lying coastal area, ESD
was an implied mandatory consideration for decision-making under the
legislation at issue and should have led to the Minister evaluating the
impacts of climate change for flood risk on the site.[36]

Indeed, Australia has been a leader globally in the development of
lawsuits regarding climate change adaptation. As in the *Walker* case
described above, most Australian adaptation cases have concerned
coastal development and the need to factor future sea level rise into
planning decisions.[37] There have also been a number of cases brought
by private property owners challenging local government actions and
policies designed to safeguard the coast in the face of likely climate
change impacts.[38] These cases have played a significant role in shaping adaptation planning and government policy, particularly in
coastal areas in Australia. More recently, the United States has
begun to see some adaptation suits as well, though mitigation ones
remain far more dominant. Like their Australian counterparts, many
of this first wave of U.S. adaptation cases involve impacts on coastal
areas, such as whether compensation is owed for government taking
property to build protective sand dunes, how the government should
handle inundation of the sewage system, whether the electricity grid
needs further storm protection, and how to address coastal water
deterioration.[39]

Petitioners in the United States also have made claims in tort, especially nuisance, and public trust,[40] although these cases are less common,

---

[35] *Walker* v. *Minister for Planning* (2007) 157 LGERA 124.
[36] Ibid., at 191–92. The Court's decision was subsequently overturned on appeal on different
      grounds, however, the appeal court agreed with the NSWLEC that consideration of the
      ESD principles of precaution and inter-generational equity would 'almost inevitably' have
      required a consideration of climate change flood risk: *Minister for Planning* v. *Walker &
      Ors* (2008) 161 LGERA 423 at 455.
[37] J. Peel and L. Godden, 'Planning for Adaptation to Climate Change: Landmark Cases
      from Australia', *Sustainable Development Law and Policy*, 9(2) (2009), 37.
[38] T. O'Donnell, 'Legal geography and coastal climate change adaptation: the Vaughan
      litigation', *Geographical Research*, 54(3) (2016), 301.
[39] For an in-depth discussion of the Australian and U.S. cases, see J. Peel and H. M. Osofsky,
      'Sue to Adapt', *Minn. L. Rev.*, 99 (2015), 2133.
[40] The public trust doctrine treats certain natural resources as owned by the government,
      which has trust obligations to the public to maintain them for public use and benefit.
      In the United States, this doctrine varies from state to state, based on their common law
      traditions, and in some states is also viewed as part of their constitutional or statutory law.

and have achieved less formal success, than statutory claims.[41] No tort or public trust claims have been brought successfully in Australia,[42] despite the growth there of a body of jurisprudence based on environmental statutory avenues.

The most successful of these U.S. cases to date has been the public trust case *Juliana* v. *United States*, which survived a motion to dismiss in November 2016 and, as of November 2018, may soon begin trial hearings.[43] The petitioners in this case argue that governmental regulators' failure to regulate GHG emissions adequately violates their constitutionally protected substantive due process rights and the government's public trust obligations.[44] However, the ultimate disposition of this case on the merits is still unclear, and a motion to dismiss has a very deferential standard of review.

In addition, numerous common law tort petitions, largely relying on nuisance law, have been brought in the United States.[45] However, the U.S. Supreme Court's holding in *AEP* v. *Connecticut* that nuisance claims under federal common law are displaced by the EPA's regulatory efforts under statute has made that pathway more difficult.[46] The *AEP* decision

---

[41] See Arnold and Porter LLP, 'Common law claims', listing 43 such lawsuits (common law and public trust) in the United States.

[42] The closest example is the case of *Gray* v. *Macquarie Generation* [2010] NSWLEC 34; [2011] NSWLEC 3; *Macquarie Generation* v. *Hodgson* [2011] NSWCA 424 heard by the Land and Environment Court and the Court of Appeal in New South Wales. The case involved a direct challenge to the lawfulness of GHG emissions from a large power station, on the basis that the power station was unlawfully disposing of 'waste' in the form of carbon dioxide without authorisation under a licence. Justice Pain in the Land and Environment Court rejected the argument that the power station's licence did not authorise the emission of GHG, but allowed an amended claim to go forward, pleading that the emitting authority granted by the licence was subject to an implied limit as to the amount of GHG emitted, which should have reasonable regard and care for people and the environment. An adverse judgment from the New South Wales Court of Appeal, overturning Justice Pain's decision, followed. The Court of Appeal found the licence was a complete defence to the argument that Macquarie Generation were wilfully or negligently disposing of waste, and therefore the case had no reasonable prospects of success.

[43] *Juliana* v. *United States*, No. 6:15-cv-01517 (D. Or., 10 November 2016) (Aiken, J.), 46 ELR 20175. For further procedural developments in this case see www.ourchildrenstrust.org/federal-proceedings (last accessed 9 March 2018).

[44] *Id.*

[45] Key cases include *Comer* v. *Murphy Oil*, 585 F.3d 855 (5th Cir. 2009); *Kivalina* v. *ExxonMobile Corp.*, 663 F.Supp.2d 863 (2009), aff'd, 969 F.3d 849 (9th Cir. 2012); *In re Katrina Canal Breaches Litig.*, 673 F.3d 381 (5th Cir. 2012). See also G. Ganguly, J. Setzer and V. Heyvaert, 'If at first you don't succeed: suing corporations for climate change', Oxford Journal of Legal Studies (in press, 2018).

[46] 131 S. Ct. 2527, 2539 (2011); see also H. M. Osofsky, 'Litigation's Role in the Path of U.S. Federal Climate Change Regulation: Implications of AEP v. Connecticut', *Valparaiso*

did not pre-empt state law nuisance claims, and those remain a potentially viable avenue.[47] In addition, as mentioned above, if the U.S. Congress eliminates the EPA's authority to regulate GHGs under the Clean Air Act, then the federal common law nuisance claims would no longer be displaced.

However, the success of the *Urgenda* case, which involved a claim of violation of the Dutch government's duty of care to safeguard its citizens from climate change risks, has spurred new interest in liability avenues in countries around the world.[48] That case was cited favourably in the Oregon District Court decision in *Juliana* v. *United States*, discussed above.[49]

The *Urgenda* case was catapulted to international public attention with the ruling of the Hague District Court on June 24, 2015, affirmed by the Hague Court of Appeal on 9 October 2018.[50] It was brought by Urgenda (the name is a contraction of 'urgent' and 'agenda'), a non-governmental organisation (NGO) providing a 'platform' for development of plans and measures to prevent climate change.[51] Urgenda brought the suit on its own behalf and on behalf of 886 Dutch citizens who authorised the NGO to act in their stead. The essence of its claim was that, under relevant provisions of the Dutch civil code and the European Convention on Human Rights, the Dutch government owed a duty of care to the NGO, to the parties it represented, and to Dutch society more generally, which was being breached by the government's inadequate climate change mitigation policy. It also argued that, through its contribution to global GHG emissions, the Dutch government had unlawfully exposed the international community to the risk of dangerous climate change,

---

U. L. Rev., 46 (2012), 447; H. M. Osofsky, 'AEP v. Connecticut's Implications for the Future of Climate Change Litigation', *Yale L.J. Online* (2011).

[47] *AEP*, 131 S. Ct. 2527 at 2540.

[48] For details of the Macquarie Generation litigation, which was the closest such example, see n. 43 above. A number of Australian environmental advocacy organisations are reportedly considering the scope for an Urgenda-style case in Australia, though prospects of success seem limited: see further F. Nelson, 'Dutch climate change case no roadmap for Aus', *Lawyers Weekly*, 16 July 2015, available at: www.lawyersweekly.com.au/news/16831-can-we-repli cate-the-dutch-climate-change-victory (last accessed 22 February 2017).

[49] *Kelsey Cascade Rose Juliana* v. *US*, 6:15-cv-1517-TC, U.S. District Court (Oregon), Order, Justice Coffin, 8 April 2016, p. 11, available at: https://static1.squarespace.com/static/ 571d109b04426270152febe0/t/576195342fe1316f09d2eb8d/1466012983313/16 .04.08.OrderDenyingMTD.pdf (last accessed 22 February 2017).

[50] *Urgenda* case.

[51] See Urgenda website: www.urgenda.nl/en/ (last accessed 22 February 2017).

with the potential for irreversible damage to human health and the environment.[52] The Court upheld Urgenda's claim that the state's 2020 emissions reduction target was inadequate when judged against the standards of climate science and international climate policy, and that this gave rise to breach of a duty of care under Dutch law.[53] The Court consequently ordered the government to ensure that Dutch GHG emissions by the year 2020 are at least 25 per cent below 1990 levels. The Dutch government unsuccessfully appealed the District Court's decision but indicated that, in the interim, it would abide by the Court's ruling.[54]

As climate change litigation has matured in countries such as the United States and Australia, and more experimentation with this tool has begun in other parts of the world, there is some evidence that we may be on the cusp of a wave of 'next-generation' climate change litigation.[55] Such litigation involves new causes of action under tort, human rights, constitutional, and corporate and financial laws; greater attention to targets such as corporate emitters and investors with significant GHG-intensive asset holdings or exposures to climate change impacts; and a broader focus on climate change risk beyond reductions in GHG emissions and adaptation measures and towards the implications of climate change for low-carbon development, loss and damage suffered by communities, and infrastructure resilience. Examples of this trend include the 2015

---

[52] Less well appreciated were the human rights arguments advanced by Urgenda in the case, although these were picked up in the appeal court's decision. For discussion of these and a potential 'rights turn' in climate change litigation, see J. Peel and H. M. Osofsky, 'A Rights Turn in Climate Change Litigation?', *Transnational Environmental Law*, 7(1), (2018), 37.

[53] *Urgenda* case, paras. 4.84–4.86.

[54] Government of the Netherlands, 'Cabinet begins implementation of Urgenda ruling but will file appeal', Press release, 1 September 2015, available at: www.government.nl/latest/news/2015/09/01/cabinet-begins-implementation-of-urgenda-ruling-but-will-file-appeal (last accessed 22 February 2017).

[55] These ideas were explored in a workshop at Melbourne Law School, University of Melbourne, on 17 November 2016, entitled 'Shaping the Next Generation of Climate Change Litigation in Australia'. See J. Peel, H. M. Osofsky and A. Foerster, 'Shaping the 'Next Generation' of Climate Change Litigation in Australia', *Melbourne University Law Review*, 41(2) (2017), 793. See also D. B. Hunter, 'The Implications of Climate Change Litigation: Litigation for International Environmental Law-Making' in W. C. G. Burns and H. M. Osofsky (eds.), *Adjudicating Climate Change: State, National, and International Approaches* (Cambridge: Cambridge University Press, 2009), pp. 357, 361 (discussing the role of improving climate change science in fostering 'the next generation of climate cases and claims').

Leghari decisions of the Lahore High Court in Pakistan, finding that the government's adaptation failures breached citizens' fundamental rights;[56] investigations launched by state Attorneys General in the United States into the climate change risk disclosures of major U.S. oil and coal companies that are alleged to have been misleading;[57] and a complaint currently being investigated by the Philippines Commission on Human Rights that claims the violation of Filipinos' human rights as a consequence of the activities of major corporate GHG polluters.[58] These emerging lawsuits suggest that climate change jurisprudence may evolve in new directions in the future, although, at this early stage, such 'new-generation' cases are far from displacing the dominant statutory law claims and, in many cases, may have significantly fewer prospects of success than more traditional climate change lawsuits.

C   Environmental Adjudication as a Regulatory Tool

Conventionally, litigation is seen as a forum for application, interpretation and enforcement of the law, rather than as a tool for achieving regulatory ends. However, there are also long traditions, particularly in common law countries, of using litigation in a strategic fashion to advance given policy outcomes and to drive behavioural shifts by key

---

[56] *Ashgar Leghari* v. *Federation of Pakistan* (W.P. No. 25501/2015), Lahore High Court Green Bench, orders of 4 September and 14 September 2015, available at: https://elaw .org/pk_Leghari (last accessed 22 February 2017).

[57] See Att. Gen E. T. Schneiderman, 'AG Schneiderman secures unprecedented agreement with Peabody Energy to end misleading statements and disclosure risks associated with climate change' (Press Release, 9 November 2015), available at: www.ag.ny.gov/press-release/ag-schneiderman-secures-unprecedented-agreement-peabody-energy-end-mis leading. J. Gillis and C. Krauss, 'Exxon Mobil investigated for possible climate change lies by New York Attorney General', *New York Times* (online), 5 November 2015, available at: www.nytimes.com/2015/11/06/science/exxon-mobil-under-investigation-in-new-york-over-climate-statements.html. A further investigation is under way in California: I. Penn, 'California to investigate whether Exxon Mobil lied about climate change risks', *Los Angeles Times* (online) 12 October 2016, available at: www.latimes.com/business/la-fi-exxon-global-warming-20160120-story.html (websites last accessed 22 February 2017).

[58] Greenpeace, Petition Requesting for Investigation of the Responsibility of the Carbon Majors for Human Rights Violations or Threats of Violations Resulting from the Impacts of Climate Change, available at: www.greenpeace.org/seasia/ph/press/releases/Worlds-largest-carbon-producers-ordered-to-respond-to-allegations-of-human-rights–abuses-from-climate-change/The-Climate-Change-and-Human-Rights-Petition (last accessed 22 February 2017). The Commission accepted the petition in December 2015 and is currently conducting its investigation.

actors, such as corporations.[59] 'Strategic litigation', in which cases are brought – usually in combination with other legal and non-legal methods – to seek legal and social change,[60] has been an approach commonly adopted by climate change litigants. It seeks to use the authority and legitimacy of court pronouncements as an avenue for promoting particular policy positions on climate change or, as one of our interviewees put it, 'you're trying to challenge the establishment through the processes of the establishment'.[61]

In our previous research on climate change litigation in the United States and Australia, we have sought to assess its 'regulatory impact'.[62] 'Regulatory' in this sense is taken to mean 'the intentional activity of attempting to control, order or influence the behaviour of others',[63] and encompasses a wide range of formal and informal action by diverse actors. Moreover, the 'impact' of litigation can be direct or indirect.[64] Direct impacts are instances of formal legal change as a result of the litigation. These may manifest as the advent of targeted rules, policies, or decision-making procedures that are mandated by a judgment or arise out of the legal interpretation developed by the court in the litigation. Indirect impacts are more diffuse and describe pathways flowing from litigation that arise due to the incentives that judgments provide for behavioural change by governmental and non-governmental actors.[65]

An example of a case with both substantial direct and indirect regulatory impacts is the U.S. Supreme Court decision in *Massachusetts* v. *EPA*. Not only did this case establish a regulatory mandate for measures to control GHG emissions under the Clean Air Act; it also had significant

---

[59] See n. 1 above.

[60] C. C. Barber, 'Tackling the Evaluation Challenge in Human Rights: Assessing the Impact of Strategic Litigation Organisations', *International Journal of Human Rights*, 16(3) (2012), 411.

[61] Interview participant 16, in-person interview 8 March 2013, Melbourne.

[62] See Peel and Osofsky, *Climate Change Litigation*. See also H. M. Osofsky and J. Peel, 'Litigation's regulatory pathways and the administrative state: Lessons from U.S. and Australian climate change governance', *Georgetown International Environmental Law Review*, 25 (2013), 207; H. M. Osofsky and J. Peel, 'The Role of Litigation in Multilevel Climate Change Governance: Possibilities for a Lower Carbon Future', *Environmental & Planning Law Journal*, 30(4) (2013), 303; J. Peel and H. M. Osofsky, 'Climate Change Litigation's Regulatory Pathways: A Comparative Analysis of the United States and Australia', *Law and Policy*, 35 (3) (2013), 150.

[63] J. Black, 'Decentring Regulation: Understanding the Role of Regulation and Self-Regulation in a 'Post-Regulatory' World', *Current Legal Problems*, 54(1) (2001), 103, 142.

[64] C. Parker and J. Braithwaite, 'Regulation' in P. Cane and M. Tushnet (eds.), *The Oxford Handbook of Legal Studies* (Oxford: Oxford University Press, 2003), p. 119.

[65] See further Peel and Osofsky, 'Climate Change Litigation's Regulatory Pathways'.

indirect effects on the public perception of climate change in the United States and on the behaviour of businesses.[66] By contrast, the tortious claims relating to climate change damage brought to date in the United States have had no direct regulatory impacts, but there is evidence of some indirect impacts in framing the public debate around GHG emissions and putting businesses on notice of the potential for corporate liability in the climate change area.[67]

In assessing the direct and indirect regulatory impacts of climate change litigation – and hence the effectiveness of environmental adjudication as a tool for achieving policy and social change – it is important also to bear in mind the differing motivations for litigation. While early-stage climate change litigation is generally 'promotive' in nature – that is, it 'seeks to promote positive environmental outcomes by way of regulatory intervention sanctioned or even required by the courts'[68] – the experience of well-established climate change litigation jurisdictions, such as the United States, demonstrates that this first wave of cases is often followed by litigation with an anti-regulatory orientation. In the United States, anti-regulatory climate change cases have been brought with the goal of delaying or dismantling existing or emerging regulatory measures for climate change mitigation, with most lawsuits involving business interests or sub-national governments that stand to lose economically as the result of climate change regulation.[69] Australia has not seen the emergence of anti-regulatory cases as such, but in response to climate change challenges brought by environmental advocacy groups there has often been significant political backlash.[70] These experiences suggest the likelihood that anti-regulatory challenges – whether in the courts or in the political system – will follow initial 'promotive' climate change litigation that achieves success in altering regulatory outcomes.

---

[66] Peel and Osofsky, *Climate Change Litigation*, pp. 49–50.

[67] Ibid., pp. 50–51.

[68] N. S. Ghaleigh, '"Six honest serving men": Climate change litigation as legal mobilization and the utility of typologies', *Climate Law*, 1 (2010), 31, 45. Ghaleigh identifies three further categories: defensive (or anti-regulatory), boundary-testing (concerned with challenging the limits of an existing regulatory regime for climate change) and perfecting (seeking improvements in an existing regulatory regime for climate change).

[69] Markell and Ruhl, 'A New Jurisprudence or Business as Usual', 65–70.

[70] Described in Peel and Osofsky, *Climate Change Litigation*, pp. 300–08.

D   Using Climate Change Litigation Strategically

Strategic litigation on climate change is now well established in jurisdictions such as the United States and Australia, where the earliest cases were brought in the 1990s.[71] Strategic climate change litigation in other parts of the world is more nascent, although the indications are that it is likely to grow as a way of driving forward action to address an increasingly urgent problem and its widespread consequences. In Europe, for example, while there had been a body of climate change cases, focusing particularly on the operation of the European Union Emissions Trading Scheme,[72] it was only with the *Urgenda* case in 2015 that climate change claims with explicit policy ends emerged. Marjan Minnesma, the executive director of Urgenda, the NGO that brought the case, described the litigation as 'a lawsuit out of love'.[73] 'Ten years ago we would not have tried this but I think things are changing', she said in an interview about the case. 'It's more clear to a broad group we are heading to a catastrophe.'[74] The *Urgenda* litigation has also inspired the launch or preparation of similar cases in other jurisdictions, including Belgium and Norway.[75]

Efforts to promote strategic climate change litigation in Europe have received a boost from a multi-year grant initiated by the Children's Investment Fund Foundation (CIFF), a philanthropic organisation based in the United Kingdom (UK). CIFF is funding the UK group ClientEarth to undertake a programme of litigation designed 'to deliver ground-breaking and impactful climate change cases.'[76] The litigation funded by CIFF relates to three key areas: 'reducing emissions from

---

[71] The first U.S. climate change case was *City of Los Angeles* v. *National Highway Transportation Safety Administration* (NHTSA) 912. F.2d 478 (D.C. Cir. 1990), a NEPA challenge to NHTSA's decision to lower fuel economy standards. Australia's earliest climate change case was *Greenpeace* v. *Redbank Power Company* (1994) 86 LGERA 143, involving a challenge to planning approval for a new coal-fired power station.

[72] Bogojević, 'EU Climate Change Litigation'.

[73] J. Queally, '"Lawsuit Out of Love" as Unprecedented Legal Action Accuses Dutch Government of Failing on Climate', *Common Dreams*, 14 April 2015, available at: www.commondreams.org/news/2015/04/14/lawsuit-out-love-unprecedented-legal-action-accuses-dutch-government-failing-climate (last accessed 22 February 2017).

[74] Ibid.

[75] Hague climate change verdict: 'Not just a legal process but a process of hope' (interview with M. Minnesma, Urgenda Director), *The Guardian*, 26 June 2015, available at: www.theguardian.com/global-development-professionals-network/2015/jun/25/hague-climate-change-verdict-marjan-minnesma (last accessed 22 February 2017).

[76] Children's Investment Fund Foundation, Climate Strategic Litigation Europe, October 2014–September 2017, available at https://ciff.org/grant-portfolio/climate-strate

existing coal plants, improving air quality and reducing emissions from the corporate sector.[77] On its webpage describing the project, CIFF declares its 'belief . . . that environmental campaigning must be coupled with using the law as a powerful tool in order to bring about social and political change for good.'[78]

With increasing interest in the use of litigation as a tool for promoting 'change for good' on climate change, understanding its effectiveness in this regard and how it interacts with other campaigning efforts is vital. In this section we consider the necessary elements of a strategic programme of climate change litigation, as well as the lessons that can be learned from the U.S. and Australian experiences of the benefits and drawbacks of litigation as a tool for addressing climate change mitigation and adaptation risks.

1   Elements of a Strategic Climate Change Litigation Programme

The tool of strategic litigation is one employed by many advocacy organisations across a wide array of social justice fields, including human rights, civil rights, labour, and environmental protection.[79] Despite its widespread use, strategic litigation, and the pathways by which it can achieve given programme goals, are under-researched, and there is no standard approach. Instead, approaches to strategic litigation selected (consciously or unconsciously) by advocacy organisations are shaped by the goals of their particular programme, the nature of the social change they wish to effect, the broader social and political context in which they are operating, legal factors (such as the causes of action available and the existence of potential legal barriers), appetite for risk, and cost.[80]

---

gic-litigation-europe/. The authors have been engaged by CIFF to evaluate the programme (last accessed 22 February 2017).

[77] Ibid. The programme has now been funded for a second phase with a similar focus but an expanded scope of activities and new target jurisdictions in Central and Eastern Europe, and China.

[78] Ibid.

[79] Public Law Project, Guide to Strategic Litigation: www.publiclawproject.org.uk/data/resources/153/Guide-to-Strategic-Litigation.pdf (last accessed 22 February 2017); P. Geary, Children's Rights: A Guide to Strategic Litigation (Child Rights Information Network, 2008): www.crin.org/en/docs/Childrens_Rights_Guide_to_Strategic_Litigation.pdf (last accessed 22 February 2017).

[80] S. L. Wasby, 'Civil Rights Litigation by Organisations: Constraints and Choices', Judicature, (1985) 337.

For some lawyers and advocacy organisations undertaking strategic litigation the preferable approach is one that focuses on legal strategy. This approach measures the success of a strategic litigation programme primarily in terms of legal success in the courtroom. The underlying thinking is that only winning cases (establishing good precedent) can effect legal change and bring about broader social and policy change. Cases that lose, on the other hand, risk the establishment of bad legal precedent and/or may entrench particular legal interpretations favoured by opponents.[81] The series of cases brought in Australia seeking to use the federal environmental impact assessment law to stop coal mining projects that contribute to climate change and damage the Great Barrier Reef vividly demonstrates the dangers of 'bad precedent' in this regard.

As a major coal exporter, many Australian climate change cases seeking to reduce the country's carbon footprint have targeted new coal mine proposals. Under Australia's federal environmental impact assessment legislation, large new developments, such as coal mines, will require assessment and approval if they have the potential to impact significantly on protected 'matters of national environmental significance.'[82] These protected matters do not include climate change but do extend to ecosystems that are highly vulnerable to climate change impacts such as the World Heritage listed Great Barrier Reef.[83] Cases challenging coal mine proposals under the federal environmental legislation have hence sought to argue that the 'impacts' to be considered in assessing such proposals include climate change impacts on protected matters resulting from GHG emitted in burning of the harvested coal, even though combustion of the mined coal generally takes place outside Australian territory.[84] In a series of cases before the Australian Federal Court including the *Wildlife Whitsunday* and *Adani Carmichael Mine* decisions, these arguments for consideration of so-called 'scope 3 emissions'[85] under the federal environment law have been spectacularly unsuccessful.

---

[81] J. Greenberg, *Litigation for Social Change: Method, Limits, and Role in Democracy* (New York:NY Bar Association, 1974).

[82] Environment Protection and Biodiversity Conservation Act 1999 (Cth) [EPBC Act], Pt 3.

[83] Ibid., s. 12.

[84] J. Peel, 'The Role of Climate Change Litigation in Australia's Response to Global Warming', *Environmental & Planning Law Journal*, 24 (2007), 90.

[85] This terminology follows that of the Greenhouse Gas Protocol, the most widely used protocol in international accounting for greenhouse gas emissions (see further www .ghgprotocol.org/) (last accessed 22 February 2017). Scope 1 emissions refer to direct, on-site emissions from an activity. Scope 2 emissions are indirect emissions from the generation of purchased energy. Scope 3 emissions are all other indirect emissions that

In *Wildlife Whitsunday*, Justice Dowsett of the Federal Court accepted a government assessment that the 'indirect impacts' on the Great Barrier Reef and other protected areas of the large export-oriented coal mines at issue in the case were 'extremely small' and 'speculative'.[86] His Honour also declared that he was 'far from satisfied that the burning of coal at some unidentified place in the world, the production of greenhouse gases from such combustion, its contribution towards global warming and the impact of global warming upon a protected matter, can be so described [as an impact of the proposed coal mines]'.[87] A similar ruling was issued by Justice Griffiths, and affirmed on appeal, in the *Adani Carmichael Mine* case,[88] with the judge accepting the government's contention that the proposed mine – which will be the largest in the Southern Hemisphere – would have no assessable impact on the Reef given various uncertainties that made the extent of that impact difficult to determine.[89] While the *Adani Carmichael Mine* litigation has garnered significant public attention,[90] the case law so far has served only to entrench the idea that the federal environmental law in Australia offers no effective avenues for remedying the climate change impacts of large emissions-intensive projects.

At the other end of the spectrum from an approach focused on winnable cases is a social/political strategy approach to designing a strategic litigation programme where the primary purpose of bringing cases is 'to inspire political action' and 'to educate the public'.[91] Success here is not measured in terms of winning or losing cases (indeed, many cases taken where this approach is followed may be legal failures) but rather by whether the litigation fosters public debate and political action,

---

occur in the value chain of the reporting entity. For coal mining, the principal source of scope 3 emissions comes from burning of the harvested coal.

[86] *Wildlife Preservation Society of Queensland Prosperine/Whitsunday Branch Inc* v. *Minister for the Environment and Heritage* (2006) 232 ALR 510, 515 and 519–520.

[87] Ibid., 524.

[88] *Australian Conservation Foundation Inc* v. *Minister for the Environment* [2016] FCA 1042; the full text of the judgment is available online at: www.judgments.fedcourt.gov.au/judgments/Judgments/fca/single/2016/2016fca1042 (last accessed 22 February 2017).

[89] Ibid., para. 174. This decision was affirmed on appeal to the Full Court of the Australian Federal Court: *Australian Conservation Foundation Incorporated* v. *Minister for the Environment and Energy* [2017] FCAFC 134.

[90] K. Murphy, 'Federal Labor feels the heat over Adani and Coalition is sweating too', *The Guardian*, 27 May 2017: www.theguardian.com/environment/2017/may/27/federal-labor-feels-the-heat-over-adani-and-coalition-is-sweating-too (last accessed 9 March 2018).

[91] J. Lobel, *Success without Legal Victory: Lost Legal Battles and the Long Road to Justice in America* (New York, NY: NYU Press, 2003), pp. 3–4.

continues protest against the *status quo*, and/or builds a movement for change.[92] An example in this vein is the 2005 Inuit petition to the Inter-American Commission on Human Rights alleging human rights violations as a result of inadequate U.S. GHG emissions reduction policies.[93] Then-chair of the Inuit Circumpolar Conference, Sheila Watt-Cloutier, acknowledged how unlikely formal success was but described the case as a basis for starting a human rights dialogue about climate change with the United States.[94] Even so, the Inter-American Commission was selected by petitioners in part because of its strong record of action on environmental rights and indigenous rights claims, making it a particularly amenable forum for legal success, even if enforcement against the United States would be difficult.

Regardless of whether a legal strategy approach or a social/political strategy approach, or (more often) some combination of the two, is pursued in climate change litigation, a key element of a well-designed strategic programme is a coherent theory of change that seeks to explain how bringing particular cases will contribute to the goals sought by the programme.[95] The difficulty that arises in attempting to construct a theory of change is how to determine the links between litigation interventions and possible flow-on effects. In particular, while direct impacts from the litigation are relatively easy to trace, indirect impacts can be more difficult to detect and to attribute to particular cases.[96] Often, tracing causal chains in this latter instance will rely on qualitative data sources such as media reports referencing the litigation, mentions of cases in subsequent cases or policy documents, or insights obtained from interviews with those involved in or closely affected by the litigation.[97]

Although elaborating causal links between cases and broader impacts is challenging, the main advantage of thinking about climate change

---

[92] Ibid.

[93] Inuit Circumpolar Council Canada, Inuit Petition Inter-American Commission on Human Rights to Oppose Climate Change Caused by the United States of America, 7 December 2005, available at: www.inuitcircumpolar.com/inuit-petition-inter-ameri can-commission-on-human-rights-to-oppose-climate-change-caused-by-the-united-states-of-america.html (last accessed 22 February 2017).

[94] H. M. Osofsky, 'The Inuit Petition as a Bridge? Beyond Dialectics of Climate Change and Indigenous Peoples' Rights', *American Indian L. Rev.*, 31 (2007), 675.

[95] S. Funnell and P. Rogers, *Purposeful Program Theory: Effective use of theories of change and logic models* (San Francisco, CA: Jossey Bass, 2011).

[96] B. J. Preston, 'The Influence of Climate Change Litigation on Governments and the Private Sector', *Climate Law*, 2 (2011), 485.

[97] This was the methodology used in compiling research on indirect regulatory impacts of climate change litigation in our book: Peel and Osofsky, *Climate Change Litigation*.

litigation as part of an overall strategic approach is that this can help in identifying the desired outcomes and impacts of the programme more systematically, and in selecting cases to meet those goals. Where cases are being brought as part of an overall approach that emphasises legal strategy, lawyers' assessment of which cases have the best prospects of success will be particularly important. A range of factors may go into this assessment, including what causes of action are available and their legal merit, whether the case is likely to create a precedent that can be built on in future cases, the potential downsides of an adverse ruling (especially in a common law system), and legal barriers that add to risk or cost, such as limitations on access to the courts and costs rules. Cases may take place concurrently with policy advocacy, public campaigns and media communications in order to create a favourable climate for legal victory or to assist with implementation of that victory. Where engaging the public and political debate is a central purpose of the litigation, an emphasis on legal prospects for success may be less important. In practice, when organisations have social change objectives, which is generally the case with strategic litigation, they are likely to be simultaneously balancing the likelihood of success with the extent to which cases could advance broader social and policy goals.

Another factor to consider in designing a programme of strategic climate change litigation and the associated theory of change is whether the aim is for cases to be transformative in their outcomes or whether advocacy organisations are content to achieve more incremental impacts. Arguably, cases such as *Massachusetts* v. *EPA* in the United States or the *Urgenda* litigation in the Netherlands have been transformational in their impact; litigants may strive for such cases in order to generate a focal point for change, even if this means losing many other cases along the way. Equally, though, a litigation and campaigning strategy may seek change through incremental and iterative processes (as in the 'Beyond Coal' Sierra Club programme in the United States that utilises litigation as part of a broader campaign and anti-coal movement designed to produce change over time as coal plants close in response to sustained social and legal pressure).[98] Again, systematically considering the desired impacts of the programme and how litigation fits into assumed processes of change will help advocacy organisations and individuals considering

---

[98] For details of the Sierra Club's Beyond Coal programme, see http://content .sierraclub.org/coal/ (last accessed 22 February 2017). See also K. Bouwer, 'The Unsexy Future of Climate Change Litigation', *Journal of Environmental Law* (2018), 30 (2018) 483.

climate change litigation to choose pathways and cases best suited to their particular goals.

2 Lessons on the Effectiveness of Climate Litigation as a Regulatory Tool

The experience of two leading climate change litigation jurisdictions – the United States and Australia – with using courts as a forum for driving social and policy change on climate change offers some salutary lessons for groups considering this strategy in other jurisdictions. Of course, local law and political-legal culture remain very important in determining the possibilities for and constraints on climate change litigation in any particular jurisdiction.[99] To give one example, the potential for adverse costs orders against a losing party has been a major obstacle to promotive climate change litigation in Australia,[100] whereas, in the United States, where more favourable costs rules apply,[101] a more significant barrier is posed by the potential for business-led anti-regulatory litigation delaying or overturning any regulatory advance brought about by pro-regulatory cases.[102]

Nevertheless, some clear themes are discernible in the experience of these two leading climate change litigation jurisdictions. The first is that although 'breakthrough' cases such as *Massachusetts* v. *EPA* capture the public attention and grab headlines, the regulatory advances brought about by climate change litigation have generally been incremental rather than transformative. This is not surprising when we consider the vehicle for change selected in a litigation approach: courts tend to be followers, rather than leaders, of social movements and sensitive to criticism that they are unduly usurping a legislative role.[103]

---

[99] D. Nelken, 'Using the Concept of Legal Culture', *Australian J. Legal Philosophy*, 29 (2004),2.

[100] C. McGrath, 'Flying foxes, dams and whales: Using federal environmental laws in the public interest', *Environmental & Planning Law Journal*, 25 (2008), 324, 335–40.

[101] The general U.S. approach to costs is that each party bears their own costs in litigation. See C. Tollefson, 'Costs in Public Interest Litigation Revisited', *The Advocates' Quarterly*, 39 (2011), 197.

[102] Peel and Osofsky, *Climate Change Litigation*, pp. 283–300.

[103] Despite the favourable ruling in the first *Urgenda* case, separation of powers arguments presented a serious concern as acknowledged by the Court in its finding ordering the Dutch government to adopt the 'minimum' 25 per cent reduction by 2020 rather than the upper limit of 40 per cent discussion in reports of the Intergovernmental Panel on Climate Change. See *Urgenda* case, para. 4.95. An argument that the District Court's decision was too political was, however, rejected by the appeal court.

A second notable theme is that anti-regulatory litigation or effects can act as a significant brake on the achievements of pro-regulatory litigation. In the United States where the seminal *Massachusetts* v. *EPA* case has been followed by a series of anti-regulatory cases challenging the extent of the EPA's authority to regulate emissions of GHG from coal plants, those cases have constrained promotive regulatory impacts somewhat, as discussed above. Similarly, challenges to state-level mitigation actions on the basis of the dormant Commerce Clause, while largely dismissed as well, constrain how regulatory programmes can be framed at that level.[104] In Australia, there has not been anti-regulatory litigation as such on climate change issues but governments – who are often the targets of pro-regulatory cases – have taken action to reduce the funding and increase the barriers for litigants who seek to take positive strategic legal actions.[105] As other jurisdictions begin along the path of climate change litigation it is worth bearing in mind the likelihood that as promotive litigation brings about regulatory advances these are likely to be opposed through the legal or political system by those most affected by the new regulatory requirements.

A third theme that emerges from the U.S. and Australian experience is that the indirect impacts of climate change litigation can often be as significant as, or even more significant than, direct legal change brought about by particular cases. Where the effect of a case or a series of cases is to establish climate change as a serious public issue or to alter business attitudes to climate change risk, these changes tend to have long-lasting, systemic effects. The indirect impacts of cases will tend to be amplified where litigation occurs as part of an overall campaign or, put another way, where it is *a* tool and not *the* tool utilised in seeking change. Once again, this points to the value of understanding climate change litigation in a strategic sense and of thinking about what the goals of the litigation are and how court action can contribute to achieving those aims.

A final theme is that litigation evolves in response to the broader political environment, and strategies must take into account both what is needed and what is possible. For example, in the United States, many of

---

[104] For examples of this litigation, see *Rocky Mountain Farmers Union* v. *Corey*, 730 F.3d 1070 (9th Cir. 2013) (upholding the California law); *Energy & Env't Legal Inst.* v. *Epel*, 793 F.3d 1169, 1173 (10th Cir. 2015) (upholding the Colorado law); *North Dakota* v. *Heydinger*, No. 14-2156, 2016 WL 3343639 (8th Cir. 2016) (ruling against Minnesota on other grounds).

[105] Examples of backlash on adaptation policy and measures are discussed in J. Peel and H. Osofsky, 'Sue to Adapt?', *Minnesota Law Review*, 99(6) (2015), 2177.

the initial statutory claims were brought during President George W. Bush's administration in response to an unwillingness to regulate GHG emissions. President Obama's administration saw more anti-regulatory suits in part because his administration used decisions such as *Massachusetts* v. *EPA* as a basis for ambitious regulation. As President Trump rolls back that regulation, promotive litigation is once again expanding in the United States. However, if the experience in the enforcement of *Massachusetts* v. *EPA* under first President Bush and then President Obama is a guide, some of those decisions may be difficult to enforce fully without another political shift.

Australia has likewise seen shifts in climate litigation activity in response to political developments, and an increase in climate change cases – designed to hold the UK government and other European actors to account – may well be a product of the Brexit vote. In sum, the general pattern seems to be one of an inverse relationship between the extent of climate change litigation and the progressiveness of governments' climate change policies. As we enter a new era of policy uncertainty at the international level and in a number of key Western countries, climate change activism and strategic litigation in this field is likely only to increase.

E   Conclusion

Despite the achievements of international treaty-making efforts, such as the 2015 Paris Agreement,[106] strategic litigation by environmental advocates seeking to use the courts to advance action on climate change is likely to remain an important part of the overall picture of climate change regulation. President Donald Trump's decision to seek withdrawal of the United States from the Paris Agreement, and the resulting uncertainties created for the international regime and U.S. participation in it, only bolster the likely role of litigation, moving forward.

First, states parties' obligations under the Paris Agreement will take effect only from 2020, and already it is evident that countries' pledged actions both pre-2020 and post-2020 are insufficient to safeguard the global climate system in the ways that the Paris Agreement requires.[107]

---

[106] Paris Agreement, n. 2 above. See also M. Doelle, 'The Paris Agreement: Historic Breakthrough or High Stakes Experiment?', *Climate Law*, 6 (2016), 1.

[107] Decision 1/CP.21, 'Adoption of the Paris Agreement', 12 December 2015, FCCC/CP/2015/L.9/Rev.1, available at: http://unfccc.int/documentation/documents/advanced_search/items/6911.php?priref=600008865 (last accessed 22 February 2017), para. 17.

Litigation can play an important role in filling this gap by maintaining pressure on governments and corporate actors to increase the ambition and effectiveness of their actions to address climate change.

Second, it is clear that government action alone will be inadequate to address the mitigation, adaptation and financing needs raised by climate change.[108] Litigation has the potential to involve and incentivise a wide range of actors, including sub-national governments, businesses and civil society actors. For example, successful cases can require the institution of more climate-friendly actions or activities by businesses and governments. Equally, the perception of 'litigation risk' created by strategic climate change litigation efforts may motivate the adoption of more effective emissions reduction or adaptation measures by government and corporate actors.[109]

Finally, while the Paris Agreement concentrates on national-level commitments and their contribution to international climate change mitigation and adaptation goals, litigation impacts both national and sub-national scale action. Cases brought before the courts in relation to specific matters allow attention to the projects, decisions and policies at multiple levels that collectively will determine whether global climate change objectives are met.

To maximise the effectiveness of its regulatory influence, climate change litigation brought by pro-regulatory groups needs to be strategic. As the experience from established climate change litigation jurisdictions surveyed in this chapter indicates, this requires attention to questions of the type of impact sought from the litigation (transformative or incremental), the way in which impacts will be achieved (directly through formal legal change or indirectly through diffuse effects on social and corporate behaviour) and the potential for positive advances to be undermined by anti-regulatory litigation or political action. Articulating a theory of change for strategic climate change litigation that identifies the overall goals of the programme and the causal pathways by which litigation might achieve those goals is a good first step along that road, which can be backed up by monitoring of outcomes and evaluation of

---

[108] The important role of 'non-party' actors was acknowledged at the Paris Conference: ibid., paras. 117–19.

[109] See further S. Shearing, 'Raising the boardroom temperature? Climate change and shareholder activism in Australia', *Environmental & Planning Law Journal*, 29 (2012), 479; Johnston et al., Climate Change Adaptation in the Boardroom;, National Climate Change Adaptation Research Facility (2013): www.nccarf.edu.au/publications/climate-change-adaptation-boardroom (last accessed 22 February 2017).

their impact to determine the effectiveness of particular litigation interventions.

While a more systematic approach to designing and implementing climate change litigation programmes will increase their chances of functioning in a strategic fashion to promote positive regulatory outcomes, advocates need to bear in mind that litigation will generally be only one tool, rather than *the* tool for effecting social change. This was stressed by one of our U.S. interviewees – a veteran of impact litigation in the climate and environmental fields: '[N]o one thing is effective in a vacuum. We could have all the grassroots organising and social movements we want. That won't be effective if we don't have laws change and court decisions. And good court decisions won't be effective unless you have the other pieces coming along.'[110]

---

[110] Interview participant 2, in-person interview 22 October 2012, San Francisco.

PART V

The Legitimacy of Non-Compliance Procedures

13

Administrative Procedures and Rule of Law Values in the Montreal Compliance System

ANNA HUGGINS

A Introduction[1]

The most successful compliance system[2] in a global multilateral environmental agreement (MEA) is arguably the Montreal Protocol[3] to the Ozone Convention,[4] which provides for the progressive elimination of ozone-depleting substances. Significantly, the Montreal compliance system at times accommodates Parties' temporary circumvention of binding legal rules en route to compliance,[5] raising questions about the extent to which international legal obligations in the Montreal Protocol circumscribe administrative action within the regime's compliance system. This contrasts with the relationship between law and administrative action in Western legal systems in which law provides the parameters for administrative

---

[1] This chapter builds upon analysis in A. Huggins, *Multilateral Environmental Agreements and Compliance: The Benefits of Administrative Procedures* (Routledge,2018), ch. 4.

[2] MEA compliance systems encompass performance review information submitted by states, multilateral non-compliance procedures, and non-compliance response measures: United Nations Environment Programme (UNEP), 'Compliance Mechanisms under Selected Multilateral Environmental Agreements' (2007), p. 9: www.unep.org/pdf/delc/ Compliance_Mechanism_final.pdf; S. Borras, 'Comparative Analysis of Selected Compliance Procedures under Multilateral Environmental Agreements' in S. Maljean-Dubois and L. Rajamani, *Implementation of International Environmental Law* (Martinus Nijhoff Publishers, 2011) p. 366.

[3] Montreal Protocol on Substances that Deplete the Ozone Layer 1987, opened for signature 16 September 1987, 1989 UNTS 28 (entered into force 1 January 1989) ('Montreal Protocol').

[4] Vienna Convention for the Protection of the Ozone Layer, opened for signature 22 March 1985, 1513 UNTS 293 (entered into force 22 September 1988) ('Ozone Convention'). On the Montreal Protocol's successes, see Section B.1.

[5] M. Koskenniemi, 'Breach of Treaty or Non-Compliance? Reflections on the Enforcement of the Montreal Protocol', *Yearbook of International Environmental Law*, 3(1) (1992), 123, 162; J. Klabbers, 'Compliance Procedures' in D. Bodansky, J. Brunnée and E. Hey (eds.), *The Oxford Handbook of International Environmental Law* (Oxford University Press, 2007) pp. 996–8, 1007–9.

action.[6] Yet there is little dispute that, politically and environmentally, the Montreal Protocol and its compliance system are international environmental law success stories.[7] A question thus arises as to whether 'this success comes at a systemic cost – the cost of giving up the rule of law in favour of a specific set of goals'.[8]

This chapter argues that although the administrative procedures and mechanisms[9] for non-compliance under the Montreal compliance system at times facilitate departure from binding legal rules, this administrative action is nevertheless constrained by administrative mechanisms for accountability, transparency, participation and reason giving. This accords with insights from global administrative law (GAL) scholarship,[10] which highlights the desirability of global regulatory action being circumscribed by administrative

---

[6] Harlow notes that: '[e]very Western administrative law system is founded on the rule of law ... the rule of law ideal forms the central background theory against which the principles of administrative law operate, while at the same time acting as the governing principle': C. Harlow, 'Global Administrative Law: The Quest for Principles and Values', *European Journal of International Law*, 17 (2006), 187, 190.

[7] In 2003, former UN Secretary-General Kofi Annan described the Montreal Protocol as 'perhaps the single most successful international environmental agreement to date': UNEP Ozone Secretariat, 'Key Achievements of the Montreal Protocol in the Past 20 Years': www.meti.go.jp/policy/chemical_management/ozone/files/pamplet/panel/07e_mp.pdf (last accessed 15 March 2018). The Montreal compliance system has also been described as a 'remarkable success': A. Cardesa-Salzmann, 'Constitutionalising Secondary Rules in Global Environmental Regimes: Non-Compliance Procedures and the Enforcement of Multilateral Environmental Agreements', *Journal of Environmental Law*, 24(1) (2011), 103.

[8] Klabbers, 'Compliance Procedures', p. 1007. Discourses on the role of the rule of law at the international level are topical in the light of the UN Secretary-General's 2012 announcement of a 'program of action to strengthen the rule of law at the national and international levels': UN Secretary-General, Delivering Justice: Programme of Action to Strengthen the Rule of Law at the National and International Levels: Report to the Secretary-General, A/66/749, 16 Mar 2012. See further Section B.3.

[9] For the purposes of this chapter, the terms 'administrative procedures' and 'administrative mechanisms' are used interchangeably.

[10] GAL can be defined as 'comprising the mechanisms, principles and practices, and supporting social understandings that promote or otherwise affect the accountability of global administrative bodies, in particular by ensuring they meet adequate standards of transparency, participation, reasoned decision, and legality, and by providing effective review of the rules and decisions they make': B. Kingsbury, N. Krisch and R. B. Stewart, 'The Emergence of Global Administrative Law', *Law and Contemporary Problems*, 68 15 (2005), 17. See also N. Krisch and B. Kingsbury, 'Introduction: Global Governance and Global Administrative Law in the International Legal Order', *European Journal of International Law* 1, and the other articles in this Symposium issue of the *European Journal of International Law*, 17(1) (2006), 1–278; S. Cassese (ed.), *Research Handbook on Global Administrative Law* (Edward Elgar, 2016).

mechanisms.[11] Such constraints are important as numerous scholars claim that procedural rigour and integrity enhance normative legitimacy in international law.[12] The adoption of administrative procedures is one way to promote right process, and thereby to address legitimacy concerns regarding MEA compliance decisions.[13]

This chapter shows that administrative mechanisms not only provide parameters for decision-making under the Montreal Protocol's non-compliance procedure, but also inject key rule of law values into compliance processes. They do this by institutionalizing ways to minimize the risk of arbitrariness in the exercise of power[14] by (1) enhancing predictability and consistency in rules and decisions, and (2) ensuring that the perspectives of those who are affected by decisions are taken into account in decision-making processes.[15] These aims are

---

[11] Kingsbury, Krisch and Stewart, 'The Emergence of Global Administrative Law', 28.

[12] See, e.g., D. Hovell, *The Power of Process: The Value of Due Process in Security Council Sanctions Decision-Making* (Oxford University Press, 2016) pp. 61–3; T. Franck, The Power of Legitimacy among Nations (Oxford University Press, 1990), p. 2; S. Cassese, 'A Global Due Process of Law?' in G. Anthony, J.-B. Auby, J. Morison and T. Zwart (eds.), *Values in Global Administrative Law* (Hart Publishing, 2011) pp. 19–20; D. C. Esty, 'Good Governance at the Supranational Level: Globalizing Administrative Law', *Yale Law Journal*, 115 (2006), 1490, 1509–14; L. Tomlinson, *Procedural Justice and the United Nations Framework Convention on Climate Change: Negotiating Fairness* (Springer, 2015) p. 74.

[13] Esty, 'Good Governance at the Supranational Level', 1509–14. Esty argues that 'the procedural rigor of administrative law is a critical tool for refining international governance and legitimizing the exercise of supranational authority': *ibid.*, 1495. Examples of legitimacy concerns in MEA compliance systems include the Russian Federation's questioning of the Implementation Committee's authority to recommend trade restrictions under the Montreal Protocol: UNEP, Report of the Seventh Meeting of the Parties to the Montreal Protocol on Substances that Deplete the Ozone Layer, UNEP/OzL.Pro.7/12, 27 December 1995, para. 44. See also Section C.1. Further, the legal basis of trade suspensions under the CITES Convention has been challenged: P. H. Sand, 'Enforcing CITES: The Rise and Fall of Trade Sanctions', *Review of European Community & International Environmental Law*, 22(3) (2013), 251, 257.

[14] This argument is adapted from Krygier's work on domestic legal systems in M. Krygier, 'Why the Rule of Law is too Important to be Left to Lawyers', *Prawo i Więź (Law & Social Bonds)*, 2(2) (2012), 30, 36.

[15] These are the obverse of Krygier's description of arbitrary power: 'Unpredictable exercise of power is one way of treating its agents arbitrarily; another is its exercise, whether predictable or not, that takes no account of the perspectives of those whom it would affect': *ibid.,* 34. A variation on these ideas is provided by Føllesdal, who argues that the two central underlying values justifying most rule of law norms are 'non-domination' and 'stable legitimate expectations': A. Føllesdal, 'Epilogue: Curb, Channel and Coordinate: The Constitutionalisation of International Courts and Tribunals' in G. De Baere and J. Wouters (eds.), *The Contribution of International and Supranational Courts to the Rule of Law* (Edward Elgar, 2015) pp. 355–69, 356.

evident in the Montreal compliance system as administrative procedures for non-compliance promote decision-making that is consistent with procedural guidelines and past practices, which has
occurred in most, but not all, instances in practice. Moreover, the
proceduralized compliance framework facilitates opportunities for
regard for the interests of states affected by compliance decisions,
which are typically developing and transition countries. Thus,
administrative procedures constrain decision-making and promote
the achievement of values that inhere in the rule of law,[16] despite
departures from strict adherence to laws legitimized by state
consent.[17]

This chapter proceeds as follows. Section 2 outlines the key elements of the Montreal compliance system, and the extent to which
they reflect rules and decisions of an administrative character.
The ways in which administrative procedures for non-compliance at
times facilitate departure from binding legal rules, which contrasts
with the relationship between law and administrative action in
Western legal systems, are canvassed. Section 3 argues that, despite
this, the non-compliance proceedings under the Montreal compliance
system represent administrative action that is circumscribed by GAL
mechanisms, which inject key values of legality into compliance
decision-making. Section 3.1 evaluates if and how administrative
procedures for non-compliance reduce arbitrariness by promoting
predictability and consistency in decision-making, and section 3.2
analyzes how these procedures allow affected states' interests to be
taken into account in compliance decisions. Concluding remarks are
offered in Section 4.

B   The Montreal Compliance System, GAL and the Rule of Law

This section summarizes the salient features of the Montreal compliance system, and outlines the extent to which they reflect rules and
decisions of an administrative character, in accordance with insights
from GAL.

---

[16] Krygier, 'Why the Rule of Law is too Important to be Left to Lawyers', 36.
[17] Accordingly, this chapter contributes to recent scholarship that seeks to illuminate and
evaluate the values associated with procedural design in global governance. See, e.g.,
Hovell, *The Power of Process*; D. Hovell, 'Due Process in the United Nations', *American
Journal of International Law*, 110(1) (2016), 1.

1   An Overview of the Montreal Compliance System

The Montreal Protocol[18] to the Ozone Convention[19] came into force in 1989, and its non-compliance procedure was adopted in 1992. The institutional and administrative apparatus surrounding the formal non-compliance procedure encompasses state reporting, the non-compliance procedure administered by the Implementation Committee, oversight by the Meeting of the Parties (MOP), and conditional funding from the Multilateral Fund and Global Environment Facility to support developing and transition country compliance, respectively.[20] Collectively, this network of institutions and procedures constitutes the Montreal compliance system.[21] The Implementation Committee is an important locus of decision-making within this system. The Secretariat plays an instrumental role in bringing non-compliance issues to the attention of the Implementation Committee, and the MOP consistently follows the advice of the Implementation Committee in relation to non-compliance matters.[22]

Despite some significant challenges,[23] both the Montreal Protocol and its compliance system are widely regarded as international environmental law success stories.[24] In 2012, it was claimed that 'the Protocol has now led to the phase-out of 98 per cent of the historic levels of production and consumption of ozone-depleting substances'.[25] In 2014, the United Nations reported that, after decades of depletion, the ozone layer was beginning to thicken.[26] A contemporary challenge for the Montreal

---

[18] See n. 3.

[19] See n. 4.

[20] For the definition of compliance system employed in this chapter, see n. 2.

[21] O. Greene, 'The System for Implementation Review in the Ozone System' in D. G. Victor, K. Raustiala and E. B. Skolnikoff (eds.), *The Implementation and Effectiveness of International Environmental Commitments* (MIT Press, 1998) p. 89. See also G. de Burca, R. O. Keohane and C. F. Sabel, 'Global Experimentalist Governance', *British Journal of Political Science*, 44(3) (2014), 477.

[22] Ozone Secretariat, *Implementation Committee under the Non-Compliance Procedure of the Montreal Protocol on Substances that Deplete the Ozone Layer: Primer for Members* (2007), p. 18: http://ozone.unep.org/Publications/ImpCom_Primer_for_parties.pdf (last accessed 15 March 2018).

[23] For example, the Montreal Protocol faced historical challenges regarding the black market in ozone-depleting substances, particularly in chlorofluorocarbons (CFCs) during the 1990s.

[24] See n. 7.

[25] UNEP Ozone Secretariat, 'Key Achievements of the Montreal Protocol in the Past 20 Years'.

[26] World Meteorological Organization and United Nations Environment Programme, *Assessment for Decision-Makers: Scientific Assessment of Ozone Depletion: 2014*, World Meteorological Organization Global Ozone Research and Monitoring Project, Report

Protocol is the phasing down of hydrofluorocarbons (HFCs), which are potent greenhouse gases and were widely used as substitutes for hydro-chlorofluorocarbons (HCFCs) as they were phased out under the Protocol. In October 2016, the Parties agreed to an amendment to the Montreal Protocol to phase down HFCs, with staged timetables for developed and developing countries beginning in 2019.[27] This 'Kigali amendment' underscores the Protocol's ongoing significance in global efforts to address both ozone-layer depletion and adverse climate change impacts.

The Montreal compliance system valuably contributes to the success of the Montreal Protocol, and has inspired institutional design choices in other MEA compliance systems.[28] The development of the formal non-compliance procedure is enshrined in Article 8 of the Protocol. Article 8 provides:

> The Parties, at their first meeting, shall consider and approve procedures and institutional mechanisms for determining non-compliance with the provisions of this Protocol and for treatment of Parties found to be in non-compliance.

At the fourth MOP in 1992, the Protocol's non-compliance procedure was formally adopted,[29] and it was subsequently amended in 1998.[30] The non-compliance procedure only consists of 16 paragraphs, yet the practice of the Implementation Committee in relation to non-compliance issues is significantly more complex than the brevity of these procedural rules would suggest.[31]

There are multiple ways in which the Montreal Protocol's non-compliance procedure can be triggered. The most common way is for the Secretariat to trigger the non-compliance procedures based on

---

No. 56, Geneva, Switzerland: http://ozone.unep.org/Assessment_Panels/SAP/ SAP2014_Assessment_for_Decision-Makers.pdf (last accessed 15 March 2018).

[27] UNEP, Decision XXVIII: Further Amendment to the Montreal Protocol, UNEP/OzL. Pro.28/CRP/10, 14 October 2016, and UNEP, Decision XXVIII: Further Amendment to the Montreal Protocol, UNEP/OzL.Pro.28/CRP/11, 14 October 2016 (together the 'Kigali amendment').

[28] Cardesa-Salzmann, 'Constitutionalising Secondary Rules in Global Environmental Regimes', 103.

[29] UNEP, Decision IV/5: Non-Compliance Procedure, UNEP/OzL.Pro.4/1, 25 November 1992 ('Non-compliance procedure').

[30] UNEP, Decision X/10: Review of the Non-Compliance Procedure, UNEP/OzL.Pro.10/9, 3 December 1998.

[31] The Ozone Secretariat notes that the Implementation Committee 'relies to a considerable extent on custom and precedent': Ozone Secretariat, *Primer for Members*, p. 4.

a Party's annual reports on the production, consumption, import and export of controlled ozone-depleting substances relative to the baseline year and the year since the Party ratified the Protocol.[32] The non-compliance procedure can also be invoked by a Party concerned about another Party's potential non-compliance,[33] and by the self-reporting of a Party which, 'despite having made its best, bona fide efforts', is, or anticipates it will be, in non-compliance.[34] Once a Party has been referred to the Implementation Committee through one of these three methods, it will usually be requested to respond in writing to the alleged non-compliance, and in complex cases, to send a representative to the Committee meeting to discuss its situation.[35] The causes of non-compliance can be either procedural, such as a failure to report on relevant data and baselines,[36] and/or relate to substantive obligations pertaining to phasing out the production and consumption of ozone-depleting substances, and controlling international trade in such substances.[37] If a Party is found to be in non-compliance with its treaty obligations, it is normally requested to submit to the Committee a plan of action for its return to compliance.[38]

In relevant circumstances, the Multilateral Fund and Global Environment Facility may be invited to advise both the Implementation Committee and the Party concerned in relation to financial and technical assistance available to support the Party's return to compliance. The Multilateral Fund and the Global Environment Facility have played pivotal roles in the success of the compliance system by providing financial incentives for non-compliant developing and transition countries, respectively, to co-operate with the Implementation Committee as they work towards achieving compliance. In the light of the difficulties faced by some developing countries in meeting their obligations under the Montreal Protocol, the Multilateral Fund financial mechanism was established to reduce the burden of 'incremental'[39] compliance costs and provide technical assistance for

---

[32] Montreal Protocol, Art. 7.

[33] Non-compliance procedure, para. 1.

[34] *Ibid.*, para. 4.

[35] Ozone Secretariat, *Primer for Members*, p. 11; Non-compliance procedure, para. 10.

[36] See the procedural requirements in: Montreal Protocol, Arts. 7 and 9.

[37] *Ibid.*, Arts. 2, 3 and 4, and annexes.

[38] Ozone Secretariat, *Primer for Members*, p. 11.

[39] The 'incremental costs' are 'the extra costs between the costs of the alternative case and the baseline case': G. M. Bankobeza, *Ozone Protection: The International Legal Regime* (Eleven International Publishing, 2005) p. 228 at fn. 39; see also UNEP, Indicative List of

these countries. In most instances, only developing countries are eligible for funding from the Multilateral Fund.[40] Accordingly, since 1991, the Global Environment Facility has provided financial assistance to support phase-out activities for ozone-depleting substances in countries with economies in transition (CEITs) that are experiencing difficulties in meeting developed countries' phase-out schedules under the Protocol.[41] In sum, therefore, the Secretariat, the Implementation Committee, the MOP, the Multilateral Fund and the Global Environment Facility can be seen as 'subsidiary bodies of an administrative character'[42] which comprise the Montreal compliance system, and are responsible for identifying and responding to non-compliance with the Montreal Protocol.

2   The Montreal Compliance System and Global Administrative Law

Global administrative law is an apposite framework for conceptualizing and analyzing the emergent principles and practices in international law and global governance that reflect characteristics of administrative law. GAL can be defined as:

> comprising the mechanisms, principles and practices, and supporting social understandings that promote or otherwise affect the accountability of global administrative bodies, in particular by ensuring they meet adequate standards of transparency, participation, reasoned decision, and legality, and by providing effective review of the rules and decisions they make.[43]

Thus, GAL scholarship identifies norms and practices for accountability, transparency, participation, reason giving and review[44] in the 'global administrative space'.[45] GAL scholars claim that the legitimacy and

---

Categories of Incremental Costs, Report of the Fourth Meeting of the Parties to the Montreal Protocol, UNEP/OzL.Pro.5/15, 25 November 1992, Annex VIII.

[40] As Art. 5 of the Montreal Protocol defines eligibility in terms of per capita consumption of ozone-depleting substances, a small number of CEITs are eligible for Multilateral Fund assistance: Bankobeza, *Ozone Protection*, p. 235.

[41] O. Yoshida, 'Soft Enforcement of Treaties: The Montreal Protocol's Noncompliance Procedure and the Functions of Internal International Institutions', *Colorado Journal of International Environmental Law and Policy*, 10(1) (1999), 95, 100.

[42] Kingsbury, Krisch and Stewart, 'The Emergence of Global Administrative Law', 21.

[43] *Ibid.*, 17.

[44] *Ibid.*, 28.

[45] See n. 10.

accountability concerns associated with global governance[46] may be ameliorated by incorporating 'new mechanisms of administrative law at the global level to address decisions and rules made within intergovernmental regimes'.[47]

There are two main ways in which GAL aptly accounts for processes within the Montreal compliance system. First, a key premise of GAL is that many contemporary global governance practices can be viewed as 'administrative action',[48] which includes elements of rule-making, adjudication and other decision-making that fall short of formal treaty-making and adjudicative dispute settlement between Parties.[49] This descriptor aligns with the processes within the Montreal compliance system as the rules and decisions governing the regime depart from consent-based treaty practices.[50] Moreover, the preference for endogenous and facilitative processes to support Parties' return to compliance was a deliberate design choice, which recognized the limitations of adversarial channels of dispute settlement for optimally responding to the inherently multilateral nature of the global environmental concerns that are the focus of co-operative action in MEAs.[51]

Secondly, GAL mechanisms play an important role in enhancing the normative legitimacy of the administrative action in the Montreal compliance system.[52] Over time, there has been evidence of the adoption of

---

[46] GAL allows legitimacy questions to be revisited in a more 'specific and focused way': Kingsbury, Krisch and Stewart, 'The Emergence of Global Administrative Law', 27.

[47] *Ibid.*, 16.

[48] *Ibid.*, 17; N. Krisch, 'Global Administrative Law and the Constitutional Ambition' in P. Dobner and M. Loughlin (eds.), *The Twilight of Constitutionalism* (Oxford University Press, 2010), p. 255.

[49] Kingsbury, Krisch and Stewart, 'The Emergence of Global Administrative Law', 17.

[50] This is part of a broader trend in which the primacy of formal state consent in 'regime-based law-making processes' in international environmental law is diminishing: J. Brunnée, 'Common Areas, Common Heritage, and Common Concern' in D. Bodansky, J. Brunnée and E. Hey (eds.), *The Oxford Handbook of International Environmental Law* (Oxford University Press, 2007) p.569; A. Peters, 'Compensatory Constitutionalism: The Function and Potential of Fundamental International Norms and Structures', *Leiden Journal of International Law*, 19 579 (2006), 587–9.

[51] See, e.g., Cardesa-Salzmann, 'Constitutionalising Secondary Rules in Global Environmental Regimes', 111–3; A. Chayes and A. Handler Chayes, *The New Sovereignty: Compliance with International Regulatory Agreements* (Harvard University Press, 1998), pp. 201–28; M. A. Fitzmaurice and C. Redgwell, 'Environmental Non-Compliance Procedures and International Law', *Netherlands Yearbook of International Law*, 31 (2000),35.

[52] A. Huggins, 'The Desirability of Administrative Proceduralisation: Compliance Rules and Decisions in Multilateral Environmental Agreements', unpublished PhD thesis, University of New South Wales (2015), ch. 4.

a limited set of administrative procedures for accountability, transparency, participation and reason giving in the Montreal compliance system, but avenues for review are circumscribed.[53] As previously mentioned, numerous scholars draw a link between right process, which is enhanced by the adoption of administrative procedures, and the legitimacy of decision-making in international law and global governance.[54] The extent to which rule of law values are also promoted warrants further examination.

3   The Montreal Compliance System, GAL and the Rule of Law

Proponents of GAL argue that the adoption of administrative procedures contributes to the achievement of various normative aims in global governance.[55] One such aim that has been identified by numerous GAL scholars is promoting the rule of law.[56] For example, Stewart argues that a:

> modest but viable role for global administrative law would be to develop the tools of transparency, participation, reason giving, and review to promote greater consideration by decision makers to disregarded interests *and promote the rule of law* over regimes of power and bargain.[57]

In order to evaluate such claims, analytical clarity regarding what it means to achieve the rule of law – a contested concept in both domestic[58] and international contexts[59] – is required.

---

[53] *Ibid.*

[54] See n. 12.

[55] For example, Kingsbury, Krisch and Stewart identify three normative foundations for GAL: 'internal administrative accountability', protection of rights of private or state actors, and 'promotion of democracy': Kingsbury, Krisch and Stewart, 'The Emergence of Global Administrative Law', 43.

[56] See, e.g., R. B. Stewart, 'Remedying Disregard in Global Regulatory Governance: Accountability, Participation, and Responsiveness', *American Journal of International Law*, 108 (2014), 211, 220; R. B. Stewart, 'Part I Courts, Institutions, and Access to Justice: Legitimacy and Accountability in Global Regulatory Governance: Global Administrative Law and Developing Countries', *Jindal Global Law Review*, 1 (2009), 41, 59; E. Benvenisti, *The Law of Global Governance* (Hague Academy of International Law, 2014) pp. 89–99; M.-S. Kuo, 'The Concept of "Law" in Global Administrative Law: A Reply to Benedict Kingsbury', *European Journal of International Law*, 20(4) (2009), 997.

[57] Stewart, 'Part I Courts, Institutions, and Access to Justice', 59 (emphasis added). See also Stewart, 'Remedying Disregard in Global Regulatory Governance', 220.

[58] See, e.g., J. Waldron, 'Is the Rule of Law an Essentially Contested Concept (in Florida)?', *Law and Philosophy*, 21 (2002), 137, 164.

[59] See, e.g., S. Chesterman, 'An International Rule of Law?', *American Journal of Comparative Law*, 56(2) (2008), 331, 355–6.

While international law scholarship is 'replete' with the use of the term 'international rule of law', definitions of this concept are sparse.[60] Often, understandings of the international rule of law implicitly or explicitly encompass adherence to international laws legitimized by state consent.[61] However, as Cogan asserts, a narrow, formalist understanding of the international rule of law may well be a 'myth' in light of the many obvious examples of its breach.[62] Indeed, this paradigm has limited purchase in accounting for the relationship between law and administrative action across much of the global regulatory governance landscape. There is a range of global regulatory bodies that are not circumscribed by international laws, or for which legal rules only partially constrain administrative discretion.[63] Even for formal intergovernmental institutions, such as the Montreal Protocol, binding international commitments in multilateral agreements between states may not provide legal parameters for the action of 'autonomous institutional arrangements',[64] such as compliance bodies. Unlike in Western administrative law systems, there is no doctrine of ultra vires at the international level, which, if present, would mean that intergovernmental organizations are bound by the treaties that established them.[65] Thus, the notion that public power must be exercised in accordance with state-made law, which is central to the nexus between law and administrative action in Western legal systems,[66] does not transpose neatly to administrative practices in global governance.

[60] R. McCorquodale, 'Defining the International Rule of Law: Defying Gravity?', *International and Comparative Law Quarterly*, 65(2) (2016), 277, 278.

[61] See, e.g., J. Waldron, 'The Rule of International Law', *Harvard Journal of Law and Public Policy*, 30 (2006), 15. A focus on enhancing states' conformity with international law is also a focus of much compliance theorizing in international law: see, e.g., Chayes and Handler Chayes, *The New Sovereignty*; G. W. Downs, D. M. Rocke and P. N. Barsoom, 'Is the Good News About Compliance Good News About Cooperation?', *International Organization*, 50(3) (1996), 379; H. H. Koh, 'Why Do Nations Obey International Law?', *Yale Law Journal*, 106 (1997), 2599.

[62] J. Katz Cogan, 'Noncompliance and the International Rule of Law', *Yale Journal of International Law*, 31 (2006), 189, 206.

[63] These bodies include: (1) formal intergovernmental institutions, (2) transnational networks of national regulatory officials, (3) distributed administration in which domestic regulatory bodies take decisions on issues of international concern, (4) hybrid intergovernmental-private institutions, and (5) private bodies: Kingsbury, Krisch and Stewart, 'The Emergence of Global Administrative Law', 20–2.

[64] R. R. Churchill and G. Ulfstein, 'Autonomous Institutional Arrangements in Multilateral Environmental Agreements: A Little-Noticed Phenomenon in International Law', *American Journal of International Law*, 94 (2000), 623.

[65] Benvenisti, *The Law of Global Governance*, pp. 90–2.

[66] See n. 6.

As in other pockets of global governance, international laws do not always constrain administrative action in the Montreal compliance system.[67] In particular, non-compliant Parties are able to negotiate plans for return to compliance with the Implementation Committee, which are based on meeting agreed targets, rather than treaty obligations. These accountability arrangements for states' return to compliance circumvent the rules in the Montreal Protocol, including the binding emissions reduction commitments in Article 2,[68] compliance with which is required under general international law. Moreover, the accountability arrangements for conditional funding for developing countries and CEITs, which are endorsed by the Implementation Committee, may be seen as actively facilitating temporary circumvention of binding commitments as funds are paid to countries that are not in substantive compliance with Article 2, but are deemed to remain 'in good standing'. For instance, the Russian Federation was in non-compliance with its emissions reduction commitments under the Montreal Protocol from 1996 to 2000,[69] and did not return to compliance until 2002.[70] Despite this, from 1995 to 2002, Russia continued to receive financial assistance from the Global Environment Facility as a 'country in good standing'.[71] This ongoing favourable treatment stands in contrast to the traditional rules of state responsibility for a breach of an international obligation under general international law.[72]

This is not to say that the rule of law has no purchase in this context. In his influential work on domestic legal orders, Krygier posits that an essential, but not sufficient, pre-condition of the rule of law is that law rules.[73] Kingsbury persuasively argues that GAL reflects a new paradigm

---

[67] See, e.g., Katz Cogan, 'Noncompliance and the International Rule of Law', 206.

[68] UNEP, Report of the Implementation Committee under the Non-Compliance Procedure for the Montreal Protocol on the Work of its Twentieth Meeting, UNEP/OzL.Pro/ ImpCom/20/4, 9 July 1998, para. 26.

[69] UNEP, Decision XIII/17: Compliance with the Montreal Protocol by the Russian Federation, UNEP/OzL.Pro.13/10, 26 October 2001, para. 2.

[70] UNEP, Report of the Fourteenth Meeting of the Parties to the Montreal Protocol on Substances that Deplete the Ozone Layer, UNEP/OzL.Pro.14/9, 5 December 2002, para. 133.

[71] See UNEP, Decision VIII/25: Compliance with the Montreal Protocol by Russian Federation, UNEP/OzL.Pro.8/12, 19 December 1996; UNEP, Decision IX/31: Compliance with the Montreal Protocol by the Russian Federation, UNEP/OzL.Pro.9/ 12, 25 September 1997; UNEP, Decision X/26: Compliance with the Montreal Protocol by the Russian Federation, UNEP/OzL.Pro.10/9, 3 December 1998; UNEP, Decision XIII/17.

[72] Koskenniemi, 'Breach of Treaty or Non-Compliance?', 134.

[73] M. Krygier, 'Rule of Law' in M. Rosenfeld and A. Sajo (eds.), *The Oxford Handbook of Comparative Constitutional Law* (Oxford University Press, 2012), pp. 233–5.

of legality premised on a social fact conception of law and principles of 'publicness'.[74] If, as Krygier submits, the achievement of the rule of law requires more than legal constraints on power,[75] this raises the question of what else is required. Krygier contrasts approaches premised on 'anatomical' characterizations of the rule of law, which specify certain indicia of legal institutions, rules and practices that together are seen to constitute the rule of law,[76] with an explicitly 'teleological' approach, which begins with reflections upon the purposes and values of the rule of law.[77] This latter approach differs from conventional accounts of the rule of law, which frequently start with means rather than ends.[78] According to Krygier, a focus on ends is preferable as the 'rule of law occurs when and to the extent that there is a social *achievement* to which law contributes'.[79]

Krygier posits that the *telos* of the rule of law in domestic legal systems is its opposition to arbitrary power, irrespective of the specific legal and institutional features that accompany it.[80] That is, the rule of law is valuable as it institutionalizes constraints on arbitrariness in the exercise of power.[81] It does this by (1) enhancing predictability[82] and consistency

---

[74] B. Kingsbury, 'The Concept of "Law" in Global Administrative Law', *European Journal of International Law*, 20(1) (2009), 23. This approach is not without its critics, who claim, inter alia, that such a conceptualization raises difficult questions about how to distinguish law from non-law in global governance: see, e.g., A. Somek, 'The Concept of "Law" in Global Administrative Law: A Reply to Benedict Kingsbury', *European Journal of International Law*, 20(4) (2009), 985, 988; M-S Kuo, 'A Reply to Benedict Kingsbury'.

[75] Krygier, 'Rule of Law', pp. 233–5.

[76] Krygier argues that the work of Dicey, Fuller and, to a lesser extent, Waldron reflects this approach due to their focus on 'particular institutions such as common law courts (Dicey), particularly formal qualities of rules, such as prospectivity, clarity, etc. (Fuller), or even traditions and procedures, such as defences, *habeus corpus*, and so on (Waldron), though the last is getting closer to explicit concern with the specific value of the rule of law': Krygier, 'Why the Rule of Law is too Important to be Left to Lawyers', 33.

[77] Krygier, 'Rule of Law', p. 235.

[78] *Ibid.* In the international law context, see, e.g., Chesterman, who advocates 'seeing the rule of law as a means rather than an end': Chesterman, 'An International Rule of Law?', 361.

[79] Krygier, 'Why the Rule of Law is too Important to be Left to Lawyers', 33 (emphasis in original).

[80] See, e.g., M. Krygier, 'The Rule of Law: Teleology, Sociology and Legality' in G. Palombella and N. Walker (eds.), *Relocating the Rule of Law* (Hart, 2009) p. 45; M. Krygier, 'Four Puzzles about the Rule of Law: Why, What, Where? And Who Cares?' in J. E. Fleming (ed.), *Getting to the Rule of Law* (New York University Press, 2011). p.64; Krygier, 'Rule of Law'.

[81] M. Krygier, 'Why the Rule of Law is too Important to be Left to Lawyers', 36.

[82] See also J. Waldron, 'The Rule of Law in Contemporary Legal Theory', *Ratio Juris*, 2(1) (1989), 79, 84–5.

in rules and decisions, and (2) ensuring that the perspectives of those who are affected by decisions are taken into account in decision-making processes.[83] The first reduces arbitrariness by allowing those subject to power to choose how to act in advance in the light of foreseeable rules and consequences, and the second achieves this end by facilitating rules and decisions that are responsive to the interests of those they affect.[84]

I argue that the *telos* of the rule of law can be conceived similarly in both domestic and global settings, yet fundamental contextual differences shape the challenges to the rule of law and the legal and institutional responses in each realm. As Waldron notes, there is no overarching government in international law and 'the subjects of [international law] – sovereign states – are not vulnerable to power exercised against them or upon them at this level in the same way as natural individuals are vulnerable to the power of national governments'.[85] For Waldron, this raises questions as to whether states need and are entitled to rule of law protections.[86] However, the 'problem of disregard' for the interests of less powerful states and other marginalized actors in international settings is well documented[87] and, I contend, highlights the desirability of rule of law protections in global regulatory governance, as in domestic legal contexts.

In the Montreal compliance system, states are the creators and enforcers, as well as the subjects and agents, of rules and decisions.[88] In this state-centric context, North–South power imbalances create a risk that rule-making and decisions will be strongly shaped by differences in power between states. This risk is manifest in the operation of the CITES[89] compliance system, for example, in which developing country Parties have been more likely to be subject to compliance proceedings and trade sanctions than their developed country counterparts.[90]

---

[83] See n. 15. On the second point, see also Dyzenhaus, who claims that the 'central aspiration of the rule of law [is] the subjection of public power to controls that ensure it is exercised in the interests of those affected by it': D. Dyzenhaus, 'The Rule of (Administrative) Law in International Law', *Law & Contemporary Problems*, 68 (2005), 127, 129–30.

[84] Krygier, 'Why the Rule of Law is too Important to be Left to Lawyers', 34.

[85] J. Waldron, 'Are Sovereigns Entitled to the Benefit of the International Rule of Law?', *European Journal of International Law*, 22 (2011) 315, 322–3.

[86] *Ibid.*, 322–43.

[87] For an overview, see Stewart, 'Remedying Disregard in Global Regulatory Governance'.

[88] Kingsbury, Krisch and Stewart, 'The Emergence of Global Administrative Law', 36.

[89] *Convention on International Trade in Endangered Species of Wild Fauna and Flora 1973*, opened for signature 3 March 1973, 993 UNTS 243 (entered into force 1 July 1975) ('CITES').

[90] See, e.g., Sand, 'Enforcing CITES', 261; Huggins, *Multilateral Environmental Agreements and Compliance*, ch. 6.

As Sand observes, this comes as something of an 'empirical surprise', as compliance gaps and loopholes are unlikely to exist in export-oriented developing countries alone – rather, they can be anticipated in export, transit and import countries, which include developed countries.[91] Thus, the risk of arbitrary power in global regulatory bodies stems from states' unequal bargaining power, which is a product of economic and political disparities between developed and developing states that have their origins in colonialism.[92] Rule of law protections are therefore important as the 'weak's counterweight to the powerful',[93] especially in the context of the North–South divide.

Despite the fact that the Montreal Protocol's administrative arrangements for non-compliance at times accommodate departure from binding treaty commitments, such arrangements are nonetheless constrained by GAL mechanisms, which may contribute to the achievement of rule of law values by opposing arbitrariness in decision-making. Specifically, to the extent that administrative law mechanisms promote predictability and consistency in decision-making practices, and help to level the playing field for less powerful states by ensuring that their interests are taken into account in decision-making, they oppose arbitrary power. These normative aspirations provide benchmarks against which the roles played by administrative procedures in the Montreal compliance system can be evaluated. This evaluative process is important as it is by no means certain that administrative procedures do promote these ideals in practice. In particular, concerns have been raised that GAL mechanisms may serve to entrench and perpetuate existing power imbalances,[94] which would undermine the aim of minimizing arbitrariness. For example, Chimni claims that 'from a third world perspective, GAL has a limited role to play in injecting the elements of democracy, equity, and justice into international law and institutions. Indeed, GAL can be co-opted by powerful states to their advantage'.[95] As shall be shown, these critiques do not have strong traction in the case of the Montreal

---

[91] Sand, 'Enforcing CITES', 261.
[92] See generally A. Anghie, *Imperialism, Sovereignty and the Making of International Law* (Cambridge University Press, 2005); S. Alam, S. Atapattu, C. G. Gonzalez and J. Razzaque (eds.), *International Environmental Law and the Global South* (Cambridge University Press, 2015).
[93] Katz Cogan, 'Noncompliance and the International Rule of Law', 207.
[94] Kingsbury, Krisch and Stewart, 'The Emergence of Global Administrative Law', 51–2; Stewart, 'Part I Courts, Institutions, and Access to Justice', 43–4.
[95] B. S. Chimni, 'Co-option and Resistance: Two Faces of Global Administrative Law', *New York University Journal of International Law and Politics*, 37 (2005), 799, 826.

compliance system, in which GAL mechanisms play roles that consistently, though not invariably, promote rule of law values.

Before proceeding, it should be noted that this chapter's approach to analyzing rule of law values implies that the Montreal Protocol and its institutional bodies are a largely 'self-contained regime', primarily influenced by emergent rule of law constraints generated within the regime, rather than being governed by the external dictates of general international law regarding, for example, breach of treaty.[96] A distinction drawn by De Baere, Chane and Wouters is useful here. As these authors note, 'The sources of *internal* rule of law constraints are the legal orders themselves whose public authorities are to be constrained', and can be contrasted with *external* rule of law constraints from 'legal orders that include but are broader in scope than the legal order whose public authorities they are meant to constrain'.[97] In this chapter, an internal rule of law lens is applied. While critiques of the 'fragmentation' of international law are acknowledged,[98] internal rule of law constraints warrant further examination in light of the limits of general international law norms in effectively constraining regulatory practice in many global governance contexts.[99]

C   GAL Mechanisms and Rule of Law Values in the Montreal Compliance System

1   GAL Mechanisms and Predictability

As noted above, a key value of the rule of law and antidote to arbitrariness is predictability in the exercise of power.[100] This section demonstrates that administrative mechanisms for accountability, participation and reason giving in the Montreal compliance system have, in most instances, led to greater predictability in compliance decision-making. Specifically, a consistent pattern of accountability arrangements for responding to

[96] Koskenniemi, 'Breach of Treaty or Non-Compliance?', 134, 162.
[97] G. De Baere, A.-L. Chane and J. Wouters, 'The Contribution of International and Supranational Courts to the Rule of Law: A Framework for Analysis' in G. De Baere and J. Wouters (eds.), *The Contribution of International and Supranational Courts to the Rule of Law* (Edward Elgar, 2015) p. 45 (emphasis in original).
[98] See, e.g., M. Koskenniemi, 'The Politics of International Law – 20 Years Later', *European Journal of International Law*, 20(1) (2009), 7, 15; M. Koskenniemi, 'Miserable Comforters: International Relations as the New Natural Law', *European Journal of International Relations*, 15 (2009), 395, 406.
[99] Kingsbury, Krisch and Stewart, 'The Emergence of Global Administrative Law', 20–3.
[100] See n. 15.

non-compliance, and supporting Parties' return to compliance, has emerged.[101] These accountability arrangements have promoted greater consistency and predictability in compliance decision-making; however, this is tempered with leeway to consider the merits of individual cases – in this instance, the circumstances of each country.[102] This predictability is *internal* to the compliance system: as previously noted, at times the compliance system does not operate in a way that is consistent with the rules in the Montreal Protocol itself. There have been rare departures from the past practices and procedural guidelines governing the compliance system in which more overtly politicized decision-making practices are evident. However, on balance, GAL mechanisms have played a positive role in enhancing predictability, and thus reducing the risk of arbitrary power, in this setting.

Within the Montreal compliance system, the Implementation Committee constitutes the locus of compliance decision-making,[103] and its processes reflect GAL principles and practices of accountability and participation in particular. This Committee, which is composed of ten Party representatives elected for two-year terms, meets twice annually, and its responsibilities include managing the Protocol's non-compliance procedure. The Implementation Committee's processes foster accountability as states are required to justify their conduct, and are answerable to the Committee for deficient performance.[104] A potentially non-compliant Party may be requested to attend the next meeting of the Implementation Committee in order to discuss and explain its situation. These discussions are intended to be 'non-confrontational but frank', underpinning a style of decision-making that favours pragmatism and flexibility over legal argumentation.[105] In addition to these participatory

---

[101] Y. Shigeta, *International Judicial Control of Environmental Protection: Standard Setting, Compliance Control and the Development of International Environmental Law by the International Judiciary* (Wolters Kluwer, 2010), p. 120.

[102] Cardesa-Salzmann, 'Constitutionalising Secondary Rules in Global Environmental Regimes', 131–2. See, generally, Ozone Secretariat, *Primer for Members*.

[103] See n. 22.

[104] This accords with Stewart's narrow definition of accountability mechanisms characterized by three structural elements: '(1) a specified accounter, who is subject to being called to provide account for his conduct; (2) a specified account holder who can require the accounter to render account; and (3) the ability and authority of the account holder to impose sanctions or other remedies for deficient performance': Stewart, 'Remedying Disregard in Global Regulatory Governance', 253. A similar definition of accountability is found in J. Black, 'Constructing and Contesting Legitimacy and Accountability in Polycentric Regulatory Regimes', *Regulation and Governance*, 2 (2008), 136, 150.

[105] Klabbers, 'Compliance Procedures', 996–7.

rights for non-compliant Parties, the Multilateral Fund and Global Environment Facility may be invited to advise both the Implementation Committee and the Party concerned in relation to financial and technical assistance available to support the Party's return to compliance.[106]

The style of administrative decision-making evident in the Implementation Committee is predictable, yet some flexibility to take into account the merits of individual cases remains. This approach is reflected in the *Primer for Members,* which was produced by the Ozone Secretariat for Implementation Committee members in 2007.[107] This document lists sixteen 'routine procedural non-compliance matters' and recommended responses to each of these types of matters. In some instances, the text of recommendations approved by the Implementation Committee at previous meetings is employed as a precedent for the new matters before it, ameliorating the need for extended deliberation or fact finding.[108] This approach is referred to as a 'blanket approval' process.[109] In other non-routine instances warranting a tailored response, the Implementation Committee undertakes an individual review to gain a nuanced understanding of the particular circumstances of the non-compliant Party.[110] This approach to responding to non-compliance simultaneously fosters predictability for routine cases, yet preserves a discretionary role for decision-makers in the light of the national circumstances of non-compliant Parties.

Similarly, the Implementation Committee's response to supporting Parties' return to compliance is largely proceduralized and consistent. In the early 1990s, a practice of making the ongoing receipt of financial assistance from the Multilateral Fund contingent upon satisfying the benchmarks that Parties have negotiated with the Implementation Committee and specified in their compliance action plan emerged. These arrangements developed in response to concerns about developing countries' accountability for the financial assistance they were receiving to support their implementation of the Protocol.[111] Significantly, as

---

[106] Multilateral Fund representatives first participated in an Implementation Committee meeting in September 1992: see UNEP, Report of the Fourth Meeting of the Implementation Committee, para. 2.

[107] Ozone Secretariat, *Primer for Members.*

[108] *Ibid.,* 14.

[109] *Ibid.*

[110] *Ibid.,* 15.

[111] Shigeta, *International Judicial Control of Environmental Protection,* pp. 131–2; Bankobeza, *Ozone Protection,* pp. 234–6; D. G. Victor, 'The Early Operation and

foreshadowed above, these negotiated benchmarks fall short of Parties' obligations to reduce the production and consumption of ozone-depleting substances under the Montreal Protocol, and instead reflect incremental targets Parties have agreed to meet en route to full compliance with their treaty commitments. After the non-compliance proceedings against Belarus, Bulgaria, Poland and Russia in the mid-1990s, a variation of this prototypical response was offered to CEITs that were eligible for funding from the Global Environment Facility. This, in turn, created a precedent for subsequent proceedings against CEITs in 1998 and 1999.[112] In this way, the accountability arrangements governing the conditional financial assistance provided by the Multilateral Fund and Global Environment Facility facilitated a standardization of the responses to substantive non-compliance by developing countries and CEITs.

These standardized responses are also reflected in the formulaic reasons provided in compliance decisions. There are a number of common elements reflected in these reasons: (1) a detailed acknowledgement and explanation of the non-compliance in question, (2) a statement that, as long as compliance benchmarks specified in the compliance action plan are met, a Party in non-compliance with its emissions reduction commitments specified in the Montreal Protocol will remain a 'member in good standing' that is eligible for international financial assistance, and (3)

Effectiveness of the Montreal Protocol's Non-Compliance Procedure' (1996), p. 12: http://pages.ucsd.edu/~dgvictor/publications/Victor_Article_1996_Early%20Operation %20and%20Effectiveness.pdf (last accessed 15 March 2018).

[112] Specifically, Azerbaijan, Belarus, the Czech Republic, Estonia, Latvia, Lithuania, the Russian Federation, Ukraine and Uzbekistan in 1998, and Bulgaria and Turkmenistan in 1999: UNEP, Decision X/20: Compliance with the Montreal Protocol by Azerbaijan, UNEP/OzL.Pro.10/9, 3 December 1998; UNEP, Decision X/21: Compliance with the Montreal Protocol by Belarus, UNEP/OzL.Pro.10/9, 3 December 1998; UNEP, Decision X/22: Compliance with the Montreal Protocol by the Czech Republic, UNEP/OzL. Pro.10/9, 3 December 1998; UNEP, Decision X/23: Compliance with the Montreal Protocol by Estonia, UNEP/OzL.Pro.10/9, 3 December 1998; UNEP, Decision X/24: Compliance with the Montreal Protocol by Latvia, UNEP/OzL.Pro.10/9, 3 December 1998; UNEP, Decision X/25: Compliance with the Montreal Protocol by Lithuania, UNEP/OzL.Pro.10/9, 3 December 1998; UNEP, Decision X/26: Compliance with the Montreal Protocol by the Russian Federation, UNEP/OzL.Pro.10/9, 3 December 1998; UNEP, Decision X/27: Compliance with the Montreal Protocol by Ukraine, UNEP/OzL.Pro.10/9, 3 December 1998; UNEP, Decision X/28: Compliance with the Montreal Protocol by Uzbekistan, UNEP/OzL.Pro.10/9, 3 December 1998; UNEP, Decision XI/24: Compliance with the Montreal Protocol by Bulgaria, UNEP/ OzL.Pro.11/10, 17 December 1999; UNEP, Decision XI/25: Compliance with the Montreal Protocol by Turkmenistan, UNEP/OzL.Pro.11/10, 17 December 1999.

a warning regarding the punitive measures that may be resorted to if non-compliance persists.[113] This type of precedent-based approach reflects rule of law values of predictability and consistency. The conditional funding arrangements also take into account the capacity constraints experienced by developing countries and CEITs, which indicates regard for less powerful states' interests – the focus of the following section.

These tendencies towards realizing rule of law values are, however, at times under strain from, and on occasion overridden by, competing forces and values at play in this setting. For example, the Russian Federation's non-compliance proceedings in the mid-1990s represent one instance in which a politicized – and arguably arbitrary – compliance solution appeared to prevail over a more procedurally-constrained variant. Non-compliance proceedings concerning the Russian Federation commenced in the Implementation Committee in 1995.[114] The Implementation Committee interpreted a statement that Russia made on behalf of itself and four other Parties (Belarus, Bulgaria, Poland and Ukraine) as self-reporting on non-compliance, triggering paragraph 4 of the non-compliance procedure. Annex V of the non-compliance procedure contains the following Indicative List of Measures for non-compliance that the MOP may recommend, in most instances acting on the advice of the Implementation Committee:

a) appropriate assistance, including assistance for the collection and reporting of data, technical assistance, technology transfer and financial assistance, information transfer and training;
b) issuing cautions;
c) suspension, in accordance with the applicable rules of international law concerning suspension of the operation of the treaty, of specific rights and privileges under the Protocol, whether or not subject to time limits, including those concerned with industrial rationalization, production, consumption, trade, transfer of technology and institutional arrangements.[115]

---

[113] Parties that do not meet these commitments are threatened with stronger measures such as export restrictions and a temporary cessation of funding assistance from the Multilateral Fund or Global Environment Facility: see A. Gillespie, *Climate Change, Ozone Depletion, and Air Pollution: Legal Commentaries with Policy and Scientific Considerations* (Martinus Nijhoff Publishers,2006), pp. 221–6.

[114] J. Werksman, 'Compliance and Transition: Russia's Non-Compliance Tests the Ozone Regime', *Zeitschrift fur Auslandisches Recht und Volkerrecht*, 56 (1996), 750, 764.

[115] UNEP, Decision IV/5, Annex V.

In this list, responses are arranged in ascending order of intrusiveness, which may be seen as a type of 'flexible pyramid' of non-compliance responses.[116]

The restrictions on trade in ozone-depleting substances imposed upon the Russian Federation, Belarus and Ukraine[117] at the 7th Meeting of the Parties in Vienna in 1995 do not appear to fall within the abovementioned Indicative List of Measures for non-compliance. Fitzmaurice argues that the MOP's recommendations represent 'the imposition of a new restriction on the countries' right to trade with other Parties which they enjoyed quite independently of the Protocol, not the suspension of a right conferred by the Protocol'.[118] In Russia's view, these 'discriminatory measures and sanctions' were 'unacceptable'[119] as other less intrusive measures specified in the Indicative List of Measures had not been resorted to before trade restrictions were imposed.[120] The perception that this was a case of serious and deliberate violation of the Montreal Protocol may help to explain the MOP's departure from procedural guidelines and past practices in this instance.[121]

This atypical response highlights the political dimensions of this non-compliance decision, which appears to be inconsistent with minimizing arbitrariness in decision-making. However, the MOP's stance does send a strong message about the importance of complying with international

---

[116] B. Kingsbury, 'The Concept of Compliance as a Function of Competing Conceptions of International Law', *Michigan Journal of International Law*, 19 (1998), 345, 364, citing I. Ayres and J. Braithwaite, *Responsive Regulation: Transcending the Deregulation Debate* (Oxford University Press, 1992), pp. 35–40.

[117] UNEP, Decision VII/17: Compliance with the Montreal Protocol by Belarus, UNEP/OzL.Pro.7/12, 27 December 1995; UNEP, Decision VII/18: Compliance with the Montreal Protocol by Russia, UNEP/OzL.Pro.7/12, 27 December 1995; UNEP, Decision VII/19: Compliance with the Montreal Protocol by Ukraine, UNEP/OzL. Pro.7/12, 27 December 1995.

[118] M. Fitzmaurice, 'Non-Compliance Procedures and the Law of Treaties' in T. Treves et al. (eds.), *Non-Compliance Procedures and Mechanisms and the Effectiveness of International Environmental Agreements* (Cambridge University Press, 2009), pp. 472–3. Cf. J. Werksman, 'Compliance and the Kyoto Protocol: Building a Backbone in a Flexible Regime', *Yearbook of International Environmental Law*,9(1) (1998), 48, 72.

[119] Brack notes that the Russian delegation walked out of the 1995 MOP at which these issues were being discussed: D. Brack, 'Monitoring the Montreal Protocol' (2003) *Verification Yearbook*, pp. 209, 219. See n. 13.

[120] UNEP, Report of the Seventh Meeting of the Parties, paras. 128–9.

[121] See, e.g., J. Peel, 'New State Responsibility Rules and Compliance with Multilateral Environmental Obligations: Some Case Studies of How the New Rules Might Apply in the International Environmental Context', *Review of European Community and International Environmental Law*, 20(1) (2001), 82, 94.

legal obligations. As is discussed in the following section, Global Environment Facility funding provided to Russia was provided alongside these more punitive trade restriction measures, which in tandem operated to facilitate Russia's return to compliance with its Protocol commitments in 2002. Providing a proceduralized route for Russia's return to compliance is congruent with promoting rule of law values through regard for an affected Party's circumstances, even if departure from the procedural guidelines for non-compliance undermined predictability in decision-making in this instance.

2   GAL Mechanisms and Regard for Affected States' Interests

A second way to reduce arbitrariness is by taking into account the perspectives of those affected by regulatory decisions.[122] This may be conceptualized as 'procedural regard', as defined by Stewart:

> As an ideal, regard requires that the decision-maker review available information about the effects of proposed decisions on the various groups, individuals, interests, and concerns entitled to consideration; weighs the benefits for and burdens on them of alternatives; and determines that decisions that impose disadvantage or harm on some affected groups and individuals are justified by relevant decisional norms.[123]

This section illustrates that the GAL mechanisms for accountability and reason giving employed in the Montreal compliance system are well suited to promoting procedural regard for affected states' interests, including those of less powerful states. The design of the compliance apparatus reflects an emphasis on understanding the reasons for Parties' non-compliance in order to support their return to compliance through flexible yet procedurally standardized approaches. Thus, GAL mechanisms inject key values of legality into the administrative apparatus for non-compliance by enhancing predictability and procedural regard.

The Secretariat's practices reflect a strong focus on understanding the situation and interests of Parties that appear to be in non-compliance with their treaty commitments. When the Secretariat is alerted to a possible instance of non-compliance, considerable effort is made to investigate, comprehend and report upon its possible causes. The Secretariat provides oral and written reports to the Implementation Committee on the apparent extent of non-compliance,

---

[122] See n. 15.
[123] Stewart, 'Remedying Disregard in Global Regulatory Governance', 224–5.

and any response the Secretariat has received from the Party concerned providing an explanation for its causes.[124] Moreover, the Secretariat reports other information regarding the Party's situation that may be relevant for the Committee's deliberations, such as the amount of funding the Party has received from the Multilateral Fund or the Global Environment Facility, and the impacts of, inter alia, civil unrest and natural disasters, on the Party's capacity to comply.[125] There is thus extensive reason giving in the Secretariat's referral process for potential non-compliance matters. In addition to this information provided by the Secretariat, the Implementation Committee's deliberations may be informed by submissions provided directly by the Party concerned, and the Multilateral Fund or the Global Environment Facility.[126] This reason giving and opportunity to be heard facilitates the Implementation Committee's regard for the individual circumstances of non-compliant Parties,[127] which is consistent with rule of law values.

The financial assistance provided by the Multilateral Fund and the Global Environment Facility reinforces the procedural regard for non-compliant states' interests demonstrated by the Secretariat and Implementation Committee by helping to respond to the cause of Parties' non-compliance. As previously indicated, these accountability arrangements are premised on Parties meeting the benchmarks specified in their individually tailored plan to return to compliance in order to continue to receive financial assistance.[128] Hence, the accountability arrangements for conditional financial assistance are procedurally constrained, and reflect regard for the capacity constraints that frequently underpin Parties' non-compliance. As Chayes and Handler Chayes note, developing countries' implementation and compliance issues are generally attributable to 'a severe dearth of the requisite scientific, technical, bureaucratic, and financial wherewithal to build effective domestic enforcement systems'.[129] Indeed, the procedural regard afforded to non-compliant Parties, which are typically developing countries and CEITs,

---

[124] Ozone Secretariat, *Primer for Members*, p. 14.
[125] *Ibid.*
[126] *Ibid.*, pp. 31, 44.
[127] Cardesa-Salzmann, 'Constitutionalising Secondary Rules in Global Environmental Regimes', 115; Klabbers, 'Compliance Procedures', pp. 996–7.
[128] UNEP, Report of the Implementation Committee under the Non-Compliance Procedure for the Montreal Protocol on the Work of its Twentieth Meeting, para. 32.
[129] Chayes and Handler Chayes, *The New Sovereignty*, p. 14.

reflects a form of differential treatment[130] for these countries, in line with the principle of common but differentiated responsibilities in international environmental law.[131] Therefore, the conditional funding arrangements negotiated between the Implementation Committee and non-compliant Parties buttress the procedural regard that is a prominent characteristic of the Montreal compliance system.

D   Conclusion

The administrative arrangements for non-compliance in the Montreal compliance system are in tension with understandings of the international rule of law premised on conformity with rules legitimized by state consent. This tension is exemplified by the practice of paying funds to countries that are not in compliance with treaty obligations and have negotiated new targets for their return to compliance.[132] Despite this, the foregoing analysis illustrates that administrative procedures play an important role in constraining administrative action. Such procedures enhance procedural rigour in the Montreal compliance system, which promotes the normative legitimacy of compliance decision-making.[133] Franck posits that legitimacy can be assessed 'only by reference to a community's evolving standards of what constitutes right process'.[134] According to this logic, ensuring that compliance decision-making is predictable and gives voice to affected interests will

---

[130] Rajamani, for example, outlines that two of the primary ways differential treatment is reflected in international environmental law are: 'Provisions that differentiate between industrial and developing countries with respect to *implementation*, such as delayed compliance schedules, permission to adopt subsequent base years, delayed reporting schedules, and soft approaches to non-compliance; and [p]rovisions that grant *assistance, inter alia*, financial and technological' : L. Rajamani, *Differential Treatment in International Environmental Law* (Oxford University Press, 2006), p. 93.

[131] According to this principle, 'all states have common environmental responsibilities, but the manner in which each state meets its responsibilities should vary according to country-specific economic, historical, social and ecological variables': A. Huggins and S. Karim, 'Differential Treatment and Substantive and Procedural Regard in the International Climate Change Regime', *Transnational Environmental Law*,5(2) (2016), 427.

[132] Klabbers, 'Compliance Procedures'; see also Section B.1 above.

[133] See n. 12

[134] Franck, *The Power of Legitimacy among Nations*, p. 26.

promote practices that accord with relevant community values,[135] and hence 'lead to legitimacy'.[136]

This chapter has shown that administrative procedures for compliance mitigate arbitrariness by (1) increasing predictability and consistency in decision-making processes, and (2) providing affected Parties with an opportunity for their interests to be heard and taken into account in compliance decisions. The design of the compliance system supports decision-making that allows for a degree of discretionary leeway in the light of national circumstances, yet is circumscribed by administrative mechanisms. This procedurally constrained decision-making provides an option for promoting the achievement of rule of law values in global governance, without necessarily insisting on strict and rigid adherence to binding treaty rules.[137] This simultaneously allows flexibility to facilitate state compliance in a consent-based international legal system, and provides procedural safeguards for minimizing arbitrariness in decision-making.

---

[135] Hovell, *The Power of Process*, p. 62.

[136] Cassese, 'A Global Due Process of Law?', pp. 19–20; Wirth also observes that 'procedural integrity is itself an important source of authority and legitimacy for international law': D. A. Wirth, 'Reexamining Decision-Making Processes in International Environmental Law', *Iowa Law Review*, 79 (1994), 769, 798.

[137] This point is informed by the work of Selznick, who argues that: '[a]s the authority of purpose moves to the foreground of legal culture, accountability is measured by fidelity to ends and values, not rules alone, and to pragmatic criteria of problem-solving and achievement': P. Selznick, 'Legal Cultures and the Rule of Law' in M. Krygier and A. Czarnota (eds.), *The Rule of Law after Communism: Problems and Prospects in East-Central Europe* (Ashgate, 1999), p. 29.

14

Legitimacy Questions of Non-Compliance Procedures: Examples from the Kyoto and Montreal Protocols

ZERRIN SAVAŞAN

A Introduction

The compliance mechanisms (CMs) created under multilateral environmental agreements (MEAs) have evolved in three stages, involving three
aims: a stage of reporting/monitoring/verification, with the aim of preventing non-compliance; a stage of institutional procedural structure,
and assessment of the compliance status within this structure with the
aim of facilitating compliance; and a stage of response measures with the
aim of responding to non-compliance. Hence, the CMs are usually
assessed with three components complementing and supporting each
other: gathering information that reviews parties' performance, institu-
tionalized multilateral non-compliance procedures (NCPs) and multilateral response measures.

The legitimacy of each component can be discussed according to its
relationship depending on the conception of legitimacy, such as descrip-
tive-normative legitimacy (legal-based, participatory-based, expert-
based);[1] or source-based, process-based, outcome-based.[2] However, it
would be an overly ambitious task to illustrate and analyze in detail all

[1] D. Bodansky 'The Concept of Legitimacy in International Law' in R. Wolfrum and
V. Röben (eds.), *Legitimacy in International Law* (Springer, 2008); D. Bodansky,
'The Legitimacy of International Governance: A Coming Challenge for International
Environmental Law?', *The American Journal of International Law*, 93(3) (1999),
596–624; R. Wolfrum 'Legitimacy of International Law from a Legal Perspective: Some
Introductory Considerations, On Legitimacy in General' in Wolfrum and Röben (eds.),
Legitimacy in International Law, pp. 1–24.

[2] Process-based, procedural-substantive and outcome-based: T. M. Franck, *The Power of
Legitimacy Among Nations* (Oxford University Press, 1990); source-based, procedural,
result-oriented: Wolfrum 'Legitimacy of International Law from a Legal Perspective';

those aspects in each component. This chapter therefore aims not to provide a complete account of legitimacy on these mechanisms, but to draw a framework of the concerns related to NCPs; it is restricted to a pure normative-conceptual analysis in terms of NCPs referring to examples from the Kyoto and the Montreal Protocol.

Indeed, this chapter is particularly concerned with the normative dimension of legitimacy (including legal legitimacy, participatory legitimacy, and expert legitimacy). This is because the descriptive dimension of legitimacy requires empirical analysis, and it is highly challenging to make an objective measurement in this kind of analysis for legitimacy-related issues. So, instead of conducting research on the outcomes of the procedures through an examination of submissions related to non-compliance cases and decisions given on them, or on the perceptions or beliefs of the parties on the justification of the authority, it inquires the justification of authority provided in accordance with law, with transparent and participatory processes, or based on experts' decisions under these procedures in proper to the concept of normative legitimacy.

In this regard, it focuses first on the conceptual and theoretical basis of both CMs under MEAs and the legitimacy question. Then, it examines the NCPs under these mechanisms in terms of legitimacy concerns under five sub-sections: the legal basis of the decision-making power, the legal basis of the NCP, the institution of the NCP (the Committee), the procedural safeguards, and the legal character of measures applied to non-compliant parties.

B Conceptual and Theoretical Basis: Compliance and Compliance Mechanism

Within the current literature, the concepts of both compliance and the CM have different definitions, yet the concept of compliance is generally understood as an actor's behaviour in conformity with legal rules.[3] The CM, on the other hand, may be identified as an international

procedural and substantive: I. Clark, *Legitimacy in International Society* (Oxford University Press, 2005).

[3] A. H. Chayes, A. Chayes and R. B. Mitchell, 'Active Compliance Management in Environmental Treaties' in W. Lang (ed.), *Sustainable Development and International Law* (Graham & Trotman/M. Nijhoff, 1995), pp. 75–89; A. H. Chayes, A. Chayes and R. B. Mitchell, 'Managing Compliance: A Comparative Perspective' in E. B. Weiss and H. K. Jacobson (eds.), *Engaging Countries: Strengthening Compliance with International Environmental Accords* (MIT Press, 1998), pp. 39–62; A. H. Chayes, and A. Chayes, *The New Sovereignty: Compliance with International Regulatory Agreements* (Harvard University Press, 1995); R. Fisher, *Improving Compliance with International Law*

mechanism created under MEAs involving three components: gathering
information that reviews national performance, the NCP (NCP), and
non-compliance response measures, excluding the dispute settlement
procedure (DSP).[4]

With respect to the theoretical basis, both international law and
international relations literature display that the most featured
theories on compliance can be widely grouped into two categories
based on the distinction introduced by March and Olsen[5] between
two different logics of behavior (the logic of consequences (LoC)
and the (LoA)[6]): the rationalist and normative theory.[7] In line with
this division, under the rationalist theory it is assumed that actors
weigh costs and benefits of their behaviour and act in accordance
with their interests following the LoC. The normative theory, on
the other hand, accepts that they act in accordance to identities,
legal obligations, shared discourses and conceptions of appropriate
action   (involving   elements   of   both   socialization   and
internationalization).[8]

Realism, among the rationalist approaches, refusing the 'legalist-
moralist' approach of Woodrow Wilson (or 'Wilsonian liberal
internationalism'[9]), puts forward that laws are made by states as the
basic actors of the international system in accordance with their interests

(University Press of Virginia, 1981); H. K. Jacobson and E. B. Weiss, 'A Framework for
Analysis' in Weiss and Jacobson (eds.), *Engaging Countries: Strengthening Compliance
with International Environmental Accords*, pp. 1–18; R. B. Mitchell, 'Regime Design
Matters: Intentional Oil Pollution and Treaty Compliance', *International Organization*,
48(3) (1994), 425–58.

[4] United Nations Environmental Programme (UNEP), *Comparative Analysis of Compliance
Mechanisms under Selected Multilateral Environmental Agreements* (UNEP, 2007).

[5] J. G. March and J. P. Olsen, 'The Institutional Dynamics of International Political Orders',
International Organization, 52(4) (1998), 943–69.

[6] International Network for Environmental Compliance and Enforcement (INECE),
Principles of Environmental Compliance and Enforcement Handbook (2009).
R. B. Mitchell, 'Compliance Theory, Effectiveness, and Behaviour Change in
International Environmental Law' in B. Bodansky, J. Brunnée and E. Hey (eds.),
The Oxford Handbook of International Environmental Law (Oxford University Press,
2007), pp. 893–921.

[7] D. Zaelke and T. Higdon, 'The Role of Compliance in the Rule of Law, Good Governance,
and Sustainable Development', *Journal for European Environmental & Planning Law*, 3(5)
(2006), 376–84; K. Raustiala, 'Compliance and Effectiveness in International Regulatory
Cooperation', *Case Western Reserve Journal of International Law*, 3(2) (2000), 387–440;
INECE, *Principles of Environmental Compliance and Enforcement Handbook*.

[8] Mitchell, 'Compliance Theory, Effectiveness, and Behaviour Change', p. 902.

[9] A.-M., Slaughter 'International Law and International Relations Theory: A Dual Agenda',
American Journal of International Law, 87 (1993), 207.

or powers.[10] Accordingly, 'considerations of power rather than of law determine compliance and enforcement'.[11],[12] Thus, holding an instrumental view of law, realists deny the existence of a moral obligation to improve the rule of law, referring to the nature of international relations in which in their understanding the concept of justice has no application.[13] In Kenneth Waltz's neo-realism as well, there is no causality between law and politics.[14] Therefore, in general, for realist theory, laws as well as issues such as legality or legitimacy have little or no impact on the acts of the states.[15] In fact, the ideology is designated as source of power rather than legitimacy for being accepted by a member of the international system.[16] This is in contrast with the legal process scholars whose views will be elaborated below. Therefore, the concept of legitimacy does not play a leading role in the works of realist theorists.[17] Under the liberal theory, in contrast with realism, other actors than states such as international organizations (IOs), non-governmental organizations (NGOs), multinational corporations, and distinct types of norms made by different actors attain importance.[18] The characteristics of representative governments, the protection of civil and political rights, and a judicial system guided by the rule of law as the main features of

---

[10] E. H. Carr, *The Twenty Year Crisis, 1919–1939:Introduction to the Study of International Relations* (Palgrave, 2001).

[11] H. J. Morgenthau, *Politics Among Nations: The Struggle for Power and Peace* (Alfred A. Knopf, 1960), p. 296.

[12] In contrast with Carr, Ku argues that Carr fell short in understanding the framework for political discourse that law provides, in that international law has been an important element for adaptation and political change in international relations evolving from a passive reflection of power in the voluntarist period, to the interventionist effort to manage power in the institutionalist period, and to the civil society period of diffused power: C. Ku, 'Global Governance and the Changing Face of International Law', *Acuns Reports & Papers*, 2 (2001).

[13] A. Buchanan 'Legitimacy of International Law' in S. Besson and J. Tasioulas (eds.), *Philosophy of International Law* (Oxford University Press, 2010), p. 89.

[14] Slaughter 'International Law and International Relations Theory', 205–39.

[15] A. T. Guzman, 'International Law: A Compliance Based Theory', *UC Berkeley Public Law Research Paper*, 47 (2001), 14; B. Kingsbury, 'The Concept of Compliance as a Function of Competing Conceptions of International Law', *Michigan Journal of International Law*, 19(2) (1998), 350.

[16] S. V. Scott, 'International Law as Ideology: Theorizing the Relation Between International Law and International Politics', *European Journal International Law*, 5 (1994), 313–25.

[17] See Morgenthau, *Politics Among Nations*; K. N. Waltz, *Theory of International Politics* (Addison-Wesley, 1979); R. Gilpin, *War and Change in World Politics* (Cambridge University Press, 1981).

[18] Kingsbury, 'The Concept of Compliance', 345–72.

a liberal state are shown as significant elements leading states to be in compliance with international law.[19]

In contrast with rationalist theories, in normative theories, as they are based on the LoA, the issues related to the legitimacy and legal processes gain greater importance and find a quite significant place in the relevant scholars' studies. Of those, in Henkins'[20] consent theory, legal process arguments are applied to explain how international law enables states to comply with their commitments, while consent of states is underlined as the key tool for binding states to legal norms.[21]

Transnational legal process theory, developed by Koh,[22] assumes the compliance of states with laws through the transnational legal process involving a process of 'interaction', 'interpretation' and 'social, political and legal internalization'[23] of international norms to domestic legal structures. As different from Henkins' approach, here, the process of interaction and internalization is constructive, as it is assumed that the interests of the participants are reconstructed in the process.

However, the concept of legitimacy arises as the key factor of the theory itself under Franck's legitimacy theory.[24] Franck defines legitimacy by four elements: 'textual determinacy' (the clarity and transparency of the rule),[25] 'symbolic validation' (regularized practices and rituals),[26] 'coherence' (consistency with the rules)[27] and 'adherence' (linkage between the primary and secondary rules).[28] When these four

---

[19] Slaughter, 'International Law and International Relations Theory', 205–39.

[20] Ibid., 205–39.

[21] L. Henkin, *How Nations Behave? Law and Foreign Policy* (F. A. Praeger, 1968).

[22] H. Koh, 'How Is International Human Rights Law Enforced?', *Indiana Law Journal*, 74 (1999), 1397–417; H. H. Koh, 'Why do Nations Obey International Law?', *Yale Law Journal*, 106(8) (1997), 2599–659.

[23] Koh, 'How Is International Human Rights Law Enforced?', 1413–14.

[24] T. M. Franck, 'Legitimacy in the International System', *American Journal of International Law*, 82(1988); T. M. Franck, *Fairness in International Law and Institutions* (Clarendon Press, 1995); Franck, *The Power of Legitimacy Among Nations*.

[25] Franck, 'Legitimacy in the International System', 713; Franck, *The Power of Legitimacy Among Nations*, pp. 30 and 52; Franck, *Fairness in International Law and Institutions*, p. 30.

[26] Franck, *The Power of Legitimacy*, pp. 34 and 92–94; Franck, *Fairness in International Law and Institutions*, p. 34.

[27] Franck, *The Power of Legitimacy*, pp. 38 and 142–48; Franck, *Fairness in International Law and Institutions*, p. 38.

[28] Franck, *The Power of Legitimacy*, pp. 41 and 184; Franck, *Fairness in International Law and Institutions*, p. 41.

elements are present, they form 'right process',[29] which will provide those to whom the rule is addressed with the perception of that rule as being legitimate.[30] With regard to the current compliance approach applied under MEAs in general, Franck argues that it has the potential to create 'legitimate and legitimating regimes'.[31] As for him, the primary element that determines the rules' 'compliance-pull' on states is put forth as legitimacy; thus, he forms a mutual relationship between legitimacy and compliance, which support each other. However, compliance-based theory advanced by Guzman, which is founded on a model of rational self-interested states, notes that, just in case,

> legitimacy theory is embedded in a reputational model, however, the motives for compliance become clear. As international commitments become more clearly defined, they are perceived to be more binding, thereby increasing the reputational stake of participating countries. Thus, as the level of legitimacy rises, the costs of violation also rise, making compliance more attractive.[32]

Within the scope of a constructivist account, Young's works on regimes' social and constitutive impacts (the impacts of legitimacy, capacity, socialization, legalization, and standard operating procedures (SOPs)) can also be shown as an example of the works relating to the legitimacy issue.[33] Indeed, he stresses the significance of a knowledge system or a discourse, habits or SOPs but also perceptions of legitimacy as sources of behavior.[34] Actors are motivated by not only self-interest, enforcement and inducements, but also pressure from society, legitimacy, knowledge system, and habits. In line with Young's social-practice perspective, many international environmental regimes aim not only to promote their 'utilitarian' impacts, but also 'non-utilitarian' impacts involving capacity, socialization, legalization, and SOPs) besides legitimacy.[35]

In addition to the theories explained, there two basic explanatory models on compliance mechanisms are also created under MEAs: enforcement and management models. The enforcement model

---

[29] Franck, 'Legitimacy in the International System', 706; Franck, *The Power of Legitimacy*, pp. 26–29; Franck, *Fairness in International Law and Institutions*, p. 26.

[30] Franck, 'Legitimacy in the International System', 706.

[31] Franck, *Fairness in International Law and Institutions*, p. 412.

[32] Guzman, 'International Law: A Compliance Based Theory', 66.

[33] O. R. Young, *The Effectiveness of International Environmental Regimes, Causal Connections and Behavioral Mechanisms* (MIT Press, 1999).

[34] H. Breitmeier, O. R. Young and M. Zürn, *Analyzing International Environmental Regimes: From Case Study to Database* (MIT Press, 2006), pp. 234–35.

[35] Breitmeier *et al*, *Analyzing International Environmental Regimes*, p. 149.

argues that high compliance with international agreements is an indicator of the shallowness of that agreement. That means that, if compliance with an international agreement is high, it is because the agreement requires not more much from the states than what they would do in the absence of such an agreement.[36] Within this model, it is argued that, in order to deter non-compliance and to sustain cooperation, the free-rider problem has to be resolved through stronger sanctions (retaliatory, monetary, political, or reputation-based punishments). Deeper cooperation can be rendered just with a stronger enforcement tool. Without strong enforcement, they can be managed only if 'there [has been] less incentive to defect from a given agreement ... [such as] changes in technology, relative prices, domestic transitions'.[37] However, the legitimacy challenge regarding these sanctions and enforcement tools is not apparently responded to; it is even asserted that the legitimacy of the punishment strategy identified as 'any threatened action or combinations of actions ... operate to offset the net benefit a potential violator could gain from noncompliance' is 'rarely an issue' under international law.[38]

In contrast with the enforcement approach, the management approach assumes that there is a 'general propensity of states to comply with international law' originating from three factors: efficiency, interests, and norms.[39] If, despite all these, there is still non-compliance, this would be an exception. Non-compliance would occur mainly because of three reasons: ambiguity of the treaty language, lack of adequate capacity for compliance, or time delays between commitments and the implementation.[40] However, for the enforcement model, ambiguity is

---

[36] G. W. Downs and M. A. Jones, 'Reputation, Compliance, and International Law', *Journal of Legal Studies*, 31(2002),95–114; G. W. Downs, K. W. Danish and P. N. Barsoom, 'Transformational Model of International Regime Design: Triumph of Hope or Experience', *Columbia Journal Transnational Law*, 38 (2000), 465–514; G. W. Downs, 'Enforcement and the Evolution of Cooperation', *Michigan Journal of International Law*, 19 (1998), 319–44; G. W. Downs, D. Rocke and P. Barsoom, 'Is the Good News about Compliance Good News about Cooperation?,' *International Organization*, 50(3) (1996), 379–406.

[37] Downs et al., 'Is the Good News about Compliance Good News about Cooperation?', 397–98.

[38] G. W. Downs, 'Enforcement and the Evolution of Cooperation', *Michigan Journal of International Law*, 19 (1998), 321.

[39] Chayes and Chayes, *The New Sovereignty*, p. 3; Chayes, Chayes and Mitchell, 'Managing Compliance: A Comparative Perspective', 78.

[40] Chayes and Chayes, *The New Sovereignty*, pp. 9–17.

to some extent endogenous,[41] because states can deliberately choose the ambiguity of agreements that they make, and the incapacity that they employ in connection with a given agreement.

Current CMs are based on a preventive approach that aims to determine possible non-compliance and to prevent it before damage occurs, through cooperation between parties.[42] When one of the parties is faced with the procedure of the CMs, it usually chooses to cooperate with the other parties and the mechanism itself. The developing states are also provided with facilitation tools, such as financial, technical assistance, or capacity building. The management model's proposal involves similar components, such as transparent information system (reporting-monitoring-verification), dispute settlement, capacity building, adaptation, responses, to those of the CMs (gathering information, NCPs (NCP), response measures, and DSP).

Overall, it may be argued that 'in considering the possible convergence of the differing theories along the compliance continuum, legitimacy emerges as a crucial consideration',[43] most strongly, however, for normative theories. Of all the theories and models discussed above, only normative theories, particularly Franck's legitimacy theory, acknowledge legitimacy as a basis. Others, and in particular Chayes and Chayes, also point out the challenge of legitimacy under circumstances requiring the use of enforcement tools, while, under the enforcement model fundamentally founded on the use of enforcement tools, legitimacy is not taken into account adequately and discussed in depth. Breitmeier, Young and Zürn,[44] in line with hypotheses derived from the legitimacy perspective, also find that none of the explanatory models can explain patterns of compliance. Therefore, there is an urgent need for a different perspective integrating incentives, institutional design, the rule of law and also legitimacy.

---

[41] Downs, 'Enforcement and the Evolution of Cooperation'; Downs et al., 'Is the Good News about Compliance Good News about Cooperation?'.

[42] J. Klabbers, 'Compliance Procedures' in B. Bodansky, J. Brunnée and E. Hey (eds.), *The Oxford Handbook of International Environmental Law* (Oxford University Press, 2007), pp. 995–1009; A. Tanzi and C. Pitea, 'Non-Compliance Mechanisms: Lessons Learned and the Way Forward' in T. Treves, A. Tanzi, L. Pineschi, C. Pitea and C. Ragni (eds.), *Non-Compliance Procedures and Mechanisms and the Effectiveness of International Environmental Agreements* (Asser Press, 2009), pp. 569–80.

[43] T. E. Crossen, 'Multilateral Environmental Agreements and the Compliance Continuum', *Berkeley Electronic Press Legal Series*, 36 (2003), 35.

[44] Breitmeier et al., *Analyzing International Environmental Regimes*, p. 104.

C   Legitimacy Question under Non-Compliance Procedures

To question whether the justification of authority is provided in accordance with law, with transparent and participatory processes or based on experts' decisions under these procedures in line with the concept of normative legitimacy, the following examination will be made under five sub-sections: the legal basis of the decision-making power, the legal basis of the NCP, the institution of the NCP (the committee), the procedural safeguards, and the legal character of measures applied to non-compliant parties.

1   Legal Basis of the Decision-Making Power

The CMs created under MEAs generally operate through the committees (implementation committees or compliance committees), a secretariat, one or more subsidiary advisory bodies (technical or scientific bodies), a financial mechanism and a conference or meeting of the parties (COP/ MOP). Of those, the COP is the ultimate decision-making-body on all matters, involving both substantive and procedural ones, and also both internal and external ones, relating to the functioning of the MEA in question. The legal basis for the decision-making power of compliance committees derives from the COP in some cases in which the NCP has been established following a decision by the contracting parties – that is, by MOP/COP (e.g. the NCP of the Montreal Protocol is established through a MOP decision).[45]

In the decision-making procedures of the MEAs, the general rule in decision-making is 'consensus'; majority voting is very rarely used. Even if it is accepted, the possibility of the parties (who do not want to be bound by the decision) objecting to the decision is not allowed in order to prevent the decision-making procedure's coming into deadlock. So, as it does not include an 'objection procedure in its scope',[46] the only example that can be shown of the agreement using the majority voting successfully so far has been the Montreal Protocol. In fact, the Montreal Protocol has previously employed both a form of weighted voting and double

---

[45] MOP 4, Decision IV/5, Copenhagen, 23–25 November 1992. UNEP/OzL.Pro.4/15 (1992). Retrieved March 25, 2017 from: http://ozone.unep.org/Meeting_Documents/mop/04mop/4mop-15.e.pdf

[46] R. R. Churchill and G. Ulfstein, 'Autonomous Institutional Arrangements: A Little Noticed Phenomenon in International Law', American Journal of International Law, 94(4) (2000), 643.

majorities. Under Article 2(9) of the Protocol, it is stated that decisions on the 'adjustment' of the timetable for phasing out the production and consumption of ozone-depleting substances that could not be reached by consensus could be taken by the favorable voting of the two-thirds of the parties representing at least 50 per cent of the consumption of the substances in question. In 1990, this provision was altered and double majority voting was accepted instead of weighted decision making. Thus, decisions to be taken started to require a two-thirds majority including a majority of developing countries and a majority of developed countries.

Regarding the legal character of COP decisions, there are three theories:[47]

1. Theories that accord binding force to COP decisions as deriving from the intention of the parties.
2. Theories that attempt to find some intermediate (soft or *de facto*) status for them.
3. Theories that seek an alternative basis from outside the law of treaties for their binding character.

Yet, neither of them is singly adequate for explaining every case that can arise in relation to the decision making, so it is fairly essential to examine each case together with its own conditions.[48] Yet, primarily because of the nature of CMs relying on the cooperation of the parties, the decisions are regarded as 'more recommendatory than legally binding':[49]

The decision-making power of the COP on amending the MEA, or on adopting new protocols and annexes to it, is based on the general procedures for amending agreements that is set out in the Vienna Convention on the Law of Treaties(VCLT). However, the amendment procedures in some MEAs can also require different conditions, such as ratification by a certain number of parties to enter into force.[50] The requirement of ratification by parties is not provided for the amendment of the annexes to the MEA (e.g. see the Montreal Protocol), so, the power of COP here can be assessed as a 'genuine law-making power'.[51]

---

[47] M. Fitzmaurice, 'NCPs and the Law of Treaties' in Treves et al. (eds.), *Non-Compliance Procedures and Mechanisms and the Effectiveness of International Environmental Agreements*, p. 464.

[48] Ibid., pp. 453–82.

[49] Ibid., p. 474.

[50] E.g., see Art. 9(5) of the Vienna Ozone Convention.

[51] Churchill and Ulfstein, 'Autonomous Institutional Arrangements', 638.

With regard to its requirements and authorities in the external sphere, even if it is controversial whether the COP has powers to act on matters, such as concluding agreements with other entities of international law (states, organizations etc.), – due to the fact that it is also controversial whether it has an international legal personality –,[52] it is possible to argue that it can act on those matters on the basis of an examination on 'the wording of MEAs, the doctrine of implied powers and the practice'.[53]

With respect to the wording of MEAs, the opinion of the UN Office of Legal Affairs of November 4, 1993 (UNOLA I)[54] can be shown as a reference.[55] According to this opinion, the COP of the Climate Change Convention has the legal capacity, within the limits of its mandate, to conclude agreements with other entities under Article 6 of the 1986 Vienna Convention on the Law of Treaties Between States and International Organizations or Between International Organizations. It states that the United Nations Framework Convention on Climate Change (UNFCCC) establishes 'an international entity with its own separate legal personality, statement of principles, organs and a supportive structure in the form of a Secretariat',[56] although the UNFCCC does not include (and most MEAs in general do not include) any explicit provision constituting international legal personality or capacity for making agreements.

The doctrine of implied powers can also be applied to infer the ability of the COP to act at the external level. That is, even if the related MEA does not contain any explicit provision establishing the international legal personality or their bodies' capacity for making agreements, the powers given to COP by the agreement are to be assessed in order to determine whether the COP has such personality and capacity.[57]

---

[52] For the view stating that there is a 'parent/subsidiary relationship' between the COP and the MOP, implying that '[t]he extent to which the subsidiary body (the MOP) can operate on the international plane will depend upon legal capacity being delegated, either explicitly or implicitly, by the parent institution [the COP]', see J. D. Werksman, 'Procedural and Institutional Aspects of the Emerging Climate Change Regime: Improvised Procedures and Impoverished Rules?', FIELD (1999), 25.

[53] Churchill and Ulfstein, 'Autonomous Institutional Arrangements', 647.

[54] UN Juridical Yearbook (1993, Chapter 5, B, para.50), Arrangements for the Implementation of the Provisions of Article 11 of the UN Framework Convention on Climate Change Concerning the Financial Mechanism (1993), para. 4.

[55] For the same view with the Office of Legal Affairs, see also Werksman, 'Procedural and Institutional Aspects'.

[56] UNFCCC, Arts. 3 and 7–10.

[57] Churchill and Ulfstein, 'Autonomous Institutional Arrangements', 623–59.

Finally, an examination on practice – that is, on the arrangements made with the host organization, with financial institutions, with the host state, and with other MEAs by the COP, can also support the conclusion that the COP has international legal personality and power to enter into agreements.[58]

2 Legal Basis of the Non-Compliance Procedures

The NCP can be established directly by an MEA or by a Protocol thereto adopted after its entry into force. Sometimes, the NCP has been established following a decision by the contracting parties – that is, by a MOP/COP if, in the treaty, it was mandated to develop such an NCP.

To illustrate, the NCP of the Montreal Protocol is established through an MOP Decision[59] on the basis of Articles 8 and 11(3.d) of the Montreal Protocol, not through an amendment of the Protocol itself or an annex to it. Though in the first report of the Ad Hoc Working Group on Non-Compliance,[60] it is suggested that decisions of the MOP should be recommendatory rather than mandatory, in the third report,[61] non-compliance with decisions of the MOP is also counted as one of the possible situations of non-compliance.[62]

The method followed in the Kyoto Protocol reflects a 'compromise solution' that could be employed to other mechanisms.[63] It stipulates the adoption of a decision on a provisional basis, with the view of adopting a subsequent amendment afterwards, if necessary. In fact, according to Article 18, the MOP should approve appropriate and effective procedures and mechanisms to determine and to address cases of non-compliance with the provisions of the Protocol and also develop an indicative list of

---

[58] Ibid., 623–59.

[59] MOP 4, Decision IV/5, Copenhagen, 23–25 November 1992. UNEP/OzL.Pro.4/15 (1992). Retrieved March 25, 2017 from: http://ozone.unep.org/Meeting_Documents/mop/04mop/4mop-15.e.pdf

[60] Ad Hoc Working Group on Non-Compliance (Ad Hoc WG 1), 'Report of the First Meeting of the Ad Hoc WG', 14 July 1989, Geneva, UNEP/OzL.Pro.LG.1/3 (1989), p. 4 para. 9i, retrieved March 11, 2017 from: http://ozone.unep.org/Meeting_Documents/adhoc/adhoc-nc-1-3-report_of_the_first_meeting.89-07-11.pdf

[61] Ad Hoc Working Group on Non-Compliance (Ad Hoc WG 3), 'Report of the Third Meeting of the Ad Hoc WG', 9 November 1991, Geneva, UNEP/WG.3/3/3 (1991), p. 6, para. 41, retrieved March 11, 2017 from: http://ozone.unep.org/Meeting_Documents/adhoc/adhoc-nc-3-3.91-04-08.pdf

[62] Ad Hoc WG 1, 10, situation vii, Annex II.

[63] A. Fodella 'Structural and Institutional Aspects of NCMs' in Treves et al. (eds.), Non-Compliance Procedures and Mechanisms and the Effectiveness of International Environmental Agreements, p. 358.

measures and consequences for the effective operation of these procedures. Based on this provision, the provisions regarding such a procedure were established by a decision of the COP,[64] and then approved by the MOP.[65] The same article also stipulates the amendment to the Protocol for the adoption of any procedures and mechanisms entailing binding measures.

With respect to an NCP created on the basis of a COP/MOP decision, two different legal bases can be mentioned:

- The first consists in an 'enabling clause' set out in an MEA provision which clearly confers this mandate on the COP/MOP.
- The second stems from general provisions of the MEA on the competence of the COP/MOP on compliance-related issues, when it is not clearly stated in the agreement. Yet, the absence of clear provisions on the power of a COP or an MOP to establish these procedures makes the question of the binding effect of the decisions establishing them a complicated one.

The adoption of the procedure in the form of a decision makes its operation faster and more flexible, but it can make the decisions' binding status blurred. In fact, what forms their binding status becomes controversial.

In line with the above-mentioned division, if the MEA explicitly gives the power to the COP to establish a non-compliance mechanism, or implicitly to review compliance matters, then it can be argued that merely the agreement (the Protocol as well) under international law forms the legal basis, and so the parties should follow the rules of the NCP.

If the mechanism is established by a COP or a MOP decision, it has a 'softer' character. Its outcomes are non-binding and the parties are merely expected to follow the decision because of the principles of cooperation with the other parties and respecting the agreement in good faith.

However, if it is a harder mechanism, with binding outcomes in the sense of creating obligations not involved under the agreement, the issue probably becomes more complex to resolve.[66] This is because, as shown under the Kyoto Protocol, under these circumstances, the amendment to

---

[64] COP 7, Decision 24, 'Report of the COP on its Seventh Session, Part Two: Action taken by the COP at its Seventh Session', Volume III, Marrakesh, 29 October–10 November 2001, FCCC/CP/2001/13/Add.3 (2001), retrieved May 11, 2017 from: http://unfccc.int/resource/docs/cop7/13a03.pdf

[65] MOP 1, Decision 27, 'Report of the COP serving as the MOP to the Kyoto Protocol on its First Session', Montreal, 28 November–10 December 2005 (2005), retrieved May 5, 2017 from: http://unfccc.int/resource/docs/2005/cmp1/eng/08a03.pdf

[66] Fodella, 'Structural and Institutional Aspects of NCMs', pp. 357–58.

the Protocol may be required for the adoption of any procedures and mechanisms entailing binding measures. Therefore, it can be argued that COP decisions can hardly be used as a legal basis for specifically hard mechanisms with binding outcomes.[67] (See Table 14.1 for an overall summary on the legal basis of NCPs).

Table 14.1 *A brief explanation on the legal basis of the NCP*

Legal Basis: COP/MOP Decisions
1. Enabling clause in the MEA/giving power to the COP
2. Relying on general provisions of the MEA

Binding Effect of COP Decisions	
if the MEA includes an enabling clause giving power to the COP/MOP to establish NCP which can produce binding effects.	The parties would be obliged to follow and respect.
if the MEA does not include an enabling clause, and if the COP decision establishes a soft NCP of which outcomes are non-binding.	The parties are expected to respect due to the principle of cooperation and respect the agreement in good faith.
if the MEA does not include an enabling clause, and if the COP decision establishes a hard NCP of which outcomes are binding and have effects in the sense of creating obligations beyond the agreement (new obligations or amending existing ones).	The **problem** emerges, as the COP decision cannot be used as a legal basis for this situation.
Solution to the Problem: Kyoto Protocol's method can be used as a response to this problem. That is, to adopt a decision on a provisional basis, with the view of adopting a subsequent amendment afterwards, if necessary. Yet, any amendment to the Protocol requires ratification by at least three-quarters of the parties to the Protocol (Art.20.4, KP).	

Note: Table prepared by the author.

3 The Institution Created under the NCP: the Committee

Most NCPs have an elected permanent Committee (which can be called a 'Compliance Committee' (ComplCom) or 'Implementation Committee'

---

[67] Ibid., p. 358.

(ImplCom)), which is usually made up of representatives from the contracting parties of the respective MEA (or, rarely, independent experts).

Various ways can be adopted to form a committee under different MEAs,[68] such as the election of representatives of the parties to the MEA by the COP/MOP;[69] the election of independent experts serving in their personal capacity and elected by the COP/MOP;[70,71] the election of representatives of the parties to the MEA to serve in their individual capacities[72] (who should have legal experience),[73] or to 'serve objectively and in the best interest' of the Convention,[74] or the acceptance of the avoidance of any possible 'conflict of interest' during their performance as a key requirement,[75] or the inclusion of additional provisions supporting the independency and impartiality of the Committee.[76,77]

It is supposed that the impartiality, objectivity, and reliability of the body improves by the use of independent experts rather than representatives of the parties as members of the committee.[78] Mostly, however, committees are rarely composed of independent experts. Still, it is promising that, in almost all MEAs, the members of the committee are required 'to have a specific legal or technical background in order to

[68] Ibid., p. 360.
[69] E.g., MP NCP, para. 5; MP, MOP 3, Decision III/20, Kyoto Protocol (KP), Section IV.I and V.1, Kyoto Protocol to the United Nations Framework Convention on Climate Change (1997), retrieved May 12, 2017 from: http://unfccc.int/resource/docs/convkp/kpeng.pdf. Montreal Protocol on Substances that Deplete the Ozone Layer (1987), retrieved April 2, 2017 from: http://ozone.unep.org/new_site/en/Treaties/treaties_decisions-hb.php?sec_id=5. MOP 3, 'Report of the COP serving as the MOP to the Kyoto Protocol on its First Session. Montreal', Nairobi, 19–21 June 1991, UNEP/OzL.Pro.3/11(1991), retrieved March 25, 2017 from: http://ozone.unep.org/Meeting_Documents/mop/03mop/3mop-11.e.pdf
[70] E.g., the nomination of experts by NGOs is possible under the Aarhus NCP.
[71] T. Stephens, *International Courts and Environmental Protection* (Cambridge University Press, 2009); T. Treves, 'Introduction' in Treves et al. (eds.), f1–10.
[72] E.g., Montreal Protocol, for the Enforcement Branch under the Kyoto Protocol CM, they should both serve in their personal capacities (NCP, Section II (6); RoP, 4).
[73] NCP, Section V(3).
[74] E.g., Basel Convention, Terms of Reference, para. 5.
[75] E.g. Kyoto Protocol, Section III; 2(d).
[76] Consolidated Rules of Procedure of the Compliance Committee of the Kyoto Protocol (RoP). Decision 4/MOP 2; Decision 4/MOP 4, retrieved May 12, 2017 from: http://unfccc.int/files/kyoto_protocol/compliance/background/application/pdf/rules_of_procedure_of_the_compliance_committee_of_the_kp.pdf
[77] E.g., the suspension of membership if he violates the independency and impartiality of the committee (Kyoto Protocol RoP, 4).
[78] Fodella, 'Structural and Institutional Aspects of NCMs', p. 361.

ensure that the requirements for a "due process" are respected, in particular in terms of recognized competence and impartiality'.[79]

The committees can be made up of a limited number of members[80] or can
be open to the participation of all parties.[81] The form in which all parties can
join increases the perception of legitimacy and transparency by providing
a chance to all to share their views others, and to contribute to the decisions
taken by the body. However, this raises other challenges such as time
management; the scope of matter (if not wide in scope, it is better to have
a small group to discuss);[82] providing funding for the regular participation of
all members, and not merely of members from developing countries and
from some low-income countries with economies in transition.[83,84]

In order to deal with this problem, such bodies are generally not
entrusted with final decision-making power, but they can make recommendations to the plenary organ that has the final authority for decision-
making. Yet, it should be kept in mind that, in general, the MOP's
decision is usually based on the ImplCom's report prepared on the
circumstances of the related matter.[85,86] Furthermore, for the members
of the committee, the principles of rotation and equitable geographical

---

[79] M. Montini, 'Procedural Guarantees in NCMs' in Treveset al. (eds.), *Non-Compliance Procedures and Mechanisms and the Effectiveness of International Environmental Agreements*, p. 401.

[80] E.g. ImplCom under the Montreal Protocol.

[81] E.g. ComplCom under the Kyoto Protocol.

[82] G. Handl, 'Compliance Control Mechanisms and International Environmental Obligations', *Tulane Journal of International and Comparative Law*, 5, (1997), 39.

[83] ComplCom 2, 'Annual Report of the Compliance Committee to the Conference of the Parties serving as the Meeting of the Parties to the Kyoto Protocol', 26 September 2007, FCCC/KP/CMP/2007/6 (2007), para. 5; ComplCom 3, 'Annual Report of the Compliance Committee to the Conference of the Parties serving as the meeting of the Parties to the Kyoto Protocol', 31 October 2008. FCCC/KP/CMP/2008/5 (2008), 4f; ComplCom 4, 'Annual Report of the Compliance Committee to the Conference of the Parties serving as the meeting of the Parties to the Kyoto Protocol', 2 November 2009, FCCC/KP/CMP/2009/17 (2009), para. 4c.

[84] S. Oberthür and R. Lefeber, 'Holding Countries to Account: The Kyoto Protocol's Compliance System Revisited After Four Years of Experience', *Climate Law*, 1(1) (2010), 133–58.

[85] The proposal raised by the United States on the amendment of the NCP of the Montreal Protocol (involving allowing increased continuity in the participation in the ImplCom, speeding up the timing for communication between the Secretariat and parties, urging parties to submit information according to Art. 7(3) within a shorter time period and to participate in all meetings of the ImplCom, and removing language difficulties) was not accepted, because of the lack of agreement on its all elements (MOP 14, 'Report of the COP serving as the MOP to the Kyoto Protocol on its First Session. Montreal', Rome, 25–29 November 2002). UNEP/OzL.Pro.14/9 (2002), 13, paras. 83–88, retrieved March 26, 2017 from: www. unep. org/ozone/mop/14mop/I4mop-9. e.pdf

[86] See Montreal Protocol NCP, para. 9, para. 14.

distribution can also be applied to decrease the possible question marks in minds regarding the legitimacy of the decisions.[87,88]

4   Procedural Safeguards

Basically, four procedural phases in NCPs are applied for the functioning of the CMs: submission (triggering) phase, preliminary phase, substantive phase (including consideration and recommendation phases) and final phase (including decision-making and final resolution phases). The procedure applied for the functioning of the compliance mechanism of the Montreal Protocol can also be illustrated in these four phases. Even if it can be divided into different phases in CMs of different MEAs, e.g. Kyoto Protocol CM's NCP phases under the facilitative and enforcement Branches, with the opportunity of triggering by the expert review teams' (ERTs') reports under Article 8, Protocol (NCP, Section VI(3), Kyoto Protocol), the logical sequence of the process is the same for all.

In NCPs, it is possible to assert that one or more parties of the MEA has not complied with its obligations, and it is possible to bring the parties' compliance problems to the attention of the related bodies of the MEA. This kind of assertion can be made by the non-compliant party itself ("self-trigger"), which has compliance problems,[89] by other parties, by the related bodies of the MEA (more often by the Secretariat), and very rarely by third-parties to the agreement (such as Aarhus Convention NCP, para. 18).

In the preliminary phase, a prior consultation is made between the parties concerned. The Secretariat sends a copy of that submission to the party alleged to be in violation of a particular provision of the relevant MEA. Then, the concerned party has to send a reply. As soon as the Secretariat receives the reply, it transmits the submission, the reply and other necessary information to the committee for its consideration. The committee assesses the submission on the basis of the criteria (procedural and substantive) established under the related MEA, then drafts and adopts appropriate recommendations on the parties submitted

[87] E.g. Montreal Protocol MOP 3, Decision III/20; Kyoto Protocol, Section IV.I and V.1.
[88] M. Ehrmann, 'Procedures of Compliance Control in International Environmental Treaties', *Colorado Journal of International Environmental Law and Policy*, 13(2) (2002), 377–444.
[89] F. R. Jacur, 'Triggering Non-Compliance Procedures' in Treves et al. (eds.), *Non-Compliance Procedures and Mechanisms and the Effectiveness of International Environmental Agreements*, p. 374.

for consideration and reports them to the COP/MOP. After receiving the committee's report, the COP/MOP adopts a decision or a recommendation on the matter and can apply measures to bring the non-compliant party to full compliance. As long as the party in question has not fulfilled its obligations, the committee continues to monitor the party's progress.

Under these phases, the experience and sense of procedural unfairness may erode the connection or trust between the parties and the NCP and its related bodies concerned. To provide a 'due process' for the parties involved in these different phases of the procedure, and to respond to the legitimacy concerns at least to some extent, some rights and safeguards which may be expressed as the indicators of the 'right process or legitimacy (referring to Franck's legitimacy theory)'[90] are provided for the parties which can be highly influential in ensuring the parties' voluntary compliance. The parties are more likely to comply with their commitments, largely with the effect of the legal or procedural formalities, seeing them as legitimate because the outcome that they generate are also seen by them as being likely to be fair and just.

The rights granted to the parties can be revealed in two different respects: the rights provided to the parties under scrutiny and the rights provided to the submitting/triggering parties. Determining specific deadlines for both the submission of the parties and the decisions to be taken by the compliance bodies can also be mentioned for improving the fairness of the procedures. In addition, despite the usage of English as a working language in the procedures, the MEAs' bodies also allow the usage of other languages 'for submissions, communications as well as other relevant documents to be filled by the parties'.[91] The rights of confidentiality and transparency of publicity within the procedures are also prerequisites of assuring fairness in NCPs. The impartiality and independence of the work of the committee,[92] the possibility of appeal, the application of fixed measures and consequences, assuring proportionality between response measures and different situations of non-compliance, can also be counted as other safeguards on which an NCP should be built.

---

[90] Franck, 'Legitimacy in the International System'; Franck, *The Power of Legitimacy Among Nations*; Franck, *Fairness in International Law and Institutions*.
[91] Montini, 'Procedural Guarantees in NCMs', p. 397.
[92] As already mentioned above while discussing the composition and the number of the committee, and will not be demonstrated again in this part.

With respect to the rights of the parties in question, e.g. under the CM of the Montreal Protocol, the party can receive a copy of the submission; reply and send any related information to the secretariat and to the relevant other parties[93] can explain the reasons of non-compliance;[94] can be represented during the consideration of the ImplCom of that submission-but not in the phase of the elaboration and adoption of recommendations.[95] Under the CM of the Kyoto Protocol, the procedure applied by the ComplCom for the resolution of non-compliance by the parties under both branches –the Facilitative and Enforcement Branches – includes similar rights provided for the parties.[96] Additionally, it is also possible to access any information considered by the committee, and also to decisions made by the MOP and to comment on such information and to present its views or expert testimony.

The procedures applied by the ImplCom under the Montreal Protocol's CM and by the ComplCom under the Kyoto Protocol's CM both require certain timetables for the different phases. For example, under the Montreal Protocol, transmitting the submission, the reply and the information provided by the parties to the ImplCom should be made as soon as the reply and information from the party are available – not later than six months after receiving the submission:[97] or under the Kyoto Protocol, the allocation of question of implementation (QoI) by the bureau should be in seven days from receipt of the QoI.[98]

Several means for ensuring transparency can also be provided under these mechanisms. To illustrate, the ImplCom's reports under the Montreal Protocol are available to anyone upon request;[99] the information considered by the Enforcement Branch under the Kyoto Protocol,[100] decisions,[101] consequences,[102] hearings,[103] all meetings of plenary and branches- except adoption of decisions[104] – are available for the public.

---

[93] NCP, paras. 2 and 3, Montreal Protocol.
[94] NCP, para. 4, Montreal Protocol.
[95] NCP, para. 11, Montreal Protocol; NCP, para. 10, Montreal Protocol.
[96] NCP, Sections VIII (general procedures), IX (procedures for the Enforcement Branch), X (expedited procedures for the Enforcement Branch).
[97] NCP, para. 2, Montreal Protocol.
[98] NCP, Section VII, 1; RoP 19.1.
[99] NCP, para. 16, Montreal Protocol.
[100] NCP, Section VIII, 6.
[101] NCP, Section VII, 6; Section VIII, 7; NCP, Section IX, 6–10.
[102] RoP 22f.
[103] NCP, Section IX, 2.
[104] RoP, 9.1.

Nevertheless, though they require transparency in their different stages, there are still a few shortcomings on achieving transparency under those procedures, e.g. although not applied to date,[105] until the conclusion of the proceedings – on request of the party being investigated and at the discretion of the Enforcement Branch – the information may be kept from the public under the Kyoto Protocol's CM (NCP Section VIII(6); similarly, under the Montreal Protocol's CM, the protection of the confidentiality of information under the reports raises as a feature of the procedure restricting its openness(NCP, paras.15, 16, Montreal Protocol). Additionally, the role of NGOs in CMs fails to meet the needs of improved transparency, which can help and support the legitimacy (or at least the perception of its existence) ensuring information to the related parties and their exchange of views.[106] To illustrate, under the Montreal Protocol, they can participate to the ImplCom proceedings as 'observers' only if the secretariat notifies and no party objects.[107] Under the Kyoto Protocol, they are permitted to provide relevant information to the relevant branch, to monitor and assess certified clean development mechanism (CDM) and sink projects.[108] Yet, they are still not allowed to initiate the NCP, despite the existence of suggestions indicating that the 'formalised possibility' of triggering an NCP should be attainable for NGOs;[109] and they face many problems in the field in the process of the compliance of the parties.[110]

Appeal opportunity given to the parties is also expressed as being one of the elements of providing due process under the NCP. The Kyoto Protocol CM can be given as an example of the mechanism in which the appeal procedure is also applied in the case of the denial of the due

---

[105] M. Doelle, 'Early Experience with the Kyoto Compliance System: Possible Lessons for MEA Compliance System Design', 1 Climate Law, 258.

[106] For details on strengthening the role of NGOs in CMs, see Z. Savaşan, 'Coping with Global Warming: Compliance Issue Compliance Mechanisms Under MEAs' in X. Zhang and I. Dincer (eds.), Energy Solutions to Combat Global Warming, Series Title: Lect. Notes Energy, Vol. 33 (Springer International Publishing, 2017).

[107] RoP, 6–7.

[108] NCP, Section VIII, paras. 4–5.

[109] A. Epiney, 'The Role of NGOs in the Process of Ensuring compliance with MEAs' in U. Beyerlin, P. T. Stoll and R. Wolfrum (eds.), Ensuring Compliance with Multilateral Environmental Agreements: A Dialogue between Practitioners and Academia (The Koninklijke Brill NV, 2006), p. 344.

[110] See S. Andresen and L. H. Gulbrandsen, 'The Role of Green NGOs in Promoting Climate Compliance' in O. S. Stokke, J. Hovi and G. Ulfstein (eds.), Implementing the Climate Regime, International Compliance (The Fridtjof Nansen Institute, 2005), pp. 169–86 for details on environmental organizations' contributions.

process, and so not related to the matters involving the violations on the substantive content.[111] Under the Montreal Protocol, as the decision-maker is the plenary organ MOP or COP and no other body superior to the MOP can decide on its decisions, there is no opportunity of this sort and also no support for creating such a mechanism.[112]

5   Legal Character of Measures

The application of fixed response measures or consequences, assuring proportionality between response measures and different situations of non-compliance is also regarded as one of the factors providing the due process under the NCP, minimizing its unfairness, and thus accelerating the legitimacy.

In line with the identification of Werksman of the components of response measures, the need for improvement of the non-compliance response measures can be discussed in three sub-groups: their 'prescriptiveness', their 'punitiveness' and their 'legal character'.[113]

With regard to prescriptiveness, under the Montreal Protocol system, there is an indicative list of measures for compliance in the form of positive measures (e.g. financial and technical assistance) and negative measures (e.g. suspension of some rights). However, the NCP does not define the situations of non-compliance, yet, it is expected that, in applying the appropriate measures to those non-compliance situations, to ensure the proportionality, the nature, degree and reason behind non-compliance, as well as the importance of the provision itself should be taken into account.[114] On the other hand, under the Kyoto Protocol system, there are predetermined measures with predetermined circumstances of non-compliance with different commitments, e.g. NCP, Section XIV defining which ones should be applied by the Facilitative Branch; and Section XV defining which ones should be applied by the Enforcement Branch . Moreover, it is stated that 'the development of an indicative list of consequences, taking into account the cause, type,

---

[111] NCP, Section XI,1.

[112] Ad Hoc Working Group on Non-Compliance, 'Report on the Work of the Ad Hoc WG', 18 November 1998, Geneva, UNEP/OzL.Pro/WG.4/1/3 (1998), 10, para. 57, retrieved May 12, 2017 from: http://ozone.unep.org/Meeting_Documents/adhoc/adhoc-nc-4-1-3.e.pdf

[113] J. D. Werksman, 'The Negotiation of a Kyoto Compliance System' in O. S. Stokke, J. Hovi and G. Ulfstein (eds.), *Implementing the Climate Regime, International Compliance* (The Fridtjof Nansen Institute, 2005), pp. 19–20.

[114] NCP, para. 9, Montreal Protocol.

degree and frequency of non-compliance',[115] thus, safeguarding the respect of the principle of proportionality between the nature of the non-compliance and the type of measure. So, it may be argued that this method of the Kyoto Protocol's NCP renders 'credibility and legitimacy' for the parties, advancing the predictability of both non-compliance situations and measures to be applied to them in such a well-designed system, including the principle of proportionality.[116]

Regarding the punitiveness of the measures, when we turn back to the theories on compliance, particularly the ones discussing the concept of legitimacy in their studies, it is seen that, for example, for Franck, though not fully thought out in some areas of international law, e.g. collective security,[117] it is already not at the core of the analysis, and not even a very significant issue. In fact, for him, if a rule is perceived as being fair, then coercive enforcement is already not necessary; and if enforcement is somehow applied, to be effective the mechanism already needs legitimacy. On the other hand, for Chayes, '[a] ... The effort to devise and incorporate such sanctions in treaties is largely a waste of time'[118] and sanctions for coercive enforcement are too costly and are too difficult to mobilize (similarly Brunnée and Toope define them as 'adversarial, backward-looking and coercive'[119]). So, it may be argued that 'illegitimacy was one of the primary justifications for [some] theories against the use of stronger enforcement mechanisms'.[120] Additionally, it is generally argued that, in accordance with the management approach, the punitive measures are rarely able 'to make much of a *difference* in a country's decision about whether to return to compliance'.[121] This is because, only in cases in which there is '*incomplete information*', i.e. the non-compliant party does not anticipate the application of punitive measures, and cannot estimate their costs both of them can exist together.[122] Under

---

[115] Kyoto Protocol, Art.,18.

[116] G. Ulfstein and J. Werksman, 'The Kyoto Compliance System: Towards Hard Enforcement' in Stokke et al. (eds.), *Implementing the Climate Regime, International Compliance*, p. 59.

[117] Franck, *Fairness in International Law and Institutions*, p. 290.

[118] Chayes and Chayes, *The New Sovereignty*, p. 2.

[119] J. Brunnée and S. J. Toope, 'International Law and Constructivism: Elements of an Interactional Theory of International Law', *Columbia Journal of Transnational Law*, 39 (2000), 46.

[120] Crossen, 'Compliance Continuum'.

[121] J. Hovi, C. B. Froyn and G. Bang, 'Enforcing the Kyoto Protocol: Can Punitive Consequences Restore Compliance?', *Review of International Studies*, 33 (2007), 438.

[122] Hovi et al., 'Enforcing the Kyoto Protocol', 444.

the Kyoto Protocol's system, as there are predetermined measures,[123] the cost of these measures can easily be estimated by developed country parties to which those measures are applied.[124] Under the Montreal Protocol's system, there is an indicative list of measures – not a complete list. So, the MOP can apply different measures not identified in this list, but all should necessarily be 'advisory and conciliatory'.[125]

Because of such cases increasing the possibility of the failure in deterring the parties from non-compliance, Hovi et al. suggest external enforcement imposing the means not addressed by the relevant agreement or taken by a non-signatory party to punish the non-compliant party so as to accomplish its return to compliance, rather than applying punitive measures. It is argued that external enforcement may enhance the deterrent effect of a compliance system, but it may also undermine its legitimacy, and so should be applied in line with the rules of international law. Only if it can be applied within such rules and can improve the deterrent effect of internal measures will it enhance compliance without undermining the system's legitimacy.[126]

On the legal character, under the Montreal Protocol's system, decisions of the MOP are accepted as advisory though there is an ongoing debate on the possible binding status of the measures;[127] and, under the Kyoto Protocol's system, any compliance procedures and mechanisms entailing binding measures should be adopted by means of an amendment to the Protocol.[128] Yet, any amendment to the Protocol requires a long period for ratification by at least three-quarters of the parties to the Protocol and this can cause some parties to stay out of the amendment process.[129] Therefore, if the measures revoked against the non-compliant party are regulated explicitly by the Agreement itself as a binding measure, or they are in conformity with general international law (e.g.

---

[123] NCP, Section XIV for the Facilitative Branch, and in Section XV for the Enforcement Branch.

[124] Hovi et al., 'Enforcing the Kyoto Protocol'.

[125] MOP 3, Decision III/2, Nairobi, 19–21 June 1991, UNEP/OzL.Pro.3/11(1991), retrieved March 25, 2017 from: http://ozone.unep.org/Meeting_Documents/mop/03mop/3mop-11.e.pdf

[126] Hovi et al., 'Enforcing the Kyoto Protocol'; J. Hovi, 'The Pros and Cons of External Enforcement' in Stokkeet al. (eds.), *Implementing the Climate Regime, International Compliance*, pp. 129–46.

[127] See Ad Hoc WG 1, 4, para.9i; Ad Hoc WG 3, 6, para.41; Ad Hoc WG 1, 10, situation vii, Annex II.

[128] See also MOP 1, Decision 2, 'Report of the COP serving as the MOP,' para. 5.

[129] Kyoto Protocol, Art. 20.4.

suspension of treaty rights and privileges can be assessed as being binding in line with Article 60 of the VCLT);[130] then, there is no problem about the binding status of that measure. However, the problem arises if there is no explicit provision in the Agreement, and if there are special rights and privileges established under COP/MOP decisions not subject to Article 60 of the VCLT. In fact, in such a case, whether a decision of the COP/MOP on the application of a response measure is legally binding for the parties concerned forms an important problem that should be resolved. So, it is argued that except the measure requiring deductions of assigned amounts at a penalty rate (equal to 1.3 times the amount in tonnes of excess emissions);[131] the other measures can be thought to be within the competence of the Enforcement Branch.[132]

D   Conclusion

The aim of this chapter was to scrutinize legitimacy concerns that may be posed under compliance mechanisms in the field of non-compliance procedures. In this regard, it first provided a brief conceptual and theoretical basis for compliance: CMs. Then, it elaborated the questions on NCP, focusing on tissues relevant to legitimacy, referring to the examples of both the Kyoto and Montreal Protocols.

Relying on the normative dimension of legitimacy (including legal, participatory and expert legitimacy), the main research question was whether the justification of authority is provided in accordance with law, with transparent and participatory processes or based on experts' decisions under these procedures.

Based on the findings made, five sub-sections – the legal basis of the decision-making power, the legal basis of the NCP, the institution of the NCP (the committee), the procedural safeguards, and the legal character of measures applied to the non-compliant parties – it may be argued that, although there are controversial issues elaborated above regarding the COP's decision-making power and its tasks and authorities at the external sphere, the legal basis of the NCP, the composition (expert-based or not) and the number of the committee (limited or unlimited), safeguards (such as pre-determined deadlines for both submissions/decisions, transparency, the impartiality and independency of the committee, fixed

---

[130] VCLT (1969), retrieved April 11, 2017 from: http://untreaty.un.org/ilc/texts/instruments/english/conventions/1_1_1969.pdf

[131] NCP, Section XV, 5a.

[132] Ulfstein and Werksman, 'The Kyoto Compliance System', pp. 39–64.

consequences, possibility for appeal), and the response measures discussed under with three components (prescriptiveness, punitiveness and legal character), it appears to a large extent that these NCPs are built to serve to vindicate the normative elements of legitimacy, at least examples from the Kyoto and Montreal Protocols give signals in this line.

However, the concept of legitimacy is a very complicated and complex concept involving many aspects and discussions in itself; it results in a diverse research area. This diversity related to the legitimacy issue apparently shows that there is a substantial need further examinations and empirical studies on the distinctive characteristics of different institutions and to develop a legitimacy perspective for each one of those.[133] Indeed, for CMs, their three components – gathering information, NCPs and response measures – require to be analyzed separately within the distinctive dimensions of legitimacy, in addition to the each component. It is also necessary to study the outcomes of these mechanisms through analyzing non-compliance cases conducted under them. Given the fact that different MEAs have different mechanisms, the need for further research increases, but, as they are built similarly to each other, with only slight differences. Yet, in short, more detailed analysis, including not only normative but also descriptive dimensions of legitimacy, is of paramount significance.

---

[133] Wolfrum, 'Legitimacy of International Law.' Bodansky also calls for further work on how to legitimize international environmental regimes ('The Legitimacy of International Governance', 623); Bodansky 'The Concept of Legitimacy,' p. 317.

PART VI

The Limits of Environmental Justice through Courts: Balancing Legitimacy with the Need for Creativity

15

Environmental Ombudsman: Its Role in the System of Accountability Mechanisms for Administrative Environmental Decision Making*

MAHITO SHINDO

A Introduction

As the Aarhus Convention shows,[1] the role of accountability mechanisms is crucial to ensuring executive accountability in administrative environmental decision making at the national level. In many jurisdictions, the system of accountability mechanisms, which reviews the legality and appropriateness of first-instance administrative decisions, comprises three layers – namely, judicial review, merits review and ombudsman review. Further, certain jurisdictions have a specialised environmental ombudsman.[2] However, in the environmental field, the role of ombudsman review has not been well researched. Consequently, the role of an environmental ombudsman has not been well articulated, which suggests that clarifying the roles of such institutions can further improve the system of accountability mechanisms for administrative environmental decision making.

Based on this recognition, this chapter discusses the role of an environmental ombudsman in the system of accountability mechanisms. The focus is on its ability to improve the legitimacy of administrative

---

* This chapter is based on the author's PhD thesis: Mahito Shindo, 'The Environmental Ombudsman and Administrative Decision Making: An Assessment of its Suitability for Japan', unpublished PhD thesis, Macquarie University (2013). The author would like to express his deepest gratitude and appreciation to Professor Brian Opeskin and the Honourable Justice Brian Preston for their wonderful supervision of his PhD.

[1] Convention on Access to Information, Public Participation in Decision-Making and Access to Justice in Environmental Matters, opened for signature 25 June 1998, 2161 UNTS 447 (entered into force 30 October 2001) ('Aarhus Convention'), art. 9.

[2] George Pring and Catherine Pring, *Greening Justice: Creating and Improving Environmental Courts and Tribunals* (The Access Initiative, 2009), pp. 67–69.

environmental decision making. To achieve this objective, a series of research questions must be answered. The first question is related to the position of ombudsman review in the system of accountability mechanisms to elucidate the general role of this layer in the accountability system. The second question is related to the effect of an absence of ombudsman review on the environmental field to highlight the significance of this layer in the system of accountability mechanisms. The third question focuses on the role played by an environmental ombudsman within the accountability system to address the objectives of this chapter. To answer these questions, the role of environmental ombudsman offices must be examined. Hence, this chapter examines three jurisdictions that have such offices (Australian Capital Territory (ACT), New Zealand and Hungary) and one jurisdiction that does not have ombudsman review (Japan). All four jurisdictions are parliamentary democracies. Since environmental ombudsman offices have not been widely researched, an examination of their role cannot rely only on a doctrinal method. Thus, empirical research was conducted to obtain the necessary data. In Hungary, as a result of the change of constitution on 1 January 2012, the office of environmental ombudsman was merged into that of the general ombudsman.[3] However, this does not diminish the value of analysis of the empirical data collected through field research to clarify the role of an environmental ombudsman. Thus, in this chapter, the situation of Hungary at the time of field research in 2011 is described and analysed.

Regarding the research methods, this chapter has recourse to comparative administrative law. The selection of jurisdictions to be compared is of central importance to comparative administrative law research, because common law and civil law systems in public law vary considerably.[4] Among the selected jurisdictions, the ACT and New Zealand belong to the common law system and Hungary belongs to the German-style civil law system.[5] Meanwhile, the Japanese administrative

---

[3] 2011. évi CXI. törvény az alapvető jogok biztosáról [Act CXI of 2011 of the Parliamentary Commissioner for Fundamental Rights] (Hungary), 26 July 2011, *Magyar Közlöny*, No. 2011/88, 25435.

[4] John S. Bell, 'Comparative Administrative Law' in Mathias Reimann and Reinhard Zimmermann (eds.), *The Oxford Handbook of Comparative Law* (Oxford University Press, 2008), pp. 1264–65; John Bell, 'Comparing Public Law' in Andrew Harding and Esin Örücü (eds.), *Comparative Law in the 21st Century* (Kluwer Law International, 2002), pp. 243–44; Peter de Cruz, *Comparative Law in a Changing World*, 3rd edn (Routledge-Cavendish, 2007), pp. 105–08.

[5] Herbert M. Kritzer (ed.), *Legal Systems of the World: A Political, Social, and Cultural Encyclopedia* (ABC CLIO, 2002), pp. 322, 670, 1153.

law system is a hybrid of the common law and German-style civil law systems, but is heavily influenced by the latter.[6] Hence, the comparability of systems of accountability mechanisms between the common law and German-style civil law systems must be considered. Because the global diffusion of Ombudsman institutions occurred in the late twentieth century, substantial differences are not observed in ombudsman review between the two legal families.[7] Although the basic features of merits review and judicial review in the common law system and German legal system – the basis of the German-style civil law system – are quite different, the overall effectiveness of the system of accountability mechanisms in each legal system does not differ significantly.[8] Thus, a comparison of accountability systems in these jurisdictions is meaningful.

To obtain empirical data on the jurisdictions to be compared, field research centred on interviews with relevant stakeholders.[9] To assess the role of environmental ombudsman offices, elite interviewing was performed, in which participants were chosen based not on their demographic characteristics but rather on their expertise in the area.[10] The method involved employing semi-structured interviews, which enabled the researcher to collect specific information from the participants.[11] Field research in the four jurisdictions was conducted from 27 May to 29 July 2011. The data on these jurisdictions, detailed below, are for 2011. The results of the interviews were transcribed, coded and analysed utilising qualitative analysis methods.[12]

---

[6] 藤田宙靖 [Tokiyasu Fujita], 行政法 I ： 総論 [Administrative Law I: General Remarks], 4th revised edn (青林書院 [Seirin Shoin], 2005), pp. 23–24, 363–65; 原田尚彦 [Naohiko Harada], 行政法要論 [Essence of Administrative Law], 6th edn (学陽書房 [Gakuyo Shobo], 2005), pp. 23–24, 350–51; 塩野宏 [Hiroshi Shiono], 行政法 II ： 行政救済法 [Administrative Law II: Administrative Remedy Law], 4th edn (有斐閣 [Yuhikaku], 2005), pp. 63–64.

[7] For a review of basic common features of the parliamentary ombudsman, which is the central institution of ombudsman review, see International Bar Association Resolution, Vancouver, 1974.

[8] Martina Künnecke, Tradition and Change in Administrative Law: An Anglo-German Comparison (Springer, 2007), pp. 69–71.

[9] Ethical aspects of this study were approved by the Macquarie University Human Research Ethics Committee. Reference No. 520100378(D).

[10] Teresa Odendahl and Aileen M. Shaw, 'Interviewing Elites' in Jaber F. Gubrium and James A Holstein (eds.), Handbook of Interview Research: Context & Method (SAGE, 2002), pp. 299–300.

[11] Sharan B. Merriam, Qualitative Research: A Guide to Design and Implementation, 2nd edn (Jossey-Bass, 2009), pp. 89–90.

[12] Hennie Boeije, Analysis in Qualitative Research (SAGE, 2010), chs 5 and 6.

This chapter is divided into five sections. This section introduces the study in the context of administrative environmental and comparative law and provides an overview of these areas. The second section provides background information on the positioning of ombudsman review in the system of accountability mechanisms. The third section examines a Japanese case, with a focus on the impacts of a lack of ombudsman review on ensuring executive accountability in administrative environmental decision making. The fourth section examines the role of an environmental ombudsman within ombudsman review, and analyses the role of an environmental ombudsman and its relationship with that of a general ombudsman. Finally, the fifth section discusses the role of an environmental ombudsman in the system of accountability mechanisms.

B   Ombudsman Review in the System of Accountability Mechanisms

This section provides background information on the positioning of ombudsman review in the system of accountability mechanisms. The role of ombudsman review in the accountability system can be divided into theoretical and practical aspects. This section clarifies the positioning of ombudsman review in the system of accountability mechanisms from a theoretical standpoint and from a practical standpoint.

1   Ombudsman Review in the Environmental Field

In public law contexts at the national level, a widely accepted definition of executive accountability is as follows: examining governmental activities when undertaking formal processes and remedying faults when necessary.[13] The objective of accountability, in this sense, is to control public power responsible for government action or inaction. In the environmental field, executive accountability plays a critical role in improving the quality of administrative environmental decision making. The development of environmental policy over the last four decades has required decision makers to consider environmental values that, historically, have been undervalued. Such a practice also increases the

---

[13]   Andrew Le Sueur, 'The Nature, Powers and Accountability of Central Government' in David Feldman (ed.), *English Public Law*, 2nd edn (Oxford University Press, 2009), p. 190; Dawn Oliver, 'Law, Politics and Public Accountability. The Search for New Equilibrium', *Public Law* [1994], p. 238, 246.

legitimacy of administrative environmental decisions.[14] However, in conservative bureaucratic culture, decision makers have experienced difficulty in adjusting to such a paradigm shift without the help of an external driving force. Executive accountability is expected to drive the diffusion of the paradigm shift and promote behavioural change in decision makers.[15] Furthermore, remedies, such as sanctions, provide decision makers with incentives to follow newly imposed norms. Executive accountability also provides a pragmatic training and learning process for decision makers, thereby assisting them in acclimatising to new situations and concepts.[16]

With the increased diffusion of the concept of executive accountability, an awareness of the importance of ombudsman review has grown in the area of public law.[17] Although the role of ombudsman review in the environmental field has not been well researched, this does not mean that executive accountability is not considered in the environmental field. Rather, as the Aarhus Convention is focused on the promotion of executive accountability,[18] its importance is widely emphasised in the environmental field. However, the anticipated role of the three layers in the accountability system here appears to be stereotypical, which is largely because the Aarhus Convention indicates that the resolution of individual disputes is the primary role of accountability mechanisms.[19]

---

[14] Jonas Ebbesson, 'The Notion of Public Participation in International Environmental Law', *Yearbook of International Environmental Law*, 8 (1997), pp. 58–59, 64, 76–79, 95; United Nations Environment Programme (UNEP), *Putting Rio Principle 10 into Action: An Implementation Guide* (UNEP, 2015), pp. 58–59, 76.

[15] François Bregha and Philippe Clément, *A Renewed Framework for Government Accountability in the Area of Sustainable Development: Potential Role for a Canadian Parliamentary Auditor/Commissioner for the Environment* (National Round Table on the Environment and the Economy, 1994), 4; UNEP, *Putting Rio Principle 10 into Action*, pp. 55, 68–69.

[16] Mark Bovens, Thomas Schillemans and Paul T Hart, 'Does Public Accountability Work?: An Assessment Tool', *Public Administration*, 86 (2008), p. 232.

[17] Michael Purdue, 'Investigations by the Public Sector Ombudsman' in David Feldman (ed.), *English Public Law*, 2nd edn (Oxford University Press, 2009); Andrew Le Sueur, Maurice Sunkin and Jo Eric Khushal Murkens, *Public Law: Text, Cases, and Materials* (Oxford University Press, 2010), pp. 697–721; Mark Elliott and Robert Thomas, *Public Law* (Oxford University Press, 2011), ch. 16; Mark Elliott, 'Ombudsmen, Tribunals, Inquiries: Re-fashioning Accountability Beyond the Courts' in Nicholas Bamforth and Peter Leyland (eds.), *Accountability in the Contemporary Constitution* (Oxford University Press, 2013), pp. 245–47.

[18] *Aarhus Convention*, preamble.

[19] Ibid., art. 9(1).

Traditionally, the most important accountability mechanism has been the court. Thus, the basic features of individual layers in the accountability system are frequently described based on their capacities to resolve individual disputes. The following serves as a typical example. Merits review examines 'what . . . "correct or preferable decision" should be by "standing in the shoes" of the original decision-maker'.[20] Judicial review examines whether the activities of governmental officials are legally correct, performed within the legal boundaries to which they are confined and exercised in a manner required by law. Ombudsman review examines whether the activities of public officers are appropriate, just or legal, especially when the solutions by means of the other processes are unavailable or unsuitable. Each accountability mechanism is limited in scope and influence, based on its nature and objectives.[21] Reflecting this tendency, the roles of the three layers in the environmental field are frequently discussed with a focus on their capacities to resolve individual disputes.[22]

However, the resolution of individual disputes is not the only way to ensure executive accountability and the legitimacy of administrative decisions. Considering the nature of the system of accountability mechanisms based on the doctrine of the separation of powers, a broader perspective emerges regarding the roles of individual layers. In a parliamentary democracy, the parliamentary ombudsman, which is the central institution of ombudsman review, is an officer of Parliament.[23] The main function of the parliamentary ombudsman is to assist Parliament in holding the executive accountable. Hence, the parliamentary ombudsman can specifically address systemic problems of administrative proceedings, policy and law.[24] The parliamentary

---

[20] William B. Lane and Simon Young, *Administrative Law in Australia* (Lawbook Co., 2007), p. 2 (emphasis in original).

[21] Ibid.; Robin Creyke and John McMillan, *Control of Government Action: Text, Cases and Commentary*, 2nd edn (LexisNexis Butterworths, 2009), pp. 14, 16; Le Sueur, 'The Nature, Powers and Accountability of Central Government', pp. 191–92; Linda C. Reif, 'Conceptions of Justice in Ombudsman Dispute Settlement: From the Classic Ombudsman to the Human Rights Ombudsman Model' in Peter Collin (ed.), *Justice without the State within the State: Judicial Self-Regulation in the Past and Present* (Vittorio Klostermann, 2016), pp. 336–39.

[22] UNEP, *Putting Rio Principle 10 into Action*, pp. 102, 121, 127–28.

[23] International Bar Association Resolution, Vancouver, 1974.

[24] Marten Oosting, 'The Ombudsman: A Profession' in International Ombudsman Institute and Linda C. Reif (eds.), *The International Ombudsman Yearbook*, vol. 1, 1997 (Kluwer Law International, 1998), pp. 7–9; Anita Stuhmcke, 'Ombudsman and Integrity Review' in Linda Pearson, Carol Harlow and Michael Taggart (eds.), *Administrative Law in*

ombudsman is able to address systemic problems because of its power to conduct self-initiated investigations.[25] Although recommendations issued by the parliamentary ombudsman are not legally binding, they can shape future law reform.[26] This is another type of contribution to ensuring executive accountability that is no less important than the resolution of individual disputes, especially in the environmental field.

2   Composition of Systems of Accountability Mechanisms in the Examined Jurisdictions

On a practical aspect, the positioning of ombudsman review within the composition of actual systems of accountability mechanisms must be understood. Hence, this subsection examines basic features of individual layers that compose the accountability system in each jurisdiction to be examined. Although the Japanese legal system does not have ombudsman review, the composition of its system of accountability mechanisms must be understood as a control. Thus, all four jurisdictions are examined. However, for simplification, accountability mechanisms for disputes on information disclosure are excluded. The objective of this subsection is to examine whether each accountability system can sufficiently address individual cases as well as systemic problems, and to provide expert review.

In the ACT, merits review was exercised by the ACT Civil and Administrative Tribunal (ACAT) and judicial review was conducted by the ACT Supreme Court.[27] The ACAT was the external merits review body for general purposes, and consisted of lawyers and other experts. Although the employment of environmental experts was not mandated, some members were responsible for examining certain kinds of

---

a Changing State; Essays in Honour of Mark Aronson (Hart, 2008), pp. 354–55; Reif, 'Conceptions of Justice in Ombudsman Dispute Settlement', pp. 329–30.

[25] Gabriele Kucsko-Stadlmayer, 'The Legal Structure of Ombudsman-Institutions in Europe: Legal Comparative Analysis' in Gabriele Kucsko-Stadlmayer (ed.), European Ombudsman-Institutions: A comparative legal analysis regarding the multifaceted realisation of an idea (Springer, 2008), pp. 21–22; Roy Gregory, 'The Ombudsman: "An Excellent Form of Alternative Dispute Resolution"?' in Linda C. Reif (ed.), The International Ombudsman Yearbook, vol. 5, 2001 (Kluwer Law International, 2002), pp. 115–15; Oosting, 'The Ombudsman: A Profession', pp. 8–9.

[26] Lane and Young, Administrative Law in Australia, p. 2; Creyke and McMillan, Control of Government Action, p. 16;Kucsko-Stadlmayer, 'The Legal Structure of Ombudsman-Institutions in Europe', pp. 44–51.

[27] Environmental Defender's Office (ACT), Challenging environmental decisions (2010), pp. 2–5.

environmental cases.[28] Another route was to complain to the ACT
Ombudsman or the Commissioner for Sustainability and the
Environment (CSE).[29] In the ACT, systemic problems were addressed
by ombudsman review and merits review, and ombudsman review provided expert review.

In New Zealand, the main accountability mechanisms for environmental disputes were merits review and judicial review. In general, environmental cases were first sent to the local council's merits review, which
was a panel of three trained independent experts. Any remaining issue
was then appealed to the Environment Court, which conducted both
merits review and judicial review.[30] The Environment Court was
a specialist institution of environment judges and environmental experts,
who were referred to as Environment Commissioners.[31] Further appeals
were made to the Supreme Court.[32] Alternatively, complaints could be
lodged with the Parliamentary Ombudsman or the Parliamentary
Commissioner for the Environment (PCE).[33] In New Zealand, systemic
problems were addressed by ombudsman review, and all three layers
provided expert review.

In Hungary, the binding review system consisted of internal merits
review and judicial review. The internal merits review had two levels
that corresponded to local authorities and the central ministry.[34]
The examining boards of local authorities usually did not include
legal experts, whereas those of the central ministry included a lawyer
(but not a trained judge) and an environmental expert.[35] Judicial
review was conducted on two levels: county courts and the Supreme

[28] ACT Civil and Administrative Tribunal Regulation 2009 (ACT), reg. 6; interview with
Linda Crebbin, General President, ACT Civil and Administrative Tribunal (Canberra,
27 May 2011).
[29] Environmental Defender's Office (ACT), *Challenging environmental decisions*, pp. 2–5.
[30] Interview with Justice Craig Thompson, Principal Environment Judge, Environment
Court of New Zealand (Wellington, 13 June 2011).
[31] Ministry for the Environment (NZ), *Your Guide to the Environment Court*, 2nd edn
(Ministry for the Environment (NZ), 2009), p. 5.
[32] Interview with Justice John McGrath, Supreme Court of New Zealand (Wellington,
13 June 2011).
[33] Interview with David McGee, Ombudsman (Wellington, 8 June 2011); interview with
Sarah Clark, Office Manager, Parliamentary Commissioner for the Environment
(Wellington, 9 June 2011).
[34] Interview with Justice Péter Darák, Supreme Court of Hungary (Budapest, 24 June 2011);
interview with Justice Fruzsina Bögös, Metropolitan Court of Budapest (Budapest,
24 June 2011); interview with Csaba Kiss, Director, Environmental Management and
Law Association (Budapest, 22 June 2011).
[35] Interview with Bögös J.

Court.[36] Complaints could also be lodged to the Parliamentary Commissioner for Civil Rights (Ombudsman) and the Parliamentary Commissioner for Future Generations (PCFG).[37] In Hungary, systemic problems were addressed by ombudsman review and merits review, and ombudsman review provided expert review.

In Japan, the basic framework of dispute resolution was a combination of internal merits review and judicial review. Although not in every case, in many cases, the exhaustion of merits review was required prior to the commencement of judicial review.[38] No single internal merits review institution reviewed all types of environmental disputes. Rather, individual administrative offices exercised merits review according to their jurisdictions.[39] In practice, officers who conducted internal review were often not properly trained as reviewers.[40] Regarding judicial review, all environmental disputes were reviewed by the judicial court. The judicial court operated on three levels: district courts, high courts and the Supreme Court.[41] While district courts and high courts exercised the power to examine facts, the Supreme Court mostly examined questions of law.[42] There was no ombudsman review in Japan, where systemic problems were not addressed and expert review was not specifically provided.

---

[36] Interview with Darák J.; Interview with Bögös J.

[37] Interview with Justice Barnabás Lenkovics, former Ombudsman (Budapest, 23 June 2011); interview with Sándor Fülöp, Parliamentary Commissioner for Future Generations (Budapest, 28 June 2011); interview with István Sárközy, Legal adviser, Office of the Parliamentary Commissioner for Future Generations (Budapest, 28 June 2011).

[38] 行政事件訴訟法 [Code of Administrative Procedure] (Japan), 16 May 1962, Law No. 139 of S37, art. 8; Shiono, *Administrative Law II: Administrative Remedy Law*, pp. 11–12; Harada, *Essence of Administrative Law*, p. 393.

[39] 行政不服審査法 [Administrative Appeal Law] (Japan), 15 September 1962, Law No. 160 of S37, arts. 3, 8, 40(5), 47(3) and 51(3).

[40] 宮崎良夫 [Yoshio Miyazaki], 行政争訟と行政法学 [*Administrative Dispute and Administrative Law Studies*], enlarged edn (弘文堂 [Kobundo], 2004), pp. 142–46; 大橋真由美 [Mayumi Ohashi], 行政による紛争処理の新動向: 行政不服審査ADR 苦情処理等の展開 [*New Trend in Dispute Management by the Administrative Branch: Developments in Administrative Appeal, ADR, Complaint Handling and Others*] (日本評論社 [Nippon Hyoron Sha], 2015), pp. 39–40.

[41] Supreme Court of Japan, 裁判所の組織: 概要 ['Organisational Structure of the Courts in Japan'] (2015): www.courts.go.jp/about/sosiki/gaiyo/index.html (accessed 28 June 2017).

[42] 民事訴訟法 [Code of Civil Procedure] (Japan), 26 June 1996, Law No. 109 of H8, arts. 311–12 and 318.

In summary, in the ACT, New Zealand and Hungary, the systems of accountability mechanisms addressed both individual cases and systemic problems, and provided expert review. In contrast, the Japanese system of accountability mechanisms addressed individual cases only and did not address systemic problems or provide expert review. The following sections reveal that the difference in the accountability systems between the former three jurisdictions and Japan were related to the ability to address systemic problems and the provision of expert review. However, the practices of the Japanese accountability system must be examined before determining whether such differences had any significant influence on the legitimacy of administrative environmental decisions.

C   Absence of Ombudsman Review in Japan and Environmental Consequences

The previous section shows that the Japanese system of accountability mechanisms in the environmental field was unique because it did not provide systemic and expert reviews or have ombudsman review. These features strongly suggest structural vulnerability when reviewing the appropriateness of first-instance environmental decisions. To illustrate whether such vulnerability occurs, this section examines the impacts of a lack of ombudsman review in the environmental field. Specifically, the actual practice of the Japanese accountability system for nuclear safety is examined. To provide background information, Subsection 1 reviews the underlying causes of the second worst nuclear disaster in human history that occurred in Japan in 2011. Then, Subsection 2 examines the actual practices of Japanese system of accountability mechanisms and considers why merits review and judicial review in Japan failed to ensure executive accountability. Furthermore, Subsection 3 addresses another problem caused by a lack of ombudsman review in the post-nuclear accident phase. Finally, Subsection 4 discusses the lessons learnt from the lack of ombudsman review in the Japanese case.

1   Regulatory Capture Revealed by the TEPCO Nuclear Disaster

On 11 March 2011, a massive earthquake and subsequent tsunami triggered the Tokyo Electric Power Company's complex nuclear accidents in Fukushima (TEPCO nuclear disaster). Official investigative committees at both at the legislature and executive levels have reported that insufficient emergency preparedness for a severe nuclear accident provoked the TEPCO nuclear disaster and exacerbated its damage.[43] The National Diet of Japan Fukushima Nuclear Accident Independent Investigation Commission (NAIIC) was Japan's first parliamentary institution to have statutorily mandated investigatory power.[44] The NAIIC attributed the insufficient emergency preparedness to regulatory capture. Due to the lack of independence, transparency and necessary expertise, the Japanese nuclear regulator had been captured by the nuclear industry and administrative nuclear promoters. These nuclear promoters had strongly lobbied not to entrench emergency preparedness measures, which would have increased nuclear power plant operational costs. The regulators had recognised the need for the entrenchment of emergency preparedness measures but sabotaged their implementation for the sake of the nuclear promoters. Academic societies had also been captured by nuclear promoters and had cooperated to prevent the entrenchment of emergency preparedness. As a result, a safety culture, which forms the basis of nuclear security, had not been established in Japan. Therefore, levels of emergency preparedness for a severe nuclear accident in Japan were far below global standards.[45]

This insufficient emergency preparedness for a severe nuclear accident caused absolute chaos in the emergency response to the TEPCO nuclear disaster. The Cabinet and the very top echelon of the government were unable to make sound decisions because of a lack of information. As a result of the poor emergency preparedness measures, the government's emergency response centre was unable to collect and deliver vital site-level information to the Cabinet for the first four days after the accident. On site, insufficient equipment was available to stabilise the accident, and operators had not been sufficiently well trained to manage such a severe accident. Off site, the government failed to implement iodine prophylaxis and provide timely and appropriate information for

[43] National Diet of Japan Fukushima Nuclear Accident Independent Investigation Commission (NAIIC) (JPN), *The Official Report of the Fukushima Nuclear Accident Independent Investigation Commission* (2012), Intro, pp. 10–13; Investigation Committee on the Accident at the Fukushima Nuclear Power Stations of Tokyo Electric Power Company at the Cabinet Office (ICANPS) (JPN), *Final Report (Main Text)* (2012), pp. 424, 429, 456 and 464–69.

[44] 東京電力福島原子力発電所事故調査委員会法 [Law on the Tokyo Electric Power Company's Fukushima Nuclear Power Plant Accident Independent Investigation Commission at the National Diet] (Japan), 7 October 2011, Law No. 112 of H23 (NAIIC Establishment Law), arts. 10–14.

[45] NAIIC, *The Official Report of the Fukushima Nuclear Accident Independent Investigation Commission*, Intro., p. 16; ch 5, pp. 14–15; ch. 5, pp. 23–30; ch. 5, pp. 46–60.

evacuation. As a result of the TEPCO nuclear disaster, massive volumes of radioactive materials were released into the environment; 1,800km^2 of land was seriously contaminated with radioactive materials; and nearly 150,000 people were evacuated from the contaminated area.[46] At the time of writing, the destroyed nuclear power plants were still emitting radioactive materials into the atmosphere.[47]

2   Functionality of the System of Accountability Mechanisms in Japan

The importance of establishing a safety culture has been emphasised and globally recognised since the Chernobyl nuclear disaster in 1986.[48] However, the lesson of Chernobyl had not been learnt in Japan. The inadequate emergency preparedness measures were based on the illogical assumption that such a severe nuclear accident would not occur in Japan.[49] Faced with this reality, the question why such a typical case of maladministration and systemic corruption as that described above was overlooked in a parliamentary democracy until 2011 must be examined. In particular, the question of how the existed accountability system failed to ensure executive accountability must be clarified.

As noted in the previous section, the Japanese system of accountability mechanisms consisted of two layers: internal merits review and judicial review. In nuclear disputes, the first-instance decisions were made in the name of the Prime Minister.[50] Since the Prime Minister is the highest administrative body, the merits review body was essentially equivalent to the first-instance decision maker. However, the effectiveness of merits

[46] Ibid., Intro., p. 15; h. 3, p. 2; ch. 3, pp. 30–45; ch. 3, pp. 59–63; ch. 4, pp. 2–4; ch. 4, p. 71; ch. 4, pp. 78–85; ICANPS, *Final Report (Main Text)*, pp. 429–34, 441–46, 448–50 and 471–75.

[47] 東京電力株式会社 [Tokyo Electric Power Company (TEPCO)], 原子炉建屋からの追加的放出量の評価結果 (2017年5月) [*Examination Results on Additional Radioactive Emission from Reactor Buildings at Fukushima Daiichi* (May 2017)] (2017).

[48] International Atomic Energy Agency (IAEA), *Safety Culture* (Safety Series No. 75-INSAG-4, 1991); Ministry of Ukraine of Emergencies (UKR), *Twenty-five Years after Chornobyl Accident: Safety for the Future* (National Report of Ukraine, 2011), pp. 14, 19, 278–80, 300 and 313.

[49] NAIIC, *The Official Report of the Fukushima Nuclear Accident Independent Investigation Commission*, Appx 3, p. 73; ICANPS, *Final Report (Main Text)*, p. 527.

[50] 北口星 [Sei Kitaguchi] and 繁松祐行 [Masayuki Shigematsu], 原発判決全点検—福島事故は裁判で防げた ['Reexamination of All Nuclear Power Plant Cases: Fukushima Accident Could Have Been Prevented by Judgment'] in 斎藤浩 [Hiroshi Saito] (ed.), 原発の安全と行政 司法 学界の責任 [*Safety of Nuclear Power Plants and Responsibility of the Executive, Judiciary and Academy*] (法律文化社 [Houritsu Bunka Sha], 2013),pp. 14, 17–18, 20 and 28–29.

review conducted by the same body was called into question.[51] In actuality, merits review on nuclear safety had not properly reviewed the first-instance decisions on nuclear matters.

Regarding judicial review, in Japan, since the 1970s, the rationality of planning approval for nuclear power plants, of which safety was doubtful, had been litigated.[52] Through these litigations, the court established its stance as follows. First, the court declared that the issue of nuclear safety required extremely high expertise on scientific technology. Then, the court noted that first-instance decisions should be made based on the results of examinations performed by an expert panel, and regarded such decisions as reliable. Accordingly, the court limited its review of first-instance decisions to the determination of whether decision-making processes were irrational or unreasonable.[53] However, the court had never acknowledged the presence of such mistakes in decision-making processes and denied potential safety risks posed by the expert witnesses of plaintiffs.[54] Consequently, the rationality of first-instance decisions on nuclear safety had not been properly reviewed.

Even prior to the TEPCO nuclear disaster, the court's stance had been criticised, especially regarding the ambiguity of standards, the lack of examination of the impartiality of the expert panel utilised by the first-instance decision maker, and the court's tendency blindly to trust the first-instance decisions.[55] In addition, Professor Sonobe, who is a former Supreme Court judge, a former professional judge with a speciality in administrative disputes and an administrative law scholar, had proposed the introduction of a quasi-judicial expert tribunal in

---

[51] 南博方 [Hiromasa Minami], 紛争の行政解決手法 [*Methods of Administrative Dispute Resolution*] (有斐閣 [Yuhikaku], 1993), pp. 106–10.

[52] Kitaguchi and Shigematsu, 'Reexamination of All Nuclear Power Plant Cases', pp. 12–31.

[53] 伊方原発事件 [Ikata Nuclear Power Plant Case], Supreme Court of Japan, 昭和60(行ツ) 133, 29 October 1992, reported in (H4) 46(7) Supreme Court Reports (civil cases) 1174; 宮田三郎 [Saburou Miyata], 行政裁量とその統制密度 [*Administrative Discretion and Its Control Density*], enlarged edn (信山社 [Shinzan Sha], 2012), pp. 345–46.

[54] Kitaguchi and Shigematsu, 'Reexamination of All Nuclear Power Plant Cases', pp. 12–31 and 48–51.

[55] Shiono, *Administrative Law II: Administrative Remedy Law*, pp. 143–44; Harada, *Essence of Administrative Law*, pp. 268–72; Miyata, *Administrative Discretion and Its Control Density*, pp. 332–33, 337; 稲葉馨 [Kaoru Inaba] and others, 日独における行政裁量の現状比較：日独行政法シンポジウム『行政裁量とその裁判的統制』討論第一部 ['Comparison of Administrative Discretion in Japan and Germany: Panel Discussion Part 1 at the Japan-German Administrative Law Symposium on "Administrative Discretion and its Judicial Control"'], *Law Cases Reports (JPN)*, 1935 (2006), pp. 6–9.

order to fulfil the court's lack of expertise in highly technical and complex cases.[56]

After the TEPCO nuclear disaster, it became obvious that judicial review had failed to ensure nuclear safety, and the court was strongly criticised. On this issue, Professor Fujita, another former Supreme Court judge and a leading administrative law theorist, claimed that the court was able to review highly technical and complex cases without receiving input from experts. He criticised the court's over-reliance on first-instance decisions in cases of nuclear safety, for the following three reasons. First, the court had been able to evaluate the appropriateness of technical decisions made by experts in a variety of cases. Secondly, the court was not required to solicit expert knowledge from the expert panel as a first-instance decision maker, and did not rely on this knowledge in other environmental cases that were not related to nuclear safety. Thirdly, regarding potential nuclear safety risks, the court had to evaluate which party's claim was more rational, based on a comparison of arguments made by experts for both parties.[57] If his reforms were adopted, the quality of judicial review on highly technical and complex cases would be improved.

Still, it should be noted that the assumption of Fujita's argument is that the role of judicial review is to resolve individual cases:[58] in other words, judicial review is not necessarily suitable for addressing systemic problems. In actuality, for the TEPCO nuclear disaster, the NAIIC revealed that the nuclear regulator's independence from nuclear promoters had not been secured.[59] The NAIIC's findings were crucial in showing that the court's over-reliance on the first-instance administrative decisions was naive, irrational and wrong. Without the presence of an accountability mechanism designed to resolve systemic problems, such as the NAIIC and an ombudsman, the rationality of the reasoning widely employed by judicial review could not be ascertained.

---

[56] 園部逸夫 [Itsuo Sonobe], 最高裁判所十年 *[Things seen in Supreme Court of Japan]* (有斐閣 [Yuhikaku], 2001), pp. 284–85, 353 and 358–59; interview with 園部逸夫 [Itsuo Sonobe], former Supreme Court judge (Tokyo, 22 July 2011).

[57] 藤田宙靖 [Tokiyasu Fujita], 裁判と法律学：『最高裁回想録』補遺 *[Trial and Jurisprudence: Supplement to 'Reminiscence about Supreme Court of Japan']* (有斐閣 [Yuhikaku], 2016), pp. 148–58 and 178–82.

[58] Ibid., pp. 130–33 and 177–78.

[59] NAIIC, *The Official Report of the Fukushima Nuclear Accident Independent Investigation Commission*, Intro, pp. 16 and 39.

3   Post-TEPCO Nuclear Disaster Law Reform

The corrupted nuclear regulator was abolished in an attempt to take responsibility for the chaos in the emergency response of the TEPCO nuclear disaster. It was the NAIIC's statutory mandates to secure nuclear safety and to rebuild the collapsed administrative mechanisms and related institutions.[60] To fulfil its statutory mandate, the NAIIC issued seven recommendations in its report. On the matter of nuclear safety, it recommended the fundamental revision of the framework of emergency preparedness and response to a severe nuclear accident, the establishment of a new nuclear regulator that is completely independent of any nuclear promoter and accountable to the Diet, the upgrading of outdated nuclear regulations to global standards, the establishment of a succession institution of the NAIIC at the Diet, and the establishment of special committees at the Diet that oversee the activities of the new nuclear regulator.[61] It was clear that the NAIIC intended to introduce a parliamentary control scheme to ensure executive accountability.

Although special committees that scrutinise the activities of the new nuclear regulator were established in both houses of the Diet,[62] the NAIIC's other recommendations have not been fully implemented.[63] Moreover, the statutory mandates were ignored because of political considerations regarding the smooth resumption of nuclear power plant

---

[60] *NAIIC Establishment Law* (JPN), art. 1.

[61] NAIIC, *The Official Report of the Fukushima Nuclear Accident Independent Investigation Commission*, Intro, pp. 18–21.

[62] Japan, *Diet Debates*, House of Representatives, 27 January 2013, 1–2 (伊吹文明 [Bunmei Ibuki], Speaker); Japan, *Diet Debates*, House of Councillors, 26 January 2015, 1 (山崎正昭 [Masaaki Yamazaki], Speaker). Nevertheless, some MPs have utilised these Committees for nuclear promotion. 南彰 [Akira Minami], 国会事故調、進まぬ開示 ['The Diet Has Not Disclosed the Investigation Record of the NAIIC'] *Asahi Shimbun* (Tokyo, 25 September) 1.

[63] In May 2017, an Advisory Board of the Special Committee was established by the House of Representatives of Japan, based on a recommendation of the NAIIC. The president of the advisory board is the former Chair of the NAIIC, and the board's role is to provide expert advice to the Special Committee. However, it would be difficult to regard this board as a succession institution of the NAIIC because it was not established as an institution. Individual members of the board are expected to occasionally provide expert advice at the request of the Committee. Japan, *Diet Debates*, Special Committee on Investigation of Nuclear Power Issues at the House of Representatives, 25 May 2017, 1 (三原朝彦 [Asahiko Mihara], Chair of the Special Committee); Japan, *Diet Debates*, Special Committee on Investigation of Nuclear Power Issues at the House of Representatives, 12 June 2017, 1 (三原朝彦 [Asahiko Mihara], Chair of the Special Committee).

operations.[64] Before the establishment of the NAIIC, the government prepared its own proposals and promoted the legislation process.[65] Although the NAIIC protested such an under-evaluation of its authority,[66] the legislation process proceeded and the Law for Establishment of the Nuclear Regulation Authority (NRA Establishment Law) was enacted in June 2012.[67] The NAIIC then published its report in July 2012. As a result of political compromise, a revision of the NRA Establishment Law was promised within three years in order to reflect the contents of the NAIIC report and the latest global standards.[68] At the time of writing, this promise has not been fulfilled.

The new nuclear safety framework established by the NRA Establishment Law is not under parliamentary control. The newly established Nuclear Regulation Authority (NRA) is the key institution of the new framework, and it plays important roles in emergency preparedness and response to a severe nuclear accident.[69] The NRA is an agent of the Ministry of Environment and, relative to other Japanese administrative bodies, it is a highly independent body.[70] However, with regard to global standards, the NRA presents several weaknesses in terms of its independence from nuclear promoters.[71] This agency was designed to be

---

[64] 塩崎恭久 [Yasuhisa Shiozaki], ガバナンスを政治の手に：「原子力規制委員会」創設への闘い [To Realise Control of the Administrative Branch by the Legislature; Political Battles for Establishment of the Nuclear Regulation Authority of Japan] (東京プレスクラブ [Tokyo Press Club] 2012), pp. 109–10.

[65] 原田健成 [Tatenari Harada], 原子力規制委員会設置法について ['About the Law for Establishment of the Nuclear Regulation Authority'] Research Bureau Ronkyu (JPN), 9 (2012) pp. 209–14; 梶山知唯 [Tomotada Kajiyama], 法律解説 国会　内閣：原子力規制委員会設置法 平成二四年六月二七日法律第四七号 ['Commentary on the Law for Establishment of the Nuclear Regulation Authority', 27 June 2012, Law No 47 of H24] Source Book on Law Commentary (JPN), 373 (2013) p. 4.

[66] 黒川清 [Kiyoshi Kurokawa], Chair of the NAIIC, 'Statement of the Chair of the NAIIC on the Cabinet Decision on the Bills for Reform of Nuclear Safety Organisations' (Statement, 2 February 2012).

[67] 原子力規制委員会設置法 [Law for Establishment of the Nuclear Regulation Authority] (Japan) 27 June 2012, Law No. 47 of H24 (NRA Establishment Law); Harada, Essence of Administrative Law, pp. 215–19; Kajiyama, 'Commentary on the Law for Establishment of the Nuclear Regulation Authority', pp. 4–5.

[68] NRA Establishment Law (JPN), supplementary provision no. 5; Shiozaki, To Realise Control of the Administrative Branch by the Legislature, pp. 109–10.

[69] NRA Establishment Law (JPN), arts. 3, 4 and 22; Kajiyama, 'Commentary on the Law for Establishment of the Nuclear Regulation Authority', p. 5.

[70] NRA Establishment Law (JPN), art. 2.

[71] NRA Establishment Law (JPN), supplementary provision no. 6(2); Shiozaki, To Realise Control of the Administrative Branch by the Legislature, pp. 222–27; 松岡俊二

primarily accountable to the executive.[72] Thus, the extent to which the NRA can ensure executive accountability apart from governmental policies is questioned.[73] After the change of government in December 2012, the governmental policy returned to a focus on the promotion of nuclear energy. The NRA then excluded the effectiveness of emergency preparedness measures applied for a severe nuclear accident off site, which had been the assumption for resuming nuclear power plant operations after the TEPCO nuclear disaster, according to the new regulation criteria on nuclear safety.[74] Consequently, at the time of writing, five nuclear power plants were operating in Japan without effective emergency preparedness measures off site.[75] As such, the essence of the NAIIC's recommendations is not reflected in the new nuclear safety framework.

This outcome can be attributed in part to the fact that the NAIIC was a temporary institution that operated from December 2011 to October 2012. The NAIIC referred to the investigation commission scheme of the United States Congress as its model.[76] Thus, after the submission of its report, the NAIIC was quickly dissolved. When it was concluded that the NRA Establishment Law would be revised, the dissolution of the NAIIC was anticipated. Without the presence of an official

[Shunji Matsuoka], 師岡慎一 [Shinichi Morooka] and 黒川哲志 [Satoshi Kurokawa], 原子力規制委員会の社会的評価：3つの基準と3つの要件 [*Social Evaluation of Nuclear Regulation Authority: Three Standards and Three Requisites*] (早稲田大学出版部 [Waseda University Press], 2013), pp. 36–40.

[72] *NRA Establishment Law* (JPN), art. 24.

[73] Shiozaki, *To Realise Control of the Administrative Branch by the Legislature*, pp. 228–29; Matsuoka, Morooka and Kurokawa, *Social Evaluation of Nuclear Regulation Authority*, pp. 33, 40 and 48–51.

[74] 原子力規制委員会 [Nuclear Regulation Authority (NRA) (JPN)], 平成25年度年次報告 [*Annual Report for Financial Year 2013*] (2014), 33–36; 小池拓自 [Takuji Koike], 新規制基準と原子力発電所の再稼働：川内原発再稼働をめぐる論点を中心に ['New Regulation Criteria for Nuclear Safety and Restarting Operation of Nuclear Power Plants: Centring the Arguing Points about the Restarting Operation of Sendai Nuclear Power Plant'], *Issue Brief (JPN)*, 840 (2015) pp. 3–5 and 10–11.

[75] 電気事業連合会 [Federation of Electric Power Companies of Japan], 国内の原子力発電所の再稼働に向けた対応状況 ['Current Situation of Restarting Operations of Nuclear Power Plants in Japan'] (2017): www.fepc.or.jp/theme/re-operation/ (accessed 15 July 2017).

[76] 塩崎恭久 [Yasuhisa Shiozaki], 国会原発事故調査委員会：立法府からの挑戦状 [*Parliamentary Investigation Commission on Tokyo Electric Power Company's Fukushima Nuclear Power Plant Accident: The Legislature's Challenge to the Bureaucracy*] (東京プレスクラブ [Tokyo Press Club], 2011), pp. 36–51; Japan, *Diet Debates*, Permanent Committee on Budget at the House of Representatives, 16 May 2011, 12–13 (塩崎恭久 [Yasuhisa Shiozaki], Liberal Democratic Party: 菅直人 [Naoto Kan], Prime Minister).

follow-up mechanism, public pressure to implement the NAIIC's recommendations did not last over the long term. Although the former chair of the NAIIC has occasionally appealed to the importance of implementing the NAIIC's recommendations,[77] the influence of his appeal has been relatively limited.

4   Lessons Learnt from the TEPCO Nuclear Disaster Case

The TEPCO nuclear disaster case shows that the Japanese system of accountability mechanisms failed to ensure executive accountability. Both layers of the Japanese accountability system had an influence on the resolution of individual cases. However, the root cause of the TEPCO nuclear disaster was systemic, i.e. regulatory capture. Neither internal merits review nor judicial review was effective in correcting such systemic problems of maladministration, which is the very area of a parliamentary democracy in which ombudsman review is the most effective. Although the institution that revealed such systemic problems of maladministration acted as a parliamentary investigative commission, due to the lack of the layer of ombudsman review in the Japanese accountability system, Japan failed to hold the executive accountable in the area of nuclear safety. The consequence was the TEPCO nuclear disaster.

More importantly, regardless of the fact that the TEPCO nuclear disaster left vast financial and environmental debts to both current and future generations, the NAIIC's recommendations have not been fully implemented. This highlights the limitations of temporary institutions. If the NAIIC had been a permanent institution, such as an ombudsman, a different outcome may have resulted. Therefore, one of the most important tools of ombudsman review is its follow-up function, which increases the likelihood that recommendations will be implemented.[78] Moreover, ombudsman review can utilise relevant reports from other investigative

---

[77] 黒川清 [Kiyoshi Kurokawa], Former Chair of National Diet of Japan Fukushima Nuclear Accident Independent Investigation Commission (JPN), '討論会 「福島原発事故から3年経つ今、われわれは何を学んだか」 [Discussion: 'What we have learnt in these three years since the Fukushima Nuclear Accident']' (speech at the Japan National Press Club, Tokyo, 10 March 2014).

[78] Marc Hertogh, 'Coercion, Cooperation, and Control: Understanding the Policy Impact of Administrative Courts and the Ombudsman in the Netherlands', Law & Policy, 23 (2001), p. 63; interview with John McMillan, former Commonwealth and ACT Ombudsman (Canberra, 27 May 2011).

bodies.[79] In a socially significant case, such as the TEPCO nuclear disaster, ombudsman review would have played an important role. Thus, a lack of ombudsman review in the Japanese system of accountability mechanisms is believed to be a key factor that prevented the full implementation of the NAIIC's recommendations.

The TEPCO nuclear disaster case clearly highlights the importance of ombudsman review in securing the legitimacy of administrative environmental decisions. Without ombudsman review, systemic problems that can mislead judicial review are not easily identified and serious consequences are less likely to be curtailed. Without ombudsman review, addressing systemic problems in an appropriate way becomes more difficult and the same mistakes are likely to be repeated. Therefore, ombudsman review is vital in the environmental field.

D   Role of an Environmental Ombudsman in Ombudsman Review

This section examines the role of an environmental ombudsman within ombudsman review. An environmental ombudsman is a specialised body that conducts ombudsman review. Whether a specialised body must be established is not clear, and several arguments have been made for both sides. Representative arguments by proponents of such bodies suggest that a specialised body is able to improve the quality of reviews on first-instance decisions through the utilisation of expertise, thereby enabling better case management and entrenching new concepts. In contrast, representative arguments by opponents of such bodies suggest that expertise is not essential for qualitative reviews, the running costs of a specialised body and caseload are not always balanced and a specialised body can be dominated by the subject of review.[80] Accordingly, whether there is a need for the specialised body in ombudsman review is also arguable. On this point, a lesson could be learned from the Japanese case. In the case of the TEPCO nuclear disaster, the expert body revealed the root cause of the man-made disaster within seven months. On the other hand, the general body failed to recognise

---

[79] See, e.g., André Marin, *Oversight Undermined: Investigation into the Ministry of the Attorney General's implementation of recommendations concerning reform of the Special Investigations Unit* (Ombudsman Ontario (ONT), 2011), pp. 7, 11, 15, 33–34, 41–42, 49–50, 55–56 and 59–63.

[80] Pring and Pring, *Greening Justice*, pp. 13–18.

structural problems for four decades, because it refused to review the appropriateness of first-instance decisions due to its lack of expertise. This finding clearly shows the effectiveness and efficiency of the specialised bodies. Furthermore, the root cause was found to be systemic. Thus, the involvement of specialised bodies in ombudsman review is vital.

The above findings indicate that the expected role of an environmental ombudsman is to address systemic problems with expertise on environmental issues. However, whether individual environmental ombudsman offices actually fulfil this role must be examined. As noted in Subsection B.1, an ombudsman generally addresses systemic problems through self-initiated investigations.[81] Thus, it is assumed that, to fulfil this role, an environmental ombudsman must be able to conduct expert review of self-initiated investigations. Hence, the question whether the environmental ombudsman offices in the ACT, New Zealand and Hungary have had bestowed on them the power to exercise these abilities is examined in the following section. In cases in which these offices have the requisite power, whether such powers are actually exercised is also examined. Then, because an environmental ombudsman participates in ombudsman review, its relationships to general ombudsman operations are addressed.

1 Abilities of an Environmental Ombudsman

Of the abilities required of an environmental ombudsman to fulfil its role, expertise on environmental issues is fundamental to conducting expert review. All three environmental ombudsman offices clearly had sufficient expertise. In the ACT, the CSE was tasked with enhancing the accountability of environmental outcomes to balance economic and environmental interests.[82] In New Zealand, the PCE was established to oversee environmental administration.[83] In Hungary, the PCFG was established to protect the constitutional right to a healthy environment.[84]

---

[81] Gregory, 'The Ombudsman', p. 117.
[82] Australian Capital Territory, *Parliamentary Debates*, Legislative Assembly, 16 June 1993, 1957 (Lou Westende).
[83] New Zealand, Parliamentary Debates, House of Representatives, 15 July 1986, 2980 (P. B. Goff, Minister of Housing, Minister for the Environment).
[84] *1993. évi LIX. törvény az állampolgári jogok országgyűlési biztosáról* [Act LIX of 1993 on the Parliamentary Commissioner for Civil Rights (Ombudsman)] (Hungary), 1 June 1993, *Magyar Közlöny*, No. 1993/81, 4433, art. 27/A.

Regarding the power to conduct self-initiated investigations, the three institutions, had such power bestowed on them, directly or indirectly. In the ACT, the CSE investigations proceeded as follows: based on complaints regarding issues of administrative environmental management in the territory; based on matters directed by the minister; and based on matters with substantial environmental impacts according to its own initiative.[85] In New Zealand, the PCE reviewed the systems of agencies and their administrative procedures to report results to Parliament and other appropriate bodies or persons. The office investigated the effectiveness of the environmental planning and management of public authorities and advised on any remedial actions. It also investigated any matter that adversely affected the environment, advised on preventive measures and recommended remedial actions to the appropriate public authority and to any other person or body. In addition to executing these self-initiated actions, the PCE had the following duties. At the request of Parliament, the office reported on any petition, bill or other matter that might have a significant effect on the environment.[86] In Hungary, a wide range of powers, including the authority of self-initiated investigation, was bestowed on the PCFG. In handling complaints, in addition to the powers of the ombudsman, the PCFG was given a wide range of authorities to ensure sustainability and improve the quality of the environment.[87] Further, the PCFG functioned as a 'parliamentary advocate'. For this purpose, the office holder had duties at both national and international levels. At the national level, the office holder expressed opinions on environment-related bills or other draft instruments, proposed legislation, and expressed opinions on long-term plans and local government development plans. At the international level, the office holder expressed opinions on obligatory international environmental agreements, contributed to the preparation of national reports to be submitted on such agreements, and monitored the incorporation of these agreements into the Hungarian legal system. The office holder also participated in the elaboration of the Hungarian stance on environmental issues in the European Union.[88]

---

[85] Commissioner for the Environment Act 1993 (ACT), s. 12(1).

[86] Environment Act 1986 (NZ), s. 16(1)(a)–(d).

[87] Act LIX of 1993 on the Parliamentary Commissioner for Civil Rights (HUN), arts. 27/B(1)–(2).

[88] Act LIX of 1993 on the Parliamentary Commissioner for Civil Rights (HUN), arts. 27/B(3)(e)–(h).

However, such authorities do not automatically mean that the three institutions fully exercised these bestowed powers. Thus, the practices of each institution are reviewed by examining statistical data on each environmental ombudsman, to reveal how each office exercised its power to conduct self-initiated investigation. In the ACT, the CSE rarely launched self-initiated investigations but conducted a few investigations directed by the minister,[89] which was attributed to the CSE's focus on the resolution of individual cases.[90] However, as part of the ministry, the CSE's discretion to conduct self-initiated investigations was undeniably limited by the minister's policies and resources.[91] In New Zealand, the PCE conducted certain number of self-initiated investigations.[92] In actuality, the PCE focused on systemic review of policy matters and was less focused on resolution of individual cases.[93] In Hungary, the PCFG eagerly conducted self-initiated investigations.[94] In actuality, it regarded the resolution of systemic problems as a major focus.[95]

The above findings show that bestowed powers, as well as independence, are crucial for environmental ombudsman offices to fulfil their expected roles.

---

[89] Commissioner for Sustainability and the Environment (ACT), *Annual Report 2008–09* (Office of the Commissioner for Sustainability and the Environment 2009), 14; Commissioner for Sustainability and the Environment (ACT), *Annual Report 2009–10* (Office of the Commissioner for Sustainability and the Environment 2010), 48; Commissioner for Sustainability and the Environment (ACT), *Annual Report 2010–11* (Office of the Commissioner for Sustainability and the Environment 2011), 11.

[90] Interview with Sarah Burrows, Senior Manager, Commissioner for Sustainability and Environment (Canberra, 31 May 2011).

[91] Interview with Ian Baird, Principal Policy Officer, ACT Department of the Environment, Climate Change, Energy and Water (Canberra, 30 May 2011).

[92] Parliamentary Commissioner for the Environment (NZ), *Annual Report for the year ended 30 June 2009* (The Parliamentary Commissioner for the Environment 2009), pp. 7–13; Parliamentary Commissioner for the Environment (NZ), *Annual Report for the year ended 30 June 2010* (The Parliamentary Commissioner for the Environment 2010), pp. 7–14; Parliamentary Commissioner for the Environment (NZ), *Annual Report for the year ended 30 June 2011* (The Parliamentary Commissioner for the Environment 2011), pp. 7–16.

[93] Interview with Clark.

[94] Parliamentary Commissioner for Future Generations (HUN), *A Jövő Nemzedékek Országgyűlési Biztosának Beszámolója 2008–2009 [Report of the Parliamentary Commissioner for Future Generations of Hungary 2008–2009]* (Office of the Parliamentary Commissioners (HUN) 2010), pp. 283–84; Parliamentary Commissioner for Future Generations (HUN), *Beszámoló: A Jövő Nemzedékek Országgyűlési Biztosának 2010. évi Tevékenységéről [Report of the Hungarian Parliamentary Commissioner for Future Generations 2010]* (Office of the Parliamentary Commissioners (HUN) 2011), pp. 330–32.

[95] Interview with Fülöp.

2   Relationship with the General Ombudsman

The establishment of an environmental ombudsman does not automatically mean that a general ombudsman does not review environmental cases. Thus, the role of a general ombudsman in environmental matters in each jurisdiction must be clarified. To understand the role of an environmental ombudsman in ombudsman review, it is also necessary to examine the relationships between general and environmental ombudsman offices.

In the ACT, the ACT Ombudsman had no limitation in investigating environmental matters.[96] Conversely, the CSE was obliged to refer complaints that overlapped with the ombudsman's jurisdiction to the general ombudsman.[97] However, based on an agreement between both institutions, the CSE handled such cases in practice.[98] Even so, the ombudsman accepted a small number of environment-related cases, and some of them were investigated,[99] which could be attributed to differences in the focuses of investigations. While the ombudsman was focused on procedural matters, the CSE covered substantive issues.[100] Furthermore, the ombudsman welcomed the CSE's assistance in resolving problems caused by the general ombudsman office's limited capacities with its specialised focus.[101] Thus, in the ACT, there was no conflict over the jurisdictions of the CSE and the ombudsman.

In New Zealand, the Parliamentary Ombudsman was not limited in their capacity to investigate environmental cases.[102] The general ombudsman was not particularly active in environmental issues, which was partly due to limited resources.[103] However, in practice, many environmental complaints were brought to the ombudsman. For instance, ombudsman David McGee explained that approximately 5 per cent of total complaints related to challenging planning

---

[96] Ombudsman Act 1989 (ACT), s. 5.

[97] Commissioner for the Environment Act 1993 (ACT), s. 25.

[98] Australian Capital Territory Ombudsman (ACT), *Annual Report 2010–2011* (ACT Ombudsman 2011), p. 35.

[99] Australian Capital Territory Ombudsman (ACT), *Annual Report 2008–2009* (ACT Ombudsman 2009), p. 33; Australian Capital Territory Ombudsman (ACT), *Annual Report 2009–2010* (ACT Ombudsman 2010), p. 33; ACT Ombudsman, p. 41.

[100] Interview with Julia Pitts, Chair, Environmental Defender's Office (ACT) (Canberra, 30 May 2011).

[101] Interview with McMillan.

[102] Ombudsmen Act 1975 (NZ), s. 13(1), ch. 1.

[103] Sir Brian Elwood, 'Session 2 Plenary' in Gary Hawke (ed.), *Guardians for the Environment* (Institute of Policy Science, Victoria University of Wellington, 1997), p. 70.

decisions.[104] In addition, a few of these environment-related complaints were thoroughly investigated and referenced in annual or special reports.[105] However, such investigations focused on issues of administrative management or on damage to individuals rather than on environmental damage itself. The ombudsman recognised that expert review of environmental matters was the PCE's responsibility.[106] Further, a strong belief in the separation of functions among parliamentary officers was observed at the institutional design level. McGee described the rationale when noting that preventing the 'danger of duplication of the work ... [is] a better use of public resources'.[107] In relation to the PCE, the ombudsman emphasised the necessity of the distinction between advocacy and complaints-handling roles.[108] As the most notable reflection of this philosophy, the ombudsman did not focus on systemic issues in order to concentrate on managing individual cases that were not covered by other specialist reviewers.[109] In addition, the two institutions cooperated to maintain these divisions. For instance, complaints submitted to the PCE could be dispatched to the ombudsman according to their content.[110] Furthermore, the PCE and the ombudsman met approximately six times each year to share experiences and prevent jurisdictional conflicts.[111]

In Hungary, the jurisdiction of a special ombudsman was strictly distinct from that of the general ombudsman,[112] so that the jurisdictions did not overlap. The PCFG was established in the 2008 financial year.[113]

---

[104] Interview with McGee.

[105] Parliamentary Ombudsmen (NZ), *Report of the Ombudsmen for the Year Ended 30 June 2007* (Office of the Ombudsmen 2007), pp. 21–22; Parliamentary Ombudsmen (NZ), *2007/2008 Report of the Ombudsmen for the Year Ended 30 June 2008* (Office of the Ombudsmen 2008), pp. 22–23; Parliamentary Ombudsmen (NZ), *Report of the Opinion of Ombudsmen Mel Smith on Complaints Arising from Aerial Spraying of the Biological Insecticide Foray 48B on the Population of Parts of Auckland and Hamilton to Destroy Incursions of Painted Apple Moths, and Asian Gypsy Moths, Respectively During 2002–2004* (2007).

[106] Elwood, 'Session 2 Plenary', p. 70; interview with McGee.

[107] Interview with McGee.

[108] Elwood, 'Session 2 Plenary', p. 70.

[109] Interview with McGee.

[110] Interview with Clark; interview with Morgan Williams, former Parliamentary Commissioner for the Environment (Wellington, 10 June 2011).

[111] Interview with Williams.

[112] Act LIX of 1993 on the Parliamentary Commissioner for Civil Rights (HUN), art. 2(2).

[113] Parliamentary Commissioner for Future Generations (HUN), *Comprehensive Summary of the Report of the Parliamentary Commissioner for Future Generations of Hungary 2008–2009* (Office of the Parliamentary Commissioners (HUN) 2010), p. 7.

The statistical data show that, after the establishment of the PCFG, the number of environmental cases investigated by the Parliamentary Commissioner for Civil Rights dramatically declined.[114] Moreover, the establishment of the PCFG strictly divided the jurisdictions between ombudsman offices. However, this division also encouraged daily disputes between the general ombudsman and other specialised ombudsman offices, about which institutions should handle complaints from the public.[115] Under this setting, the general ombudsman initiated the reform of the ombudsman scheme to eliminate disputes between ombudsman offices over jurisdiction and establish overall control.[116] This decision was deeply related to the institution's philosophy. The general ombudsman's main concern was the balancing of environmental and other rights with a focus on the interests of the current generation. This approach was advantageous because it allowed for compromise and consensus.[117] Conversely, the PCFG's priority was the protection of environmental rights with a focus on protecting the environment for future generations.[118] Unfortunately, clashes over this difference in philosophy provoked the abolition of the PCFG.

These findings show that relationships with a general ombudsman are central to an environmental ombudsman's capacity to fulfil its role. Even when sufficient powers are bestowed upon it and it is fully independent from the subject of oversight, an environmental ombudsman is likely to face difficulties in exercising its powers when a good relationship is not maintained with a general ombudsman.

---

[114] Parliamentary Commissioner for Civil Rights (HUN), *Beszámoló: az Állampolgári Jogok Országgyűlési Biztosának Tevékenységéről 2007 [Annual Report on the Activities of the Parliamentary Commissioner for Civil Rights in 2007]* (Office of the Parliamentary Commissioner (HUN) 2008), pp. 257–76; Parliamentary Commissioner for Civil Rights (HUN), *Beszámoló: az Állampolgári Jogok Országgyűlési Biztosának 2008. évi Tevékenységéről [Report on the Activities of the Parliamentary Commissioner for Civil Rights in the Year 2008]* (Office of the Parliamentary Commissioner (HUN) 2009), pp. 1141–52; Parliamentary Commissioner for Civil Rights (HUN), *Beszámoló: az Állampolgári Jogok Országgyűlési Biztosának 2009. évi Tevékenységéről [Report on the Activities of the Parliamentary Commissioner for Civil Rights in the Year 2009]* (Office of the Parliamentary Commissioner (HUN) 2010), pp. 1575–86.

[115] Interview with Vajk Farkas, Lawyer, Ministry of Public Administration and Justice (Budapest, 28 June 2011); interview with MP Benedek Jávor, Chair, Sustainable Development Committee at the National Assembly of Hungary (Budapest, 24 June 2011).

[116] Interview with Farkas.

[117] Interview with Lenkovics.

[118] Interview with Fülöp.

E   Role of an Environmental Ombudsman in the System of Accountability Mechanisms

In conclusion, the role of an environmental ombudsman in the system of accountability mechanisms is to provide expert review on systemic problems of administrative environmental decision making. This role is central to ensuring executive accountability and the legitimacy of administrative decisions in the environmental field. As is shown in the Japanese case, when this function is not present, serious environmental disasters can occur. This role cannot be substituted by either judicial review or merits review institutions. Even in ombudsman review, the role should be played by an environmental ombudsman as a specialised body. However, to fulfil this role, an environmental ombudsman must be afforded sufficient powers and independence and must build a strong relationship with its general ombudsman. Otherwise, environmental ombudsman offices may not be able to play, or continue to play, this essential role in society. For jurisdictions, such as Japan, that do not currently conduct expert review and review of systemic problems, it is reasonable to examine the feasibility of introducing of this legal institution.

16

The Role of NGOs in Monitoring Compliance under the World Heritage Convention: Options for an Improved Tripartite Regime

EVAN HAMMAN

A   Introduction

Global governance today involves more than just governments.[1] Non-State actors, such as non-governmental organisations (NGOs), have emerged as powerful forces on the international stage including in setting global agendas and shaping conservation outcomes.[2] As outsiders (and sometimes as insiders[3]) NGOs have the capacity quickly to absorb and disseminate information and to promote compliance with standards set by international protocols, treaties and other norms.[4] In the literature, the role and legitimacy of NGOs under multilateral environmental agreements (MEAs) is increasingly well studied.[5] Most recently, scholars such as Nasiritousi and Bäckstrand have focused on NGO presence and

---

[1] J. Rosenau and E. Czempiel, *Governance without Government: Order and Change in World Politics* (Cambridge University Press, 1992), p. 4.

[2] See N. Gunningham et al., *Smart Regulation: Designing Environmental Policy* (Oxford University Press, 1998); and A. Gillespie, 'Facilitating and Controlling Civil Society in International Environmental Law', *Review of European, Comparative & International Environmental Law*, 15 (2006), 327–338.

[3] See the language of 'inside' and 'outside' track strategies used in H. Stokke, *Taking the inside or outside track – or both? NGO advocacy in State reporting under the Child Rights Convention: a case study from Kenya* (CMI Report, 2015): www.cmi.no/publications/file/5529-taking-the-inside-or-outside-track-or-both.pdf (accessed 13 July 2017).

[4] B. Gemmill and A. Bamidele-Izu, 'The Role of NGOs and Civil Society in Global Environmental Governance' in D. Esty and M. Ivanova (eds.), *Global Environmental Governance: Options and Opportunities* (Yale, 2002), pp. 77–100.

[5] B. Arts, *The Political Influence of Global NGOs: Case Studies on the Climate and Biodiversity Conventions* (Utrecht, 1998); and C. Pitea, 'The Compliance Procedure of the Aarhus Convention: Between Environmental and Human Rights Control Mechanisms' in N. Ronzitti (ed.), *XVI The Italian Yearbook of International Law* (Martin Nijhoff Publishers, 2007), pp. 85–116; and F. Cumming, 'The Role of NGOs in

influence under the climate change regime.[6] Others, such as Green, have focused on the place of non-State actors as 'governors' in transnational environmental frameworks, predicting that, in the future, 'we should [expect to] see more, not less delegation'.[7] But how legitimate and effective are the activities of NGOs? Can they contribute meaningfully to questions of compliance under international environmental law?[8] And, if so, what mechanisms and measures do NGOs use to exert such influence?

This chapter explores the role of NGOs in monitoring State Party compliance under the Convention Concerning the Protection of the World Cultural and Natural Heritage (hereafter the 'World Heritage Convention' or simply the 'Convention').[9] The chapter begins by defining the concept of regulation and setting out clearly what is meant by 'monitoring'. This discussion is followed by an overview of the World Heritage Convention, including setting out the main duties and obligations under the Convention and the regulatory bodies that

---

multi-lateral environmental agreement compliance', *New Zealand Journal of Environmental Law*, 17 (2013), 41–80.

[6] See N. Nasiritousi et al., 'The roles of non-State actors in climate change governance: understanding agency through governance profiles', *International Environmental Agreements: Politics, Law and Economics*, 16(1) (2016), 109–126; T. Böhmelt et al., 'Civil society participation in global governance: Insights from climate politics', *European Journal of Political Research*, 53(1) (2013), 18–36; and J. Kuyper and K. Bäckstrand, 'Accountability and Representation: Non-State actors in UN climate diplomacy', *Global Environmental Politics*, 16(2) (2016).

[7] J. Green, 'Transnational delegation in global environmental governance: When do non-State actors govern?', *Regulation & Governance* 1 (2017), 1–14, 14.

[8] It should be noted that compliance is not the same as 'implementation'. Nor, for that matter, is it the same as 'effectiveness'. Generally, implementation refers to what is done by the State at a domestic level 'to live up to [its] international commitments', whereas compliance refers to the provisions 'elaborated at the international level' and the actions taken by States to meet them. See P. Haas, S. Andresson and N. Kanie, 'Introduction: Actor Configurations and Global Environmental Governance' in N. Kanie, S. Andresson, and P. Haas (eds.), *Improving Global Environmental Governance: Best Practices for Architecture and Agency* (Routledge, 2014), p. 15. For the distinction between implementation, compliance and effectiveness, see H. Jacobson, and E. B Weiss, 'Strengthening Compliance with International Environmental Accords: Preliminary Observations from a Collaborative Project', *Global Governance*, 1(2) (1995), 119–148.

[9] As noted above, compliance is separate from effectiveness and implementation, but it is able to be dissected further. Jacobson and Weiss, for example, talk about the differences between 'procedural compliance', 'substantive compliance' and 'spirit of the treaty compliance'. This chapter is concerned largely with procedural compliance – that is, the question of whether and how a State is able to meet the reporting and other administrative requirements of the regime. See P. Le Prestre, *Governing Global Biodiversity: The Evolution and Implementation of the Convention on Biological Diversity* (Routledge, 2017), ch. 3.

administer them. The chapter then moves on to give examples of ways in which NGOs have used petitions as a mechanism for monitoring State behaviour. In its most basic form, a petition is a written instrument given from an individual to a State to address a grievance.[10] In the case of World Heritage, petitions have been used by NGOs to bring issues of non-compliance to the attention of the World Heritage Committee (the primary decision-making body under the regime). While the Committee eventually accepted their petitions, there is no formal process or format for their use and thus the legal status and impact of petitioning are highly questionable.

Accordingly, this chapter argues that the World Heritage system needs stronger and clearer mechanisms for enrolling NGOs in regulatory activities. To do this, NGOs need to be authorised and incentivised to take part. The text of the Convention need not be changed, but some of the institutional bodies that administer the framework will need to relinquish some regulatory power. The arguments in this chapter are drawn from broader regulatory theory (or theories) such as tripartism,[11] surrogate regulation[12] and regulatory enrolment.[13] These theories make the case for a more 'hands on' role for NGOs as 'regulatory partners' as opposed to mere observers or 'consultants'.[14] Questions about accountability and legitimacy of NGOs will likely raise their heads, but the politics and 'diplomatisation' of World Heritage[15] urgently require new ideas about how to improve State compliance with the regime. One way of doing that is to consider bringing a broader suite of actors into the regulatory game.

---

[10] See *Encyclopaedia Britannica*, 'Petition': www.britannica.com/topic/petition-law (last accessed 13 July 2017).

[11] I. Ayres and J. Braithwaite, 'Tripartism: Regulatory Capture and Empowerment', *Law and Social Inquiry*, 16(3) (1991), 435–496.

[12] N. Gunningham, M. Phillipson and P. Grabosky, 'Harnessing Third Parties as Surrogate Regulators: Achieving environmental outcomes by alternative means', *Bus. Strat. Env.*, 8(4) (1999), 211–224.

[13] J. Black, 'Enrolling Actors in Regulatory Processes: Examples from UK Financial Services Regulation', *Public Law*, 1 (2003), 62–90.

[14] This is a shift that appears to have been taking place for some time. See P. Willetts, 'From "consultative arrangements" to "partnership": The changing status of NGOs in diplomacy at the UN', *Glob. Gov.*, 6(2) (2000), 191–212.

[15] H. Hølleland, 'Practicing World Heritage: Approaching the changing faces of the World Heritage Convention', unpublished PhD thesis, University of Oslo (2013), p. 87.

B   NGOs and Their Role as Regulators

In the past, understanding exactly what NGOs were doing in world politics was not an easy task.[16] Were they consultants? Were they watchdogs? Were they partners? Or were they simply there to further their own agenda? Part of the problem was (and still is) that the term 'NGO' is an amorphous concept, and any attempts to define it have been met with criticism and uncertainty.[17] Underlying this is the fact that NGOs come in many different shapes and sizes. Some are concerned with human rights, others with conservation, and others still with broader principles such as transparency, access to justice and accountability. The main difficulty in categorising NGO activities is thus due to the 'tremendous diversity found in the NGO community'.[18] Or, as Beer and others succinctly put it, 'rigid definitional schemes [about NGOs tend to] break down under the diversity of organisations [that exist]'.[19]

Nevertheless, over the last twenty years, various discourses in international relations, environmental law and the social sciences have explored the link between NGOs and improved forms of governance. New and impressive analytical frameworks are being developed and fine tuned, including, for example, concepts such as New Environmental Governance[20] and Biermann and others' research into Earth System Governance.[21] These ideas are related, conceptually at least, to theories of decentralised and pluralistic governance in which NGOs play a role over and above mere observers in environmental affairs. Theories such as tripartism, surrogate regulation and enrolment (mentioned in the introduction) claim that NGOs act not only as lobbyists, advocates and campaigners, but can also be 'service providers' and even 'regulators'.[22]

---

[16] T. Princen and M. Finger, *Environmental NGOs in World Politics: Linking the Local and the Global* (Routledge, 1994).

[17] K. Martens, 'Mission Impossible? Defining Nongovernmental Organizations', *International Journal of Voluntary and Non-profit Organizations'*, 13(3) (2002), 271–285.

[18] T. Princen and M. Finger, *Environmental NGOs in World Politics: Linking the Local and the Global* (Routledge, 1994), p. 43.

[19] C. Beer, T. Bartley and W. Roberts, 'NGOs: Between Advocacy, Service Provision and Regulation' (chapter 23) in D. Levi-Faur (ed.), *The Oxford Handbook on Governance* (Oxford University Press, 2012), p. 326.

[20] C. Holley et al., 'The New Environmental Governance', *Journal of Environmental Law*, 25 (2013), 161–163.

[21] Biermann et al., 'Accountability and Legitimacy in Earth System Governance: A Research Framework', *Ecological Economics*, 70 (2011). 1856–1864.

[22] See C. Beer, T. Bartley and W. Roberts, 'NGOs: Between Advocacy, Service Provision and Regulation' in D. Levi-Faur (ed.), *The Oxford Handbook on Governance* (Oxford University Press, 2012). For non-State actors as regulators generally, see B. Hutter,

But what do we mean by the concept of regulation? And what regulatory role could (or do) NGOs play in World Heritage?

Regulation is defined functionally in this chapter as having three core elements: (1) standard setting; (2) monitoring; and (3) enforcement (or some form of 'behaviour modification'). These three elements seem to be common across most definitions of regulation in the literature.[23] The term 'standards' refers generally to the 'norms, goals, objectives, or rules' around which a regime is structured.[24] Thus, the action of standard setting refers to the activities surrounding the creation or development of suitable goals or objectives. Standards are central to the definition of regulation, such that, without standards, there can be no regulation.[25]

The second element of regulation, monitoring, covers actions such as inspections, requests and provision of information, analyses of trends or unexplained issues or impacts. In short, monitoring (or 'compliance monitoring' as some refer to it[26]) involves: 'checking up on whether those covered by [standards] are doing (or not doing) what is required of (or forbidden to) them'.[27] A similar definition of monitoring is provided by Tandon and Kak: 'the checking, collecting and analysis of information about current projects'.[28] Other definitions of monitoring

'The role of non-State actors in Regulation', *CARR Discussion Chapters* DP 37 (2006); and J. Black 'Legitimacy and the Competition for Regulatory Share', 14/09 LSE Working Chapters (2009): www.lse.ac.uk/collections/law/wps/WPS2009-14_Black.pdf (last accessed 13 July 2017).

[23] See, for example, D. Levi-Faur (ed.), *Handbook on the Politics of Regulation* (Edward Elgar, 2011), p. 6; and B. Hutter, 'The role of non-State actors in Regulation'. Hutter refers to the third element (enforcement) as some form of 'behaviour modification'.

[24] C. Scott, 'Standard Setting in Regulatory Regimes' in R. Baldwin, M. Cave, and M. Lodge (eds.), *The Oxford Handbook of Regulation* (Oxford University Press, 2010), p. 104.

[25] Non-State actors can, of course, play a role in standard setting, and many of the MEAs that exist today, such as the Convention on Biological Diversity (CBD), the Convention on International Trade in Endangered Species of Wild Fauna and Flora (CITES) and the Ramsar Convention on Wetlands of International Importance (Ramsar) are the result of attention from global organisations such as the World Wildlife Fund for Nature (WWF) and the International Union for the Conservation of Nature (IUCN).

[26] R. Mitchell, 'International Environmental Agreements; A Survey of Their Features, Formation, and Effects', *Annu. Rev. Environ. Resources*, 28 (2003), 429.

[27] C. Russell, 'Monitoring and Enforcement' in P. Portney (ed.) Public Policies for Environmental Protection (Resources for the Future, Washington, D.C., 1990). See also C. Dion, P. Lanoie and B. Laplante, 'Monitoring of Pollution Regulation: Do Local Conditions Matter?', *Journal of Regulatory Economics*, 13 (1998), 5.

[28] R. Tandon, and M. Kak, *Citizen Participation and Democratic Governance, in Our Hands* (Concept Publishing, 2007), p. 175.

make reference to 'indications of the achievements (or lack thereof) of [intended] results' by regulated parties.[29]

Finally, the third element of regulation, enforcement, involves more than merely checking up on a regulated body's behaviour. As Russell points out, it includes actions that seek to 'force violators to mend their ways'.[30] As Peel and Sands point out, in the context of international environmental law, enforcement also entails a 'right' to take measures to 'ensure the fulfilment of international legal obligations or to obtain a ruling [by an appropriate Court or other recognised body]'.[31] It might be added that enforcement must involve an actor, whether State or non-State, with some level of 'authority' to 'perforce violators' in relation to a breach. Presumably this is what Peel and Sands refer to when they talk about 'a right [to take measures]'.

By and large, this chapter is concerned with NGOs as monitors in World Heritage. In other words, it is concerned with how NGOs calibrate (or attempt to calibrate) State behaviour against the duties and obligations set out in the regime. The next section of the chapter gives background to the World Heritage framework. It discusses the operation and structure of the Convention, the powers of the World Heritage Committee and the role of the Advisory Bodies and the Secretariat. It also covers the main duties under the Convention and the non-compliance tools available to these bodies.

C The World Heritage Convention

1 Background and Context

The World Heritage Convention was adopted on 16 November 1972 and came into force in December 1975. The Convention has been widely ratified and now has 193 Member States. In the years leading up to the Convention, international concern had grown about the depletion of natural resources around the world as well as destruction of or damage to cultural property during the Second World War.[32] Several further

---

[29] See C. Nelson, 'Exploring monitoring and evaluation within a good governance perspective: A case study of Stellenbosch Municipality', unpublished Masters' thesis, Stellenbosch University (2016), p. 9.

[30] C. Russell, (1990), p. 243.

[31] J. Peel and P. Sands, *Principles of International Environmental Law* (Cambridge University Press, 2012), p. 144.

[32] For a history of the development of the Convention, particularly the early years, see M. Batisse and G. Bolla (eds.), *The Invention of World Heritage* (Association of Former UNESCO Staff Members (AFUS), 2005).

events, in particular, had caused the international community great concern, especially the construction of the Aswan High Dam in Egypt and the resultant risk to the great historical monuments of Nubia (including the Abu Simbel temples).[33]

The World Heritage Convention creates a list of sites (i.e. the World Heritage List) that have 'Outstanding Universal Value' (OUV).[34] Prospective sites must first be put forward by the State where they are located, on a Tentative List.[35] Thereafter, sites may progress to be included on the World Heritage List for either their natural values, their cultural values, or both (known as 'mixed sites'). The final decision is made by an intergovernmental body known as the World Heritage Committee upon advice from its three Advisory Bodies: The International Union for the Conservation of Nature (IUCN); the International Council on Monuments and Sites (ICOMOS) and the International Centre for the Study of the Preservation and Restoration of Cultural Property (ICCROM). There are currently 1,092 sites on the World Heritage List: 845 cultural sites; 209 natural sites; and 38 mixed sites. Statistically, therefore, natural and mixed sites make up only 22 per cent of all World Heritage sites. The World Heritage List has thus been considered 'imbalanced'.[36]

The term 'OUV' is the cornerstone of the Convention and refers specifically to sites that are: 'so exceptional as to transcend national boundaries and to be of common importance for present and future generations of all humanity'.[37] In practice, however, inclusion on the World Heritage List provides for more than just an expression of OUV. As Webb remarks, World Heritage listing creates a 'complex map of organisational and individual meanings'.[38] It can be a recognition of the

---

[33] See B. Lausche, *Weaving a Web of Environmental law* (Schmidt, 2008). See also ibid., p. 15.

[34] See Article 11(2) of the Convention. See also chapter 2 of UNESCO World Heritage Centre, *Operational Guidelines for the Implementation of the World Heritage Convention* (revised July 2016). For a thorough commentary on the concept of OUV, see S. Titchens, 'On the construction of outstanding universal value: UNESCO's World Heritage Convention and the identification and assessment of cultural places for inclusion in the World Heritage List', unpublished PhD thesis, Australian National University (1995).

[35] UNESCO World Heritage Centre, Operational Guidelines, para. 63.

[36] P. Figgis, A. Leverington, R. Mackay, A. Maclean and P. Valentine (eds.), *Keeping the Outstanding Exceptional: The Future of World Heritage in Australia* (Australian Committee for IUCN, 2012), p. 50.

[37] UNESCO World Heritage Centre, Operational Guidelines, para. 49.

[38] T. Webb, 'The meanings of World Heritage: a study of environmentalists and World Heritage managers with respect to the Great Barrier Reef World Heritage Area', unpublished PhD thesis, James Cook University (2000), p. 6.

value or quality of place,[39] a 'status symbol' or 'accolade' for the State,[40] a badge of honour,[41] or indeed 'just another layer' in an already complex and overcrowded domestic regulatory framework.[42] Whether and which of these conceptions applies are largely empirical questions which will vary from site to site. An iconic World Heritage property such as Australia's Great Barrier Reef, for instance, might start as a badge of honour, but, over time, transition towards a sense of obligation.[43]

2   The World Heritage Bodies

Several key institutional bodies play a role under the Convention. The World Heritage Committee (the 'Committee') is the chief decision-making body. It is a rotating body of twenty-one State Parties, which operates according to certain Rules of Procedure.[44] The Rules of Procedure set out, for example, details about voting rights and which bodies (including NGOs) can attend as 'observers' or 'consultants' at Committee meetings.[45] The Committee has several functions under the Convention, including: deciding on whether proposed sites should be included on the World Heritage List; examining the ongoing State of conservation of sites; and deciding whether sites could be added to the List of World Heritage In Danger (the 'In Danger List'). The Committee has been described as an 'executive authority' that enjoys a degree of 'coercive' power over the Convention.[46] In another light, we might also consider the Committee to have a quasi-judicial role, given its power to decide on key compliance issues such as whether to include a site on the In Danger List, or delete it from the World Heritage List altogether (see below).

---

[39] Ibid., p. 210.

[40] Ibid.

[41] Ibid., p. 212.

[42] Ibid., p. 216.

[43] Ibid., p. 204.

[44] Intergovernmental Committee for the Protection of the World Cultural and Natural Heritage, Rules of Procedure of the World Heritage Committee, adopted by the General Conference of UNESCO at its seventeenth session on 16 November 1972 and most recently revised by the World Heritage Committee at its thirty-ninth session (Bonn, 2015).

[45] Ibid., rules 7 and 8.

[46] See E. Goodwin 'The World Heritage Convention, the environment, and compliance', Colorado Journal of International Environmental Law and Policy, 20(2) (2009), 157–179, 157.

The World Heritage Centre, established in 1992, is a part of the United Nations Educational, Scientific and Cultural Organization (UNESCO) and is the official secretariat for the Convention. The Centre has several specialised roles, which include: organising the meetings of the Committee; implementing the decisions of the Committee; organising the periodic reporting process, and coordinating and partaking in reactive monitoring missions where required. Periodic reporting and reactive monitoring are forms of monitoring activity under the Convention and are referred to in greater detail below. The Convention also authorises the services of three non-State actors – IUCN, ICCROM and ICOMOS – to act as 'advisory bodies'.[47] The advisory bodies evaluate potential World Heritage listings as well as conduct monitoring activities in the event that a World Heritage site is under threat. In recent years, technical advice from the advisory bodies has increasingly been ignored and Committee decisions are being driven by politics. Many new sites, for instance, though 'not yet ready to be inscribed' have nevertheless been rushed in.[48] Meskell has termed this the 'rush to inscribe'.[49] These politics have created 'unprecedented challenges' for the operation (and legitimacy) of the regime.[50]

3   State Party Obligations

The obligations of States under the Convention are built around the concept of a duty. Article 4 of the Convention stipulates that States have a duty to ensure the 'identification, protection, conservation, presentation and transmission to future generations' of their World Heritage sites. Moreover, Article 6 provides for an additional duty on the international community 'as a whole' to co-operate in the protection of heritage. In modern terms, we might equate these duties as something akin to

---

[47] J. W. Thorsell, World Heritage Convention 1992–2002: Effectiveness and lessons for governance, paper prepared for Parks Canada Conference (2003): www.iucn.org/content/world-heritage-convention-effectiveness-1992-2002-and-lessons-governance (last accessed 13 July 2017), 1.

[48] K. Buckley, 'The World Heritage Convention at 40: Challenges for the work of ICOMOS', Historic Environment 26(2) (2014), 38, 42.

[49] L. Meskell, 'The rush to inscribe: Reflections on the 35th Session of the World Heritage Committee', Journal of Field Archaeology, 37(2) (2012), 145.

[50] L. Meskell, 'UNESCO's World Heritage Convention at 40: Challenging the Economic and Political Order of International Heritage Conservation', Current Anthropology, 54(4) (2013), 483.

'stewardship', a concept which itself is highly ambivalent.[51] In the case of the Convention, duties are said to create a 'shared commitment' to preserve heritage for future generations and the rest of the world.[52] But the Convention also respects the principle of State Sovereignty and does not 'replace' or otherwise usurp the authority of State Parties in their own domestic decision-making.[53] Thus, following inscription of a site on the List, the Convention is said to act like 'a burden' on the State in whose jurisdiction the site is situated.[54] More specifically, Battini writes, it is 'a burden of taking into account the global interests affected by their decision'.[55]

Whereas the text of the Convention sets out the broad (and mostly aspirational) obligations of States, a secondary document – the Operational Guidelines for Implementation of the Convention – provides specific guidance on how to implement the text. When the Operational Guidelines were first drafted, in 1977, they consisted of twenty-eight short paragraphs. Today, they boast almost 300 paragraphs in total over some 60 pages (plus annexures). Next to the text of the Convention, the Operational Guidelines constitute the most important regulatory document in the framework. They represent, as Redgwell points out, 'a code of good practice for the effective implementation of the Convention'.[56] But more than that, the Operational Guidelines also set out the procedural obligations that States need to abide by. Parties are required, for instance, periodically to report, every six years, on their implementation of the Convention. In addition, all States are required, under paragraph 172 of the Operational Guidelines, to alert the Committee to any intention they have to any new activities (e.g. developments) that may affect the OUV of one of their sites. Over the years, there have been several instances of non-compliance with paragraph 172,

---

[51] E. Barritt, 'Conceptualising stewardship in environmental law', *Journal of Environment Law*, 26(1) (2014), 1, 2.

[52] Meskell, 'UNESCO's World Heritage Convention at 40', 483.

[53] S. Battini, 'The procedural side of legal globalization: The case of the World Heritage Convention', *International Journal of Constitutional Law*, 9(2) (2011), 340.

[54] B. Gaillard, 'The Legal Effects of World Heritage Listing under the 1972 Convention Concerning the Protection of the World Cultural and Natural Heritage: The example of the Dresden Elbe Valley in the Federal Republic of Germany (special edition), *Primitivetider* (2014), 37, 43.

[55] S. Battini, 'The procedural side of legal globalization: The case of the World Heritage Convention', *International Journal of Constitutional Law*, 9(2) (2011), 340, 342–343.

[56] C. Redgwell, 'Article 2 – Definition of Natural Heritage' in F. Francioni and F. Lenzerini (eds.), *The 1972 World Heritage Convention, A Commentary* (Oxford Commentaries on International Law, 2008), p. 79.

including: the ancient city of Thebes and its Necropolis (Egypt);[57] the Old Town of Regensburg with Stadtamhof (Germany);[58] Kaziranga National Park (India);[59] Ibiza (Spain);[60] the Ancient City of Nessebar (Bulgaria);[61] and the Great Barrier Reef (Australia).[62]

4   Monitoring and Enforcement under the Convention

It is apparent from the previous section that the World Heritage system creates duties (or, to use a regulatory term, 'standards') on Member States to identify and conserve their common heritage. These duties are aspirational (e.g. Articles 4 and 6 of the Convention) as well as procedural (e.g. periodic reporting, paragraph 172 of the Operational Guidelines). The responsibility for monitoring these requirements is largely outsourced to the World Heritage Centre and the advisory bodies (IUCN, ICCROM and ICOMOS). Through their work, they seek to involve NGOs (many NGOs are members of IUCN, for example) but NGOs are not explicitly authorised, without specific invitation, to inform the Committee of instances of non-compliance.

One of the most obvious forms of monitoring that the advisory bodies undertake is reactive monitoring. Reactive monitoring (not to be confused with the six-yearly 'periodic reporting' mentioned above) involves the Centre and the Advisory Bodies collecting information and reporting back to the Committee 'on the state of conservation of specific World Heritage properties that are under threat'.[63] Reactive monitoring can also involve 'ground-truthing' claims about the dangers to a site and meeting with State and non-State representatives to understand fully how the values of a site might be at risk. The objective of reactive monitoring is said to: 'prevent the deletion of a property from the [World Heritage] List' and 'offer technical co-operation' to State Parties'.[64] It may be the case, for instance, that a party that breaches the paragraph 172 requirement will be asked to 'invite' a reactive monitoring mission to their site.

---

[57] World Heritage Committee decision 30 COM 7B.46 (2006).
[58] World Heritage Committee decision 31 COM 7B.98 (2007).
[59] World Heritage Committee decision 32 COM 7B.12 (2008).
[60] World Heritage Committee decision 33 COM 7B.41 (2009).
[61] World Heritage Committee decision 34 COM 7B.81 (2010).
[62] World Heritage Committee decision 35 COM 7B.10 (2011).
[63] UNESCO World Heritage Centre, Operational Guidelines, para. 169.
[64] Ibid., para. 170.

This occurred recently, for instance, in the case of Australia's Great Barrier Reef, which was under threat from fossil fuel developments.[65]

In terms of enforcement procedures ('forcing' violators to mend their ways), there is no international court to adjudicate disputes, although creative arguments have been made to bring cases in the International Court of Justice (ICJ).[66] Green Martinez has pointed out that the obligations of States under the Convention are *erga omnes* in nature (that is, owed to everyone), and, accordingly, he argues that any State should have standing 'to invoke the responsibility of other State parties for alleged breaches of [World Heritage] obligations'.[67] Green Martinez's arguments are compelling but, as he freely admits, despite recent developments in jurisprudence around *erga omnes* the ICJ has never granted its jurisdiction solely on such a basis. On the other hand, the World Heritage Committee can and does play something of a quasi-judicial role in punishing states in instances of non-compliance. There appear to be two main options open to the Committee in such a case. First, it can threaten to place a site on the In Danger List, or, secondly, it can delete it from the World Heritage List altogether.

Some nations, though not all, are spurred into compliance to avoid an In-Danger listing. Australia, for instance, went to great lengths to avoid an In-Danger listing of the Great Barrier Reef between 2010 and 2015. But not all reactions from States follow this pattern of diplomatic resistance. Some, such as the United States[68] and Honduras,[69] have actively called for In-Danger listings to ensure that appropriate conservation strategies take place. In fact, as Buzzini and Condorelli write, it appears that 'in the majority of cases', sites have been placed on the In Danger List at the time of inscription, including making an immediate request for financial assistance.[70] There are several examples of where this has occurred, including Angkor Wat in Cambodia and the Minaret of Jam in Afghanistan.[71] Removal of sites from the World Heritage List altogether

---

[65] See World Heritage Committee decision 35 COM 7B.10 (2011).

[66] S. Green Martinez, 'Locus Standi before the International Court of Justice for Violations of the World Heritage Convention', *Transnational Dispute Management*, 5 (2013), 1.

[67] Ibid., 1.

[68] World Heritage Committee decision: 34 COM 7B.29 (2010)

[69] World Heritage Committee decision: 35 COM 7B.31 (2010)

[70] Buzzini and Condorelli, 'Article 11 List of World Heritage in Danger' in F. Francioni and F. Lenzerini (eds.), *The 1972 World Heritage Convention, A Commentary* (Oxford University Press, 2008), p. 182.

[71] B. Boer, 'Article 3 Identification and Delineation of World Heritage Properties' in (ibid.), 101.

is rare. There have only been two known instances of this occurring, and the World Heritage bodies seem particularly reticent about going down this path.[72]

D   NGO Petitioning as a Form of Monitoring

This next section of the chapter describes how NGOs have attempted to engage in regulatory (monitoring) behaviour by complaining directly to the World Heritage Committee about the condition of certain sites. The filing of petitions is a recent phenomenon in World Heritage, and it seems to reveals how NGOs feel left out of the formal regulatory processes under the existing framework.

1   The 'Climate Change' Petitions (2004–07)

Between 2004 and 2007, several petitions were lodged with the World Heritage Committee, seeking inscription of World Heritage sites on the In Danger List due to the impacts of climate change. First, in September 2004, a petition was sent to the Committee by the Australia-based Climate Justice Programme, requesting that the Great Barrier Reef World Heritage Area be placed on the In Danger List. Two months later, in November 2004, petitions were also sent to the World Heritage Committee requesting that Sagarmatha National Park (Nepal) Belize Barrier Reef (Belize) and the Huascaran National Park (Peru) be listed for similar reasons. The Huascaran National Park petition was the result of Foro Ecologico del Peru as well as other NGOs.[73] At the 29th Session of the Committee (in 2005), the Committee took note of all four petitions (29 COM 7B.a). Though it refused to list the identified sites In Danger, the Committee did request that a working group of experts, in consultation with the World Heritage Centre, the Advisory Bodies and other relevant United Nations (UN) bodies, prepare a joint report on 'Predicting and managing the effects of climate change on World Heritage' (29 COM 7B.a). Shortly thereafter, a document entitled 'Predicting and Managing the Effects of climate change on World Heritage' and another entitled 'a Strategy to Assist States Parties to the

---

[72] Only two sites have ever been deleted from the World Heritage List: Oman's Arabian Oryx Sanctuary (2007) and Germany's Dresden Elbe Valley (2009).

[73] L. Malone and S. Pasternack, *Defending the Environment: Civil Society Strategies to Enforce International Environmental Law* (Island Press, Washington D.C., 2006), p. 203.

Convention to Implement Appropriate Management Responses' were prepared and subsequently endorsed by the Committee.[74]

In 2006, a separate petition was sent to the Committee on behalf of twelve NGOs from the United States and Canada, requesting the inclusion of the Waterton-Glacier World Heritage site on the In-Danger list. The petition for the site, which borders the United States and Canada, was noted by the Committee in the 33rd session in 2009. The Committee considered, among other things, the 'high level of public concern' regarding the effects of climate change and requested a joint conservation report on the property and a monitoring mission from experts from the World Heritage Centre and the IUCN.[75] Finally, in 2007, another petition was lodged with the Committee, signed by several NGOs including the Climate Action Network Australia, Greenpeace, the NSW Nature Conservation Council and Friends of the Earth. That petition sought the inclusion of the Greater Blue Mountains World Heritage Area (Australia) on the In Danger list. On this occasion, the Committee did not formally respond, though, in 2008, the Committee did note 'the real danger from climate change' faced by many World Heritage properties and adopted criteria proposed for assessing properties that are most threatened by climate change for inclusion on the In Danger List.[76]

2   The 'Black Carbon' Petition (2009)

In January 2009 United States-based EarthJustice and the Australian Climate Justice Program petitioned the Committee to consider 'the Role of Black Carbon' in threatening various World Heritage sites. The forty-four-page submission made lengthy and impressive legal and scientific arguments and made several requests including that the Committee place the sites identified on In Danger List.[77] The Black Carbon petition attempted to distinguish itself from the previous climate petitions, which had been successful in spurring policy action on climate change among World Heritage bodies, but not to have the sites listed as in danger:

---

[74] World Heritage Committee decision 30 COM 7.1 (2006).
[75] World Heritage Committee decision 33 COM 7B.22 (2009).
[76] World Heritage Committee decision 32 COM 7A (2008).
[77] O. Quirico, 'Disentangling Climate Change Governance: A Legal Perspective', *Review of European, Comparative & International Environmental Law*, 21(2) (2012).

> This petition requests that the Committee take action that is specific, that does not overlap with the work of other international bodies, and that falls squarely within the Committee's mandate under the Convention.[78]

In 2009, the Committee responded formally to the Black Carbon petition but again, decided not to list the sites In Danger. The Committee did, however, note the NGOs' efforts and encouraged all States Parties 'to exchange information on existing national policies, regulations and opportunities for immediate voluntary action to control the generation of black carbon that can affect World Heritage properties'.[79]

3   The Wood Buffalo Petition (2014)

In December 2014, the Mikisew Cree First Nation Peoples (consisting of about 2,800 First Peoples) sent a petition to the World Heritage Committee, requesting that the Wood Buffalo National Park (inscribed in 1983) in the north east of Alberta (Canada) be listed as In Danger. Their reasons included, among other things: the presence of hydroelectric dams affecting the hydrology and biodiversity of the park and the industrial development of Alberta's oil sands region and proposed mining nearby. The World Heritage Committee responded directly to the Wood Buffalo Petition (in 2015), refusing to list the site as In Danger but requested 'the State Party to undertake a Strategic Environmental Assessment (SEA) to assess the potential cumulative impacts of all developments on the OUV of the property'.[80] The Committee also asked Canada, as is the protocol, 'to invite' a reactive monitoring mission to the site. In September 2016, a mission was undertaken to investigate the effects of the dam, the oil sands, and other relevant issues. The report highlighted the importance of the petition:

> In the view of the [IUCN/UNESCO] mission, the Petition constitutes a legitimate, well-reasoned and technically strong contribution. The mission carefully considered the many calls to recommend the inscription of WBNP on the List of World Heritage in Danger.[81]

---

[78] Earth Justice, 'Petition to the World Heritage Committee: The Role of Black Carbon in Endangering World Heritage Sites Threatened by Glacial Melt and Sea Level Rise' (29 January 2009), 40.

[79] World Heritage Committee decision 33 COM 7C (2009).

[80] World Heritage Committee decision 39 COM 7B.18 (2015).

[81] Ibid., 42.

E   Discussion

1   The Legality of 'Petitioning'

The word 'petition' derives from the Latin *petitio*, meaning 'aimed at' or 'sought' or 'laid claim to'. The *Encyclopaedia Britannica* defines a petition as a 'written instrument directed to some individual, official, legislative body, or court in order to redress a grievance or to request the granting of a favour'. Some jurisdictions, such as China, have a long history of petitions (*xinfang* or *shangfang*), which date back to Imperial times.[82] Other earlier concepts are said to date back to Roman times, in which a commoner might request that a grievance be managed by the emperor.[83] A more popular legal use of the term is most clearly displayed in seventeenth-century England in the conflict between the English Parliament and Charles I.[84] In 1628, the Petition of Right (which pre-dated the enlightenment period, and also gave rise to provisions in America's Bill of Rights) was sent to King Charles I, seeking, among other things, no taxes without Parliament's consent and no imprisonment without proper cause (i.e. *habeas corpus*).

Today, petitions have a variety of meanings, some more legally significant than others. Article 1 of the United States Bill of Rights allows citizens to petition the government 'for a redress of grievances'. In 1995, Canada introduced a system of petitions under its Auditor General Act (section 22). Likewise, the European Parliament has a modern system for petitioning under the Treaty on the Functioning of the European Union. Article 227 allows any citizen of the Union to lodge a petition to the Parliament on a matter 'which comes within the European Union's fields of activity and which affects him, her or it directly'. Indigenous Peoples in Australia have also long used petitioning processes to demand justice from the monarchs in England with respect to land and other rights in colonised Australia.[85]

Under international law, the petitioning system has had strong recognition and an interesting history, based largely on individual complaints and human rights. The League of Nations, formed after the First World

---

[82] C. Minzner, and Xinfang 'An Alternative to Formal Chinese Legal Institutions', *Stanford Journal of International Law*, 42 (2006), 103.

[83] A. Schiller, *Roman Law: Mechanisms of Development* (Mouton, 1978).

[84] L. Reeve, 'The legal status of the Petition of Right', *The Historical Journal*, 29 (1986), 257–277.

[85] B. Attwood and A. Markus, *The Struggle for Aboriginal rights: a Documentary History* (Allen & Unwin, 1999)

War, had a prescriptive system of petitioning that allowed for the handling of 'minority complaints'.[86] The Permanent Mandates Commission (PMC) – the League's principal body responsible for territories of the [former] Ottoman Empire and Germany – adopted a petitioning system for inhabitants of mandated territories.[87] From this, the 'trend' towards individual petitioning under international law can be traced to Article 87(b) of the UN Charter and the [then operational] Trusteeship Council which oversaw the process of decolonisation throughout the world.[88] The practice of petitioning thus had its roots in decolonisation, the abuse of sovereign power, and the prevention of discrimination of minority groups and individuals.

It perhaps comes as no surprise, then, that there is a formal petitioning system under the 1969 International Convention on the Elimination of All Forms of Racial Discrimination as well as the Optional Protocol to the International Covenant on Civil and Political Rights and Optional Protocol to the Convention on the Elimination of all Forms of Discrimination Against Women.[89] Regional human rights arrangements also allow for petitioning to occur. For example, the Inter-American Commission on Human Rights allows for petitioning where there are potential breaches of human rights. Likewise, Article 25 of the European Convention on Human Rights has been described as one of the 'most successful petition system stories'.[90]

Yet petitions have had no such equivalent history in international environmental law, and their legal relevance today is highly questionable. The evolution of international environmental law developed largely after the 1970s, and petitioning from individuals and NGOs scarcely makes a mention. The World Heritage Operational Guidelines make no mention of a petition, nor does the Convention itself, nor the Committee's Rules of Procedures. The secretariat of the Convention (the World Heritage Centre) can 'receive information' from parties other than State

---

[86] P. Hibbeln, 'Supervising Imperialism: Petitions to the League of Nations Permanent Mandates Commission, 1920-1939', *Proceedings of the Ohio Academy of History* (2001), 21

[87] Ibid.

[88] L. Chen, *An Introduction to Contemporary International Law: A Policy-Oriented Perspective,* 3rd edn. (Oxford University Press, 2015).

[89] L. Burgess and L. Friedman, 'A Mistake Built on Mistakes: the Exclusion of Individuals under International Law', *Macquarie Law Journal,* 11 (2005), 221.

[90] L. Chen, *An Introduction to Contemporary International Law: A Policy-Oriented Perspective, 3rd edn.* (Oxford University Press, 2015), p. 130.

Parties,[91] though a proper NGO grievance mechanism is not prescribed or elaborated upon any further. The strategy of petitioning is thus something which has evolved and might be said to be customary, but not in the strict legal sense. That is to say, it is doubtful that petitioning under MEAs forms part of customary international law (CIL). For that to be the case, it would require States to recognise petitioning under MEAs as widespread, general and consistent practice. This is unlikely to occur, given that petitioning has no equivalent history to human rights abuses, and petitions vary wildly in the form, content and requests that they make under the various MEAs. Further, different MEAs have different governing bodies and procedures, which makes customary practice of petitioning across MEAs too difficult to accept.

2   The Impact of Petitioning

The legal status of petitioning as a form of NGO monitoring and engagement is, of course, separate to its impact. The impact of NGO petitioning under the Convention is far more debatable and difficult to quantify. It is perhaps helpful to understand the impact of petitioning through the broader-lens of influence.[92] In other words: what influence have NGOs had on the World Heritage framework by using petitions? Wood suggests that the concept of influence can have two meanings. First, we can understand influence in terms of impact – that is, where an actor's activities or relationships are causing or have caused some kind of result.[93] A related notion, says Wood, is 'impact-based responsibility', which involves 'an organization's direct and indirect contributions to social or environmental impacts'.[94] Alternatively, we can view influence in terms of how much leverage an actor has had through its activities.[95] The idea of leverage is largely synonymous with NGOs having 'some kind of power' to affect

---

[91] UNESCO World Heritage Centre, Operational Guidelines, para. 174.

[92] S. Wood, 'The Case for Leverage-Based Corporate Human Rights Responsibility', *Business Ethics Quarterly*, 22(1) (2012), 63–98. See also B. Richardson, 'Are Social Investors Influential?', *European Company Law*, 9(2) (2012), 133–140; and E. Hamman, 'The influence of environmental NGOs on project finance: a case study of activism, development and Australia's Great Barrier Reef', *Journal of Sustainable Finance & Investment*, 6(1) (2016), 51–66.

[93] S. Wood, 'The Case for Leverage-Based Corporate Human Rights Responsibility', *Business Ethics Quarterly*, 22(1) (2012), 3.

[94] Ibid.

[95] Ibid.

a course of events.[96] If we were to look at the actions of NGO petitioning, we would see that all the case studies elicited some form of response from the World Heritage bodies and thus exhibited a degree of power over decision-making bodies. Hence, we can say that there was at least some leverage exhibited by NGOs as well as some degree of impact of their petitions.

Online platforms have created an ideal environment to use petitions as a form of influence.[97] Through social media, NGOs are able to exert a degree of leverage (i.e. power) over World Heritage institutions. The true impact of petitioning, however – that is, causing some result to occur – is probably less certain. The result that was intended by NGOs in the case studies, at least on paper, was for the sites to be listed 'In-Danger.' At no point did this occur. Nevertheless, by following the decisions and actions of the World Heritage bodies subsequent to the petitions, it is clear that climate change has now become a major concern of the Committee and advisory bodies. In terms of issue raising or agenda setting, then, climate groups were influential in engaging the Committee process to at least acknowledge the impacts on World Heritage.[98] The Committee and other bodies have recognised the 'need for proper coordination' between the climate change regime and the World Heritage Convention (Decision 29 COM 7B.a). In a far narrower sense, they were less influential in gaining traction on the identified sites In Danger.

In Bonn, Germany, in 2015, several years after the climate petitions were first lodged, the Committee acknowledged that: 'World Heritage properties are being increasingly affected by Climate Change.'[99] In 2016, UNESCO, the United Nations Environment Program (UNEP), and the Union of Concerned Scientists (UCS) released a joint report on World Heritage and Tourism showing the sites most at risk from climate change. UNESCO continues to acknowledge the role of NGOs in bringing climate change to the attention of the Committee at its 29th Session in

---

[96] B. Richardson, 'Are Social Investors Influential?', *European Company Law*, 9(2) (2012), 134.

[97] L. Malone and S. Pasternack, *Defending the Environment: Civil Society Strategies to Enforce International Environmental Law* (Island Press, Washington D.C., 2006), ch. 4.

[98] B. Gemmill and A. Bamidele-Izu, 'The Role of NGOs and Civil Society in Global Environmental Governance' in D. Esty and M. Ivanova (eds.), *Global Environmental Governance: Options and Opportunities* (Yale, 2002), pp. 77–100.

[99] World Heritage Committee decision 39 COM 7 (2015).

2005.[100] The impact of their activities has also been considered by the academic community as well.[101]

Outside the examples above, not all petitions to the Committee are seeking an In Danger listing. In 2012, a Petition to save the Tigris River in Mesopotamia urged the Committee to assess the particular impacts of proposed development on a 'potential' World Heritage site. The Tigris River Petition asked the Committee to 'insist on the State Party to refrain from any action infringing upon any sites bearing the potential to become a World Heritage Site'. Likewise, in 2015, a Petition to Save the Pitons in St Lucia, Caribbean signed by only a few hundred people, asks that the Committee deny the pending sale of undeveloped beachfront land to a private individual. Petitions that ask the Committee to 'investigate' or 'assess' particular activities at the World Heritage site appear to misconstrue the role and jurisdiction of the Committee.

F   Options for Improved NGO Engagement

The above analysis suggests not only that petitioning is legally obscure but that its impact as a regulatory activity is debatable. What seems clear, however, is that NGOs have resorted to petitioning as a means to raise the profile of ecological risks at certain sites, not out of choice, but out of necessity. With no formal protocol processes for NGOs (unlike human rights treaties), the practice of petitioning is hardly unsurprising. After all, petitions have long been used as a 'last resort' or an 'appeal' to the monarch or colonial powers where all other avenues have failed. In short, they are desperate tactics by those desperate to engage more fully with conservation issues. We ought not only to recognise that but to embrace and facilitate such interest in the Convention through more established lines of communication.

As noted in the introduction to this chapter, it is well accepted that global governance is no longer the sole domain of governments.[102] Effective handling of environmental disputes, which includes monitoring

[100] Perry and Falzon, *Climate Change Adaptation for Natural World Heritage Sites: a Practical Guide* (UNESCO, 2014), p. 6.
[101] See A. Huggins, 'What Obligations Do States Parties to the World Heritage Convention Have to Protect World Heritage Sites from the Adverse Impacts of Climate Change?', *Australian International Law Journal*, 14 (2007), 121–136; and S. Shearing, 'Here Today, Gone Tomorrow? Climate Change and World Heritage', *Macquarie Law Working Chapter, No. 2007–11* (2007).
[102] K. Brand and F. Reusswig, 'The Social Embeddedness of the Global Environmental Governance' in G. Winter (ed.), *Multilevel Governance of Global Environmental Change:*

and enforcement, is best handled by partnerships, both formal and informal, between NGOs, private and other non-State actors.[103] Moreover, it is described as 'best practice' that NGOs should be encouraged to take part in decision-making processes at the international level.[104] The involvement of NGOs in a wide variety of ways is part of the 'preconditions for successful institution building'.[105] These principles are as relevant to global environmental governance as they are to domestic regulatory settings.[106]

Non-State actors, such as NGOs, can be made 'fully fledged' third players of regulatory regimes.[107] Their participation need not be limited to consultation. Rather, they can be 'enrolled', as Julia Black might say,[108] to carry out regulatory tasks that the World Heritage bodies lack the resources to police. Many global NGOs are, in fact, perfect for this role. They already play a fundamentally different role to States under global governance regimes.[109] NGOs are not bound by State interests or, in the context of international law, by 'non-intervention principles'.[110] While States are often hamstrung by bureaucracy and domestic politics, NGOs can be opportunistic and move quickly to address new agendas in World politics.[111]

If such a course is to be accepted, the first thing to do is a comparison of other MEAs and their mechanisms for more meaningful NGO

Perspectives from Science, Sociology, and the Law (Cambridge University Press, 2006), p. 80.

[103] Ibid.

[104] A. Gillespie, 'Facilitating and Controlling Civil Society in International Environmental Law', *Review of European, Comparative & International Environmental Law*, 15 (2006), 327–338.

[105] K. Brand and F. Reusswig, 'The Social Embeddedness of the Global Environmental Governance' in G. Winter (ed.), *Multilevel Governance of Global Environmental Change: Perspectives from Science, Sociology, and the Law* (Cambridge University Press, 2006), p. 104.

[106] N. Gunningham et al., *Smart regulation: designing environmental policy* (Oxford University Press, 1998).

[107] I. Ayres and J. Braithwaite, 'Tripartism: Regulatory Capture and Empowerment', *Law and Social Inquiry*, 16(3) (1991), 439.

[108] J. Black, 'Enrolling Actors in Regulatory Processes: Examples from UK Financial Services Regulation', *Public Law*, 1 (2003), 62–90.

[109] A. D. Tarlock, The 'Role of Non-Governmental Organizations in the Development of International Environmental Law – Chicago-Kent Dedication Symposium', *Environmental Law, Chi.-Kent. L. Rev.*, 68 (1992), 61.

[110] Ibid., 73.

[111] B. Gemmill and A. Bamidele-Izu, 'The Role of NGOs and Civil Society in Global Environmental Governance' in D. Esty and M. Ivanova (eds.), *Global Environmental Governance: Options and Opportunities* (Yale, 2002), p. 11.

engagement. To a large extent, this has already been attempted.[112] Secondly, NGOs must be 'accredited' under the Convention. Currently, no clear accreditation procedures for NGOs are available. The current wording for NGO involvement is by no means acceptable. Consider, for instance, Article 8(3) of the Convention, which States that NGOs with similar objectives to IUCN, ICOMOS and ICCROM may attend Committee meetings in an advisory capacity. Article 13(7) of the Convention also talks about cooperating with NGOs who have 'objectives similar to those of *this Convention*'. It is plain to see that objectives similar to the advisory bodies and objectives similar to the Convention are not one and the same. In fact, IUCN and ICOMOS have a far wider range of duties and interests than just World Heritage. The role of ICOMOS, for example, as defined under the Operational Guidelines, is 'to promote the application of theory, methodology and scientific techniques to the conservation of the architectural and archaeological heritage', though it also has a specific role under the Convention which is far narrower.[113]

Accreditation procedures can be modelled on other Conventions. For example, the Operational Directives for the Implementation of the Convention for the Safeguarding of the Intangible Cultural Heritage provide accreditation procedures (in Chapter III) as do the Operational Guidelines for the protection of underwater heritage (in Chapter VI). It should, of course, be noted that UNESCO already has directives that cover partnership with NGOs.[114] There are dozens of civil society organisations that have an official partnership with UNESCO in consultative status, and many that have an associate status with UNESCO (including ICOMOS and IUCN). But those directives are not specific to UNESCO's role as secretariat of the World Heritage Convention. Nor do they specify the types of monitoring roles NGOs might play under the Convention. Furthermore, the directives deal only with UNESCO's relationship with NGOs and not the other regulatory bodies such as IUCN, ICOMOS and the Committee. Currently, if an NGO wishes to present in front of the Committee, for instance, it must be nominated by a Committee member and are only allowed two minutes to address the assembly.

---

[112] S. Oberthür et al., *Participation of Non-Governmental Organisations in International Environmental Co-operation: Legal Basis and Practical Experience* (Erich Schmidt Verlag GmbH & Co, 2002).

[113] UNESCO World Heritage Centre, Operational Guidelines, paras. 34 and 35.

[114] A. Chechi, 'Non-State actors and cultural heritage: friends or foes?', *Anuario de la Facultad de Derecho de la Universidad Autónoma de Madrid*, 19 (2015), 473.

In addition to the above, it must be clearly considered what role NGOs are to play in monitoring the Convention. In other words, what leverage and formal power should NGOs be afforded under the Convention (over and above just consultation on identified issues)? As a starting point, NGOs can add great value in monitoring certain key provisions of the Convention framework, for instance compliance with paragraph 172 of the Operational Guidelines. There are, of course, problems with what is being suggested here. One problem might be that the greater participation and range of actors makes consensus building more difficult.[115] It can create something of a competition between non-state regulators.[116] Although the current problems of the Convention seem to rest not with consensus or lack thereof (between the regulators), but on a drain in resourcing and political will (from states on the Committee) to confront the Convention's ongoing challenges.

The legitimacy of NGOs as regulators under the regime would also provide a sticking point. Questions arise, for example, over their transparency and accountability to undertake regulatory tasks such as monitoring and enforcement. As Black remarks, non-State actors have a particular problem with legitimacy, as, unlike States, they cannot rely on the natural authority of law to support them. She writes:

> unlike State-based regulators whose actions are supported by law, non-State regulators cannot necessarily rely on the authority of law to motivate people to behave, or derive their legitimacy from their position in a wider legal order and constitutional settlement.[117]

How, then, might they gain a legitimacy to act in a regulatory role? Jepson has suggested that NGOs can create a legitimacy, as it were, by leveraging their legitimating assets (their support networks, information, public profile etc.).[118] But such questions are more empirical than normative, and the assets (and legitimacy) are likely to differ significantly between NGOs themselves. The regulatory legitimacy of an organisation such as Greenpeace (which has national branches), for example, would likely

---

[115] See S. Bernstein, 'Legitimacy in intergovernmental and non-state global governance,' *Review of International Political Economy*, 18(1) (2011), 17–46.

[116] J. Black 'Legitimacy and the Competition for Regulatory Share' LSE Working Chapters 14/09 (2009): www.lse.ac.uk/collections/law/wps/WPS2009-14_Black.pdf (last accessed 13 July 2017).

[117] Ibid., 13.

[118] P. Jepson, 'Governance and accountability of environmental NGOs', *Environmental Science & Policy*, 8 (2005), 515–524.

differ significantly from a group such as WWF (which also has national branches). To a certain extent, the accreditation process could address these concerns, but what if the policies and management of NGOs change? How could that be accommodated in such a system? Another problem is that NGOs make up a substantial membership base of both IUCN and ICOMOS, the formal advisory bodies (and major regulatory agencies) under the Convention. As Battini suggests, it is possible that NGOs can influence the decisions of the Committee via their membership of such bodies.[119] Opportunities for communications, influence and leverage through those organisations raises interesting questions about how and which issues of World Heritage compliance come to the attention of the regime. In the end, these issues would need to be considered thoroughly before any changes could be made.

From a practical viewpoint, incremental or administrative amendments to the framework are not difficult. As noted above, the Operational Guidelines have been zealously expanded by the Committee from some twenty-seven paragraphs in 1977 to close to 300 paragraphs today. Going forward, such an approach would require explicit and deliberate acknowledgement of the role of NGOs in far clearer terms than what the Convention currently provides and what the Operational Guidelines currently support. Amendments to the existing Operational Guidelines or even a protocol process, similar to that of the International Covenant on Civil and Political Rights (ICCPR) or the Nagoya Protocol to the Convention on Biological Diversity (Nagoya Protocol) might also suffice. A subsidiary compliance body might be useful as well such as the Implementation and Compliance Committee established under the Basel Convention or the Compliance Committee established under the Convention on Access to Information, Public Participation in Decision-making and Access to Justice in Environmental Matters (the Aarhus Convention). Certainly the Committee has the power to create such a body. Article 10(3) of the Convention allows the Committee to create such consultative bodies as it deems necessary for the performance of its functions. Rules 20 and 21 of the Rules of Procedures of the World Heritage Committee do likewise.

---

[119] S. Battini, 'The procedural side of legal globalization: The case of the World Heritage Convention', *International Journal of Constitutional Law*, 9(2) (2011), 352.

G   Conclusion

This chapter has explored the role of NGOs under the World Heritage Convention and, in particular, their efforts in using petitions to monitor State behavior under the regime. Petitions have turned out to be a vague and legally ambiguous method of airing grievances in international environmental law. Accordingly, a fuller role for NGOs in monitoring World Heritage sites should be better formulated than it is currently. This would deliver enormous benefits in terms of legitimacy and resources to a regime struggling with both. Moreover, a framework like World Heritage is a prime candidate for a tripartite approach in which NGOs are not just consulted but fully fledged third players in the regulatory game. Understandably, NGOs are seeking, and ought to be afforded, a clearer degree of traction in monitoring events at existing sites. That role ought to be made explicit, first by way of accreditation through the Convention's Operational Guidelines (or other document) and possibly supported by the creation of a subsidiary body or 'sub-committee'.

Any changes to the framework for NGO involvement could be modelled on existing MEAs, including related-heritage treaties that already have established NGO accreditation processes in their operational guidelines. There is every motivation for cash-strapped and over-committed institutions such as UNESCO, IUCN and ICOMOS to draw more heavily on the resources of civil society. As potential surrogate regulators, NGOs could increasingly be 'brought into the regulatory conservation'.[120] Certainly, UNESCO and the Advisory Bodies are spoilt for choice as to how best to go about it. Arguments for NGO interventions and multi-stakeholder governance are well established in the literature, and various practical suggestions exist for their fuller involvement.[121] The biggest challenge for change is not theoretical, but a practical one: how best to navigate the politics of the World Heritage Committee?

In the end, as former UNESCO Director General Koichiro Matsuura noted: "[A formal role of NGOs] is something the 1972 Convention should have more carefully looked into."[122]

---

[120] C. Ford, 'Prospects for Scalability: Relationships and Uncertainty in Responsive Regulation' in *Regulation & Governance* 1 (2012), p. 12.

[121] S. Oberthür et al., *Participation of Non-Governmental Organisations in International Environmental Co-operation: Legal Basis and Practical Experience* (Erich Schmidt Verlag GmbH & Co., 2002).

[122] M. Rössler and C. Cameron (eds.), *Many Voices, One Vision the Early Years of the World Heritage Convention* (Routledge, 2013), p. 218.

It is definitely not too late. If NGOs are to be expected and accepted as a major part in promoting compliance with World Heritage, as this chapter suggests they should, the processes of third-party involvement in monitoring need to be better defined, easier to navigate and more often encouraged.

17

Beyond Litigation: the Need for Creativity in Working to Realise Environmental Rights*

LISA CHAMBERLAIN

A Introduction

South Africa is one of the jurisdictions in the world that enjoy the benefit of a justiciable constitutional environmental right.[1] The significance of the existence of this right was recorded in the early judgment of *Director: Mineral Development, Gauteng Region and Another* v. *Save the Vaal Environment and Others*, in which South Africa's Supreme Court of Appeal noted that:

> Our Constitution, by including environmental rights as fundamental, justiciable human rights, by necessary implication requires that environmental considerations be accorded appropriate recognition and respect in the administrative processes in our country. Together with the change in the ideological climate must also come a change in our legal and administrative approach to environmental concerns.[2]

However, in comparison with other rights in the South African Constitution, there has been relatively little jurisprudence on the environmental right.[3]

---

* This is an open access article published under the terms of the 'Creative Commons Attribution-Non Commercial-Share Alike 3.0 Unported License', reprinted with permission: www.lead-journal.org/content/17001.pdf

[1] Section 24 of the Constitution of the Republic of South Africa (1996) reads as follows:
Everyone has the right

    a. to an environment that is not harmful to their health or well-being; and
    b. to have the environment protected, for the benefit of present and future generations, through reasonable legislative and other measures that
        i. prevent pollution and ecological degradation;
        ii. promote conservation; and
        iii. secure ecologically sustainable development and use of natural resources while promoting justifiable economic and social development.

[2] 1999 (2) SA 709 (SCA) [20].

[3] The right has been considered in only a handful of cases, which include: *Fuel Retailers Association of Southern Africa* v. *Director-General: Environmental Management, Department of Agriculture, Conservation and Environment, Mpumalanga Province and Others* 2007 (6) SA 4 (CC); *HTF Developers (Pty) Ltd* v. *The Minister of Environmental Affairs and Tourism* (2006) 5 SA 512 (T); *BP*

It has been suggested that some of the possible reasons for this include the novelty of the subject-matter, a lack of judicial familiarity with environmental law and a failure by litigating lawyers to raise the environmental right.[4] In addition, many of the cases that can be categorised as environmental cases are not cases brought in the public interest.[5] There has certainly been criticism of the public interest legal community for not using both the framework of environmental justice and the environmental right itself in the courts.[6] In this chapter, I would like to respond to such criticism by addressing a slightly different point, which is why, in practice, litigation is not an ideal strategy for communities seeking to realise either environmental rights or environmental justice. Instead, I introduce, for consideration and critique, some non-litigious strategies emerging out of a civil society campaign to protect the Mapungubwe World Heritage Site in South Africa.

Southern Africa (Pty) Ltd v. *MEC for Agriculture, Conservation, Environment and Land Affairs* 2004 (5) SA 124 (W); *Hichange Investments (Pty) Ltd* v. *Cape Produce Co Ltd t/a Pelts Products* 2004 (2) SA 393 (E); *Save the Vaal Environment* 1999 (2) SA 709 (SCA); *Minister of Health and Welfare* v. *Woodcarb (Pty) Ltd* 1996 (3) SA 155 (N); and *Minister of Public Works & Others* v. *Kyalami Ridge Environmental Association* 2001 (3) SA 1151 (CC).

[4] L. Ferris, 'Constitutional Environmental Rights: An Under-Utilised Resource', SAJHR, 24 (2008), 29, 38; A. du Plessis, 'South Africa's Environmental Right (Generously) Interpreted: What is in it for Poverty?', SAJHR, 27 (2011), 279, 289. See also T. Madebwe, 'Carving Out a Greater Role for Civil Litigation as an Environmental Law Enforcement Tool in Zimbabwe's 2013 Constitution', *Law, Environment & Development Journal*, 11(2) (2015), 106, 108, in which the author comments on the dearth of environmental cases brought before the courts in Zimbabwe.

[5] Consider, for example, the *Fuel Retailers* case 2007 (6) SA 4 (CC), in which the Constitutional Court pronounced definitively and in detail on the principle of sustainable development. This case was brought by a fuel company seeking to build a petrol station. This dearth of public interest environmental litigation is despite the fact that South African standing provisions in environmental cases are extremely generous. See, for example, T. Murombo, 'Strengthening Locus Standi in Public Interest Environmental Litigation: Has Leadership Moved from the United States to South Africa?', *Law, Environment & Development Journal*, 6(2) (2010), 163; and M. Kidd, 'Public Interest Environmental Litigation: Recent Cases Raise Possible Obstacles', PER, 13(5) (2010), 27.

[6] M. Murcott, 'The Role of Environmental Justice in Socio-economic Right Litigation', SALJ (2015) 875 and J. Dugard and A. Alcaro, 'Let's Work Together: Environmental and Socio-economic Rights in the Courts', SAJHR, 29 (2013), 14. Dugard and Alcaro argue, at 31, that 'environmental organisations have been playing it safe; going for the winnable points in court and not really pushing the boundaries of s 24 of the Constitution, let alone venturing into the brown and red components contained in the socio-economic rights clauses'.

B   The Challenges of Public Interest Litigation in the Environmental Sector

Although mitigation is sometimes possible, environmental degradation is often irreversible.[7] This means that there is usually a small window of time in which to prevent permanent environmental harm and exercise principles of environmental good governance, such as the precautionary principle.[8] Litigation, however, is not known for its speed. Preparing court papers and securing a hearing date from over-burdened courts are time-consuming exercises, and the timeframes involved are typically much longer than the time available to prevent environmental damage that cannot later be undone.

Such time-sensitive issues are further complicated by the fact that there are often multiple levels of judicial, or quasi-judicial, processes to go through. In South Africa, for instance, before a party can review a decision to grant environmental authorisations and mining rights before a court, it is necessary first to go through an internal administrative appeal process.[9]

This is not to suggest that there are no legal mechanisms that try to address this very problem. Courts can be approached on an urgent basis for remedies such as interdicts.[10] Interim interdicts are specifically designed to buy the time needed to resolve other legal disputes (such as the resolution of administrative appeals, for example). Nevertheless, interim interdict proceedings pose a different kind of challenge when litigating environmental issues, particularly in a public interest context. In South Africa, one of the requirements for successfully obtaining an interim interdict is proving that the 'balance of convenience' favours the party asking for the interdict.[11] Essentially, this requires the applicant to

---

[7]   See M. Kidd, *Environmental Law*, 2nd edn. (Juta, 2011), p. 37, discussing the framework principles contained in s. 2 of the National Environmental Management Act 1998.

[8]   This is one of the foundational principles of global environmental governance, and is enshrined in many international legal instruments such as principle #15 of the Rio Declaration on the Environment and Development (1992), which provides that '[i]n order to protect the environment, the precautionary approach shall be widely applied by States according to their capabilities. Where there are threats of serious or irreversible damage, lack of full scientific certainty shall not be used as a reason for postponing cost-effective measures to prevent environmental degradation'. It is also contained in s. 2(4) of the National Environmental Management Act 1998.

[9]   National Environmental Management Act 1998, s. 43; Mineral and Petroleum Resources Development Act 2002, s. 96.

[10]   An interdict is referred to as an 'injunction' in many jurisdictions.

[11]   *Hix Networking Technologies* v. *System Publishers (Pty) Ltd* 1997 1 SA 391 (SCA).The requirements for obtaining an interim interdict are: first, a prima facie right in terms of substantive law must be established (*Eriksen Motors (Welkom) Ltd* v. *Protea Motors*

convince the judge that, on balance, more harm will be caused to the applicant if the interdict is *not* granted than that caused to the respondent if it *is* granted.

Let us consider for a moment what this might look like in practice. Say, for instance, that a multinational mining company is planning to construct a new coal mine in rural South Africa, and has obtained a mining right from the South African Department of Mineral Resources. The community currently living on the land above the minerals may face the risk of relocation, and polluted air and water that could result in health problems and loss of livelihoods, as well as the possible destruction of ancestral graves and other sacred sites. The mining company is not required to obtain the consent of the community in order to mine legally. However, it is required to consult them.[12] Let us assume that, as is so often the case,[13] the company has consulted with a small fraction of the community that the rest of the community claims does not legitimately represent them. The bulk of the community is either outright opposed to mining in the area, or opposed to mining unless they receive some tangible benefit such as permanent, secured jobs or a guaranteed share of the profits. Unlike many communities in this situation, this community manages to access pro bono legal assistance from a local non-governmental organisation (NGO), which lodges an appeal with the relevant authorities against the granting of the mining right. In order to prevent any further construction on site, the NGO acting on behalf of the

---

Warrenton 1973 3 SA 685 (AD) and *Knox D'Arcy Ltd* v. *Jamieson* 1996 4 SA 348 (SCA)); secondly, there must be a reasonable apprehension that the continuation of the conduct will cause irreparable harm to the applicant if the interim relief is not granted (*Setlogelo* v. *Setlogelo* 1914 AD 221, 227 and *Braham* v. *Wood* 1956 1 SA 651 (D)); thirdly, the balance of convenience must favour the granting of the interim interdict (*L F Boshoff Investments (Pty) Ltd* v. *Cape Town Municipality, Cape Town Municipality* v. *L F Boshoff Investments (Pty) Ltd* 1969 1 All SA 430 (C)); and, lastly, there must be no other satisfactory remedy available to the applicant (*Van Niekerk* v. *Van Rensburg* 1959 2 SA 185 (T) and *Candid Electronics (Pty) Ltd* v. *Merchandise Buying Syndicate (Pty) Ltd* 1992 2 SA 459 (C)).

12 Mineral and Petroleum Resources Development Act 2002, ss. 10 and 23.
13 See, for example, the experience of the Bakgaga Ba-Kopa community, discussed in a publication by the Centre for Environmental Rights entitled 'Community Case Book on Mining and Environmental Rights' (February 2014), at 19: http://cer.org.za/wp-content/uploads/2014/03/CER-Casebook-on-Mining-Final-Web.pdf (accessed 9 February 2017) and the discussion of consultation in a report by the Centre for Applied Legal Studies entitled 'The Social and Labour Plan Series Phase 1: System Design Trends Analysis Report' (March 2016): www.wits.ac.za/media/wits-university/faculties-and-schools/commerce-law-and-management/research-entities/cals/documents/programmes/environment/resources/Social%20and%20Labour%20Plans%20First%20Report%20Trends%20and%20Analysis%2030%20March%202016.pdf (accessed 9 February 2017).

community also launches an application for an interim interdict, seeking an order that construction be stopped until the mining right appeal is resolved. It must now satisfy the elements of an interim interdict, including the 'balance of convenience' requirement mentioned above.

For the mining company to prove the prejudice that it will experience if the interdict is granted is probably a fairly straightforward process. The company is likely to have entered into a number of contracts with construction sub-contractors, each of which may have a penalty clause in the event of contractual default (which will kick in if construction is halted). In addition, the company will presumably have done thorough economic feasibility modelling exercises before applying for the mining right and will therefore be able to quantify its projected loss of profit fairly quickly. Furthermore, it is likely to be able to make arguments based on possible job losses necessitated by a halt in construction. All of this can probably be done in a matter of days by actuaries and other experts whom the company has on retainer already.

On the other side of the fence, the community is required to show what prejudice it will suffer if construction continues.[14] This means having to demonstrate the value of their connection to the land. When that connection is one rooted in culture and spiritual significance, this is a very difficult thing to do. Putting a monetary value on something so sacred can also sometimes be an undesirable, if not abhorrent, process.[15] On the ecological front, proving possible harm resulting from pollution is also extremely difficult. Causation issues in environmental cases are notoriously challenging – especially in those involving water and air pollution. In addition, to make such an argument convincingly in court, it is

---

[14] In determining whether the balance of convenience favours the granting of the order the court must weigh up the prejudice to the applicant if the interdict is not granted against that to the respondent if it is granted (*Dorbyl Vehicle Trading & Finance Company (Pty) Ltd* v. *Northern Cape Tour & Charter Service CC* 2001 1 All SA 118 (NC)). The exercise of the court's discretion usually resolves itself into a consideration of the prospects of success and the balance of convenience: the stronger the prospects of success, the less need for such balance to favour the applicant, whereas the weaker the prospects of success then the greater the need for it to favour the applicant (*Olympic Passenger Service (Pty) Ltd* v. *Ramlagan* 1957 2 SA 382 (D)).

[15] For a discussion on environmental economics in the South African context, see H. A. Strydom and N. D. King (eds.), *Fuggle and Rabie's Environmental Management in South Africa* (Juta, 2009), pp. 44–51. Sharife and Bond warn that if we relegate the environment to mere natural capital, what follows is to convert value into price and then to sell nature on the market: K. Sharife and P. Bond, 'Payment for Ecosystem Services versus Ecological Reparations: The 'Green Economy' Litigation and a Redistributive Eco-debt Grant', SAJHR, 29 (2013), 144, 150.

advisable for the community to have contracted some scientific experts to assess impact. Even assuming that they are able to commission such experts (which is unlikely, and is a further challenge that will be discussed in more detail below), impact assessments take time and the community is unlikely to have had the time necessary for a credible one to be produced. We must remember that they are applying for an *urgent* interim interdict. In addition, in the midst of the antagonism that characterises litigation, the mining company is unlikely to allow the community's experts access to the site itself in order to conduct what will be perceived by the company as a 'rival' impact assessment.

So how, then, does the community quantify projected environmental harm in order to satisfy the requirements for an interdict and convince a judge to grant them the relief that they seek? Quantifying environmental degradation is extremely complex. Although it is an emerging area of expertise and there are promising developments in this field, very few experts are yet equipped to perform this kind of analysis, at least in South Africa.

The process of securing scientific experts is a further reason for litigation in the environmental context being very difficult, at least from a community and civil society perspective. In South Africa, scientific experts work on a consultancy basis. This means that most of them earn their living working for the corporate sector, i.e. for developers. It is therefore very difficult for an NGO to find an expert willing to work on behalf of a community. First, communities and civil society organisations rarely have the funds necessary to pay consultants at the going rate. Even if they do, the second, and more insurmountable, problem is that, in the Centre for Applied Legal Studies' (CALS')[16] experience, very few experts are willing to go on record in a case opposing a large development (such as a mine) for fear of being 'blacklisted' by industry and thereby cutting off future workstreams. Even though, in theory, consultants act independently and so who they work for should not matter, because the science is neutral, the reality is that it does. In CALS' experience, the result is that typically there are a handful of underpaid and overworked experts trying to assist all civil society litigation in the environmental context.

One possible solution to this problem is to turn to universities in order to source experts. Experts working at universities are usually more amenable to working pro bono or on reduced rates, and are also less

---

[16] A human rights organisation based at the School of Law at the University of the Witwatersrand in Johannesburg, South Africa.

likely to be concerned about 'conflict of interest' because their consultancy work is not their only income stream. The risk, however, is that university-based experts may be more academically inclined and lack the practical experience enjoyed by full-time consultants. When litigation gets ugly, this is exactly the kind of thing that a company will use in an attempt to discredit inconvenient expert reports.

Lastly, even assuming that our hypothetical community has managed to overcome all the obstacles discussed above, their lawyers remain faced with the challenge of translating complex and technical scientific subject-matter (such as groundwater models and biodiversity offsets) into language accessible for a judge, who may not have any background in environmental issues.[17] So if litigation is not the answer, or at least not the whole answer, what is? Several alternative strategies are discussed in the next section.

C Alternative Strategies: Lessons from Mapungubwe[18]

1 Background to the Campaign

In 2010, an Australian company called Coal of Africa Limited (CoAL) was granted a licence to build an opencast and underground coal mine in northern South Africa, a few kilometres away from Mapungubwe, which is a United Nations Educational, Scientific and Cultural Organization (UNESCO) World Heritage Site and a place of enormous cultural and ancestral significance for large numbers of people from Southern

---

[17] K. J. Park, 'Judicial Utilization of Scientific Evidence in Complex Environmental Torts: Redefining Litigation Driven Research', *Fordham Environmental Law Review*, 7 (2011), 483, 484; T. Greiber (ed.), 'Judges and the Rule of Law: Creating the Links: Environment, Human Rights and Poverty', IUCN Environmental Policy and Law Paper No 60 (2006), 8–9; United Nations Environmental Programme, 'UNEP Global Judges Programme' (2005) www.doe.ir/portal/file/?116502/Unep-Global-Judges-programme.pdf 54; and G. Pring and C. Pring, 'Specialised Environmental Courts and Tribunals: the Explosion of New Institutions to Adjudicate Environment, Climate Change and Sustainable Development', invited paper at 2nd Yale-UNITAR Global Conference on Environmental Governance and Democracy (17–19 September 2010) 12.

[18] Much of this material is derived from a publication by the Centre for Applied Legal Studies, entitled 'The Mapungubwe Story: A Campaign for Change': www.wits.ac.za/media/wits-university/faculties-and-schools/commerce-law-and-management/research-entities/cals/documents/Mapungubwe%20Report%20Updated%2019%20March%202015.pdf (accessed 30 March 2017). I am indebted to my colleagues Louis Snyman and Robert Krause – the primary authors of that publication – for their contribution to this chapter in this regard.

Africa.[19] It is also located in an extremely water-scarce area and sits atop rich mineral deposits. In response to CoAL's proposed mining development, a group of civil society organisations concerned about the impact of the proposed mine in this sensitive and sacred place formed themselves into a coalition[20] and secured legal representation.[21]

Over the next few years, CoAL, the Save Mapungubwe Coalition and the various government regulators involved[22] would work – sometimes against each other and sometimes collaboratively – to answer the question of what kind of development was appropriate in this sensitive area, and who would benefit. This journey is not a unique one, as sensitive areas increasingly come under threat in the growing global drive towards mineral extraction. The events that unfolded at Mapungubwe hold many lessons, including about the use of litigation in the environmental context, and about the array of alternative strategies available.

2   Connecting the Dots between an Advocacy Campaign and Company Share Price

In the early stages of the campaign, the Coalition launched several prongs of litigation. These included an administrative appeal against the granting of the mining right, an appeal to the Water Tribunal against the granting of a water use licence, an administrative appeal against the (retrospective) granting of environmental authorisations, and an interim interdict to halt construction of the mine pending resolution of the legal battles.[23] Ultimately, this litigation paved the way for the parties to enter into negotiations. But it also provided content for press releases and media coverage in a way that would turn out to be immensely significant.

---

[19] For more on Mapungubwe, see http://whc.unesco.org/en/list/1099 (accessed 5 May 2017); N. Swanepoel and M. Schoeman, 'Mapungubwe Matters' South African Archaeological Bulletin, 65(191) (2010), 1–2.

[20] Consisting of the Mapungubwe Action Group, the Endangered Wildlife Trust, WWF South Africa, the Association of Southern African Professional Archaeologists, Birdlife South Africa and the Wilderness Foundation.

[21] From CALS and the Centre for Environmental Rights. This dual legal representation model was one of the key successes of the campaign. Unfortunately, discussion of this model is beyond the scope of this chapter, but it is outlined in CALS' publication 'The Mapungubwe Story: A Campaign for Change'.

[22] Which included the Department of Mineral Resources, the Department of Water Affairs (as it then was), the Department of Environmental Affairs, the Department of Agriculture, Forestry and Fisheries, the South African Heritage Resources Agency, South African National Parks and two municipalities.

[23] 'The Mapungubwe Story: A Campaign for Change', 49.

As has been highlighted by McCann, legal mobilisation can provide 'leverage to supplement other political tactics'.[24]

At the beginning of the campaign, CoAL's share price on the Johannesburg Stock Exchange was 1,455 points. Then began a pattern that looked something like this: every time CoAL was awarded a licence by one of the government regulators, it would issue a press statement to announce that. Its share price would spike as a result. The Coalition would then issue a counter press release indicating either that it had lodged an appeal against the licence concerned, or that it intended to. The share price would dip a little in response. CoAL would then sometimes respond with a further press release indicating that such an appeal did not suspend the validity of the licence – meaning business as usual. Its share price would then sometimes recover slightly.[25] This pattern repeated in response to many of the licences involved in this case.

The net result was a steady decline in share price. By February 2015, CoAL's share price was down to 35 points.[26] While this steady decline occurred due to a range of factors, including a weak global coal market, CoAL's overestimation of the quality of the coal in the area, and enforcement action taken by government, the Coalition's campaign contributed to the cauldron of troubles undermining confidence in the company. The Mapungubwe campaign thus provides some evidence that unsustainable practices by companies compromise their profitability.[27]

Such linkages are illuminating for all those involved in development projects. For human rights lawyers, and their community partners, this is a signal that speaking the language of profit and reputation can be far more effective in practice than human rights discourse. For mining companies and their investors, the lesson is one of vulnerability – a small group of people with fairly limited resources can leverage

---

[24] M. W. McCann, *Rights at Work: Pay Equity Reforms and the Politics of Legal Mobilisation* (University of Chicago Press, 1994); J. Dugard 'Rights, Regulations and Resistance: The Phiri Water Campaign', SAJHR, 24 (2008), 593, 611.

[25] 'The Mapungubwe Story: A Campaign for Change', 50–2 and Centre for Applied Legal Studies, 'Changing Corporate Behaviour: the Mapungubwe Case Study' (2014), 25–8: www.wits.ac.za/media/wits-university/faculties-and-schools/commerce-law-and-man agement/research-entities/cals/documents/Changing%20corporate%20behaviour-The% 20Mapungubwe%20case%20study.pdf (accessed 9 February 2017).

[26] www.coalofafrica.com/investors-and-media/share-price-information (accessed 5 May 2017).

[27] 'The Mapungubwe Story: A Campaign for Change', 50–2 and 'Changing Corporate Behaviour: the Mapungubwe Case Study', 24.

government enforcement action and bad publicity in a way that has a serious impact on a company's bottom line.

3 Community Learning Exchanges

At the heart of the unequal experience of mining lies a power imbalance.[28] Companies have ready access to a team of lawyers, a dedicated public relations office to manage public image and the resources to build and maintain relationships with government decision-makers. Communities often cannot afford legal representation and will certainly not have a dedicated communications office. Members of rural communities may have to travel far to reach government officials. Further, the culture of secrecy in the mining sector means that it is very difficult for the public to access information about planned developments and their environmental impacts.[29]

The result of these asymmetries of knowledge and resources is that the conditions of a true contract – equality of arms and access to the same information – are not typically present in engagements between mining companies and communities. Many of these resource disparities are rooted in centuries of exploitation and systemic inequality,[30] meaning that trying to disrupt them can be quite overwhelming. However, that does not mean that there is not scope for communities and civil society organisations to be creative in trying to reduce the asymmetries of knowledge that otherwise keep them on the back foot.

NGOs involved in environmental justice work tread a precarious line between trying to provide communities affected by mining with the knowledge to make informed choices on the one hand, and improperly trying to influence community responses to mining development on the

[28] John Knox, UN Special Rapporteur on Human Rights and the Environment, has emphasised the particular vulnerability to environmental damage experiences by indigenous peoples. See 'Report of the Independent Expert on the issue of human rights obligations relating to the enjoyment of a safe, clean, healthy and sustainable environment', December 2012.

[29] See, for example, Centre for Environmental Rights, 'Turn on the Floodlights: Trends in Disclosure of Environmental Licenses and Compliance Data' (March 2013): http://cer.org.za/wp-content/uploads/2013/03/Turn-on-the-Floodlights.pdf (accessed 9 February 2017). See also the series of shadow reports produced by the Promotion of Access to Information Act Civil Society Network, available at: www.saha.org.za/projects/national_paia_civil_society_network.htm (accessed 5 May 2017).

[30] B. Meyersfeld, 'Empty Promises and the Myth of Mining: Does Mining Lead to Pro-Poor Development?', *Business and Human Rights Journal*, 2(1) 2007, 31.

other hand. Specifically, mining offers the potential for job creation, which often means that it is welcomed by local communities, notwithstanding the environmental price that they may pay down the line.[31] What is important is that a community's agency to decide for themselves whether they will support or oppose a proposed development is respected and deferred to. One of the ways for NGOs to do so with integrity, while still chipping away at the information asymmetry described above, is by facilitating community learning exchanges.

The concept of a community learning exchange is that a community that is likely to be affected by mining in the near future is introduced to a one that has already been affected by mining. In this way, those best placed to comment – people who have lived through the experience themselves – can *directly* share their knowledge about what it means to live near and/or work for a mine. Importantly, such exchanges can also include a site visit so that 'yet-to-be-affected' communities can see at first hand what a mine looks like and what kind of impact it can have on the surrounding area, whether it be positive or negative.

This can facilitate an exchange of insights into the impacts of mining, strategies for engaging with companies and government regulators, and success stories to inspire soon-to-be-affected communities. The ultimate objective is to support communities grappling with mining to access information with which they can become more powerful in their engagements with state and corporate repositories of power.[32] Importantly, community learning exchanges also have the advantages of limiting the intermediary role often occupied by NGOs and instead placing value on the knowledge that exists within communities.

At the time of writing, a number of community learning exchanges had taken place in the context of the Mapungubwe campaign.[33] Through this exchange of peers, communities were able to share learning,

[31] A. du Plessis, 'South Africa's Environmental Right Generously Interpreted: What is in it for Poverty?', *South African Journal of Human Rights*, 27(2) 2011, 279. See also Centre for Environmental Rights, 'Zero Hour: Poor Governance of Mining and the Violation of Environmental Rights in Mpumalanga': http://cer.org.za/wp-content/uploads/2016/06/Zero-Hour-May-2016.pdf (accessed 30 March 2017).

[32] For an example of similar methodology used in the water and sanitation sector in South Africa, see: http://livinglands.co.za/enviro-champs-workshop-community-learning-eachange-from-mpophomeni-township-to-kayamandi/ (accessed 5 May 2017).

[33] See www.wits.ac.za/cals/our-programmes/environmental-justice/community-learning-exchanges/ (accessed 9 February 2017).

LISA CHAMBERLAIN

information and ways of attenuating the exploitation of mining companies.[34] These are groups who, historically, had neither engaged nor organised as a collective, and such exchanges have provided the platform for them to do so. In fact, some of the communities involved have gone on to organise additional exchanges on their own initiative, without the need for facilitation by lawyers or NGOs. From the perspectives of both sustainability and agency, this is a most welcome outcome.

Furthermore, the second such exchange involved a community that opposes another CoAL mine in another part of the country. This has meant that, in addition to general learning about mining, the participating communities could also engage directly about the particular company involved, its business practices and what strategies are likely to be most successful with respect to this company in particular.[35] Community learning exchanges are thus a potentially powerful and effective alternative (or complement) to the more traditional litigious mechanisms in environmental justice work.

4 Collaborative Compliance Monitoring: The Case of the EMC

After progressing through a litigation and negotiation phase (an analysis of which is beyond the scope of this chapter), the Mapungubwe Coalition embarked on the third and most interesting phase of the campaign: participation in a collaborative compliance-monitoring body. In South Africa, the monitoring of a mining company's compliance with its environmental and other licences consists primarily of self-reporting by the company.[36] Occasionally, capacity permitting, government regulators will send out inspectors to conduct a site visit.[37] However, there are always many more mines than there are inspectors.

---

[34] Participating communities included the Machete, Vhangona, Tshivula, Mudimeli, Bessie, Balemba, Makgatho, Bathlabine and Tshikondeni communities in Limpopo province.

[35] See T. Murombo, 'Regulating Mining in South Africa and Zimbabwe: Communities, the Environment and Perpetual Exploitation', *Law, Environment and Development Journal*, 9(1) (2013), 31, 38, in which the author discusses the impact of mining on this particular community (the Mudimeli community).

[36] Mineral and Petroleum Resources Development Act 2002, s. 25.

[37] These inspectors – colloquially known as the Brown Scorpions (for mining), the Green Scorpions (for environmental issues) and the Blue Scorpions (for water issues) – are established in terms of the Mineral and Petroleum Resources Development Act 2002, s. 92 and the National Environmental Management Act 1998, ss. 31A–31Q.

Against this backdrop, the model piloted in the Mapungubwe case is particularly significant, as a special body was established to monitor CoAL's compliance with its licences. This body – which is known as the Vele Colliery Environmental Management Committee (EMC) – was formally established by the conditions of both the environmental licences granted by the Department of Environmental Affairs, and the water use licence granted by the Department of Water Affairs. The objective of the EMC is to monitor compliance with the provisions of these licences, as well as to promote improved decision-making and environmental practices using the information gained from monitoring.[38] Its operations are informed by the work of two technical sub-committees –dealing with water, and heritage and biodiversity, respectively.[39] But what is most striking is how broadly representative the EMC is. On it sit a number of government departments[40] at both national and provincial levels, local municipalities,[41] state agencies,[42] farmers' unions,[43] and, for the first time in the history of the mining industry in South Africa, civil society.[44]

CALS has represented the Save Mapungubwe Coalition on the EMC since 2011. It has not been an easy road, and the decision to join the EMC, and then repeated decisions to stay on it, have not been taken lightly.[45] However, during this time, the EMC has transformed from a body plagued by procedural issues (such as membership and logos) into a dynamic watchdog that continues to hold CoAL accountable. While impact on Mapungubwe has not been prevented, it has at least been mitigated. Along the way, many lessons have been learned.[46] Chief among these are that effective EMCs need trust, transparency and teeth.

[38] Vele Colliery Environmental Management Committee Terms of Reference, clause 2.

[39] The designation of specialist sub-committees has allowed detailed, technical interrogation to take place in each sub-committee, chaired by an expert in the field, which then reports to the main EMC.

[40] Including the Departments of Mineral Resources, Environmental Affairs, Water and Sanitation and Agriculture, Forestry and Fisheries.

[41] The Blouberg and Vhembe Municipalities.

[42] Such as SANParks and the South African Heritage Resources Agency.

[43] The Weipe Farmers' Cooperative.

[44] In the form of the Save Mapungubwe Coalition and their legal representatives, the Centre for Applied Legal Studies.

[45] In particular, CALS and the Coalition have had to assess regularly whether their participation in the EMC in any way legitimises inappropriate mining development at Mapungubwe.

[46] See also 'The Mapungubwe Story: A Campaign for Change', ch. 11, which outlines in more detail suggested prerequisites for effective EMCs.

a) Trust

One of the most valuable attributes of this kind of collaborative body is that the broad range of stakeholders involved can bring very different skills and experience to the table. Unlike in litigation, this knowledge is collectively pooled rather than set up in opposition. To do this effectively requires trust. In the context of Mapungubwe, it was not easy for parties who had been litigating against each other to change the nature of their relationship into something more collaborative. Inevitably, it took time to build this kind of trust.[47] Anyone wishing to set up a collaborative compliance-monitoring body should therefore factor in considerable time at the beginning of the process to allow such relationships to develop.

b) Transparency

Natural resources are common goods and must therefore be managed in the public interest. Members of the public can hold an EMC-type body accountable only if they are aware of the manner in which it is addressing environmental issues. In addition, public scrutiny can create a sense of accountability, as participants in an EMC want to be seen to be doing the right thing. A lack of readily available and sufficiently detailed information can lead to a number of misgivings about the role of an EMC, including concerns that it has been concealing non-compliance. It is therefore critical that the default position is one of transparency – which should apply to minutes of all meetings, as well as to as scientific and impact-related data. The Vele EMC has had some heated debates about whether raw data can be disclosed (as opposed to interpretations of that data), and remains divided on this issue.

c) Teeth

An EMC is inherently a watchdog body. Its power is to observe, highlight any issues of concern, provide a forum in which those issues can be discussed and make recommendations to both the government regulators and the mining company. Such a body is not a regulator itself and cannot therefore take enforcement action. This is probably as it should be, given the participation of non-government actors on this body.[48]

---

[47] Similar issues of trust have been discussed in the context of co-management of protected areas in South Africa. See, for example, T. Kepe, 'Land Claims and Co-management of Protected Areas in South Africa: Exploring the Challenges', *Environmental Management*, 41 (2008), 311.

[48] Such as the Save Mapungubwe Coalition and the Weipe Farmers Union.

However, the fact that the full range of government regulators is represented in the EMC is enormously useful, as any instances of licence non-compliance or other environmental issues of concern can be brought fairly quickly to the attention of the government department involved. It also provides an opportunity for different government departments, or different units within the same department, to put principles of co-operative governance into practice.

Another important component of 'teeth' is the necessity for institutional independence. Although EMCs can be established in terms of the conditions of government-issued licences, they are designed to operate independently of the government departments that created them. Were this not the case, the functioning of an EMC would be severely hampered, as EMCs are effective only if they can make recommendations without fear or favour.[49]

So the Vele EMC certainly presents a model for consideration. Whether it would be sustainable to use such a structure in relation to all mines is questionable, given the significant investment of resources required. Another, largely unexplored, issue that should be debated is how such structures might address the cumulative impact of mining activity. Highly invasive activities such as mining, especially when conducted on a large scale, have an impact on the socio-ecological environment that extends far beyond the project area. Further, mineral deposits (such as coal seams) often cover a significant geographical area, which means that there is the potential for there to be a large number of mining projects in close proximity. Thus, while the individual impact of a particular mine on water, soil and air might seem moderate, the combined impact of all the potential mines in the area might lead to a state incompatible with health, wellbeing and livelihoods. If each mine had an EMC set up to monitor only its activities, the big picture of the cumulative environmental, economic and social impact of all the mines operating in a particular area would be lost. One possibility is that where there is a real likelihood of a concentration of mining projects in a particular geographical area, a regional EMC should be established. This approach

---

[49] One example of where this went wrong at Mapungubwe is when high level politicians, who themselves did not participate in the EMC, overturned the EMC's election of a Coalition representative as chairperson. While the replacement chairperson has done an excellent job, the principle to be conscious of is: if such political interference is possible with regard to the EMC's choice of chairperson, would it also be possible in relation to a more serious instance of environmental non-compliance?

could address both the sustainability problem and the cumulative impact issue.

D Conclusion

Litigation is often part of the strategy to address human rights violations, and environmental rights violations are no exception. Yet litigation is not a strategy that is well suited to the environmental sector. Some of the reasons for this are applicable to human rights work generally, such as the difficulties that affected communities face in accessing legal representation. However, there are peculiarities involved in addressing environmental issues in particular, which make environmental litigation challenging in fairly unique ways. These include the small window of time available in which to take action before irremediable environmental damage is caused, the difficulties in quantifying environmental harm, the challenges in securing scientific experts willing to work 'against' industry, and the need to translate complex technical data into language accessible to a judge.

Those seeking to advance environmental rights must therefore look beyond litigation. The Mapungubwe campaign offers a number of alternative strategies for critique and discussion. This chapter has examined three of these: targeting company share price through media and other advocacy initiatives; the methodology of community learning exchanges; and the innovative piloting of a collaborative compliance-monitoring model in the mining industry. What is clear is that communities affected by environmental harm, and the lawyers who support them, will have to devise and experiment with creative strategies outside the conventional litigious box. The realisation of environmental rights depends on it.

INDEX